CW01496391

A Variorum Commentary on the Poems of John Milton

Samson Agonistes

A Variorum Commentary on the Poems of John Milton

GENERAL EDITOR:

Albert C. Labriola

ASSOCIATE GENERAL EDITOR:

P. J. Klemp

CONTRIBUTING EDITORS:

Archie Burnett
W. Gardner Campbell
Claudia Champagne
Stephen B. Dobranski
Richard J. DuRocher
Cheryl Fresch
Edward Jones
Jameela Lares
John Leonard
John Mulryan
Stella Revard
Louis Schwartz

A Variorum Commentary on the Poems of John Milton

VOLUME THREE

Samson Agonistes

By
STEPHEN B. DOBRANSKI

Introduced by
ARCHIE BURNETT

Edited by
P. J. KLEMP

DUQUESNE UNIVERSITY PRESS
Pittsburgh, Pennsylvania

Published in the United States of America by
DUQUESNE UNIVERSITY PRESS
600 Forbes Avenue
Pittsburgh, Pennsylvania 15282

LCCN 70129962
ISBN 978-0-8207-0415-9

∞ Printed on acid-free paper.

This volume is supported, in part, by a grant from the Calgon Corporation.

For my parents,
Irene B. Dobranski
and
Stephen Dobranski

Contents

Abbreviations of Milton's Writings

Animad	*Animadversions*
Apol	*An Apology against a Pamphlet*
Arc	*Arcades*
Areop	*Areopagitica*
BrNotes	*Brief Notes upon a Late Sermon*
Bucer	*The Judgement of Martin Bucer*
Canz	*Canzone*
CharLP	*Character of the Long Parliament*
Circum	"Upon the Circumcision"
CivP	*A Treatise of Civil Power*
Colas	*Colasterion*
ComBk	*Commonplace Book*
DDD	*The Doctrine and Discipline of Divorce*
Def 1	*Pro populo anglicano defensio*
Def 2	*Pro populo anglicano defensio secunda*
Defpro Se	*Pro se defensio*
DocCh	*De doctrina Christiana*
Educ	*Of Education*
Eikon	*Eikonoklastes*
Eli	*In obitum Praesulis Eliensis*
EpDam	*Epitaphium Damonis*
EpWin	"An Epitaph on the Marchioness of Winchester"
FInf	"On the Death of a Fair Infant Dying of a Cough"
HistBr	*The History of Britain*

Hor	"The Fifth Ode of Horace, Lib. I"
IlPen	*Il Penseroso*
L'All	*L'Allegro*
Log	*Art of Logic*
Lyc	*Lycidas*
Mask	*A Mask Presented at Ludlow Castle (Comus)*
Nat	"On the Morning of Christ's Nativity"
OAP	*Observations on the Articles of Peace*
PE	*Of Prelatical Episcopacy*
PL	*Paradise Lost*
PR	*Paradise Regained*
Procan	*In obitum Procancellarii medici*
Prol	*Prolusions*
Ps	Psalm
QNov	*In quintum Novembris*
RCG	*The Reason of Church-Government*
Ref	*Of Reformation*
REW	*The Readie and Easie Way*
Rous	*Ad Joannem Rousium*
SA	*Samson Agonistes*
SolMus	"At a Solemn Music"
Sonn	Sonnet
Tetr	*Tetrachordon*
TKM	*The Tenure of Kings and Magistrates*
TR	*Of True Religion*

Preface

P. J. KLEMP

A Variorum Commentary on the Poems of John Milton has been a work in progress for more than half a century. The first step in bringing closure to that monumental work, this volume on *Samson Agonistes* is a tangible sign of the scholarly continuity that exists between a new generation of Miltonists and our esteemed predecessors. Commentary about Milton's poems extends back to his own century, and the first variorum edition—*cum notis variorum,* which translates "with the notes of various people"—of *Paradise Lost* appeared in 1749 and that of *Paradise Regained, Samson Agonistes,* and many of the shorter poems in 1752, both edited by Thomas Newton. Although the new installments of a *Variorum Commentary* on *Samson Agonistes* and *Paradise Lost* (the latter to appear during the next few years) look back to those landmarks of scholarship, our main goal is to continue and complete the Columbia University Press *Variorum Commentary,* published between 1970 and 1975.

Although that *Variorum Commentary* appeared as one war ended, its inception occurred fully two decades earlier, in 1949, in the shadow of another war. Merritt Y. Hughes, the *Variorum Commentary*'s general editor, explains the process by which that scholarly project took shape. Following a survey of the Modern Language Association's members, in December 1949, the "interested section" of that organization "commissioned" the new *Variorum Commentary.* The editors selected were some of the twentieth century's finest Milton scholars, starting

I want to acknowledge the diligent work of two student assistants, Jeri Capek and Kelley Duhatschek; the support of Duquesne University and the University of Wisconsin, Oshkosh; and the vision and generosity of Al Labriola.

with J. Milton French, who conducted the initial survey and declined the offer to become general editor. The rest of the participants were of the same stature, many of them joining French in being named Honored Scholars of the Milton Society of America: Merritt Y. Hughes (assigned to annotate *Paradise Lost*), Walter MacKellar (*Paradise Regained*), William Riley Parker (*Samson Agonistes*), A. S. P. Woodhouse (the so-called minor English poems), Douglas Bush (the Latin and Greek poems), and James E. Shaw (the Italian poems). If this epic catalog of scholars shines so brightly as to intimidate future generations who toil in the variorum's fields, it soon grew shorter.

For this generation of Milton scholars faced mortality, some well before their time. The opening volume of the Columbia University Press *Variorum Commentary* refers to the deaths of William Riley Parker, whose work on *Samson Agonistes* would be carried on by John Steadman, and of James E. Shaw, whose work on the Italian poems was updated by A. Bartlett Giamatti. The second volume refers to more departures—including that of A. S. P. Woodhouse, whose commentary on the minor English poems was completed by Douglas Bush. In his preface to that volume, Bush expresses his grief over the death of Merritt Y. Hughes, the general editor and annotator of *Paradise Lost,* which would mark perhaps the greatest impediment to the completion of the *Variorum Commentary.* If some of the *Variorum Commentary*'s charter members left scholarly work for others to complete almost immediately, Hughes's work on *Paradise Lost* and Parker's on *Samson Agonistes* would need to wait for future generations.

Because no one except John Steadman had expressed any interest in completing the *Variorum Commentary,* the indefatigable Albert C. Labriola stepped in, prompted by his respect for the labors of Hughes and Parker, a respect that also motivates the new contributing editors. Having seen the *Variorum Commentary* languish in an unfinished state for decades, Al first located the typescripts that had been collecting dust in boxes. With the help of John Steadman, who held the draft of Hughes's annotations to *Paradise Lost* (and had done some minor revising of them) as well as Parker's introduction and annotations to *Samson Agonistes,* Al gathered up these typescripts and secured Columbia University Press's permission to complete the *Variorum Commentary.* In mid-1997, the editorial process officially began when a delivery van brought seven boxes of this material to my doorstep.

Because more than three centuries of scholarship have accumulated about Milton's poems, much of that scholarship rich and perceptive, no variorum commentary could synthesize and present all, or even the bulk, of it. The term *variorum,* as demonstrated by the Columbia University Press volumes and, more recently,

Acknowledgments

William Riley Parker had begun composing a variorum commentary on *Samson Agonistes* when he passed away in 1968, and the hundreds of pages of notes and introductory material that he assembled served as this book's foundation. My numerous citations to Parker's unpublished annotations can only begin to suggest the debt I owe to his hard work and acumen. He identified many of the passages in *Samson* that echo Milton's other works, and I often found myself agreeing with the key words that he singled out and the quotations from secondary sources that he selected.

I am also grateful to John M. Steadman and Edward Weismiller for their exacting contributions to Parker's commentary. They first edited Parker's papers, compiling a list of further readings, proposing new topics for the introduction, and supplementing Parker's observations with quotations from additional sources. Edward Weismiller also incorporated his own insights on Milton's prosody, which I have quoted and cited in the following pages.

Among the many people with whom I worked directly on this book, Albert C. Labriola and Paul J. Klemp deserve my deepest gratitude. As the editors of *A Variorum Commentary on the Poems of John Milton*, Al and Paul have undertaken the enormous task of completing the Milton variorum begun by Columbia University Press in the 1970s. I am grateful that they invited me to compose the commentary for *Samson Agonistes* and that they have been so helpful through each stage of the writing process. From start to finish, Al has worked with characteristic ardor, pursuing possible sources of funding, organizing regular meetings of the Milton variorum's contributors, and commenting on early drafts of my annotations and bibliography. Paul Klemp's support and his suggestions on my drafts have also been invaluable. Paul oversaw the transfer of Parker's notes to computer files, and, in the later stages, he read the complete manuscript so many times that I lost count. He pored over matters of substance and style; I could not ask for a more gracious, keen-eyed editor.

I am also grateful to Al and Paul for teaming me on this book with Archie Burnett. Archie has written a thorough, insightful introduction that crystallizes many of the points of contention surrounding the critical legacy of *Samson Agonistes.* I received support from Archie and the Milton Variorum's other contributors: W. Gardner Campbell, Richard DuRocher, Cheryl Fresch, Edward Jones, Jameela Lares, John Leonard, John Mulryan, Stella Revard, and Louis Schwartz.

Much of my research for this book was conducted at Emory University and Georgia State University. In particular, the resourceful librarians at Georgia State's Interlibrary Loan Department tirelessly filled my many requests for obscure editions and hard-to-find dissertations. Additional research was facilitated by the helpful staffs at the Bodleian Library, the British Library, and the Harry Ransom Humanities Research Center at the University of Texas at Austin. I remain grateful to past and present members of these staffs for their friendly assistance. One of my research trips to England was funded in part by a grant from the Department of English at Georgia State University, and, during the final summer of revision, the department generously awarded me a second grant that helped me to complete work on the manuscript. I am particularly grateful to Matthew Roudané and Randy Malamud for supporting my research even in fiscally challenging times.

Finally, I wish to thank my parents for their unwavering encouragement during the ten years that I was researching and writing this book. And to my brilliant wife, Shannon: thank you for helping me in more ways than you realize and in more ways than I can express. Any faults that remain are my own.

—*Stephen B. Dobranski*

Introduction

Archie Burnett

Samson Agonistes is probably John Milton's most controversial poem. Virtually everything about it has been open to dispute: its composition date, how we are to regard the principal characters, whether Samson undergoes regeneration, and whether it is a work to be read politically or typologically. This introduction aims to give an outline of the principal critical debates, and, rather than merely summarize the contents of everything published on the poem up to this volume's cutoff date of 1970, to do so selectively and critically, highlighting key developments, weighing up evidence, and forming judgments.

Date

The statement made by Milton's nephew Edward Phillips in 1694 still stands in 1970: "It cannot certainly be concluded when he [Milton] wrote his excellent Tragedy entitled *Samson Agonistes,* but sure enough it is that it came forth after his publication of *Paradice lost,* together with his other Poem call'd *Paradice regain'd.*" Phillips also suggests that *Paradise Regained* (*PR*) was written between 1667 (when *Paradise Lost* [*PL*] was first published) and 1670: it "doubtless was begun and finisht and Printed after the other was publisht, and that in a wonderful short space considering the sublimeness of it" (Darbishire, *Early Lives* 75). This alone is

This introduction is dedicated to the memory of a dear friend, Milton bibliographer Calvin Huckabay.

I wish to acknowledge the collaboration of associate general editor Paul Klemp, whose tactful promptings and vigilance have effected improvements on nearly every page.

1

enough to lead William Riley Parker to conclude that it is "quite clear" that Phillips, "for one, does not believe the *Samson* to have been written after *Paradise Lost*" ("Date" 147). Phillips, however, expresses no such belief. Parker assumes that if Phillips believed that *SA* was written at the same time as *PR* he would have said so. But one can as readily assume that Phillips's "cannot certainly be concluded" suggests that he did think *SA* written at the same time as *PR* but that he could not be certain. For similar reasons, Ernest Sirluck's question, "If Edward Phillips thought *Samson Agonistes* written before *Paradise Lost*, why did he not say so?" (776), may be answered, "Because he did not know for certain when it was written." The facts that Sirluck (778) adduces for a late date—that Phillips was away from London in 1664–65 and 1650–51, and that Milton was in hiding in 1660 and at Chalfont St. Giles in 1665—do not constitute firm evidence for any date of composition. Suppositions and speculations as to why Phillips says what he does—or no more than he does—establish nothing and cannot dislodge the fact that Phillips does not know for sure, says so, and says nothing more: "Edward Phillips' admission of not knowing when *Samson Agonistes* was composed may be understood as being just that—an admission of ignorance" (Oras, *Blank Verse* 3).

The Anonymous Biographer (probably Cyriack Skinner) affirms that *SA* and *PR*, and several other works, were "finish'd after the Restoration" (Darbishire, *Early Lives* 29). This leads Parker to conclude that *SA*, like some other works mentioned by the Anonymous Biographer, was begun before it ("Date: A Postscript" 202). But, again, he presses the witness too hard: the Anonymous Biographer is telling what he believes to be true, which is of course not everything that may, in an ideal world, be known: Parker himself (202) notes omissions from his account. And, in any case, "finish'd after" does not imply "begun before": it may also have been begun after, for all he knows. And this is so even if other works finished after the Restoration were begun before it. Other early biographers offer little help: John Toland mentions *SA* but says nothing about composition date; John Aubrey and Anthony à Wood do not even mention the poem (Parker, "Date" 145).

Parker's aggressive cross-examination of Phillips and the Anonymous Biographer is oddly inconsistent with his neglectful or curtly dismissive treatment of two other early witnesses: Jonathan Richardson (1734) and Thomas Newton (1752), both of whom, in disagreement with Parker, happen to regard *SA* as Milton's last composition. Sirluck (775) notes that Richardson had questioned many people who were acquainted with Milton during his later life, and that he therefore had some authority. Milton's time, Richardson reports, "was Now Employ'd in Writing and Publishing, particularly *Paradise Lost*. and after That, *Paradise Regain'd*, and *Samson Agonistes*" (Darbishire, *Early Lives* 275). Newton (1:liv), who, Sirluck (776) reminds us, read and compared all written accounts of Milton's life and work, collected some particulars from "credible tradition," and talked to Milton's granddaughter Elizabeth and others, states of *SA:* "This I conceive to be the last of his poetical pieces."

The traditional date for *SA* is a post-Restoration one, in the 1667–70 period. Newton in 1752 speaks for the eighteenth-century consensus. David Masson, along with his nineteenth-century predecessors, accepts the traditional date (*Life* 6:662). The problem with the whole tradition, however, is that it largely rests on supposed autobiographical and political allusions and parallels in the poem. Thus, William Hayley in 1796 concludes that *SA* "probably flowed from the heart of the indignant poet soon after his spirit had been wounded by the calamitous destiny of his friends, to which he alludes with so much energy and pathos" (*Life* 167–68; Todd 5:350). Charles Dunster (in Todd 5:350) and A. J. Church (viii–x) argue on narrower biographical grounds that the poem was composed between 14 June 1662 and 24 February 1663, these being the respective dates of the execution of Henry Vane (likely to upset and depress Milton) and of Milton's third marriage (preceded by domestic unhappiness like Samson's). The inferential shakiness and unwarranted specificity of such claims are easily exposed by John Aubrey's account (Darbishire, *Early Lives* 13), as told to him by Edward Phillips, that it was at this very time that *PL* was brought to completion ("finished about 3 yeares after the K[ing]'s Restaurac[i]on"): how, one wonders, would the epic be tied down to such events? But a larger objection exists, at which Parker hints ("Date" 154): it is a deeply flawed procedure in which *SA* is interpreted as evidence of Milton's thoughts and feelings after the Restoration, and such thoughts and feelings are, in turn, interpreted as evidence of the poem's post-Restoration date.

This would, however, disqualify the use of such a procedure to arrive at an earlier dating, too, and Parker's flirtations with trying it out show him at his weakest ("Date" 152–53, 160–63). The "deep personal conviction" he finds significant in *SA* can be found in works written just before, during, and after the Restoration (Sirluck 777). And the fact that there is a similarity of spirit between *SA* and the Psalms Milton versified in 1648 and 1653 does not guarantee any date for *SA* or render Psalm 88 and *SA* "an expression of deep personal woe": as Ants Oras contends, "the spirit of the psalms...is of the kind that may have recurred to him during any part of his later years" (*Blank Verse* 4). George Muldrow points out that the theme of God's unexpected return to aid and to bear witness to his own, though present in the first group of Milton's paraphrases of the Psalms, is in fact absent from the second (244–45). Nor is it the case, despite Parker's instincts, that Milton could not late in his career have chosen to write a prophetic work any more than a didactic one — or even a work at once prophetic and didactic. And the eloquence and harrowing conviction of Samson's speeches on blindness do not, as Parker believes, have to derive from "newly-met reality": "the feeling behind them is powerful but it is transmuted into great art, much like the treatment of the same experience in the exordium to *PL* III" (Oras, *Blank Verse* 5). A further criticism of Parker ("Date" 156–57) is that Milton's contemplation in *RCG* (1642) of the possibility (no more) of writing a tragedy, and titles and sketches for plays and a brief mention of Samson in the Trinity Manuscript (Parker, "Trinity Manuscript" 225–32), do not constitute evidence of his working on *SA* during the 1645–48 period when he was free from pamphleteering: as Sirluck (778) points out, *Pro populo anglicano defensio* (*Def 1*), though it even mentions the incomplete *The History of Britain* (*HistBr*) as well as published works, makes no mention of *SA*. And when Parker alleges that the style and characterization of *SA* indicate that "its composition was several times interrupted" ("Date" 159), he needs to present evidence.

A. S. P. Woodhouse's suggestion that *SA* was composed between May 1660 and May 1661 cannot avoid the autobiographical approach, however much he disavows it ("*Samson Agonistes*"). He draws parallels between Samson's career and Milton's (169–70), and claims that the poem reflects "a state of depression not very difficult to imagine in the poet whose world had collapsed around him and who was blind, disillusioned, ill, and essentially alone. Such must have been the prevailing mood of 1660–1" (170–71). He then goes on to propose that, through Dalila, Milton is reflecting back on his first marriage to Mary Powell, which "left a permanent scar" (172). So in one case the poem reflects a contemporary mood of a specific time, but in another it can be made to reflect experience from long ago. But why does the composition date have to reflect immediate experience in one case but not in another? On such grounds might one not suggest a date around the time when the first marriage had (temporarily) gone wrong? Woodhouse interprets Samson's confession of error and sin — for which it is difficult to find a biographical parallel — as symptomatic of the poet's "state of depression"; and though he admits that "there can be no direct external evidence in support of this hypothesis," he still finds it difficult to avoid the impression that "to Milton's introspective and retrospective gaze error and humiliation have somehow taken on the colouring of sin" (170–72). Somehow, then, but there is no knowing how, or even if.

Allan H. Gilbert's attempt in "Is *Samson Agonistes* Unfinished?" to locate the poem in the early 1640s has not proved convincing. Gilbert alleges that there are discrepancies between the Argument and the events of the poem; that Dalila and Harapha are comic characters who do not fit in with Milton's condemnation in the prefatory note of the practice of mixing comedy and tragedy; that Samson's visitors are abruptly introduced; and that there is much idle repetition of word, image, and idea. These are, for Gilbert, symptoms of a general lack of care, and warrant for the hypothesis that Milton revived, but did not revise, an early work for publication in 1671. Sirluck (780–81) readily counters: there are no discrepancies; Dalila and Harapha are not comic; printed errata such as "Page 16. verse 127. for Irresistable, r. *Irresistible*" (Patterson, *Works* 1:2:605) do not square with a lack of care or failure to revise; and it is inconceivable that Milton did not publish in 1645, or mention in 1654, a *SA* that he thought good enough to publish without revision in 1671. In addition, it can be argued that the abrupt introduction of Samson's visitors as they "break in upon him" (*SA* 116) accords perfectly with his blindness, and that such repetition as there is serves many rhetorical purposes, not least the dramatization of Samson's vexed obsession with his failure.

Several attempts have been made to date *SA* according to stylistic criteria. Parker argues that the use of rhyme in one-eleventh (154 lines) of the poem cannot be reconciled with Milton's attack on rhyme in the 1668 headnote to *PL,* and that Milton, when writing *SA*, could therefore not have felt about rhyme as he did in 1668 ("Date" 147–49). Accordingly, Parker rules out the years immediately before or after 1668 as a composition date for *SA*. In this, he is curiously narrow: the publication in 1671 of a poem containing so much rhyme would still be flagrantly at odds with the 1668 headnote, as would the publication of a second edition of Milton's (pervasively or intermittently rhymed) earlier poems in 1673.

The fact that Sirluck, building on John Diekhoff's 1934 article "Rhyme in *Paradise Lost,*" can affirm that there are "well over four hundred line-end rhymes close enough together to be picked up by ear, and a very large number of caesural rhymes" (777) urges more careful attention to the 1668 headnote than it customarily receives. In it, Milton claims that rhyme is "no necessary Adjunct or true Ornament of Poem or good Verse, in longer Works especially, but the Invention of a barbarous Age, to set off wretched matter and lame meeter"; he argues that "the jingling sound of like endings" is "as a thing of it self" not the source of "true musical delight," "which consists only in apt Numbers, fit quantity of Syllables, and the sense variously drawn out from one Verse into another"; he alleges that some modern poets, carried away by the custom of rhyming, have experienced "vexation, hindrance, and constraint to express many things otherwise, and for the most part worse then else they would have exprest them"; and he champions "ancient liberty recover'd to Heroic Poem from the troublesom and modern bondage of Rimeing" (Patterson, *Works* 2:1:6). The emphasis is on rhyming as customary, dysfunctional, and, above all, constraining: a fad that curbs expression and is, in any case, not the principal resource of truly musical verse. It is not the case that his remarks constitute "a more eloquent protest than he would have allowed on more sober reflection" (Beum 177): Milton is not opposed to rhyme *tout court,* and his position is not inconsistent with the use of rhyme in *SA* after the Restoration any more than in his poems published before it or reissued after it. Instead, therefore, of taking rhyme as evidence for a composition date, it would be more profitable to consider the poetic uses to which it is put, in *SA* as elsewhere. Robert Beum, for instance, suggests that Milton uses rhyme in *SA* "to heighten the force of passionate or sententious utterances" (178), and he notes that in the speeches of the Chorus, where most rhymes are (178–79), it "marks the symbolic, the interpretive, as distinguished from the dramatic, presence of the chorus. It gives the chorus, in that role, a superior language: more mnemonic, more incantatory—in short, a stronger and more evocative language, just the sort of discourse suited to gnomic, interpretative, rather than participant, voices" (180). Beum is right to concede that he is not making a hard-and-fast distinction (181): the Chorus can be at once a participatory dramatic presence and an interpreter of the action, and its range of tone and effect is greater than he suggests. But Beum is at least thinking about tone and effect rather than about composition date.

Oras attempts to support the traditional composition date by conducting a statistical analysis of the blank verse of *Comus, PL, PR,* and *SA* ("Milton's Blank Verse"). Unfortunately, as John Carey (Carey and Fowler, *Poems* 332) affirms, "much of his evidence goes against it (e.g., the relative percentages of terminal and medial strong pauses are exactly the same in *Comus* and *SA;* the percentage of run-on lines in *SA* is nearer to that in *Comus* than to that in *PL* or *PR;* the relative percentages of feminine and masculine pauses in *SA* are nearer to those in *Comus* than to those in *PL* or *PR;* the frequency of feminine line-endings in *SA* is nearer to that in *Comus* than to that in *PL* or *PR*)." To which it might be added that among Oras's statistics for the distribution of polysyllables over the verse line, the difference between *Comus* and *SA* is, by his own admission, exceeded by that between individual books of *PL* ("Milton's Blank Verse" 154–55). And, similarly, his figures for pyrrhic verse endings (181) are 127.5 per 1,000 lines in *Comus* and 51.6 in *SA,* but 53.9 for *PL* 1, 49.3 for *PL* 8, 27.8 for *PL* 9, 46.2 for *PL* 10, 31.9 for *PR* 1, and 78.1 for *PR* 2. How can conclusions about chronology possibly be drawn from such data?

John T. Shawcross ("Chronology") modifies Oras's data and draws the conclusion that both *SA* and *PR* (with the possible exception of book 1) predate *PL*. The study is so thoroughly statistical that it is difficult to see how it could stand up without hypotheses of the kind advanced by Parker and Gilbert. Like Oras, Shawcross does not counter the objection to dating according to statistical criteria that Parker voices ("Date" 155): that it fails to take into proper account the influence of decorum or genre. Oras, who at least attempts an answer, manages only a feeble one: certain aspects of Milton's style would, he says, "appear to be too deep-seated" to be influenced by decorum and are therefore "likely to have survived" ("Milton's Blank Verse" 129). This prompts another objection to Oras and Shawcross: that they are bound to assume that an author's style will manifest a clear, usually linear development, irrespective of the aesthetic requirements of whole individual works or of structures within them. Oras, for instance, finds clusters of pyrrhic verse endings in certain passages of *PL* and in Dalila's speeches (185, 189) but seems unwilling to concede that it is artistic design (rather than some mysteriously independent instinct in Milton, or something that he could not help) that determines the stylistic distribution. In his later study, *Blank Verse and Chronology in Milton,* Oras criticizes Shawcross for failing adequately to relate form to meaning (38, 39). But his own practice is to stick closely to the generalities and approximations of his statistics; and though he expands his earlier findings, he adheres to the same assumptions and draws the same conclusion, that "the old chronology in its main outlines seems unassailable" (40). Parker, who believes that "most stylistic tests" are "largely inconclusive" ("Date" 155), astonishingly also believes that metrical experiments in *SA* and in the Latin poem *Rous* suggest a date of 1647 (156): but this would be so only if Milton were incapable of metrical experimentation at different times; which is, in Milton's case especially, absurd. And this applies also to Shawcross's contention that a similarity between prosodic experiments in Milton's translation of Horace's fifth ode (*Hor*) and *SA* "implies a closeness of composition date" ("Prosody" 88). Implies? "What, precisely, can a comparison of the metrics of poems in different languages prove?" (Sirluck 777).

Muldrow (240–62) tentatively suggests a date after 1661, when revisions were made to *De doctrina Christiana* (*DocCh*) through amanuensis "N" that show that "Milton would have had to battle within himself to renew his faith just as Samson does" (255). But this can hardly establish the date of *SA,* which could stand in anticipatory, contemporary, or retrospective relation to Milton's revisions. Back to Edward Phillips: "It cannot certainly be concluded."

PUBLICATION AND TEXT

No manuscript of *SA* survives. Francis Atterbury, in his letter of 15 June 1722 to Alexander Pope, mentions one belonging to the printer Jacob Tonson, but no one records having seen it. *SA* was licensed for publication by Thomas Tomkyns on 2 July 1670, but it was not entered in the Stationers' Register until 10 September 1670 and not published, jointly with *PR*, until at least late 1670. The volume was advertised in the Michaelmas Term catalog for 1670, and the date on all copies of the first edition is 1671. The reason for the delay in publication is not known. Possibilities (all speculative) include the slowness of the blind Milton's superintending proof correction of the 528 pages of the two poems and *HistBr* (1670) taken together, illness, and revisions to the texts. *SA* was printed for John Starkey, the bookseller who also published the second edition in 1680. The printer was "J. M.," identifiable as John Macocke, owner of one of the largest print shops in London, who also printed *HistBr*. Lines 1526–39 were omitted but printed as *Omissa* on page 101, there were ten errata printed on the unnumbered page 103 (but they did not include *sent* for *scent* in *SA* 720), and the speech prefix for Samson was given variously as *Sa.*, *Sam.*, and *Sams.* The principal textual authority for *SA* is the first edition with the *Errata,* but it is a far from reliable authority. Harris Francis Fletcher's collation of sixty copies (*Complete Poetical Works* vol. 4) reveals twenty-two corrections made during the printing process, only a few of which are of editorial interest. Carey (Carey and Fowler, *Poems* 332) notes eight differences in the states of the first edition and, in every case, corrects the first state, which contains clear errors (indentation of line 306, a full stop after *pure* in 548, a semicolon and a full stop for a question mark in 1093 and 1337 respectively), and what seem to be missing commas (after *nothing* in 1033, *Gath* in 1078, *encounters* in 1086, and *feats* in 1340). Parker ("Notes") observes that the 1671 text omits some of Milton's known or supposed spelling preferences, which are reinstated, but with different results, in the editions by Helen Darbishire (*Poetical Works*) and B. A. Wright (*John Milton*); that there are internal spelling inconsistencies, which may be attributed to the use of several amanuenses for the manuscript sent to the printer or to the printer's compositor; that capitalization is inconsistent throughout; and that there are errors in punctuation. However, he also notes:

> Despite all the carelessness and confusion suggested by the foregoing observations, it should not be overlooked that the 1671 text contains a number of examples of what students have come to recognize as distinctively "Miltonic" spellings. For most of these the compositor could not have been solely responsible; they are present because

the compositor was working with a manuscript that was either written by persons aware of *some* of the poet's orthographical preferences, or partly in the handwriting of the poet himself. (697)

Sources, Models, and Analogues

Only general influences are considered here. Milton's mind was famously well stocked with literature, and details such as phraseology came readily to him. The more particular influences are documented in Stephen Dobranski's annotations.

Judges

Milton's principal source is the account of Samson in chapters 13–16 of Judges. Parker (*Milton's Debt* 4) estimates that he uses "almost half" of the biblical material. He adds the visits to Samson of the Chorus, Manoa, Dalila, Harapha, and the Officer (9); he invents the Chorus, Harapha, the Officer, and the Messenger who relates the catastrophe; and he develops the characters of Manoa and Dalila. The possibility of paying a ransom for Samson is not presented in Judges, and may serve to make the Philistines seem more reasonable, to suggest an alternative to tragedy, and to constitute a misguided attempt to divert Samson from his mission. In *SA* 857–61, but not in Judges, a priest ever at her ear, of whom Milton would not have approved, encourages Dalila to betray Samson, making her seem more vulnerable to the pressure of "powerful arguments" (862). In Judges, Samson is not under any prohibition to reveal the secret of his strength, whereas in *SA* the disclosure constitutes a weak-minded betrayal of a secret entrusted to him by God. Such additions bring complexities suited to drama.

The omissions and substitutions in Milton's account are instructive. Some of them seem little more than details that could without much loss be discarded in any reworking of the story: God's sending water after the slaughter at Ramath-lechi, the number of people who visited Samson on the rock, or the number of Philistines on the temple roof. However, by omitting any reference to Judges 15:20 ("And he judged Israel in the days of the Philistines twenty years"), Milton is able to represent Samson's fall to Dalila as all the more sudden and devastating. Other omissions seem designed to focus attention more centrally and unwaveringly on Samson and his present plight (Parker, *Milton's Debt* 5): the substantial reduction of the accounts of his birth in Judges 13:4–23 and of the conduct of his first wife in Judges 14:16–17. By excising Samson's return to his unfaithful first wife, the giving of her to his companion, his setting fire to the tails of three hundred foxes, his patronizing of the harlot at Gaza, a detailed account of Dalila's three unsuccessful attempts on his strength, and the cause and form of his riddle at the feast and the trivial part played by his parents in the affair, Milton confers dignity appropriate to a tragic hero (Parker, *Milton's Debt* 6–8, 83). Similarly ennobling are the replacement of the lad with a vaguer guide to lead Samson to the temple pillars, and of his final prayer for vengeance with a silent prayer. Woodhouse finds Samson "remote indeed from the sanctified barbarian of the Book of Judges" ("*Samson Agonistes*" 162), and Chauncey B. Tinker concludes that, by removing "traces of barbarism, murder, and torture . . . as well as the foolish and ostentatious examples of the hero's eccentric and scoffing genius," Milton has made Samson, "as a result of the sufferings which he has endured, a person whom it is possible not only to pity but to admire and even love" (62). Not everyone has gone as far as admiration and love, as will be seen, but there is general agreement that Milton's modifications of his source materials take the reader in that direction.

Job

Milton's familiarity with the book of Job is beyond question. In *RCG* he views it as a "brief model" of the "Epick form" (Patterson, *Works* 3:1:237), and in *PR* Job is referred to six times by name. In *SA*, James Holly Hanford ("*Samson Agonistes*" 173–74) notes "marked similarities" to the book of Job "throughout the dialogue": Samson and Job are both "loyal to the truth and . . . maintain their positions against the apparent facts"; the Chorus and Manoa resemble Job's visiting friends who "sharpen Job's agony by their mistaken comfort"; Samson's resistance to the shaking of his convictions parallels Job's "passionate denial of the imputation of unrighteousness"; and, finally, the constancy of both is rewarded by a manifestation of divine approval. Geoffrey Bullough and Margaret Bullough agree that the book of Job "probably suggested" the "stream of visitors" in *SA*, though they find a closer influence in some of the choral odes (48, 52). To this may be added John M. Steadman's view that, "Like Job, Milton's protagonist is a hero of faith, whose patience and constancy are tried and perfected in suffering" ("Tragic Glass" 113), as well as the fact that the thoughts of both of them at various times turn toward death (Job 6:9, 11; 7:15–16; 10:20–21; *SA* 575–76, 598, 629–30, 649–51).

Against such possible influence must be set marked differences. Job is "perfect and upright" and "sinned not" (Job 1:1, 22), whereas Samson's awareness of his misdemeanors and follies smites him again and again with remorse and anger. The principal difference between the two works lies, however, in their conclusions: Job is rewarded materially with "twice as much as he had before" and dies "being old and full of days" (42:10, 17), whereas Samson kills himself and the Philistines. Much of the book of Job is tragic, as Murray Roston contends (165); but, as he readily concedes, its ending is not tragic.

Greek Tragedy

John Payne Collier reported that Samuel Taylor Coleridge thought *SA* "the finest imitation of the ancient Greek drama that ever had been, or ever would be written" (qtd. in Brinkley, *Coleridge* 606; Wittreich 195–96). Parker's *Milton's Debt to Greek Tragedy in* Samson Agonistes (1937), which drew upon several of his earlier articles, is the all-but-comprehensive authority on the subject: a stunned Carey (*John Milton* 150) remarks that the book "pummels its chosen aspect into complete submission." Parker's thesis is directed at the claim made in a paper by Sir Richard Jebb read posthumously to the British Academy in 1908: that though *SA* "may fairly be called classical both in language and in structure," "neither as poem nor as drama is it Hellenic" (341, 348). Rather, Jebb announced, the spirit of the poem "is the spirit of Hebraism" (344). He was not without followers, each of whom made his own individual emphases (principally, Elbert N. S. Thompson 148; Baum 365–71; Curry 350; Stoll 226, 232–33). Jebb's main contention is that "Hellenism contrasts man with fate. Hebraism contrasts God and His servants with idols and their servants" (345), so that whereas "Samson in his death triumphs over the Philistines; Herakles in his last agony is the victim of fate" (346).

Parker's counterarguments in *Milton's Debt to Greek Tragedy* are powerful. He contends that labels such as *Hebraic* and *Hellenic* (or *Puritan*) are vague, and may either fail to discriminate or be applied undiscriminatingly: "there are also 'Hebraic' and 'Puritan' features in Aeschylus," he remarks mischievously (193), before going on to demonstrate that, in its incorporation of the idea of unmerited suffering, *SA* is "more like the 'Hellenic' Sophocles than the 'Hebraic' Aeschylus" (218). Spirit, another vague term, cannot be pinned down to "a specific belief at all" (193). Parker draws a valuable distinction between "the tone or temper [of a work] resulting from certain animating or controlling *artistic* principles" and what may result from "dominant ideas *other than artistic*" (194). Milton, he then maintains, is not concerned with ideas so much as with the impression made by them (197), and *SA* and Greek tragedy are alike serious, thoughtful, didactic, religious, and, in their elevation of the spirits, sublime. Parker's case is at its most convincing when he presents evidence in *SA* of what Arthur Haigh in *The Tragic Drama of the Greeks* (323) had highlighted in Greek tragedy as the "pervading sense of the dark mystery of existence" and the "wistful craving for knowledge concerning the ways of providence, and the destiny of mankind": Samson's repeated probing of such matters (*SA* 23–29, 30–36, 44–46, 83–85, 90–97, 205–9, 521–22, 562–65, 606–15, 633–51); the choral ode beginning "Many are the sayings of the wise" (652), "as dark an interrogation of divine justice as anything Greek tragedy can offer" (Parker, *Milton's Debt* 203); the fact that God remains not only "th' interminable" but also "th' unsearchable" (*SA* 307, 1746); and that, significantly, the question of whether Samson's punishment was "Too grievous for the trespass" (691, 430–31) remains unanswered. As for "Fate," it is "a mysterious divine decree, to both Milton and the Greeks" (217).

Parker (*Milton's Debt* 168–76, 177–85) cites two Greek tragedies as particular sources for *SA:* Sophocles' *Oedipus at Coloneus* and, to a lesser extent, Aeschylus's *Prometheus Bound.* His insights into the former far surpass those of P. H. Epps and Wilmon Brewer, and into the latter those of J. P. Mahaffy (49), Frank L. Lucas (116), and Brewer. The parallels with *Oedipus at Coloneus* are so striking that Parker suspects "a certain amount of conscious imitation" on Milton's part (168). There are similarities in length and proportion, dramatis personae, unity of action, sequence of events, dramatic incident, sentiment, and prevailing tone, and both plays focus centrally on a "long-suffering hero" who is blind, helpless, and pathetic, and who finds at last "a not inglorious death" (168). The influence of *Prometheus Bound* is largely to be detected in the slightness of the action, the plot as a series of visits, and the central figure of the lamenting hero, though there are also details such as the hero in each play suspecting that the Chorus has come to gaze at his affliction (*SA* 112–13; *Prometheus Bound* 118). Parker stresses that the influence of these two plays does not necessarily constitute "the whole — or even the greater part — of Milton's 'best example'" (185), but rather that Milton's debt to Greek tragedy is altogether more miscellaneous.

Taking his cue from Milton's Preface, where it is stated that "Division into Act and Scene referring chiefly to the Stage (to which this work never was intended) is here omitted" (Patterson, *Works* 1:2:333). Parker (*Milton's Debt* 17) provides a convincing outline of the formal structure of *SA* as a Greek tragedy: prologos (*SA* 1–114); parodos, or entrance song (115–75), 1 epeisodion, following the entry of the Chorus (176–292); 1 stasimon, or stationary song (293–325); 2 epeisodion (326–651); 2 stasimon (652–709); 3 epeisodion (710–1009); 3 stasimon (1010–60); 4 epeisodion (1061–1267); 4 stasimon (1268–99), 5 epeisodion (1300–1426); 5 stasimon (1427–40); and exodos, following the last stasimon (1441–1758), incorporating kommos, or dirge (1660–1758). J. B. Broadbent structures his commentary on these divisions (*Milton* 39–59). Parker (60–61) also highlights structural symmetry by dividing the work into five parts, nearly all of the same length: Samson alone and with the Chorus (*SA* 1–325), Samson and Manoa (326–709), Samson and Dalila (710–1060), Samson with the two instruments of force (1061–1440), and Samson at the feast (1441–1758). Jebb (341) had included the prologos and exodos with the first and fifth "acts" respectively, but whatever the precise divisions, such outlines give a strong sense of the episodic sequence of arrivals and departures, the linear series of intense encounters, characteristic of *SA*.

P. W. Timberlake, whom Parker oddly ignores, highlights Euripidean influence in the litigious element, in the sententiousness, and in the role of the Messenger in heightening suspense, and he also records numerous verbal similarities. J. C. Maxwell concedes a structural influence of *Prometheus Bound* on *SA* but finds a dearth of convincing verbal parallels ("Milton's Knowledge" 366–71). He notes, however, that in *SA* 1388–89 — "This day will be remarkable in my life / By some great act, or of my days the last" — "Milton has taken the idea of alternative destinies, and given it the same sort of irony as attaches to the prophecy of 'release from toils' [*Women of Trachis* 79–81] in Heracles' speech, by making them not really alternative but complementary" ("Milton's Samson" 91).

Dubia

In chapter 8 of book 5 of *Antiquities of the Jews,* Josephus retains much of what Milton removes from the Judges account of Samson. In other respects, too, he proves an implausible influence on *SA*. He improvises a comic Manoa who is madly attracted to his beautiful wife and therefore jealous of the angel who announces the birth of Samson to her; he has Samson divorce the woman of Timna; Dalila, not the woman of Gaza, is a harlot; and Samson's hair is shorn while he is "disordered in drink and asleep" (Hone 75). Josephus's possible significance in relation to *SA* lies in his attempt — difficult to reconcile with what he retains — to ennoble Samson by stressing his "magnanimity at his death" and his "extraordinary virtue" (Hone 76). But this is in line with the only other biblical mention of Samson outside of Judges, Hebrews 11:32–35, where he is numbered among the heroes of faith who accomplished great things.

The case for Italian influence may gain credibility from the fact that Milton in his Preface on tragedy twice mentions the Italians, in each case in relation to the introduction of the Chorus and as a modern example of ancient practice still extant. But the specific influence of Italian neoclassical tragedy is all but erased by the fact that *SA* demonstrably shares with the Italians a common cultural heritage from ancient Greece.

In 1885, George Edmundson boldly developed the identification of *Samson, of de Heilige Wraek* (1660) by Joost van den Vondel as the "literary parent" of *SA,* puffing his case as "indisputable" and "practically unassailable" (15, 190), and ingeniously promoting its credibility by rendering passages from Vondel into Miltonic blank verse. A. W. Verity (158–68) duly disputed and assailed it on the grounds that, as there is no external evidence that Milton studied Vondel, and as both poets independently chose Greek models, Edmundson's parallels merely show that "writers who treat the same theme in much the same style are sure to meet in periodic points of similarity" (168). Postmortem examinations of Edmundson are conducted by Martin W. Sampson (279), Elbert N. S. Thompson (172–73), Herbert Grierson ("Note" 55–63; *Milton* 141), and Watson Kirkconnell (178–80).

George Wesley Whiting (*Milton's Literary Milieu*) alleges Milton's "indebtedness" to Francis Quarles's "elaborate, uninspired, and pious" *Historie of Samson* (1631), but warns the reader that the "startling parallelism of thought" is often "disguised" by "the great contrast in style" (253, 256–57). However, F. Michael Krouse's *Milton's Samson and the Christian Tradition* makes it clear that Whiting is merely adducing commonplaces. Bullough and Bullough, in their edition of *Milton's Dramatic Poems* (49), suggest that Quarles's "Meditation 22" is "in similar strain" to Milton's parodos (*SA* 115–75), but, once again, Quarles's pedestrianism is no precursor of the responsive flexibility of Milton's verse.

A debt to Shakespeare is much exaggerated by George Coffin Taylor, and Alwin Thaler also amasses alleged parallels and verbal echoes ("Shakespearian Element"; "Shakespeare and Milton"). Only a very few are close enough in phrasing to suggest that Milton may have remembered Shakespeare's words, and the evidence, taken as a whole, does not indicate the notable influence of any particular Shakespeare play, plot, scene, character, or theme. Such influence as exists is dispersed and limited to phraseology.

Characters

Chorus

The Chorus plays a prominent part in *SA*. Parker (*Milton's Debt* 139) notes that it is given about 27 percent of the 1,758 lines of the play, and that 18 percent comprises choral odes. Only two plays by Euripides (*Rhesus* and *Hercules Furens*), he notes, and none by Sophocles, devote more lines to the Chorus, whereas in each of the tragedies of Aeschylus except *Prometheus* the Chorus is given more than 40 percent of the lines (139–40). The proportion in *SA,* he estimates, is closest to that in Euripides' *Hercules Furens* and *Alcestis* (140). However, Milton follows "the general practice of the Attic tragedians" (142) in the length of the choral odes, in keeping the Chorus on stage, and in giving the Chorus the last word in the drama; and for his choice of a male Chorus there is a precedent in eleven Greek tragedies (143). Milton's Chorus "owes something to all three of the great tragedians" (150), but his inclusion of "ten speeches of the Chorus between five and ten lines in length" is a practice "extremely rare" in Greek tragedy (140). While identifying an Aeschylean precedent for the lengthy conversations with the protagonist (150), Parker views the function of the Chorus in *SA* as distinctly Sophoclean (145): it is excluded from any important share in the action, apart from playing a slight part in Samson's development; it ignores its own personal fortunes and directs attention to the words of the protagonist (145–46); and it is genuinely relevant to the drama, and truly belongs in the play (148–49).

The Argument describes the Chorus as "certain friends and equals" of Samson's tribe (Patterson, *Works* 1:2:334), and the Chorus announces itself as his "friends and neighbours" (*SA* 180). Both Manoa (332) and Samson (1413, 1445) address it as "brethren." The Chorus refers to itself both in the first-person singular and first-person plural, sometimes alternating fluently, and with no great sense of significance, between the two (116, 124, 151, 170, 178–83, 215). The plural form is often symptomatic of an impulse to generalize impersonally about humankind (309, 554, 667, 1745); but sometimes it may refer to Israel (309, 667), sometimes specifically to the Chorus and Manoa (1522–26, 1539–40). Thus, the Chorus is given the illusion of individuality and subjectivity while giving voice to a consciousness by turns philosophical, national, and social.

The Chorus performs several functions, acting as "impersonal mouthpiece of some of the general moral ideas in the play" (Daiches 238); "following almost always a step behind" and playing "a kind of descant on the central problems" (MacCaffrey xxxiv); and "interpreting the emotions appropriate to the successive moments in the action, . . . clarifying the larger significance of the whole, and . . . rounding out the story by allusions to Samson's past" (Hanford, *Handbook* 236).

One primary function of the Chorus in relation to Samson is identified in the Argument: they "seek to comfort him what they can" (Patterson, *Works* 1:2:334). This at once suggests the difficulty of comforting Samson but also some deficiency in the Chorus's ability; it suggests limitations as well as limits. Parker (*Milton's*

Debt 147–48) observes that though the Chorus is largely a "sympathetic witness" capable of great kindness, and resembles its Greek prototype in "its piety, its readiness to sympathize with what is noble, its essential loyalty to its leaders, and its belief in moderation" (147–48), it is not without shortcomings: it is tactless, easily influenced, irresolute in opinion, and readily deceived, and it sees "no more clearly through the events of the drama than do any of the other characters" (147). Louis L. Martz equates poor verse with poor insight in the Chorus's speech at *SA* 277–89 and believes that the rhymes and partial rhymes in lines 300–14 "create an effect of something like triviality" (121). Other commentators have emphasized the Chorus's intermittent ineptitude. Arnold Stein (*Heroic Knowledge* 157) notes its "license to digress" and characterizes lines 541–46 as "a kind of musical-comedy aria on the theme of Samson's alcoholic abstinence." John Huntley also sees these lines as comic: "It is as though a man should finally see the blackness of his soul and cry out, 'I have betrayed my father for a whore.' Then his true friends cluster around to say, 'Well, don't worry; at least you never smoked or drank'" (138). More generally, Huntley judges that the Chorus is lacking in "admirable truths and emotions" and unable to perform "the classical functions of detached observation and trustworthy comment" (132). However, he notes that, toward the end of the play, "The Chorus gradually develop an understanding midway between Samson and Manoa in that the Chorus reintegrate themselves (as Manoa does not) with their newfound understanding of Samson and Israel's God" (143). On *SA* 210–18, Alan Rudrum (26) comments: "The reply of the Chorus is very human, embracing a Jewish commonplace (Don't call God into question); a universal cliché (Many wise men have been deceived by women); and something like vulgar curiosity (But why did you do it?)." Balachandra Rajan (135) finds the Chorus obtuse and inconsistent, particularly when it warns Samson not to tax "divine disposal" (when he has not in fact done so) and then proceeds to tax that disposal itself. Rudrum interprets the Chorus's speech at lines 237–40, beginning with balm and ending with gall, as "a perhaps unconscious invitation to Samson to despair completely" (29). Line 240, "Yet *Israel* still serves with all his Sons," E. M. W. Tillyard finds "sceptical" (*Milton* 287) and Hanford "somewhat malicious" (*Milton Handbook* 239). Rudrum comments on the Chorus's later speech on the necessity of female subjection (*SA* 1053–60), that it "is not merely twisting the knife in Samson's wound; for he has just demonstrated that he is not going to commit that error again" (50). And Franklin R. Baruch believes that when "shiftings of temporal reference mingle with fusions of material and spiritual image and connotation" in the Chorus's thinking, it demonstrates "both sympathetic feeling and poor understanding" (329).

The dramatic implications of the fact that the Chorus does not always share Samson's outlook have been remarked. Rajan notes that it is "neither spectator nor actor, standing somewhere in between them in detachment" (143). Martz believes that the impoverished speeches of the Chorus serve to offset Samson's heroic dignity and distinction from ordinary men, and he contrasts Samson's "grandeur of despair" and the "ordinary, commonplace musings of the chorus" in lines 633–51 and 667–76 (122, 125). Lines 1010–17 and 1025–60, also spoken by the Chorus, he judges to be "the feeblest lines and the weakest rhyming of the entire play" (129–30), and he suspects that the heavy rhyme in lines 1660–68 likewise suggests that the Chorus's view "is not to be taken as the whole truth" (132). Certainly, when the Chorus's view differs from Samson's, it dramatically clarifies or challenges, prompting new recognitions. It is important, then, that the Chorus be humanly fallible; that when David Daiches observes that all Samson's visitors "are tempters in one way or another" (236), the Chorus should be regarded as a visitor.

Manoa

The character and role of Manoa in *SA* are largely Milton's invention. In Judges, Manoa is named as Samson's father (his mother is not named). He is represented as being devout and practical-minded: he does not disbelieve the angel's prophecy of Samson's birth but is nevertheless careful to check it over. Manoa and his wife disappear after the episode with the woman of Timna and Samson's riddle of the honey in the carcass of the lion, which is before Samson meets Dalila. And though it is stated that Samson was buried "in the buryingplace of Manoah his father" (Judg. 16:31), it is not disclosed whether Manoa was even alive at the time of Samson's death.

In the absence of a developed biblical precedent, critics have looked elsewhere for sources and models. Parker (*Milton's Debt* 119–21) finds no close parallels in Greek tragedy, and the dearth undermines his assertion that Milton's treatment of the aged father owes a debt to Sophocles. Tillyard thinks that "Milton may well have had his own father in mind" (*Milton* 288), and Ernest Brennecke Jr. (x) agrees. But such surmise cannot establish influence, let alone illuminate it.

The two episodes involving Samson's father (*SA* 326–605, 1441–1744) occupy a substantial portion of Milton's poem and serve to establish Manoa as, in Don Cameron Allen's phrase, "probably Milton's broadest irony" ("Idea as

Pattern" 87). "His well meant attempts to alleviate the suffering of his son," Allen explains, "have invariably an effect of contrary intent," and, as a result of his imperfect comprehension of his son's destiny, his "love and devotion—emotions good in themselves—have the attributes of temptation" (87, 86). Rudrum comments that Samson "receives as an astringent what Manoah offers as balm" (33). His disillusionment with divine providence and his inclination to blame God for subjecting Samson to "foul indignities" (*SA* 350–72) prompt Samson to take responsibility for his past actions, blame himself, and feel that he deserves his punishment (373–419, 448–59, 488–501, 532–40). Acutely, Rudrum notes that, when Samson describes himself as "Sole Author" and "sole cause" (*SA* 376) of his woes, "he takes to himself two words which were often applied to God" (35). Manoa's kindly visit to his son paradoxically leaves him utterly despondent and longing for death (558–76, 606–51), "more despairing…than he was at the beginning" (Summers 160). The name *Manoa* in Hebrew (*manowach*) means "a home, a place of rest," and, albeit well meaningly, he in effect offers an active hero a temptation to idleness (Broadbent, *Milton* 46; Barker 178; MacCaffrey xxxiv; Muldrow 187). Ever mindful of dignity and honor, be it Samson's (*SA* 372), his family's (446–47, 1717), or Israel's (440–43, 1714–15), Manoa is single-minded about paying a ransom (481–83, 601–4, 1457–71, 1476–80) and taking Samson home (516–20, 579–80, 1490–94); but, though motivated by a generous tenderness, his concerns and actions turn out to be wholly misguided. Ann Gossman finds him "limited in insight" but meaning only kindness, "human and plausible, practical, and reasonable as the world judges" ("Ransom" 11–12); Marcia K. Landy remarks on his "more customary way of regarding life" and his inability to "see the larger issues at stake" ("Character" 243); and Nancy Y. Hoffman notes the "finite quality" of his mind, "forever reaching, never apprehending, forever stating truths not understood" (197). Rajan's witty comment that he has a "talent for changing the subject" (137) catches the unwitting obtuseness exactly. The only "ransom" (*SA* 1572–73) is paid by death: Samson will be taken home dead to his father's house (1733), and it is in death that he acquits himself with honor that Manoa regards as being at once personal, familial, and national (1709–17). Manoa's joy turns out to be not what he anticipated should he secure Samson's freedom (1505), but joy at the slaughter of the Philistines (1531, 1564). Though he has hopes that God will restore Samson's sight and strength to some purpose or other (581–89, 1495–1503), and he agrees with Samson that God will triumph over Dagon (461–78), Manoa cannot foresee Samson's involvement: "But for thee what shall be done?" (478) is, by hindsight, the most powerful (and poignant) moment of blind solicitude. His questions when Samson pulls down the temple, "O what noise! / Mercy of Heav'n what hideous noise was that!" (1508–9), mark the supremely ironic moment for Manoa. Martin Mueller ("*Pathos*" 248) argues that the whole scene constitutes "a little complex tragedy with Manoa as the tragic hero, Samson's death as the *pathos,* and the messenger's arrival as the *peripeteia* through *anagnorisis,*" and that Manoa ultimately experiences catharsis (247). Mueller's case for tragedy founders with Manoa's distinctly untragic joy, however, and he readily concedes that Manoa's is "not a real tragedy" (251). Manoa's teeming questions (*SA* 1520, 1579, 1580–81, 1583, 1584, 1584–86) emphatically set him apart from Samson's tragic destiny, and it remains for him only to carry out the arrangements for his son's funeral and commemoration.

The poem is kinder to Manoa than some critics have been. The fullness of Milton's portrayal has not seemed full enough for some: Tillyard, for instance, takes the view that Manoa announces "with a certain satisfaction" that Samson will have to appear at the feast of Dagon, that he "hopes to make more important" his offers of mediation with the Philistines, and that he succeeds in depressing Samson "beyond his expectations" (*Milton* 288). In a similar vein, Daiches (238), echoed by Nicolson (359), believes that Manoa "comes to rub salt into his son's wound, though of course not intentionally," and that he reminds his son of his original fault "almost smugly" (240). Such novelistic improvisations invent a derogatory psychology that is not explicitly there in Milton's poem.

Manoa is not blamed in the poem. He may have his faults: "a full human share of pride and resentment" (Stein, *Heroic Knowledge* 160); "a platitudinous obviousness" and a tendency to overemphasize his own misfortune (Rudrum 33, 36); a "talkative insensitivity" (Rajan 131). But though "he is not heroic or tragic," "he is not corrupt" (Stein, *Heroic Knowledge* 161), and his hopes, though mistaken, are not ignoble (Rudrum 61). Even his "silly illusions" are "reasonable and justified in the world he lives in" (Mueller, "*Pathos*" 250). Rajan (131) notes fairly that he is not alone in his shortcomings. Stein identifies Manoa's as "the most human voice" in the drama (*Heroic Knowledge* 148), and Hoffman views him as "the human parallel, at times the human antithesis, always the human continuum, of the more distant, mythic Samson" (195).

Dalila

Compared to Judges, Milton's account assigns Dalila an altogether more significant role. In Judges 16:4 she is merely a woman Samson loved; in *SA* she is his wife (*SA* 227). (This despite the fact that the Chorus calls her "unchaste" [321], that Samson in anger calls her a "concubine" [537], and that in *PL* 9.1060 she is a harlot.) Further, whereas in Judges 16.19 "she called for a man" to shave Samson's head, in *SA* she cuts off his hair herself (537–40). Of all the figures in the poem, she is perhaps the most puzzling. Her very appearance is something of a surprise, and not only to Samson: she pays a visit neither in Judges, where she disappears from the narrative after the betrayal, nor in Christian tradition. Parker, noting that Clytemnestra, Deianira, and others had deceived their husbands, looks, as always, to Greek tragedy for a precedent (*Milton's Debt* 125). He finds Dalila's characterization Euripidean (126), and notes a striking parallel to her visit in the *Troades* 895–1059, where Helen, who had deceived Menelaus and profaned their marriage, comes before her husband in finery bought with Trojan gold (1023) and attempts to justify herself. In the debate that ensues, she pleads a patriotic and a religious excuse (930–37, 941–50), tries to anticipate her husband's objections, and concludes by asking for pardon. Hecuba's reply, with which the wronged husband later agrees, is much like Samson's: her excuses are slander; what she really wanted was the Trojan gold and glory. Menelaus, regarded by all Greece as "effeminate" (1035), refuses to forgive her (Parker, *Milton's Debt* 126–28). Crucially, however, what could not have been influenced by the Euripidean episode, and what therefore weakens Parker's case, is the reason for Dalila's visit or any motivation she may have had. In the *Troades,* Helen is a captive, like Samson; she confronts her husband after the successful siege of Troy; and her lust had been for Paris, not for the man she betrayed.

Dalila in Milton's poem is a more enigmatic figure than she is in Christian tradition, where she was "well known from poem, broadside and sermon as a deceitful, a treacherous, a dangerously clever sort of woman, skillful in blandishment and importunity" (Krouse 102). Samson himself treats her very much in the spirit of this tradition, showing no sympathy or compassion, and appearing not to believe a word she says. He thinks she has come through malice (*SA* 821), to trap, betray, humiliate and enslave him again (931, 946–48). He berates her as the typical false woman (748–65), too weak to resist gold (830–31), out to satisfy her "lust" (836–37), and eager to please the Philistine gods (896). To him, she is a "Hyæna," a "poysnous bosom snake," a "viper" (748, 763, 1001); and he has had to learn enough of "Adders wisdom" to protect himself against her "sorceries" (936–37). She is also a "sorceress" with a "fair enchanted cup, and warbling charms" (819, 934). (Steadman relates her to the temptresses of Odysseus as Renaissance mythographers had conceived them ["Dalila" 560–65; *Milton* 74, 133].) Dalila, with some justice, concludes that Samson is "implacable" (960). His final explanation of her visit is: "God sent her to debase me, / And aggravate my folly" (999–1000). However, though he thinks she has sought forgiveness so that she might again transgress (758), and though he says he will no more forgive her than forgive himself for his folly (825–27), he finally does forgive her (954).

The Chorus, prompted by the strength of Samson's emotions, registers something of Dalila's attractiveness. It may satirize her as a fully rigged ship (710–19, 1072), but it is also moved by her weeping "Like a fair flower surcharg'd with dew" (728). After her departure, it reflects Samson's imagery by pronouncing her "a manifest Serpent" (997), but it observes too that "beauty" has "strange power" "to regain / Love once possest, nor can be easily / Repuls't," and concludes that Samson must have felt the "secret sting of amorous remorse" in resisting her (1003–7). Even after the choral ode reflecting on the deficiencies of woman and the need for her to be curbed in marriage by man's God-given "despotic power" (1054), she remains "The sumptuous *Dalila*" with the "inchanting voice" (1072, 1065).

Some critics, picking up on the Chorus's satire, have regarded Dalila as being to some degree a comic figure (Gilbert, "Is *Samson Agonistes*" 100, "Milton's Defense" 68–69; Tinker 67; Stein, *Heroic Knowledge* 167, 168, 173, 177; Nash 28–29); others, like Samson, have taken her seriously and reacted vehemently to her. Unflinching opposition of the kind found in the Christian tradition begins in 1788 with William Mickle, who finds her insincere, boastful, and insulting, the very embodiment of "the unfaithful wife and female tyrant" (401–6; Shawcross, *Critical Heritage* 344–49, especially 346 and 349). This becomes a marked trend in nineteenth-century criticism, and particularly in school editions of the poem, where Dalila is routinely accused or dismissed: Verity, for instance, finds in her nothing but "hardened, heartless unrepentance" and "moral callousness," and concludes that "Milton, no lover of women, puts his best work and strongest feelings into the picture" (lv–lvii). Wildest of all is John Churton Collins, who surpasses Samson and calls her a "syren-tigress" (7).

Such views give too little account of, and take too little into account, Milton's dramatic representation. Dalila can hardly speak for weeping (*SA* 727–31); she affirms that "conjugal affection" has made her wish to see Samson and alleviate his suffering in whatever way she can (739–45), and she eventually offers to intercede with the Philistine lords so that she can take him home to care for him (917–27); she admits that she misjudged the outcome of her misdeed (736–37, 747), having been led to believe that the Philistines intended only "safe custody, and hold" (802), and contends, plausibly enough, that she was "Adjur'd by all the bonds of civil Duty / And of Religion" to "entrap / A common enemy, who had destroy'd / Such numbers of our Nation" (853–57); she professes contrition (732–39) and confesses to weakness, sexual jealousy, foolishness, rashness, and miscalculation (773–89, 790–810, 907–8). With some point, she maintains that Samson was weak too (781, 785–89, 843–44). Only when Samson has rejected her utterly does she decide not to humble herself to no avail, and to claim that her defamation among the Israelites will be countered by fame among her own people (960–94).

By attending to the complexities of the drama, the twentieth century has, on the whole, regarded Dalila more compassionately than the nineteenth did. J. Mac-millan Brown, the author of the first book-length study of the poem, *The* Samson Agonistes *of Milton* (1905), believes that Milton, albeit unconsciously, "is so eager to be impartial to her that he almost overstates her case," and that he gives her "perfectly valid" arguments and appeals, with the result that many readers are left with a "pitying if not sympathetic mood" toward her (60, 99, 97). James Waddell Tupper attributes to Milton a similar—though similarly unverifiable—unconscious impulse: "Milton tried to depict her as a hypocrite and just could not do so. He could not make her words betray her into actual insincerity" (382). Cleanth Brooks (*Complete Poetry* xvi), Daiches (241, 243, 244), and William Empson (*Milton's God* 224) do not think her a liar, and for Allen everything she says is "seriously spoken" and every speech except her last is "filled with verbal tones of contrition" ("Idea as Pattern" 88). Charles Mitchell (617) notes her repeated pleas for pardon. Empson, her strongest advocate, detects in her words a "cool sad dignity" and even a "generous-minded assurance of being in the right" (*Milton's God* 223, 220): "what ambitious or deceitful purpose could she have," he argues, "in offering to spend the rest of her life as nurse to a blind and (from her point of view) totally discredited husband?" (224). Allen ("Idea as Pattern" 90) and Carey (*John Milton* 142) agree. Landy notes her persistence, but judges her to be, like Manoa, "not inherently evil" but "a bundle of contradictions" ("Character" 244–46). Similarly sympathetic is Virginia R. Mollenkott, who maintains that, on a human level, "Samson's conduct is at least as reprehensible as Dalila's." Milton's portrayal of Dalila she regards as "unusually fair" because of his "sympathetic recognition of the complexity of being fallible" and his "unusually modern emphasis upon the partial validity of everybody's point of view" (98, 100, 102, 91).

Simply believing and admiring Dalila, like simply dismissing or vilifying her, diminishes the dramatic characterization. In the twentieth century, reactions to her have been mixed, mindful of her complexity rather than uniformly sympathetic.

Paull F. Baum finds her "rather subtly characterised," though his particular appreciation of subtlety is not free of misogyny: "At least, she is so much a woman as almost to leave us in doubt whether or no she is sincere. Perhaps she even deceived herself for a while" (360). Behind her wealth and finery Tillyard (*Milton* 290), Carey (*John Milton* 142), and Muldrow (191) catch the glint of the gold she took to betray Samson. Her love, however sincere it may be, has proved problematic: Daiches judges it to be "a dangerous kind of love," one that does not accord with Milton's ideal of marriage but rather with a tradition of courtly love (the man as prisoner) that Milton attacked elsewhere (241–42); Ernest S. Gohn accuses her of subverting the order of nature "by misconceiving sensual delight for true love" (265); while, for Isabel Gamble MacCaffrey, her love is "imprisoning and untrustworthy" (xxxiv). Carey (*John Milton* 142) and Rudrum (44) note that she makes excuses while insisting that she is without excuse (*SA* 734), though Carey also notes that Samson does the same.

Some critics remain firmly rooted in the nineteenth-century critical tradition. G. Wilson Knight oversimplifyingly sees *SA* as "one massive tirade against feminine wiles and guiles" ("Frozen Labyrinth" 81). Gilbert, while noting that Milton makes Dalila Samson's wife, finds that "her temperament, with its lust, avarice, and infidelity, is whorish enough" ("Milton's Defense" 68). W. B. C. Watkins finds her "too glib, full of too many explanations . . . transparently shallow" (144). Mary Ann Nevins Radzinowicz, tracing what she takes to be "the stages in Dalila's growth into a hard-hearted taunter" ("Eve" 168), ignores Samson's hard-heartedness altogether as well as the fact that only when Dalila finds that all else has failed to assuage Samson's implacable anger does she decide to part from him and enjoy her fame among her own people: as Mason Tung has argued (483), her last outburst is "understandable under the circumstances, and should not be used to infer that all her previous speeches were nothing but lies." Thomas Kranidas, though sensitive to the complex shifts in tone and attitude in her speeches, treats such shifts as calculated on her part and finally judges her to be "both strong and culpable" and therefore deserving of Samson's outraged responses (125). Hanford finds her approach "insidious," her plea "specious" (*Milton Handbook* 240), and, for Rajan, she merely "strikes many poses" (138). Muldrow, though he shows signs of sensing her complexity and mystery, is obliged to regard her as wholly wicked because he is rigidly committed to a process of repentance for Samson that requires her to represent the "departure from evil" stage (190). No one, however, goes so low as Logan Pearsall Smith, who draws the Rymerish moral from both *PL* and *SA* that "a husband must keep his wife in her proper place" (48). And never, never let her give you a haircut?

Dalila's motives in visiting Samson have been the focus of most critical attention. Nicolson takes the view that she is merely sent to report back to the Philistine lords, who are taking no chances before demanding Samson's attendance at their feast (365–66): this, however, does not begin to reflect on the significance of the length of her visit or attend to a word she says. Tillyard, Samson-like, is alone in thinking she returns out of cruelty and curiosity (*Milton* 290). Along with Woodhouse ("Tragic Effect" 453), George Williamson (94), and Stanley Fish (244), Carey (*John Milton* 142) finds her motives obscure, but he inclines toward thinking that possessiveness seems likeliest. Other motives attributed to her may be related to this or to each other: lechery (Allen, "Idea as Pattern" 88; Carey, *John Milton Poems* 142–43); "sincere but perverse love" (Daiches 244); simple selfishness (Broadbent, *Milton* 50); love of power (Stein, *Heroic Knowledge* 176–77; Nash 29; Landy, "Character" 246; Kranidas 136; Rudrum 48; Muldrow 200).

The range of interpretations of Dalila, and their attendant indeterminacies, should alert us to the quality of Milton's characterization that Max Beerbohm identified when, reviewing a theatrical performance in 1908, he singled out Dalila as "the one dramatically imagined person in the play" ("Agonising Samson" 528). Is it not characteristic of true drama to prompt questions that prove difficult to answer and speculations that do not resolve themselves into certainties?

Whatever the complexity of Dalila or the obscurity of her motives, the effects of her visit to Samson have been largely beyond dispute. Watkins finds Samson "purged of gloom and self-pity and despair" (146), and is thus in agreement with Broadbent's view that Samson moves out of the Slough of Despond (49). Samson is able at last to resist venereal love, and his "uxorious weakness…goes with Dalila's exit" (Allen "Idea as Pattern" 88, 90): with some effort, he rejects "the blandishments of a pretty woman, luxury, and lust," and when she leaves his nerves are "on edge but roused" (Tillyard, *Milton* 289, 290). For G. A. Wilkes, Samson's rejection of her, though seeming negative, has its positive side: "while Samson still does not know *what* he is to do, he at least knows that he is not to do what Dalila urges" (372). "She seems not to know that she actually creates in Samson the will to contest," comments Jon S. Lawry (380), mindful of the complexities and indirections of motivation and outcome. Only James Waddell Tupper goes against the critical consensus in feeling that the Dalila episode affects neither Samson's despondency nor the spiritual course of the drama (380–81, 384). Critics since Dr. Johnson have largely elaborated on his comment that Dalila's visit has the effect of "raising the Character of *Samson*" (*Rambler* 16 July 1751). Woodhouse, for instance, comments that the function of the Dalila episode "is to demonstrate by her powerlessness to reassert her sway the completeness of Samson's repentance" ("*Samson Agonistes*" 165).

Harapha

Harapha does not make an appearance in Judges, and he is, in that respect, Milton's invention. He is not, however, without precedent, and commentators have argued for influences from biblical, classical, and chivalric traditions. Steadman ("Milton's Harapha") relates him to another heavily armored Philistine giant, native of Gath, and enemy of Israel: his son Goliath (*SA* 1247–49), in 1 Samuel 17. He notes that Samson, like David, seems to be at a disadvantage in the encounter with the giant but, triumphantly, represents *fiducia in Deo* (trust in God) rather than *fiducia carnalis* (reliance on the flesh). In Harapha's longing to meet another famous warrior, Parker detects Greek influence, and in his language a specifically Euripidean quality: "the introduction of an insolent giant, the frank depiction of a noisy quarrel, the tendency to mix laconic insult with formal debate—these are all things which we expect from Euripides. There are bullies and blusterers in Aeschylus and Sophocles, of course; but surely the masking of cowardice with rhetoric is a trick...which we associate with Euripides alone" (*Milton's Debt* 123). Krouse sees a parallel between Harapha and Hercules' giant opponent Antaeus (130). For Gilbert, Harapha is rather the boastful knight of romance, "own brother to Spenser's Braggadocchio" ("*Samson Agonistes* 1096" 161), and for George R. Waggoner the encounter with Harapha is chivalric, revealing Milton's interest in single combat and dueling. Waggoner (85) and E. Wright (224) also note references to sieges, armor, lists, trophies, and laurels throughout *SA*.

Daniel Boughner's view of Harapha accords with Gilbert's: he finds him comic, a cowardly *miles gloriosus*. Two substantial difficulties arise immediately with such a view: Milton's remarks on comedy in his Preface to *SA* are rendered at best inconsistent (Allen, "Idea as Pattern" 91), at worst stupid; and Harapha just happens not to be funny. Boughner is aware of these, but, undaunted, explains that "even when he was trying, Milton never appears very funny" (306). This begs the question of whether Milton was in fact trying to be funny—and trying in a work he had just prefaced with an attack on the "error of intermixing Comic stuff with Tragic sadness and gravity; or introducing trivial and vulgar persons, which by all judicious hath bin counted absurd." Krouse judiciously counts Boughner's view absurd, stating flatly that Harapha is "not a comic agent" and arguing that he represents "the instrument of temptation by violence and fear" (129, 130). Steadman reminds us that "he is cast in a recognizably heroic mould. His 'stock renown'd As *Og* or *Anak*' links him with a breed notable for exploits of a conventional, though false, heroism," and suggests that, far from being simply comic, his discomfiture "exposes the *fortezza* formula to public ridicule" (*Milton* 27–28). Tinker finds Harapha "one of the most hateful characters to be found anywhere in the whole of literature" (68), a sweeping judgment that nevertheless has the merit of taking into account his cowardly disdain toward a blind opponent.

An alternative, biographical source for Harapha has been Milton's ideological adversary Salmasius. The suggestion originates with Masson's *Life* (6:675), which favors biographical readings of the poems, and it is endorsed by E. H. Visiak (*Milton* 99) and Grierson (*Milton* 221). Christian E. Kreipe, in "Milton's *Samson Agonistes*," strains to provide hard evidence by noting that Salmasius was regarded contemporaneously as a gigantic figure. However, in the absence of more specific and more substantial biographical evidence, the Harapha-Salmasius identification can be based on no more than a shadowy analogy. Harapha in Milton's poem remains intransigently unlike Salmasius in too many respects for a more precise influence to be credible: he is not a linguist, nor a Calvinist, nor a much-published scholarly author, nor a noted Royalist. For all that, the identification is no match in extravagance for H. G. Rosedale's supposition that the encounter with Harapha is to be related to an alleged—and wholly undocumented—interview between Milton and the Duke of York (Ames 164–66).

Commentators have been slow to find significance in the Harapha episode. Influenced no doubt by Dr. Johnson's affirmation that *SA* "must be allowed to want a Middle, since nothing passes between the first Act and the last that either hastens or delays the Death of *Samson*" (*Rambler* 16 July 1751), Charles Jerram in his 1890 edition of *SA* found Harapha "intrusive and hardly required for the action of the play" (x), and E. C. Knowlton in 1922 judged that the episode "does not contribute to the probability or inevitability of the catastrophe" (336). Richard Garnett in 1890 is the first to sense something of Harapha's significance when he says he "not only enriches the meagre action, and brings out strong features in the character of Samson, but also prepares the reader for the catastrophe" (183). Tillyard's view in 1930 represents a turning point: "Samson's spirit rises when he has routed [Harapha]. His despair has been conquered and he believes that God may yet pardon and employ him. But he is quite exempt from pride in all his defiance of Harapha. He is truly regenerate" (*Milton* 290). In contrast to James Waddell

Tupper, who thinks Samson "spiritually...not further advanced than he was in the interview with Manoa" (386), Parker remarks on Samson's "self-mastery" and "final spiritual victory" as he "*finds his faith completely;* all his doubts disappear" (*Milton's Debt* 45–46). Woodhouse comments that the Harapha episode "rouses Samson from the lethargy of despair and leads him, almost unawares, into the expression of a hope that perhaps God may yet pardon him and, for one final act, restore him to his service" ("*Samson Agonistes*" 166). Allen also detects a development: "Before our eyes a brave and knightly man will change into a coward and a blusterer.... Lancelot becomes Braggadocchio within the space of a hundred and fifty lines. Samson's courage grows and Harapha's melts" ("Idea as Pattern" 92). Stein sees in Samson "the return of inspiration" and a return to "the world of practical action" after "the long descent into the darkness of self" (*Heroic Knowledge* 179, 182). In broad terms, Gohn agrees: "the spiritual change in Samson is again evident" (265). Others see Harapha as clarifying Samson's development: for Landy, Harapha represents mere "reliance on physical strength or prowess" ("Character" 247), and for Albert W. Fields he is "the darker self that has come to rule Samson" and that Samson must reject (399).

Samson is roused by Harapha to offer single combat three times (*SA* 1222) to "decide whose god is god" (1176). Pathetically, but with supreme courage, he is obliged to think of "Some narrow place enclos'd" (1117) where such a fight might be possible for a blind man. Harapha, like all the protagonists, is a mixture: in his case, of pride (just and unjust), curiosity, and cowardice. He leaves "somewhat crestfall'n...in a sultrie chafe" (1244, 1246). By contrast, the Chorus celebrates God's apparent bestowal on Samson of "invincible might," "plain Heroic magnitude of mind," and "celestial vigour" (1271, 1279, 1280), while reflecting that "patience is more oft the exercise / Of Saints, the trial of thir fortitude" (1287–88) and concluding that "Either of these is in thy lot, / *Samson*" (1292–93). Both of these, it turns out, are in Samson's lot, and he approaches the catastrophe "patient but undaunted" (1623).

Public Officer

The Philistine Public Officer is clear about his orders and efficient in carrying them out. He is also civil to Samson. When Samson refuses to comply, his response — "I am sorry what this stoutness will produce" (1346) — sounds sincere; equally so, "I praise thy resolution" (1410) when Samson complies on certain conditions. Parker notes that the enemy herald Talthybius in Euripides' *Troades* shows a similar generosity and tact in his treatment of the Trojan women but concludes that "any of a dozen plays might have furnished the parallel" (*Milton's Debt* 137–38).

Messenger

Parker notes that a long narrative recited by an eyewitness of the catastrophe is a device associated with Sophocles, and, in particular, that Milton's account of the narrative in the Argument specifies a typical Sophoclean practice: "confusedly at first; and afterward more distinctly relating the Catastrophe" (*Milton's Debt* 136–37).

Samson

The central question has been whether Samson undergoes regeneration. Parker identifies the main theme of the work as "the hero's recovery and its result. In other words, it is regeneration and reward" (*Milton's Debt* 237). The process, as he sees it, is fourfold: "first, he must achieve patience; second, he must achieve faith; third, he must conquer the weakness which had led to his fall; and finally, he must recognize and obey the call to further service" (238). Woodhouse judges the whole poem to be "a study in regeneration": "From a state of unrelieved despair, incapable of action, Samson is brought to a state in which the last heroic act is not only possible but inevitable" ("*Samson Agonistes*" 162). As does Parker, Woodhouse identifies successive stages in the process of "temptation, disobedience, repentance, obedience, restoration" (161). M. M. Mahood traces the regenerative action in Samson's mind as a "descending and reascending curve represented by the three stages: thirst for glory; renunciation of glory; bestowal of glory unsought" (237). Similarly, Steadman ("'Faithful Champion'" 13) and Muldrow (165–225) align Samson's development with the progressive steps in repentance specified in *DocCh*: conviction of sin, contrition, confession, departure from evil, and conversion to good. Other notable regenerationists have been Kenneth Fell, Bullough and Bullough, Landy ("Character"), French Fogle, and John S. Hill.

Not everyone has been convinced that Samson experiences regeneration. Even Parker, though he finds Samson's predicament moving and traces at length what he sees as a spiritual recovery (*Milton's Debt* 30–54), still finds him "anything but lovable...cold, forbidding, grand...unsympathetic to an extreme" (117). Kenneth Burke dismisses him as "an aggressive, self-destructive hero" (153). Instead of the processes outlined by Parker, Woodhouse, Steadman, and Mahood, Wilkes detects an alternative pattern of "provocation, instinctive response, counter-assertion, and defiance" (374–75). Far from developing a spiritual insight, Samson, in Wilkes's view, is "an uncomprehending figure . . . who is struggling with his incomprehension" (372). Fish is also skeptical about the linearity and cause-and-effect relationship in the alleged regenerative process: "(1) Samson despairs; (2) he engages in a series of discussions with various persons; (3) he no longer despairs. Presumably the change from (1) to (3) has something to do with (2); we feel certain that it has; but we can only conjecture (with some confidence perhaps) as to what that something is. The striking thing about the affirmation of faith which Harapha draws from Samson is its unexpectedness" (252).

Samson confesses his past faults early on (*SA* 46–57), and indeed does so repeatedly (197–202, 233–34, 373–80, 824), stressing that he is punished justly (412–19, 488–91, 1168–71): as John Dale Ebbs insists, Samson "never denies that the fault rests with him" (383). Further, Samson realizes early on that it is not for him to quarrel with "the will / Of highest dispensation" (*SA* 60–61), and he rebukes Manoa by telling him "Appoint not heavenly disposition" (373). He feels that he has let God down (451–59, 497–501), and implores the divine pardon (521) that later he will not despair of receiving (1171–73). His faith is that God "will arise and his great name assert" over Dagon (467), and it is on exactly these terms that he offers to fight Harapha (1145–55, 1174–77). Lawrence Hyman notes that as late as lines 1262–64 Samson reverts to a mood of despair in which he longs for death ("Unwilling Martyrdom" 93). The stages at which these thematic concerns occur—or recur—in the text would suggest that linear formulations of Samson's "regeneration" are overschematized. By contrast, Anne Davidson Ferry regards the "sudden, mysterious, inexplicable" restoration of Samson as "a miracle which escapes demonstration or explanation" (130). Mason Tung would agree, but because Samson's sustained tragic impatience makes a sudden conversion necessary.

The main problem with Samson's regeneration, however, is not the exact sequence it may or may not follow; it is Samson's violence. Tillyard reserves patrician disdain for "Samson's tedious butcheries" (*Milton* 283): for him, one suspects, "tedious" is an indictment on a level with "butcheries." Rajan tartly observes that Samson's threat to tear Dalila apart shows "a scarcely Christian ferocity" (133), and Wilkes cannot square Samson's offer to swing Harapha in the air and dash him down to the hazard of his brains and shattered sides (*SA* 1237–41) with "the humility and contrition that are in order at this late stage of the regenerative process" (373). It is difficult, too, given the tragic catastrophe and its mass slaughter, to agree with E. L. Marilla that Samson's "temptations" are "to put personal and immediate interests above concern for ultimate and universal good" (74). Fish deplores Samson's harsh treatment of the solicitous Officer ("not the Nazarite's finest moment"), and cannot accept the slaughter of the Philistines "with equanimity" (258, 259)—a far cry from Tinker's grimly coercive argument that, as it is Jehovah's will, the reader "must feel nothing but satisfaction" at their deaths (64–65). Behind such a view is the recognition that readers have felt anything but satisfaction. One such reader is Christopher Ricks, who states the principle involved: "The things which are indeed 'given' in a work of literature, and which the reader must accept if he is to get anything at all from the work, are not matters of meaning, conscience, and profound belief, but matters of situation, incident, and convention" ("Milton" 315). Carey remarks that Christ's contempt in *PR* for "war" and "violence" which destroy "the flourishing works of peace" (3.80–91) "might make any reader think about Samson's theatre-demolition" (*John Milton* 138). Resentment, not regeneration, is for Carey the key to Samson's psyche: "There seems...no spiritual development, only a change of circumstances which eventually allows the resentment, which has been gnawing inwardly, to hit out"; "Samson's inner life consists of resentment, self-pity and hatred: intense, but negative" (139, 145).

Another problem with regeneration is that it tends to require the underpinning of a Christian theology that *SA* seems to lack. For Parker, "Samson's regeneration is not, in the strict sense of the word, Christian, for the Holy Spirit and the purifying power of Christ are missing" (*Milton's Debt* 242). There is certainly no promise of everlasting life in heaven for Samson (Parker, *Milton* 937; Goldsmith 78). God in *SA* is not loving or merciful. Joseph Frank remarks grimly that "God's only manifestation of mercy in the entire poem is that He lets Samson die" (106). God in *SA* is "to be pleased, obeyed, or feared" (*SA* 900); not one whose ways are revealed through Christ, but "the unsearchable" (1746), "a secret, incomprehensible God, whose ways call forth anxious questionings, and not precise exclamations," as in *Paradise Lost* (Saurat 199), "a God whose ways are dark to our understanding" (Hyman, "Milton's Samson" 42); emphatically "*Israels* God" (*SA* 1527) who, "favouring and assisting to the end" (1720), will through his "faithful Champion" (1751) deliver Israel from Philistine power and triumph over the false god Dagon.

The "Middle"

The hero's alleged regeneration has been the basis of critical retorts to Dr. Johnson's contention that the poem "wants that power of attracting attention which a well-connected plan produces" ("Milton" 1:189), that it "must be allowed to want a Middle, since nothing passes between the first Act and the last that either hastens or delays the Death of *Samson*" (*Rambler* 16 July 1751). William Wordsworth is reported by Henry Crabb Robinson to have agreed with Johnson (Wittreich 138). Parker's attempts to answer Johnson (*Milton's Debt* 22–54) prove unconvincing: conceding that *SA* is "weak in physical action," he maintains that "every epeisodion brings its conflict and almost every conflict brings us nearer to the catastrophe" (53). Brings us nearer, yes, but the lack of incident and the psychological nature of the conflicts can equally be seen as delaying the catastrophe; they do not directly bring it about.

It was Richard Cumberland who in 1785 inaugurated a critical tradition when he argued that it is the psychological and spiritual effects on Samson of the visits of Manoa, Dalila, and Harapha that constitute the middle (Shawcross, *Critical Heritage* 335–37). Thus, M. E. Grenander argues that the middle is taken up with restoring Samson to divine favor; Kenneth Muir alleges, not without some condescension, that Johnson "did not realize that the action takes place mainly in the mind of the hero" (178); and Nicolson even accuses Johnson of being "perversely wrong" in failing to see that "*Samson Agonistes* is preeminently a psychological study of the development of a human being" (357). Roland Mushat Frye (133) alleges that Johnson's failure was rather that he "did not recognize" a "progression through the archetypal sins" of the world, the flesh, and the devil, represented respectively by Manoa, Dalila, and Harapha (who advises Samson to abandon his faith in God). But the grounds on which Johnson's objection is made are dramatic, not theological or ideological. George Williamson acknowledges that "the arrangement of the incidents lacks any necessary concatenation" but argues that this is because "the necessary conditions of the plot are external, not within the power of the protagonist...the action must come to Samson" (96). But it would be difficult to cite a dramatic plot that was entirely within the protagonist's power, and what comes to Samson is not action in the conventional sense. As John Arthos contends, what we are presented with is "more evidently a representation of states of mind and of passions than it is an imitation of an action in any sense ordinarily accorded that word," "not...a sequence of events but of encounters" (130, 177).

Christopher Ricks ably defends Johnson, pointing out that he could see well enough that Manoa's visit tended to "animate or exasperate *Samson*" and that Dalila's visit had the effect of "raising the character of *Samson*": "It is not the presence of psychological development that Johnson deplores," Ricks concludes, "it is the absence of any other structural principle in the play, the absence of any reason *other* than the psychological development of Samson for the entrances and exits of characters" ("Milton" 312). Characteristically, Ricks goes on to argue a larger point of critical principle (and he has not been answered):

> Naturally Milton wishes to show a particular development, from Samson's despairing unfitness for doing the will of God to an upright fitness. But Milton's wish will be the more effective for not being at work upon a soft medium, and if Samson's development is truly to tell upon us, it is essential that there be some reason other than just Milton's wish to have it so which ushers in the psychological development. What is it that saves such a work from being a high-minded and high-handed manipulation, a rigging of the story in order to manifest a moral or spiritual lesson? The regeneration of King Lear, a man marred and touching in his humanity, may owe its greater tragic power to the fact that in *King Lear* the events do have cause and consequence, do hasten or retard the catastrophe. So that Lear's psychological development is not something being staged by the dramatist: it is as truthful as it is powerful, and has not simply been made up or willed into existence by Shakespeare. The convincingness of the events of the play is inseparable from its psychological acumen. (314)

The lack of a middle involving action, and the sustained concentration on Samson's psychological and spiritual struggles, would seem to have consequences for the kind of work *SA* is—or is not. Milton in his headnote states that it was never intended for the stage, and repeatedly refers to it as a poem. The critical consensus has certainly been that *SA* is, in Thomas Green's terse summing up, "a noble Poem, but a miserable Drama" (402). Beerbohm, reviewing a stage performance in 1908, is led to conclude that *SA* possesses "no dramatic quality whatsoever" ("Agonising Samson" 527), and Robert Lowell decisively pronounces that it is "the only great English play that cannot be acted" (178).

TRAGEDY

A satisfactory play for the theater it may not be; a tragedy it emphatically is. Milton's Preface is about tragedy, and at the end of the Argument, *SA* is explicitly called a tragedy. Samson is a traditional tragic protagonist: an eminent figure, a Nazarite "separate to God" (*SA* 31), renowned for his strength, who suffers and dies. Further, he suffers in tragic isolation: "outwardly isolated as a blind, helpless captive, inwardly as estranged from God," and "neither friends nor enemies understand what is going on in his soul" (Bush, "Isolation" 65–66). He is a markedly flawed character. Gossman considers whether the Aristotelian hamartia should be interpreted as an error of judgment or a moral flaw ("Milton's Samson" 528–32), but both meanings were available to Milton and, so comprehensive is Samson's self-reproach, he clearly availed himself of both. Samson insists that he made mistakes, chiefly in thinking God meant him to marry the woman of Timna and Dalila (*SA* 219–33), in allowing himself to be "Effeminatly vanquish't" (562), and in disobeying God (497–501). He berates himself for weakness (50, 235); foolishness (198, 377, 825); "foul effeminacy" (410) and "Shameful garrulity" (491); and for hubris, for going about "Fearless of danger, like a petty God" (529), and being "swoll'n with pride" (532). Moments of tragic recognition (anagnorisis) would seem to lie in his awareness of himself and of his responsibility for what has happened: "Whom have I to complain of but my self?" (46), "She was not the prime cause, but I my self" (234), "I my self have brought them on" (375), "I to my self was false e'er thou to me" (824). Any ultimate anagnorisis is, as Tillyard (*Milton* 292) judged, kept vaguely obscure, uncertain: Samson feels "Some rouzing motions" (*SA* 1382); he guesses cautiously "If there be aught of presage in the mind, / This day will be remarkable in my life / By some great act, or of my days the last" (1387–89); he cannot tell whether it will be "The last of me or no" (1426); and we are not told what he sees when "With inward eyes illuminated," with "eyes fast fixt he stood, as one who pray'd, / Or some great matter in his mind revolv'd" (1689, 1637–38). The final reversal (peripeteia) is brought about when the Philistines' demonstration of their power over Samson is suddenly turned upon them. This constitutes the catastrophe, which as in Greek drama takes place offstage, and Samson lies among his slain self-killed (1664).

The tragic emotion of pity is engaged by Samson's suffering; that of fear, principally by the closing section of the work and its bloody climax. C. M. Bowra's judgment (128) that *SA* "does not really arouse pity and fear. Samson's fault is stressed so strongly that we hardly pity him, and if we feel any fear, it is less for him than for the Philistines" seems callous. It is Samson himself in all the wretchedness of his suffering who most stresses his fault, so that his stressing it becomes part of his suffering. Fear may be for the Philistines, but for Samson too, who dies with them. And fear may be engaged in prospect, as the known catastrophe looms nearer, and in retrospect, for the extremity of blinding and enslavement. Bowra must be alone among readers in feeling nothing during the great lament of Samson for his blindness (*SA* 67–109).

Milton discusses catharsis at the beginning of his Preface as the purgation of pity and fear. His precise understanding of the term, and in particular the possible influences on his thinking, have been much disputed (see Stephen Dobranski's annotations on the Preface). A profitably broader view, and one more attentive to the tragedy itself, is taken by Mueller, who makes the connection between Milton's medical interpretation of catharsis in the Preface and an extensive use in the play of medical imagery that suggests that "it is Samson that is to be healed or purged" ("*Pathos*" 241). This is an interpretation developed by Lee Sheridan Cox ("Natural Science" 51–74), Georgia Christopher, and Sherman Hawkins, who detect a pervasive homeopathic catharsis brought about by opposition of the kind succinctly described by Parker: "Almost every intention or action indicated in Milton's drama brings about the opposite of what was meant. Manoa, for example, comes to comfort his son and cheer him with the prospect of ransom; but his visit produces a mood of despair which threatens to prevent the catastrophe. Dalila comes to make peace with her husband, but succeeds in arousing his ire; she intends to give him quiet and comfort, but actually prepares him for action. Harapha comes to humble an enemy, but leaves that enemy eager for combat" (*Milton's Debt* 234). However catharsis operates in *SA,* and however Milton understood it, he clearly believed in it, and the work ends with "calm of mind all passion spent" (1758).

Poetic Language

Dr. Johnson remarked on "the language, which, in imitation of the ancients, is through the whole dialogue remarkably simple and unadorned, seldom heightened by epithets or varied by figures" (*Rambler* 20 July 1751). Though Johnson's judgment would not apply to such passages as the flamboyant description of Dalila as a ship (*SA* 710–24) or the languorous elegiac meditation on the contrast between Samson's past and present (118–34), the critical consensus has shared his perception of a poem written predominantly in a plain, austere style (e.g., Raleigh, *Milton* 159; Jebb, "Samson Agonistes" 341; Tinker 61; Bush, *English Literature* 418). Imagery, however, has been found to be plentiful. Theodore Banks merely noted images of flowers, snakes, and animals (106, 149), but subsequent studies have demonstrated a broader range and significance, encompassing ships and tempests (Lewalski, "Ship-Tempest"); medicine, pollution, and purgation (Mueller, "*Pathos*" 241, 243–45); sea, snake, flower, and flame (Carey and Fowler, *Poems* 338–43); light and dark (Hyman, "Milton's Samson" 39–43; Carson; Sadler); and birds (Wilkenfeld; Sadler). Duncan Robertson (319–25) notes that Samson is associated with vegetation, fresh water, and the sun, which serves to endorse his cause with "the compelling glamour of natural good." Most comprehensive of all is Cox ("Natural Science"), who elaborates on these studies and includes images of imprisonment and entrapment, of money, of beasts, of sound and silence, and of deafness and hearing. Ferry notes that Milton shapes his material in the light of Samson's attitudes toward language (127–77), and Landy highlights "the basic tension between sounds and silence, words and deeds" ("Language" 185). Interpretation of the image patterns calls for careful discrimination: whereas Carey sees ironies and disturbing parallels—between Samson's shipwrecked "vessel" and Dalila "Like a stately Ship," for instance—Cox, along with Barbara Lewalski, "Ship-Tempest," and Kranidas (127), notes that "the same element may be good or evil," and that "Milton chooses images with multiple associations, all applicable to his pattern of moral comment, and fits them into a complex figurative design" ("Natural Science" 256, 276).

The handling of metaphor has come in for sharp criticism. Dr. Johnson, commenting on lines 197–201, objected that "sometimes metaphors find admission, even where their consistency is not accurately preserved. Thus Samson confounds loquacity with a shipwreck" (*Rambler* 20 July 1751). Ricks develops the insight (*Milton's Grand Style* 50–53), noting how a coin changes abruptly into a swarm (*SA* 189–92), how a "deadly swarm / Of Hornets" is made to "present / Times past, what once I was, and what am now" (19–22), how a "Plant" is "Ensnar'd, assaulted, overcome, led bound" (362–65), and how a shorn sheep is "disarm'd" (537–40). When the metaphors do not live along the line, but instead are switched on and suddenly switched off like this, one may, with Carey, detect in their mixture something of the disorientation of Samson's (or in lines 362–65, Manoa's) anguish, and also note that the individual components of the metaphors are "only isolated if viewed in isolation from the rest of the work" (Carey and Fowler, *Poems* 339). But the jarring changes do still jar; and a representation of anguish need not open itself to allegations of absurdity. Ricks also demonstrates how "give the rains" (*SA* 1578) and "flower" (144, 1654) remain curiously inert expressions (*Milton's Grand Style* 54–56). In this last example, in which the temple roof falls upon the "heads" of "Thir choice nobility and flower," the crushing of the flower heads seems consistently enough conceived. But the life of the expression is short: the duplication in "nobility and flower" spoils the effect by asking us to think of "flower" merely as a tired equivalent of "nobility," and in the ensuing passage— "Thir choice nobility and flower, not only / Of this but each *Philistian* City round / Met from all parts"— "'city' and 'Met' ensure that the word 'flower' is dead" (56).

Though *SA* has been dismissed as a work for the stage, its style has been recognized as dramatic. Dr. Johnson (*Rambler* 16 July 1751) memorably notes the "graceful abruptness" of the very opening. Coleridge recognizes a broader propriety, in that "colloquial language is left at the greatest distance, yet something of it is preserved, to render the dialogue probable" (qtd. in Brinkley, *Coleridge* 607; Wittreich 274).

What commentators have stressed most, however, is how responsive the language is to suffering. Walter Savage Landor's suggestion that in "Eyeless in *Gaza* at the Mill with slaves" (*SA* 41), "there ought to be commas after *eyeless*, after *Gaza*, and after *mill*" may lack textual authority, but its insight is sure: "the grief of Samson is aggravated at every member of the sentence" (5:295; Wittreich 330). John Bailey (227, 225) remarks on an "intense omnipresent emotion," instancing "the triple stab of passionate agony in the thrice repeated, strongly accented 'dark, dark, dark'" and "the spasmodic disorder of violent grief" in the inverted stresses of "Irrecoverably dark" (*SA* 80–81); and George Steiner registers "sharp as a whiplash, the hurt and tension of the successive assaults on Samson's bruised integrity" (32).

More technically, Seymour Chatman observes that the poem uses past participles heavily: "A great deal of what is said either rehearses the past, informal exposition [*SA* 361–67], or reflects the peculiarly helpless—that is passive—situation in which Samson finds himself [118–23], or predicts his future, but still in passive terms: he will be the object, not the agent, of future actions [1490–94]" (1393). The cumulative power of "short disjunctive lists of adjectives, nouns, or verbs" is noted by Leonard Moss (300). More comprehensively, Carey notes the gain in internal vigor from a whole range of rhetorical figures involving repetition (Carey and Fowler, *Poems* 337–38). Carey also provides detailed and perceptive accounts of the intensification resulting from the promotion of adverbs, adverbial phrases, clauses, or objects of verbs to leading positions, of the clarification of the internal nature of Samson's struggle when activity is repeatedly delegated to abstract nouns, and of the ubiquity of questions and commands (336–39).

Viewing the entire work as a "sustained continuous musical composition," Una Ellis-Fermor highlights its rhythmic variety, from "the rhythms of flat, inert despair" and "those of restless conflict and turmoil" to "the swinging, marked rhythms of exultation" and "the level verse of serenity, plain and relatively unvaried" (31). The accounts surveyed here seem altogether more attentive to the poetic language than F. R. Leavis, who could not bring himself to acknowledge its merit. On the lines "The Sun to me is dark…Among inhuman foes" (86–109), he comments: "It might, of course, be said that the jerky, ejaculatory stiffness is dramatically appropriate, expressing an arid, exhausted, uneloquent desperation of agony. Yes, it is true that general unsatisfactoriness of the verse has a peculiar expressive felicity" (66). But if what is (infelicitously) termed "ejaculatory stiffness" is "dramatically appropriate" and does possess "expressive felicity," what test is Milton failing that renders the verse unsatisfactory?

The versification of *SA* has received much attention, most of it focused on the choruses. What Dr. Johnson found "often so harsh and dissonant, as scarce to preserve, whether the lines end with or without rhymes, any appearance of metrical regularity" (*Rambler* 20 July 1751), Gerard M. Hopkins, himself a notable experimenter, thought the "highwater mark" of Milton's versification (*Correspondence* 13). That Hopkins disapproved of Milton, the advocate of divorce, as "a very bad man" (*Letters* 39), only guarantees his enthusiastic respect for the rhythmic complexity of the choruses: "the choruses of *Samson Agonistes* are in my judgment counterpointed throughout; that is, each line (or nearly so) has two different coexisting scansions. But when you reach that point the secondary or 'mounted rhythm,' which is necessarily a sprung rhythm, overpowers the original or conventional one and then this becomes superfluous and may be got rid of; by taking that last step you reach simple sprung rhythm. Milton must have known this but had reasons for not taking it" (*Correspondence* 15). He elaborates slightly in a letter of 21 August 1877: "The choruses in *Samson Agonistes* are intermediate between counterpointed and sprung rhythm. In reality they are sprung, but Milton keeps up a fiction of counterpointing the heard rhythm (which is the same as the mounted rhythm) upon a standard rhythm which is never heard but only counted and therefore really does not exist" (*Letters* 45–46). Robert Bridges, crediting Hopkins with having discovered the principle of the versification, provides a clearer, more technical account of it: "The whole of the 'dactylic' and 'trochaic' effects are got by the placing of inversions, elisions, &c.; and where the 'iambic' system seems entirely to disappear, it is maintained as a fictitious structure and scansion, not intended to be read, but to be imagined as a time-beat on which the free rhythm is, so to speak, syncopated, as a melody" (*Milton's Prosody* 55). T. S. Eliot, while not faulting Bridges's analysis, extends its scope:

> It is the period, the sentence and still more the paragraph, that is the unit of Milton's verse; and emphasis on the line structure is the minimum necessary to provide a counter-pattern to the period structure. It is only in the period that the wave-length of Milton's verse is to be found: it is his ability to give a perfect and unique pattern to every paragraph, such that the full beauty of the line is found in its context, and his ability to work in larger musical units than any other poet—that is to me the most conclusive evidence of Milton's supreme mastery. ("Milton II" 271)

Hopkins's views on counterpoint have not always been accepted (Prince, *Italian Element* 161–62; Weismiller 127), but his esteem of the versification has found general agreement: metrically, *SA* is for S. Ernest Sprott "the pinnacle of its author's achievement" (131); for Bridges it contains "Milton's most elaborate and artificial versification" (*Milton's Prosody* 46). The adventurousness of the prosody continues to astonish those who have investigated it most. Edward Weismiller finds many lines metrically ambiguous (121, 125), and observes how in the choral odes "the strangeness of rhythmical effect...arises principally from the fact that, in them, lines of differing length occur together in combinations to which the ear trained in rhythms of English stanzaic poetry is little accustomed" (134). Stead- man ("'Verse without Rime'" 386, 398) traces the use of rhyme in the choruses to Italian models (Trissino and his followers), and F. T. Prince (*Italian Element*) finds similar precedents for certain effects in Tasso, Guarini, and Andreini. Prince, however, also remarks on the "almost wanton variety of rhythms" in the choruses (161), on shifts from chanted verse to spoken (156), and on the unusual effect of "rhymed verse which does not rhyme, or unrhymed verse which seems to do so" (167). Between the extremes of alexandrines and lines of only four or five syllables, he observes, Milton "allows himself every variety of length and movement" (161). It is a measure of the complexity of the versification that Shawcross can open up the question of parallels between the scansion of the Chorus in *SA* and that of Greek drama ("Prosody" 86–88), and that Frank Kermode can supplement classical and Italian precedents by suggesting correspondences between the lyric portions of *SA* and Hebrew measures and rhymes.

Those who study versification often regard it as an end in itself, with arid results. Thus, for instance, Weismiller:

> Similar comments could be made on Milton's use, in *Samson Agonistes,* of the seven syllable line, the acephalous tetrameter. This line had been used, in English poetry, as the occasional variant-equivalent of the full octosyllable (or iambic tetrameter) since the thirteenth century; in Chaucer we find it so used in the *Romaunt of the Rose* (at, e.g., line 133), in the *Book of the Duchesse* (line 5), and in the *Hous of Fame* (line 40, etc.)—and with a presumed feminine ending, so that it counterfeits a full trochaic tetrameter, in such a line as *Hous of Fame* 35. (135)

The occurrence here of *use* and *used* reminds us that we are not in fact being told how, or to what poetic end, the device has been used. It is refreshing, therefore, when Bridges remarks of line 115 ("This, this is he; softly a while") that "the sibilants are hushing," or of line 127 ("No strength of man, or fiercest wild beast could withstand") that the "heavy twelve-syllable line" is "descriptive of Samson's strength," or of line 122 ("In slavish habit, ill-fitted weeds"), where Milton "puts his hero in rags he must have been conscious that he was putting his verse into rags" (*Milton's Prosody* 62, 63, 63–64). And it is a merit of Prince's account too that he transcends mere technicalities to provide literary-critical insight: "Rhyme becomes more frequent and obtrusive in the chorus on the deficiencies of women and in the concluding choruses, which celebrate the triumph of Samson's death: in the first of these Milton wishes to gain the effect of sardonic animation, and in the others a note of exalted finality" (*Italian Element* 158).

INTERPRETATION

Autobiographical, Political, Psychological

The view that Milton in *SA* is writing about himself is first articulated in 1746 by John Upton, who takes the view that Samson "imprisoned and blind, and the captive state of Israel, lively represents our blind poet with the republican party after the restoration, afflicted and persecuted" (162). It has proved to be a very influential reading, perpetuated through editions by Newton (1752), Thomas Warton (1785, 1791), William Cowper and William Hayley (1794–97), and Henry John Todd (1801–42). Hayley in his *Life of the Author* (168) attributed the fact that *SA* was singularly moving to the "marvellous coincidence" between Milton's lot and Samson's: "first (but we should regard this as the most inconsiderable article of resemblance) he had been tormented by a beautiful but disaffectionate and disobedient wife; secondly, he had been the great champion of his country, and as such the idol of public admiration; lastly, he had fallen from that heighth of unrivalled glory, and had experienced the most humiliating reverse of fortune.... In delineating the greater part of Sampson's sensations under calamity, he had only to describe his own." Thomas de Quincey in 1847 also saw parallels between Samson and Milton: "He (like Milton) was—1. blind, 2. in a city of triumphant enemies, 3. working for daily bread, 4. herding with slaves,—Samson literally, and Milton with those whom politically he regarded as such" (qtd. in Wittreich 490). The title of H. T. Wolff's book *On Milton's* Samson Agonistes *Both as a Drama and as an Illustration of the Poet's Life* (1871), and Hiram Corson's printing the whole of *SA* in 1899 among a collection of autobiographical passages in Milton's works, bear witness to the durability of the biographical interpretation. Masson, in his monumental *Life* (1881), believes that Milton, in choosing his subject, has not "overstrained it for a personal purpose," but still regards the play as "profoundly and intensely subjective" and "a metaphor of the tragedy of his own life" (6:670, 664). More recently, F. E. Hutchinson even believes that Milton writes the poem so that "he can deliver himself freely under cover of the story of Samson" (144).

There have been strong dissenting voices. *SA,* Hanford insists ("*Samson Agonistes*" 178), "is a work of art and not a disguised autobiography" (though this, as will be seen, does not inhibit him from offering elaborate conjectures about Milton's psyche). Parker reflects that "the marvel is that the drama was ever printed, even as late as 1671. The last thing in the world that the poet wished was for readers to identify Samson with John Milton" ("Date" 150). Parker pertinently invokes Milton's own caution in the matter: in *Apol* (1642) he maintains that "the author is ever distinguisht from the person he introduces" (Patterson, *Works* 3:294), and, consistently, in *Def 1* (1651) that "we must not regard the poet's words as his own, but consider who it is that speaks in the play, and what that person says; for different persons are introduced, sometimes good, sometimes bad, sometimes wise men, sometimes fools, and they speak not always the poet's own opinion, but what is most fitting to each character" (Patterson, *Works* 7:307). Another problem with autobiographical interpretations that merge into political allegory and personal psychology is that they depend upon a post-Restoration composition date for *SA,* and it is not known when the poem was written.

Steadman suggests that in *SA* Milton is presenting a broader view of the human condition in all its misery and dignity, not merely expressing subjective feelings ("Tragic Glass" 104). This seems wise, for parallels between Milton's Samson and Milton all have their breaking point. Though Milton and Samson were both blind, Samson is suddenly blinded by avenging enemies and as a punishment for sin (*SA* 1170–71), whereas Milton's blindness was gradual, accompanied (he believed) by insight, and in no sense a punishment. Williamson observes that in his attitude to blindness "Samson becomes the antithesis of Milton" (89). Eleanor Gertrude Brown, in *Milton's Blindness,* argues against Milton's conscious voicing of his own feelings through Samson, on grounds that "he would most certainly know that every expression referring to blindness would be construed as personal.... He would have been mentally blind ... to have afforded such boundless satisfaction to those who would most delight in his downfall" (94).

The differences between Milton and Samson outweigh the similarities. Both made marriages with women of different political allegiance. But Samson thought his marriage with the woman of Timna was "of God" in giving him an occasion for beginning Israel's deliverance (*SA* 221–26), and she proved false. Samson marries Dalila with disastrous consequences, whereas Milton's first marriage was to a seventeen-year-old girl from a family with Royalist sympathies, and though her desertion of him no doubt caused him anguish, they were later reconciled and had four children, and the marriage seems not to have had any political significance or the remotest connection with Milton's loss of sight. Samson's calling to deliver Israel ends with his own death in an act of mass slaughter. By contrast, Milton's attempts to reform England were carried out through his prose writings, and he enjoyed both a measure both of success, in the years 1641–42 and 1649–55, and of failure in 1643–45 and 1659–60. The Restoration that blighted his political hopes marked the release of poetic energies that resulted in his greatest poem, *PL*. Both Samson and Milton were imprisoned. However, Samson suffered utter degradation in prison, whereas Milton, after a brief imprisonment, was pardoned and returned to private life politically silenced but otherwise free to write. Parker provides additional evidence for the claim that Samson's story was in its essentials by no means Milton's story: "He had not disobeyed God's command, and his eyes had not been put out as a punishment for anything. He had not revealed God's holy secret to a woman, nor had his own wife betrayed him to his enemies. He had never been glorious like Samson, and he was not possessed of strength without wisdom. Unlike the Hebrew champion, he had not dishonoured his God; he felt no need for repentance and regeneration" (*Milton* 314). It is difficult, given such a range of differences, to agree with, say, Hilaire Belloc when he states that "Samson is altogether Milton, without overlap and without exception. He is Milton in every particular" (272), or with Denis Saurat when he alleges that "Milton is more intimately present in *Samson Agonistes* than in any of his other poems. Here he put the history of his own life" (200).

There is a strong tradition of reading the poem as political allegory. Masson is a committed, and influential, exponent: "The Hebrew Samson among the Philistines and the English Milton among the Londoners of the reign of Charles the Second were, to all poetic intents, one and the same....Who are the Philistine lords and ladies, and captains, and priests...but Charles himself, and the Duke of York, and the whole pell-mell of the Clarendons, Buckinghams, Killigrews, Castlemaines, Moll Davises, Nell Gwynns, Sheldons, Morleys, and some hundreds of others" (*Life* 6:670, 676). Garnett agrees, though without the overparticularizing naming of names: "Old, blind, captive, helpless, mocked, decried, miserable in the failure of all his ideals, upheld only by faith and his own unconquerable spirit, Milton is the counterpart of his hero" (184). (For further discussion of autobiographical readings, see Stephen Dobranski's annotations on lines 30–33, 67–109, and 563–68.) With alarming versatility, Garnett suddenly decides that "Samson seems no less the representative of the English people in the age of Charles the Second" (184), a view shared by Verity (lxii), and, more recently, by Muir, who sees Samson as "amongst other things, a symbol of England...the England of the Restoration, enslaved to monarchy, and spiritually blind" (181, 179). Muir's interpretation, like Garnett's, can shift with the greatest of ease: when Samson blames himself for the evil that has befallen him, "Milton is referring not to his personal misfortunes but to the failure of the English people; but when the chorus complain that God seems to desert his chosen, Milton may be thinking of himself" (178). Radzino-wicz, like the others, assumes a post-Restoration date for *SA,* and, reading it against the background of Milton's prose, sees it as "a moral analysis of political failure with the possibility of personal deliverance contained in it," with Samson as "the representative of the defeated Puritan cause" ("*Samson Agonistes*" 464, 465). A great deal of the tragedy has to be filtered out to maintain such a view: when, for instance, she insists that *SA* is "not a program of action," we are asked to forget that Samson's return to bloody action results in a catastrophe involving his own death and that of his enemies. And it is difficult to discern how this can constitute "a vision of how one might face the facts of human defeat with some kind of intelligible hope" (471). Lewalski maintains that "there is basis in Patristic and Medieval typological theory for associating Samson and the Christian Elect," and that seventeenth-century English Puritans "were disposed to see the Book of Judges as an image of their own times, with Samson and their own leaders as correlative types" ("*Samson Agonistes*" 1055, 1057). But she does not establish evidence that Milton in *SA* shares or invokes this disposition. Long before, Bailey (231) found a larger, double identity for Samson: "a type in which Milton can see himself and the Cromwellian saints who lie ground under the heels of the victori-ous Philistines of the Restoration." J. Macmillan Brown went one better: Samson is Milton himself (the play is "almost autobiographic"), "a Hebrew Cromwell," and "the Restoration Puritan" (vi, ix, 78). As can be further seen in Stephen Dobranski's annotations on lines 272–76, the most striking characteristic of the allegorical interpretations is their tendency to metamorphose, from one interpreter to another and even within a single account.

Within these interpretations there is, in the twentieth century, a tendency to offer a psychological explanation of events in the poem. Grierson alleges that "Milton had his own life and fate in mind, was finding relief for his pent-up feelings in a dream, a wish-fulfilment" ("Note" 62). Rose Macaulay, reading *SA* as "almost a crypto-autobiography and jeremiad on current affairs," also finds Milton "releasing himself in that glorious wish-fulfilment of the pulling of his enemies' city upon their heads" (131, 133). Hanford offers a full diagnosis:

> The self-reproaches which Milton never allows himself to utter in his own person find free expression through the dramatic personality.... Samson, then, is Milton as he might have been without the spiritual resources he had built up within himself or, to put it differently, he is Milton in his moods of depression and vain rebelliousness.... The drama thus becomes his unconscious confessional.... His two successful marriages have done nothing to wipe away the memory of his earlier experience.... The drama becomes... in its central incident a last imaginative gratification of the poet's will to power. (*John Milton* 248, 249, 252, 255, 256)

The force here of the sequence "then...becomes...becomes" can be little more than that of a rhetoric for maintaining the consistency of the conjectures: there is no logic, and no basis in external evidence. In the 1953 revision of his *Poems of John Milton,* Hanford writes of the poet: "It is hard to believe that he was ever a prey to fear or to the sense of guilt. The soul-searchings and the protestation themselves tell another story. It is no wonder that *SA* should seem to bring us closer to the real Milton than any of the preceding works" (548). Some may feel that such access through a dramatic work to "the real Milton" (as distinct from other perfectly accessible Miltons who seem just as real) is wonderful indeed.

Prevaricating, vacillating, and disclaiming feature tellingly in the conjectural interpretations: note J. Macmillan Brown's "almost autobiographic" (vi), Macaulay's "almost a crypto-biography" (134), Hanford's "seem to bring us closer to the real Milton" (*Poems* 548), and Muir's "may be thinking of himself" (178). And yet such interpretations, so hedged or not, emerge as overdefined and overconfidently asserted. Milton certainly knew blindness, something of the woe (as well as the weal) that is in marriage, as well as political defeat and imprisonment; and *SA* as a poem is no doubt the more powerful for its feeling representations of such experiences. However, the range, partialities, inconclusiveness, and kaleidoscopic transmutations of the autobiographical, allegorical, political, and psychological interpretations may be seen as indicating that Milton's own experience is not so much reflected in *SA* as refracted through it; that the poet's life, circumstances, and outlook can yield no more than flitting adumbrations of the poem. Thus, when Burke hypothesizes that Milton found in Samson an outlet for his own blocked rage and resentment, "a figure fit to symbolize both aggressive and in-turning trends," he runs into difficulties with Samson's aggressive and in-turning suicide, for "Milton's religion strongly forbade suicide" (154). Grierson's emphasis (*Milton* 145), albeit relegated to parentheses, is a just one: "Into no poem has he [Milton] put more of his deepest feeling, his own sufferings physical and mental (but dramatised and so held at a distance)." Mark Pattison, though sympathetic to Masson's political reading, expressed the strong reservation that the "nominal persons of the drama almost disappear behind the history which we read through them" (192); which prompted H. D. F. Kitto to add "exactly; and the nominal poetry and the nominal drama disappear too" (325). Pattison does qualify his position, however, by suggesting that the resemblance between the incidents in Samson's life and Milton's life or the Puritan cause "lies in the sentiment and situation, not in the bare event" (196). It is at such a general level that Émile Saillens finds parallels between *SA* and the history of the Commonwealth and of Milton: in the themes of "divine election, exceptional gifts, incredible victories, pride, weakness born of pride, divine disavowal, the triumph of the wicked" (330). And Edward Wagenknecht is similarly discriminating in outlining the personal significance of the poem to the poet: "It is nonsense to suppose that he [Milton] meant Samson as an image of himself, but if he wrote *Samson Agonistes* after losing his sight, it is equally silly to suppose that he was unaware of the very personal, poignant meaning which some of Samson's utterances had for him" (18). Like all great poems, *SA* required a transcendence of mere subjectivity and immediate historical circumstance, as well as literary knowledge and linguistic skill. As Parker contends, "An artist does considerably more than express his own feelings; he colors them, heightens them, modifies them, distorts them, to achieve the effects he has in mind. . . . In *Samson Agonistes* Milton is a dramatist" ("Date" 165).

Typological

In this mode of interpretation, Samson is taken to be a "type" of Christ. As we have seen in considering the question of Samson's regeneration, there are difficulties in finding a Christian theology in the poem or in discerning in Samson a newfound ability to turn the other cheek and love his enemies. However, for T. S. K. Scott-Craig ("Concerning" 46–47), the "central meaning" of *SA* is a Christian one: the "liturgical" poem celebrates the atonement, "Samson Agonistes is really Christus Agonistes," and "the celebration of the agony of Samson is a surrogate for the unbloody sacrifice of the Mass." (Note that this is an interpretation that can sustain itself in the face of the poem's insistence upon Samson's body "Sok't in his enemies blood" and encrusted with "clotted gore" [*SA* 1726, 1728].) For Northrop Frye, there can be no final "calm of mind all passion spent" if Samson is not "a prototype of the rising Christ" (*Anatomy* 215). But catharsis has hardly always depended on Christian theology or borne Christian meanings, and Frye's requirement must hinge on an interpretation of the phoenix as an image of Christ's resurrection (*SA* 1699–1707)—on exactly the interpretation advanced by Roger B. Wilkenfeld, for whom "every word of the great emblem looks forward to the New Testament's mythology and Christ" (167). The poem, however, makes explicit reference only to the bird's recovered vigor and lasting fame, as William G. Madsen, attempting a typological reading, has to concede (111). (His final concession is larger still, when he notes "the harshness of the contrast between Samson's ethic and Christ's" [114].) Robert H. Goldsmith adumbrates Christian themes in *SA:* "exaltation of the humble, strength gained through weakness, and triumph through defeat and humiliation" (80). But, stated so vaguely, such themes are not exclusively Christian, and if *through* is replaced by *after* or *despite,* which is arguably the case with Samson, they are not at all Christian. The "rite generally analogous to a Christian liturgy" which Thomas B. Stroup (55) detects in Samson's last day may be no more than the ritual of Greek drama.

The chief exposition of the Christian-typological view is Krouse's *Milton's Samson and the Christian Tradition.* Krouse, however, finds in *SA* "no trace at all of analogical (i.e., theological or mystical) interpretation" of Scripture, and "no specific suggestion of what is known as tropological interpretation" (88), and he is led to think that Milton's interpretation of the Samson story is "ostensibly an example of rationalistic literalism" (89). He persists in reading the poem as Christian allegory on the grounds that in Christian tradition, from the fourth century on, there was a tendency, manifest in the works of Augustine, Isidore of Seville, and many others, to develop analogical parallels between Samson and Christ (41–43). Astonishingly, Krouse concedes that in *SA* there is "almost no vestige of this aspect of the tradition" (120). He faithfully (but weakeningly) demonstrates that the tradition was a troubled one, and that Rupert of St. Heribert, for instance, who "contributed more than anyone else in the scholastic period to the allegorical interpretation of Samson...wondered whether Samson's deeds could be reconciled at all with Christian ethics" (52–53). The mention of Samson slaying his enemies with the jawbone of an ass (*SA* 142–45, 262–64), interpreted from Gregory the Great onward as an allegory of the conquering power of the gospel, is seized on by Krouse as the "one shred of palpable internal evidence" that Milton intended the poem to be read as Christian allegory (120). If, as Krouse finds, "one looks in vain for more tangible internal evidence of allegorical interpretation in *Samson Agonistes*" (122), then this one scrap has to be made to serve as "part of—perhaps even the center of—the meaning which the poet intended the tragedy to have" (123).

Krouse's concessions inflict severe damage on his thesis. Roston's counsel against reading a tradition into a work that does not draw upon it (156) seems apposite. Several commentators on the poem have even remarked on the fact that Milton seems not to have availed himself of possible Christian meanings. Saurat exclaims,

"No allusion, no prophecy on the subject of Christ in *Samson,* and yet, what a rich and tempting poetical theme was there!" (238), and Hanford concludes that the story of Samson must have had for Milton "an independent human value, neither implying nor prefiguring the life of Christ" ("*Samson Agonistes*" 268). Burton O. Kurth echoes this: Milton's emphasis is on Samson as "an independent historical figure" who is not given "the support of the larger meaning of Christ in universal history" (131). Nicolson finds *SA* "the least Christian of all Milton's major works"—indeed, "Christianity plays almost no part in it" (352), and Lewalski reasons that "since there is no explicit reference to the crucifixion in *Samson Agonistes* there is no clear evidence that Milton intended to invoke the antitype of Christ's sacrificial death" ("*Samson Agonistes*" 1054). Sister Margaret Theresa, in one of the numerous reviews of Krouse's book that rejected the theory of Christian allegory, is more blunt still: if Milton "were thinking Christ,...he would have said Christ" (138).

Christian readings of *SA* are difficult to square with tragedy. George Steiner puts it baldly: "Christianity is an anti-tragic vision of the world" (67). Death to a Christian is victory (1 Cor. 15:22, 54–57), and not a victory over earthly enemies, who are instead to be loved (Matt. 5.44). Thus, while death to Christians may involve human sorrow, they "sorrow not, even as others which have no hope" (1 Thess. 4:13). It is for such reasons that David Daiches regards the idea of Christian tragedy as "a contradiction in terms": "nothing to a Christian can be tragic if seen in its proper perspective" (247). Woodhouse, a leading exponent of the Christian tragedy view, may therefore seem to make concessions so large as to undo his interpretation: "The question has often been asked whether a Christian tragedy is really possible. No doubt on a total view Christianity presents the drama of existence as a divine comedy—or at most a divine tragicomedy—in which the overruling power is the Supreme Goodness....If a Christian tragedy is possible, then its subject will be the saved, or those on the way to being saved, not the utterly lost" ("Tragic Effect" 463). This seems a far cry from the bloody conflict of *SA* and its violent hero lying among his slain self-killed. Of all Milton's poems, *SA* cannot be read without a sense everywhere of dark perplexity and mystery.

A Note on the Annotations

All long annotations in the following commentary for *Samson Agonistes* (hereafter, *SA*) are organized topically, according to, for example, a passage's versification, historical context, or autobiographical overtones. Within these broader categories, I have attempted to arrange chronologically individual authors who address related ideas. In some cases, however, the logic of pairing authors whose ideas are closely related has superseded chronology.

While some annotations are attached to single lines, I have elsewhere grouped together lines that commentators interpret as a single passage, such as lines 365–66 or 368–72. I have also paired or grouped together lines where the glosses of individual words are related to one another, such as lines 363–64, where *Select, Sacred,* and *miracle* seem usefully connected.

If a commentator quotes an outside text in her or his work, I have included, with few exceptions, that quotation in the commentary and provided both the appropriate citation and, when necessary, a translation. Alternatively, if a commentator includes a citation but does not quote the relevant passage from an outside text—whether from Scripture, Sophocles, or Shakespeare—I have not added the quotation. All parenthetical citations to secondary and reference works are to page numbers, unless otherwise indicated. Citations to classical works are to the Loeb editions published by Harvard University Press. Citations to editors' line-by-line commentaries do not include page numbers except in a few instances in which I quote from the editor's introductory material or from a section of the editor's commentary that does not correspond to the lines I am annotating.

A definition followed by "so *OED*" indicates that the passage in *SA* is cited in the *Oxford English Dictionary,* 10 vols., ed. James A. H. Murray et al. (Oxford: Clarendon Press, 1884–1928). There are approximately 640 such citations, although not all *OED* citations from *SA* are reported here. References in these notes to *OED* without the word *so* indicate that *SA* has not been cited.

In writing this commentary, I have also often consulted (but not cited) William Ingram and Kathleen Swaim, eds., *A Concordance to Milton's English Poetry* (Oxford: Clarendon Press, 1972). I have used the text of *SA* in volume 1 of *The Works of John Milton,* ed. Frank Allen Patterson (New York: Columbia University Press, 1931); all references to line numbers in the Preface and Argument correspond to the line breaks in that edition. I have also made frequent use of one other uncited work: Frank Allen Patterson and French Rowe Fogle, *An Index to the Columbia Edition of the Works of John Milton,* 2 vols. (New York: Columbia University Press, 1940).

COMMENTARY

The Title

Samson: Parker notes that in naming his drama after the leading character, instead of after the Chorus ("the Danites"), Milton followed the example of more than half of the extant Greek tragedies ("Variorum"). Verity specifically observes that "the form 'Samson' comes from the Septuagint Σαμψών, the Hebrew being *Shimshôn*" (57). Although Josephus says that the word means "one that is strong" (*Antiquities of the Jews* 5.8.4), Krouse (42) notes that throughout the patristic period the accepted etymology of the name was *sol ipsorum* ("their sun"), which he traces as far back as Jerome's *Commentarii in epistolam ad Philemonem* (Migne 26:644): "Totam Samson fabulam, ad veri solis (hoc quippe nomen ejus sonat) trahere sacramentum"; and finds also in Augustine's *Enarrationes in Psalmos* (Migne 37:1041) and Isidore of Seville's *Etymologiae* 7.6 (Migne 82:278). Krouse (42) notes further the allegory that Augustine derived from this etymology, which makes Samson a prefiguration of *Sol Justitiae* or Christ. Some modern scholars give the meaning of the name as "solar," "sun hero," or "sunny," from *shemesh*, "the sun"; other editors interpret it as meaning "the strong," from *shamam*, "to waste." Parker instead asserts that for Milton's contemporaries the name signified "there the second time" (*Milton's Debt* 13); he cites Blount's *Glossographia* (1656), William Camden's *Remaines* (1605), and Phillips's *New World of Words* (1658). Parker adds, "this etymology supports—and may even have suggested—the theme of regeneration which runs through Milton's version of the story. It may also have suggested elements of the plot: Samson, whose birth was twice prophesied by an angel (*SA* 24, 361, 635), is given a second chance to resist Dalila; the Public Officer 'came now the second time' to fetch Samson (Argument); and Manoa makes two appearances" ("Variorum").

Agonistes: in adding a distinguishing epithet to the name of his protagonist, Milton followed the example, among others, of three of the greatest Greek tragedies, Aeschylus's *Prometheus Bound,* Sophocles' *Oedipus Rex,* and Euripides' *Hercules Furens.* Newton suggests that *Agonistes* designates Samson as an "actor" or as one represented in a play (sig. P2r); Stebbing, e.g., repeats this interpretation, but Dunster (in Todd) eschews it and explains that an Agonist was an "athlete" (competing in public games). Accepting this, Masson (*Poetical Works* 3:88) and Verity add the meaning "wrestler," which subsequently prompts Hughes to explain that Samson "wrestles with the pillars" (*John Milton* 537). The word αγωνιστής means more than "athlete," however; it means also (as A. J. Church notes [68]) "performer" and "player," and (as Percival notes [60]) "champion" (cf. 705, 1152, 1751). Bush writes that the word means "a contestant in public games," which "applies—both literally and ironically—to Samson's last acts in the Philistine temple and applies also to his spiritual wrestlings with himself" ("John Milton" 412); adds Tinker, "it may be applied to an athlete but not to a professional athlete. The contestant may very likely have a rival or opponent," whom Tinker here identifies as Dagon (72–73). Bush suggests that the word also has "the Miltonic overtone of 'God's champion'" (*Milton*). Sellin instead emphasizes the idea of "Samson 'dissembling,' Samson 'assuming a mask,' or Samson 'playing a part'" ("Milton's Epithet" 157). Parker observes also that "*agon,* in the Christian tradition, connotes moral struggle for virtue" (*Milton* 319). Rudrum writes, "the arena of the combat is his [Samson's] own soul, and the enemy to be defeated is the 'deadly swarm' [19] of his own thoughts" (22). Phillips defines *agonize* as "to play the Champion or valiant Combatant" (*New World* sig. Eee1r). Parker thinks it may be "significant that Milton used neither *agony* nor *agonize* in his play, despite countless opportunities offered" (*Milton's Debt* 13). Cf. Milton's early intention "to sing the victorious agonies of Martyrs and Saints" (*RCG* [Patterson, *Works* 3:238]). Rudrum is reminded of "the related word 'agonistic,' which is a rhetorical term denoting the attempt to overcome an adversary in argument"; he adds that much of *SA* "hinges upon discussions which often become 'arguments'" (18); see also Moss (297, 298).

Among *SA*'s other commentators, Krouse proposes that the epithet *agonistes* is especially significant, inviting us "to think of Samson as a model of virtue, as a hero, as a champion of God, as a saint, a martyr, and a counterpart of Christ" (124). From such early literal meanings as "the contest for a prize at public games," the word ἀγών came to mean any "struggle or trial" and, increasingly, "a spiritual struggle, an inner conflict" (109–10). Krouse traces the development of this meta-phorical meaning in Greek literature: although ἀγωνιστής "usually meant 'hero' or 'champion,'" it was "often used figuratively" (e.g., by Plutarch, who called Socrates ἀγηθείας ἀγωνιστής, "the champion of truth"); and in educational theory (e.g., by the Sophists and especially by Isocrates), it "signified the finished product of educa-tion, one fully prepared to take his place in the *agon* of life" (112). Krouse notes that Stoic thought did much to develop what he calls "the *agon*-idea," a concept in which conflict becomes "the essence of moral life" (113–14); early Christian writers then adopted this concept, St. Paul's "good fight of faith" being perhaps the most familiar illustration (114). Athletic, military, forensic, or dramatic terms came to be used to express the spiritual struggles and victories of saints and martyrs (Samson exclaims, "My race of glory run, and race of shame" [597]), and of Christ in his mission against Satan. Thus, Krouse reasons, "the *agon*-idea took its place very close to the heart of Christianity" (114). He cites many examples, including Augustine's *De agone christiano* (117); he concludes by arguing that, because of the Christian tradition, *SA* is inescapably allegorical and "Samson and his story are a figure of Christ and His story" (123). Northrop Frye similarly writes, "the ultimate author of the story of Samson was Christ himself, and the tragedy of Samson is thus one of Christ's parables" (Paradise Lost *and Selected Poetry* xxi).

Preface

Title: "Of that sort of Dramatic Poem which is call'd Tragedy" is the heading of Milton's Preface or "Epistle" to *SA*. The first forty-two of the seventy-six lines are a vindication of tragedy as a poetic form; the remaining part is an explanation of the "Greek manner" of this particular tragedy. Langdon observes that the heading "implies an expression of a general theory" (98). Sellin describes it as "the most complete piece of Miltonic criticism" but cautions that, given Milton's rhetorical purpose here, "one cannot expect the Preface to cover even the most salient points of tragic theory, or develop those raised beyond the minimum requisite for an apology" ("Milton on Tragedy" 166). Commentators note the Preface's largely apologetic tone. Moody writes that its "elaborateness...proves that he did not consider himself, even when following in the footsteps of Sophocles, safe from the attacks of zealous brethren" (284). Masson observes that Milton "concerns himself not at all with the matter of the poem, or his own meaning" (*Poetical Works* 3:88).

Commentators also read Milton's Preface as a response to the period's new dramatic form, the rhymed heroic tragedy. In 1668, Dryden had crystallized the critical attitudes of his time in *Essay of Dramatick Poesie,* and a controversy followed over the relative merits of blank verse and rhymed verse as a vehicle for tragedy. Although the Preface to *SA* exhibits no explicit recognition of any of these developments, many readers have considered it (with Verity [58]) "intended as a retort" to Dryden's essay. Freedman offers the fullest argument that the Preface was "stimulated" by Dryden: he asserts that *SA* was, in part, "Milton's creative contribution to the contemporary symposium on tragedy," and he finds in Milton's Preface many indirect or implicit comments on points made by Dryden ("Milton" 73, 76). A. J. Wyatt and A. J. F. Collins (14) as well as Grieve (v) suggest that Milton wrote the

Preface to "put the censor off the track," or, perhaps, in whole or in part, it was penned before the Restoration. Parker specifically notes that its argument echoes a similar one in *RCG* of 1641/42 ("On Milton's" 51); Buchanan argues that, because the Preface and *RCG* have so many parallels in both phrasing and idea, they are near each other in time of composition (47–49). For possible additional evidence or suggestion of early composition, see the prosodic analysis offered by Shawcross ("Chronology" especially 349–52, 356) and the notes on Preface 1–2, 18–19, 22–24, 31, 32–34, 42, 47, 53; but cf. those on Preface 29, 57.

1. *Tragedy, as it was antiently compos'd:* "the emphasis in the first part of Milton's Preface is on the *content* of classical Greek tragedy as a poetic form; its 'Greek Manner' becomes the subject of the second part" (Parker, "Variorum"). Ellis-Fermor, however, classifies *SA* not as a tragedy but instead discusses it as a "religious drama": "We are accustomed to associate with tragedy a balance between…the sense of pain, grief, or terror on the one hand, and, on the other, something that triumphs and illuminates. But in Milton's play we find instead a progression towards triumph and illumination which gradually subdues the sense of pain, grief, and loss and at the end transcends and utterly destroys it" (17). Scott-Craig instead discusses *SA* as a "Catholic tragedy," a "poetic surrogate celebration of the victorious and redeeming death of Christ" ("Miltonic Tragedy" 104–9). Bowra suggests that Milton's choice of genre is rhetorical: "protected by the objective form of drama and helped by the respect which his generation felt for anything classical, Milton could say certain things which could not be safely expressed in the first person by a rebel and a regicide" (113).

    antiently: "in ancient times"; Parker notes that the spelling follows the Latin rather than the French ("Variorum").

1–2. *hath been ever held:* this statement is open to question. Renaissance criticism, for the most part, did not follow Aristotle in ranking the epic after tragedy (*Poetics* 26), and critics disagree over whether Aristotle himself believed that tragedy serves a social, moral function. Parker ("Variorum") notes that "Milton's own attitude toward the socially instructive function of drama (at least in the period 1641–44) is clear from *RCG* and *Educ*, and Milton may have known that Aristophanes agreed (*Frogs* 1009–93)." On the status of tragedy, Phillips writes, "Next to the *Heroic Poem*, if not as some think equal, is *Tragedy*" (*Theatrum* sig. **7v). In the address to the reader in the tragedy of *Orbecche* (1541), Giraldi

Cinthio begins with a sweeping assertion like Milton's and then goes on to say that tragedy is no longer in esteem and that its name is even odious to many.

gravest: "most serious" and/or "most important" (*OED* s.v. *grave* 2). Parker finds Milton's superlatives here "interesting," in part because they were published in the same volume in which Christ dismisses Greek tragedy as "Thin sown with aught of profit or delight," replying to Satan's praise of "the lofty grave Tragœdians" as "teachers best / Of moral prudence" (*PR* 4.345, 261–63). Parker adds, "Christ contrasts, of course, Greek with Hebraic poetry, but Milton's words in this Preface refer to 'all other Poems'" ("Variorum"). Cf. Milton's *ComBk,* probably written during the 1640s: "what in the whole of philosophy is more impressive, purer, or more uplifting [*gravius aut sanctius aut sublimius*] than a noble tragedy, what more helpful [*utilius*] to a survey at a single glance of the hazards and changes of human life?" (Patterson, *Works* 18:206–7).

moralest: "[most] beneficial in moral effect" (so *OED* 3c, the sole citation). In his *Apol,* Milton speaks of "those *Attick* maisters of morall wisdome" (Patterson, *Works* 3:347). Flower writes that "the emphasis on morality even more than delight is Horatian [*De arte poetica,* ll. 333, 343–44]...and a commonplace of the Renaissance and later" (410); but, she adds, Milton's idea of tragedy's moral function "differs from all these others in being concerned, not with teaching an attitude, but with effecting a change in the emotional constitution" (412).

most profitable: cf. Christ's words quoted in Preface 1–2n s.v. *gravest.*

3. *of all other Poems:* the construction is a Latinism (Parker, "Variorum"); cf. *PL* 4.323–24.

   said by Aristotle: the reference is to the passage in the *Poetics* quoted in part on the title page of the first edition of *SA.* Prince observes, "He cites Aristotle's definition as what it was, an observation on the ancient Greek dramas, and not a rule according to which they were constructed" (*Samson Agonistes*). Arthos suggests this is "more a nod of respect than deference, and the play itself makes it clear that Milton's doctrine is a revision and even a transformation of Aristotle's" (130). See also Preface 59n.

4. *of power:* in *RCG* Milton writes that poetical abilities are "of power...to allay the perturbations of the mind, and set the affections in right tune" (Patterson, *Works* 3:238). See Preface 5–6n.

   pity: this word occurs only once in *SA,* in a speech by Dalila (814).

fear, or terror: the word *terror* does not occur in *SA;* but the Chorus eventually fears for Samson (e.g., 1250–52, 1300, 1348–53, 1380), as it earlier pities him. On the title page, Milton translates Aristotle's dictum as *per misericordiam et metum.* Parker notes, "this rendering, with *metus* having the meaning, or at least the connotation, of religious awe or dread (cf. *lustratio* for *katharsis*), was also that of Pietro Vettori, and it was less Senecan in coloring or influence than the *terror* or *horrore* of other translators (see Vettori, *Commentarii in primum librum Aristotelis de arte poetarum* [1560]). Here in his Preface, however, Milton seems aware of the variation among translations" ("Variorum"). Penn adds that Milton's translation "exactly accords" with Gotthold Lessing's sense of Aristotle's dictum and that "what is translated 'terror' means only a selfish alarm on imagining ourselves in the danger or distress we see" (2:221–22). But Bowra suggests that *SA* "does not really arouse pity and fear. Samson's fault is stressed so strongly that we hardly pity him, and if we feel any fear, it is less for him than for the Philistines" (128).

purge: commentators note that there are two principal ways of interpreting *katharsis,* either "purgation" (a medical meaning) or "purification" (a moral or religious meaning): whereas Milton seems to suggest "purgation" in the Preface, the Latin on the title page instead translates Aristotle's κάθαρσις not as *purgatio* but *lustratio.* Langdon describes Milton as "wavering" between the two notions (90); Hawkins argues that, in fact, the two senses are "complementary aspects of the same tragic and redemptive process," both in Milton's poem and in the tradition behind it (219); Flower similarly suggests that "to Milton, the moral function and the aesthetic function are inseparable" (412). Parker adds that the word *purge* means the partial removal of excess "humours" so that the passions are reduced to a healthy, balanced proportion. Behind this theory of the moderation of the passions as a function of tragedy, which Milton may have first encountered in the works of Mazzoni and Tasso, was the widespread idea of the Aristotelian mean ("Variorum").

Other commentators compare Milton's rhetoric with the poem itself. Thus, Gray writes, "Milton expresses his intention of aiming at a catharsis of the emotions of pity and fear, but because there are two acts of *hybris* present there may be some doubt as to the accomplishment of this aim"; Gray identifies the Philistines' pride, error, and subsequent punishment as one possibility, but he decides on Samson's defeat by Dalila as "the more natural act of *hybris*," even though it occurs before the play begins (144). Arthos instead suggests that if the ending of *SA* effects the catharsis, "it must be doing this not merely through awe but in the accompanying assurance of God's working for good through the catastrophe. And if this is so, then…the play is partaking of comedy, and the theory of *lustratrio* may be another way of justifying it" (145).

5–6. *such like passions:* Hawkins notes that the phrase implies that there may be other passions in addition to pity and fear; he suggests that grief is the third tragic passion in *SA* (222). Parker ("Variorum") suggests that Milton may have meant "all passions," as Corneille did in his "Discours du Poème Dramatique" (1660).

   to temper and reduce them to just measure: commentators dispute the sources of Milton's notion of catharsis. Gilbert (*Literary Criticism* 517n15) notes a similarity with Giambattista Guarini's *ridotti a vertuoso temperamento* (*Il pastor fido…con un compendio di poesia* [1602]). Sellin argues against Guarini as an influence on Milton's concept of catharsis ("Sources" 721–24), and instead calls attention (727) to Daniel Heinsius's *quemadmodum oportet* (*De Tragoediae Constitutione Liber* [1643]). However, Mueller ("Sixteenth-Century Italian Criticism" 145–49) responds that Sellin minimizes the general influence of sixteenth-century Italian criticism, not only on Milton (who seems to have assimilated it during the time of his Italian journey), but also on Heinsius (who, e.g., frequently cites Vettori). Also, Milton's concept of catharsis as a reduction of the passions to a mean was developed at least as early as *RCG* (see Preface 4n s.v. *of power*). In reply, Sellin continues to make the case for Heinsius as a significant influence for Milton's concepts of catharsis and tragedy ("Milton and Heinsius"; "Milton on Tragedy"). Flower, while not arguing about influence per se, agrees with Sellin that Milton's concept of catharsis as a tempering and reduction of passions is closer to Heinsius's theory than it is to Minturno's: she adds, "Both Heinsius and Milton link catharsis closely to the moral purpose of tragedy: it is because tragedy effects catharsis that it is moral" (411). Rajan observes, "This is a view of catharsis which is still respectable but it is also of a piece with Milton's firm conviction that all things in the created order are good to the extent that they serve that order and its ends" (143).

   with: Sellin suggests that this word should "be interpreted not as 'by means of' but 'accompanied by,'" which he traces to "Greek datives predominating in corrupt Renaissance texts" and, he notes, also parallels Heinsius's use of the Latin ablative ("Milton on Tragedy" 171).

kind of delight: Sellin thinks that Milton means only delight at "skillful imitation of an object" ("Sources" 718). But, Mueller argues, the "cautious phrasing" of *kind of* suggests that Milton was not limiting delight to imitation alone by following an unambiguous interpretation of Aristotle: "It is difficult to establish the exact relationship between imitation, purgation, and delight in this sentence, but it is clear that purgation is itself conceived as pleasurable" ("Sixteenth-Century Italian Criticism" 149). Mueller adds that Milton may be remembering Aristotle's οἰκεῖα ἡδονή ("intimate pleasure") (150). Flower suggests that "the delight results from the quality of the poet's mimesis and causes the audience's catharsis" (412).

7. *reading or seeing:* Parker ("Variorum") writes, "Aristotle insists that plays must be considered primarily without reference to their representation on the stage (*Poetics* 6.19; 7.6; 14.1–2; 26.3)." See also Preface 52–53n.

   passions well imitated: Arthos discusses this as a shift of focus from Aristotle's *Tragœdia est imitatio actionis,* quoted by Milton on the title page: "I think this is because he conceived of the affections and energies of man's nature as in themselves possessing the disposition to obey God.... The play would not treat of an event and its consequences as the imitation of an action, but, rather, the way in which, through a series of repressions and challenges, a sentient being is raised from depression to purposefulness" (152). See also Preface 3n.

9. *in Physic:* commentators largely agree that Milton was indebted to Italian criticism in describing his theory of catharsis by comparing it to medicine. At least three Italian critics whom Milton probably read present explicitly medical theories of catharsis: Antonio Minturno, Lorenzo Giacomini, and Giambattista Guarini. Mueller notes that Giacomini comes very close to modern concepts, discussing purgation at length and explaining "that the passions are purged by exteriorization"; Giacomini likens the effect of tragedy to that of medicinal purgatives, which naturally drive out physiological humors ("Sixteenth-Century Italian Criticism" 147–48). Mueller adds that it is Guarini, however, who combined the homeopathic theory with the more common theory of moderating the passions (147). Spingarn first calls attention to this passage in Minturno's *L'arte poetica* (1564): "Nè più forza haura il Physico di spengere il feruido ueleno della infermità, che'l corpo afflige, con la uelenosa perturbationi con lo empito degli affeti in uersi leggiadramente espressi" ("As a physician eradicates,

by means of poisonous medicine, the perfervid poison of disease which affects the body, so tragedy purges the mind of its impetuous perturbations by the force of these emotions beautifully expressed in verse") (*Critical Essays* 1:251; *History* 78–81). Spingarn notes, "Like Milton, Minturno conceived of tragedy as having an ethical aim; but both Milton and Minturno clearly perceived that by *katharsis* Aristotle had reference not to a moral, but to an emotional effect" (*History* 81). Langdon, however, points out that Minturno, "before formulating his definition, explains the effects of pity and fear on the spectator, and lays the stress, not on purgation through and of these emotions, but on the assistance they give toward avoiding personal suffering and disaster" (93). Verity notes that the ancient maxim, *similia similibus curantur* ("like cures like"), was "applied in isolated cases by Hippocrates" and eventually developed into the theory of homeopathy by Samuel Hahnemann (1755–1843). Bywater also suggests Antonio Scaino da Salo and Tarquinio Galluzzi as possible sources for Milton's explanation of his theory (270–74)—two possibilities that Mueller ultimately finds unconvincing ("Sixteenth-Century Italian Criticism" 147). Sellin is dismissive of Italian sources in general; he suggests that Milton's homeopathic analogy "really is no more than an analogy" and instead recommends Daniel Heinsius's theory of catharsis for its similarity to Milton's ("Sources" 716, 724–30; see also Preface 5–6n).

Beyond discussions of sources for Milton's theory, Gilbert comments, "Milton's wording implies that the pity and fear are imitated by the actors rather than felt by the audience; it seems that he must have had in mind the imitation of actions that would produce such passions. Milton's theory is apparently medical to such an extent that it does not contemplate the complete expulsion of pity and fear, just as it would not be well to expel from the human body any of its natural fluids or humors" (*Literary Criticism* 593n1). Hanford instead emphasizes what he sees as "The difficulty of incorporating such a principle in the general theory of tragedy": "How is the delight of seeing the passions well imitated related to the emotional identification demanded by the theory of like curing like? Milton raises basic aesthetic questions but by no means solves them" (*Poems* 553). Christopher argues, however, that the homeopathic analogy broadly informs the drama's plot and structure: "natural medicine works inexorably in *Samson Agonistes* and points to Milton's major themes.... That ferocious patient Samson is returned to spiritual health by application of the very arguments and attitudes which constitute his disease" (361); Hawkins similarly argues that Samson is cured "homeopathically, employing 'like against like' "

(221–22). Prince finds Milton's choice here "very characteristic. . . . He chooses to interpret the spiritual effects of tragedy in terms of individual experience, claiming that there is a scientific explanation of the way in which our emotions are 'purged' by the representations of human sufferings which tragedy offers. This is in accordance with his rational approach to religious dogma and practice" (*Samson Agonistes*).

melancholic hue: editors note (e.g., Church 67) that Milton may refer here to the medical doctrine of "signatures" developed by Paracelsus (see *Labyrinthus medicorum errantium* ch. 9), according to which plants and other natural objects have distinctive colors and shapes that are an indication of their curative qualities; thus, saffron was considered good for the liver, lungwort for the lungs, quinces (a hairy fruit) for baldness. Bywater remarks that Milton's language has "a Helmontistic colouring" (267).

11. Flower notes that a similar justificatory strategy occurs in Sidney's *Defence of Poesie:* that both works appeal to past authorities is "no accident . . . , for both were defenses against philistine detractors, and affirmations of the traditional honor accorded to poetry, and to tragedy in particular" (413).

    humours: see *SA* 600n.

12. *Cicero:* Verity writes that Cicero indeed cites tragic poets "often in his works"; e.g., in *Tusculanae quaestiones* 2.10, Cicero translates twenty-eight lines from Aeschylus's *Prometheus Bound.*

    Plutarch: Verity suggests, "many instances might be quoted from the *Moralia.*"

13. *thir:* the second edition (1680) alters this Miltonic spelling to *their* here, twice in the Argument, and in *SA* 13, 15, 114, 137, 140, 141, 176, 251, 257, 259, 262, 269, 274, 279, 286, 304, 343, 345, 443, 693, 1026, 1188. At 1214 it alters *their* to *thir.* See *SA* 190n.

14–15. *Paul . . . Euripides:* Verity notes the iambic verse in question is 1 Cor. 15:33: φθείρουσιν ἤθη χρηστὰ ὁμιλίαι κακαί ("evil communications corrupt good manners"). Milton's Latin version in *DocCh* is: "mores bonos commercia corrumpunt mala" (Patterson, *Works* 17:278); without mention of any author, Tertullian gives it another form: "bonos corrumpunt mores congressus mali"

(Verity). The saying is found not only among the fragments of Euripides but also among the *Thais* of Menander (Lynch 477). It had been attributed to Euripides by, among others, Clement of Alexandria and Socrates the historian (Parker, "Variorum"); to Menander, by Jerome and Grotius (Newton and Todd), and in 1622 by Henry Peacham, *The Compleat Gentleman* (Spingarn, *Critical Essays* 1:118). Page suggests that "Milton is here defending himself against the objections of Puritans"; so also Patterson, *Student's Milton*. Roston similarly writes that the space Milton devotes to Christian authority in the Preface (see also Preface 26–28n) "confirms the suspicion that Milton...felt qualms about writing a biblical drama even in so venerable a tradition as that of the Athenian stage" (153). Tillyard adds that Milton also wrote the Preface "to prove to the academic reader that he was following the rules of Aristotle" (*Miltonic Setting* 164). Verity and other commentators compare *Areop:* "in *Paul* especially, who thought it no defilement to insert into holy Scripture the sentences of three Greek Poets, and one of them a Tragedian" (Patterson, *Works* 4:306).

16–18. *Paraeus:* David Paré or Wängler (1548–1622), a German Calvinist theologian and author of *A Commentary upon the Divine Revelation of the Apostle and Evangelist John*. In this work, Pareus describes the dramatic form of the book of Revelation, which, he writes, "may truely be called a *Prophetical Drama*, show, or representation" (sig. C4v). Lewalski discusses both Pareus's treatment of the Apocalypse as a tragedy and his influence on Milton's depiction of Samson as a type of the Christian Elect ("*Samson Agonistes*" 1051–54); Cook examines Pareus's treatment of Revelation, along with some eighteenth-century commentaries ("Milton's View" 74–80). Cf. *RCG:* "And the Apocalyps of Saint *John* is the majestick image of a high and stately Tragedy, shutting up and intermingling her solemn Scenes and Acts with a sevenfold *Chorus* of halleluja's and harping symphonies: and this my opinion the grave autority of *Pareus* commenting that booke is sufficient to confirm" (Patterson, *Works* 3:238). See also Hughes, *Complete Poems* 669.

Revelation: Lewalski compares the book of Revelation (according to seventeenth-century Protestant exegesis) with Milton's tragic portrayal of Samson's last day: "The Saints' story, as recorded in the Book of Revelation, is a tragedy of suffering and struggle, yet at its conclusion the providence of God visits the tragic catastrophe not upon the suffering faithful but upon their enemies and persecutors" ("*Samson Agonistes*" 1054).

18–19. *Heretofore Men in highest dignity:* Parker writes, "if the wording implies that this was no longer true, contemporary readers could have named the exceptions, e.g., the Earl of Orrery" ("Variorum"). Cf. *DDD:* "to be wise and skilful in these matters [imaginative writing], men heretofore of greatest name in vertue, have esteemd it" (Patterson, *Works* 3:402).

20–22. *Dionysius the elder:* the tyrant of Syracuse, ca. 430–367 BC. Verity and other editors note that he contended often for the prize of tragedy at Athens and finally, it is said, won first prize at the festival of Lenaea with a play called *The Ransom of Hector.*

22–24. *Augustus Cæsar:* the first Roman emperor; he lived 63 BC to AD 14. The story Milton refers to is told by Suetonius (*Vita Augusti* 2.85) and by Macrobius (*Saturnalia* 2.4). Asked by his friends how his tragedy was progressing, Augustus is said to have replied that *his* Ajax had committed suicide by falling on a sponge (Verity).

    begun, left it unfinisht: so Milton ends his explanation of his own unfinished *Passion* in his volume of *Poems* in 1645.

24–26. *Seneca:* Lucius Annaeus Seneca (died AD 65), Stoic philosopher and tutor to Nero, is almost certainly the author of *Hercules Furens, Medea, Troades, Phaedra, Agamemnon, Oedipus Rex, Hercules Oetaeus, Phoenissae,* and *Thyestes,* all based on Greek originals; Carey (*Complete Shorter Poems*) notes that a tenth play, *Octavia,* is now ascribed to a later imitator. Milton's nephew Edward Phillips writes: "*Medea,* and some others are generally believed not to be his, if the rest or part of the rest be" (*Theatrum* sig. F7r). Gilbert suggests: "Possibly Milton did not admire Seneca so much as some earlier authors had.... Doubts about authorship go hand in hand with unfavorable remarks on quality" (*Literary Criticism* 593n3). Carey instead suggests, "The doubt as to authorship of the tragedies is due to a mistake of Sidonius Apollinaris, *Carmen* ix 230-38, who clearly distinguishes between Seneca the philosopher and Seneca the tragedian." Parker asserts that Seneca's plays had a tremendous influence on the Renaissance, in England perhaps most conspicuously on *Gorboduc* (1562) and the tragedies of Ben Jonson ("Variorum"). Verity notes that Milton refers to "*Seneca* the Tragedian" in *TKM,* where he also cites some verses (Patterson, *Works* 5:19); see, too, *Def 1* (Patterson, *Works* 7:327).

by some thought: Parker offers specific examples: "Crinitus, *De Poetis Latinis* (1505), had declared: 'Scripsit Tragoedias X.'; J. J. Scaliger excepted the *Octavia;* Daniel Heinsius and Lipsius postulated three or four authors for the ten plays. Milton reflects the uncertainty felt by the scholarship of his age" ("Variorum").

26–28. *Gregory Nazianzen:* St. Gregory Nazianzen, or Gregory Theologus (ca. 330–90), was one of the four fathers of the Greek church and Catholic bishop of Constantinople. Verity comments that the *Christus patiens,* in 2,061 lines, "contains passages from most of Euripides' plays (especially the *Bacchae* and *Medea*)," and is an attempt to Christianize Greek drama. Verity also notes that some Elizabethan apologists for the stage, like Milton, cited it as proof that the church had supported the drama. Phillips does not mention it in his account of Gregory (*Theatrum* sig. E10r), but in his account of Apollinarius the Elder he mentions "his devine poems, among which some reckon *Christus patiens,* which is generally ascrib'd to *Gregory* of *Nazianzene*" (sig. B12r). Scholars no longer ascribe the piece to Gregory; linguistic evidence points instead to some Byzantine Greek of the twelfth century. Verity adds a long note on the problem of authorship (137–38) where he explains that J. G. Brambs, the editor of the play in Teubner's *Bibliotheca scriptorum medii aevi* (Leipzig, 1885), ascribes the piece to Theodorus Prodromos (1143–80), but that there is no general agreement as to the author.

Christ suffering: among his own plans for dramatic composition, Milton had listed "Christus patiens" (Patterson, *Works* 18:240), and as a youth he had begun a poem on "The Passion."

29. *vindicate…from: OED* 3c dates this construction from 1664.

30. *infamy:* see Preface 34n.

31. *at this day:* this phrase raises the question of when the Preface was written (see also "still in use" [Preface 42]). Browne, Collins, et al. think the passage "an oblique allusion" to the tragicomedies of Dryden and his contemporaries; Church (68) does not, as Dryden's first play was performed in 1663, when Milton was already blind. See Preface 32–34n. Cf. *Educ:* "that sublime Art which in *Aristotles Poetics,* in *Horace,* and the *Italian* Commentaries of *Castelvetro, Tasso,*

Mazzoni, and others, teaches what the laws are of a true *Epic* Poem, what of a *Dramatic.*...This would make them soon perceive what despicable creatures our common Rimers and Playwriters be" (Patterson, *Works* 4:286).

    Interludes: "(popular) stage plays"; Phillips, however, defines them as "a kind of Stage-Play, that which is sung, or represented between the several Acts" (*New World*). In *Ref,* Milton speaks of church ceremonies as an "Enterlude to set out the *pompe* of *Prelatisme*" (Patterson, *Works* 3:6); in *Colas,* he calls his opponent "the lowest person of an interlude" (Patterson, *Works* 4:237). More pertinent is *RCG:* "what we know of the corruption and bane which they [our youth and gentry] suck in dayly from the writings and interludes of libidinous and ignorant Poetasters, who having scars ever heard of that which is the main consistence of a true poem, the choys of such persons as they ought to introduce, and what is morall and decent to each one" (Patterson, *Works* 3:39).

32–34. *intermixing Comic stuff...vulgar persons:* Gilbert finds it "difficult to suppose that Milton penned his attack on comic scenes in tragedy when fresh from writing of Dalila and Harapha" ("Is *Samson Agonistes*" 101). But Allen finds *SA* consistent with the Preface because Harapha, he argues, is not a comic character: the giant enters as "a genuinely valorous man" who devolves into a blusterer only when Samson confronts him ("Idea as Pattern" 91). Commentators also discuss whether this statement in the Preface applies to Restoration tragedy or to the tragedies of Shakespeare and early seventeenth-century dramatists. Edmund K. Chambers suggests, "This criticism covers nearly every popular play, from Marlowe onwards" (19), and Masson thinks, "It is impossible not to see a reflection here upon the practice of Shakespeare and others of the Elizabethans" (*Life* 6:665; *Poetical Works* 3:89); adds Hales, "it would be a mistake to suppose that these convictions, so trenchantly enounced and so nobly illustrated, belonged only to Milton's senescence, or can be explained by his disgust with the theatre of the Restoration. Years and years before Milton had made up his mind on this matter" (201). Thaler, however, notes that in the paragraph "The Verse" of *PL* (composed ca. 1668), Milton seems to praise "our best *English* Tragedies" because they rejected rhyme. Thaler argues that Milton's "imaginative sympathy with...Elizabethan dramatic poetry" can be supported in part by the various Shakespearian "echoes" and "overtones" in *SA* ("Shakespearian Element" 143–44); he adds that Milton's criticism in the Preface is directed specifically at recent tragedies "rather than...the conditions and circumstances of dramatic performance" ("Milton in the Theatre" 212). Bullough and Bullough think "it is hard to imagine" that, after blindness (1652), Milton ever attended a stage performance, "but he may have done" (61); adds Parker, "Milton could also have had a published play by Dryden or one of his contemporaries read to him" ("Variorum"). On the sentiment, cf. *Colas:* "I had rather, since the life of a man is likn'd to a Scene, that all my entrances and *exits* might mixe with such persons only, whose worth erects them and their actions to a grave and *tragic* deportment, and not to have to doe with *Clowns* and *Vices*" (Patterson, *Works* 4:271). Cf. also Phillips's condemnation of "that *Linsie-woolsie* intermixture of *Comic* mirth with Tragic seriousness, which being so frequently in use, no wonder if the name of Play be apply'd without distinction as well to *Tragedy* as *Comedy*" (*Theatrum* sig. **8r). On the extent to which comic relief figures in Greek tragedy, see Parker, *Milton's Debt* 199.

33. *sadness:* "seriousness" (*OED* 2 [1611]) and/or "sorrowfulness" (*OED* 5).

34. *by all judicious:* e.g., Philip Sidney, *Defence of Poesie* (1595), who criticizes plays that are "neither right Tragedies, nor right Comedies; mingling Kings and Clownes, not because the matter so carrieth it, but thrust in Clownes by head and shoulders, to play a part in maiesticall matters, with neither decencie nor discretion: So as neither the admiration and commiseration, nor the right spiritfulnes, is by their mungrell Tragy-comedie obtained" (cited by Wyatt and Collins; see also Gilbert, *Literary Criticism* 593n4). Flower also suggests that Milton here aligns himself with neoclassical taste: "However, Milton goes beyond the usual neoclassical attitude when he insists that the mixture of genres is the cause of the 'infamy' [Preface 30] of the contemporary drama" (413).
    bin: see *SA* 874.

35. *discretion:* Flower writes that "the word...seems to be used both in its aes-thetic sense, as propriety..., and in its moral sense, as good judgment (as the following adverb, 'corruptly,' shows)" (415).
    to gratifie the people: "Milton may have remembered that Aristotle too had expressed some contempt for the contemporary theater (e.g., *Poetics* 13), especially for playwrights who catered to the low tastes of audiences" (Parker, "Variorum").

36. *no Prologue:* that is, "no address from the author to the audience asking their indulgence, such as Plautus and Terence used" (Verity). See *PL* 9.854 and cf. *SA* 1554. Editors (e.g., Onions; Prince, *Samson Agonistes;* et al.) note that Milton's use of *prologue* here should not be confused with prologos, or that part of Greek tragedy that preceded the entrance of the Chorus (cf. *Poetics* 12.2). Prince adds, "he may have had in mind such prologues in verse as were common on the Restoration stage and had also been used by Marlowe, Shakespeare (*Troilus and Cressida* and *Henry V*) and Ben Jonson" (*Samson Agonistes*).

   yet using sometimes: no commentator names any "antient Tragedy" using the equivalent of an "Epistle."

37. *self defence:* Parker ("Variorum") notes that *OED* dates the word from 1651, but Milton uses it twice (with a hyphen) in *TKM* (Patterson, *Works* 5:8, 55).

38. *Martial...Epistle:* see Preface 36n. The Roman epigrammatist Martial (ca. 40–ca. 104) prefixed an *epistola* in prose or verse to ten of the fifteen books of his *Epigrams,* some *ad lectorem,* some to friends, and two to his patron Domitian. Editors quote illustrative passages; e.g., "Nunc video quare tragoedi et comoedi epistolam faciant" (Church 68); "Video quare tragoedi epistolam accipiant, quibus pro se loqui non licet" (Collins).

39. *after the antient manner:* Hanford notes, "Milton touches on the essential points of superiority claimed by Renaissance criticism of classical as opposed to modern drama: (1) purity of genre, violated by the mixture of comic and tragic; (2) decorum in the dramatis personae, violated by the portrayal of common men; (3) concentration of action and unity of time; (4) the use of chorus" (*Poems*).

40. *Epistl'd:* "written as a preface or introduction." Apparently Milton's coinage; cf. *OED.*

41. *Chorus:* Parker notes the absence of an article ("Variorum"). Cf. Phillips, who writes: "I shall only leave it to consideration whether the use of the *Chorus*...would not rather by reviving the pristine glory of the *Tragic pall,* advance then diminish the present" (*Theatrum* sig. **8r).

42. *but modern:* commentators speculate whether it is significant that Milton omits any reference to French classical dramatists. E.g., Finney notes that Corneille was "the century's model for tragedy without chorus" (650); Landor discusses the merits of French drama and suggests Milton ought to have paid more attention to it (5:296). Freedman argues that Milton ignored the French and mentioned the Italians because Dryden, in his *Essay of Dramatick Poesie* (1668), had mentioned the French and ignored the Italians ("Milton" 77–78). Parker writes, "the French Senecans of the sixteenth century differed from the Italian Senecans in their use of biblical stories and in their thinking of plays as things to be read rather than acted—two respects in which Milton, consciously or unconsciously, followed them" ("Variorum"). He adds that Milton also omits any reference here to the Countess of Pembroke's group, which was influenced by Robert Garnier.

still in use among the Italians: Finney discusses the classical use of a chorus in Italian musical dramas of the early seventeenth century as well as in a later popular musical form, the oratorio. She notes that in musical dramas "the use of chorus waned after 1640," and she doubts that Milton was familiar with oratorio composed after his Italian journey. Since "of the Latin oratorios not even a libretto was published, apparently, before 1678," she concludes "that Milton used the expression 'still in use' on the basis of his acquaintance with Italian 'melodramma' and oratorios till and during his visit to Italy" (659, 663). See Preface 31n. (Her conclusion does not lead her to any inferences about the date of the Preface and of *SA*.) On *melodramma* and *SA*, see also Arthos 168–87.

Other critics suggest that Milton was referring to such dramas as Politian's pioneering fifteenth-century *Orfeo* (Wyatt and Collins), or to early-sixteenth-century works such as Trissino's *Sofonisba* and Rucellai's *Rosmunda* (Verity; Gilbert, *Literary Criticism* 214n2), or to the late-sixteenth-century pastoral dramas, Tasso's *Aminta* and Guarini's *Il pastor fido* (Prince, *Italian Element* 145–68; Verity; et al.). Spingarn (*Critical Essays* 1:252) claims that Italian tragedy continued to use the chorus during the seventeenth century, e.g., Andreini's *Adamo* (1613), Chiabrera's *Angelica in Ebuda* (1615), and Dottori's *Aristodemo* (1657). Prince, however, writes, "The expression 'still in use' is somewhat misleading, since it suggests that the use of the Chorus in sixteenth- and seventeenth-century Italian dramas continued a tradition ascending to ancient times. There was no such continuous tradition" (*Samson Agonistes*). Kastner and Charlton assert, "there never was, and never could have been, a really Greek influence in the shaping of typical Renaissance tragedy" (1:li); they add, "In the whole vernacular tragedy of the Renaissance there is but one small group of authors, the Italian Trissino and his followers, Rucellai, Pazzi, and Martelli, whose plays [in the first four decades of the sixteenth century] are marked by a specifically Greek influence of considerable weight and deliberate discrimination" (1:xxix). For Flower, "The important point…is that Milton is consistently following classical practice rather than the post-Senecan choric tradition, in which the chorus was the observer and commentator rather than a participant" (416).

43. *with good reason:* see Preface 63–64n s.v. *and best example.*

45. *The Measure of Verse us'd in the Chorus:* Milton's explanation has puzzled, and occasionally disturbed, commentators. E.g., Cumberland notes, "there is a harshness in the metre of his chorus, which to a certain degree seems to border upon pedantry and affection: he premises that the measure is indeed of all sorts, but I must take leave to observe that in some places it is no measure at all" (333). Parker responds that Milton does not use *measure* in the usual sense of "metre, poetical rhythm" (*OED* III.16), nor is he talking primarily about the grouping of lines; instead, Parker proposes, this statement indicates that Milton has abandoned all regular stanzaic or strophic divisions, and therefore felt free to vary the line length and write in irregular stanzas to suit either the sense or the effect wanted ("Variorum"). Even so, Epps suggests that the choral odes, "though incapable of strict arrangement into strophe and antistrophe, do yet give a marked strophic and antistrophic effect" (191). See *SA* 115n.

46. *Monostrophic:* μονόστροφος, "single stanza." *OED,* which dates usage of the word from Milton's Preface, defines *monostrophic* as "consisting of repetitions of one and the same strophic arrangement." But, Parker writes, "this does not give the sense here. The word…is slightly misleading as a description of successive stanzas which vary, not only in length, but also in measures; the word is useful only as emphasizing an abandonment of the usual Greek arrangement of strophe and paired antistrophe, corresponding metrically" ("Variorum"). See Preface 47n.

47. *Apolelymenon:* ἀπολελυμένος, "loosed, set free"; "freed from the restraint of any particular stanza," i.e., with each line of any measure the poet chooses.

Edmund K. Chambers suggests that Milton is thinking of the "more irregular form of lyric" introduced by Euripides; Phillips, however, writes about "the *Monostrophic,* or *Apolelymenon,* used in the Chorus's of *Æschylus* his Tragedies" (*Theatrum* sig. **4r). These descriptions correspond to Milton's earlier explanation of the stanzas and meter of *Rous*: "Alioquin hoc genus rectius fortasse dici monostrophicum debuerat. Metra partim sunt κατὰ σχέσιν partim ἀπολελυμένα"; "Otherwise [i.e., had the ode not divided into three strophes, three antistrophes, an epode purely for convenience in reading], it would have been more proper perhaps to call this sort of writing 'monostrophic.' The meters are partly 'responsive, in correlation,' partly 'apolelymenon' or free from any restraint of correlation." The technical term *apolelymena* appears in the *Encheiridion* (1553) of the metrist Hephaistion, in the second century of the Christian era. Parker finds evidence of Milton's interest in irregular stanzas (during 1646–47) in his praise of William Cartwright's "Ariadne Deserted by Theseus" in line 11 of his sonnet to Lawes ("Variorum").

49. *Music:* Parker writes, "in view of Milton's lifelong love of music, it may be thought surprising that he did not regret the loss of music to choral songs. He here sounds severely Aristotelian (in the *Poetics* music is near the bottom of the list of the elements of tragedy), and unlike Monteverdi and other Italians" ("Variorum"). Sellin suggests that Milton's omission of both musical considerations and scenic arrangements, two elements that Milton deems "not essential," parallels Heinsius's classification of tragedy's components ("Milton on Tragedy" 167).

50. *therefore not material:* Parker finds this passage "interesting as showing Milton's attitude toward 'rules' and formal elements in poetry" ("Variorum"). The regular stanzas in Greek tragedy had a practical reason for their existence; they were put to music. With the disappearance of the reason, Milton felt free to write irregular stanzas. See Preface 63–64n.

51. *Allaeostrophe:* ἀλλὸιόστροφος, "different stanza"; "strophes not consisting of alternate strophe and antistrophe," i.e., stanzas of varied form. Masson defines "divers-stanzaed" (*Poetical Works*).

52. *Division into Act and Scene: SA* has but a single scene, described as "*before the Prison in* Gaza." Langbaine suggests that Milton's precedent for avoiding act and

scene divisions was Sophocles, "whose Plays are not divided into Acts" (376). Parker notes that division of *SA* into acts has tempted critics and editors from the time of Johnson onward, with a resultant confusion that Parker describes and deplores (*Milton's Debt* 14). See also Preface 54–55n.

52–53. *the stage (to which this work was never intended):* commentators dispute whether Milton intended this statement literally. J. Macmillan Brown asserts, "Milton thus abandoned from the beginning the central principle of Greek dramatic art" (56). But Langdon suggests, "the statement amounts only to this, that Milton did not expect forcibly to produce *Samson Agonistes* under theatrical conditions in the time of the Restoration, and had therefore made no mechanical preparation against such an emergency" (99). Masson similarly writes, these words "do not imply that Milton would not willingly have consented to the production of his *Samson* on the stage had it been possible. My belief is that he would have regarded such a production as an example towards the restoration of the stage to its right uses" (*Life* 6:665–66). Beerbohm agrees, although he believes that *SA* "has none of the qualities which make production tolerable to more than a very few even in the inner ring of the faithful" ("*Samson Agonistes*" 489). Lawry proposes that Milton may have wanted readers to envision *SA* "as being 'for' and of a vaster stage—that on which a part of the great poem of God's design is enacted...by all humankind" (352). To Summers, the drama need not be staged because the "significant action" occurs "within Samson's mind and heart"; nevertheless, he adds, "there is an imaginary 'stage' and...we will be compelled, at certain moments, to imagine gestures which are of the greatest importance for the internal drama" (155). Thaler discusses eighteenth-century dramatic and musical adaptations of Milton's *SA,* most notably Handel's oratorio *Samson.* He adds that this parenthetical aside does not support claims that Milton disdained the theater: "Nor is there any real contradiction involved in a great poet's enjoying the theatre and yet, in a sense, shrinking from personal contact with the stage" ("Milton in the Theatre" 213).

54–55. Grierson attempts to improve the paragraphing: he adds a colon to the end of the preceding paragraph and moves the clause "It suffices...beyond the fift Act" so that it concludes the penultimate paragraph; the final paragraph thus begins, "Of the style and uniformity" (*Poems* 1:xxxiv, 317).

    beyond the fifth act: Horace, *Ars poetica* 188–90, claimed that a play should consist of five acts, advice that "was taken seriously by Renaissance writers"

(Gilbert, *Literary Criticism* 134n30). Flower adds, "Both in Horace and here, the statement refers not to mere mechanical structure, but to something like Aristotle's 'as having magnitude, complete in itself,' and therefore, by implication, also includes his remarks on what constitutes being a whole: having a beginning, middle, and end" (418). *Beyond* means "apart from" (Tinker 65).

    style and uniformitie: Sellin observes that Milton lists these two components of tragedy and three more (plot, music, and scene), whereas Aristotle listed six: "It is possible that he replaced Aristotelian 'character' and 'thought' by the single aspect 'uniformitie' on the authority of *Ars poetica* (99–125)" ("Milton on Tragedy" 167). Flower infers from Milton's coordination of these two terms "that the latter term does refer to rhetorical decorum, a concept of artistic harmony closely linked with style" (420).

56–58. Arthos interprets this to mean that "the ordering of the events of the play is to be governed, not by necessity (as it is when the poet subscribes to the conception of beginning, middle, and end in necessary sequence), but by an ordering of a composition in conformance with notions of the decorous and the lifelike" (130). Grenander alternatively describes *SA*'s plot as "multilinear" but with an essential unity that "derives from the ratio which is set up among four sets of relations: those between Dagon and the Philistines, Samson and the Philistines, Samson and God, and God and Dagon" (380).

    intricate or explicit: cf. Aristotle's categories in *Poetics* 10.1452a14–18. Sellin interprets this phrase to mean that, for Milton, "tragedy imitates a 'serious' action involving a single change of fortune" ("Milton and Heinsius" 132). Langdon deems *SA* to be "explicit" (i.e., "simple"): "there is no main discovery, and, for the hero, no 'reversal of situation'" (105).

    disposition . . . decorum: these terms, according to Sellin, "suggest that, as in Heinsius, criteria for judging a work rest ultimately on principles obtained from the study of actual life and nature, a conjecture supported by Milton's epigram on William Marshall, where failure is attributed to the engraver's inability to represent his model within the range of possibilities governing not artistic forms but the natural species" ("Milton and Heinsius" 132; "Milton on Tragedy" 174).

    verisimilitude: Langdon explains this as "the technical name applied in the Renaissance both to elements of realism in epic and dramatic art and to the observance of probability in the incidents and logical sequence in the events of the epic or dramatic fable. It is in the latter sense alone that Milton feels it

important in the 'economy and disposition' of the plot of *Samson Agonistes*"
(108–9).

    decorum: cf. Aristotle's πρέπον ("the appropriate" or "proper"; *Poetics*
7.1455a25; 18.1456a14; 22.1459a4). Langdon traces the term's context from
Aristotle to Dryden (109–12), noting the "considerable freedom" in its interpretation; she concludes that "Milton paired 'verisimilitude' and 'decorum' to
the confusion of both" but "undoubtedly" intended *decorum* to mean "fitness
in imitation" (111, 114). Flower suggests that *decorum* also "had a rhetorical
sense, the harmony or consistency of the work of art itself," but she adds that
decorum and *verisimilitude* were "seldom so clearly distinguished in seventeenth-century criticism" (418–19). Sellin notes that Milton "does not link
these doctrines with delight...and in so doing radically differs from critics like
Dryden" ("Milton on Tragedy" 174).

59.   Commentators debate Milton's faithfulness to his Greek models. Among those
who think that Milton closely follows ancient models, Steiner argues that *SA*
(along with Schiller's *Braut von Messina* and Hölderlin's *Empedokles*) "come[s]
nearest in European literature to a reincarnation of the Greek ideal" (232).
Coleridge reportedly made a similar comment in conversation: "[he] said, with
becoming emphasis, it was the finest imitation of the ancient Greek drama that
ever had been, or ever would be written" (qtd. in Brinkley, *Coleridge* 606). Prince
similarly observes, "the intensity of his religious convictions gave his tragedy
a quality which later attempts to follow Greek tragedy, like Swinburne's, have
usually lacked—a seriousness which is related to the point of view of the Attic
dramatists" (*Samson Agonistes* 17). Hanford also discusses "a thoroughgoing
conscious classicism, which extends far beyond such matters as the ordering of
the incidents and the employment of ancient devices like the messenger. It is
shown in a more philosophic and intrinsic way in the subtle turns which the
poet gives to the interpretation of his theme in order to bring it more nearly
into conformity with the spirit of ancient tragedy" ("*Samson Agonistes*" 183;
see also Hanford, *Poems* 549). For Cumberland, Milton's "close adherence to
the model of the Greek tragedy is in nothing more conspicuous than in the
simplicity of his diction: in this particular he has curbed his fancy with so tight
a hand, that, knowing as we do the fertile vein of his genius, we cannot but
lament the fidelity of his imitation" (333). On the other side, Jebb argues that
SA in "spirit" is Hebraic and "neither as poem nor as drama is it Hellenic"

("*Samson Agonistes*" 344, 348); Curry also writes that *SA* "has no relation with Greek tragedy in either spirit or structure, except for a superficial resemblance in form"; instead, he argues, it is Christian in spirit and resembles a modern drama in which "the tragic struggle is transferred to the soul of the criminal" (350–51). Bailey responds to Jebb: "the broad division which separates the world's drama into two kinds is a real thing, and . . . Milton's drama belongs in spite of differences unquestionably to the Greek kind and not to the other, both by its method and by its spirit. There can be no real doubt that it is far more like the *Prometheus* or the *Oedipus* than it is like *Hamlet* or *All for Love*" (243). See also Preface 3n. Bush thinks that *SA* is remarkable for "avoiding overt reference to any specifically Christian belief or idea. . . . If there is any violation of Greek tragic decorum, it is in Samson's sense of responsibility to God, yet that is not felt as a violation" (*Milton* 514). Writing on this specific line from the Preface, Flower (421) detects an echo of Horace's advice ("Vos exemplaria Graeca / nocturna versate manu, versate diurnal" [*Ars poetica* 268–69]) as well as Crites's encomium in Dryden's *Essay of Dramatick Poesie*.

   Æschulus: referring to the Greek tragedians in *RCG* (Patterson, *Works* 3:237) and *Educ* (Patterson, *Works* 4:286), Milton mentions only Sophocles and Euripides. Maxwell asserts, "Aeschylus was not a popular writer, even among scholars, in the seventeenth century, and Milton was exceptional in ranking him with Sophocles and Euripides" ("Milton's Knowledge" 366). Milton's only other specific reference to Aeschylus in all his extant writings occurs in a comment on a quotation from Salmasius in *Def 1* (Patterson, *Works* 7:307). The matter of this seeming neglect is discussed by Parker (*Milton's Debt* 245–49). The *Index* to Patterson's *Works* lists thirty-four alleged references to Aeschylus, but these are examined by Maxwell, who reports: "There is not a single one where it can be said with confidence that Milton must have had, or even that he very probably had, Aeschylus in mind whether consciously or unconsciously" ("Milton's Knowledge" 367). Bush asserts more generally that "the 'epic' predominance of the protagonist and the strongly religious conception of sin and righteousness are Aeschylean" (*Milton* 513). Prince adds, "Milton's reference to the three great Attic dramatists, as well as an analysis of his tragedy, shows that he is following no one dramatist, and still less any one play" (*Samson Agonistes*).

60. *Sophocles:* Milton refers to Sophocles about eight times in five separate works (Parker, *Milton's Debt* 247). Bush suggests, in general, "the efforts of successive

interlocutors to break down the protagonist's resolution, the pervasiveness of irony both general and particular, and the handling of the chorus are Sophoclean" (*Milton* 513).

Euripides: Parker notes that Milton makes eighteen references to him in twelve separate works: he adds, "Both *Areop* and *Tetr* have passages from Euripides on their title pages, and contain, in addition, three specific allusions.... Euripides is the only tragedian and one of the few Greeks quoted in *DocCh*" (*Milton's Debt* 245–46). In 1634, Milton purchased a two-volume edition of Euripides (published in Geneva, in 1602), which is now in the Bodleian Library. The relationship between the two poets is studied by Timberlake, 334–38. Bush asserts in general, "the strain of ratiocination and the presence and self-exculpation of a masterful 'bad' woman suggest Euripides" (*Milton* 513).

61. *unequalled yet by any:* Landor regrets the implications of Milton's diction "because it may leave a suspicion that he fancied he, essentially undramatic, could equal them, and had now done it; and because it exhibits him as a detractor from Shakespeare" (5:297). Steiner writes that "the judgment [these words] convey and the tragedy which they introduce are the great counterstatement in English literature to Shakespeare and to all 'open' forms of tragic drama" (31). Alternatively or also, Parker suggests that Milton may be alluding, not to his own drama, but to Seneca, whom many Renaissance critics (e.g., Scaliger, Cinthio, Cavalcanti, Riccius) considered equal or even superior to the Greeks ("Variorum"). See Preface 24–26n.

62–64. *The circumscription of time:* the "limitation of time" is the only part of "the ancient Law of tragedy" that Phillips emphasizes (*Theatrum* sig. **8r). Note that Milton mentions only one of (and does not use the expression) "the three unities"; the expression occurs, perhaps for the first time in English, in Dryden's *Essay of Dramatick Poesie* (1668; cf. *OED*). Parker suggests that this rule does not "spring from practical necessity in the same sense as does the rule of place. An audience with imagination enough to think of two hours as being twelve or twenty-four, is likewise capable of imagining two hours as being a week" (*Milton's Debt* 19). Parker observes that all extant classical tragedies follow the limitation of time except for five: Aeschylus's *Persians, Agammemnon,* and *Eumenides;* Sophocles' *Women of Trachis;* and Euripides' *Suppliant Women*—with *Andromache* another possible exception; Parker (*Milton's Debt* 19, 20) adds that Milton actually used only about seven of the twenty-four hours that he mentioned as permissible—from sunrise (11) to noon (1612).

63–64. *antient rule:* Spingarn notes, "The only 'ancient rule' for the unity of time is Aristotle's casual reference" (*Critical Essays* 1:252). See Aristotle, *Poetics* 5.4: "Tragedy endeavours, as far as possible, to confine itself to a single revolution of the sun, or but slightly to exceed this limit; whereas the Epic action has no limits of time....[A]t first the same freedom was admitted in Tragedy as in Epic poetry" (qtd. in Parker, *Milton's Debt* 19). Carey lists five surviving Greek tragedies that do not follow these rules: Aeschylus's *Persians, Agamemnon,* and *Eumenides,* Sophocles' *Women of Trachis,* and Euripides' *Suppliant Women* (*Complete Shorter Poems*). Spingarn adds that, in England, the first mention of the unities of time and place occurs in Sidney's *Defence of Poesie,* where, Spingarn claims, they are derived directly from the Italian critic Castelvetro (*History* 290). Kastner and Charlton summarize French and Italian opinions on the three unities (1:cxxiv–cxxxiii). Langdon infers from Milton's list of possible subjects for tragedy in the Trinity Manuscript "that he intended a rigorous observance of unity, not only in the action, but also in place and time" (116). Kellett suggests that "much" in *SA*—including this reference in the Preface—"is not merely *in* the Restoration era, but *of* it....[Milton] followed their favourite rules with more utter hardihood and more uncompromising faithfulness than any other had the knowledge, the gifts, or the daring, to show" (87–88).

and best example: Parker notes, "In a time when 'antient rule' was being blindly followed merely because it was rule, this poet dared to talk about 'best example' as well....Milton must always be reasonable: rules had to be known, but they were guides to be modified by experience" (*Milton's Debt* 19). Routh calls this attitude *rationalism* and suggests that Milton furnishes "perhaps the neatest example of it" in his age (627). See *SA* 1641n. Langdon adds, "In taking this ground, Milton, if he is more exacting than Aristotle, speaks much in his tone, and quite escapes the absurdity of the Italian [critical] position" (119).

The Argument

The Argument: commentators have comparatively little to say about this opening section, mostly discussing how accurately it represents *SA*'s narrative. E.g., Gilbert identifies various discrepancies between the Argument and the poem (see the notes for Argument 10, 15–16, 20, 24–25, 27–28); he concludes that the Argument was written before Milton completed *SA* and represents an early outline ("Is *Samson Agonistes*" 98–100). But Hanford insists, "The crucial steps in the action are clearly indicated" (*Poems*). Grierson also asserts that the Argument is "doubtless the last thing written" because it emphasizes the poem's "main intention," which Grierson identifies as divine inspiration "by latent impulsion to do certain things which in normal morality are forbidden" (*Milton* 139).

2–3. *Gaza:* see *SA* 41n.

    a common work-house: see *SA* 6n. Parker ("Variorum") notes that after 1652 the word *workhouse* acquired the meaning, inappropriate here, of "a house established for the provision of work for the unemployed poor of a parish" (*OED* 2).

    Festival: see *SA* 1598.

4. *comes forth:* Parker notes, "actually, he is led" ("Variorum").

    place: see *SA* 17, 333.

6. *at length:* i.e., after his opening soliloquy; cf. "to sit awhile" (5). See Argument 20n.

7. *equals:* Latin *aequales,* "one who has lived as long; a contemporary" (*OED* B.1c); Page suggests that it also refers to the person's rank. The word is not used in the poem itself.

    tribe: see *SA* 217.

9. *Manoa:* see *SA* 328n.

10. *procure:* Parker notes that this word, repeated in Argument 24, is not used in the poem itself ("Variorum").

    lastly: Wyatt and Collins write that the order of the Argument is the reverse of that of the poem: Manoa tells about the feast in 434–47, about the plans for ransom in 481–86, and, upon Samson's deprecation of that proposal, he tries to comfort his son in 502–20. Gilbert adds, "in reality neither Manoa nor the Chorus make much effort at comfort" ("Is *Samson Agonistes*" 98).

11. *proclaim'd:* so *SA* 435, 1598.

    Philistins: so also Argument 27. Parker ("Variorum") observes that Milton's spelling is *Philistims* in the Trinity Manuscript plans for tragedies (Patterson, *Works* 18:236 is in error), *Ref* (Patterson, *Works* 3:45), *RCG* (Patterson, *Works* 3:276), *Areop* (Patterson, *Works* 4:327–28), *Ps 83* 27 (composed April 1648), and *Eikon* (Patterson, *Works* 5:179). However, the word is spelled *Philistine* twice and *Philistines* eight times in the text of *SA*. All three spellings occur in Phillips's *New World: Philistines* five times (s.v. *David, Goliah, Sampson, Saul, Shamgar*), *Philistins* once (s.v. *Abimelech*), and *Philistim* once (s.v. *Haraphah*). See also *SA* 577.

11–12. *day of Thanksgiving:* Parker writes, "such public celebrations were proclaimed from time to time in England from 1641 on" ("Variorum"). See *SA* 12n s.v. *Feast.*

    deliverance: so *SA* 437. Nash notes the punning irony that "the great deliverer [40] has been delivered to his enemies and Philistia now celebrates her 'deliverance'" (31).

    thir: so also Argument 18; this spelling first occurs in Preface 13 and predominates in the text. See *SA* 190n.

14. *prosecute:* see *SA* 603.

Philistian: Parker writes, "so spelled elsewhere in Milton (e.g., *Animad* [Patterson, *Works* 3:122] and *Tetr* [Patterson, *Works* 4:160]) except in *PL* 9.1061, where it is 'Philistean,' accented on the third (instead of the second) syllable" ("Variorum").

15–16. *redemption:* see *SA* 1482.

visited by other persons: commentators discuss why Milton here does not name Samson's specific visitors. Gilbert objects that this "colorless phrase" describes the 555 lines, nearly one-third of the tragedy, given to Dalila and Harapha's visits: "If the Argument were composed later than the tragedy, is it possible that characters so important...would not have been named?.... [T]he development of these visits appears to have been an afterthought" ("Is *Samson Agonistes*" 98, 101). Sellin, however, thinks that the omission here of Dalila and Harapha indicates that these scenes are "'episodes,' ...admitted to the tragic poem for the sake of embellishment, ornamentation, or sheer bulk"; he proposes that the visits of these characters are not directly related to the final catastrophe and "need not be connected with the 'action' according to criteria of unity thought to govern the parts" ("Milton on Tragedy" 175; "Milton's Epithet" 142). Scott-Craig argues instead that Milton's phrase here links Dalila's and Harapha's visits and thus "they should be viewed together in the structure of the developing action" ("Concerning" 48). Baum alternatively suggests that Milton sums up these scenes here because he "seems to have been curiously aware" that the entrance and exit of Dalila and Harapha do not follow a probable or necessary sequence, as Aristotle's principles require (362).

require: see *SA* 1314.

17. *People:* Parker suggests *commonalty* ("Variorum"); so *SA* 1421; cf. *PR* 3.48–49.

18. *play:* see *SA* 1340, 1448.

20. *at length:* meaning either "in the end" or "after a long time." If the latter, Gilbert objects that Samson's debate is actually short, indicating further, he reasons, that the Argument was written before the poem was completed ("Is *Samson Agonistes*" 99). Cf. Argument 6.

perswaded inwardly: see *SA* 1381–83. The persuasion is "inward," but Gilbert asserts that "the Argument calls for a casuistical discussion in verse, not furnished by the tragedy" ("Is *Samson Agonistes*" 99). Grierson finds in this phrase the "main intention of the poem" and compares the "latent impulsion" that inspired the execution of Charles I and the election of Oliver Cromwell (*Milton* 139). Cf. *RCG:* "an inward prompting which now grew daily upon me" (Patterson, *Works* 3:236); cf. also *Def 2:* "some diviner monitor within" (warning him that his "destiny" included blindness for the sake of duty [Patterson, *Works* 8:69]); and Milton's panegyric to Cromwell in *Def 2:* "a man who is upheld by divine help, who is admonished and taught by little less than divine converse" (Patterson, *Works* 8:229); see also *DocCh:* "the inward persuasion of the Spirit working in the hearts of individual believers" (Patterson, *Works* 16:279).

22–23. *the Chorus yet remaining:* Gilbert reasons that because the Chorus's continued presence is evident to any reader, perhaps this clause was one of Milton's directions to himself while writing ("Is *Samson Agonistes*" 99).

23–24. *joyful hope:* see *SA* 1504–5, 1574–75.

24–35. *deliverance:* see *SA* 603; cf. *SA* 1505, 1575.
  in the midst of which discourse: Gilbert notes that no mention is made of the offstage noise heard by Manoa and the Chorus: "This is important in the effect of the play when read, and would be still more so in performance.... If Milton before writing his summary had decided on a noise off stage, ...would he not have mentioned it?" ("Is *Samson Agonistes*" 99).

25. *Ebrew:* on this spelling, see *SA* 1308n.
  haste: cf. the spelling *hast* in *SA* 1027, 1441, 1678.

26. *more distinctly:* see *SA* 1595.
  the Catastrophe: Parker defines this as "the change which produces the final event of the drama; λύσις or dénouement" ("Variorum"). Scott-Craig notes that the word "does not imply just dreadful misfortune.... Indeed the word *lusis* in Aristotle's *Poetics,* which we usually translate either as 'denouement' or 'catastrophe,' is simply 'loosing,' and is derived from the same primitive root from which *lustrum* and *lustratio* in Latin, and *lutron* in Greek also come" ("Concerning" 48).

27–28. *by accident:* "by chance or fortune" (Parker, "Variorum").

   wherewith the Tragedy ends: Gilbert finds here yet another discrepancy between the Argument and poem: the tragedy actually ends, not with the speech of the Messenger, but, a hundred lines later, after choral odes and a speech by Manoa ("Is *Samson Agonistes*" 99).

The Poem

1–114. The part of a Greek tragedy that preceded the chorus's entrance was called the πρόλογος, or "prologos" (Aristotle, *Poetics* 12.2). Parker notes that only Aeschylus's *Suppliant Maidens* and *Persians* do not have the prologos (not to be confused with a prologue in the modern sense); both plays instead begin with a processional ode by the chorus (*Milton's Debt* 15). Parker finds ancient precedent for other aspects of Milton's prologos and compares both Euripides (e.g., thirteen of his tragedies begin, like *SA*, with a soliloquy) and Sophocles (e.g., his plays, like *SA*, "begin quickly" and are dominated by their principal characters). Parker, however, emphasizes the unique characteristics of *SA*'s prologos: "[it] is longer by twenty-seven lines than the longest opening speech in the extant plays.... There is also no ancient model for a soliloquy which grows out of words addressed to a silent companion" (*Milton's Debt* 94, 96).

Commentators discuss various precedents for Samson's opening speech. Cumberland writes that "Samson possesses all the terrific majesty of Prometheus chained, the mysterious distress of Œdipus, and the pitiable wretchedness of Philoctetes" (337). Sheppard alternatively offers a detailed analysis of what he calls the "Aeschylean symmetry" of the prologos (157–59); Brewer also compares Samson's opening lament with Prometheus's soliloquy in *Prometheus Bound* (914–15); Kitto similarly suggests that Samson's opening speeches echo Prometheus's speeches to the chorus from Aeschylus: in both cases, "the essential drama" is the character's "present mind" (60). But Hill discusses how "Samson is more than a fallen Hercules or Prometheus, more than a tragic image of despoiled strength; he is spiritually dead.... [and] he realizes that he is" (152). Arthos also writes that Milton begins with "the heart of the matter" and foregrounds "the fatigue of the spirit," whereas, in contrast, "the characteristic note of the opening of the classical tragedies approximates the note of proclamations, before a temple or before the king's palace"; Arthos suggests that the "manner" of Samson's words "and what they point to is a play to proceed as *melodramma* does" (171, 172, 174). Ralli finds in this soliloquy "a quality present in no other of Milton's poems": "The utter loneliness of a defeated human soul is what strikes us first, but as we read and meditate we discover that to this soul, defeated yet repentant, God is present" (141–42). But Christopher argues that "the bulk of Samson's opening soliloquy implicitly accuses God. . . . He complains of nothing less than a divine betrayal" (363). On Samson's remorse, see 46n.

Discussing the versification, Ellis-Fermor writes: "The prevailing movement [lines 1 to circa 65] . . . is slow, lifeless, and inert. The lines drag, like the thought. Sometimes they are deliberately unmusical and formless; they seem again and again about to drift into silence. . . . This is the natural musical opening for the play. . . . Passages of more vigour, in thought as in movement, break in here from time to time, but the inertia re-asserts its weight throughout the opening phases and even at intervals up to the entry of Dalila" (148). See 67–109n.

1–11. Commentators discuss the beauty and biographical implications of these lines. Johnson (*Rambler* 16 July 1751) finds "the beginning . . . beautiful and proper, . . . with a graceful abruptness" (218). Mahood is reminded of the invocations to the Holy Spirit in *PL* and thinks Milton intended the "echo" to "prepare us for the autobiographical character of the tragedy" (318). Charles Williams similarly thinks Milton alludes to his own writing of poetry (*English Poetic Mind* 143), and J. Macmillan Brown more emphatically suggests that "it is Milton himself who appears at the beginning . . . ; he is a prisoner in Philistine or Restoration London" (34). But Hughes thinks "Samson is less the mouthpiece for his creator's lyric cry than he is the representative of all blind humanity" (*John Milton* 425), and Upton earlier dismisses interpretations that cast Samson as a surrogate for Milton after the Restoration: "these mystical and allegorical reveries have more amusement in them, than solid truth; and savour but little of cool criticism" (sig. M1v). Lawry thinks Samson's opening speech is more evocative and inclusive, addressed not only to a "literal Greek *kophon prosopon* [silent face] . . . but also to the approaching chorus; to his 'guide' in the temple of Dagon; to his tempters . . . ; to his own restless mind; to God; and to the audience . . ." (353). See also 1n. Parker remarks on the symmetry: the eleven lines addressed to the guide constitute a single sentence that is exactly balanced by a following sentence of eleven lines explaining the occasion (*Milton's Debt* 61). Penn in his edition of *SA* cuts various passages so as to provide "that rational as well as theatrical rapidity of march...for the purpose of showing the true nature of the drama" (2:213); here, for example, he makes the first of his many omissions, lines 2, 7–11.

Other commentators offer various comparisons for the opening speech. They are especially reminded of the opening scenes of Sophocles' *Oedipus at Colo-neus,* where the blind old man is conducted to a resting place by his daughter Antigone, and of Euripides' *Hecuba,* where the Trojan dames lead forward their former queen; also of the scene in Euripides' *Phoenician Women,* 834–40, where blind Tiresias is led on by his daughter (e.g., Richardson [in Newton]). Cf. *Def 2* (Patterson, *Works* 8:75). Martz writes that the phrasing also has a "redemptive overtone" taken from Luke 1, where Zacharias prophesies the redemption of God's people (118). Watkins (142–43) compares Samson's state of mind with that of Adam after the Fall (*PL* 10.720–844) and also detects "a weariness reminiscent of Hamlet's exhausted fatalism" (*Hamlet* 5.2.222–40)—but with the "significant difference in Samson's readiness." Robertson, discussing Samson as a figure for Adam, compares this request for a guiding hand with the final image of Adam and Eve, hand in hand, at the end of *PL* (330). Arthos finds a similarity with the opening of G. F. Busenello's Renaissance opera *L'incoronazione di Poppea* (173–74). To MacCaffrey, Samson is here "a Gulliver among Lilliputians" (xxx). Tinker compares Milton's Samson with Samson's depiction in Judges and finds these opening lines "indicative of the new quality of patience, which is the direct product of his suffering in prison" (63). Van Doren (104) suggests that this passage influenced the scene with Manto and Tiresias in Dryden and Nathaniel Lee's *Oedipus.* Ferry thinks this latter comparison revealing: Milton allies readers with Samson by leaving them in the dark. The opening lines of *SA,* in contrast to Dryden's play, "make virtually no effort to compensate to the reader for the visual effects that would be supplied automatically by performance, to an audience watching in a theatre" (132–33). See also 3n.

1. Carey cites this line to illustrate the "common" disruption of English word order in *SA* by "the promotion of adverb or adverbial phrases or clauses to the start of a clause, sentence or, sometimes, speech" (*Complete Shorter Poems* 334; see also 6, 79, 472, 547–50, 590, 594, 732–33, 819).

   onward: Parker ("Variorum") notes a mournful echo in *on* (2) and *yonder* (3) and *wont* (4).

thy: spoken to the unidentified guide who leads Samson "on stage." Cf. Judges 16:26, where his guide at the end is a "lad" (a detail not used by Milton). This person is not listed among the dramatis personae; the Greeks would have called him a κωφὸν πρόσωπον, or "mute character, silent actor" (Edmund K. Chambers; Parker, *Milton's Debt* 30); Milton alludes to such in *HistBr* (Patterson, *Works* 10:185). See 721n.

guiding hand: Bush thinks the line indicates Samson's "immediate relationship with God" (*John Milton* 200); Ferry similarly argues that *guiding hand* refers to both "the hand of the unseen companion, and . . . the leading spirit of divine grace guiding Samson unawares toward a final goal of rest for his tortured spirit" (154). Arthos writes, "Milton strikes the note of general charity along with the note of poignancy. . . . Here the tone is that of one who is identified sympathetically with a figure whose renewal is taking place in the public view" (184). Broadbent (*Milton* 40) compares Psalm 43 and notes the foreshadowing of the hand that guides Samson to the pillars at the climax (1629–30). For other references to hands, both literal and figurative, see 142, 259, 359, 438, 507, 593, 668, 684, 951, 1105, 1159, 1185, 1230, 1233, 1260, 1270, 1299, 1302, 1306, 1526, 1581, 1584. See also 1306n.

2. Bush writes that the poem's first two lines, as well as the title, "inaugurate the dramatic irony and ambiguity that run throughout" (*Milton*).

    these: "my," imitating the Greek use of ὅδε (Percival, Blakeney) or τοῖσδε (Collins).

    dark: "not able to see, . . . blind" (*OED* 9), transferred from the eyes to the feet. The words *caecus* and τυφλῶ have the same meaning in Latin and Greek; Church notes that *caecus* "has exactly this double sense of that which cannot see and that which cannot be seen." Commentators offer various possible precedents. Verity, Timberlake (335), et al. suggest Milton is remembering Euripides' *Phoenician Women* 834–35: ὡς τυφλῶ ποδὶ / ὀφθαλμὸς εἶ σύ ("since to the blind foot ['sightless feet'] thou art an eye"); both A. D. (555) and Fogel (115–17) suggest instead that Milton is remembering Sidney's *Arcadia* 2.10.3, where the King of Paphlagonia protests, "no bodie daring to shewe so much charitie, as to lende me a hande to guide my darke steppes" (see also Carey, *Complete Shorter Poems;* Bush, *Milton*). Fogel further compares this expression to the catachresis "Blind mouths" from *Lyc:* in *SA,* "not the physical disability itself but the effect of the disability—darkness of vision—is transferred. The resultant more strenuous mental leap demanded of the reader intensifies and actualizes Samson's state of total eclipse amid the blaze of noon" (116). Rajan suggests, "The blindness is both a dramatic fact and a symbolic presence, a reminder to all of us of what we cannot see" (128).

   a little further on: Parker notes the pathetic repetition and balanced phrasing ("Variorum"). Darbishire (*Poetical Works*) and B. A. Wright emend to *furder,* which seems to have been Milton's normal spelling; the word recurs in 520, 1252, and 1499 spelled as here. For some reason, however, neither Darbishire nor Wright changes the spelling in 520, and Wright also does not emend the spelling of this word in 1252. Writing about these and other editorial inconsistencies, Parker concludes that the spelling of Milton's poetry is less important than the "sounds and rhythms Milton meant to be heard" and that "the most careful scholars will forever disagree on Milton's orthographical intentions" ("Notes" 690).

3. *yonder bank:* blind Samson directs his guide. Newton recalls that blind Oedipus sat upon a little hill near Athens, "but yet I think there is scarcely a single thought the same in the two pieces." Ferry notes the "special relationship" that Milton forges between readers and Samson: e.g., we learn that Samson has reached this bank "only in a manner roughly parallel to the ways Samson himself learns it, by recording the different sensations caused upon the skin by 'Sun,' 'shade,' and 'fresh' breezes" (136). Arthos suggests, "This evident staginess we accept as no distraction because it fits with Samson's blindness, and it also serves the immediate situation of the play in which a blind man is groping his way" (184).

   hath: "affords, offers" (Parker, "Variorum"); the next line explains how Samson knows this.

   Sun or shade: although these words describe a literal situation, commentators note that they may also express symbolically the alternatives of Samson's fate (see, e.g., Wilkenfeld 162; Lawry 354); cf. 1389, 1426. Following Masson's lead (*Poetical Works* 3:87–88), some editors also find here "an autobiographical touch" (Blakeney); they quote Richardson's account of blind Milton sitting outdoors in sunny weather, enjoying the fresh air (Darbishire, *Early Lives* 203); cf. 10n. See also Page (13), as well as Banks's suggestion that 1–11 reflect Milton's experience of being released from a prison in 1660 (136). Northrop Frye writes, more generally, that the poem "sums up Milton's life" (Paradise Lost *and Selected Poetry* xx). Grierson agrees, proposing that Milton "was finding relief for his pent-up feelings in a dream, a wish-fulfilment" ("Note" 338–39); elsewhere, though, Grierson adds, "one will never be fair to Milton...if one thinks of him as complaining simply of his *own* unhappy lot as a man. He is thinking of himself as identified with 'the Good Old Cause' which has gone under" (*Milton* 137). Bush agrees that Milton is "reliving his own career as a great deliverer now in subjection." But he cautions "that Milton—always, under the keenest stress, an impersonal classical artist—sublimated his own experience and emotions; and that everything in the drama that suggests a Miltonic parallel is an integral part of the story of Samson" (*Portable Milton* 22; cf. "John Milton" 412; *Milton* 515). Roston traces Milton's "passionate identification" with Samson to the Reformation's "new and deep respect" for Old Testament Jews "as men closer to the purity of divine revelation than the saints and martyrs of the Catholic church" (161).

4. Percival notes that this statement and the subsequent one about the growth of his hair (568–69) imply "that Samson has been some time in prison"; see also 929 ("long since") and 938n.

    wont: "accustomed, used" (Parker, "Variorum"). Hunter writes, "this is the past participle of the Saxon verb *wunian,* which signified to dwell, to be accustomed."

    chance: Carey suggests that often activity in *SA* is delegated to abstract nouns such as this one: "They carry the weight of the action, either as the subjects or as the objects of the verbs.... This abstraction might be thought a way of conveying Samson's blindness, if it were not prominent in the speeches of the other characters also" (*Complete Shorter Poems* 336); e.g., in Samson's first speech, see 14–15, 36–37, 43–44, 52, 57, 60–61, 64–66, 111, 112–13.

5. *my task of servile toyl:* see 35, 41. Samson's *labor servilis* ("work performed by slaves") is grinding corn. Percival and Verity cite references to show that this was, among both the Jews (e.g., Exod. 11:5, Lam. 5:13) and the Greeks and Romans, a task for slaves, often a punishment, and a degrading labor. Note Milton's use of the phrase "slavish toyle" in *Ps 81* 21.

6. Weismiller (in Parker, "Variorum") scans this line as follows: the second and third syllables are coalesced, read as one through *pronunzia congiunta* or synaloepha; the line begins then with a trochee; it ends with the simulated trochaic

movement of an unstressed ending (the last syllable an unaccented particle). Parker adds, "the marked variation from the established iambic rhythm calls attention to the sense" ("Variorum").

Daily: so also 76, 114; Parker finds the iteration "moving" ("Variorum"). Cf. 1261.

common Prison: Harapha, repeating this phrase (1161–62), names slaves and asses as Samson's "comrades" (Parker, "Variorum"). The prison is a "gaol" (949), a "dungeon" (69, 367), and a "public Mill" (41, 1327, 1393). See 922n. Whiting (*Milton's Literary Milieu* 254) notes that Quarles in *Historie of Samson* (1631) uses this same phrase (sig. S2v).

else: "otherwise" (*OED* 4); but at least six editors read it as having a rare temporal use and meaning "at other times." Lockwood overlooks this occurrence of *else;* cf. 315, 586, 604, 770, 1163, 1524.

7. *Prisoner:* Darbishire (*Poetical Works*) and B. A. Wright emend to *Pris'ner* (as in 1308, 1460); Parker agrees ("Notes" 693).

chain'd: so also 68, 1238. Oras notes that the *-ed* participle is placed after the noun, an inverted word order that is "exceptional" in Milton's early poetry but "becomes the rule" in his later compositions (*Blank Verse* 17, 22). See also 20, 347, 385, 520, 729, 884, 1079, 1083, 1117, 1224 (twice), 1231, 1357, 1494, and 1556.

draw: "breathe" (*OED* II.23a); cf. *Lyc* 126.

8. *air imprison'd also:* Percival detects a play on words: "stuffy, ill-ventilated," and (pathetic fallacy) "put in prison." Johnson (*Rambler* 20 July 1751) censures this as "verbal quaintness" (221), Landor as a "prettiness" (5:295). Percival defends the expression as an imitation of the Greek practice; Martin W. Sampson adds: "under powerful emotions inanimate objects may be spoken of in terms that might be mere 'conceits' were they uttered in cold blood." Cf. 94.

9. *draught:* "that which is inhaled at one breath" (so *OED* V.16); cf. *draw* (line 7); in apposition to *air* (line 8).

amends: "improvement in health, recovery" (so *OED* 4b); cf. 745.

10. Muldrow writes, "the imagery of the 'breath of Heav'n' introduces the theme of recovery. The contrast between the 'air imprison'd' [8] and air of Heaven . . .

suggests the need for change on Samson's part" (171). But Hawkins suggests that, while "Samson thinks of his cure in terms of opposites," this imagery points to how he is actually cured homeopathically, using "like against like" (221); see 606–51n. McCall discusses how this line fits within the poem's imagery of disease (89–93); Cox writes of the implied imagery in this line and the next: "there is not only the implication of equation between two elements (fire and water), but also the declaration that fire and air come from the same source" ("Natural Science" 52–53). Hanford suggests instead, "So Milton, long in populous city pent, was wont to seek the country air" (*John Milton* 213).

   breath: cf. 628; also *Arc* 56 and *PL* 4.641, 650.

   Heav'n: this seems to have been Milton's preferred spelling from at least 1645 on; it recurs in 36, 150, 525, 549, 565, 632, 1046, 1212, 1217, 1509; but cf. 23, 373, 635, 1035, 1134, 1438, where it is *Heaven* or *Heavenly* (see Parker, "Notes" 693).

11. *day-spring:* "early dawn" (so *OED*); see also *PL* 5.139; 6.521; Job 38:12; Luke 1:78. Church and Verity observe that a breeze often springs up at daybreak. Cf. 1597. Carson suggests that the sun's morning rays symbolize Samson's dawning spiritual renewal (174); Bush also finds in this and the preceding line "a hint of divine inspiration and aid" ("John Milton" 504n).

   born: "brought into existence" (Parker, "Variorum").

   respire: "to take breath; to rest or enjoy relief from toil" (so *OED* 4). Commentators note that the guide seems now to leave the scene because Samson wishes to be alone. In view of what follows, the word may have the additional meaning of "recover hope" (*OED* 3; Parker credits Victor A. Doyno for suggesting this latter meaning to him ["Variorum"]).

12. See 1–11n. Samson's long soliloquy begins, candidly (by convention) revealing his state of mind. Milton here observes "unity of action" by mentioning at once the occasion "upon which the entire drama hinges" (Percival; also Parker, *Milton's Debt* 31).

   This day: so also 434, 1311, 1388, 1574, 1600. Parker writes, "It is Samson's last day on earth" ("Variorum").

   solemn: "religious," "sacred" (*OED* 1); Le Comte (45) writes that "solemn feast" is a "Biblical phrase" and notes it is repeated at 1311; cf. Milton's Elegy 6.9 *solennes epulas;* see also *PL* 1.390. Verity and Meiklejohn suggest the meaning "recurring annually" (Latin: *solemnis*); Edmund K. Chambers thinks that "the more ordinary English sense suits just as well."

Feast: Parker ("Variorum") defines this as "a religious anniversary appointed to be observed with rejoicing, in honor of someone" (here Dagon) or in commemoration of some event (so also with this anniversary, as the Argument and 434–39 reveal; *OED* 1a). Krouse argues that Milton intends the latter meaning only: "This choice...followed the classical principle of economy and also permitted Milton to wring more tragic irony from the predicament of Samson: it is deeply humiliating for the hero to take part in the celebration of his own ruin; and it also greatly enhances Samson's final triumph" (107).

13–14. *Dagon thir Sea-Idol:* editors note that Dagon, a vegetation and fertility god, was among the oldest Akkadian deities and was worshiped throughout the Euphrates Valley as early as the twenty-fifth century BC. To Luther and others the name meant "wheat," and Dagon worship meant gluttony (Bullough and Bullough 45); Dodd writes that the name "signifies corn, as if he was the inventor of it" (sig. I2v). But Milton's conception of him (cf. *PL* 1.462–63) was based on an earlier, no longer accepted derivation of his name from a Semitic root, *dag*—"fish" (*OED* 2)—and from a marginal reading for 1 Samuel 5:4. Thus, Blount in 1656 writes: "It had the upper part like a man, the neather part like a fish" (sig. M4r). Dagon is not listed in Phillips's *New World;* Éstienne in his *Dictionarium* refers to him as "*magnifico pisce*" (sig. 3G1v). Parker notes that the god had a temple at Ashdod (1 Sam. 5:2–3) as well as one, presumably, at Gaza (Judg. 16:21–23); the Philistines worshiped other gods; cf. 859, 896, 1231, 1242 ("Variorum"). Carey (*Complete Shorter Poems* 337) suggests that this reference to the sea initiates the poem's larger pattern of marine imagery: e.g., Dalila's entrance with the simile of a ship (714–19).

forbid / Laborious works: Parker finds this ironic, in view of what they finally require of Samson ("Variorum").

rest: also ironic: "The feast of the Philistines now does in a small way what it will do in a final way" (Stein, *Heroic Knowledge* 139).

15. *Superstition:* "false, pagan, or idolatrous religion" (so *OED* 2).

16–22. Ferry notes how, as in this simile, Samson "uses language ordinarily referring to the body to form figures of speech expressing his condition of spirit." Such passages are a reminder, she argues, "that his mind or soul exists within a body which he cannot see but cannot escape from feeling" (138). Cf. *PR* 1.196–200. Gohn is reminded of Adam and Eve after the fall (262). Prince suggests that if *popular* is elided, line 16 can be read as pentameter (*Samson Agonistes* 135).

 popular: "constituted or carried on by the people" (so *OED* 2); cf. 434, and *PL* 2.313; 7.488; 12.338; *PR* 2.227. Adams writes, "The adjective carries, and is meant to carry, all sorts of contemptuous feelings from Latin *populus;* the contempt is interestingly augmented by inverting the conventional adjective-noun, attribute-substance relationship, so that the noise seems to outweigh the people who make it" (191). Stein adds, "At the end of the play it is in the frequented place amid the popular noise that he seeks and finds ease, to body and mind" (*Heroic Knowledge* 139).

17. *This unfrequented place:* see 16–22n s.v. *popular.* In the Argument 4–5, Milton describes it as "a place nigh, somewhat retir'd."

18. See the choral comment on this thought (1297–99). Krouse writes that during the medieval and Renaissance periods, "Samson's fall and misery had been internalized, with the result that the mere physical aspects of his fall…were minimized; while the spiritual aspects of his ruin…were magnified" (84). E.g., in *A Commentary upon Judges* (1615), Richard Rogers speaks of Samson "sitting in the irksome prison in paine of body, but greater of mind" (qtd. in Krouse 84).

 Ease: Carey notes that the rhetorical figure in which the word (or phrase) occurring at the end of one line of poetry is used to begin the next was known as anadiplosis; he also cites 247–48, 376–77, 878–79 (*Complete Shorter Poems* 335). For other patterned repetitions, also called figures in sound, cf., e.g., 1–3, 37, 270–71, 414–15, 829–31, 1369–72, 1508–22. Weismiller (in Parker, "Variorum") adds that Milton's schoolmaster at St. Paul's, Alexander Gil, discusses "De figuris in sono" in chap. 21 of *Logonomia Anglica* (2nd ed.; 1621), and illustrates these repetitions from the poetry of the time, particularly from *The Faerie Queene.* More generally, Carey discusses the various uses of repetition and other rhetorical figures to heighten "moments of tension" in *SA* (*Complete Shorter Poems* 335–36). Dryden and Raleigh (see *Milton* 206) thought this form of expression rare in Milton. Landor defends the rhythm of this line against Johnson's objections: "Milton's ear happened to be satisfied with these pauses; and so will any ear be that is not…nine fair inches long" (5:254).

19–21. The construction: "thoughts that…no sooner (am I) found alone but (they) rush upon me" (see Hunter). Cf. 623, where this simile is repeated. Marilla compares Samson's distress with Adam's reaction as he reawakens after the Fall: "he, too, recognizes that his condition signifies a defection which in its true import far transcends its consequences in mere personal tragedy" (71).

    restless thoughts: Parker notes that the phrase occurs also in *PL* 2.526 ("Variorum").

    swarm: cf. *PR* 1.196–97 (Verity). Todd notes that the figure of thoughts swarming and stinging occurs in, among other places, Sidney's *Arcadia* (1593) and *Macbeth* (3.2).

    Hornets: "insects dreaded in Palestine and commonly regarded as a divinely ordained scourge (e.g., Exod. 23.28; Deut. 7.20; Josh. 24.12)" (Parker, "Variorum").

    found: Verity et al. observe that this word agrees with *me* (21), not with *Hornets.* Ricks criticizes Milton's figure here as "disappointing" because "the sentence rushes forward to something incongruous…. Since the last dozen words…have nothing to do with hornets, then the sentence itself is not a living tissue" (*Milton's Grand Style* 52). Cf. 192–93n, 198n, 362n.

22. A line consisting of monosyllables (see also 59, 66, 79, 86, 92, 110, etc.). Cf. Sophocles, *Oedipus at Coloneus* 109–10; Verity also compares *PL* 4.24–25, writing that a "self-conscious contrast between the past and the present is often the essence of pathos." Jerram finds this a "pathetic reference" to the poet's own past; Hedley Vicars Ross similarly writes, "these words…came forth from the inmost heart and experience of Milton" (46).

23. Grenander finds Samson's recollection of his former glory crucial for the play's structure: he suggests that it is the play's true beginning. If the drama had not included these details about Samson early on, Grenander reasons, "his change would be from misery to triumph, and the play would either not be a tragedy at all, or at best a very inferior one" (382).

    wherefore: the first of a series of troubled questions which Samson asks himself; cf. 30, 40, 44–45, 46, 53–54, 85, 93–94. Parker writes that these questions "add psychological and dramatic interest to the recollection of past incidents" ("Variorum"). Here, he suggests, "the conflict of the play begins. The catastrophe, which we know to be impending, is obviously not to be brought about so long as the hero is in this state of mind" (*Milton's Debt* 31). Allen adds, "It is the way the good man talks in his tribulations. Job asked questions of this sort, and Milton knew that it was the first move in the gambit of doubts about the wisdom and validity of Providence" ("Idea as Pattern" 84). Other characters, later, ask other questions. Charles Williams writes, "The persons, if they do not exactly accuse God, at least indicate to God the unanswered questions.... [T]he humility consists in believing that there may be an answer" ("Introduction" xxi).

Heaven: see 10n, and cf. 525.

foretold: this fact is referred to again in 525 (cf. 44, 1662); Parker ("Variorum") detects a parallel with the life of Christ (cf. *PR* 1.238). In 1648, Diodati identifies the angel with "the Son of God himself" (sig. L5r), an identification that Milton evidently ignores.

24. *Twice:* first to the mother alone (Judg. 13:3–21). Cf. *PR* 1.238. Hoffman thinks this detail significant for *SA:* "Milton depends upon his audience to remember that the angel comes twice for a reason: Manoa calls him back to learn the best way to raise this special child.... And the angel apparently does not answer Manoa's question, for he only repeats his injunctions about eating and drinking to Manoa's wife.... Thus, before Manoa ever comes on stage his figure suggests the faith that is not quite enough, the fear of God greater than the love, the father who...cannot quite make contact with the angel of annunciation" (197).

25–26. *all:* "completely." Empson suggests that this word, used 612 times in *PL*, appears in nearly every scene with "any serious emotional pressure" ("Emotions" 597–98). The word occurs 103 times in *SA*.

flames: Carey traces a larger pattern of fire imagery; e.g., see also 27, 80, 262, 549, 1351, 1419–22, 1433, 1434–35, 1688–92, 1699–1707 (*Complete Shorter Poems* 340–41).

Off'ring burn'd: Judges 13:16, 23: "burnt offering."

27. *as:* "as if" (*OED* B.10).

fiery column: Judges 13:20: "it came to pass, when the flame went up toward heaven from off the altar, that the angel of the Lord ascended in the flame of the altar." *OED* 3 (cf. 1d) cites this as the earliest use of *column* in this sense. Bullough and Bullough also compare the "pillar of fire" in Exodus 13:21.

charioting: "carry[ing] or convey[ing] in a chariot" (so *OED* 1). Cf. 2 Kings 2:11: "behold, there appeared a chariot of fire...and Elijah went up by a whirl-wind into heaven" (Collins; Verity; Prince, *Samson Agonistes;* et al.). Cf. *Passion* 36–37; *PR* 2.16–17; *Apol* (the "fiery Chariot" [Patterson, *Works* 3:314]). But some commentators think Milton was here remembering Josephus, *Antiquities of the Jews* 5.8.3: "the angel, borne on the smoke as on a chariot, was plainly seen by them ascending into heaven" (Todd; Browne; Church; Grieve vii; Percival; Hughes, *Complete Poems* and *John Milton;* et al.). See also 1431–35. For other passages possibly influenced by Josephus's account of Samson, see notes to 139, 318, 349, 352–55, 386, 529, 581–82, 637, 850, 1020, 1196, 1479, 1613. (Other references to Josephus are in notes to the title, 218, 227, 321, 328, 472–86, 550, 715, 934, 1068, 1184, 1186, 1195–1200.) Osgood briefly discusses Milton's other references to astronomical chariots (xxv); Robertson sees this and other references to light and fire as part of Samson's more general association with the sun (324).

28. *Godlike:* "divine" (*OED* 1); cf. Judges 13:22; *PL* 7.110; etc.
  presence: "actual person," "embodied self" (so *OED* 4), or, the opposite, "incorporeal being" (*OED* 6). "This use of the abstract for the concrete to invest a personage with awe is frequent in Milton" (Percival).
  and from some: Verity and Moody gloss this line: "ascended from the altar...and from (the revelation of) some great act." Other commentators prefer, "ascended...as charioting...and (as) from" (Newton, Percival, Martin W. Sampson), which would make the sense "as *though* (if) he had revealed" (Church; Collins; Wyatt and Collins; Prince, *Samson Agonistes;* Bullough and Bullough). Hunter writes, "the preposition is here used for *after,* as *ex* or *ab* in Latin"; Upton suggests *from,* "on account of" (sig. X7v).

29. *Abraham's:* pronounce as two syllables (as in 465); cf. *PL* 12.152 (Parker, "Variorum").

30–33. Commentators find these lines to be biographical: Elbert N. S. Thompson, "It may well be of himself that he is thinking" (39); Bailey, "obviously here...the poet is already thinking of himself" (232); Edward J. Thompson, "Nowhere does Milton more clearly speak in his own person" (246); and Visiak, "the voice is Milton's" (*Milton* 61). Among other responses, O'Connor emphasizes that Samson "is an instrument, not a victim, of Providence. He may question the means of expressing but not the *end* of God's design" (80). But Fogle believes that Samson here "descends to self-pity and comes close to blasphemy in questioning the justice of Providence for permitting this abysmal descent" (191). See 60–62n.

    breeding: "education, youthful bringing up" (Parker, "Variorum"). See 31n, 318n, and Judges 13:5.

    order'd: "regulate[d]," "ordain[ed]" (so *OED* 2d); cf. 362. Judges 13:12: "And Manoah said,...How shall we order the child...?"

    prescrib'd: "laid down, appointed, or fixed beforehand" (*OED*).

31. *separate:* "separated" (past participle; so *OED* A), "set apart." Parker ("Variorum") cites Numbers 6:2–5: "When either man or woman shall separate themselves to vow a vow of a Nazarite, to separate themselves unto the Lord: He shall separate himself from wine and strong drink.... All the days of the vow of his separation there shall no rasor come upon his head:...he shall be holy, and shall let the locks of the hair of his head grow." Parker ("Variorum") adds that St. Paul was "called to be an apostle, separated unto the gospel of God" (Rom. 1.1); and the word *Nazarite* is from Hebrew *nazar,* "to separate...oneself, to refrain from anything" (*OED* 2); see 318n, 520n, 634n, 1199n.

32. *great exploits:* cf. 525, 1221, 1492; the phrase occurs also in *PL* 11.790 (see Le Comte 45, 174).

    if I must dye: see 764–65n, 1225n.

33–38. Stein suggests, "The facts of blindness and imprisonment are fiercer [here] than in their first expression" (*Heroic Knowledge* 140). Carey cites this as one of fifteen examples of polysyndeton or asyndeton in the first five hundred lines of *SA,* "and the figure is regularly repeated until the conclusion" (*Complete Shorter Poems* 336).

    Betray'd: see 378–79n.

    Captiv'd: accent the second syllable, as in 694 (Fleming; Hanford, *Poems*). For precedent, editors cite, among others, Spenser's *The Faerie Queene* 2.4.16.1: "Thus when as *Guyon Furor* had captiu'd." Weismiller (in Parker, "Variorum") observes that *Captiv'd* is oxytone also in Cowley's *Davideis* 2.634, 4.123.

    put out: so also 1103, 1160, and Judges 16:21: "and put out his eyes."

34. *scorn:* "object of mockery or contempt" (so *OED* 3b).

    gaze: "an object eagerly looked on" (Lockwood, I.a), "public spectacle" (Bullough and Bullough), or "that which is…stared at" (so *OED* 1); so also 567; cf. *Macbeth* 5.8.24: "And live to be the show and gaze o' th' time!" (Parker, "Variorum").

35. *Brazen:* Judges 16:21: "and bound him with fetters of brass; and he did grind in the prison house." Cf. 132.

    under task: "under the command of a taskmaster; by compulsion" (so *OED* 4c); cf. 5; possibly "under orders imposing a certain amount of daily work" (Church; Collins; et al.).

36–38. Moss notes that this passage offers "concise examples of *ecphonesis, antitheton, synonymia,* and *simile*" (298). Lawry writes, "with a great serpentine involution of labials and liquids and sibilants, the verse coils around Samson's self-condemnation, which becomes our own" (355).

    Heav'n-gifted "given, bestowed" (so *OED*, the only example cited). Krouse argues that this idea comes from the extra-biblical tradition, not from Judges (93).

    strength: the word is used forty times in *SA.* Robertson argues that Samson's "physical virtue…is of interest in the poem chiefly as a symbol of…*moral* virtue" (320). Carey notes that the rhetorical figure *ploce* (repetition with intervening words) occurs "constantly" in *SA,* as here, "strength…strength"; e.g., in Samson's opening speech, 73–74, 80–81, 90–91 (*Complete Shorter Poems* 335).

37. *labour of a Beast:* see 1162; asses were employed to turn mills; Percival cites Matthew 18:6: μύλος ὀνικὸς ("millstone of asses") and Ovid, *Fasti* 6.318: "et quae pumiceas versat asella molas" ("and the she-ass that turns the millstones of pumice").

    debas't: cf. 1335 (*debas'd*).

38–42. For Le Comte, "this is the key passage dramatically, for it has the promise, has the past accomplishment…and gives us the agonizing present" (45).

    bondslave: Parker ("Variorum") recalls that the Philistines carried on a lucrative slave trade, which Amos denounced (Amos 1:6). See also 41, 122, 367, 418, 485, 1162, 1224, 1392. Weismiller notes the emphasis given the self-contempt by the explosive *b* in *Beast, debas't…bondslave* (in Parker, "Variorum"). Cf. 411

(*Bond-slave*). Moody calls this a "contracted expression, due perhaps to the fact that the intervention of the concrete word 'beast' [37] has obscured the speaker's recollection of the abstract word 'strength' [36]."

Promise... deliver: Judges 13:5. Samson here exaggerates; later, he states the "promise" accurately (225–26). Cf. 292, 1213, 1661–62, 1714–16. Because Samson's "political career" was the fulfillment of this promise—making "the entire action..., in a sense, *Israel Delivered*"—Nash (23–25) proposes that Milton recognized an affinity with Tasso's *Gerusalemme liberata;* see also 556n. Regarding the specific word *deliverer,* Nash writes, "No word in the poem is more plangent..., and no idea is more recurrent or subject to more ironic variations" (31). As in Judges 13:5, 15:18, Milton's Samson is spoken of as a "deliverer" of his people in 39–40, 225, 246, 274, 292, 1214—as are Gideon (279–80) and unnamed others (1270, 1289). Manoa's proposed ransom of his son is "deliverance" (603) or "delivery" (1505, 1575); the Hebrews had once "delivered" Samson to his enemies (437, 1158, 1184); and Dagon "deliver'd" (438) Philistia out of the hands of Samson. Carey notes that the repetition of a word in a different grammatical form—here, "deliver" (39) and "deliverer" (40)—is called *traductio* and occurs throughout *SA;* see, e.g., 113–14, 1508–22, 1686–87, 1709–10 (*Complete Shorter Poems* 335–36).

Israel... Philistian: these are the first of thirty-five or thirty-six (cf. 628) place-names, or adjectives derived from place-names, used in *SA* (Parker, "Variorum"). See Argument 14n. Belloc discusses Milton's "masterly use of place names," particularly in *PL* and *SA:* "It is Milton's most characteristic gift to English letters" (121, 257).

40. *Ask for:* "inquire about," "ask" (so *OED* 7).

great Deliverer: cf. 279 and 38–42n s.v. *Promise... deliver.* Arthos notes Samson's continuous mingling of first and third person: "he seems to want to distinguish, for himself and for us, between what he is and what he was" (185). So also Broadbent, who interprets the line-ending stresses on *I* and *him* as "a little sign" that Samson "hasn't fully identified his innermost self with the failed Samson he is contemplating" (*Milton* 41). Muldrow detects perhaps "a touch of his old weakness, pride, in his description of himself" (171).

and: old use indicating contingent consequence (Percival; Blakeney). Dunster (in Todd) finds in 40–42 a political allusion to the fate of the "lately victorious" republican party after the Restoration. (For the next alleged political allusion, see 240n.)

41. *Eyeless...slaves:* cf. 365–67. This line has been much praised. As Raleigh notes, "the sense of humiliation and abasement is intensified at every step" (*Milton* 204). Because each phrase sets forth, in graduating climax, a distinct cause of Samson's misery, Landor suggests punctuating the line thus: "Eyeless, in Gaza, at the Mill, with slaves" (5:295), so also Patterson, *Student's Milton*. Stein writes, "The friction of self-hate and detachment gives a special tone" to the words (*Heroic Knowledge* 140). Collins compares "an equally admirable climax" in Cicero's *Verrine Orations* 2.5.62; Krouse has a note on the "ancient echoes" in the line (106); Raleigh hears a "parallel to the manner of Virgil" (*Milton* 203); Lawry (356) compares it with Jesus' cry on the cross (Matt. 27:46); and Broadbent associates this line with "the dark Satanic mills" in William Blake's "The New Jerusalem," a passage which, according to Broadbent, similarly describes "the punitive repression of genius in all its forms" *(Milton* 39). See also 1151n.

  Gaza: the southernmost of the five cities of the Philistines—the others being Ashdod (Azotus), Ashkelon (Ascalon), Ekron, and Gath—Gaza is a few miles from the Mediterranean Sea (cf. 13) and is called *Azzah* in Deut. 2:23 (Gilbert, *Geographical*); see 147n. Parker writes ("Variorum") that here, in Samson's concise catalog of humiliations, "it presumably suggests both Dagon-worship and a scene of former triumph [Judg. 16:1–3]."

42. *Himself in bonds:* Parker ("Variorum") notes that this is an ironic contrast with "this great Deliverer" (40).

  Philistian yoke: ironic repetition (cf. 39).

43–44. Cf. 60–62. Steadman ("'Faithful Champion'" 22) calls this a temptation to distrust God (as opposed to a temptation to doubt God; see, e.g., 23, 350–72). Stein writes, "This, the first expression of justice and individual responsibility, interrupts the main theme of the promise ruined, and gives temporary pause to the expression of the personal. But not for long, since the feeling has too much force to remain still" (*Heroic Knowledge* 140–41). Rajan finds foreshadowing here but also describes how this phrase and 60–61 "put a brake on the emotion, holding it adequately short of self-destruction" (134). Roston describes this "clash...between reason and emotion" as "the Jobian clash between a longing for theodical affirmation and the dreadful suspicion that theodicy is merely a figment of the imagination" (169).

  Yet stay: so also *Mask* 819.

  rashly: cf. Dalila's confessions (747, 907).

44. *what if:* "what (wonder) if" (Percival). Cf. 790. Samson answers this question later (1217–19).

45. *been:* see 874n s.v. *bin.*
   fulfilled: cf. 1661.
   but: "except, save," i.e., "were it not" (Parker, "Variorum").
   default: "failure in duty," "culpable" (so *OED* II.4; cf. *PL* 9.1145). Keightley changes the comma following this word to an exclamation point (*Poems*); Masson changes it to a question mark (*Poetical Works*).

46. Commentators discuss here the significance of Samson's admission of blame and the reason for his failure. Edmund K. Chambers asserts, "This is the keynote of the tragedy. Samson…failed through his own fault; and though after repentance he has a new opportunity, yet it carries with it his own destruction." Percival writes, "He checks himself and acknowledges that it was his own frailty (the ἁμαρτία of Aristotle) that was to blame" (62); but Langdon claims, "The tragic flaw upon which the catastrophe…depends is not so much an instance of the Aristotelian ἁμαρτία ('a mistake or error in judgment'…) as of an inherent frailty or tendency toward error" (123). Bush detects in Samson's recognition of his responsibility "the seed of ultimate recovery" (*Milton* 197); Christopher similarly claims, "something of the champion still remains to plague him" (363). Woodhouse, however, writes that Samson's remorse in the poem's first section is "not yet repentance" ("Tragic Effect" 208); similarly, Hill suggests, "although it is a step in the right direction, Samson's sense of guilt is too self-oriented to be true repentance" (153). Baum is even more critical, arguing that Samson's admission undermines his heroic stature: "Most of what is 'heroic' in Samson springs from his opportunity for greatness, thwarted by inherent defects which are sub-heroic and almost below the common strength of man…. This makes his failure come a little short of tragic failure" (365). Bowra accordingly notes that Samson differs from Oedipus: "Samson is largely responsible for his own sufferings, whereas Sophocles' Oedipus falls and suffers not from any fault of his own but because the gods will it so" (117). Hanford instead finds further signs of the poem's autobiographical significance: in this speech, "the self-reproaches which Milton never allows himself to utter in his own person find free expression" (*John Milton* 214).
   complain of: so also 67; cf. 157.

my self: so also 234, 375, 824. Tickell changes the question mark following this word to a semicolon.

47–49. Editors paraphrase the passage: "myself, who could not keep under the seal of silence this high gift of strength committed to me, in what part (it was) lodged, how easily (it could be) bereft me." Cf. 394–95. But Fish finds these lines ambiguous: "'Who' is likely to be taken as a relative pronoun with an unclear referent...or, less probably, as an interrogative.... Either reading points to God as the agent referred to, and however the lines are finally resolved, He remains implicated in the action.... 'In what part lodg'd' merely continues the ambiguity; does the phrase qualify 'strength'...? or is it another interrogative...? or both?" (238). Carey cites this passage to illustrate the "insistent disturbances of English word order"; here, he writes, "the imitation of the Latin initial copulative relative is followed by an inverted construction in which the object and indirect questions connected with it precede the verb which, as often in Latin, occupies the final position" (*Complete Shorter Poems* 334).

  this high gift of strength: cf. *DDD:* "this high gift of wisdom" (Patterson, *Works* 3:378). Cf. also 1354–55.

  committed: "entrusted"; cf. 1000.

  easily: so also 409.

  bereft: "taken from"; cf. 85, 1294. Fish continues (see 47–49n) to develop the passage's ambiguity: he wonders "who...or what *is* the subject of 'bereft'? If 'bereft' is a participle, and requires no subject, 'how' (the question is there in the line) has the action of berefting been effected? by what agency? and why 'easily'?" (238).

49–50. *silence:* "secrecy"; so also 236, 428. Ricks complains that the phrase "'Seal of silence' ought to be metaphorical," but is "merely words" (*Milton's Grand Style* 54). See also 144n, 1578n; Ferry (127–77) thinks this phrase fits within a larger interpretive pattern: see 236n.

  a woman: so also 236, 379, 1114. Verity suggests it is "the emphatic word"; Blakeney writes, "said sneeringly."

  must: ironic (Parker, "Variorum").

51. *importunity:* "troublesome pertinacity in solicitation" (*OED* 4); cf. 379, 775, 779, 797, and Judges 16:16.

tears: cf. 200, 728–30, 735. The Timnian wife had "wept before him" (Judg. 14:16–17). Tickell changes the period following this word to a question mark.

52. This idea recurs in 206–9, but cf. 1010, 1279. Some critics have deemed it a peculiarly Miltonic emphasis, but Krouse writes that "it is entirely in keeping with the whole of the Samson tradition"; he adds, "I have found no document in the exegetical literature in which Samson is treated as having been endowed with remarkable intellectual capacity" (100). But A. B. Chambers challenges this assertion (315–20). See 206–7n.

53–54. Commentators offer various sources for this thought. Following Jortin and Richardson (both in Newton), most editors quote Horace, *Odes* 3.4.65 ("vis consili expers mole ruit sua" ["Brute force bereft of wisdom falls to ruin by its own weight"]), and Ovid, *Metamorphoses* 13.363 ("tu vires sine mente geris" ["You have force without intelligence"]). Hughes (*Complete Poems; John Milton*) points out that the thought goes back to Pindar's *Pythian Odes* 8.15; commentators also mention Sophocles, *Ajax* 1250–53 (Collins; Percival) and Aeschylus, *Prometheus Bound* 214–15 (Parker, *Milton's Debt* 180). Carey notes that the Chorus's subsequent estimation of Dalila—"'outward ornament' but 'judgment scant'"—echoes Samson's assessment here of himself (*John Milton* 145). See 1025–33n. On double references in *SA*, see 153n.
    share: notice the rhyme with *Hair* (59); cf. 55, 58 (Parker, "Variorum").
    wisdom: some editors (e.g., Tickell; Bohn; William Aldis Wright) change the comma following this word to a question mark.
    unwieldy: "characterized by clumsy massiveness...or ponderousness" (so *OED* 2b); thus, "difficult to use or manage" (Lockwood).

55. *secure:* "careless or over-confident" (*OED* la; Latin: *securus*), "rash." On this line, some editors cite Sophocles, *Ajax* 1078–79.

56. *weakest suttleties:* "wily stratagem[s] or trick[s]" (so *OED* 4 s.v. *subtlety*) that are weak, or, perhaps, contrived by the weakest—which some commentators gloss as "by a woman" (Keightley, *Poems;* Fleming; Percival; Blakeney); Parker, however, notes that elsewhere (e.g., 50, 235, 499, 785) the weakness is Samson's ("Variorum").

57. On the sentiment, cf. *Tetr:* "the wiser should govern the lesse wise, whether male or female" (Patterson, *Works* 4:77).

    subserve: "act in a subordinate position" (so *OED* 3a, the only example given); Percival cites its Latin use in Plautus's *Menaechmi* 5.2.

    command: "control, sway" (*OED* 3).

58–59. See Judges 16:17. Although the earliest biblical commentators believed, as this passage suggests, that Samson's strength really *resided* in his hair, 1140–44 seem to indicate that Milton agreed with later commentators that the unshorn hair symbolized Samson's adherence to his Nazaritic vows. Parker ("Variorum") describes the assertion in these lines as "an example of Samson's grim humor (possibly with a sexual double entendre)"; Krouse, however, finds 59 and 1140–44 "contradictory" and reflecting "two opposed views in biblical exegesis" (94–95). Daiches also takes these lines seriously and thinks they reveal Samson's momentary "self-pity": Samson already accepts God's justice, "but intellectual assent is not the same thing as emotional conviction, and . . . the thought of his former strength leads him to reflect bitterly on the fact that it lay only in his hair, so easily sheared" (234). Haller interprets this passage to mean that "the gift was nothing in itself. . . . The intention behind the gift is all that matters, and any action which makes toward the achievement of that intention is already victory" (210).

    withal: "at the same time" (*OED* 1b); "in addition, moreover, likewise" (Lockwood).

    slight: "unimportant, trifling" (*OED* 5b).

    Hair: Percival recalls, "on a single golden hair growing in the head of Nisus, king of Megara, depended his life" (Ovid, *Metamorphoses* 8.8–10; see 1494n), and "on a single hair of his head depended the life of Orillo, the magician of Egypt" (Ariosto, *Orlando Furioso* 15.85–90). Browne quotes Bacon's contrasting thought: "God doth often hang the greatest weights on the smallest wires" (*Advancement of Learning,* book 2). Todd quotes from the account of Samson in *Patriarchae sive Christi servatoris genealogia per mundi ætates traducta* (1657).

60–62. Bullough and Bullough assert, "This is the text of the whole drama"; Larson agrees that these lines contain the poem's message, which he paraphrases as, "If we but throw ourselves upon God with unquestioning faith, all will terminate happily" (198). Allen instead suggests, "For a moment Samson is on the edge of error, but he saves himself with a quick admonition" ("Idea as Pattern" 84). Woodhouse writes, "these lines give us our first clue to the inner tension between man's freedom and God's Providence which only the final words of the poem will resolve" ("Tragic Effect" 207). For Rudrum, Samson's statement here does not "indicate a belief that God may still be able to use him" but instead belongs "to that species of dramatic irony in which the protagonist speaks very much more than he knows" (24–25). See also 43–44n.

 peace: cf. *Mask* 358. Some editors (e.g., Bohn, William Aldis Wright) change the comma after this word to an exclamation point; Tickell changes it to a semicolon.

 quarrel: "find fault" (so *OED* 1a), with a legal complaint perhaps connoted (Parker, "Variorum").

61. *highest dispensation:* "the ordering . . . of events by divine providence" (so *OED* 5). Parker writes, "this is Samson's meaning here; but it is divine 'dispensation' in another sense that had confused Samson about marrying Philistines and will eventually send him to a Philistine feast" ("Variorum"). Shawcross also detects an etymological pun "on its being 'hung' in his hair" (*Complete English Poetry*). Rajan suggests that Milton's use of *dispensation* and, elsewhere, *disposal*—instead of *providence*—illustrates his "adherence to the properties of a pre-Christian event" (181). See 210, 373, 506, 1746.

62. Tragic irony. Wilkes detects here a "hint that the divine plan may still be fulfilled" (369). Sheppard notes, "After each act of confession there comes a gleam of light, followed—as anyone may understand from Bunyan's allegory, if not from experience—by a relapse into despondency" (157).

 Happ'ly: "perhaps, perchance" (*OED*); Darbishire (*Poetical Works*) and B. A. Wright emend to *Haply.*

 reach: "capacity or power of comprehension" (so *OED* 7b); so also 1380; cf. *PL* 5.571–72; 10.793.

63. *Suffices:* "it is enough," i.e., for me to know (so *OED* 2b).

 me: Darbishire (*Poetical Works*) and B. A. Wright emend to *mee;* see 219–20n s.v. *Mee.*

bane: "ruin," "instrument of woe" (*OED* 4–5); so also 351, where Manoa decries God's gift. Parker notes that Sophocles, *Ajax* 1250, makes physical strength a source of danger (*Milton's Debt* 31).

64. *miseries:* Hughes writes that Milton "in general...did not intend to syncopate many syllables," and thus in this case the *e* should be sounded (*John Milton* 424–25).

65–66. *each:* Edmund K. Chambers suggests that this word is used both as the subject of *ask* and the object of *wail;* Wyatt and Collins as well as Grieve suggest "(be) wail (it in)."
    ask: "need," "call for" (*OED* 23).
    wail: "bewail, lament" (*OED* 5).
    but: Parker notes that the following forty-three and a half lines (66–109), all devoted to Samson's present blindness, balance the exactly equal number (23–66) which were devoted to his lament for the past (*Milton's Debt* 61).
    chief: cf. 457.

67–109. *O loss of sight:* cf. *PL* 3.22–55. Commentators find in these lines a reference to Milton's own calamity and situation (e.g., Church: "without doubt"; Collins: "obvious to everyone" [8–9]; Meiklejohn: "autobiographical"; Alden Sampson: "must have been" [221]). Hanford calls this passage "Milton's one untrammeled expression of rebellion at the fate which has deprived him of his sight.... Here through the unreasoning voice of Samson he gives us the naked truth of his bittersweet emotion" (*John Milton* 214). Masson thinks that the reference "will strike the reader at once," and adds: "some parts of it receive painful illustration from the domestic circumstances of Milton in his old age and blindness" (*Poetical Works*). Parker, too, while stressing that we do not know when this and Samson's other speeches on blindness were written, nevertheless notes that "they have about them the eloquence and conviction of newly met reality" ("Date" 241; *Milton* 431). Woodhouse, however, writes, "the question at issue between him [Milton] and his opponents was whether his blindness was a punishment for his political beliefs and actions, a question not raised in the case of Samson at all" ("*Samson Agonistes*" 170).
    Since 1791, when the testimony in connection with Milton's nuncupative will was published by Warton (sigs. d2r–e4v [1791 ed.; not in 1785 ed.]), com-

mentators have also seen in these lines (especially 76) a reference to the poet's mistreatment by his daughters. Hayley writes "perhaps" (*Life* 1:lxxxix); Garnett questions the veracity of the daughters' alleged mistreatment but nevertheless blames Milton for their unhappiness and finds in these lines "how deep the iron had entered into his soul" (141); and on the strength of the supposed allusion, Dunster (in Todd 5:350) and Church (viii–x) argue for a date of *SA*'s composition circa 1662. If we may believe the testimony of a maidservant who worked for Milton about a year before his death, he had confided to her (on the evidence of a former maidservant, she says) the intimate facts that his daughters had tried to sell his books and to cheat him in marketing, and in 1663, his daughter Mary had wished him dead. This possibility gains some support from Christopher Milton's testimony that the daughters were "undutiful and unkind" to their father, "careless of him being blind, and made nothing of deserting him" (J. Milton French 5:214). Masson, therefore, asserts that "it is impossible not to remember" these things, now that we know them (*Poetical Works*).

However, other commentators have raised doubts about an autobiographical reading. Parker notes, e.g., that "we are dealing with gossip, that Samson had no daughters and could not, in context, be talking about any form of *domestic* life, and that he is plainly and appropriately speaking of his treatment in a prison. Also, Milton's loss of sight came gradually upon him and was not a violent punishment for sin" ("Variorum"). Eleanor Gertrude Brown is also unconvinced by autobiographical readings of this passage: "This wail, if considered autobiographical by his enemies, would have been a source of fiendish satisfaction to them. Such satisfaction Milton would never willingly have afforded.... Consciously or unconsciously expressed, the plaint remains utterly out of keeping with the spirit evinced by Milton in his other works" (97). Tinker cautions against the "seductive but dangerous theory" of emphasizing the similarities between Milton and Samson: e.g., "Milton's blindness, whatever its cause, was not the result of any mutilation by his enemies, and is in no sense indicative of a state of mental blindness like Samson's" (71). Ricks similarly emphasizes this latter connection: "the greatest thing in *Samson Agonistes,* its evocation of the hideous deprivation which is blindness, is at once spiritual and physical, and a great tragedy would show how intimately and indissolubly the spiritual is often related to the physical" ("Milton" 313).

On the versification of this passage, Ellis-Fermor writes: "As Samson's mind tosses between dejection and sharp protest, the verbal music flashes from one extreme to the other of tempo and cadence, alternating between heavy, dragging verse and lines of the utmost irregularity, harsh in the pitch and relation of their sounds. . . . There is more vigour, in sound as in feeling, than in the opening lines, but it is still undisciplined, restless, unsustained" (148–49). Daiches also finds the opening versification aptly reflective of Samson's mental anguish: "The repetitions of individual words, the very occasional rhyme, startling and emphatic because of its rarity, the many hints of rhymes and deliberate echoes of sounds, the short lines thrust out with moving force between the longer lines, the dwindling down of hopelessness at the end—all contribute to the bodifying forth of the speaker's emotion as it rocks to and fro between self-reproach and self-pity, between resignation and despair" (235). See also Hanford, *Poems* 551–52. Burney records that Handel, who composed music for Newburgh Hamilton's adaptation of these lines on blindness, was, in his own blindness, "always much disturbed and agitated" upon hearing this part performed (31). (Handel was not blind, however, in 1741 when he composed "the affecting air" that later so moved him [Burney 31].)

68–69. *enemies:* Masson (*Poetical Works*) and William Aldis Wright change the comma after this word to an exclamation point.

    chains: cf. 7, 1238.

    Dungeon: so also 367; cf. 156 ("dungeon of thyself").

    decrepit: "feeble," "worn out" (*OED* 1). Calton's suggested emendation (in Newton), "beggary *in* decrepit age," has not been adopted by some editors. Cf. 570–73.

70. *Light:* the word is repeated in 71, 75, 84, 90, 92, 98, 99.

    prime: "first in order of time or occurrence" (*OED* 1; see Gen. 1:3); perhaps also "chief" (*OED* 3; Grieve). Raleigh, followed by Blakeney, thinks that the original and derivative senses of the word "are united in the conception" (*Milton* 210). See 83–85, and cf. 234, 388.

    me: Darbishire emends to *mee* (*Poetical Works*); see 219–20n s.v. *Mee*.

    extinct: "extinguished, quenched" (*OED* 1); cf. 95, 1688.

71–72. *her:* Latin *lux* is feminine. For other examples of Milton observing Latin gender, see 93, 173, 612–13, 1706 (Parker, "Variorum"). Hunter suggests,

"Milton uses *her* for *its,* when the old neuter possessive *his* would not harmonize well with the idea for which it would be pronominal."

Anull'd: "reduced to nothing" (so *OED* s.v. *annul* 1).

73. *Inferior:* Church writes that this adjective must agree either with *me* (70) or, according to the Latin construction, with the personal pronoun latent in *my* (72).

vilest: "meanest" or, perhaps, "most repulsive" (*OED* 5b, 3).
become: cf. 155.

74. *Of man or worm:* cf. Psalm 22:6: "But I am a worm, and no man"; Gossman refers to this as a "traditional image of vileness," which also occurs in Job ("Samson, Job" 215). Low observes that this image is also traditionally interpreted as prefiguring Christ's passion and death: "The danger in going directly to the Christian analogue, however, is that one will lose sight of the tragic significance of this pattern" ("Tragic Pattern" 927–28). The author of the abusive *Clamor* (1652) professed to wonder whether Milton was a man or a worm (*Def 2* [Patterson, *Works* 8:112]).

here: "in this particular," i.e., of sight (Parker, "Variorum").

75. *dark in light:* an oxymoron; cf. 100 ("a living death"). Percival notes a similar oxymoron in Sophocles, *Ajax* 394–95: ἰὼ / σκότος, ἐμὸν φάος; "O woe is me! / Darkness, my light!"

76. See 67–109n.

77–78. *still:* "always" (*OED* 3).

fool: "dupe" (*OED* 3), and/or, more likely in view of line 78, "a weak-minded person." Bullough and Bullough note, "imbeciles were often legally handed over to guardians who controlled their property and used them as jesters."

In power of others: Hanford identifies the feeling of helplessness, here and in line 87, as Milton's own; but, he emphasizes, "all this is heightened and idealized for purposes of art" ("*Samson Agonistes*" 179).

80–109. Martz (118–19), among others, notes that Samson's lament now becomes a lyrical passage, with a more impassioned tone (note, e.g., the pathetic repetition), irregular meter, and some lines with only three or four stressed syllables. Todd, Collins, and Percival recall Oedipus's lament on his blindness (*Oedipus Rex* 1313–18). Timberlake finds this sudden introduction of a lyrical passage Euripidean in inspiration (335–36); Prince notes its Italian analogues, describing it as a transition "from chanted verse to spoken" (*Italian Element* 155–56). See 606–51n. For Coleridge's manuscript scansion of 80–114, see Brinkley, *Coleridge* 607–8. Bush scans 80–82 and offers the following interpretation: "The first four syllables, all long, depict Samson's condition, in contrast with the three following iambs that depict the bright world about him. In the second line the rising—one might say struggling—rhythm of the first half (an anapest and two iambs) shifts to a trochee in 'total'; and the juxtaposition of two stressed syllables at the caesura explosively shatters the rhythm and intensifies the emotion. The third line links itself in sense and rhythm to the second half of the first, but with the negation that belongs to Samson's darkness" (*Milton* 195; cf. "John Milton" 411). Prince (*Italian Element* 156–57) notes that Milton uses rhyme in this speech to enrich the verse's music "out of all proportion to the number of words which actually rhyme"; here, the rhyme words are discretely placed—*noon* (80) with *Moon* (87), and *night* (88) with *sight* (93), *light* (98), and *light* (99). See 134–35n.

O dark, dark, dark: Charles Williams compares this line with the description of blindness in *PL* 3.40–50: "Neither is more moving that the other; but the one awakens in us a knowledge of our capacity for realizing that we are blind; the other a knowledge of our capacity for blindness" (*English Poetic Mind* 144). Bailey writes that the "effect of three strongly stressed syllables following immediately upon one another" makes a "triple stab of passionate agony" (225); Le Comte describes the line as an example of epizeuxis expressing Samson's fear of darkness "as a kind of death, an end of usefulness" (20); Rajan suggests that the repetition of *dark* "ring[s] like blows of entombment sealing Samson into the dungeon of himself," while the "flaring out into 'blaze' of the same vowel that the repetition locks in, makes us all the more keenly aware of the constriction" (130). Cf. *Mask* 383; cf. also *Ps* 6 13–14: "mine Eie / . . . is waxen old and dark."

    amid: cf. 683.

    noon: Sadler discusses various typological implications of the drama's setting: "noon as the brightest part of the day symbolizes full understanding of the divine," but it also represents "the period of greatest temptation" because the sun's proximity causes intense heat and because, as a still point, noon "interrupts the cycle of nature" (199). Cf. 1612n.

81. *Irrecoverably dark, total Eclipse:* the scanning of this line offers difficulties. Sprott lists this line as the first of fifteen in the poem in which the first and second feet are inverted (trochaic); the others are as follows: 126, 175, 298, 618, 1268, 1269, 1271, 1280, 1686; 341, 443, 842, 1533, 1601 — "the last five cited being in pentameter context" (132). Bridges also reads the fourth foot in this line as trochaic (*Milton's Prosody* 56); Edmund K. Chambers prefers to call the first foot an anapest (and not to elide the *e*). Bailey hears the "spasmodic disorder of violent grief" in "the inversion of three out of the five stresses" (225). See also Bush in 80–109n.

  Parker notes there was a great solar eclipse on Mirk Monday, 29 March 1652, but Milton, probably by then totally blind, would not have witnessed it ("Variorum"). Carson detects here the beginnings of a light-dark "imagistic pattern" that recalls Samson's origin as a pagan solar deity; Carson specifically interprets this "total Eclipse" as suggesting Samson's "loss of his special relationship with the true Sun" (171, 174). Madsen instead proposes here "an oblique allusion to the Crucifixion" (197).

82. *all:* "any whatever" (*OED* A.I.4), perhaps like Latin *omnis* (Parker, "Variorum"). See 25.

83–84. Cf. 70, Genesis 1:3, and *PL* 3.1–2 and 7.243–44. Percival suggests that Milton partly follows the Targum on Genesis 1:3 and partly John 1:1–3. Church suggests that Milton slightly alters the end of this quotation from Genesis "for the sake of the verse; grammatically the whole line is an apposite of 'Thou great Word.'" Sheppard is reminded of Prometheus—but adds, "how new is the effect" (159). Johnson (*Rambler* 20 July 1751) compliments these and the following lines for containing a "very pleasing train of poetical images, . . . concluded by such expostulations and wishes, as reason too often submits, to learn from despair" (222).

  Word: "divine communication, command, or proclamation" (*OED* 11a); possibly also an allusion to the Johannine account of creation (see John 1:1–5), which, according to Goldsmith, would be the poem's single anachronism (79). The word *word* (used thirteen times) is capitalized only here.

  there: Darbishire (*Poetical Works*) and B. A. Wright emend to *ther;* Darbishire calls it "the unemphatic form" and compares *PL* 7.243.

85. *Why:* Samson questions again; cf. 23, 30, 44–46, 53, 93.
    bereav'd: "deprived, dispossessed of" (Parker, "Variorum"); cf. 48, 1294.
    prime: see 70.
    decree: "command, edict" (cf. *OED*).

86. *The Sun to me is dark:* Parker ("Variorum") reasons that, if Milton here echoes
    Dante, Samson implies that he is in a kind of hell; *Inferno* 1.60: "Mi ripingeva
    là, dove 'l sol tace" ("I hid myself there where the sun is silent"). See 87n.

87. *And silent as the Moon:* both sun and moon are always, presumably, noiseless,
    but Warburton (in Newton) notes that Milton expects readers to recall the Latin
    phrase *silens luna,* referring to the moon in the period when it does not shine
    (*interlunium*), between the waning of the old moon and the rising of the new
    moon. Editors cite Pliny, *Naturalis historia* 16.74: "quem diem alii interlunii,
    alii silentis lunae appellant" ("the date which some call the interlunar day and
    others the day of the moon's silence"); also *Naturalis historia* 18.75; Columella
    2.10.11; Cato, *De re rustica* 29.40; etc. Warburton (in Newton) and Stebbing
    also compare *2 Henry VI* 1.4.17: "the silent of the night."
        silent: "not shining" (*OED* 5a [pre–1646]); perhaps the meaning here is "invis-
    ible" (Parker, "Variorum"); Bush suggests, "not performing its function, i.e.,
    dark" ("John Milton" 505n). Cf. Virgil, *Aeneid* 2.555; Dante, *Inferno* 1.60, 5.28
    (Bush, "John Milton" 505n; *Milton*). Tillyard asserts: "No English poet . . . had
    ever called the sun silent, and the conjunction of the two words is not only
    new but has a dramatic relevance to the blind speaker. In the monotony of his
    blindness he must, to be expressive, do more than reiterate the fact of darkness;
    so he translates the visual *dark* into the aural *silent*." Tillyard adds that Milton
    may be echoing Dante's *Inferno,* but "he gives the notion quite another point
    by putting it in the mouth of a blind man" (*Miltonic Setting* 101; see also Ferry
    140). Landy notes that sight and sound in *SA*'s early speeches are often coupled
    together (see, e.g., 112–13, 161–62): "This focus on the conjunction of seeing
    and hearing draws the reader further into the circumscribed world of Samson's
    psychic condition, and therefore defines more clearly the close interconnection
    between intrinsic and extrinsic reality"; the combination of sight and sound,
    she adds, becomes a "metaphor for working out the nature of language and
    its limitations" ("Language" 178). Brooks, commenting on this magnificently
    "daring and illogical" statement, writes that eighteenth-century critical theory

could not condone such irrationality (*Modern Poetry* 232). MacCaffrey calls the conflation of sight and sound "surrealistic" (xxxvi).

88. *deserts the night:* as Todd notes, Milton may be remembering Seneca, *Hippolytus* 309–10: "arsit obscuri dea clara mundi / nocte deserta" ("The radiant goddess of the darksome sky [Diana or Luna] burned with love and, forsaking the night"); and Catullus 7.7 has the expression *cum tacet nox.* Parker adds that Milton's reference to "the dark of the moon" is singularly appropriate in a story of Samson: "the moon had been a significant factor in the lives of the Hebrews during their nomadic period, since, to avoid the intense heat, flocks were customarily moved by night, and the appearance of the new moon was an occasion of feasting and rejoicing (1 Sam. 20:5, 24–29, and Amos 8:4[–5])" ("Variorum").

    night: sight (93) and *light* (98, 99) may be intentional rhymes (Parker, "Variorum").

89. *vacant:* "undisturbed by business or work" because the moon is then vacant "at leisure" (*OED* 4c, 4b); the epithet is transferred to the cave (Verity). Parker ("Variorum") adds that the sky is also in a sense vacant, i.e., "empty" (so *OED* 2). Meadowcourt (in Newton and in Todd) compares Pliny, *Naturalis historia* 16.74. Tillyard explicates: "It means 'where the moon is in vacation, where she has nothing to do and can't get on with her proper job of lighting the world.' It is Samson's own anguish that dictates the word, for Samson is thinking of his own 'vacancy,' his own utter impotence of doing those things for which he is best fitted.... '[V]acant' does more than lead up to 'interlunar'; it insists on sharing the emphasis with it. And the two words interact. The chill remoteness, the utter inhumanity of 'interlunar' quench the human appetencies implied by 'vacant'" (*Miltonic Setting* 102).

    interlunar: "pertaining to the period between the old and new moon" (so *OED*). Martin W. Sampson calls it "a peculiarly daring expression because literally it means only 'between moons'... but the tautology disappears under the strength of the adjective." Parker notes that not only will the moon return and shine again, but also Samson's "light"—reflected from a greater source—will also be renewed ("Variorum").

    cave: cf. *PL* 6.4–8. Grieve notes, "the cave into which the *vacant* (= unemployed) moon is supposed to retire is mentioned in the Homeric hymn to

Demeter [22–26], where the moon is identified with Hecate" (also Percival; Wyatt). Tillyard comments: "It suggests barrenness, but it is there partly because the ancients supposed the moon to retire into one [cave] during the intervals of her appearance, and it was well bred to repeat their supposition. . . . I don't think the word will carry a very heavy load of meaning" (*Miltonic Setting* 101–2). Bush, commenting on this same tradition, notes that the moon's retirement to a cave was only temporary: "Lines 86 –99 may suggest to the reader that God, like the sun or moon, has only seemed to desert Samson and will return" ("John Milton" 505n). Overlooking this allusion, Keightley (*Poems*) and Meiklejohn call this line "a fancy of Milton's own," and Eliot, while pronouncing *interlunar* a "stroke of genius," thinks that it "is merely combined with 'vacant' and 'cave,' rather than giving and receiving life from them" (*On Poetry* 159). Stein writes of these lines, "the light not seen is felt as silence and lonely space" (*Heroic Knowledge* 142–43).

90–93. Church quotes Matthew 6:22–23: "The light of the body is in the eye: if therefore thine eye be single, thy whole body shall be full of light. But if thine eye be evil, thy whole body shall be full of darkness. If therefore the light that is in thee be darkness, how great is that darkness!" Alden Sampson (226–27) discusses what he calls the "three orders of light" in *SA:* visible light, light as meaning life (e.g., 591–92), and light as "the spiritual essence of God and of man's soul"; this passage refers to the third order. Broadbent connects this passage to what he describes as the "pan-vitalism of the angels" in *PL* (*Some Graver Subject* 214–15). Percival finds a parallel to Milton's thought in John Davies's "Of the Soule of Man": "So doth the piercing soul the body fill / Being all in all, and all in part diffused" (737–38); Bullough and Bullough instead quote Henry More's *Psychathanasia* 2.2.32; but, according to Arnold Williams, the doctrine that the soul is *tota in qualibet parte corporis,* "entire in every part of the body" (so Augustine, *De Trinitate* 5.6), was a "psychological commonplace" expressed by many medieval and Protestant authorities (537). In *DocCh* (Patterson, *Works* 15:46) Milton approves it (but misattributes it to Aristotle).

92. Cf. *PL* 3.51–53.

93–97. *She:* Latin *anima* is feminine; cf. 71. B. A. Wright emends to *Shee;* Darbishire does not make this change (*Poetical Works*); see 219–20n s.v. *Mee.* Parker

("Variorum") paraphrases: "(and that) all of the soul is (diffused) in every part (of the body)." Spencer and Willis (387) find a parallel thought in Arnobius's *Libri septem adversus Gentes* 2.59 (Migne 5:903): "Cur cum esset utilius oculis nos illuminare compluribus ad periculum caecitatis, duorum sumus angustiis applicati?" Percival quotes Plotinus, *Ennead* 4.2. Svendsen finds similar sentiments in contemporary sources and concludes, "Samson's agonized query was a current physiological commonplace" (*Milton and Science* 185). Tillyard comments: "This is the very height of sensuousness, the body conscious of itself with its own consciousness. D. H. Lawrence might have said that the solar plexus rather than the head created the last line" (*Miltonic Setting* 103). Cox notes that Samson here equates the senses of sight and hearing: here and later, Cox writes, "the sound and hearing imagery...emphasize[s] the need for right assessment of the element received by the senses and the need for proper use of and differentiation between the physical and the spiritual senses, while at the same time suggesting that they feed one another" ("Natural Science" 60, 63).

94–95. In the first edition, 94 ends with a question mark and 95 with a comma; some editors (e.g., Fenton; Bohn; Verity; William Aldis Wright) switch this punctuation, so that 94 ends with a comma and 95 with a question mark. Tickell ends 94 with a comma and 95 with a semicolon.

th': elision of *th* recurs in 246, 307, 331, 443, 506, 592, 611, 644, 660, 715, 768, 822, 973, 1153, 1216, 1272, 1318, 1746. Cf. 727.

obvious: "exposed or open *to* (action or influence)" (*OED* 2; Latin: *obvius,* "in the way"; cf. *PL* 11.374).

quench't: "put out, extinguish[ed]" (*OED* 1; cf. 1c); cf. *extinguished* (1688) and *extinct* (70) and *PL* 3.25.

96–97. Bullough and Bullough quote John Davies's "Of the Soule of Man": "the feeling power.../ Through every living part itself doth shed" (877–78). Cf. 90–93. J. Macmillan Brown finds here evidence of Milton's familiarity with early modern philosophers: "This is the reasoning of the age of Descartes and Hobbes, Newton and Locke; already philosophy had begun to analyse the senses on the basis of physiology and observe their special functions and qualities" (76).

not as feeling: "not, as the sense of touch (is)." Prince finds "a strange intensity and daring in this idea" (*Samson Agonistes*).

she: now *sight;* cf. 93.

99–105. Johnson (*Rambler* 20 July 1751) thought these lines "too elaborate to be natural" (221).

land: "realm, domain" (so *OED* 3c). Blakeney sees a reminiscence of Job 10:22: "A land of darkness, as darkness itself; and of the shadow of death, without any order, and where the light is as darkness." Cf. also *Ps 88* 49–52. Greenlaw, Osgood, and Padelford (2:274) note a passage "not very unlike" these lines in *The Faerie Queene* 2.8.16.8–9. Stein comments, "The movement turns back to the personal grief, uniting the themes of light and dark, life and death" (*Heroic Knowledge* 143). Parker notes that the word *light* occurs eight times in 70–99: "the iteration suggests self-torture" ("Variorum").

darkness: cf. *PL* 7.27.

100. Cf. 79. "With this [sense of abandonment] the death-thought comes, for the darkness of his physical affliction symbolizes for Samson the darkness of the pit of death" (Allen, "Idea as Pattern" 85).

living death: "a state of misery not deserving the name of life" (so *OED* 2f). This oxymoron, used also in *PL* 10.788 (Le Comte 67), is a poetical commonplace, and editors quote more than a dozen examples. Of lines 100–9, Ellis-Fermor writes: "the cadences of despondency recur with increased effect, after the vigorous protest and grief that have gone before" (149).

101. The caesura effectively emphasizes "And buried" (Percival xlvii; Bailey 226).

buried: Todd quotes Donne's "The Progress of the Soul" 160: "living buried man."

102. "The rising anguish . . . is achieved by the sequence of three rhythmic phrases each longer than the preceding one" (Daiches 235). Cf. 156. And, as Bush notes, the parallel structure of 1334 helps to measure, by comparison, Samson's developing confidence (*Milton* 199). *Mask* 382–84 offers a curious parallel to the thought here (Parker, "Variorum").

moving Grave: Percival thinks that Milton intends a serious pun, with the secondary meaning "a grave the sight of which (whom) is harrowing." Todd notices the phrase "liuing graue" in Sidney's *Arcadia* (1593) and Sylvester's *Divine Weekes and Workes of Du Bartas* (1621), and "a walking Grave" in Robert Howard's *Vestal Virgin* (1665) 5.1, where the blind Artabaces is the speaker.

The idea that the body is the grave of the soul is an ancient one (Percival cites, e.g., Plato, *Cratylus* 17 [400B] and *Gorgias* 47 [493A]).

105. *evils:* so also 194, 374, 648, 1169.

   pains: "punishments" (*OED* 1); so also 485, 501. Percival reads "pains and wrongs" as "wrongful punishments," making the phrase a case of hendiadys, or expression of a complex idea by two nouns connected by *and* (or *of*). Cf. 535, 1394.

106. *obnoxious:* "open," "exposed," "liable" (*OED* 1a); "vulnerable" (MacCaffrey); for this Latin sense of the word, cf. *PL* 9.170, 1094, and *RCG* (Patterson, *Works* 3:212).

108–09. Percival writes, "Each thought occupies a line by itself. This slowness of rhythm is meant to express the intensity of grief that each thought by itself causes."

110–14. Moss notes "how closely Milton follows the conventional method of Aeschylus, Sophocles, and Euripides...for preparing the entrance of a new actor" (296); Wilkenfeld cites these lines to describe *SA* as a "dramatic poem" (instead of a "play") because, here and elsewhere, "words...replace stage actions" (161). See also 326, 710, 1067, 1301, 1390, 1539. Ferry suggests that Milton intends Samson's question here to emphasize his "separation from the unseen world of other human beings, whose threat to him is repeatedly associated in his imagination with the ability to look at his body while he, though imprisoned in darkness, is exposed" (141). Fish similarly writes, "the tone here is nine parts self-pity...and the focus of Samson's fear is entirely physical" (250). Kermode identifies 110 (*hear*) and 114 (*more*) as the first imperfect rhyme in *SA*, a style, he suggests, that Milton may have deliberately incorporated in imitation of Hebrew prosody (62). See also 125 and 126; 146 and 147; 277 and 281; 285 and 286; 318 and 320; 325 and 338; 625 and 627; 688 and 691; 711, 717, 720, and 722; 713 and 718; 1019 and 1020; 1025 and 1027; 1046 and 1048; 1527 and 1528.

   joint pace: "joint step"; Church notes that it depends on "stearing" (111). Parker sees a resemblance to the Greek rhythmic style of choral movement: "Milton, although professedly not writing for the stage, visualizes his Chorus stepping together, moving in time" ("Variorum"). Verity compares *PL* 4.866 and *Mask* 145–46 (cf. *Mask* 91–92); other commentators quote Virgil, *Aeneid* 2.731–32: "subito cum creber ad auris / visus adesse pedum sonitus"; "when suddenly, crowding on my ears, seemed to come a tramp of feet." For other possible echoes of the *Aeneid*, see notes on 118, 340, 501, 700, 727–28, 973, 1122, 1637, and cf. 133, 270–71.

111. *many feet:* "the Greek tragic chorus seems to have had from twelve to fifteen members" (Parker, "Variorum").

   stearing: "shap[ing] one's course" (*OED* s.v. *steer* 4); cf. *Nat* 146 and *Mask* 307–9. Warburton (in Newton and in Todd) thinks the metaphor "extremely hard and abrupt." Cf., e.g., 198–200, 459; Cox discusses the poem's many nautical images: they, along with other image patterns, "enable Milton to explore the relation between the microcosm and the geocosm" ("Natural Science" 57–58).

112–13. Parker calls this an ironic guess ("Variorum").

   enemies: cf. *Ps 6* 13–15: "mine Eie / . . . is waxen old and dark / Ith' mid'st of all mine enemies that mark."

   stare . . . insult: Todd and Columbia *Index* cite Sophocles, *Ajax* 79: οὔκουν γέλως ἥδιστος εἰς ἐχθροὺς γελᾶν; "What mockery sweeter than to mock at foes?" And also 368: ὤ μοι γέλωτος, οἷον ὑβρίσθην ἄρα; "Ah me! The mockery, the scorn, the shame!" Parker (*Milton's Debt* 179) quotes *Prometheus Bound* 118: πόνων ἐμῶν θεωρός; "to stare upon my sufferings." Jerram is reminded of Psalm 35:15.

   affliction: "misery, distress" (so *OED* 2); cf. the use of the word in 503.

   to insult: Weismiller speculates whether this word should be emended to *t' insult* (in Parker, "Variorum"). Cf. 944.

114. *Thir daily practice:* "in apposition with 'to stare' and 'to insult'" (Church). Carey notes that the repetition of "affliction . . . afflict" is an example of *traductio* (*Complete Shorter Poems* 335); see 38–42n.

115–75. The first utterance of the Greek chorus is called the πάροδος, or parodos ("entrance song"). Parker notes only two examples of the parodos following, as here, an opening soliloquy and only four examples of its following an opening speech: Aeschylus's *Agamemnon* and *Choephori,* and Euripides' *Bacchae* and *Suppliant Women.* Parker argues that Sophocles' *Oedipus Rex* and *Antigone* provide the most "probable model" for *SA*'s parodos, while he also notes a "striking" resemblance to the opening of the *Choephori* (*Milton's Debt* 16, 95, 99, 102). Epps (191) numbers this speech the first chorus and divides it into strophe (115–34), antistrophe (135–50), and epode (151–75); but see 117n.

More generally, commentators discuss how Milton's Chorus resembles and/or differs from its classical precursors. Cumberland writes, "Milton's Chorus subscribes more to the dialogues, and harmonises better with the business of the scene, than that of any Greek tragedy we can now refer to" (335). Lawry similarly suggests that the Chorus is "more directly concerned in the play than is the usual Greek Chorus, but in another sense it has surrendered its unitary function and become individuated—members of an Israelite group, rather than collectively a Chorus" (347). Kermode proposes that Milton in writing such irregular lines—"exceedingly free in accent, and occasionally rhyming"—is not imitating Greek choruses: "this was the practice also of the Psalmist and the author of Job" (61). Adams also suggests that Milton's choruses lack Euripides' "verbal swordplay or rhetorical display"; he describes these passages as "not high points but relaxations of the verse. After flashes of exultation, often barbarically rhythmic, sometimes rising to vindictiveness, the choruses of Milton's drama generally return to a stolid, literal level of flat, discursive assertion, almost as a defence against the intensity of expectation" (195–96). Moody suggests, "Milton follows Sophocles rather than his favorite Euripides in making the Chorus cling closely to the thought and emotion of the play itself, instead of allowing it to wander away into philosophic generalizations" (285).

Other commentators find echoes of various contemporary writers. Freedman ("*All for Love*" 515; "Milton" 104–5) notes the similarity between the Chorus's description of Samson at the start of this passage and Ventidius's description of Antony in Dryden's *All for Love* 1.1. (On Milton and Dryden, see also 183–86n, 951n, and Preface Title, 31n, 42n, 56–58n, 62–64n.) Whiting (*Milton's Literary Milieu* 256) finds here a "startling parallelism of thought" with Quarles's *Historie of Samson* (see sig. S2r–S3r). Kirkconnell (164–67, 178–81) compares and contrasts Milton's Danite chorus with the chorus of Hebrew maidens in both Marcus Andreas Wunstius's *Simson, tragoedia sacra* (1600) and Joost van den Vondel's *Samson, of Heilige Wraeck, Treurspel* (1660). Edmundson (171–72) also compares the Chorus's opening lines with a similar passage in Vondel's drama (2.184). Verity, however, challenges at length Edmundson's conclusion that such parallels reveal "that Milton was much indebted to the language of Vondel's *Samson*" (190); Grieve also dismisses such "verbal coincidences" (vii). See Verity's counterargument (159–69).

Commentators emphasize the Chorus's status as an interpreter of the drama—although they disagree about the Chorus's reliability. Stein, e.g., notes, "With the coming of the Chorus we have an external measure for the internal revelation of the monologue, and the first external help arrives for the internal deliverance.... We accept, as we must, the first physical account and the brilliantly contrasting history of what he was" (*Heroic Knowledge* 143; see also Grenander 384). For Verity, the ode not only increases our sympathy for Samson but also supplements the story of his past (125–50)—thus skillfully avoiding too long an opening speech by Samson and yet successfully meeting a difficulty imposed by the unity of time. Percival adds, "through this ode runs a parallelism with Samson's last speech"; Charles Williams similarly describes the Chorus as "self-awareness personified" and claims that "a great deal of what the Chorus says might be uttered by Samson himself" (*English Poetic Mind* 145). But Ferry notes a significant difference between the Chorus and Samson: here (118, 123), as elsewhere (326, 1065), the Chorus's language "seems designed...to make us aware that they apprehend through their eyes"; Milton presents the Chorus, as the play's other characters, "as observers of Samson's outward appearance" to emphasize "the contrast between the experience of the blind man encased within his dark body and the ways of men in the unseen world surrounding him" (142, 143).

Among other, more general observations on the Chorus in *SA,* Verity asserts that "without it the play would fall to pieces"; it serves primarily to "illustrate" Samson's character, "partly by contrast, for the Chorus has a caution and self-restraint impossible to the protagonist; partly by sympathy—by sharing in his feelings, by taking up his words and enlarging on them, by extending the train of his thought" (xxxvii). To Summers, the Chorus "represents the 'conventional wisdom' of the drama; but the premise of the poem is that conventional wisdom is inadequate" (163). Woodhouse instead suggests "it is Hebrew in its outlook and offers...a Hebraic commentary" that Milton presents "consistently though unobtrusively, from a Christian standpoint, and thus it serves the purposes of historical realism; it is not the mouthpiece of the poet: it does not run ahead of events, but like the audience follows them step by step and learns from them what it can" ("Tragic Effect" 208). Fish suggests that commentators may go too far in discussing the Chorus's limited perspective: "the important point here is not the correctness of what the Chorus say, but the startling precision with which they articulate the misgivings we ourselves have felt, both as men and as readers" (247). Rajan describes the Chorus as "neither spectator not actor, standing somewhere between them in detachment, so that the reader interprets an interpretation that is continually reformulating itself" (143). Radzinowicz describes how the "Chorus applies Samson's experience to themselves and generalizes it to apply to mankind and the future, always a step behind Samson in his recovery, but by their plain, sensible, something wondering words showing what Milton wants them to learn and apply" ("*Samson Agonistes*" 467). Eleanor Gertrude Brown cites the Chorus's description of Samson's appearance in this passage to show that Samson "could hardly be said to portray Milton" (98). Lawry writes, "the Chorus increases the agony for Samson even as it begins its own agon by duplicating his progress in self-awareness" (358). Hanford thus concludes that the Chorus (and Manoa) "are the antagonists of the drama, however much they may come ostensibly to comfort and sustain" ("Temptation Motive" 191); elsewhere, Hanford compares the Chorus (along with Manoa) to the friends of Job who "sharpen [his] agony by their mistaken comfort" ("*Samson Agonistes*" 173). Similarly, Tung observes, "the Chorus finds itself unable to make its comforts lasting or its counsel effective," but this failure "precisely realizes its artistic function of pointing up Samson's lack of patience" (480).

As for the meter, Hanford writes, "no other chorus goes to the lengths of this one in illustration of Milton's statement in his preface that the verse is 'of all sorts.' But even here the prevailing pattern is iambic" (*Poems* 558). He adds, "The trochaic measures of the first two short lines yield to long sweeping iambics, quickened here and there by trochees, anapests, and dactyls, or slowed down by spondees" (552). Sprott notes that the choruses are composed by prosodic rules "quite similar to" the rest of the poem: "the so-called lyric choruses are essentially heroic blank verse which has thrown off the bondage of preserving a uniform length of line" (130).

Some commentators find fault with the choruses. E.g., Johnson (*Rambler* 20 July 1751) complains that the Chorus's speeches "are often so harsh and dissonant, as scarce to preserve...any appearance of metrical regularity" (221). Ralli complains that the choruses, with only a few exceptions, are "prosaic, and point to a failing command over verse rather than the appearance of any new power" (141). Garnett regrets their "frequent harshness...some strophes are almost uncouth" (182). Belloc writes that the choruses "are much too long and still more too formless. They are not carried on, as were the Greek choruses, by a surge of metre" (275). Jebb writes that the "irregularity" of the choruses has "a certain grandeur, but it is not the grandeur proper to a tragedy on the Greek model; it is rather the sublimity of some of the bursts of eloquence in the Hebrew prophets" ("*Samson Agonistes*" 341).

Among the commentators who appreciate the choruses, Hopkins praises the "rhythm and metrical system" of the Chorus's speech: "it is amazing that so great a writer as Newman should have fallen into the blunder of comparing the first chorus...with the opening of *Thalaba*.... Milton having been not only ahead of his own time as well as aftertimes in verse-structure but these particular choruses being his own high-water mark." In the choruses, Hopkins finds early examples of what he termed "sprung rhythm" and "counterpoint rhythm" (*Correspondence* 13–15, 17; *Letters* 45–46). Prince, however, disagrees with this latter claim: "there is none of that rhythmic counterpointed which comes from the mounting of one particular rhythm on a presumed norm"; Prince instead describes Milton's verse as "disciplined improvisation" exhibiting a "freer ebb and flow" and "greater variety" than the rhythmic counterpoint characteristic of Italian prosody (*Italian Element* 161–62). Weismiller similarly takes issue with Hopkins: "the trochaic overlay in the choral odes...is...[only] an occasional effect" (127). Edward J. Thompson finds the verse's rhythmic variations meaningful: "For conscious control and intimate oversight of words this is perhaps the most masterful passage in the language. If any line has a syllable more or less than another, there is a reason" (246). For Coleridge's detailed scansion of 115–50, see Brinkley, *Coleridge* 607–8. Analyzing the prosody of the parodos, Ellis-Fermor suggests: "The choric verse at this point has a significant and organic relation to the verse of his [Samson's] speeches" (149); she adds that this first speech, not heard by Samson, is important, "both arousing the sympathies of the audience and enriching their knowledge (or memories) of the past and its contrast with the present" (26).

115. Bridges describes this as "an eight-syllable line, with third foot inverted [trochaic]; the sibilants are hushing" (*Milton's Prosody* 62). Daiches remarks that the Chorus "speak[s] first in tones of exaggerated quiet, appropriate to someone entering a sick chamber" (236). Bailey comments: "Not even Milton ever made the arrangement and sound of words do more to enforce their meaning" (232).

This, this is he: an echo of Ben Jonson's *Satyr* (Verity) and *Arc* 5, 17 (Le Comte 174). Darbishire emends to *hee* (*Poetical Works*); see 219–20n s.v. *Mee*.

softly: "wait"; an exclamation with imperative force, enjoining silence or deprecating haste (so *OED* 10). The situation resembles that in Euripides, *Oresteia* 140–45, where Electra warns the chorus not to disturb her brother (Dunster [in Todd]; Browne; Jerram; Percival; Hughes, *John Milton* and *Complete Poems*). Timberlake calls it "a plain echo.... Even the rhythm is similar" (337).

a while: so also 363, 1632, 1636.

116. Sprott lists this line as the first of seventeen, all in the lyrical sections of the poem, that exhibit "the most drastic relaxation of principles...with the appearance of a new rule which permits monosyllabic feet....It is difficult to say whether Milton would have regarded the lines as being trochaic with the last foot catalectic, or as iambic with the first foot catalectic" (132). The other examples are as follows: 125, 172, 606, 607, 610, 614, 652, 1280, 1430, 1436, 1669, 1699, 1701, 1745, 1746, 1749. Bridges calls this "a perfect four-foot line in falling rhythm" (*Milton's Prosody* 62).

break in: Ferry notes that this phrase "suggests penetration by some outer force. Here and throughout the poem words spoken to him [Samson] by others are like alien bodies, existing outside the hero's private world" (144).

117. Bridges describes this as a "ten-syllable line, metre reflective: the fourth foot inverted for wonder" (*Milton's Prosody* 62). Epps suggests that here the "real chorus comment begins," because the first two lines of the strophe are "used rather as a signal for the chorus to begin"; he observes, "this leaves the strophe only two lines longer than the antistrophe—a fact which bears out Milton's assertion in the preface that he did not regard the division as essential, but which is also a rather forceful indication of...his classical learning" (192).

change: so also 340.

beyond report: editors gloss as "worse, greater that rumor (had represented)"; *beyond:* "surpassing" (*OED* B.8); cf. 527.

thought: "conception, imagination" (so *OED* 4c).

118. The first of thirty twelve-syllable lines (alexandrines) in the lyrical parts of the poem (there are thirteen in this ode); "in describing great Samson stretched on the bank, it describes itself" (Bridges, *Milton's Prosody* 62). As listed by Sprott

(131), the other alexandrines are as follows: 124, 127–28, 138, *141,* 144, 146, 157, *169, 630, 644,* 648, 654–55, 658, 672, 684, *689,* 695–96, 706, 708, *1035, 1297,* 1429, 1666 (italicized numbers are those that Bridges describes as "continuous lines without any break" [*Milton's Prosody* 60, to which *689* is added]). Three other apparent alexandrines, not listed by Sprott, are lines 131 and 148–49; Bridges (*Milton's Prosody* 60) counts a total of only twenty-six and does not list them all. Cf. 80 ("dark, dark, dark") and 1626, which perhaps should be read as hexameter (Parker, "Variorum"). In pentameter and nonlyrical contexts, there are few twelve-syllable lines that, according to Bridges (*Milton's Prosody* 61), should be taken as pentameter "with extrametrical endings"; Bridges lists 132, 374, 445, 705, 797, 868, 1361, 1517; Sprott (131) lists 445, 603, 783, 868, 893, 1361, to which may be added 497, 797, and possibly 911. Prince finds a Spenserian influence in Milton's use of alexandrines; he thinks they reveal, more generally, "the degree to which his [Milton's] whole conception of English verse had been founded upon Spenser's achievement" (*Italian Element* 163–64). Weismiller counts thirty alexandrines or hexameters in *SA* and adds these observations: "not one concludes a choral ode, or even a section of a choral ode; three are followed by semicolons and five by periods or exclamation marks, but the rest occur in mid-sentence as in mid-paragraph, and many of them are strongly enjambed or run on" (134–35).

On the Chorus's specific observation in this line, Muldrow notes, "the Chorus has the peculiarly human way of judging by externals" (175). Low develops this idea in discussing Samson's isolation: although the Chorus is sympathetic to Samson in his suffering, "his appearance leads them to misjudge him. His dirt, his rags, and his careless posture, as well as his blindness, make Manoa and the Danites assume that God has abandoned his champion, that Samson is no longer a hero" ("Tragic Pattern" 921).

at random: "carelessly, heedlessly" (*OED* 3a): Latin: *temere* (Keightley, *Poems;* Collins). Northrop Frye compares *languished* in 119 (Paradise Lost *and Selected Poetry*).

diffus'd: "extended or spread out" (so *OED* 3), with the suggestion of the literal Latin meaning "poured out," as though the tired Samson were inanimate (Parker, "Variorum"). Cf. 96 and 1141. Editors quote, among others, Spenser, *The Faerie Queene* 1.7.7.2: "Pourd out in loosnesse on the grassy grownd"; Ovid, *Ex ponto* 3.3.8: "fusaque erant toto languida membra toro"; "my inert limbs stretched about the couch"; Virgil, *Aeneid* 6.422–23 (of Cerberus): "immania terga resolvit / fusus humi"; "with monstrous frame relaxed, sinks to earth."

119. Bridges finds the brevity of this six-syllable line meaningful: "its shortness is the want of support" that the Chorus is describing (*Milton's Prosody* 62).

languish't: "reduced to langour" (so *OED*), "drooping" (from lost vitality or suffering [Verity]); "relaxed" (Hughes, *Complete Poems; John Milton*). Cf. *Mask* 743, *EpWin* 33, and *Prol 1* (Patterson, *Works* 12:138–39). Le Comte (62) recalls the simile in Homer, *Iliad* 8.306–8. Cf. also *PL* 9.427–33.

120–21. Bridges describes these as "two six-syllable lines, with extrametrical final syllables suggestive of negligence" (*Milton's Prosody* 62). Landor cites these and the following lines to support his criticism that "it must have been the resolution of Milton to render his choruses as inharmonious as he fancied the Greek were, or would be, without the accompaniments of instrument, accentuation, and chaunts" (5:295).

past hope: the phrase occurs in Shakespeare, *Romeo and Juliet* 4.1.45 (Thaler, "Shakespeare and Milton" 83). Cf. 912 ("past cure"). Allen suggests, "His face becomes the mirror of his mind" ("Idea as Pattern" 85). But Stein here questions the Chorus's assessment: "The moral gestures toward responsibility and Providence indicated a stage well this side of despair.... [Samson] is no more abandoned than he is resigned. His grief is fresh enough to hurt. The anger and self-contempt are too powerfully felt and expressed to represent despair.... The Chorus will soon make the occasion for the correcting of its error" (*Heroic Knowledge* 143–44). See 241–76n.

abandon'd: "desert[ed]," "[left] without one's presence, help, or support" (so *OED* II.8); see 121n.

121. *given over:* "abandon[ed]" (*OED* 63); so also 629. Darbishire (*Poetical Works*) and B. A. Wright emend to *giv'n;* Parker agrees ("Notes" 693). Cf. 359, 378, 578, 629, 1135, 1697.

122. This is the first of fourteen lines in *SA* (only three found in *PR*), which Bridges argues would not have been admitted into *PL* because they are exceptions to rules he finds observed there (*Milton's Prosody* 47). The other lines are 524, 577, 651, 748, 997, 1171, 1378, 1383, 1470, 1480, 1545, 1670, 1726. From this evidence Bridges concludes that Milton "did not keep quite strictly to his laws of 'elision' [that he established in *PL*], but that he approved of the great rhythmical experiments which he had made, and extended these" (46). Bridges

scans this as an eight-syllable line with elision in the third foot: "where Milton
puts his hero in rags he must have been conscious that he was putting his verse
into rags; for he always rejected such a garment as he here weaves as unworthy
of his Muse" (62, 63–64). Edmund K. Chambers (127) describes the middle of
the line as an unstressed rhythm—although, he admits, forced elisions would
sustain the regular iambic meter; he similarly describes 399, 429, 579, 748,
842. Weismiller finds the compression in this line "more violent than almost
any other in Milton's poetry" and suggests a precedent in Chaucer, *Romance
of the Rose* 4913–14: "And eke abyde thilke day / To leve his abt, and gon his
way" (in Parker, "Variorum").

    habit: "attire," "dress" (*OED* 1); so also 1073, 1305.
    weeds: "clothes" (*OED* 5b).

123. *O're worn:* editors gloss as "threadbare, the worse for wear." A four-syllable
line; "its shortness and simple diction are the poverty of the subject" (Bridges,
Milton's Prosody 62); see 321n. Percival calls this line "a touch of Euripides,
who is fond of dwelling upon the rags and squalor of misery, for which he is
ridiculed by Aristophanes." Cf. 415; see 1107n.

124–34. A twelve-syllable line (alexandrine; see 118n); Bridges suggests that it is
meant to evoke "the crowding of new ideas" (*Milton's Prosody* 62). Cf. 118,
127–28. Daiches compliments this passage further: "The emphatic 'hee,' the
short demonstrative line 'That Heroic, that Renowned' [125], rising to the climactic 'Irresistible *Samson*' [126], expresses brilliantly" the Chorus's "shock and
incredulity" (236). Low notes that Milton chose not to eliminate the "unheroic
or barbaric elements" from Samson's story in Judges but instead retains and
transforms them: Milton "further emphasized the contrast with chivalric heroism
by adding the contemptuous catalogue of useless weaponry and armor. (Though
by the subtle illogic of poetry he appropriates all their favorable associations to
Samson even as he dismisses them)" ("Tragic Pattern" 922).

    misrepresent: "to give a false...account of"; this is an early use of the word
(so *OED* 1).

    hee: so also in 178. The spelling of this word in Milton's manuscript is con-
sistently *he*. See 219–20n.

125. Bridges identifies this as a seven-syllable line with falling (trochaic) rhythm
(cf. 116), "heralding" the rhythm of 126 (*Milton's Prosody* 55, 62). Sprott

(132) thinks it difficult to determine whether Milton thought of the line as "trochaic with the last foot catalectic, or as iambic with the first foot catalectic" (see 116n). Kermode (62) identifies a "doubtful" imperfect rhyme in 125–26; see 110–14n.

126. Bridges identifies this as "a ten-syllable line, with first two feet inverted [trochaic; see 81n], descriptive of Samson's violence" (*Milton's Prosody* 56, 63). Fenton transposes the punctuation from the first edition so that he puts a semicolon here after *Samson* (instead of a question mark) and a question mark (instead of a semicolon) at the end of the following line.

    Irresistible: "too strong…to be resisted" (so *OED* 1). The text of the first edition has *Irresistable*, corrected in the *Errata*.

    unarm'd: Judges 14:6: "and he had nothing in his hand." See 130n.

127. "A heavy twelve-syllable line, descriptive of Samson's strength" (Bridges, *Milton's Prosody* 63; see 118n). Cf. 128.

    wild beast: the phrase recurs in 1403; also *PR* 1.310, 502. Weismiller writes, "[These] two stressed (though not quite equally stressed) syllables comprise a single accentual foot. In 127 the division of the phrase between two adjacent feet, '…or fier / cest wíld béast could / withstand,' produces a tenser rhythm, a rhythm at once more forceful and more awkward"; he finds examples of such a grammatical-accentual sequence in *PL* 2.332 and 335 as well as in George Chapman's *Illiads* 7.367–68, 9.244 and his *Odysses* 2.555 (in Parker, "Variorum").

128. A twelve-syllable line. Bridges adds, "with break disguised. Observe how the first half of the line is more powerful than the second" (*Milton's Prosody* 63; see 118n). Judges 14:5–6: "a young lion roared against him…and he rent him as he would have rent a kid."

129. A ten-syllable line, "with final extrametrical syllable. The ease of the metre after the two alexandrines is Samson's successful rush" (Bridges, *Milton's Prosody* 63).

    embattled: "drawn up in battle array, marshalled for fight" (*OED* 1); so *PL* 6.16, 550; 7.322; 12.213. Cf. *PL* 1.129 ("th' imbattelld Seraphim") and 12.213 ("thir imbattelld ranks").

Armies: Phillips writes, "it would be absurd in a *Poet* to set his Hero upon Romantic actions (let his courage be what it will) exceeding Human strength and power, as to fight singly against whole Armies, and come off unhurt, at least if a mortal man, and not a Deity or armed with Power Divine" (*Theatrum* sig. **6r–v).

clad in Iron: Todd finds the same phrase in Edward Fairfax's translation of Tasso's *Gerusalemme liberata* 8.75 ("And *Baldwin* first well clad in iron hard" [see also 533n]), and cites Horace, *Odes* 4.14.29–30: "ut barbarorum Claudius agmina / ferrata vasto diruit impetu"; "even as Claudius o'erwhelmed with destructive onslaught the mail-clad hosts of savages." Parker notes that the Philistines were in this period equipped with iron weapons, while the Hebrews apparently were not ("Variorum"); cf. 284, 1123–24, and see both the story of Goliath and 1 Samuel 14, 17. Parker adds, "The Philistines seem to have had a well-organized army; 1 Sam. 13.5 mentions 30,000 chariots and 6,000 horsemen. On the relative cultural status of the Philistines and Hebrews, see 1 Sam. 13.19–22" ("Variorum").

130. A six-syllable line; "its shortness is Samson's nakedness and singlehanded-ness" (Bridges, *Milton's Prosody* 63). Because Samson has already been described as "unarm'd" (126), the line may be thought redundant. This whole passage foreshadows, however, the Harapha episode (Steadman, "Milton's Harapha" 790).

131. Bridges writes, "a twelve-syllable line, with fourth foot inverted [trochaic], and weak ending to each half, descriptive of the failure of the preparations" (*Milton's Prosody* 63). Brydges finds this line "prosaic."

ridiculous: Adams suggests that this repeated word (see also 539, 1361, 1501) "is one sort of index to Milton's rather complicated feelings in this drama; it also provides a measure of justification for the rational, prosaic tone of the choruses" (195).

forgery: "the action or craft of forging metal" (so *OED* 1); Bullough and Bullough suggest the additional meaning "pretense." To Broadbent, the word "punningly asserts that romantic might is false" (*Milton* 59). The choral description of the useless armor of Samson's enemies (129–41) anticipates the elaborate listing of Harapha's "gorgeous arms" (1119–22); Broadbent lists this line as the first of "a series of gibes at various kinds of falsity" (e.g., 189, 533, 845, 934) that cumulatively "spread a network...of deceitful complications, which...can

be got out of only by faithful commitment to a single believed-in 'right'"
(*Milton* 59).

132. *brazen:* "made of brass." Cf. 35, where the word is capitalized. Church writes,
"of copper, a metal which iron, as being difficult to extract from ore, was long
in superseding."

　　Cuirass: "a piece of armour for the body... reaching down to the waist, and
consisting of a breast-plate and a back-plate, buckled or otherwise fastened
together" (*OED* 1). It seems to have been introduced in the fifteenth century;
Church detects a connection with corium (leather). Cf. *PR* 3.328. Bridges
cites this word as an example of a "heavier ending" than in *PL* (*Milton's Prosody*
61).

133. *Chalybean:* editors disagree on the pronunciation; most (following Newton)
accent the second syllable, but some (Dunster [in Todd]; Blakeney; Grieve; also
OED) accent the third, usually on the analogy of Milton's apparent pronunciation
of *Adamantean* (134) and *empyrean* (six times in *PL*). But Percival believes the
accentuation doubtful. Johnson (*Rambler* 20 July 1751) censures Milton for
the anachronism involved in this reference to the Chalybes—an ancient nation
of Asia Minor famous for their skill in working iron—of whom "it is not very
likely that his chorus should have heard" (220). (For other possible anachro-
nisms, Parker ["Variorum"] cites 150, 235, 389, 404, 500–1, 628, 934, 1494,
1606, 1699–1707. See also 533n and Preface 58n.) On the Chalybes, who lived
on the southern shore of the Euxine or Black Sea, editors cite Virgil, *Georgics*
1.58: "at Chalybes nudi ferrum"; "the naked Chalybes give us iron"; Percival
also notes a reference in Aeschylus, *Prometheus Bound* 134, 733.

　　temper'd: "[brought] to a suitable degree of hardness and resiliency" (*OED*
14; cf. *PL* 6.322).

　　frock of mail: "a defensive garment, armour" (so *OED* 2b).

134. *Adamantean Proof:* "proved of impregnable hardness of tested invulnerabil-
ity" (if *Proof* is an adjective; cf. "Chalybean temper'd"), or "of power proved
(to be) like adamant" or "strength like adamant" (if *Proof* is a noun). Editors
are divided: e.g., Church and Grieve make the two words a compound adjective; Wyatt and Collins call *proof* a substantive and describe *Adamantean* as
a "classically-formed adjective" (accenting it on the fourth syllable); Percival,

Verity, Edmund K. Chambers, Blakeney, and Carey (*Complete Shorter Poems*) also make *proof* a noun, as does Lockwood, who defines this usage as "impenetrability" (1.c). Masson tentatively suggests another possible reading: "proof against adamantean weapons" (*Poetical Works*). Parker asserts that, despite this disagreement, "the meaning is clear: the armor was *not* impregnable against Samson, although previous tests had proved it hard enough to resist anything" ("Variorum"). Commentators also disagree over whether Milton conceived of adamant as steel of the hardest kind, as the diamond (cf. *Apol* [Patterson, *Works* 3:314]), or as the lodestone or magnet. Johnson writes "perhaps" Milton coined the word *Adamantean* (*Dictionary*), and Todd suggests that the idea came from Ovid, *Metamorphoses* 7.104: "ecce adamanteis Vulcanum naribus" (but cf. Horace's "tunica tectum adamantina" [*Odes* 1.6.13]). Milton uses *Adamantine* in *Arc* 66 and *PL* 1.48; 2.646, 853; 6.542. In *PL* 6.254–55, Satan's shield is a "rockie Orb / Of tenfold Adamant," resembling Arthur's in *The Faerie Queene* 1.7.33.

134–35. Prince calls this "the first unmistakable rhyme in the play," notes "its structural purpose, as providing a link and a renewed impulse," and says that the "place and effect of the second rhyme here are those of the *chiave* of a *canzone*" (*Italian Element* 157). Roberts W. French is instead critical: "the first rhyme...is so prominent and so pointless as to strike the reader as a bothersome tinkle, a simply facile playing with sounds" (61). Beum (181) writes that this is one of the few passages in which the Chorus rhymes while "speaking in its humbler role" as friends of Samson (as opposed to its other, more elevated role as interpreter of the action). Cf. 159–60n. Parker uses the presence of such rhymes in *SA*—about one-eleventh of the poem rhymes, according to his calculations—as part of his argument that Milton composed *SA* earlier than *PL*, most likely in 1646–48 ("Date" 221–23; *Milton* 904). On the apparent inconsistency that Milton had disparaged rhyme in the note on "The Verse" in *PL*, Masson writes, "Milton was too exquisite a metrical artist to feel himself bound by an absolute law" (*Life* 6:667); Oras adds that in *SA* Milton uses rhyme only "intermittently,...as a means of special emphasis at points of stylistic culmination, very much in the manner of 'the Italian poets of prime note' he mentions [in *PL*'s note on "The Verse"]" (*Blank Verse* 4); Beum agrees that Milton uses rhyme for emphasis in *SA* and describes the prefatory note on rhyme in *PL* as "a hasty and a temporary animadversion" (181). Cf. rhymes in 160–61, 170–75,

224–25, 286–89, 297–98, 303–6, 610–11, 668–69, 672–75, 687–91, 1010–17, 1018–45, 1053–60, 1687–1707, 1745–58.

On Milton's use of short lines here and elsewhere in *SA,* Hanford observes, "The irregularity is made somewhat less than it appears to be to the eye by the fact that successive lines of 3 or 4 beats often go together to make a longer rhythmic unit" (*Poems*).

stood aloof: cf. *PL* 1.380 (Le Comte 174).

136. *insupportably:* "irresistibly" (so *OED*, first example cited). Following Thyer (in Newton), editors quote Spenser's *The Faerie Queene* 1.7.11.1–2: "That when the knight he spide, he gan aduance / With huge force and insupportable mayne." There may also be the suggestion of "unsupported (by arms)" (Parker, "Variorum").

advanc't: "raised" (*OED* III.9); cf. 450. Edmund K. Chambers suggests a reminiscence of Shakespeare's *Coriolanus* 2.1.160–61: "Death, that dark spirit, in's nervy arm doth lie, / Which, being advanc'd, declines, and then men die." Adams suggests that *advanc't,* first encountered, can be read as either a participle or an independent verb: "the reader must hold the sentence in suspension till the true verb, appearing with a wonderful contemptuous suddenness in 'Spurn'd,' jolts the whole sentence into resolution" (192).

137. Carey describes Samson's renunciation of violence in this line as a "quibble merely" (cf. Manoa's assertion that Samson is "Himself an Army" [346]) and argues that Milton intended Samson's violence to contrast with Jesus' contempt for war (*John Milton* 138).

arms: a possible play on words (Parker, "Variorum"). Cf. *foot* (136).

tool: "a weapon of war, *esp.* a sword" (*OED* 1b). Adds Parker, "in this sense the word was probably already an archaism; Milton may have intended a contrast with Samson's 'sword of bone' (143); any 'instrument' is a mere 'tool' without divine help" ("Variorum").

138. A twelve-syllable line (alexandrine; see 118n). Prince notes Milton's use of an essential feature from Italian prosody: "the provision, in the last place of the line, of a word which is as weighty as a rhyme-word." He adds that the expectation of a rhyme is often disappointed but "impels the verses forward," while "these

rich or heavy terminations are satisfying in themselves" (*Italian Element* 166). See also, e.g., 144.

 Spurn'd: "trample[d]" (*OED* 5).

 Ascalonite: Prince accents the second syllable (*Samson Agonistes*). Editors define as an inhabitant of Ascalon (Askelon, Ashkelon), one of the five chief cities of the Philistines, north of Gaza and on the Mediterranean. See 981, 1186–87, and Judges 14:19.

139–40. *Fled:* Parker ("Variorum") suggests these are not the Ascalonites whom Samson murdered: "Perhaps Milton is here recalling Josephus's version of the story (*Antiquities of the Jews* 5.8.6)"; see 27n, 1186n.

 Lion ramp: "lion-like threatening posture" (so *OED* s.v. *lion* 12, s.v. *ramp* 3), or, perhaps, "leap, spring" (Lockwood 1). Because *rampant* is a heraldic term, Parker pictures Samson standing in profile, his right leg raised ("Variorum"); cf. 136. But cf. *Apol:* "visag'd like a Lion to expresse power, high autority and indignation" (Patterson, *Works* 3:314); and cf. *PL* 4.343; 7.466. Todd and Bullough and Bullough suggest that in these lines Milton was thinking of "the deeds of valorous knights," and for parallels cite Spenser's *The Faerie Queene* 4.4.41 and 5.3.8 (cf. also 1.8.12).

 turn'd...heel: according to Church, Percival, et al., the sense is: "old warriors turned their plated backs (in flight, and, overtaken, were trampled) under his heel." Parker alternatively proposes that, "if the picture of Samson as a lion rampant is intentionally comic, Milton may here wish us to visualize Philistine warriors turning to flee under Samson's heel" ("Variorum"); see 141. Lockwood defines *turn* as "twist about, writhe" (II.1.c).

 plated: "overlaid, covered, or strengthened with a plate or plates of metal for ornament or defence" (so *OED* 1).

141. A twelve-syllable line (alexandrine; see 118n) without any break. Edward J. Thompson suggests, "the length of this line expresses the full length and prostrate position of the Philistian warriors" (246).

 grovling: "[lying] with the face downwards" or "mov[ing] with the body prostrate upon the ground" (so *OED* 1).

 crested: "plumed." Cf. 1244. Dunster (in Todd) cites Livy's *History of Rome from Its Foundation* 9.40.3: "galeae cristatae, quae speciem magnitudini corporum adderent" ("Their helmets were crested, to make their stature appear greater"); and Ovid, *Metamorphoses* 8.25: "cristata casside" ("crested casque").

142–45. Judges 15:15–17.

Then: perhaps a typographical error for *He;* cf. 146 (Parker, "Variorum").

with what: editors gloss as "by means of whatever."

trivial: "trifling" (*OED* 6), "such as may be met with anywhere" (*OED* II.5), with the possible suggestion of "picked up from the road" (Latin: *trivium,* "crossroad, highway" [Church]). Percival adds that the world "has a subsidiary meaning of 'seemingly inadequate for the great havoc it produced.'" The phrase "trivial weapon" is repeated in 263; on Samson's weapon, see also 1095.

came to hand: cf. *PL* 11.436.

143. Hughes cites this line to show that often in the poem "light feet . . . are imme-diately compensated by spondees" (*John Milton* 424).

144. A twelve-syllable line (alexandrine; see 118n). Carey accuses Milton in this passage of "converting" Samson "into a vehicle for his own sterile loathings" (*John Milton* 146). For other signs of "this Puritan Samson," Carey cites 1024, 1439, 1703. See also 138n.

thousand: so Judges 15:15–16; in *RCG* Milton makes it *thousands* (Patterson, *Works* 3:276).

fore-skins: "uncircumcised men," i.e., a metonymy for the Philistines (not in *OED*). Cf. 260, 1100. Keightley notes Philistines are so described in Scripture (*Poems*).

fell: "[brought] to the ground" (*OED* IX.51). Perhaps a typographical error for *fell'd;* see 142–45n s.v. *Then,* the implied subject of "pull'd up" in 146, and 263. Percival is the only editor who attempts to deal with the difficulty of this construction: he suggests "a thousand foreskins fell (died) with what trivial weapon" and adds that we should today say either "he felled" or "before (or *to*) him . . . a thousand fell."

flower: "choicest individual or individuals," "the pick" (*OED* 7); cf. 264, 1654. Ricks criticizes Milton's failure to reinvigorate this dead metaphor (*Milton's Grand Style* 55–56). Parker notes the alliteration ("Variorum").

Palestine: "Philistia"; cf. 1099 and also 380. The region over which the Hebrews and Philistines struggled, this strip of land lies between the highlands of Judea and the sea; it was first called Canaan, later Palestine — so deeply did the Philistines impress themselves upon later ages (Gilbert, *Geographical*).

145. *Ramath-lechi:* editors gloss as "hill or height of the jawbone." So Milton spells it in the Trinity Manuscript (Patterson, *Works* 18:236). Editors also observe

that the marginal note of the Authorized Version in Judges 15:17 interprets *Ramath-lechi* as "the lifting up, or casting away, of the jawbone." *Lehi* (Vulgate *Lechi*), meaning "jawbone," was the name of the place or rock where the event occurred (see Gilbert, *Geographical*). See 581–82n.

famous to this day: Landor (5:295) objects to this as a truism on the ground that such an exploit was not likely to be forgotten in the course of twenty years (according to Judges 15:20 and Archbishop James Ussher's chronology of world history [1650]). Percival responds that the allusion is rather to Samson's successful renaming of the place. Cf. 1094–95. Parker ("Variorum") notes that Samson later uses the phrase "to this day" in referring to another aspect of this same episode (1216).

146–49. Judges 16:1–3. Commentators observe that Milton here mentions Samson's feat of strength but omits the preceding incident where Samson visits the harlot of Gaza. The alexandrines in 146 and 148–49 are perhaps suggestive of ponderous effort; see 118n. Kermode (62) identifies an imperfect rhyme in 146–47; see 110–14n.

147. *Azza:* another name for Gaza (Jer. 25:20); see 41n. It is used here only; Parker suggests perhaps to avoid alliteration ("Variorum"). Sandys in 1632 defines the word as "strong" (sig. O3r). Mitford compares Beaumont, *Psyche* canto 5, stanza 71.

Post: Judges 16:3 mentions "the two posts"; Meadowcourt (in Newton) accordingly proposes the emendation *Posts*. Adds Newton, "but perhaps Milton might prefer *post* as somewhat of a softer sound."

massie: Milton uses this form rather than *massive;* see, e.g., 1633, 1648, *PL* 2.878. Verity quotes Joshua Sylvester's *Divine Weekes and Workes of Du Bartas:* "th' Iron Gates, whose hugeness wont to shake / The massie Tours of *Gaza,* thou dost take / On thy broad shoulders."

Bar: cf. *PL* 2.877.

148. *Hebron:* also called Chebron (*Def 1* [Patterson, *Works* 7:108]), or Kirjath-Arba (Josh. 14:15; Judg. 1:10). Gilbert (*Geographical*) defines: "an ancient city of Palestine about twenty miles south-southwest of Jerusalem"; when Samson took the gates of Gaza, "and put them upon his shoulders, and carried them up to the top of an hill that is before Hebron" (Judg. 16:3), he was traveling from a

city whose name meant "strong" to a city associated with giants. Gilbert traces this latter association back to the first Hebrew spies who, at Hebron, penetrated Palestine and "saw the giants…in our own sight as grasshoppers, and so we were in their sight" (Num. 13:33; cf. Deut. 9:2). Hebron was "the city of Arba the father of Anak" (Josh. 15:13).

149–50. Edward J. Thompson writes that these lines "by their rhythm express the labouring and difficult character of the operation they describe (Samson's rape of the gates of Gaza)" (246).

journey of a Sabbath day: editors gloss, "short journey." Exodus 16:29: "abide ye every man in his place, let no man go out of his place on the seventh day." According to rabbinical prescription in the time of Christ, the utmost limit of permitted travel was two thousand *ammöth* or ell (equivalent to 1,225 yards); see Acts 1:12. Diodati notes, "the Ecclesiasticall constitution had limited two thousand cubits, which are a mile" (sig. H2v). Editors offer various measurements for the distance from Gaza to Hebron: "about thirty miles" (Collins), "about thirty-five miles in a bee-line" (Wyatt and Collins), "thirty-eight miles due west" (Buttrick 2:791), about forty miles (Verity; Martin W. Sampson; Blakeney; Northrop Frye, Paradise Lost *and Selected Poetry*), or "not less than thirty miles" (Church).

and: Percival suggests that this word "has the force of 'while,'" which "brings it near a common Irish provincialism." Cf. *OED* B.9. Cf. 357, 1480.

150. *Like whom:* editors gloss, "like (him) whom"; a Latinism (see Edmund K. Chambers 134; Wyatt and Collins 18).

Gentiles: "the nations of the West" (Verity); here (and in 500) the reference would seem to be to the ancient Greeks (Wyatt and Collins).

feign: "fable," "relate in fiction," or "believe erroneously" (*OED* 3, 4b); cf., e.g., *PL* 2.627; 4.706; 5.381. Hughes thinks that this is an anachronistic reference to Hercules, which he attributes to an "established idealization of Samson" (*John Milton* 429). But most later commentators accept that the reference is instead to Atlas, one of the Titans, often described in classical literature as supporting the heavens on his head and hands, or shoulders; e.g., Aeschylus, *Prometheus Bound* 348–50. Cf. *PL* 2.306. In response to commentators who still label this line an anachronism (see 133n), Steadman argues that, by Renaissance notions, it was not ("Samson-Nisus" 451).

151–52. Parker writes that the question is a formula, both Greek and Senecan ("Variorum"). Percival writes, "the Chorus solves its own doubt almost immediately by bewailing Samson's blindness first, as the greater calamity." Cf. 66–67. The word *bewail* recurs in 182, 955, 1742.

153. Church (quoted by others) glosses, "Samson's blindness made an inner prison within that of the 'bondage' in which he lay, causing a general hopeless darkness." Cf. 236n. Cox traces the poem's various images of imprisonment ("Natural Science" 63–64); Landy thinks this reference to doubling typifies the poem's double references: "double vision, physical and psychic imprisonment, strength without a 'double share of wisdom' [53–54], seeing and hearing, and the double meanings in the crucial words, speeches, and actions in the poem" ("Language" 182). Nash suggests, however, that "the levels of imprisonment are at least triple"; here he adds that Samson is tempted to become again Dalila's prisoner of love (27–28). Metrically this line has no parallel elsewhere in the poem or in Milton's other verse (Parker, "Variorum").

154. *Inseparably dark:* Percival, citing *PL* 3.45, observes that Samson cannot separate himself from the dark of the prison of blindness. Wyatt and Collins gloss, "Samson's blindness made an inner prison within that of the bondage in which he lay."

155–56. Grenander suggests that the Chorus here develops "the spiritual nature of his [Samson's] suffering, making explicit that his external blindness is a symbol of something worse, the internal blindness of his soul" (384).

156. Cf. 102 and also *Mask* 382–84 (Le Comte 66).

157. A twelve-syllable line (alexandrine; see 118n); Parker suggests, "perhaps for emphasis and for contrast with the following line" ("Variorum"). Commentators detect here the Pythagorean and Platonic notion that the body is the soul's prison—a commonplace to Milton and his readers. Despite Milton's monism, Samuel writes, "he never completely rejected the teaching of Plato on the relative worth of body and soul" (158); see 1572n. Editors cite, among others, Plato, *Phaedo* 6.62B; Shakespeare, *3 Henry VI* 2.1.74–76; Virgil, *Aeneid* 6.733–34; Lucan, *Pharsalia* 6.720–22.

Which: "i.e., a thing which, referring to what follows—that the soul is imprisoned in the body" (Verity).

without cause: Parker wonders whether this is the opinion of the Chorus, or of Milton ("Variorum").

complain: "bewail, lament" (*OED* 1); "murmur at" (Lockwood b). The text of the first edition has *complain'd,* corrected in the *Errata.*

158. *indeed:* "truly," "in reality" (*OED* 1).

159–60. *real:* "actually existing," i.e., as contrasted with the metaphorical darkness of the soul imprisoned in the body. Pronounce as a disyllable (Parker, "Variorum").

darkness of the body: Percival reads "dark body," making this phrase a case of hendiadys (see 105n). Todd suggests a possible allusion to Matt. 6:23: "But if thine eye be evil, thy whole body shall be full of darkness. If therefore the light that is in thee be darkness, how great is that darkness!"

dwells: cf. *PL* 3.248–49.

outward light: editors gloss as "actual, physical light," i.e., as contrasted with the "inward light" of the soul (92, 162). Beum thinks the rhyme with *night* in the next line is purposeful and indicative of a larger tendency in the Chorus's rhyming in *SA:* "it identifies that body in its wiser, more passionate, more universal aspect; and at the same time it underscores the wisdom, passion, and universality of its language" (180). E.g., here *light* and *night* are "thematic words." He adds, "the interwoven rhyme patterns create a kind of lyric and incantatory analogy with the dancing and chanting of an Aeschylean chorus" (180). Cf. 134–35n.

161. *incorporate:* "unite or combine with something else so as to form one body" (*OED* II.5); cf. *PL* 10.816 (Prince, *Samson Agonistes*); "to occupy a body of darkness" (Hunter).

162. *inward light:* "the 'light' of the soul" (Verity); cf. 92, 1689, *Mask* 380, and *PL* 3.51–52. See 90–93n.

alas: some editors (e.g., Tickell; Bohn; Verity; William Aldis Wright) insert an exclamation point after this word. But Prince comments, "If punctuation is added to this interjection it spoils the flow of the lines" (*Samson Agonistes*).

163. *visual beam:* "ray proceeding from the eye [giving vision]" (so *OED* A.1); "the faculty of sight" (Verity); "ray of light" (Grieve). Cf. 83 and *PL* 3.620 (Verity). Editors also note that *visual* is here used actively. Ancient theories explained sight as "due to something emanating from the eye and falling upon the object seen" (see Hughes, *Complete Poems*).

164–65. The construction: "O mirror, unparalleled since man (has been) on earth." Cf. *PL* 1.573 ("never since created man"). Krouse, followed by Bullough and Bullough, calls 165–69 a passage that "is reminiscent of the many instances of the use of Samson as an *a fortiori* example, a device...essential to moral interpretation" (88). A. B. Chambers is more critical: "The Chorus, with a stupidity rarely equalled even by its ancestors in Greek drama, seizes this occasion for a brief dissertation on *de casibus* tragedy" (317). Steadman acknowledges that this image "is a commonplace—indeed a cliché" but insists that "the very fact that it *was* so conventional actually enhanced its argumentative force"; he suggests that the Chorus's speech helps universalize Samson's predicament and notes that Milton may be indebted to Antonio Minturno's *L'arte poetica* (1564), in which the image of a mirror is "specifically associated with tragedy as the representation of man's condition and fortune changes" ("Tragic Glass" 105). Rudrum also discusses how the Chorus "generalize Samson's case to construct a theory of tragedy" (25).

    mirror: "faithful reflection," "exemplar," i.e., of reverses of fortune (*OED* II.4b, 5 [1637]; cf. 5c [1633]); see 166 (*example*). Cf. 706. See 1407n.

    fickle state: cf. *PL* 9.948 (Le Comte 67).

166–75. Tillyard suggests that this passage justifies Samson as a hero of tragedy by Aristotelian standards (*Milton* 279; cf. Bush, "John Milton" 505n). Commentators, following Todd, find resemblances to the choral reflections on the fate of Oedipus in Sophocles, *Oedipus Rex* 1186–1221. Eleanor Gertrude Brown (100) thinks that these lines of the Chorus are "more suggestive of Milton than those of Samson" (see also 293–99, 1268–76).

    The rarer.../ By how much: "(all) the rarer...because or inasmuch as" (see Hunter); a Latinism (*exemplum tanto rarius quanto,* or *eo rarius quo*). Lockwood interprets *how* to mean "to what extent or degree; correlative to *so,* which is omitted" (I.4.b). Percival notes, "there is a slight discrepancy here if 'unparallel'd'...is interpreted in its strict sense."

    example: see 765.

167–68. For the sentiment, Percival quotes both Sophocles, *Antigone* 1158–59: τύχη γὰρ ὀρθοῖ καὶ τύχη καταρρέπει / τὸν εὐτυχοῦντα τόν τε δυστυχοῦντ ἀεί; "For Fortune with a constant ebb and rise / Casts down and raises high and low alike"; and Ariosto's *Orlando Furioso* 45.1: "Quanto più sull' instabil ruota vedi / Di Fortuna ire in alto ir miser uomo, / Tanto più tosto hai da vedergli i piedi / Ove ora ha il capo, e far cadendo io tomo"; "By how much higher we see poor mortal go / On Fortune's wheel, which runs a restless round / We so much sooner see his head below / His heels; and he is prostrate on the ground."

> *By how much:* Patterson writes, a "Latin construction, ablative of degree of difference" (*Student's Milton*).

> *glory:* Carson thinks this term is one of the key words in the poem's first 710 lines: here the Chorus associates *glory* with the sun's diurnal movement, and gradually the word "becomes invested, in the context of multiple references to the sun and to light, with its Latinate connotation" (175).

> *mortal men:* the phrase recurs in 1682; it also occurs in *DDD* (Patterson, *Works* 3:490); *PL* 1.51; 3.268; 12.248 (Le Comte 67).

169. A twelve-syllable line (alexandrine) without any break (see 118n). It "trundles along the ground, as it were" (Daiches 236).

> *pitch:* "level," "degree" (so *OED* V.22); Percival, Verity, et al. have *depth*. The phrase "lowest pitch" occurs also in *DDD* (Patterson, *Works* 3:439); Percival adds, "elsewhere Milton always use this word for 'height.'"

> *abject:* "cast down," "brought low" (so *OED* A.2; cf. *PL* 1.312). See 172 on *fortune*.

> *fall'n:* see also 414; cf. 690 ("Unseemly falls").

170–75. Commentators find fault with either the Chorus or Milton in these lines. Jerram thus writes: "even Euripides in such passages was never more dull, or less musical. It seems almost incredible that . . . Milton could have written [these lines], . . . with their miserable rhymes, and the extraordinary jumble at the end." Roberts W. French instead writes that the rhymes (abc abc) "give the passage an air of assurance and finality," a tone that he thinks the Chorus's speech does not warrant: here the Chorus seems to blame Samson for his downfall, while "only a few lines earlier the Chorus had called Samson a 'mirror of our fickle state' (164), suggesting that neither they nor Samson are entirely responsible for their fates. Not only are they miserable comforters; they are inconsistent as well" (62). Bullough and Bullough alternatively note, "Samson is not just the medieval tragic hero cast down by Fortune, but the Aristotelian hero ruined by a moral flaw."

    reckon: "consider," "regard" (*OED* 3, 5b). Darbishire emends to *reck'n* (*Poetical Works*).

    estate: "position in the world," "status," "degree of rank" (*OED* 3); editors gloss: "For I do not consider him of (truly) high status." Cf. 742 and see *PL* 12.351. On the sentiment, Percival compares Ovid, *Ex ponto* 1.9.39–40: "nec census nec clarum nomen avorum / sed probitas magnos ingeniumque facit"; "not property nor the illustrious names of ancestors, but uprightness and character render men great."

171–72. *long descent…raises:* Parker describes this as a paradox or oxymoron, and also a pun: "the Chorus ridicules the notion that descent (ancient lineage) can either 'lift up' (above others) or 'bring into existence' (*OED* s.v. *raise* 17, 9) men of 'high estate'" ("Variorum"). Lockwood (I.11) interprets *raises* as meaning "to advance to a higher rank or position, exalt in power" (*OED* 18).

    birth: "lineage." Todd and Brydges cite Juvenal, *Satires* 8.1: "quid prodest, Pontice, longo / sanguine censeri"; "What boots it, Ponticus, to be valued for one's ancient blood?"

172. Bridges identifies this as one of seventeen lines in falling (trochaic) rhythm (*Milton's Prosody* 55); see 116n. Edward J. Thompson adds, "the 'lift' given to the metre by the sudden inversion coming in the first foot expresses the upward turn of Fortune's shifting wheel" (246). But Edmund K. Chambers would scan the first foot as anapestic (129). Sprott (132) thinks it difficult to determine whether Milton thought of the line as "trochaic with the last foot catalectic, or as iambic with the first foot catalectic" (see 116n). Note the unstressed rhyme (with 175); for others see 303, 306, 668, 669, 688, 691, 1011, 1012, 1015, 1277, 1283, 1660, 1664; and cf. 622, 632. See also 1541n.

    the sphear of fortune: editors find this phrase troublesome because, as Verity notes, a *sphere* could "scarcely be said to raise." Church, followed by other editors, writes that the image of Fortune having a wheel was "the more common image, and seems to suit the text better," whereas the image of Fortune standing on a globe was meant to signify her supremacy. Percival suggests that in *SA* Milton identified, or confused, globe with wheel; Warburton (in Newton) suggests that

Milton had in mind an image of Fortune painted on a perpetually moving globe. Editors cite many illustrative passages, but none entirely clears up the difficulty; e.g., Northrop Frye compares this image to the opening of Chaucer's *Troilus* (Paradise Lost *and Selected Poetry* 167n). Parker, however, proposes that *sphere* is the right word "precisely because it most improbably 'raises' men—because it offers a picture as incongruous as the oxymoron of 'long descent' lifting up [see 171–72n]" ("Variorum"). Parker glosses this line literally: "I do not reckon of high estate one exalted above others by either ancestry or chance" ("Variorum"). The late classical Fortune was first depicted with a sphere—"globe or ball" (so *OED* 9a)—which, represented two-dimensionally as a circle, came eventually to be associated with the wheel of human affairs. Patch discusses this tradition more generally and notes, e.g., that Boethius put man on the revolving wheel and intimated that Fortune turned it (148–77). Shawcross adds, "Fortune's wheel...does not bring true glory" (*Complete English Poetry*). For other references to Fortune, see 169, 1093, 1291; and cf. *occasion* in 224, 237, 423, 1329, 1716. See also *REW* (Patterson, *Works* 6:128).

173. Editors gloss as "But (rather I reckoned) thee (in high estate), whose."
    vertue: The meaning seems to be "moral excellence" (cf. *OED* 2), and what prompts the implied criticism is suggested by 215–18, 319–21. Verity and Grieve identify virtue here with wisdom and cite 53–57 (which, however, the Chorus did not hear). Dick Taylor writes that the Chorus here knows, like Samson (206–9), "that he has used his strength improperly and capriciously" (76). On *vertue,* see also 1010, 1039, 1050, 1690, 1697, and cf. 756. Parker adds, "this line discourages any reading of the whole passage as in any sense autobiographical" ("Variorum").
    her: Latin *vis,* "strength," is feminine; cf. 71–72n (Wyatt and Collins).

174–75. *the Earth:* "the inhabitants of the earth" (Parker, "Variorum"); cf. *Ps 82* 25–26.
    Universally: Church would stress the second syllable; Verity and Blakeney, the first, making the first two feet trochaic, which is also Bridges's (*Milton's Prosody* 56), Sprott's (132), and Weismiller's (121) reading (see 81n). Hughes similarly suggests: "the art of reading such a line consists in putting just the right, deliberate stress upon *crown'd* to give it the predominance which it was...intended to have, and which marks it as the point of recovery of the iambic rhythm" (*John*

Milton 423–24). Edward J. Thompson writes that this line "with its huddled syllables expresses the tumultuous character of popular acclamation" (246).
    crown'd: "agrees with 'strength'" (Church). Cf. 1296, 1579.

176–292. Editors define as the first epeisodion, with the Chorus taking part in dialogue (e.g., Wyatt and Collins 25). Edmund K. Chambers explains that, in Greek tragedy, after the entrance of the chorus (parodos) came the ἐπεισόδιον, literally meaning, "that which follows the entry of the chorus"; the word came to designate "the intervals of dialogue between two choric songs" (84). Thus, in these notes, it is used to designate the various acts or scenes between the pro-logos and the exodos, as they are separated by odes (stasima) from the Chorus. For subsequent epeisodia, see 326–651, 710–1009, 1061–1267, 1300–1426. Baum, however, does not consider 176–292 an epeisodion (354). More gener-ally, Raleigh compliments the meter of the Chorus's speeches: here, he claims, Milton "reaches the top of his skill," varying "even the length of the line" and treating "the iambic pattern…merely as a point of departure or reference" (*Milton* 195). Brewer compares this dialogue with the similar interview between Prometheus and the Chorus in *Prometheus Bound* (915).

176. This line suggests that the choral ode was not a soliloquy; the Chorus was speaking, instead, at a distance, almost out of earshot (Parker, "Variorum").

177. *Dissolves unjointed:* Landy writes, for Samson "all sound is discordant and disjointed. The sounds, like the darkness he perceives, are indicative of his alienation from God who represents not only the light of wisdom, mercy, and love, but also order, harmony, and agreeableness" ("Of Highest Wisdom" 221). Parker specifically notices "air…e're…ear" ("Variorum"). Editors cite *1 Henry IV* 1.3.65: "This bald unjointed chat."

178–86. Parker observes that the first two speeches of the Chorus (see 210–18) are exactly balanced in length (*Milton's Debt* 62).
    Hee: Darbishire (*Poetical Works*) and B. A. Wright emend to *he;* see 124n, 219–20n s.v. *Mee.*
    Matchless…grief: Parker ("Variorum") describes as "a dubiously tactful beginning in addressing an obviously suffering friend; but the Chorus is else-

where tactless or nearly so (see, e.g., 215–18, 240, 1003–07, 1063, 1539)."
A. B. Chambers comments: "with a syntactical ambiguity it neatly summarizes
the apparent contrast.... Both then and now the might [was and] is matchless,
but Samson once played the hero and now he does not" (317). Cf. *PL* 10.404
(Le Comte 66).

The glory…now: editors notice parallels in John Fletcher's *The False One*
(1647), 2.1: "Thou glory of the world once, now the pitty" (e.g., Collins thinks
the passage "strongly recalls" this play); and Phineas Fletcher's *Piscatorie Eclogs*
(1633): "his glory late, but now his shame" (e.g., Todd writes that the line in
SA "resembles" this passage).

grief: Keightley (*Poems*) and William Aldis Wright change the semicolon following this word to an exclamation point.

180. *friends and neighbors:* Parker ("Variorum") notes that both Manoa and Samson
address them as *brethren* (332, 1413, 1445).

not unknown: "this use (litotes) of two negatives as a feeble equivalent of
an affirmative has its point here, because Samson cannot recognize his visitors
except through their voices. Imagine 178–86 divided among nine speakers"
(Parker, "Variorum").

181. *Eshtaol:* a city of Palestine in the inheritance of the tribe of Dan (Gilbert,
Geographical); see Joshua 19:41, and Judges 13:24–25: "and the child grew,
and the Lord blessed him. And the Spirit of the Lord began to move him at
times in the camp of Dan between Zorah and Eshtaol."

Zora's fruitful Vale: Parker ("Variorum") notes that Zora (Authorized Version: *Zorah*), modern Surah, Samson's birthplace (Judg. 13:2), was a town
about a mile from Eshtaol, near the eastern end of the Vale of Sorek (see 229).
Gilbert (*Geographical*) adds that it and Eshtaol were in a valley (Josh. 15:33);
the burial place of Manoa was between them (Judg. 16:31). Near Zora, according to Thomas Fuller (*A Pisgah Sight of Palestine* [London, 1651], 198; qtd.
in Gilbert, *Geographical*), was the brook of Eshcol, famous for its fruits (Num.
13:23–24). Parker adds, "both Zora and Eshtaol were about thirty-seven miles,
as the crow flies, from Gaza; Milton offers no explanation of how the Chorus
and Manoa, whose visits were made possible by the Philistine festival, arrived in
Gaza in the early morning; cf. 1596–97" ("Variorum"). Page discusses Milton's
unique ability to incorporate smoothly such place names into his poetry: "they

appear to fit into his verse as the eye dwells in the socket" (13). See also 229, 528, 716, 981, 988.

182–83. *or bewail:* Calton (in Newton) believes that Milton intended "and bewail"; Keightley (*Poems*), Jerram, Percival, Verity, Martin W. Sampson, et al. agree. Percival interprets the construction as "we come to visit and bewail, or (to see) if better (i.e., more appropriately) we may bring"; Jerram, Verity, and Blakeney take "we may bring" as a main verb. Parker adds that *visit* can mean "to go to see a person in distress in order to comfort or assist him" (see *OED* II.7b, and cf. *RCG* [Patterson, *Works* 3:257]), and so here the contrast might be "To comfort or bewail thee," with the idea of bringing *Counsel* as a further alternative ("Variorum").
   Consolation: cf. 664, 1757.

183–86. Stroup finds here the first evidence that the play's action "may involve the healing and consolation of religious service," and he specifically notes that in these lines the Chorus "suggest, if they do not invite, confession" (56–57). Low instead identifies this as the first in a pattern of "disease imagery" that serves various purposes: "It can symbolize the perils of despair, the spiritual fruits of sin, the shameful condition of slavery. It contrasts with Samson's former healthy state. It cannot be said entirely to oppose the physical to the spiritual, because Samson is impaired in both respects" ("Tragic Pattern" 924). Low further compares Samson's resulting "repulsiveness" with the incurable wound suffered by the Greek bowman Philoctetes (925–26). For other disease images, see, e.g., 480, 571–75, 579, 697–704. Freedman ("*All for Love*" 515; "Milton" 105) notes the verbal and thematic correspondence between this passage and Venditius's speech with Antony in Dryden's *All for Love* 1.1. See also 115–75n, 951n.

184. *Salve to thy Sores:* "(as) a remedy for sorrow," literally "a healing ointment for application to wounds or sores" (so *OED* 1b); a proverbial phrase. Editors cite many examples, e.g., Spenser's *The Faerie Queene* 3.2.36.5 and 6.6.5.9; Mitford describes it as "one of the most common expressions in old English poetry." Baum writes, "the Chorus, in offering 'salve to his sores' [184], only reëmphasizes the completeness of his downfall and increases his melancholy" (359); see also Lawry and Hanford in 115–75n.

apt words…mind: Thyer (in Newton), Bullough and Bullough, Hughes (*Complete Poems; John Milton*), Brewer (918), et al. quote Aeschylus, *Prometheus Bound* 379–80—a famous passage because Cicero quoted it in his *Tusculanæ quæstiones* 3.31—but, as Maxwell emphasizes, the sentiment occurs elsewhere ("Milton's Knowledge" 368–69). Editors cite, among others, Menander, *Dyscolus;* Dante, *Purgatorio* 11.119; Horace, *Epistles* 1.1.34–35; Spenser's *The Faerie Queene* 1.10.24.4–8.

    swage: "assuage," "abate" (so *OED* a); also *PL* 1.556. Cf. 627.

185–86. *tumors:* "'swelling[s]' of passion" in the mind (*OED* 4a); Latin: *tumors* (Wyatt and Collins). For Shawcross, "the word connotes the exaggeration or preoccupation arising from psychological disorder" (*Complete English Poetry*).

    as Balm: is understood (Parker, "Variorum"); cf. 651.

    fester'd: "festering" (*OED*); cf. 621.

187–209. Clark notes that the portrait of Samson in Judges "exhibits little of this filial tenderness and nothing of this neighborly love" (93). Ellis-Fermor analyzes the dramatic function of the prosody in 187–447 and finds three related movements: "short passages of dramatic verse which break in intermittently, as gusts of energy sweep over Samson's mind"; "steadier, firmer moulding of the verse…, as the defensive mood of the debate and argument develops"; and, in contrast, "the wavering, weak rhythm of some of Manoa's speech [especially 340–72]" (149–50). On the prosody in these lines, see also 241–76n, 340–72n.

    Friends: so also 193, 202, but not again until 1415 (cf. 1413).

188. Church finds in this line "the antithesis so common in the Greek tragedians and Thucydides."

    talk: Ferry suggests that this word "by its curiously colloquial sound here implies a scornful tone—'mere talk'"; she also argues that the talk Samson is criticizing "is not idle chatter, malicious slander, or the betrayal of secrets, but abstract generalizations, or moral maxims" (147). Landy adds, "The Chorus, unlike those others who crowded around Samson in more prosperous days, seems more important to him for its coming, its presence, than for the words of counsel and comfort which it brings" ("Language" 183).

189–90. One of the many sententiae in the poem—an element possibly influenced by the well-known practice of Euripides (Collins 5; Timberlake 338; Parker, *Milton's Debt* 206). Some other examples: 210–12, 268–70, 293–94, 652–53, 1008–9, 1406–7. Landor complains that "fondness for Euripides made him [Milton] too didactic when action was required" (5:295).

    counterfeit a coin: Cox traces the poem's various images of money: "money and payment are linked with a misuse of the senses and the will, with corruption, and with a sin against order. Also, money and payment images are used to describe punishment" ("Natural Science" 70). Landy alternatively discusses this and other "references to coinage, counterfeiting, and legalisms," which "all point to Samson's awakening to the appearances of things" and "the distinction between words and deeds" ("Language" 184).

    friends: editors gloss as "(the word or title of) friends." Dunster (in Todd) quotes Shakespeare's *Two Gentlemen of Verona* 5.4.53: "Thou counterfeit to thy true friend!"; and *A Mirror for Magistrates:* "A golden treasure is the tried friend; / But who may gold from counterfeits defend." Percival quotes Theognis, *Elegies* 117–18: Κιβδήλου δ'ἀνδρὸς γνῶναι χαλεπώτερον οὐδέν; "Nothing is harder than to detect a counterfeit friend." Thaler ("Shakespeare and Milton" 89) is reminded of Shakespeare's Timon, who is also disillusioned in his friendships (*Timon of Athens* 2.2.193; 3.2.79–80; 3.6.34, 99, 106). Jerram is reminded of Job 19:13–14; Psalm 41:9.

    who friends / Bear in their Superscription: Parker asserts, "Milton is surely not alluding to the Society of Friends founded by George Fox in 1648–50, though the phrasing here may have encouraged such an interpretation when *SA* was published in 1671" ("Variorum").

190. On the use of enjambment in *SA* (such as between 190 and 191), Oras observes that even it contributes to the poem's "staccato rhythm": it tends "to appear in brief phrases or abrupt parenthetical insertions splitting the text rather than adding to its continuity" (*Blank Verse* 29). See, e.g., 399–400, 735–37, 1092–93. See also 205n.

    their: Darbishire (*Poetical Works*) and B. A. Wright emend to *thir,* here and in 192. Parker observes that *their* occurs fourteen times in the poem, whereas *thir* occurs eighty-four times ("Notes" 691). Darbishire changes *their* to *thir* ten times, and *thir* to *their* once, in line 1267 (*Poetical Works*). See 880–90n, Preface 13n, and Argument 11–12n.

    Superscription: "a piece of writing or an inscription" upon a coin (so *OED* 1b); Banks (8) notes other similar images in Milton's poetry and suggests as a source Matthew 22:20: "Whose is this image and superscription?" Cf. also *Liber de amicitia qui inscribitur Laelius* (Church), and *Tetr:* "wee must either new stamp our Coine, or we may goe new stamp our Foreheads with the superscription of slaves instead of freemen" (Patterson, *Works* 4:142).

of the most: "of the majority," i.e., Samson tactfully says in effect that the Chorus is obviously excepted (Verity).

191–93. Commentators are intrigued by Samson's complaint that "most" of his former friends have deserted him. Parker notes that no illustrations are adduced, *SA* mentions no former friends (see, however, 1196), and the idea is an addition to the account in Judges ("Variorum"). Masson wonders whether this passage has autobiographical implications: "Perhaps from Milton's own experience after the Restoration" (*Poetical Works*); Martin W. Sampson says "evidently"; Fleming and Rosedale (159) sound positive about it. But Eleanor Gertrude Brown adduces various examples to show that Milton's "friends worth retaining certainly had not deserted him" (95–96), and Verity insists, "Milton himself had no cause to complain of want of loyalty in friends like Thomas Ellwood; nor did the outside world neglect him." See also, e.g., *Def 2* (Patterson, *Works* 8:72, 74) and John Aubrey's account of Milton's many learned acquaintances (Darbishire, *Early Lives* 6–7). Following Keightley (*Poems*), editors quote Ovid, *Tristia* 1.9.5–6: "donec eris sospes [felix], multos numerabis amicos: / tempora si fuerint nubila, solus eris"; "So long as you are secure you will count many friends; if your life becomes clouded you will be alone." Blakeney notes that the thought is the basis of Shakespeare's *Timon of Athens* (so also Verity) and quotes other parallels, including Euripides, *Hercules furens* 1223–25; Brydges hears an echo of these lines in Gray's "Hymn to Adversity."

understood: the first edition has no punctuation here; Tickell inserts a colon before the closing parentheses; Bohn inserts a semicolon before the closing parentheses; Verity, William Aldis Wright, et al. insert a period after the closing parentheses.

192–93. Ricks finds fault with Milton's "blurring" of metaphors in this passage: "The image of the coin, which 'Superscription' asks us to take seriously, turns within the same sentence into a swarm of something (summer flies, presumably, but where they appear from is not clear), who then *withdraw their head*—a phrase which can only dubiously be applied to a swarm and which moreover is unhelpfully apt to a coin, which has a head but cannot withdraw it" (*Milton's Grand Style* 50). Cf. 19–21n, 198n, 362n. Carey, however, objects to Ricks's criticism: "the base coin is not, from the perspective of the whole work, as lonely as he would have us suppose. Dalila as Danaë in the shower of Philistian gold (388–91, 831) keeps it company in Samson's tormented mind.... The rarity of *SA*'s imagery allows it to make connections across areas too large for Ricks's focus" (*Complete Shorter Poems* 337).

    swarm: cf. 19.

    adverse: see 1040.

    head: perhaps emend to *heads* (Parker, "Variorum").

    Yee: cf. 332, 1453, and see 219–20n s.v. *Mee.* Darbishire emends to *Ye* (*Poetical Works*). The word *you* occurs only in 1445, 1511, and 1644.

195. *that which was the worst:* see 67–69.

    least: Parker ("Variorum") glosses as "not at all" (as also in 927, 1136). Cf. *Colas:* "*least* is tak'n in the Bible, and other good Authors, for *not at all*" (Patterson, *Works* 4:264).

    now least afflicts me: Broadbent suggests this is an exaggeration: "when Samson goes back on his own ode and says it is not blindness but shame that grieves him most, it is not so much a development of his mood as an alteration in it to suit his now more public situation" (*Milton* 43). But Carey thinks this "more histrionic" statement (cf. "O loss of sight, of thee I most complain" [67]) reveals that with the Chorus's entrance Samson has begun "to think of the impression he is making" (*John Milton* 139). Nash offers another possibility: "There may be surface contradictions here, perhaps enough to make us feel that the *Agonistes* did not receive a final polishing, but there is no real confusion" (27).

197. *heave:* "lift, raise" (so *OED* 1); cf. *L'All* 145; *Mask* 884; *PL* 1.211.

198. *shipwrack't:* this metaphor, an ancient and familiar one (cf., e.g., *REW* [Patterson, *Works* 6:143]), is later echoed by the Chorus (1044–45). Commentators here discuss its origin and value. Dunster (in Todd) and Church cite both 1 Timothy 1:19 ("Holding faith, and a good conscience; which some having put away concerning faith have made shipwreck") and James 3:4–5 ("Behold also the ships,... turned about with a very small helm, whithersoever the governor listeth. Even so the tongue is a little member, and boasteth great things"). While Johnson

(*Rambler* 20 July 1751) criticizes Milton's use of this metaphor as confounding "loquacity with a shipwreck" (221), Dunster (in Todd) replies that Samson rather "ascribes his own ruin, or *shipwreck,* to . . . indiscretion." Ricks, however, agrees with Johnson that this is "a disappointing failure in metaphor": "Samson is like a bad pilot only in the respect that he has carelessly shipwrecked—loquacity has nothing to do with it. Pilots don't shipwreck because they divulge secrets. . . . Milton is, within the same sentence, asking us both to take his metaphor with tragic seriousness, and then to ignore it" (*Milton's Grand Style* 49–50). Lewalski, noting that the passage initiates the poem's "larger pattern of ship and tempest imagery," explains that this specific comparison "operates both as simile and metaphor: Samson is like the disgraced Pilot who has shipwrecked his vessel, but also, Samson's Reason has not properly piloted the strong and 'gloriously rigg'd' craft that is his body" ("Ship-Tempest" 372). For other imagery of navigation, see the entrance of the Chorus (111) and the choral introduction of Dalila (713–19); cf. *Sonn 22,* on his blindness: "but still bear up [i.e., 'sail before the wind'] and steer / Right onward." Samson is also compared to a ship in Vondel's *Samson* (Edmundson 176–77); Quarles, too, uses the metaphor of shipwreck in his *Historie of Samson* (sigs. F4v, K4r). More generally about the influence of Quarles's drama on *SA,* Kirkconnell concludes, "Parallels with Milton are few, slight, and probably accidental" (173). On Quarles, see also 386n, 960–96n, 1066n, 1605–10n, 1633n, 1634n, 1740n.

200. *a word, a tear:* Judges 16:16: "she pressed him daily with her words, and urged him." Cf. 235, 779, 905. Ellis-Fermor finds in 200–5 "something of the immediacy of emotional speech in the hands of an experienced playwright; they unite with the cadences and tempo of dramatic verse those of familiar speech" (150).

201. Krouse finds here "an interesting parallel" with the Christ of *PR,* who did not divulge to Satan his identity and the source of his power (101); Le Comte recommends various verbal echoes in Milton's prose, both English and Latin (100–1). Some editors (e.g., Tickell; Bohn; Verity; William Aldis Wright) replace the first edition's comma after *Fool* with an exclamation point.
   divulg'd: "reveal[ed]," "disclose[d]" (so *OED* 2); cf. 1248.

202–09. Tillyard writes: "These words would suit Milton's thoughts in 1643 to perfection. 'Immeasurable strength' would be his own estimate of himself the smiter of Bishops, but lack of wisdom.... [H]e must have admitted of think-ing of his foolish marriage" (*Milton* 294–95). Bowra alternatively writes of this speech, "This is not the mood in which Heracles or Ajax makes his first appear-ance. Milton's drama starts at a point which Sophocles would normally have kept for a later stage" (120).

    deceitful: cf. 537.

    Woman: cf. 50, 236, 379, 1114, and see 49–50n, 211n.

203. Low finds evidence here of Samson's isolation: "His fear of mockery, his sensitivity to appearance, are the reactions of a man who knows that he is cut off, rejected, different from other men. Formerly he could take pride in the dif-ference; now he feels shame" ("Tragic Pattern" 925). Todd et al. compare Job 30:9: "And now am I their song, yea I am their byword"; editors also compare Deuteronomy 28:37: "And thou shalt become an astonishment, a proverb and a byword"; and Psalm 69:11–12: "I am became a proverb to them. They that sit in the gate speak against me; and I was the song of the drunkards."

    proverbd: "[made] a byword of" (so *OED* 1); cf. *Romeo and Juliet* 1.4.37 (George Coffin Taylor 194) and *Antony and Cleopatra* 5.2.215–17 (Thaler, "Shakespearian Element" 167). Thaler adds that Milton may have "had in mind the scurrilous Elizabethan street-ballads" (167). Krouse, too, suggests (103) an allusion to actual ballads and broadsides on Samson with which Milton might have been acquainted (a possibility that Bullough and Bullough repeat).

204. Some editors follow Tickell (e.g., William Aldis Wright) and change the comma after *street* (in the first edition) to a question mark; a new sentence then begins with *do* (which some editors change to uppercase *Do*).

205. Oras cites this line to illustrate the poem's "special staccato rhythm" and notes that *SA*'s has the highest incidence of heavy punctuation among Milton's blank verse: "the sense...is relatively seldom 'drawn out' from line to line for any length of time" (*Blank Verse* 29). See, e.g., 235, 959, 1508, 1583, 1584. See also 190n.

    Are come upon: editors gloss as "befall, happen to"; so also 1681.

206–07. Carey writes that often in *SA*, as here, English word order is disrupted and the object of a verb occurs at the start of a sentence or clause; see also 14–15, 219, 241, 291, 521, 1640–41 (*Complete Shorter Poems* 335).

Immeasurable: Parker pronounces "im-meas´-ur-a´-ble," but also compares *PL* 1.549 and 7.211 ("Variorum").

mean: "not far above or below the average" (*OED* 6). The word can also mean "inferior" (*OED* 3n), but Church writes, "Samson does not positively disparage his own sense. It ought to have been in excess, to match his strength; it was only a mean." Lawry suggests, "the pun in 'mean' turns the charge back upon himself.... His renewed complaint, as old as that of Eve or Satan, is empty. Even a merely 'mean' wisdom must contradict it; of wisdom, he, like every man, possessed sufficient to have stood" (361). Rudrum agrees: "However plausible Samson's words are psychologically, what they imply is unacceptable. The task God had set him was not too hard for his intelligence; it merely required common prudence" (26). Huntley is similarly critical: "Samson's statement betokens more self-pity than self-understanding; it portrays a childish cry for comfort rather than a mature recognition of the enemy within who wanted the sin" (134).

208. Cf. 53–54.
    paired: "match[ed], equal[ed]" (*OED* 1); see 206–7n s.v. *mean.*

209. *transverse:* "awry"; cf. *PL* 3.487–88. Editors note that this word probably reverts to the shipwreck metaphor (198–200); it means literally "athwart," "situated or lying crosswise" (so *OED* 1, C); i.e., the imbalance of Samson's strength and wisdom caused him to swerve from his intended course (Parker, "Variorum"). Langdon (46–47), however, sees *proportioned* and *transverse* as technical terms in music, and compares *SolMus* 17–23 and *PL* 11.557–59.

210–18. See 178–86n.
    Tax: "dispute," "call in question" (*OED* 7); "find fault with, blame" (Verity et al.); the sense: "Don't blame God for not giving you enough wisdom" (Grieve); Hanford (*Poems*) compares *PL* 8.561. Parker infers from what the Chorus says next that it disagrees with Samson's view that inadequate wisdom was his undoing; cf. 173 ("Variorum"). On "Tax" cf. *Animad:* "as if a man should taxe the renovating and re-ingendering Spirit of God with innovation" (Patterson, *Works* 3:144); Le Comte (13) also finds a verbal echo of *DDD:* "of all those wild words which men in misery think to ease themselves by uttering, let him not op'n his lips against the providence of heav'n, or tax the wayes of God and his divine truth" (Patterson, *Works* 3:496).

disposal: "giving," "bestowal," i.e., of strength and wisdom (*OED* 3), or, perhaps, "control, direction," "dispensation" (so *OED* 1). Cf. 373, 506, 1746.

wisest Men: Todd, Collins, Percival, et al. think this probably an allusion to Solomon, described in *PL* 1.444–46 as "that uxorious King, whose heart though large, / Beguil'd by fair Idolatresses, fell / To Idols foul." Blakeney agrees, adding that Milton also has in mind "his own matrimonial miscarriages." Todd and Fleming quote 1 Esdras 4.27: "Many also have perished, have erred, and sinned for women"; many editors quote *Tetr:* "the best and wisest men amidst the sincere and most cordiall designes of their heart doe dayly erre in choosing" (Patterson, *Works* 4:87). Le Comte (45, 87–88) notes that the phrase recurs in 759, 867, and 1034, and also compares *DDD* (Patterson, *Works* 3:394, 461); *Tetr* (Patterson, *Works* 4:120); *Colas* (Patterson, *Works* 4:256). Parker concludes: that the Chorus here voices a Miltonic conviction strengthens, dramatically, "Samson's temptation to doubt" ("Variorum").

211. *bad Women:* Parker notes the qualifying adjective ("Variorum"); see also 202. Cf. *PL* 10.837 (Le Comte 62).

212. *pretend:* editors disagree about this word's precise meaning; possibilities are "intend," "aspire," "attempt," or "feign" (*OED* 8–9, 4); Lockwood (1.e), Percival, Verity, Edmund K. Chambers, and Martin W. Sampson favor the sense "intend, mean, aim at"; Church and Grieve suggest "the construction is explained by a reference to the Latin idiom; so we find *Hannibal aegrum simulabat* (Livy 25.8)." Wyatt and Collins gloss as "however wise they claim to be"; Verity glosses as "however wise their intentions may be."

ne're so: "ever so"; in conditional clauses denotes an unlimited degree or amount (*OED* 4); i.e., "to whatever degree" (Lockwood b). On the sentiment expressed in this line, Prince (*Samson Agonistes*) compares *PL* 10.896–908.

213. *Deject:* "dishearten," "depress in spirits," and/or "abase, humble" (*OED* 5, 3), with perhaps "weaken" (*OED* 4) as a secondary meaning (cf. *load* in 214). Cf. 338.

215–18. Parker (*Milton's Debt* 33) finds the Chorus "delightfully human" and notes that after such doubtful sort of comfort, it responds indirectly, and with more curiosity than tact, to Samson's questions (202–5). Adds Ellis-Fermor, "The chorus (like most visitations of friends from the time of Job downwards) soon falls into the question, Why did you do it?" (26). Bush, noting the same comparison to Job's comforters, suggests instead that the Chorus "contrive[s] to turn the knife in Samson's wound" ("John Milton" 506n). Huntley attempts to explain why the Chorus "introduce[s] a matter which must increase both his sorrow and his guilt.... Apparently they intend to stifle Samson's blasphemies by proving that Samson, not God, was in fact to blame because of the ill-advised marriage with Dalila" (136). Krouse notes, "Nearly every commentator who dealt with Samson asked why he had persisted in choosing Philistine women" (97).

217. *Tribe:* editors note that Samson and the Chorus were of the tribe of Dan, referred to in 332, 876, 976, 1436, 1479, 1540. See 332n.

218. Jerram thinks this "a poor line, especially as closing the passage."
 thy own: cf. "thine own" (217).
 noble: Prince interprets "as noble" as meaning "of the same social standing as yourself" (*Samson Agonistes*). Parker finds it "an ironic reflection on the moral quality of Samson's wives. If this refers to rank rather than character, Milton is without biblical or other authority implying that Samson's wives were noble; indeed, Josephus says that Dalila was a harlot (*Antiquities of the Jews* 5.8.11)" ("Variorum").

219–25. Krouse notes that the Christian tradition since Theodoret "had argued that all of Samson's apparent waywardnesses," such as marrying the woman of Timnath, were done at God's prompting: "In Milton's own age, Calvin, Brenz, Bullinger, Pareus, and others had defended Samson on that ground" (96). To explain this deviation, T. Warton (in Todd), followed by Masson (*Poetical Works*) and Percival, writes that Milton "alludes to some of the particulars" of his own first marriage, e.g., the conflicting political loyalties. Percival adds that the fact that Mary Powell left him "only a few weeks after marriage, partly at the instigation of her relatives, finds a parallel in that of Samson's first wife being withheld from him by her father." See 795n.
 Other commentators, however, are skeptical of such autobiographical readings. E.g., Parker writes in 1968 that "for more than two hundred years scholarship has lowered itself to nasty-minded and malicious gossip in its interpretation

of Milton's first marriage" (*Milton* 317). Parker adds, "Milton married three times, but his first wife, if we may credit early commentators, doubled as the model for *both* of Samson's treacherous wives. Here Milton seems to follow Judg. 14.1–4 closely in his account of Samson's first marriage" ("Variorum"). For subsequent references to Samson's first wife, see 320–25, 382–87, 795, 1018–21, 1192–1200. Gilbert finds this reiteration a flaw, one of a series of unnecessary repetitions that he believes suggest *SA* was never fully revised ("Is *Samson Agonistes*" 105).

219–20. *Timna:* Timnah (Hebrew) or Timnath, or Thamna (Josephus, *Antiquities of the Jews* 5.8.5) or Thimnathah, now identified with Tibneh, was a "City" (1194) on the north frontier of the tribe of Judah between Bethshemish and Ekron and south of Gath (Josh. 15:10–11); at one time it was counted in the territory of Dan (Josh. 19:43); see Gilbert, *Geographical;* and Wyatt and Collins. Parker adds that it was about four miles southwest of the camp of Dan ("Variorum"). Prince thinks that Milton drops the *th* of Judges 14:1 in the Authorized Version as an awkward sound (*Samson Agonistes*); but cf. *Gath* (266), *Ramath* (145), *Succoth* (278). Among the possible subjects for tragedy listed in the Trinity Manuscript, Milton wrote "Samson marriing or in Ramath Lechi Jud. 15" (Patterson, *Works* 18:236), which Parker interprets as Samson's marriage to the woman of Timnah, not Dalila ("Trinity Manuscript" 228).

  she pleas'd / Mee: Judges 14:3, 7: "And Samson said unto his father, Get her for me; for she pleaseth me well"; "And he went down, and talked to the woman; and she pleased Samson well." Milton used the spelling *mee* in the manuscript versions of *Mask* 481 and *Lyc* 56, 154; in *SA* it recurs in 252, 290, 291, 1125. Stress may or may not have been intended in some or all of these instances. Cf. *hee* (124, 178), *yee* (193), and note the absence in *SA* of *bee, shee,* and *wee,* spellings that Milton elsewhere occasionally used. Shawcross concludes that the double *e* in these words does not indicate stress ("One Aspect" 503, 506, 509). Adams similarly writes, "*Paradise Regained* and *Samson Agonistes* could not be more random in their use of 'emphatic' forms.... [They] are not evidence that Milton changed his principles; they merely make obvious that he had never had any" (66). Adams adds that *SA* has only eight such forms, only one of which (*mee* [1125]) occurs in the last 1,467 lines: "The odd distribution suggests, though not conclusively, that the copyist or compositor may, in fact, have determined the spellings.... In each poem, no more than one or at the most two of the distinctively spelled pronouns would be considered emphatic if not spelled in an unusual way" (66).

not my Parents: Parker glosses as "it did not please my parents" ("Variorum"). Cf. 420–21. The Hebrew father arranged the marriage of his son (Gen. 24:48, 28:2), and the son was under an obligation to obey his father absolutely. Parker notes that Samson nowhere mentions his mother specifically in *SA* ("Variorum"); cf. 25.

that: "in that" (so Church).

221–22. *Infidel:* "Gentile" (so *OED* 2b) or "unbeliever" (*OED* 1). In Judges 14:1 she is called "of the daughters of the Philistines."

they knew not...God: editors cite Judges 14:4: "But his father and his mother knew not that it was of the Lord, that he sought an occasion against the Philistines." Parker ("Variorum") finds an apparent contradiction in Manoa's later statement (421–23).

motion'd: "[made] a proposal," "offer[ed] a plan" (*OED* 2; cf. *PL* 9.229). The text of the first edition has *mention'd,* corrected in the *Errata* but still repeated in the 1680 text.

223. *intimate:* "inmost" (so *OED* 2). Cf. "prompted" (318), "Divine impulsion" (422), "divine instinct" (526), and "rouzing motions" (1382).

impulse: "incitement or stimulus to action" (*OED* 3b; the first occurrence of this word as a noun is traced to 1647). Grierson (*Milton* 143; "Note" 333–34) compares Augustine's defense of Samson in book 1, chapter 21 of *De civitate Dei:* "nisi quia Spiritus latenter hoc iusserat"; "unless the Spirit of the Lord had given him special intimation to do so."

therefore: Edmund K. Chambers suggests that it be taken in connection with "that...I might begin."

224. Diodati writes in 1648 that Samson "stood waiting to have the Philistims give him cause by some unjust and unworthy act to contend with them" (sig. L5r–v).

Marriage: around 1641 or 1642 Milton came to spell this word *mariage* (also *mary*), perhaps whimsically after his own to Mary Powell (Parker, "Variorum").

occasion hence: Parker ("Variorum") glosses as "opportunity" or "juncture of circumstances favourable or suitable to an end or purpose" (cf. *OED* I.1). See 221–22n. For other uses of the word *occasion,* see 237, 423, 425, 1329, 1716.

225–26. *begin:* see 38–42n s.v. *Promise...deliver.*
    work: "mission"; so also 565, 1662; cf. 680.
    divinely: "by the agency or power of God," i.e., by an angel (*OED* 1); see 24.

227. *She proving false:* Judges 14:10–20.
    took to Wife: "married." Krouse (76) calls attention to the discussion in Renaissance commentaries over whether Dalila was Samson's wife or concubine (see 537n). In making her a wife, Milton follows John Chrysostom, Joannus Cassianus, Sulpicius Severus, Benedictus Pererius, and others—and goes counter to the opinion of Josephus, Ambrose, Jerome, Benedictus Montanus, Nicholas Serarius, and many others (Krouse 76). J. Macmillan Brown thinks this choice was "for the purposes of suiting Puritan feeling and passing criticism on contemporary life" (98). See 228n, 229n, 231n.

228. *fond:* "foolish" (*OED* 2); cf. *PL* 10.834 (Le Comte 62). Parker reasons, "if Samson had married Dalila as a result of God's prompting ('intimate impulse'), he would not now wish that he had ignored divine directions" ("Variorum"); see also 231, 233–34. But Percival (commenting on 210–76) writes that "in both his marriages he was acting under divine impulse"; various commentators make this same argument: Prince (*Samson Agonistes* 102), Bowra (117), Steadman ("'Faithful Champion'"17), and Wilkes (368). Cf. 878n.
    late: editors (e.g., Tickell; Verity; William Aldis Wright) often replace the period with an exclamation point.

229. Judges 16:4: "And it came to pass afterward, that he loved a woman in the valley of Sorek, whose name was Delilah." Parker notes that nothing is said of his marrying her; of the woman of Timnath, whom he married, it is not said that he loved her ("Variorum"); see 219–20n, 724n.
    Sorec: "a valley of Palestine extending from the coastal plain eastward to the neighborhood of Jerusalem" (Gilbert, *Geographical*); possibly Surar, in the

neighborhood of Ekron (Prince, *Samson Agonistes*). The name means "choice wine" (cf. Isa. 5.2).

Dalila: Dalila (Vulgate) or Delilah (Authorized Version) or Dalala (Josephus) or Dalida (the usual spelling in the Middle Ages); the name means "pining with desire" (but cf. 727–28n). Fell instead suggests that the name, "despite possible affinities to weakness or exhaustion, probably stands for night, of which she is doubtless a personification" (146). On Milton's spelling of the name cf. *PL* 9.1060–61: "the Harlot-lap / Of *Philistine Dalilah*." Thorpe infers from Hebrew pronunciation, metrical scansion, and the general practice of recessive accentuation that the primary stress of this name should fall on the antepenultimate syllable, so that it is pronounced "Da´-li-la" (72). Verity suggests a long second syllable ("Da-lee´-la") and thinks the last two syllables are intended as a trochee.

230. This line generates a mixed response: some commentators celebrate Milton's punning—e.g., Raleigh writes, "he taxes every line to its fullest capacity, and wrings the last drop of value from each word" (*Milton* 208). But other critics seem to disapprove of the line's ambiguities—e.g., Warburton (in Todd) on quibbles.

specious: "beautiful to the sight, fair to behold" (*OED* 1; Phillips, *New World*), but also with the secondary meaning of "having a fair or attractive appearance but in reality devoid of the qualities apparently possessed" (*OED* 2).

Monster: "person of inhuman and horrible cruelty or wickedness" (*OED* 4), and possibly, "marvel," "prodigy" (*OED* A.1). Dunster (in Todd) suggests that this whole expression refers to Hesiod's Echidna, who was half serpent, half woman. Steadman instead points out that the *monster* label was conventional in Renaissance interpretations of the Sirens and the cites Alciati, Conti, and Mignault ("Dalila" 562). Cf. *TKM:* "If I make a voluntary Covnant as with a man, to doe him good, and he prove afterward a monster to me, I should conceave a disobligement" (Patterson, *Works* 5:35). Cf. also *PR* 4.100, 128.

accomplisht: "perfect, especially in attainments" (cf. *PL* 4.660), but also with the secondary meaning of "fulfilled, completed," or even perhaps, "fully informed" (*OED* 2, 1, 3). Because the word suggests calculation and practice, it also suggests, in some cases, cunning (Prince, *Samson Agonistes*). Carey, too, detects a possible pun: "The snare is accomplished in that it has fulfilled its function and caught Samson, and Dalila is accomplished because she has various accomplishments, persuasiveness, for example" (*Complete Shorter Poems*).

snare: "trap," literally for small animals or birds (*OED* 1b); so also 409, 532, 845, 931. Cf. 1 Samuel 18:21. Empson notes a potential pun: Samson avowedly married Dalila to "snare" the Philistines but was snared himself; thus, Dalila, in this line, is simultaneously "that beautiful marvel, my charming trap (for my enemies)" and "that deceptive appearing, inhuman creature who accomplished my entrapping" (*Seven Types* 102).

231. Commentators offer various interpretations of Samson's reasoning. Muldrow suggests that this "argument by analogy leaves the possibility that Samson may have been more moved by Dalila's beauty than he can now admit" (177). Stein instead emphasizes, "He has done an extraordinary thing: he has interpreted intuition by analogy!...There is more than a suspicion that the trust of God was here, perhaps for the first time, symbolically violated, and the precious, individual favor of the 'intimate impulse' rationalized in a logical analogy to indulge a 'motion' from self" (*Heroic Knowledge* 146). And yet, Empson archly observes, Samson's first marriage "was a total failure from the start, not even needed to make Samson hate the Philistines, whereas the second marriage at least leads him to his lethal triumph; so it is doubtful whether the distinction is to the credit of God, or of Samson's intuitions about God" (*Milton's God* 218). Hill thinks Samson's analogy reveals his presumption: "on a purely human level, it would be difficult to fault Samson for his decision to marry Dalila in pursuance of his divinely ordained vocation.... On the other hand,...Samson's action was fostered by spiritual blindness and feebleness, and...as such it was blameworthy" (155); cf. 532–37. See 878n.

    thought: significantly, he does not say he *knew* (Parker, "Variorum"). See 1743–44.

    lawful: "permissible," i.e., despite the law against marrying Philistine women (*OED* 1b).

    from: denotes ground, or reason, or progress from a premise to an inference (see Verity; Prince, *Samson Agonistes;* et al.). According to Parker ("Variorum"), both 228 and 234 (as well as the account in Judges) suggest that Samson knows now it was not "lawful"; his mistake was, at least in part, this error in judgment, hence his emphasis on insufficient "wisdom" (52–57, 207–9).

232. *And the same end:* i.e., "my object was the same, viz. to oppress the Philistines" (Verity).

233–34. Cf. 701 ("causless suffring"). Parker recalls here that Aristotle, discussing tragic personages in the *Poetics,* describes characters in drama whose sufferings result from a flaw or defect (ἁμαρτία); see 369 ("Variorum").

She: Darbishire emends to *Shee* (*Poetical Works*); see 219–20n s.v. *Mee.*

prime: "first in order of time or occurrence" and also, probably, "chief" (*OED* 1, 3); cf. 70, 85, 388.

my self: cf. 46, 375, 824.

235. On the line's rhythm and punctuation, see 205n.

peal: "loud outburst" (so *OED* 6), but also in view of 235 and 404, "discharge of guns or cannon so as to produce a loud sound" (*OED* 5), hence another anachronism (Verity; Grieve; et al.); see 133. Cf. 906. Greenlaw, Osgood, and Padelford (5:244) note this image's precedent in *The Faerie Queene* 5.9.39.7; Browne cites *Love's Labour's Lost* 5.1; Hunter says this anachronistic use is instead in imitation of Shakespeare, *1 Henry VI* 3.3. Robertson writes that this imagery suggests, on the one hand, "that the issues involved in a moral struggle are large, that the struggle is violent, desperate, to the death"; on the other hand, because "this particular struggle is also a battle of the sexes,...the effect of elaborating this in military terms is mock-heroic" (322). Carey adds, "A peal of guns was used as a salute or sign of rejoicing: the guns were not weapons of attack when pealing. Samson's disgrace is all the more bitter: he gave up his fort at the mere sound of guns" (*Complete Shorter Poems*). On the imagery of military siege, see also 403–5n, 560–61n, 845–46n, 906n.

(O weakness!): Grierson writes, "It is a very Miltonic repentance in which there is more of wounded pride than of Christian repentance which includes forgiveness" (*Milton* 142). Keightley alternatively suggests, "It is not impossible that the conclusion of Jonson's *Silent Woman* may have been in the poet's mind" (*Poems*).

236. Ferry thinks this line an especially significant expression of Samson's strength: in contrast to a prison, which Samson chooses earlier to describe his body (153), a fort uses "enclosure and separation for heroic defense." Ferry adds that for Samson to surrender his "fort of silence" would mean "in Samson's own interpretation to betray his destiny by admitting hostile sounds [such as Dalila's blandishments] and by uttering forbidden words, thus to violate his divinely ordained relationship to language" (163). Cox discusses how here and elsewhere

the poem's images of sound and silence "enrich and amplify the developing comment on alternatives and the difficulty of choice" ("Natural Science" 61).

fort: "fortress" (*OED* 1), and perhaps also "forte, strong part or point" (Percival; Bullough and Bullough).

silence: see 49.

Woman: Edmund K. Chambers writes, "Samson's contempt is for women as women, and not merely Dalila among women"; but, Parker responds, the modifiers used in 202 and 211 to distinguish deceitful women suggest that Samson and the Chorus do not treat all women the same ("Variorum").

237–39. "Learning that Samson's marriages were prompted by his desire to serve Israel, the Chorus admits his unflagging patriotism in the past" (Parker, "Variorum"). Rudrum writes that this speech "Psychologically...is very natural. It says the kind of thing we are all apt to say to someone to whom we are trying to be kind, but toward whom we have an underlying hostility" (27); the hostility, Rudrum suggests, finds expression in 240.

just: Parker glosses as *righteous,* and, probably, with deliberate ambiguity, *lawful* (*OED* 1, 3b); he compares 231 and recalls the Chorus's doubts about the legality of Samson marrying Philistines ("Variorum").

occasion: see 224.

provoke: "challenge, call out to a fight" (*OED* 3; Prince, *Samson Agonistes*); so also 466, 643. Lockwood (c) defines "arouse to anger."

240. Editors gloss as "yet the whole of Israel is still in subjection to the Philistines." Huntley describes the Chorus's comment as another "slap" (see 206–7n for the first one): "Thus Milton uses the Chorus to begin a change in Samson which Manoa, Dalila, Harapha, and the Philistine Officer will continue" (136–37).

Todd, Collins, Percival, Blakeney, et al. recall Jortin's assertion (in Newton) that Milton is in this passage "certainly" reproaching his countrymen with the Restoration of Charles II ("which he accounted the restoration of slavery"). Hanford thus argues, "The failure of the Israelites to maintain the freedom which has been won for them is obviously parallel to the return of the English through their own perverseness into slavery" (*John Milton* 216). Masson (*Poetical Works,* and qtd. in Edmund K. Chambers) similarly finds here "an occult reference perhaps to the conduct of those in power in England after Cromwell's death, when Milton will argue against the restoration of the King." Rosedale alternatively suggests that the Philistines represent the "Jesuit influence" at court (162). See 268–76n, the next possible political allusion.

Israel: B. A. Wright emends (as also in 1714 but not elsewhere) to *Israël,* as the meter would seem to require. Cf. *Ps 81* 35. Prince observes, "this was originally an alternative name for Jacob, father of the twelve patriarchs who were the reputed ancestors of the twelve tribes of Israel. When the Jews referred to themselves as 'Israel'..., the word kept its quality of an individual proper name, as it does in this passage" (*Samson Agonistes*).

241–76. Commentators suggest that this speech—exactly twice the length of that of 219–36 (Parker, "Variorum")—reveals Samson's growing strength. Stein writes, "The defense is positive and strong in a way we have not seen before.... Samson refuses to accept, though in the rubbish of his major ruin, the small addition of personal injustice.... He refuses, now for the first time,...the temptation to *withdraw*.... Justice toward the self is more strenuous than the acceptance of individual responsibility. It is to be one of the hero's chief trials, and will require a measure of intellectual strength he has denied having" (*Heroic Knowledge* 146–47). Tillyard also comments: "by a skilful dramatic touch, he unconsciously reveals great latent energy in his reply...an energy which prepares us for his subsequent revival" (*Milton* 287). Ellis-Fermor adds: "a steadier, firmer moulding of the verse begins to show, as the defensive mood of the debate and argument develops.... [T]here is a tendency [e.g., in 241–46]...for the lines to form into brief verse paragraphs, a rhythmic movement strictly in harmony with the growing cohesion of Samson's thought and passion" (150).

Among other responses to these lines, Summers suggests that Samson's reproach is directed at the members of the Chorus, "the alternative warriors and leaders of his own tribe of Dan, who might have been expected to feel a greater responsibility than any others to support their champion" (163–64). Mollenkott cites this passage to illustrate the poem's pervasive relativism: "From the Chorus's point of view, it is Samson's fault that Israel is still in bondage; from Samson's, it is the fault of the Israelite leaders" (93). Parker compares Samson's account of his people's ingratitude with Prometheus's story of Zeus's ingratitude in Aeschylus, *Prometheus Bound* 216–25 (*Milton's Debt* 180). Radzinowicz finds here a correlation between individuals and the state: "Israel's fate is Israel's doing and its redemption lies in its power still.... Every individual and every political group is the cause of its own fall" ("*Samson Agonistes*" 468).

Other commentators find a contemporary allusion here. Fleming writes, "Milton intended to reproach his countrymen, indirectly and as plainly as he dared, under the Restoration of Charles II"; Whiting suggests that "these lines might be applied to Milton and the other men of the Commonwealth, who, as they thought, were champions of liberty and who were repudiated at the Restoration" ("*Samson Agonistes*" 211); and Hedley Vicars Ross finds it "strange" that the licenser did not remove "this very evident allusion to the Restoration" (57). Daiches, too, finds in this passage "some obvious autobiographical elements (Milton will not reproach himself for the ultimate failure of his political pamphleteering)" and also thinks Samson's defense "reflects Milton's view that proper self-esteem is consistent with true humility, and that a good man gone astray through weakness is not showing a proper moral recovery by abjectly blaming himself for *everything* he has done" (238). Parker generally cautions against autobiographical readings of *SA* but nevertheless finds Milton drawing on his past emotions and experiences in various places such as the first part of this speech: "Milton, when he wrote these lines, must have thought of his own efforts at reform, and the cold reception they had met with from persons in authority" (*Milton* 315). Rudrum responds to these types of comments: "Such a reading is not so much incorrect as irrelevant, and dangerously irrelevant in so far as it leads our attention away from the inner drama of Milton's tragedy" (28).

242. Cf. 1183 ("Magistrates") and 1208. Parker writes that Milton says nothing about Samson's "judging" Israel for twenty years (Judg. 15:20, 16:31), for "this point does not suit the poet's conception of an unsupported leader" (*Milton's Debt* 8). But Percival thinks it is implied here (xxi), and Lewalski discusses at length the significance of Samson's role as judge ("*Samson Agonistes*" 1050–62); see also Milton's *DocCh* (Patterson, *Works* 16:362–63). Parker comments more generally that "there was no central government of the Hebrews in this period; rarely, even in time of crisis, did more than two or three tribes unite against the common enemy. Thus, the Song of Deborah condemns the tribes of Asher, Dan, Reuben, and the dwellers in Gilead for taking no part in the great battle of independence which it celebrates. The choral answer to this speech of Samson gives other examples. Milton knew that the tribes had lost the sense of nationalism which Moses had worked to develop, and he records the situation faithfully—whether or not it reflected a situation in England at or near the time he is writing" ("Variorum").

243–45. *seeing…Acknowledg'd not:* Percival compares Matthew 13:14: "and see-ing ye shall see, and shall not perceive"; also Aeschylus, *Prometheus Bound* 447: βλέποντες ἔβλεπον μάτην; "though they had eyes to see, they saw to no avail." *great acts:* the phrase occurs also in *PR* 2.412 (Le Comte 174).

244. *me…their:* Darbishire (*Poetical Works*) and B. A. Wright emend to *mee…thir.* Cf. 1125; see 190n s.v. *their* and 219–20n s.v. *Mee.*

245. *consider'd:* "[took] for," "look[ed] upon (as)," or "[gave] heed to," "regard[ed]" (*OED* 10, 3, 7). Verity glosses as *valued;* the meaning "esteemed" (Grieve; Hughes, *Complete Poems* and *John Milton;* et al.) dates from 1692 (*OED*). The commentary on the Geneva Bible puts the matter more strongly than does Samson: "Thus they had rather betray their brother, then use the means that God had given them for their deliverance." Whiting believes that this "seems to be positive evidence that the poem is related to the commentary" ("*Samson Agonistes*" 211).

246–47. *on th' other side:* the phrase is repeated in 768.
    ambition: "canvassing" (so *OED* 5); "attempt to get support" (Northrop Frye, *Paradise Lost and Selected Poetry*). Church notes, "the Latin *ambitio,* meaning literally, 'a going about,' and used for the canvassing with which candidates for office used to commend themselves to the electors." Thus the sense here: "I did not go about soliciting applause for my deeds." A. B. Chambers adds, it is "a vice opposed to magnanimity, and among other things, Aquinas informs us [*Summa Theologica* II–II, Q. 46], it refers to a desire for honor as an end in itself rather than as a means of profiting others" (317). See *DocCh* (Patterson, *Works* 17:244). Low thus suggests, "Samson's meaning is that he has refused to prostitute himself to popular wishes" ("Tragic Pattern" 923).

248. Some editors cite similar sentiments: George Herbert's saying in *Jacula prudentum:* "Neither praise nor dispraise thyself; thy actions serve the turn" (Verity); Beaumont and Fletcher's *Lovers Progress* 3.1: "Deeds, not words, / Shall speak me" (Blakeney); Shakespeare's *Henry VIII* 2.4.137–40: "If thy rare qualities…/…could speak thee out" (Wyatt and Collins).
    deeds: Carey notes that the rhetorical figure in which the word (or phrase) occurring at the end of one line of poetry is used also to begin the next is ana-diplosis (*Complete Shorter Poems* 335); see 18n.

249–50. *persisted deaf:* "continue[d] to be [deaf]" (so *OED* 2), i.e., to the loud-speaking deeds; cf. 960 and *PL* 10.874. Verity notes, "*persist* generally implies steady pursuit of a bad course"; Church finds it "analogous to the Latin *perstabat memorans,* persisted in telling (*Aen.* 2.650)."

    seem: "appear" (*OED* 4b), or perhaps, "think fit" (*OED* 9b [1610]). Wyatt and Collins interpret this word either (along with Blakeney) as "it seemed as if they would not count," or (along with Grieve) as "be seen."

    count: "reckon," "esteem," "hold" (*OED* 3); so also 949, 991.

251–64. Judges 15:8–17.

    Thir Lords: editors compare Judges 15:11: "Knowest thou not that the Philistines are rulers over us?"

    gather'd powers: cf. 1110, 1190.

252. *Judea:* the territory of the tribe of Judah, called *Judah* in Judges 15:9; it is located in southern Palestine, west of the Dead Sea (Gilbert, *Geographical*). Percival observes, "the name of 'Judea' was applied to the whole of the country inhabited by the Jews only after the return from Captivity." Cf. the spelling *Judæa* in *PR* 3.157; *HistBr* (Patterson, *Works* 10:14); *Def 1* (Patterson, *Works* 7:201); *DocCh* (Patterson, *Works* 16:306–8).

    mee: B. A. Wright emends to *me;* cf. 244, 1125, and see 219–20n s.v. *Mee.*

253. *Safe:* "safely" (Blakeney; cf. *OED* 1), or, proleptically, "in order to be safe" (Percival).

    Etham: Etam (Authorized Version) was "a rock of unknown situation in the territory of Judah" (Gilbert, *Geographical;* Josephus, *Antiquities of the Jews* 5.8.8) but apparently not far from Lehi (Judg. 15:8–14). Verity identifies it with modern Beit 'Atab, near Zora and Eshtaol. Cf. 2 Chronicles 11:6.

    retir'd: "withdraw[n] *to* or *into* a place (or a way of life) for the sake of seclusion" (*OED* 1, 5), or "withdraw[n], fall[en] back, or retreat[ed]" (*OED* 2).

254–55. Whiting (*Milton's Literary Milieu* 257–58) notes that Samson in the Bible "had ... no definite purpose" in retiring to the rock Etam; he adds that Milton, like Quarles in *Historie of Samson* (sig. N3v–N4r), emphasizes that Samson's motive for doing so was to destroy the Philistines.

fore-casting: "consider[ing] or think[ing] of beforehand" (so *OED* 1b).
   advantag'd: "might be of advantage" (Percival).

256. *men of Judah:* so Judges 15:10, 11; there were three thousand. *Judah* is also so
   spelled in 265, 976; *PR* 3.282; *PL* 1.457; *Eikon* (Patterson, *Works* 5:204, 292);
   but cf. *Juda* in *PR* 2.424, 440; *Nat* 221; *Ref* (Patterson, *Works* 3:66); *RCG*
   (Patterson, *Works* 3:25); *CivP* (Patterson, *Works* 6:25, 26); Trinity Manuscript
   (Patterson, *Works* 18:235).

257. *harrass:* "harry[ing], lay[ing] waste" (*OED* dates from 1667).
   beset: "surrounded"; cf. 194. Le Comte discusses what he calls Milton's
   "veritable obsession" with this figure (98–100).

258–59. *on some conditions:* editors cite Judges 15:12: "And Samson said unto
   them, Swear unto me, that ye will not fall upon me yourselves."
   yield: "yielded" (so Percival; Wyatt; Grieve), or, instead, a historical present
   (Verity). Wyatt and Collins add that the usual form occurs in 407; see also
   593, 868.

260. *uncircumcis'd:* the word is repeated in 640, 1364; Parker notes the Philistines
   are so termed contemptuously in, e.g., Judges 14:3, 15:18; cf. 1 Samuel 18:25
   ("Variorum"). See also 144 (*fore-skins*).

261–62. So Judges 15:13–14; cf. 1691 and *Ps* 2 7–8.

263–64. *Unarm'd:* see 126n, 130n.
   trivial weapon: see 142–45n.
   Their: Darbishire (*Poetical Works*) and B. A. Wright emend to *Thir;* see 190n
   s.v. *their.* Parker compares Milton's sketch for a drama on Lot (Patterson, *Works*
   18:233): "thire choycest youth" ("Variorum").
   choicest youth: cf. 144, 1654.

265. *Judah:* the tribe of that name; cf. 256, 976.
   or one whole Tribe: Keightley (*Poems*), Fleming, and Browne take this to mean
   a *subdivision* of the tribes of Judah and refer to Numbers 4:18; Judges 20:12;

1 Samuel 9:21, where the Hebrew *shebet* ("tribe") is so used for a subdivision. Parker suggests, "perhaps the meaning is '(any) one,' i.e., Samson would accordingly imply: 'Where was the Tribe of Dan—including you, my friends—on that day?'" ("Variorum").

266. *by this:* "by now," "by this (time)" (*OED* III.21b; Verity); cf. 483.
      possess'd: the normal Miltonic spelling is *possest* (1005); cf. 1467 (Parkcr, "Variorum").
      Gath: one of the five cities of the Philistines (see 41), and the home of giants (1068, 1078–80, 1247–49); it disappeared from history after it was captured and presumably destroyed by Uzziah (2 Chron. 26:6). Buttrick notes it "is usually identified with Tell es-Saliyeh, twelve miles inland from Ahsdod at the foot of the Vale of Ehah" and eleven miles south of Ekron (2:903). Gilbert mentions that Milton's expression, "the Towers of *Gath*," is a figure for all of Philistia; cf. 2. Samuel 1:20 (*Geographical*). At some time the Philistines took Gath away from the Jews (1 Sam. 7:14); Percival writes, "the lost chance of its recovery is here referred to."

267. *lorded over:* "ruled, acted as lords of" (their Lords); the connotation of "ruled tyrannically" or "assumed airs of grandeur" (so *OED* 1b) is absent (Parker, "Variorum"). Cf. *RCG:* "Lording over their brethren in regard of their persons" (Patterson, *Works* 3:200); also *RCG:* "the hatefull thirst of Lording in the Church" (Patterson, *Works* 3:213).

268–76. Commentators offer various interpretations of these lines. Bush remarks that the passage contains the "recurrent Miltonic conviction…that nations grown corrupt fall readily into bondage" (*John Milton* 197; "John Milton" 506n; *Milton*). Lawry suggests that "Samson's case against Israel is identical with God's case against him" (363). But Tillyard detects a difference between Samson and the Israelites: "It would almost seem as if Milton had come to believe in two forms of Fall: one for the 'common rout,' the other for the potential elect. The 'common rout' have minds so trivial that their reason is easily enslaved by the passions: the potential elect cannot be accused of mental triviality, it is the sheer strength of their passions that may lead them astray" (*Milton* 298). See also 529n. Huntley thinks this passage implicitly describes the members of the Chorus: "Blind to reality,…the Chorus grope towards their salvation. They are neither vicious nor saintly, but represent the vast ambivalent mass of mankind which neither knows what it feels nor feels what it knows" (139). Bowra writes that Milton with this speech accomplishes two ends: "First, he shows how Samson, despite his humiliations, is still at heart a great man of action, capable of facing serious issues and maintaining powerful convictions.... Secondly, the old love of glory for its own sake has been transformed into love of country" (122).

Other commentators echo or go beyond Newton's assertion, in 1752, that Milton "very probably intended" here "a secret satir upon the English nation" after the Restoration. Keightley writes that it is "evident" (*Poems*); Hedley Vicars Ross finds it "unmistakable" (58); Masson thinks it "a plain reference" (*Poetical Works*); Grieve thinks the whole passage alludes to Henry Vane's execution (v); Verity argues, "The bondage meant is the Restoration of the Stuarts"; and Collins finds "obvious" an allusion "to the collapse of Milton's party, [and] to the weakness and treachery of those republicans who joined in restoring Charles II." Landor similarly writes: "sentiments worthier of a pure, indomitable, inflexible republican, never issued from the human heart, than these referring to the army, in the last effort made to rescue the English nation from disgrace and servitude" (5:298). Wyatt and Collins caution that "more has been read into particular passages than they well can bear," but here the editors have "no doubt" about the allegory of England (14). Blakeney also sees here "a side allusion to the Restoration" and writes that "the anti-Puritan reaction had set in with a vengeance long before this passage...was penned; with it followed a train of luxury, loose-living, and corruption." Hanford similarly suggests: "Milton has carried over into the interpretation of the simple Israelite his own messianic conviction" (*John Milton* 217). See also Muir 179–80; and see 272–76n. Radzinowicz, while emphasizing that "the drama is not a simple allegory of contemporary politics showing how the common rout was let down by the irresponsibility of the leaders," nevertheless sees Samson as a contemporary symbol "representing the nation England as the chosen leader of the elect minority" ("*Samson Agonistes*" 467). Timberlake suggests that this technique is Euripidean: "As Euripides so often does, Milton puts into the mouth of a character his own reading of contemporary events" (338).

Three objections have been raised in reply to those commentators who find topical, political allusions in this passage. First, as Thyer (in Newton) observes, Milton consistently attributed the loss of liberty to a corruption of morals (e.g., *Def 2* [Patterson, *Works* 8:248, etc.]). Second, in expressing such sentiments, Milton was consciously echoing a famous body of classical literature; e.g., in the same note in which Newton sees here "a secret satir," he observes that the sentiment is "very like" that of Aemilius Lepidus in his oration to the Romans against Sulla (preserved among the fragments of Milton's favorite historian, Sallust). Third, as Krouse suggests, "Milton did not invent the political overtones of Samson's story, nor did he make changes in the material to make those overtones clearer. They were an integral part of the Samson tradition" (93)—a part that was evidently welcome to the poet, but that, Krouse believes, should not be overemphasized: "The most that we can say confidently of the political import of *Samson Agonistes* is that Milton...with a nice appreciation of contemporary applicability,...kept that element intact in his poem. But any attempt on the part of critics to make political allegory the heart of this poem is indefensible" (93). Lewalski similarly argues, "there is no basis for reading the play as political allegory of any kind. The echoes [of contemporary events]...are merely the contemporary reverberations of a universal paradigm recurring throughout history" (*"Samson Agonistes"* 1061).

269. Cf. *HistBr:* "when God hath decreed servitude on a sinful Nation, fitted by thir own vices for no condition but servile" (Patterson, *Works* 10:198).

270–71. Edmund K. Chambers compares *SA* 18 and writes, "Another instance in which the idea of one line is dwelt upon and elaborated in a second" (see also Raleigh, *Milton* 208). Broadbent calls this Samson's "first public activity in the play" but writes that it "is vitiated by its context of self-justification" (*Milton* 45). For the sentiment, cf. Mammon's speech in *PL* 2.255–57: "preferring / Hard liberty before the easie yoke / Of servile Pomp" (cited by Percival; Verity; Brinkley, *Samson Agonistes;* et al.). Church recalls Issachar, who "saw that rest was good, and the land that it was pleasant; and bowed his shoulder to bear, and became a servant unto tribute" (Gen. 49:15). Percival quotes Virgil's *Georgics* 4.564: "studiis florentem ignobilis oti"; "rejoiced in the arts of inglorious ease." Church (see 268) quotes from section 25 of "The Speech of the Consul Lepidus to the Roman People": "accipite otium cum servitio"; "accept a peace combined with servitude" (Sallust, *Histories*). See also *PL* 2.255–57n.

On the prosody of these lines, Oras writes that the pyrrhic endings—what he calls a light, secondary stress on the line's tenth metrical syllable—"breaks the monotony of the terminal full stresses"; it is an "early favorite" of Milton but is also "fairly prominent" in *PR* and *SA*, and thus does not support *SA*'s early composition (*Blank Verse* 36–42; "Milton's Blank Verse" 181). See 315–20n. Oras draws the same conclusion regarding the poem's traditional dating by analyzing the treatment of strong pauses, polysyllables, unstressed endings, and syllabized *ed* endings.

Liberty: Keightley changes the comma to an exclamation point (*Poems*).

strenuous: "vigorous, energetic," "characterized by strenuous exertion" (so *OED* 3), "accompanied by exertion and labor" (Lockwood). Knight compliments the precision of Milton's diction here and compares it with Keats's use of "strenuous tongue" (line 27) in "Ode on Melancholy" (*Chariot* 88).

272–76. Many commentators find specific allusions in these lines. To Masson (*Poetical Works*) the Deliverer (274) is Milton himself; to Collins, Martin W. Sampson, Blakeney, and Bullough and Bullough, he is Oliver Cromwell (cf. *Def 2* [Patterson, *Works* 8:210]); to Dunster (in Todd), quoted approvingly by Percival and Verity, he is John Lambert in his final republican effort against George Monck. Alternatively, Church believes that Milton "may have been thinking of the reception which Moses met with in his first endeavor to deliver his countrymen" (Exod. 2:11–14). According to Parker, however, "the 'Deliverer' is no specific person but, rather, *all* good, patriotic men whose leadership is rejected" (*Milton's Debt* 34; "Variorum"). For the next alleged political allusion, see 276n; for the specific word *deliverer*, see 38–42n and 40, 279, 1214, 1289.

273. *Whom:* "him whom, whomever" (Edmund K. Chambers, et al.); cf. 150.

274. *Deliverer:* Masson (*Poetical Works*) and William Aldis Wright change the semicolon following this word to a question mark.

276. *heap ingratitude:* Collins and Blakeney suggest that this line refers to the disinterring and disgracing of the remains of the leading regicides (in January 1661); cf. 368–72n, 693–94n. In *Eikon*, King Charles "heaps ingratitude upon the Parlament" (Patterson, *Works* 5:116); in *Def 2*, Milton notes that "those who are unworthy of liberty are commonly the first to show their ingratitude towards our deliverers" (Patterson, *Works* 8:249). Collins adds, "The reader will note the subdued intensity, the majestic self-restraint of these sublime verses";

Parker suggests that they are appropriate to Samson's point and are appropriately illustrated by the Chorus in reply ("Variorum"); cf. 280n.

worthiest deeds: the phrase is repeated in 369. Keightley (*Poems*) and William Aldis Wright change the question mark following *deeds* to an exclamation point.

277–89. Commentators discuss the appropriateness of the Chorus's comparisons. Parker writes that in sympathetically recalling other examples of rejected deliverers, the Chorus implies "complete agreement with Samson's statement of his case" (*Milton's Debt* 34). Rudrum similarly suggests, "The immediately relevant point is that Gideon and Jephthah, like Samson, deserved better of their countrymen than they received"; that these examples "do not fully agree with Samson's case...emphasise[s] the fact that Samson is special" (31, 32). Krouse notes that Gideon and Jephthah are linked as saints with Samson in Hebrews 11:32–34 "and countless times thereafter in the literature of Christianity...always with the Epistle to the Hebrews as part of the connotation" (98); Edmund K. Chambers also observes, "It is a frequent function of the Greek chorus to illustrate the immediate story of the play by reference to similar situations in other familiar legends." Christopher sees the Chorus's sympathetic response here as part of Samson's homeopathic recovery: "When...the weak-minded chorus forgets its nostrums and joins for a moment the current of Samson's thinking, they unwittingly administer the first drop of physic" (364). Cf. *Antigone* 945–87. But Roberts W. French finds fault with what he calls the Chorus's "smug complacency" in these lines: the speech's rhymed conclusion "is firm and confident; but when the reader looks closely he sees that what the Chorus is concluding so firmly is an outright evasion of a serious charge which Samson has brought against his people and their leaders, the Chorus included" (62). Gideon and Jephthah are also spoken of together in *PR* 2.439 and *DocCh* (Patterson, *Works* 16:362–63).

remembrance bring: cf. *PL* 4.38.

278–81. Judges 8:4–9. Verity, Edmund K. Chambers, Prince (*Samson Agonistes*), et al. note that the men of Succoth and of Penuel refused food to Gideon and his ridiculously small army of three hundred because they had not yet captured the kings of Midian whom they were pursuing. Kermode (62) identifies an imperfect rhyme in 277–281; see 110–14n.

Succoth: Buttrick explains, "modern Tell Deir 'alla, just north of where the Jabbok breaks through the eastern highland to the Jordan Valley" (2:745). Gilbert adds that in Milton's time its exact location was unknown; it was simply "a place in Palestine east of Jordan" (*Geographical*).

Fort: Judges 8:9 and 8:17 speak of a tower, which Milton evidently assumes to have been fortified (Verity; Wyatt and Collins).

Penuel: editors explain as a place several miles east of Succoth on the Jabbok.

280. *The matchless Gideon:* Parker refers to him as one of Israel's greatest rulers in peace, a notable military commander delivering his people from the Midianites: "He abolished idolatry. Early in his career he narrowly escaped the murderous wrath of his own countrymen. Like Oliver Cromwell, he refused the crown (Judg. 8.23), but Milton here makes nothing of this or other such parallels" ("Variorum"); cf. *Def 1* (Patterson, *Works* 7:135); *DocCh* (Patterson, *Works* 17:241); *BrNotes* (Patterson, *Works* 6:154). As did Samson, Gideon had divine signs and pledges of God's special favor (Judg. 6:11–12, 36–40). Milton at one time jotted down "Gideon Idoloclastes" and "Gideon persuing" as possible subjects for a drama (Patterson, *Works* 18:236).

281. *Madian:* so Acts 7:29 (Authorized Version), the Vulgate, and the Septuagint; but in *Ps 83* 33, as in the Authorized Version of Judges 8 and elsewhere, it is *Midian* (see Edmund K. Chambers; Prince, *Samson Agonistes*). Gilbert adds that the Midian was a nomadic Arabic tribe (*Geographical*).

her vanquisht Kings: Zebah and Zalmunna (Judg. 7:22, 8:5); so also *Ps 83* 43.

282–89. Judges 11:15–27, 12:1–6 (chapters that immediately precede the story of Samson). Prince (*Samson Agonistes*) and Bullough and Bullough summarize: after a fruitless exchange of messages with the king of the children of Ammon, Jephthah defeats him without seeking the aid of the men of Ephraim, who, angry and ungrateful, threatened to burn down Jephthah's house. He not only vanquished them in battle but, afterward, caught and killed many who had escaped, detecting them, as they tried to cross the Jordan River, by their pronunciation of the word *Shibboleth* as *Sibboleth*. Cf. 988–90n, 1674n. Parker ("Variorum") recalls that in *Eikon* Milton refers to Ireland as King Charles's Ephraim (Patterson, *Works* 5:204).

283–84. *Had dealt:* "would have dealt" (Verity; et al.); Judg. 12:1.

    by argument...spear: Judges 11:15–27. Parker comments, "although Jephthah discussed with force and ingenuity the Israelite right to the country, the negotiation was abortive; therefore it is interesting to note Milton's inclusion of this detail, which had almost nothing to do with the ingratitude of Ephraim. Without even breathing the suggestion of an allusion, one might recall Milton's praise of Sir Henry Vane for statesmanship in peace" ("Variorum").

285. *Ammonite:* cf. *PL* 1.396 and *Ps 83* 25. Kermode (62) identifies an imperfect rhyme in 285–286; see 110–14n.

286–89. Belloc thinks that this "quatrain of verse" is "ridiculous," "grotesque," and "not tolerable at all" (278). Prince thinks the rhymes are "used for sonorous emphasis" (*Samson Agonistes* 138). Martz suggests that the lines' "flatness...may convince us that these are men of no particular insight, whose utterances are mainly commonplaces and not, for the most part, expressed by Milton in distinguished poetry" (121).

    quell'd thir pride: cf. *PL* 5.740 (Le Comte 174).

    sore battel: Parker ("Variorum") notes that the expression is biblical (e.g., Judg. 20:34).

    so many: forty-two thousand (Judg. 12:6).

    Reprieve: "delay," "respite...from impending punishment" (so *OED* 1, 4), "suspension of the execution of a death sentence" (Lockwood).

    adjudg'd: "sentence[d]," "deem[ed]" (so *OED* s.v. *adjudge* 3).

    Shibboleth: see 282–89n, 1674n.

290. Rudrum thinks this is dramatic irony: Samson "does not yet know that God will enable him to transcend these predecessors" (32).

291. Editors gloss as "my people ('mine') may neglect me easily indeed." A Latinism (cf. the parallel in 1169) with which Verity takes issue: "the possessive pronouns in English, being uninflected, are ill adapted to this idiom."

    Mee: Parker writes, "he means 'me as a person,' but not 'me as God's agent'" ("Variorum"). On the emphatic form here and in 290, see 219–20n.

    easily: "with little exertion...or difficulty," or "without pain, discomfort, or anxiety" (*OED* 4, 1); Church et al. suggest "without harm or evil consequences."

Mahood comments: "the implication of the play's opening act...is that the hero had experienced a kind of religious *hubris*, a certainty that his own election made him indispensable to God" (237).

292. *Gods propos'd deliverance:* Parker comments, "there is a threat implied here" ("Variorum").

    not so: "not so (easily)" (Prince, *Samson Agonistes*).

293–325. Editors identify this as the first stasimon. Parker writes, "in Greek tragedy, after the entrance song or first utterance of the chorus (*parodos*) came στάσιμα ('stationary songs'), so called because the chorus has then taken up its position in the orchestra. *SA* has five *epeisodia* separated by *stasima,* and with a *stasimon* separating the fifth from the *exodos*" ("Variorum"). For subsequent stasima see 652–709, 1010–60, 1268–99, 1427–40. On the use of such terms, Sprott cautions that Milton preferred an "open form" and that "those critics who deal in parode and stasimon and epode and their like should beware that they do not go further than their author would go with them" (131). Epps (192) numbers this speech the second chorus and proposes two possible ways of dividing it into sections: strophe (293–306), antistrophe (307–21), and epode (322–29); or strophe (293–99), antistrophe (300–06), strophe (307–14), antistrophe (315–21), strophe (322–25), and antistrophe (326–29). Stroup describes this first stasimon as "a sort of canticle echoing Revelation 15 and Psalms 14 and 8" (57); Sheppard compares the passage with the first ode of *Agamemnon,* where "the Chorus brood on the just, harsh ways of Zeus" (160). Fish (246) detects here "the confusion of the Chorus's thought (a confusion which the reader shares)." Eleanor Gertrude Brown (100) thinks that these lines of the Chorus are "more suggestive of Milton than those of Samson" (see also 166–69, 1268–76).

293–94. *Just are...to Men:* most editors recall here the broad purpose of Milton's epic (*PL* 1.25–26); Le Comte (67, 85) notes that a similar phrase also occurs at *SA* 300, *PL* 8.226, *Tetr* (Patterson, *Works* 4:164), and *CivP* (Patterson, *Works* 6:39). Daiches observes that this passage "is really less a vindication than an expression of the nature of the problem. Here the Chorus speak no longer as visitors to Samson...but rather as the impersonal mouthpiece of some of the general moral ideas in the play" (238); Gray similarly argues that "here the Cho-

rus mirrors the spectators' thoughts" (143). Grierson suggests, "The interest
for Milton is the thought of God as directly inspiring men by latent impulsion
to do certain things which in normal morality are forbidden" (*Milton* 139).
Ellis-Fermor calls this ode "a debate on the justice of God" and a revelation
of "the thought that is in Samson's mind" (26). J. Macmillan Brown suggests
that here "the chorus speaks like a Puritan pastor chastising or consoling some
stray sheep of his flock" (60).

But Parker proposes that this ode "has a very limited, almost legalistic subject,
namely, the justification of a Nazarite's marriages to two Philistine women. The
Chorus had been puzzled (173, 215–18, 237–40), Samson had explained briefly
(222–26, 231–33), and now the Chorus tries to summarize the *implications*
of what it has learned" ("Variorum"). Parker further discusses the Chorus's
concerns here as a "a structural anticipation of two extremely important later
developments. First, Samson cannot go to the Philistine feast without again doing
something apparently 'unclean' and therefore sinning; he must face this whole
problem once more and be completely certain that God wishes him to go. See
1320–21, 1357–62, 1377–79, 1381–86.... Second, Samson cannot without
sinning intend his own death; *mors voluntaria* is forbidden to Christians. But
as St. Augustine and St. Thomas Aquinas had argued, Samson can be excused
if he acted on the direct inspiration and guidance of God" ("Variorum").

295. *think:* "believe in the existence of" (so *OED* 13); editors gloss as "unless there
be (those) who think (there is) no God at all." Hughes (*Complete Poems; John
Milton;* also Church) writes that Milton uses "a Greek construction...familiar
to him in many authors, from Herodotus to Plato, in expressions of disbelief
in the gods"; editors quote specific examples. Landor sees this construction as
a "blemish" because it is not English (5:298).

296. Note the short, four-stress line of regular rhythm (Parker, "Variorum"); see
321n.

If any be: cf. 452–53 ("op't the mouths / Of...Atheists"). Cf. also *DocCh:*
"there be not a few who deny the existence of God" (Patterson, *Works* 14:25);
TR (1673): "it is a general complaint that this Nation of late years [has]...bold
and open Atheism every where abounding" (Patterson, *Works* 6:178). In 1641,
Milton believed that "the Englishman of many other nations is least atheisticall"
(*RCG* [Patterson, *Works* 3:224]).

walk: "to live or act in any particular manner, pursue any course of life" (Lockwood II.1.e). Parker suggests that it may be an implied contrast to Aristotle, the Peripatetic ("Variorum").

obscure: "inconspicuous," "unnoticed," i.e., because they are only a few, isolated individuals, and also "devoid of or deficient in light" (*OED* 6, 1).

297. *School:* "a body or succession of persons who . . . are disciples of the same master, or who are united by a general similarity of principles," or more probably (in view of *walk* and *heart*), "a place in which an ancient Greek or Roman philosopher taught his hearers" (*OED* 5, 2). The sense is that there has never been a systematic philosophy or sect of atheism (Verity; Bullough and Bullough).

298. *But the heart of the Fool:* an echo of Psalm 14:1 or 53:1: "The fool hath said in his heart, There is no God"; this quotation introduces the chapter "Of God" in Milton's *DocCh* (Patterson, *Works* 14:24–25). Editors notice "the peculiar effect of contempt" (Masson, *Poetical Works*) given by the sudden introduction of rhyme in 297–98 and by the anapestic rhythm in this two-stress line following three lines of regular iambic rhythm. Bailey, e.g., writes that here "rhyme is called in to give its touch of impatient contempt at the folly of the atheist" (234); and Bradshaw (in Verity) similarly comments, "the rhyme and rapid rhythm . . . may have been intended to have a contemptuous effect" (80). Sprott (132) suggests the first two feet are inverted (trochaic); Weismiller (148) instead suggests that the first two syllables are unstressed, followed by a trochee, then an iamb (see 81n).

299. *therein:* accent the first syllable (Lockwood). Cf. *thereof* (1314), *thereon* (1505).

Doctor: "a learned man" (*OED* 2; and so Percival; Verity; Lockwood; et al.), but also "teacher," i.e., in the "School" of the "heart" (*OED* 1). Parker glosses, "no one makes an atheist of another through instruction" ("Variorum"). Thyer (in Newton), Keightley (*Poems*), and Landor (5:298) think this is a too "quaint conceit," out of place in such a serious speech; Landor also objects, "the chorus knew nothing of schools and doctors."

300. Editors gloss as "yet there is a more numerous group than the atheists, who believe in the existence of God but doubt that his ways are just." Bullough and

Bullough cite Job 8:3, 16:11–21. Hanford comments: "The Arminian modification of Calvinistic theology was designed to preserve God's justice, which seemed imperiled by the strict doctrine of predestination. Calvinists, on the other hand, feared the diminution of God's glory in any limitation of his power by man's free will. Milton tended to treat these problems simply...taking his stand on the Bible texts" (*Poems*).

   there: Darbishire emends to *ther*—what she considers "the unemphatic form"—here and in 84 and 297 (*Poetical Works*).

   doubt: "suspect" (*OED* II.6b) or, possibly, "fear" (Hanford, *Poems*). Percival suggests that "this and the following line refer to the Skeptic."

301. Editors note the play on words, "*edicts*...contra*dict*ing." Roberts W. French finds this aural repetition "ugly and awkward" (63). Cf. 1278, and see 1118n. Martz writes that the rhymes and partial rhymes in this speech "create an effect of something like triviality in the chorus.... The [broader] effect is thus to stress, by contrast, the grandeur of Samson, the glory of his poetry, the greatness of his mind: his difference from ordinary men" (121). Masson comments that the use of rhyme and "peculiar versification" in this and the following lines reminds him of Goethe's *Faust* (*Poetical Works*). See 303n, 1010–60n.

   edicts: the few editors who mention the construction in this line seem to disagree: Church says that *found* belongs to *who* (300); Collins interprets *as to* as meaning "with regard to"; Percival and Blakeney explain *to* as used on the analogy of the Latin *contradico,* which governs the dative. Verity, Edmund K. Chambers, Prince (*Samson Agonistes*), et al. scan this as "*e-dicts'*" as in *PL* 5.798.

   edicts...contradicting: cf. 898. For Milton's ideas about God contradicting himself, see *Tetr* (Patterson, *Works* 4:85, 130); *DocCh* (Patterson, *Works* 14:68–69, 342–43).

302. *give the rains:* cf. 1578, where this expression recurs. Parker ("Variorum") compares *DDD:* "to give a little the rains" (Patterson, *Works* 3:372).

   wandring: "random," "not directed by reason or fixed purpose," but also "erring" (*OED* 2b, 3a); Bullough and Bullough add, "thought uncontrolled by faith (hence error)." Cf. *PL* 2.561.

303. *diminution:* "lessening," "belittling" (*OED* 3). Following Richardson (in Newton), editors find this phrase a Latinism, expressing the *majestatem minuere*

or *crimen laesae majestatis* of Roman law—offenses equivalent to high treason. Le Comte (100) compares *Areop:* "the diminution of his glory" (Patterson, *Works* 4:294). Of the rhymes in 303–6 (abba), Roberts W. French writes: "The Chorus has little patience with those who vainly search for certitude; their own serene assurance is indicated by the finality of the rhymes" (63). See 301n.

304–05. *perplexities:* "in the metaphor that develops, this word takes on the additional meaning of 'entanglements'" (Parker, "Variorum").

   ravel: "inquire" (*OED* 4) and hence, as editors note, "become entangled or confused" (so *OED* 1); the metaphor is that of the unwinding of a thread. Editors compare Shakespeare's *Two Gentlemen of Verona* 3.2.51–52: "Therefore as you unwind her love from him, / Lest it should ravel."

   resolv'd: "free[d]...from doubt or perplexity," with the suggestion of "untie[d], loosen[ed]" (*OED* 15, 10).

306. Fletcher (*John Milton's Complete* 4:32) and Carey (*Complete Shorter Poems*) note that in the 1671 edition this line exists in two different states: in the first state, this and the next line are indented.

307–14. Huntley finds fault with the Chorus for contradicting here its earlier assertion (293–94) that God is just: "Milton represents the Chorus projecting their confusion onto God by imagining him (never themselves) to be wilful, irrational, and fickle" (137). Saurat instead asserts that "the power of God goes beyond all free wills: He directs the laws which move events and destiny which is over all; in reality, no law binds God whose will is always done" (107). Prince here analyzes Milton's prosody: "the line-endings are full of double consonants, most of them dentals and labials, and the effect of rhyme is so strongly suggested...that one has to look twice to discover that what we have here is not rhyme, but assonance, and that perhaps not wholly intentional" (*Italian Element* 166).

   th' interminable: "that [which] cannot be bounded," "the Infinite" (so *OED*). Church glosses as "incomprehensible (ἄπειρος) of the Athanasian Creed."

   prescript: "law," "command" (*OED* 1).

309. *Who made our Laws to bind us, not himself:* Samuels notes that "Milton's God in *Paradise Lost* is the God of laws, while in *Samson Agonistes* He is a God above the laws" (496). See also Milton's note (circa 1644) on this subject in

his *ComBk* (Patterson, *Works* 18:189). Parker ("Variorum") recalls Milton's views in the second edition of *DDD* (1644), where he insists that "God being a pure spirit could not command a thing repugnant to his own nature" and thus "binds himself like a just lawgiver to his own prescriptions, gives himself to be understood by men, judges and is judg'd, measures and is commensurate to right reason" (Patterson, *Works* 3:438–40).

    our Laws: cf. 1320, 1386, 1409, 1425, where the phrase has *Law* (singular).

311. The sense: "to exempt whomever it please him (to), chosen (from others who must obey the law)" (see Hunter).

312. *obstriction:* "state of being morally or legally bound; obligation" (so *OED*), hence "restrictive laws" (Milton's coinage from Latin *obstrictus*). Editors also note that the "National obstriction" referred to here is the Mosaic law forbidding Jews as a people from intermarrying with Gentiles (Exod. 34:16; Deut. 7:3)—specifically cited by Milton in *DocCh* (Patterson, *Works* 15:152–53). Northrop Frye writes that Dalila was, according to this law, "unclean...as well as unchaste" (Paradise Lost *and Selected Poetry*); see 321. Edmund K. Chambers paraphrases the Chorus's argument: "God was entitled to exempt Samson from this obligation, and to allow his marriage with Dalila, in order to bring about the deliverance of Israel." But, Chambers adds, this leaves unanswered how Samson's marriage worked to this end. Parker instead poses two related questions: "Did God actually prompt Samson to marry his *second* wife?"; and, "Did either of Samson's marriages actually begin Israel's deliverance?" ("Variorum"); see 228, 231, 234, 241–76, 320.

313. *legal debt:* Verity, Edmund K. Chambers, Carey (*Complete Shorter Poems*), et al. connect this term with "exempt...From" and gloss it as "debt, obligation, or duty to fulfill the Mosaic law." Parker instead treats it as part of a compound object of the preposition *of* and interprets it as "offense or trespass against law." He compares "the interchange of the words 'debts' and 'trespasses' in versions of the Lord's Prayer" ("Variorum").

314. To "dispense with" is here "to give special exemption or relief from" (*OED* s.v. *dispence* 10). Verity suggests, "abrogate, cancel." Cf. 1377. Hanford writes,

"It was a congenial thought with Milton that God might grant a dispensation from the letter of the law to an individual who came to know his will 'by intimate impulse,' and this, in Samson's case, even before the abrogation of the law under Christ" (*Poems*); but see 309n.

315–20. Oras notes the "austere dignity" of Milton's pyrrhic endings here and elsewhere in the odes and lyrical monologues (also, e.g., 638–41): the effect of these endings, which have "none of the semioperatic aria atmosphere of *Tamburlaine* and parts of *Comus*," suggests that *SA* was one of Milton's later compositions ("Milton's Blank Verse" 189–90). See 270–71n, 770–808n, 1604n.

wanted: "lacked" (*OED* s.v. *want* 2). Parker comments, "the point is that Samson as a person was not the *only* means by which God could have acted" ("Variorum").

in respect of: "as relates to or regards," "with reference to" (*OED* s.v. *respect* 4a).

the enemy: Darbishire (*Poetical Works*) and B. A. Wright emend to *th' enemy*. Parker counts nineteen instances of Milton creating regular meter by marking elision with *the* followed by a word that begins with a vowel; here and in other lines (361, 640, 672, 695, 696, 893, 1241), editors must decide whether to use an apostrophe similarly ("Notes" 694).

318. Kermode (62) identifies an imperfect rhyme in 318–320; see 110–14n.

Nazarite: Grieve defines as one who is devoted to or has separated himself for God's service, taking the vows of abstinence given in Numbers 6:1–21 (see also 31n, 520n, 634n, 1199n). These involved (1) no cutting off hair from "the head of his consecration," (2) no use of wine or strong drink, and (3) no contact with the dead. Grieve comments, "The added regulations concerning intoxication and ceremonial defilement...really originated long after Samson's day." Only the first restriction is mentioned in the story of Samson in Judges (13:5, 16:17). Parker notes, though, that the second was required of Samson's mother by the angel (Judg. 13:4, 14) and Milton assumes (541–52), as does Josephus (*Antiquities of the Jews* 5.8.2), that it applied to Samson as well ("Variorum"). On the third requirement, see 1199n. Scott-Craig discusses the term *Nasarite* as applied to both Samson and Christ ("Concerning" 51). Whiting suggests that the concept of Nazarite (being "separated" and dedicated to God) represents a Puritan idea ("*Samson Agonistes*" 209).

319. *purity:* "ceremonial cleanness," or, possibly, "chastity" (*OED* 3). Although the vows of the Nazarite (see 318n) include no reference to marriage or celibacy, the idea of separation may have seemed to Milton to imply celibacy (Masson, *Poetical Works*). Editors (Northrop Frye, Paradise Lost *and Selected Poetry;* Prince, *Samson Agonistes;* et al.) note that a Philistine woman was, by Mosaic law, ceremonially unclean (see 321).

320. *fallacious:* "deceitful" (*OED* 2a); also 533, and cf. 537.

   that...Bride: Parker ("Variorum") notes that the Chorus had asked about Samson's marrying Philistine "women" (216), but here and in 320–21 it speaks of a single "Bride" (cf. 1018, 1196, 1198). Collins, Masson (*Poetical Works*), Edmund K. Chambers, Blakeney, Krouse (97), Hughes (*Complete Poems*), et al. think that it was Dalila. But Bush (*Milton*), Carey (*Complete Shorter Poems*), Bullough and Bullough (47), et al. suggest that the Chorus may refer to the woman of Timna, whom Samson sought in marriage (220) but who deceived him and proved "false" (227). See also 321n s.v. *unchaste,* and 325n. Rudrum writes more generally, "We are too cocksurely post-Freudian if we imagine that Milton cannot have been sardonically amused at the degree of interest shown by the Chorus in Samson's sex-life" (33).

321. A four-syllable line; Prince suggests that Milton replaces the traditional Italian prosody with "a freer ebb and flow, which enables him to bring under one rule a greater variety of lyric measures" (*Italian Element* 161).

   Unclean: Parker defines as "taboo" (Hebrew: *tâmê*); he adds, "the word does not mean 'impure' or 'dirty, foul' in the sense it usually has for us; it is a ritual term for something that must not be touched, in this case a non-Hebrew woman" ("Variorum"). Cf. 324, 1362–64. Cf. also *PR* 2.328.

   unchaste: editors dispute whether this term applies to Dalila or to the woman of Timna; see also 320n, 325n. Samson's bride from Timna "was given to his companion, whom he had used as his friend" (Judg. 14:20); and even the Philistines recognized that Samson had been wronged in this instance (Judg. 15:6); see 1020n. The basis of Dalila's unchastity, by comparison, is a subject of debate. Keightley writes that "it is nowhere expressly said in the Bible narrative that she [Dalila] was unchaste; yet perhaps it presented her as a harlot" (*Poems*). But Edmund K. Chambers insists, "There is nothing to identify her with the 'harlot' [of Judges 16:1]"; he argues that Dalila was "only unchaste after she deceived Samson" and adds that "there is an inconsistency throughout in Milton's view of Dalila." To support the idea that the Chorus is neverthe-less referring here to Dalila, Browne and Collins argue that "in Milton's stern code" repeated headstrong behavior constituted fornication and thus unchastity; Blakeney argues that Milton's moral code was so "unbendingly severe" that Dalila's falseness to the "trust reposed in her" becomes a form of unchastity; and Percival and Grieve cite Josephus, who calls Dalila a harlot (*Antiquities of the Jews* 5.8.11). Grieve adds, "'unchastity' may here mean general faithless-ness to the marriage vow." Various editors quote here Milton's reference in *PL* 9.1060–61 to "the Harlot-lap / Of *Philistine* Dalilah," where *Harlot* may be simply a term of opprobrium (see *OED*) and not a charge of unchastity. Parker also compares the account of Samson in *RCG:* "laying down his head among the strumpet flatteries" (Patterson, *Works* 3:276); and the *Cursor Mundi* 7247–50, where, unlike *SA*, Dalila marries after betraying Samson, who, blind, is led to her bridal ("Variorum").

322. Woodhouse writes: "After his bold applications of the canons of logic in his writings on liberty, and (in the *De doctrina*) on Christian dogma, the pronounce-ment on reason suggests a new development in Milton's thought" ("*Samson Agonistes*" 170).

   Down: adverb with ellipsis of a verb (so *OED* VI.23); Prince glosses as "let Reason then submit" (*Samson Agonistes*); Wyatt and Collins paraphrase this pas-sage, "[God] has…full right to exempt Samson from the taint of uncleanness in marrying a heathen woman. Down, then, with Reason, or rather with vain reasonings; albeit Reason points out that there was no offence against morality, but only against the Jewish law." Grierson comments on the distinction made in this line: "Reason is at work in many people who are quite incapable of con-scious reasoning. For reasoning demands at once a clear statement of premises, i.e. definitions and axioms, which few untrained people are capable of" (*Milton* 11). Grierson cites Rousseau: "The art of reasoning is not reason, often it is the abuse of reason" ("Lettres Morales" II).

323. *aver:* "affirm," "assert as a fact" (*OED* 4c); legally the term meant "offer to justify an exception pleaded" (*OED* 3).

324. *moral verdit:* following Warburton (in Newton), editors—e.g., Collins, Percival, Moody—interpret this as meaning "the law of nature" as opposed to the national Mosaic law that made a non-Hebrew woman unclean. Martin W.

Sampson explains: "as distinguished from the divine judgment." Bullough and Bullough add that Dalila ceased to be unclean when she married Samson; they quote St. Paul: "the unbelieving wife is sanctified by the husband" (1 Cor. 7:14). Samuels, cautioning that this is "a passage of the most tormented and elliptical syntax in the poem," offers the explanation that Dalila "was clean enough, by the will of God, to marry Samson, but not so clean as to mitigate her guilt" (497). Cf. also Acts 10:28 and *DocCh* (Patterson, *Works* 17:180).

    verdit: "verdict," "judgement" (so *OED* 2); cf. 1228.

    quits: "acquit[s]," "absolve[s]" (*OED* 2b).

    of unclean: "of (the charge of being) unclean" (Parker, "Variorum"); see 321.

325. Editors disagree over whether the Chorus is referring to Samson's first or second wife; see also 320n, 321n. Carey, e.g., suggests that the woman of Timna was "unclean only in a legal sense, as a Gentile"; she "was subsequent" unchaste because her unchastity took place afterward, when Samson merely left her temporarily—thus "her stain not his" (*Complete Shorter Poems*). Masson et al. instead think that the Chorus is here speaking of Dalila, and therefore assume that Dalila was unchaste. As Samuels puts it, "The purpose of this extraordinary speech is to utterly absolve Samson and God and to utterly blame Dalila" (497). Martin W. Sampson offers a unique reading: "unchastity must have depended on uncleanness: of what avail, then, for reason to acquit her of uncleanness?" Johnson (*Rambler* 16 July 1751) complains that "at the conclusion of the first act there is no design laid, no discovery made, nor any disposition formed towards the subsequent event" (218). Kermode (62) identifies an imperfect rhyme in 325–328; see 110–14n.

326–651. Commentators identify this as the second epeisodion; see 176–292n. Commentators generally agree that this exchange between Samson and Manoa is significant for both the poem's narrative structure and Samson's development. Prince notes that throughout this dialogue Milton "scatters passages which complete the story," e.g., 381–409, 522–31, 541–52 (*Samson Agonistes* 106). Mickle claims that with the arrival of Samson's father, "the middle now commences in the true spirit and manner of the Greek tragedy" (401). J. Macmillan Brown adds that Manoa's entrance, here and toward the end, "reveals the dramatic power of the poet, its self-contained and self-controlling force" (62). James Waddell Tupper, while agreeing with Johnson that *SA* lacks a middle, finds Manoa's visit to be the one "incident…which has a dramatic significance in the development of the play": Manoa reveals both the religious implications of Samson's defeat and, through his failure to comfort Samson, "the depth from which the drama must rise to its triumphant close" (378–79, 388). Rajan describes the scene with Manoa as Samson's "first radical testing. It is tempting to arrange the three confrontations in an increasing order of difficulty, to see them as steps in a movement of regeneration.... [But] Perhaps the movement out of darkness into dimness is more uncertain and groping" (135–36). Hanford sees the conversation between Manoa and Samson "as an imaginary one between Milton and his parent" (*John Milton* 217); elsewhere Hanford likens Manoa (along with the Chorus) to the friends of Job who increase his suffering by his "mistaken comfort" ("*Samson Agonistes*" 173). Brewer instead compares the visit of Samson's father with the visit of Prometheus's father-in-law, Oceanus, in *Prometheus Bound:* "the second interview in each drama occurs between the hero and a venerable personage closely related to him who comes to offer sympathy" (916).

On Manoa's character (a subject that commentators have discussed comparatively little), Hoffman describes Samson's father as "the human parallel, at times the human antithesis, always the human continuum, of the more distant, mythic Samson" (195); she adds, he is also a "searching psychological study of the demands and limitations of parental love" (198). Landy writes, "Manoa...is not evil or foolish, but...one must recognize his inferiority to his son. Manoa represents a more customary way of regarding life. He cannot see the larger issues at stake" ("Character" 243). Rudrum similarly asserts, "There is a platitudinous obviousness about Manoah which should evoke an affectionate response even while the drama is educating us to reject...the temptation he offers" (33). Allen instead suggests, "Manoa has much of the pessimism and some of the world pain of a man who has lived long and seen most of his hopes thin out; hence, he has become, as much as it is possible for a Jew, a pre-Stoa stoic who sees in withdrawal...the decent and sensible conduct of life" ("Idea as Pattern" 85).

see: Parker suggests, "an ironic lapsus linguae?" ("Variorum"). Tickell, William Aldis Wright, Verity, et al. insert an exclamation point.

reverend Sire: so also 1456; the phrase appears as well in *PL* 11.719 and *Lyc* 103 (Parker, "Variorum").

326–29. Prince compares Milton's Chorus with Trissino's in *Sofonisba:* the Chorus remains on stage and "is made to open the new Act after having sung its comments on the last" (*Italian Element* 155). See also 710–15, 1060.

327. *careful:* "anxious," "full of care" (*OED* 2), "performed with care" (Parker, "Variorum"). Hoffman finds Manoa's tread "symptomatic of his age and the cautious common sense of partial truths characterizing him" (198).

    white as doune: Percival calls this "an unusual simile," because one expects instead "soft as down." Landor also objects, "whiteness is no characteristic of down" (5:299). Parker, however, responds that down can be white when called so (cf. *Mask* 250–51: "Raven doune / Of darkness"), and "for poets who had referred to the down of doves or of swans—Leda's swan in particular—white down had become a commonplace. See e.g., Chaucer's *Book of the Duchess* 250; Shakespeare's *Winter's Tale* 4.4.363; Jonson's *Triumph of Charis* 26–30; etc." ("Variorum").

328. *Old Manoah:* the father's name is so spelled in the Authorized Version, but the spelling in the Argument, the list of Persons, and elsewhere in the text (1441, 1548, 1565) is *Manoa,* as in *DocCh* (Patterson, *Works* 14:244). Parker ("Variorum") notes that Josephus makes the name (in Greek) *Manoches* or *Manochos* (*Antiquities of the Jews* 5.8.2–3). Darbishire prefers *Manoah* as rendering "the Hebrew form" (*Poetical Works*); in Hebrew, the name has the meaning of "a home, a place of rest." Thorpe infers from Hebrew pronunciation, metrical scansion, and the general practice of recessive accentuation that the primary stress of this name should fall on the antepenultimate syllable, so that it is pronounced "Ma'-no-ah" or "Ma'-noa" (72, 74). Manoa's death is not explicitly mentioned in Scripture; Hoffman infers from the reference in Judges 16:31 ("the burying place of Manoah his father") that Manoa dies long before Samson (205), but Percival (in the note for 330) as well as Wyatt and Collins write that the language in this passage is ambiguous.

    advise: "take thought, consider, reflect, ponder, deliberate" (so *OED* 6). Hoffman infers from the Chorus's advice, "This is then no warm spontaneous relationship between father and son" (198).

330–31. These lines are balanced in length by 338–39 (Parker, *Milton's Debt* 62).

    Ay me: editors compare to the frequent οἴμοι ("alas") of Greek tragedies; Todd recalls Sophocles, *Philoctetes* 1185; cf. also *Mask* 510; *Lyc* 56, 154; *PL* 4.86; 10.813. Fenton changes to *Ah me;* Keightley (*Poems*), William Aldis Wright, and Verity change the comma after *me* to an exclamation point.

another inward grief: Blakeney writes, "Samson feels that his folly has brought discredit on his father's name" (so also Percival). But Edmund K. Chambers thinks this indicates "Samson's pity for the aged father bereft of his son." Cf. Satan's "inward griefe" in *PL* 9.97.

assault: see 845–46n; cf. 365. Cf. also *PR* 4.19, 570.

332. *Brethren:* so also 1413, 1445.

Dan: editors note that Manoa, Samson, the Chorus, and the Messenger were of Dan. Gilbert defines as "one of the tribes of Israel, whose territory was northwest of that of Judah and extended to the sea" (*Geographical*). See other references in 332, 876, 976, 1436, 1479, 1540.

333–34. *uncouth:* "unfamiliar, unaccustomed, strange" (so *OED* 2b), "with the implication of unpleasant, uncanny, or fearsome" (Lockwood). Jerram suggests "unusual, wild, disorderly."

gloried: "honour[ed]," "[made] glorious," or, perhaps, "boasted" (*OED* 3, 2; Hughes, *Complete Poems*).

335. *inform'd:* "guide[d]," "direct[ed]" (so *OED* III.4d and Lockwood; so also *Mask* 179), here perhaps with the connotation "inspir[ed]" (*OED* II.3), or, as Hunter suggests, "actuated, moved." Milton provides the two earliest examples of this use of the word in *OED* (III.4d). Cf. 1229; *PL* 3.593.

336. Prince notes that Milton here supplies verisimilitude: "This explains why Manoa enters some time after the Chorus: he set out at about the same time, but walked more slowly" (*Samson Agonistes* 107). Later we hear another reason for his tardy arrival (481–83).

younger feet: Parker ("Variorum") notes that "so Milton speaks of himself in *Apol*" (Patterson, *Works* 3:304). Cf. 1442.

cast back: "impede[d]," "[held] back" (so *OED* 73c).

337. *say if he be here:* finding it "strange that the father cannot recognize his son," Percival conjectures that this "is purposely introduced to show the great change in Samson's appearance." Given that the Chorus recognized him at once (115), Hoffman suggests that there may have been distance between father and son

even when Samson was strong (198). Parker proposes instead that Samson is here lying down (118, 339, 480) with the Chorus surrounding him ("Variorum").

338–39. *signal:* "striking, remarkable, notable, conspicuous" (*OED* 1, which dates the earliest occurrence 1641). Shawcross suggests, "indicative of his present low state, he is lying down" (*Complete English Poetry*).

    earst: "not long ago" (*OED* 5b); so also 1543. But cf. Collins, Blakeney, Hunter, Lockwood, and Prince (*Samson Agonistes*), who gloss instead as "once, formerly."

340–72. Commentators discuss how Manoa contributes to his son's regeneration. Grenander thinks Manoa's visit provides "the first inkling" that Samson will "cease to blame God for his woes and take the fault upon himself" (385). Ellis-Fermor suggests that Manoa's lament "rouses Samson to defend the decrees of Heaven and to lay the blame steadily upon himself. The timing of this is exquisite. The lamentations would have been useless before the slight tonic effects of the choric dialogue had worked upon Samson's mind.... The inspired blunders of Manoa serve the same purposes throughout" (27). Williamson similarly comments that Manoa "comes to comfort Samson, but in fact adds to his distress by making him the occasion for questioning Providence" (92). Jerram, however, mentions among the poem's shortcomings, "We get tired of Manoa" (x).

    On the prosody, Ellis-Fermor discusses "the designed confusion, the wavering, weak rhythm of some of Manoa's speech," and concludes that the most important function of the passage's versification is perhaps "to emphasize the growing formal restraint and shapeliness of Samson's lines [especially 373–419]" (150). Moss analyzes the passage's "rhetorical density" and notes that "the passage as a whole illustrates *prolepsis,* detailed amplification of a general subject ('miserable change')" (299).

    change: cf. 117. Percival compares Virgil's *Aeneid* 2.274: "ei mihi, qualis erat! quantum mutatus ab illo"; "Ah me! what aspect was his! how changed from [Hector]." George Coffin Taylor (194) compares Shakespeare's *Antony and Cleopatra* 4.15.51–52: "The miserable change now at my end / Lament nor sorrow at."

341. Landor accents the third syllable in *invincible* (5:299); Masson (*Poetical Works* 3:118), Percival, Verity, Sprott (132), and Bridges (*Milton's Prosody* 56) scan the

first two feet of this line as trochaic (see 81n). Cf. 1271; *PR* 2.408; *PL* 1.140; 4.846; 6.47. Collins suggests that Milton intends the accent of the Latin and is deriving the word from the late Latin *invincibilis;* see also 775n.

far: the phrase occurs also in *PL* 1.507 and *PR* 4.46 (Le Comte 66). Here and in 755, 1038, 1467, Darbishire emends to *farr* (*Poetical Works*).

renown'd: so the Chorus (125).

342. *dread:* see also 1474, 1673.

strength: Percival quotes 2 Peter 2:11: "Whereas angels, which are greater in power and might." Cf. *PL* 5.458–59.

343–44. *Angels:* Keightley would make this a genitive (*Poems*). Church suggests it is a Grecism: "it would be usual, in English, to say, 'to *that* of angels.'"

walk'd thir streets: Krouse writes, "One of the things about the Samson story which drew rationalistic interpretation to the aid of literalism was the doubtfulness of Samson's being able to go in and out of Gaza and Sorek without being set upon by foes in those Philistine strongholds" (89). Bullough and Bullough compare Job 29:7–10.

offering: Parker proposes *off'ring* for purposes of meter, as in 26 and 519 ("Notes" 693). See also 1152.

single: so also in 1111, 1210, 1222; cf. 1092.

345. *Duell'd:* "encounter[ed] in a duel or combat" (*OED* 2); see 1102 and cf. *PR* 1.174. Parker comments, "since 'duel' normally implies a fight between two persons more or less equal, Milton's verb underlines Samson's superhuman strength" ("Variorum"). *OED* gives 1645 as the earliest recorded use of the verb; however, Todd finds it in not only Joseph Boden's *An Alarme Beat up in Sion* (1644) but also the twelfth-century romance "Horn Childe and Maiden Rimnild" (see Ritson 3:297).

proud: cf. 137.

346. See 137n.

348–62. According to Fish, Manoa concludes that God is capricious "by appealing to the law of the excluded middle: either children are a blessing or they are not.

The alternative—the possibility that they may be both and that the complexity of the world may elude the formulations of logic—is not considered.... [B]etter an irresponsible deity than one who is incomprehensible and hence unimpeachable" (245).

348. *at one spears length:* editors gloss as "Samson could not save himself from a single armed opponent (one spear contrasted with 'Armies'), even a 'coward' who would take care to kill or injure him from the safe distance of a spear's length." Prince instead interprets the phrase as "even at close quarters," which would give a different meaning (*Samson Agonistes*). Edmund K. Chambers suggests that "'one' belongs to 'spear,' not to 'length.'" Cf. 1116–21, 1235, 1237 (*coward*). Tickell, Bohn, Verity, William Aldis Wright, et al. change the period after *length* to a question mark.

349. Editors gloss this line: "what (is there) in man (that is) not."
  mortal strength: cf. 36. Parker, without offering a specific reference, suggests this may be an echo of Josephus ("Variorum").
  oh: this spelling recurs in 1268, 1516; Parker ("Variorum") notes there are twenty-eight occurrences of *O* and only one of *ah* (1565).

350–51. Church and Collins observe that the whole of Juvenal's tenth satire is a comment on these verses. See 1401–7n.
  Deceivable: "fallible," "capable of being, or liable to be, deceived" (*OED* 2, which dates this use from 1646); so also 942 (*deceivable*), although Edmund K. Chambers (132, 140) suggests the meaning "deceitful" in both passages.
  vain: Parker ("Variorum") notes the rhyme with *bane* (351).
  bane: see 63n.

352–55. Parker comments: "seeing the matter more personally" in the middle third of this speech, Manoa "indulges in self-pity—the same weakness that Samson had recently indulged and mastered. This results, as we might foresee, in questioning of God's purpose" (*Milton's Debt* 36). But Christopher thinks that Manoa is bolder in his accusations than Samson had been (see 36, 47, 63–64), which helps Samson heal: "Only when Manoa shows Samson his doubt raised to the level of mass concensus [*sic*] is Samson roused to give a ringing affirmation of God's power over history" (365). See 368–72n; cf. 448–71n.

pray'd: Percival asserts that Milton here follows Josephus, *Antiquities of the Jews* 5.8.2; cf. Judges 13:2. Calton (in Newton) quotes seven lines from a fragment of Euripides.

    Children: Darbishire (*Poetical Works*) and B. A. Wright emend to *Childern.*

    reproach: "a fact, matter, feature, or quality bringing disgrace or discredit upon one" (so *OED* 1); so also 446. Genesis 30:23: "And she [Rachel] conceived, and bare a son; and said, God hath taken away my reproach" (Church); so also Luke 1.25 (Percival). Cf. *Tetr:* "the Jews hardly could endure a barren wedlock" (Patterson, *Works* 4:82).

354. *And:* added in the *Errata* of the first edition.

    as: editors gloss as *that.* Newton thinks "in all probability" that Milton here was thinking of the "happy father in Terence" (*Andria* 1.1.69 [96–98]): "quom id mihi placebat tum uno ore omnes omnia / bona dicere et laudare fortunas meas, / qui gnatum haberem tali ingenio praeditum"; "My pleasure wasn't the only result, for all the town heaped congratulations on me for my good fortune in having a son endowed with such a character."

    hail'd: "salute[d] as" (so *OED* 1b).

356–57. *O wherefore:* cf. 23; Manoa now, like Samson earlier, is questioning providence: see 352–55n.

    And: Verity and Blakeney gloss as "And that too."

    blessing: "gift" (*OED* 4).

    pomp: "splendor" (*OED* 1).

    adorn'd: see 679.

358. *desirable:* "delectable," "to be wished for" (*OED* 1), but also "to be regretted" (*OED* 2 [1650]). Parker ("Variorum") suggests that Milton may have relished the ambiguity in this word and in *tempt,* meaning both "to invite, attract" and "to entice to do evil" (*OED* 5, 4).

360. *Graces:* editors gloss as *favours* (*OED* II.6, 8) and note the Latin *gratiae.* Grieve suggests, "free favours." Cf. 679 and *PL* 3.674.

    draw: editors gloss as "turn out to be curses in the end" (see Wyatt and Collins).

Scorpions tail: the intense pain caused by the sting of the scorpion (situated at the point of the tail) is proverbial (*OED* 1). Todd quotes both *DDD*, where Milton speaks of a "most deadly and Scorpion like gift" (Patterson, *Works* 3:448), and *Tetr*, where he speaks of man's perversity turning "this bounty of God into a Scorpion" (Patterson, *Works* 4:84). Verity et al. compare Luke 11:12: "Or if he [a son] shall ask [of his father] an egg, will he offer him a scorpion?"; and Revelation 9:10: "And they [locusts] had tails like unto scorpions, and there were stings in their tails." Svendsen summarizes the various characteristics associated with scorpions during the Renaissance (*Milton and Science* 150). Landor acknowledges the "great eloquence and pathos" in Manoa's speech but finds "inapposite" the expression "tail behind" (5:299).

361. *the:* Darbishire (*Poetical Works*) and B. A. Wright emend to *th' Angel.* See 315–16n.

    Angel twice descend: cf. 24, 635; see 24n.

362. *nurture:* "nourishment, food" (so *OED* 2), and/or "upbringing, rearing" (so Lockwood; *OED* 1); cf. 30.

    holy: Parker writes, "the word not only means 'free from sin' but also implies a separation or setting apart from secular to religious uses. Any Nazarite was 'holy unto the Lord' (Num. 6.8)" ("Variorum"). Parker also notes the possible punning of *wholly* and, in view of what follows, even *holly* ("Variorum"). Keightley inserts a question mark after this word (*Poems*).

    as of a Plant: cf. 728. Parker observes, "though a plant is presumably without sin, it is not *per se* holy, though a select plant of course receives a special kind of nurture from the gardener" ("Variorum"). On the virtue of plants, see *Mask* 620; *PL* 4.199; 9.110–11; etc. The word *plant* can also mean "nurseling, a young person, a novice" (*OED* I.1.c). Dunster (in Todd), followed by some editors, cites a variety of possible parallels: Isaiah 5:7: "For the vineyard of the Lord of hosts is the house of Israel, and the men of Judah his pleasant plant"; Isaiah 53:2: "For he shall grow up before him as a tender plant"; also Theocritus speaking of Hercules (*Idyll* 24.101), and Thetis speaking of her son Achilles in Homer's *Iliad* 18.57. A. B. Chambers (in a letter to Parker) calls attention to Psalm 1:3: "And he shall be like a tree planted by the rivers of water, that bringeth forth his fruit in his season"; Psalm 144:12: "That our sons may be as plants grown up in their youth"; and Ezekiel 34:29: "And I God will raise up for them a plant of renown" (Parker, "Variorum"). Hughes (also in a letter to Parker) suggests Coverdale's—and Luther's—translation of Psalm 47:2: "The hill of Sion is like a Fayre plante" (Parker, "Variorum"). Cox discusses more generally how Milton uses plant metaphors in *SA*: "by the plant imagery he can comment on the inseparable relation between the external elements and individual growth" ("Natural Science" 57–58). Darbishire would omit the semicolon after *Plant* (*Poetical Works*); B. A. Wright substitutes a question mark. The latter emendation would perhaps address Ricks's criticism of the sentence as it stands, in which 365–67 have nothing to do with a plant (*Milton's Grand Style* 53).

363–64. *Select:* "selected" (*OED* 1), or "put or set aside" from the Latin *selectus* (Verity; Wyatt and Collins; et al.). Verity adds, "In Elizabethan English, the form of the past participle is often influenced by the Latin."

 Sacred: Masson (*Poetical Works*) and William Aldis Wright emend the comma after this word to a question mark.

 miracle: "marvel," "a wonderful object," "a person or thing of more than natural excellence" (*OED* 2c); cf. 1528. Percival and Verity quote Shakespeare's *2 Henry IV* 2.3.33: "O miracle of men!"

 an hour: cf. 1056; cf. also *PL* 1.697.

364–67. Daiches describes Manoa's tone in these lines as "masochistic fury" (239).

365–66. Blakeney—following Todd, Collins, and Percival—remarks on what he calls the "pathetic effect produced by the piling up of participles without conjunctions (*asyndeton*)"; cf. 563 and *PL* 6.851. For similar use of asyndeta, Percival cites Aeschylus's *Prometheus Bound* 679–80 and Sophocles' *Oedipus Rex* 1314–15. Hanford writes that Manoa's speech culminates in these lines, "a spiritual outburst, expressive no longer of the hero's physical misery and obvious disgrace...but of the inner agony of the soul which springs from full contemplation of his sins" ("*Samson Agonistes*" 175). Lawry compares Manoa here to Mary of the Passion (369). Edmundson compares Manoa's words to a passage in Vondel's *Samson* (180); on Vondel, see 115–75n.

 Ensnar'd: cf. 860.

 overcome: see 51.

 Poor: cf. 1479, and for the possible autobiographical significance, see 697n. Lockwood defines "to be pitied, unfortunate, wretched"; cf. *PR* 1.411.

Slaves: some editors (e.g., Masson, *Poetical Works* and William Aldis Wright) emend the question mark to an exclamation point; Keightley prefers a period (*Poems*).

368–72. Parker writes that Manoa, having rehearsed all the matter of Samson's previous complaint (356–67), here "adds a new, more insinuating note" (*Milton's Debt* 36). Hoffman suggests that this is Manoa's "nadir": he, in effect, has asked, What did we as parents do wrong? and, because he is unable to shoulder all the responsibility, he blames God (199–200). Landor (5:300)—followed by Collins ("plainly alluded to"), Percival, Blakeney, et al.—sees here an allusion to the disgracing of Cromwell's remains. We might note, however, that Samson immediately rebukes Manoa and pronounces his punishment just. See also 276, 693–94.

Alas: some editors (e.g., Tickell; Verity; William Aldis Wright) insert an exclamation point after this word.

methinks: Hunter glosses as "It seems to me. The derivation is from the Saxon *thencan,* to seem, not from *thincan,* to think."

369. *worthiest deeds:* an echo of 276.

frailty: "moral weakness," "liability to err" (*OED* 2); cf. 783 ("womans fraility"). Percival suggests that the word means " 'a momentary weakness' as opposed to deliberate sin and vice." Cf. *Apol:* "the humane frailty of erring" (Patterson, *Works* 3:292).

err: cf. 211.

370–71. *o'rewhelm:* cf. *DocCh:* "God…assigns a limit to chastisement, lest we should be overwhelmed" (Patterson, *Works* 15:388–89).

foul: "disgraceful, ignominious, shameful" (*OED* 13); so also 410.

indignities: cf. 411, 1168, 1341.

372. *honours sake:* Buchanan glosses as "proper reward," and notes that Milton in *SA* generally seems to consider honor external, instead of (following Aristotle) as the reward of virtue: "If it is external, it consists in reputation and in external signs, offices, monuments, celebrations, etc." (174). Buchanan notes two exceptions, where Samson uses *honor* to mean "virtue," in 412 and 1424.

373. Some commentators find here an indication of Samson's regeneration. Wood-house writes, "Samson has taken his first step in the long road to recovery: he has acknowledged his fault, and the justice of God's punishment, and from this acknowledgment he will not retreat" ("*Samson Agonistes*" 163). Hanford adds, "It is now Samson who rebukes a murmur against the apparent injustice of God's ways to man. Manoa's doubts and fears are a heavy burden on Samson's faith" (*Poems*); Bush also comments, "Manoa's reproaching of God rouses Samson to condemn himself more strongly than before" ("John Milton" 508n). Similarly, Samuels argues that "the drama of the first confrontation is not how Samson withstands a tempter but how Samson argues against the easy interpretation of his plight which would criticize the will of God and set a seal on Samson's alienation" (503). Landy discusses the "contrast between Manoa's mode of expression, which is legalistic, literal, and inclusive, and Samson's, which suffers from the great strain of trying to embody in language the agonies which he suffers and which admit of no easy solution" ("Language" 186). Lawry (369) detects here an echo of God's stance from *PL* 3.122–28. Goethe reportedly praised Samson's confession of guilt, saying it was "in a better spirit than anything in Lord Byron" (qtd. in Robinson 1:371, 373).

Appoint: "impute blame (to), stigmatize, arraign" (so *OED* 18 and Lockwood 2), or "find fault with, call in question," or "fix, arrange, determine, settle" (Verity; Patterson, *Student's Milton;* et al.). G. C. Moore Smith (74) argues for "prescribe or determine the course of, pin down to a fixed course" and notes the possibly similar usage in *Areop* (Patterson, *Works* 4:350): "Neither is God appointed and confin'd"; Verity makes this same comparison. But Weekley disagrees, arriving at "arraign, challenge, call to account" by examining various uses of the French verb *appointer,* a common legal term (373–74). For other words or phrases that Milton seems to use uniquely, see 424, 551, 803 (Prince, *Samson Agonistes* 108).

disposition: "dispensation," "ordering, control" (*OED* 3), or "argument" (Verity); cf. 506, 1746. For the sentiment Percival quotes Pindar's *Olympian Odes* 9.56: λοιδορῆσθαι θεούς ἐχθρὰ σοφία; "to speak evil of the gods is a skill that is hateful."

374. Bridges cites this line as an example of a "heavier ending" than in *PL* (*Milton's Prosody* 61).

Nothing: "no part, share" (so *OED* 2).

375. Percival quotes Aristophanes, *Nubes* 1454–55: αὐτὸς μὲν οὖν σαυτῷ οὐ τούτων αἴτιος, στρέψας σεαυτὸν ἐς πονηρὰ πράγματα; "Nay, nay, old man, you owe it to yourself. Why didst thou turn to wicked practices?" Muir writes, "In such speeches, Milton is referring not to his personal misfortunes, but to the failure of the English people" (178). Eleanor Gertrude Brown agrees, "There is certainly nothing suggestive of Milton's attitude" (98).

376. *sole cause:* Le Comte (62) notes that Eve so blames herself (*PL* 10.935).
    aught: see 274.
    vile: "degrading" (*OED* 4); cf. 371, and see also 1361.

377. *vile:* "despicable on moral grounds" (so *OED* A.1). Carey notes that this is an example of anadiplosis, the rhetorical figure in which the word (or phrase) occurring at the end of one line of poetry is used also to begin the next (*Complete Shorter Poems* 335); see 18n.
    my folly: Samson repeats this phrase in 825, 1000; cf. 1043.
    profan'd: "violate[d]," "treat[ed] (what is sacred) with irreverence" (*OED* 1), or (with its Latin meaning) "disclosed, revealed, made public" (Church; Verity; Edmund K. Chambers; Prince, *Samson Agonistes;* Bullough and Bullough). Cf. the spelling *prophane* in 693, 1362.

378–79. *mystery:* "a hidden or secret thing," "something beyond human knowledge or comprehension" (*OED* 5); cf. 384.
    giv'n: Parker suggests that the meter requires " 'given' as in 121 (which is in error); the other five instances of 'giv'n' are metrical monosyllables" ("Notes" 693).
    betray'd: "reveal[ed]" (*OED* 6; cf. 5). Parker ("Variorum") comments, "Elsewhere in the poem Samson is himself 'betray'd' (33, 383, 399, 750, 840, 946, 1109)."
    woman: cf. 50, 202, 236, 1114.

380. *Canaanite:* Verity notes that the Philistines were "immigrants into Canaan, like the Israelites, and consequently distinct from the Canaanites or native inhabitants" (65). Parker ("Variorum") observes that, "strictly speaking, the land of Canaan (western Palestine) embraced Phoenicia on the north and Philistia on the

southwest (Zeph. 2.5)." But Wyatt and Collins suggest that the term *Canaanites* came to be used "of the non-Jewish inhabitants of the land generally"; so also Prince: "the term was extended to include all who were rivals or opponents to the Israelites in their mission to conquer Palestine" (*Samson Agonistes*). Hughes adds, "The Philistines might be called *Canaanites* because they were the earliest conquerors of the land of Canaan," thus giving their name to the land (*Complete Poems;* see also *John Milton*). See 144n s.v. *Palestin* and 722n s.v. *Philistian.* Cf. *DDD:* "the *Jews* were commanded to divorce an unbeleeving Gentile for two causes: first, because all other Nations, especially the *Canaanites* were to them unclean. Secondly, to avoid seducement" (Patterson, *Works* 3:406).

    faithless: "unbelieving," "without [Hebrew] faith," and/or "perfidious," "unfaithful," hence "treacherous" (*OED* 1b, 2, 3). Cf. 388 ("More faith").

381. Watkins comments: "This personal tragedy repeats in psychological detail the original situation [*PL* 9.997–99]. Each act is compulsive, against all knowledge, all true desire. And each taps a fundamental stratum of deep emotional memories, and mystery of wrong choices made with eyes open yet blind" (87–88).

    This: that a Canaanite woman would be a "faithless enemy" (Parker, "Variorum").

    surpris'd: Martin W. Sampson suggests, "in the military, rather than the psychological, sense."

382–87. Judges 14:11–18.

    oft: "frequent," "happening…many times" (so *OED* B).

    she: her name is never mentioned in the Bible.

    betray: see 378–79n.

384. *The secret:* Samson's riddle; cf. 1194–1200.

    highth: editors find that this is Milton's usual spelling (indicating his pronunciation) in thirty-two places in his poetry; Wyatt and Collins add two exceptions, in *Arc* 75 and *PL* 9.167.

385. *Love:* the noun occurs eighteen times in *SA.*

    profest: "pretend" (*OED* 3); cf. 884. Judges 14:16–17.

386. *corrupted:* "induce[d] to act dishonestly or unfaithfully" (*OED* 4); cf. *PL* 1.368.

Spies: the thirty "companions" or groomsmen; see 1197. Percival notes that Milton here follows Josephus (*Antiquities of the Jews* 5.8.6), who terms them "their chief stalwarts, ostensibly as companions, in reality as his guardians." Quarles also adopts this notion (sig. H2r).

387–91. This passage, which to Belloc is "one of Milton's rare obscurities," is explained in the individual notes that follow. Belloc asserts: "Let the reader make what he can of it; I can make nothing" (273). McCollom adds that an actor who would have to speak these lines "would surely deserve our meed of sympathy.... Milton, to be sure, was not writing for the stage, but in ignoring the actor, he has here forgotten the character whom an actor *might* impersonate" (141).

Rivals: Lockwood defines as "companions." Parker suggests that Milton refers to their competition in the solving of the riddle, for Samson had only one rival (see 1020 and Judg. 14:20) for his wife's affection ("Variorum"). Cf. 1204 (*underminers*).

388. *Faith:* cf. 750, 986, 1115.

prime: "best or most flourishing stage or state" (*OED* 9b), as in "highth" (384); or "beginning" (Lockwood 2.a). Prince also interprets this to mean "first" (*Samson Agonistes*). Cf. 70, 85, 234.

389. *embraces:* editors indicate that the word probably has its secondary meaning of "sexual intercourse" (*OED* 1; cf. *PL* 2.793, 10.994). Verity et al. suggest that "spousal embraces" is in apposition to "prime of love."

vitiated: "corrupt[ed]," but also "deflower[ed]," "violate[d]" (*OED* 2, 3); Grieve suggests "prostituted." Editors note that this word modifies *who.*

Gold: because Judges 16:5 has the Philistine lords offering her "every one of us eleven hundred pieces of silver," Church, Percival, Grieve et al. conjecture that Milton here alludes to the fable of Danaë visited by Jupiter in a shower of gold (see also 390n). Alternatively, Keightley (*Poems*) and Collins suggest a possible allusion to Juno's conception of Mars by the touch of a flower. On the offer of gold, see also 831, 849, 958, 1114.

390. *Though offer'd only:* Parker suggests that this qualification increases the probability that Milton is remembering the story of Danaë: "In a grim jest Samson

says, in effect, that Dalila went Danaë one better, becoming pregnant by merely *smelling* a shower of gold" ("Variorum"). Hunter relates an anecdote about conception through the sense of sight from James Howell's *Instructions for Forraine Travell* (1642); Jones finds a reference here to the notion that "odorous gas was believed to further the fruitfulness of women" (2:318).

   sent: Latin *sentio;* editors gloss as "by the mere offer of gold." Verity adds that Milton always used this spelling (155).

   conceiv'd: cf. the further punning on this word in 1506 and 1574.

391. *spurious:* "bastard, adulterous" (*OED* 1b).

   Treason: "treachery," "betrayal" (*OED* 1); cf. 959. Richardson (in Newton), followed by Church, et al., thinks that Milton means petty treason—here, the murder of a husband by a wife (*OED* 2b). Keightley suggests that Samson, with grim humor, names the child (in the Hebrew manner) *Treason-against-me* (*Poems*). Parker ("Variorum") finds Samson's bitter reference to the child he never had to be "a mocking echo of his father's bitter remarks about the son God gave him (352–55)."

392–407. Krouse (123) compares *PL* 1.619.

   Thrice: Judges 16:6–9, 10–12, 13–14.

   assay'd: "tried"; cf. 1625 and *PL* 1.619.

   amorous: cf. 1007.

394. *capital:* Parker ("Variorum") observes that three or four meanings of the word are probably intended: "important," "fatal," and "pertaining to the head" (*OED* A.6e, 2d, 1); the pun occurs also in *PL* 12.383. Some editors suggest the meaning "chief" (so also *OED* A.6d). Cf. 1225. Adams describes the effect of this pun: "Samson may be seen as making reference to the importance of his secret and the fact that it resided in or on his head, as well as to the fact that like the capitol in Rome it was the center of his power and the residence of a deity. The effect...is that of an overlay; one sees and responds to the English word at the same time that one is aware of a Latin word behind the English, with its own impact and impetus" (191). Hedley Vicars Ross describes such possible wordplay as true to the book of Judges, where Samson is depicted as "given betimes to riddling and sly humor"; Ross also finds such jesting psychologically realistic: "Samson here attempts a witticism...because he would fain dispel some of the gloom that overcasts the brow of old Manoa on his account" (153–54).

395. *in what part:* the repetition (here and in 394) suggests Dalila's importuning (Parker, "Variorum").

    summ'd: "to collect into or embrace in a small compass" (*OED* 3); cf. *PL* 9.454. McCollom suggests that this is an additional pun, Latin *summus,* "top" (140); see 394n.

396–99. Judges 16:9–15. Noting that Milton omits Dalila's three attempts on Samson's strength, Parker speculates that they may have "seemed rather ridiculous for a hero of tragedy" (*Milton's Debt* 7–8); to Tinker, however, this is "the most surprising of all Milton's omissions" (61). Clark observes that here "Milton's hero is less credulous, more sophisticated, than Samson of old; he is 'not at all surprised' at Dalila's assaults," and he is more truthful, resorting to "cunning shifts" instead of outright "lyes" (92, 95). Parker additionally compares Milton's Samson with Adam in *PL:* he argues that both understand their decision at the moment of their respective falls, "but a big difference between the two is that Adam so deeply loves his wife that he cannot face a future without her" ("Variorum").

    deluded: "mock[ed]," "play[ed] with…under pretence of acting seriously" (so *OED* 1a).

    sport: "jesting," "merriment" (so *OED* 2b); Lockwood defines "a laughing-stock" (1.d). Judges 16:15: "thou hast mocked me these three times."

    importunity: see 51.

399–400. On the use of enjambment in *SA,* see 190n. Edmund K. Chambers (127) detects an unstressed rhythm in the middle of 399—although, he adds, forced elisions would sustain the regular iambic meter; he similarly describes 122, 429, 579, 748, 842.

401. Cf. Shakespeare's *Comedy of Errors* 3.2.162: "Hath almost made me traitor to myself" (Percival).

402. *mustring:* "summon[ing], gather[ing] up" (so *OED* 3b), but also, according to editors, "enlisting, assembling (like troops)" as they note the extension of the metaphor in 403–05. Cf. 235–36, 906.

403–05. Landy discusses the martial and militant context used to describe Dalila's words: "Milton here conceives of language as a form of aggression. This dramatizes a reversal of masculine and feminine roles which betokens . . . an inversion of the proper nature of things. Samson is the passive tower or fortress who allows himself to be taken and victimized by Dalila, the active battering ram" ("Language" 185). Ferry also describes the effect of this military language on Samson: "Dalila's words 'storm' him as weapons bombard besieged ramparts" (162). On the imagery of military siege, see also 235n, 236n, 560–61n, 845–46n, 906n.

> *blandisht:* "invested with flattery or blandishment" (so *OED;* the only occurrence of this word recorded in *OED*), or "coaxing, gently flattering" (Prince, *Samson Agonistes*).

> *parlies:* "talk," "argument[s]," but also (continuing the metaphor) "conference[s] with an enemy, under a truce" (*OED* 1, 2); cf. 785.

> *feminine assaults:* see 845n. Cf. *PR* 2.192–95.

404. *Tongue-batteries:* on the coinage, cf. *tongue-doubtie* (1181) and also *DDD: tongue-fence* (Patterson, *Works* 3:502). Todd, followed by Mitford, Fleming, Percival, and Verity, thinks this "probably suggested" by Shakespeare's *1 Henry VI* 3.3.78–79: "I am vanquished! These haughty words of hers / Have batt'red me like roaring cannon-shot." Todd quotes also from the anonymous play, *The History of the Tryall of Cheualry* (1605): "[ears] Pearst with the volley of thy battring words." Verity quotes *Colas:* "To this position I answer, that it lays no battery against mine, no, nor so much as faces it" (Patterson, *Works* 4:241).

> *surceas'd:* "cease[d]," "stop[ped]" (so *OED* 1c).

405. Judges 16:16: "she pressed him daily with her words, and urged him, so that his soul was vexed unto death."

> *storm:* "attempt to take by storm (a fortified position)" (*OED* 6 dates from 1645).

> *over-watch't:* editors gloss as "weary or exhausted from want of sleep" (*OED* 3). Parker specifically finds here the suggestion of a sentinel standing guard ("Variorum"). Cf. *PL* 2.288.

> *out:* the first edition has a period here, but because the sentence continues, Newton et al. substitute a comma.

406–07. *At times:* editors gloss as "at one time and another."

unlock'd: "explain[ed], provide[d] a key to" (*OED* 3b); cf. *Mask* 755. Judges 16:17: "he told her all his heart"; also Judges 16:18: "he hath shewed me all his heart."

408. *manhood:* cf. 410, 417, and see 537n.
  resolv'd: "determin[ed]" (*OED* 14).

410. *foul:* see 371.
  effeminacy: "addiction to women" (cf. *OED* 2), and/or "unmanly weakness" (Lockwood; *OED* 1); cf. 408, 417, 562, and also *PL* 11.634 and *PR* 4.142. Parker comments, "Milton may have had in mind the *mollities* of Aristotle and Aquinas, the softness which contrasts with constancy, patience, and also chastity" ("Variorum"). McCall suggests that this word here has a triple meaning: "it refers to Samson's unmanliness in submission, to the fact that the yoke was imposed by a woman, and to Samson's attachment to a woman (uxoriousness is a possible synonym) that has trapped him" (60). Cf. *Eikon:* "effeminate and Uxorious Magistrates. Who being themselves govern'd and overswaid at home under a Feminine usurpation" (Patterson, *Works* 5:139). See 537n.

411–19. Following Mickle, who describes this passage as "strikingly pointed" (401), Moss offers a detailed analysis of the rhetorical style: the passage "exemplifies *epanodos,* expansion of a statement by repeating and amplifying key words. In addition, it contains a logical scheme (*proportion*) based upon the analogy between two comparisons in time and degree: . . . present servitude is less serious than past, just as past blindness was more serious than present" (299). Roston describes how the "theme of profaned vocation is brilliantly suggested . . . by Milton's distinction between *service, servitude* [416], and *servility* [412, 413]. . . . In the Hebrew Bible, *'avodah* ('service') in isolation denotes the purity of Temple worship, but in conjunction with *zarah* ('foreign') is transformed to mean idolatry and hence whoring after strange gods and strange women; the word *'eved* ('slave') is a derivative. For Milton, then, to serve truly was to submit to no yoke other than that of the King of Kings; and servitude to woman constituted idolatry, leading appropriately enough to physical enslavement" (171–72). For uses of *service,* see 686, 1163, 1499.

411. Thyer (in Todd) describes the "sudden gust of indignation and passionate self-reproach upon the mentioning of his weakness."

> *O indignity:* so Satan exclaims in *PL* 9.154 (Le Comte 65).
> *blot:* "disgrace" (so *OED* 2); so also 978 and *FInf* 12.

412. *servile:* also used in 5 and 1213.

413–19. Carey thinks Samson's claims here "sound affectedly noble" and, while "it would be hugely insensitive to suggest that Samson is putting on an act," he argues that the Chorus's presence forces Samson "to turn against himself indignation which he desperately wants to divert elsewhere" (*John Milton* 140). Verity and Edmund K. Chambers quote Bishop Joseph Hall's account of Samson in *Contemplations* (1617): "he was more blinde when hee saw licentiously then now, that he sees not; He was a greater slaue when he serued his affections, then now in grinding for the Philistins." Parker ("Variorum") also compares Milton's description in *Tetr* of a bad marriage as "the ignoblest, and the lowest slavery...an unmanly task of bondage" (Patterson, *Works* 4:121).

> *base...base:* "degrading, despicable, befitting a person of low degree" (Lock-wood 2.c).
> *degree:* "stage or position in the scale of dignity" (*OED* 4).
> *rags:* cf. 122–23.
> *grinding:* Parker suggests that the word may have sexual connotations ("Variorum"). Cf. *DDD:* "to grind in the mill of an undelighted and servil copulation" (Patterson, *Works* 3:403).

417. Peck cites this line to illustrate Milton's characteristic use of a "continuative epithet," that is, three epithets to compose a single line of verse (sig. P4r). See also 827, 1364, 1422. Edmund K. Chambers cites other examples of this stylistic device from the Greek tragedians, from earlier English poets, and from *PL*. Moss catalogs other examples of this rhetorical technique from *SA;* he calls it *synonymia,* "short disjunctive lists of adjectives, nouns, or verbs, all of which mean almost the same thing but which in tandem exert a cumulative power" (300).

> *Unmanly:* see 537n.

418. *that blindness:* cf. 1686. Parker notes that the tradition insisted upon Samson's *caeca mens,* "mental blindness" ("Variorum"); see 413–19n.

420. Stein describes Manoa's reply as a "shocking descent from the objective 'I' of the tragic hero to the subjective 'I' of the comic parent repeating an ancient domestic pattern" (*Heroic Knowledge* 151). Belloc thinks this line "flat" and "deplorable," with "an element of *meiosis* [or litotes]...which is not without attraction, but it is a little overdone" (273, 274). For other examples of litotes in *SA*, Parker cites 180, 970, 1642 ("Variorum"). Martz instead suggests that the flatness in the first part of Manoa's speech may be deliberate: "The distance between Samson and ordinary men is at once emphasized by Manoa, as he proceeds to ignore the power of Samson's self-castigation and answers at first by a feeble, querulous, and half-comic rebuke of Samson's willful choice of foreign wives" (123). Sadler uses this line to develop a typological interpretation: "Manoa's regret only of Samson's marriage choice parodies Samson's marriage with the Lamb" (203). Watkins instead suggests that Milton may have been drawing from his own father's reaction to his marriage to Mary Powell: "the line...must have cost Milton pain, for at times he opens in a frenzy of self-torture his deep domestic injury which never heals" (134). Perhaps developing such a biographical reading, Rowse thinks it a "plain fact" that "Milton was marrying above him" (95).

    Son: so Manoa addresses him in 503; in 438 and 445, he addresses him by name (Parker, "Variorum").

421–23. Editors note that Milton here departs from Scripture: "Then his father and his mother said unto him, Is there never a woman among the daughters of thy brethren, or among all my people, that thou goest to take a wife of the uncircumcised Philistines? And Samson said unto his father, Get her for me; for she pleaseth me well. But his father and mother knew not that it was of the Lord, that he sought an occasion against the Philistines" (Judg. 14:3–4). Cf. 221–22, where Milton follows Scripture closely.

    plead: cf. *urg'd* (223). Fish suggests that Manoa is indirectly criticizing his son: "one need not overread to hear the sneer in 'plead / Divine impulsion'" (243).

422. *impulsion:* "instigation, incitement" (*OED* 2a); cf. 223, 526, 638.
    prompting: "suggest[ing]," "inspir[ing]" (*OED* 3); cf. 318. Verity comments, "it qualifies 'impulsion'; for the allusion, see 222."

423. *occasion:* see 224 and 425n.

    infest: "harass," "molest by repeated attacks" (*OED* 1).

424. *state:* "assign a value to, have an opinion upon" (so *OED* 2b, giving this as its single use of the word in this meaning), or "to set out (a question, problem, etc.) in proper form" (*OED* 7), or "to represent (a matter) in all the circumstances of modification" (*OED* 8). Editors gloss Manoa's statement as "I shall not go into the details of that"; Verity adds, "he passes to a point on which there can be no dispute." Sheppard infers that "Manoah doubts—and so, of course, does Milton—whether God really prompted the affair with the woman of Timna" (161). For other words or phrases that Milton seems to use uniquely, see 373, 551, 803 (Prince, *Samson Agonistes* 108).

425. *occasion:* Church and Grieve note the satirical repetition of this word; cf. 423. Carey suggests that this repetition approaches *antimetabole* (repetition with inversion): "occasion...foes / foes...occasion"; see also 462–63, 686 (*Complete Shorter Poems* 335). Parker adds that "soon" in this line echoes "some" in 423 ("Variorum"). Lockwood considers "soon" an adverb meaning "in a short time, before long, presently, shortly, quickly" (1.a).

    thereby: Lockwood accents the first syllable; cf. 941.

    thee: Parker thinks this pronoun is emphasized ("Variorum").

426–27. *triumph:* "subject of triumph" (so *OED* 2b, the only example cited); cf. 1312. Lockwood defines "a cause of rejoicing" (I.e); Prince glosses as "an occasion for them to triumph" (*Samson Agonistes*).

    thou the sooner Temptation found'st: Parker ("Variorum") writes, "with these blunt words Manoa helps us to see how Samson's unconscious error (228, 231) led to the committing of a conscious error (233–36)."

    charms: the word recurs in 934, 1040; cf. 1134.

428. *sacred trust:* the phrase is repeated in 1001. Cf. 49.

    silence: see 49, 236.

429. Edmund K. Chambers (127) detects an unstressed rhythm in the middle of this line—although, he adds, forced elisions would sustain the regular iambic meter; he similarly describes 122, 399, 579, 748, 842.

430. *Tacit:* "unspoken" (*OED* 1), "covered in silence" (Hughes, *Complete Poems; John Milton*). Jerram thinks this word superfluous.

   true: cf. 408–9. Percival and Blakeney remark that the word is emphatic, not concessive, here: "Too true, alas," or "It is true" (*OED* 3b).

431. *Enough:* Milton's normal spelling was *Anough;* cf. 455, 1468, 1592 (Parker, "Variorum").

   more: Percival glosses, "'more (than enough),' the punishment has been heavier than the fault deserved." Krouse notes that Jacobus Salianus in his *Annales* (1620) makes this same point (84, 105). Cf. 368–72, 687–91.

   burden: "load of...blame," and also "heavy lot or fate" (*OED* I.2, III.8); Percival suggests "heavy consequences."

432. McCall writes that this "legal-financial imagery" makes concrete "the abstract notion of man's relationship to God" (79). Landy also briefly addresses this imagery ("Of Highest Wisdom" 234–35).

433. *rigid:* "harsh, severe" (*OED* 3).

   score: "obligation," "reckoning" (*OED* 11b), "record of a debt" (Hughes, *Complete Poems; John Milton*).

   A worse thing yet remains: commentators see this as a turning point in the poem. With this line, writes Percival (94–95), ends the first motif of the piece, Samson's marriage and its consequences; he adds that the announcement of the Philistine celebration "is appropriately made through one who, next to Samson, feels most keenly the dishonour it brings.... Samson already knows the *fact* that the feast is going to be held (12), but, we may suppose, not its *object.*" Edmund K. Chambers similarly comments, "At last the real action of the play begins"; he adds that Manoa's announcement "is the first thing that urges Samson to his great deed." Collins also writes that this remark (and 468–71) is "paving the way for the catastrophe" (5). Cumberland, in reply to Johnson, contends that Manoa's announcement and Samson's response make the whole epeisodion an "incident" and "middle" (335–36). Hanford agrees: "Here, then, is the 'middle'.... The crisis comes at this point, technically at the end of the second act. The trial is over and Samson has emerged from it unscathed" ("Temptation Motive" 192). Grenander similarly emphasizes the passage's significance: "the conflict is thus raised from the level of a human one between Samson and the

Philistines to a personal contest between God and Dagon, and the enormity of the consequences of Samson's crime is made manifest" (385). Baum (359) and Hanford ("Temptation Motive" 192) believe that Manoa tells Samson he "must take part in the Philistine holiday." Tillyard suggests that Manoa's announcement is made "with a certain satisfaction" (*Milton* 288); Daiches believes that the "very excess" of the "conscious cruelty" in Manoa's speech "helps to calm Samson" (240); Lawry suggests that Manoa sounds "like the Miltonic God of popular misconception, berating his son Adam in smug mercilessness" (370); Mickle, however, thinks this "condemning" speech contains a "mixture of paternal tenderness" (402).

434. Editors cite Judges 16:23: "Then the lords of the Philistines gathered them together for to offer a great sacrifice unto Dagon their god, and to rejoice: for they said, Our god hath delivered Samson our enemy into our hand."
   popular: "public" (*OED* 1); cf. 16.

435–36. *proclaim:* cf. 1598.
   Pomp: "triumphal or ceremonial procession," "splendid display or celebration" (*OED* 1, 2); cf. 1312 and *PR* 1.457 (Le Comte 67).
   Sacrifice: cf. 1312, 1612.
   Praises loud: so said of Cromwell in *Sonn 16* 8 (Le Comte 65).

437–78. *Dagon:* in this passage, as again in 1145–77, Dagon is treated as the antagonist (see 433n), but Parker notes that in 859, 896, 1231, and 1242 other Philistine gods are mentioned; he compares 13, 1297, 1311, 1360, 1370, 1672, where Dagon is simply the local god whose feast is being celebrated ("Variorum"). Cf. also 861, 1463.
   Their: Grierson (*Poems* 1:xxix) asserts that this line's rhythm requires *their* (as opposed to *thir*); Fletcher also thinks the word is stressed (*John Milton's Complete* 4:212).

439. *Them . . . thine:* the construction: "who hath delivered them out of thy (hands)." Dagon is now a "Deliverer" (Parker, "Variorum"); see 38–42n.
   who slew'st them many a slain: editors note the construction probably is "who slew a slain," with *them* an ethical dative (or dative of reference) and the adjective *many* used distributively to designate a great indefinite number, i.e., "who

slew many of them to their loss." Percival, however, reads "who slew (at the cost of) them many a (man who was thus) slain." Landor thinks this expression "absurd" (5:300); Prince instead suggests that the unusual word order in 438–39 "gives emphasis" (*Samson Agonistes*). Cf. Judges 16:24: "And when the people saw him, they praised their god: for they said, Our god hath delivered into our hands our enemy, and the destroyer of our country, which slew many of us." Verity suggests that Dryden imitates Milton in *Alexander's Feast* (1697): "thrice he routed all his foes, and thrice he slew the slain."

440–41. *magnifi'd:* "extoll[ed]," "glorif[ied]" (*OED* 1). Newton notes that Milton invents this reproach and that it comes naturally from a father, whereas it would have sounded insulting in the mouth of the Chorus.
    Besides: "other than," "except" (*OED* B.3); the word is elsewhere an adverb (214, 845, 1361).

442. *Disglorifi'd:* "deprive[d] of glory," "treat[ed] with dishonour" (so *OED*, which finds the word also in John Dee's *A True and Faithful Relation* [1659]). Muir comments: "After the Restoration, from the point of view of the Puritans, God had been blasphemed.... The position of Samson resembles that of the defeated Puritans" (177).
    had in scorn: cf. *Ps 4* 8.

443. Commentators have difficulty scanning this line. The text of the first edition has "By th' Idolatrous," but Bridges thinks that the elision was a printing mistake; he proposes scanning *By the* as a trochee, scanning *idol* as an iamb, and eliding the *atr* in *idolatrous* (*Milton's Prosody* 65). Bridges also acknowledges the possibility of retaining the elision as printed and reading "do'-la" as a second inverted foot; Sprott (132) favors this latter possibility; see 81n. Church instead suggests that we emphasize the *a* in *Idolatrous,* although note 1364 and *PR* 1.444.
    rout: "rabble" (*OED* 7b), or "a disorderly crowd" (Edmund K. Chambers 144); so also 674; cf. *Ps 3* 16.
    wine: cf. 1418, 1613, 1670.

444. *Which to have come:* a Greek (Collins) or Latin (Church) construction; editors paraphrase it as "And that this has come" or "Which things having come."

445. *sufferings:* Parker proposes *suff'ring,* as regular meter would seem to require ("Notes" 693). See 701.

 heaviest: Oras identifies this word as one of the poem's dactylic endings—although, he adds, it "permits at least fictive diphthongization of the vowels involved" ("Milton's Blank Verse" 168). Bridges similarly cites this line as an example of a "heavier ending" than in *PL* (*Milton's Prosody* 61). See 603n.

446–47. *all reproach:* editors gloss as "the most shameful of all reproaches that could have befallen thee." See 353; Verity comments, "'reproach' is a collective word for 'disgrace,' 'infamy.'"

 ever: cf. 1336.

 Father's house: Parker notes the ironic echo in 1717 ("Variorum").

448–71. Commentators identify this passage as a significant transition for Samson. Ellis-Fermor comments: "The news..., which a little earlier in the play would have led to despair, falls upon a mind now capable of being roused...to draw a distinction between his fortunes and those of...[God]. Despairing for and still condemning himself, he perceives, in a sudden leap of the mind forward, the power of God to accomplish His own purposes.... A preliminary climax, a foretaste of exultation is reached" (27–28). Bush similarly argues that "Manoa's account of the glorification of Dagon enlarges the significance of Samson's fall and deepens his grief...for the dishonor he has brought on the God of Israel" ("John Milton" 509n). Christopher also suggests that the "ringing tones" of Samson's speech here "are far different from the uncertain way in which Samson had earlier defended national providence with a qualifying 'haply' [62].... From this time forth Samson never blames God nor doubts his power"—even though his "cure" remains "far from complete" (365–66); Woodhouse agrees that "this is a step forward, though for the time being it only deepens Samson's despair" ("Tragic Effect" 209). Mickle, too, compliments Samson's "generous contrition" in these lines and adds, "progressive impressions on the mind of Samson have...been artfully delineated" (402). But Carey (*John Milton* 141) is suspicious of Samson's sincerity: Samson may agree with Manoa about God's dishonor—Samson now even claims that it is his "chief affliction" (457)—but "so far as we can see...it has not occurred to him before," and, "once he has collected his wits, he...returns to belabouring himself (487–501) and soon forgets about how God will get on without him."

Among other responses, Garnett cites the first part of this passage to illustrate Samson's remorse, his "heaviest burden"; he adds, "as in the Hebrew prophets Israel sometimes denotes a person, sometimes a nation, Samson seems no less the representative of the English people in the age of Charles the Second" (184). Of the versification, Ellis-Fermor writes that this is the first complete verse paragraph: "a continuous passage of thought is now for the first time co-terminous with a speech. As the thought rises to a climax of conviction its mood is reflected in…the gradual quickening of pace and increase of emphasis and tension, in the momentary restlessness [458–59]…and in the sudden exhilaration [460–65].… There is relaxation at the end…as the music and the emotion sink down again to quiescence" (150–51).

acknowledge and confess: Blakeney writes, "so in the opening exhortation of the English Prayer Book" and comments on the formula's essential bilingualism; see also Stroup 57–58. Cf. 735, 1170 (*acknowledge*), 753, 829 (*confess*).

449–50. *pomp:* "celebration" (Parker, "Variorum"). See 436, where the word is capitalized, and cf. 357.

advanc'd: "magnif[ied]" (*OED* III.12), or "promoted, raised aloft" (Verity; et al.). Cf. 136.

praises: see 436, where the word is capitalized, and cf. 1621.

451. *Among the Heathen round:* so also 1430 and see *PL* 10.579, *PR* 2.443 (Le Comte 67). Cf. Leviticus 25:44: "of the heathen that are round about you" (Verity).

452. *Dishonour, obloquie:* cf. *PR* 3.131 (Le Comte 67). Parker comments, "in what follows (452–56) Samson goes beyond his father's bitter summary (440–43) and mentions other evils for which he is responsible. He ignores his father's impious suggestions in 426–27, 431" ("Variorum").

453. *Idolists:* editors gloss as "worshipers of idols." Milton was not the first to use this word, as has been thought (e.g., Wyatt and Collins); *OED* quotes from Joshua Sylvester's *Bethulia's Rescue* (1614) and Francis White's *Replie to Jesuit Fishers Answere* (1624). Cf. *PR* 4.234. Parker ("Variorum") notes that Samson's tribe of Dan first introduced idolatry into Israel (Judg. 18).

Atheists: see 296n.

scandal: "discredit to religion," and also, or particularly, "perplexity of con-science occasioned by the conduct of one who is looked up to as an example" (*OED* 1). Wyatt and Collins gloss in its Greek sense of "cause of stumbling."

454–56. *diffidence:* "distrust," "doubt" (*OED* 1; Latin: *diffidentia*). Steadman observes, "in contrast to numerous references to doubt, the drama contains only one explicit allusion to distrust" ("'Faithful Champion'" 23).
   propense: "inclined," "prone," "ready" (so *OED* 1).
   fall off: "become a backslider, apostatize" (Verity; et al.).

457. *Which:* the antecedent is the whole of what Samson here confesses (Parker, "Variorum").
   chief: cf. 66.

459. To Stein this is the drama's "darkest moment," Samson's "psychological low point so far," but even here "in the darkness" Stein detects "the subtle movements of light preparing under the surface" (*Heroic Knowledge* 153, 228). Eleanor Gertrude Brown (98) cites this passage, among others, to support her argument that Milton has not created Samson in his own image (see also 489–96, 563–68).
   eie: Parker observes, "this spelling (also found in *IlPen* 141 and *Mask* 328) recurs in 584, 636, 690, 726; but 'eye' also occurs (nineteen times). There is irony in blind Samson's expressing himself in such terms" ("Variorum").
   harbour: "entertain," "shelter" (so *OED* 1); cf. *PL* 1.185 (Verity). Cf. also 111 (*stearing*), 198–200.
   sleep: cf. 629.

460. Stroup detects a significant transition in this line: "Samson's confession to his father follows the general structure of confessions, in that it comes to a turning, a 'but' or 'on other hand' or 'now therefore,' or 'yet,' or some such construction either expressed or implied" (58). Rajan notes that Samson's "sense of abandon-ment," expressed in this and the following two lines (as well as at 631–32), is "reversed in the encounter with Harapha" (133).
   only: "single, one" (*OED* 3).
   hope: Sheppard comments, "As always, the new stage in self-knowledge brings hope" (161–62). But Stein interprets the emphasis otherwise: "Samson's

answer...is *withdrawal*. The temptation he refused from the Chorus, and that, in another form, he is about to refuse from his father, he now embraces for the moment and calls it hope.... His piety...is irreproachable but not in character" (*Heroic Knowledge* 153–54).

    relieves: Lawry suggests "an unwitting pun" in Samson's retreat—*relieves* instead of *revives* (371).

461–62. *With me:* Grieve as well as Wyatt and Collins gloss as "as far as I am concerned"; Bullough and Bullough suggest, "that through me the strife comes to its climax." Darbishire (*Poetical Works*) and B. A. Wright emend to *mee;* cf. 63, 463, 1125; see 219–20n s.v. *Mee.*

    contest: Verity suggests that the accent falls on the second syllable, as in 865; he compares *PL* 11.800. See also *PL* 4.872.

    now / 'Twixt God and Dagon: Knight (*Chariot* 90) suggests that this, what he calls the main conflict in *SA,* "is also Milton's old conflict of Puritanism and the Prelacy"; accordingly, the pagan worshipers of Dagon are associated with revelry and "licentious debauchery" (see 440–43, 1418–20, 1669–74). Hill instead sees signs of Samson's presumption: "In saying that the battle for Israel's freedom is *now* between God and Dagon, he is assuming that before his fall the battle was between Dagon and himself"; Hill notes the irony that in this same line Samson accuses Dagon of presumption (159). Carey notes that this repetition approaches *antimetabole* (repetition with inversion): "God...Dagon / Dagon...God"; see also 423–25, 686 (*Complete Shorter Poems* 335).

463. *Me overthrown:* absolute participle construction (so *OED* 6c; Masson, *Poetical Works* 3:78), in imitation of the Latin ablative absolute (Hunter). Darbishire (*Poetical Works*) and B. A. Wright emend to *Mee;* cf. 63, 461, 1125; see 219–20n s.v. *Mee.* Bullough and Bullough interpret this to mean that Samson's "failure, by encouraging Dagon to boast, will cause God to act directly against the latter [i.e., instead of through Samson]."

    list: "place or scene of combat or contest" (so *OED* 9b); a tournament is connoted (Bullough and Bullough). Cf. 1087. On related terms, see 556n.

464. *Deity:* "godhood," "estate or rank of a god" (*OED* 1a); so also 899 (*deity*); cf. 1153.

    comparing: "bear[ing] comparison," or, perhaps, "rival[ling]" (*OED* 4b).

preferring: "set[ting] or hold[ing] (one thing) before others in favour or esteem" (*OED* 7); so also 1374, 1672. Lockwood has "promoting, advancing."

465. *Abraham:* see 29n.
   be sure: so Samson again in 1385, 1408.

466–67. *connive:* "remain dormant" (so *OED* 5), or "shut [his] eyes to" (*OED* 1), or "be long-suffering" (Prince, *Samson Agonistes*); cf. *PL* 10.624. Edmund K. Chambers (140) sees an allusion to Acts 17:30: "And the times of this ignorance God winked at."
   provok'd: editors gloss as "challenged"; so also 237.
   arise: Percival writes, "a frequent biblical expression."
   assert: "defend," or "vindicate" (*OED* dates from 1649); see *PL* 1.25, 6.157.

468–71. Bush identifies this passage as one of several "general premonitions that build toward the climax" ("John Milton" 508); Collins also writes that this remark (in conjunction with 433–37) is "paving the way for the catastrophe" (5); J. Macmillan Brown similarly suggests, "It is from this unhesitating confidence that the first gleam of light comes, the faith that his own God will put into his hands...the power to avenge" (81); so also Hughes, "we have a foretaste of the fall of Dagon's temple and a foretaste of Manoa's role as the unconscious prophet of the catastrophe" (*Complete Poems* 536). Parker adds, "perhaps the recollection of this prophecy helps to influence Samson when the summons from the lords is brought" (*Milton's Debt* 37). Alternatively, Moody describes these lines as the first instance of tragic irony in the poem: Samson does not realize, as we do, the part he will play in what he is here prophesying (286). See also 433n.
   stoop: Keightley (*Poems*) and Percival conjecture that Milton remembers here (as in *PL* 1.457–66) the later and literal fall of Dagon (1 Sam. 5:3). Nash points out that *stoop* (Italian *chinarsi* or *abbassarsi*) is another term from chivalric combat (37); cf. 463, 469–70.

469. *discomfit:* "defeat," "discomfiture" (so *OED*); cf. Judges 4:15. Nash (37) notes that *discomfit* (Italian *sconfitta*) and *despoil* are terms from chivalric romance, as is *Trophies* (470). On related terms, see 556n.

470. *Trophies:* "token[s] or evidence of victory" (*OED* 2b); see 469n, and cf. 1736. Samson refers to the consequences confessed in 448–55.

    on: "from" (so *OED* III.23); but Verity has *over.*

471. *confusion:* "overthrow, ruin" (*OED* 1).

    blank: "confound," "nonplus" (*OED* 2), or "blanch," "make pale [with terror]" (*OED* 1; and so Church; Masson; Percival; Bullough and Bullough; et al.). Todd, followed by Mitford, Grieve, et al., compares *Hamlet* 3.2.230: "Each opposite that blanks the face of joy." Parker compares *Ps* 6 21–22: "Mine enemies shall all be blank and dash't / With much confusion" ("Variorum"). Church further notes "the extravagance of the diction of the whole passage, indicating, possibly, that 'blank' was not in common use."

    Worshippers: cf. *PL* 1.461.

472–86. Parker (*Milton's Debt* 62) observes that this speech of fifteen lines is exactly balanced by Samson's reply (487–501).

    this hope relieves thee: Parker ("Variorum") notes that Manoa echoes Samson's words (460).

    these words...receive: "regard" (so *OED* 14b). Johnson (*Rambler* 16 July 1751) writes, "this part of the dialogue, as it might tend to animate or exasperate *Samson,* cannot, I think, be censured as wholly superfluous" (219). Parker attributes even more weight to this passage: with 472–78 "the high point of the epeisodion is reached" (*Milton's Debt* 37). Editors cite various precedents for the taking of omens from spoken words: 1 Samuel 14:1–14 (Percival); Virgil, *Aeneid* 7.117 (Browne; Collins; et al.); Sophocles, *Electra* 668 (Verity); Euripides, *Ion* 562 (Hughes, *John Milton* 436). Percival observes that Josephus (*Antiquities of the Jews* 5.8.4) also says of Samson that "it was plain...that he was to be a prophet." Milton may also be remembering here Judges 13:12, where Manoa, not realizing that he was talking with an angel, had accepted readily that prophecy of Samson's birth ("Now let thy words come to pass") and then had turned immediately to the practical concerns of the child's training and the feeding of his guest. Parker adds, "for Manoa's prompt acceptance here of Samson's words is, we should recognize, a facile optimism, totally unwarranted by anything in the actual situation" ("Variorum"). Bullough and Bullough comment that "the reader knows better than Manoa that it *is* prophetic."

474–75. *certain:* Allen writes, "The ultimate victory of Jehovah is never doubted by either Samson or his father, but they are both totally unaware of the instrument" ("Idea as Pattern" 86). See 460n, 472–86n.
    vindicate the glory: cf. *PR* 2.47–48.

477. *Endure it, doubtful:* i.e., "tolerate" it to remain doubtful (*OED* 4). Jerram compares 1 Kings 18:21. Some editors (e.g., Newton; Verity; Edmund K. Chambers; William Aldis Wright) omit this comma.

478–81. Manoa's mind, suggests Ellis-Fermor, "like that of Dr. Johnson's, interprets Samson's story in terms of events and not of inner experience" (28).

479. *forgot:* Allen comments about Manoa, "By implying that God has no further use for Samson, he presses his son against the sharp blade of despair" ("Idea as Pattern" 86).

481–86. Manoa's attempt to ransom his son is Milton's innovation, without warrant in either Scripture or tradition (Krouse 99); see also 601–4n. Commentators discuss the irony of Manoa's efforts and identify possible precedents and parallels. Johnson (*Rambler* 16 July 1751) doubts the passage's importance: the dispute about ransom "is only valuable for its own beauties, and has no tendency to introduce any thing that follows it" (219). Mickle replies that such an assertion "is perverseness indeed" (403). Adds Edmund K. Chambers, "With this ... motive begins the irony of the play, for Samson's liberty will be secured in a very different fashion" (88). Williamson describes the irony this way: "Samson's true course is to bear his lot with patience, not to buy his release; thus spiritual and physical deliverance are fundamentally opposite, except as the latter becomes an 'accident' of the former" (87). Daiches suggests there is irony also because Manoa's "facile optimism succeeds only in depressing Samson" (241). Allen writes: "Manoa unwittingly substitutes himself for God, and seeks to persuade his son to accept the plans of a loving father instead of awaiting those of a loving God. If there is a temptation in this scene, it revolves about this substitute proposal. Had Samson, who has already fallen into sloth through lechery ..., accepted his father's plans, he would have plunged deeper in the slough of sloth" ("Idea as Pattern" 85–86); Barker more bluntly calls it a "well-intentioned but senile offer of juvenile ransom" (178). Prince explains: "By introducing the possibility of ransom...[Milton] obtains a two-fold dramatic effect: since the question remains to be settled, it impels the plot forward; and, by giving Samson a clear impression of what is after all the best he can hope for, it precipitates in him a deeper sense of sorrow and a deeper conviction of his guilt" (*Samson Agonistes* 107). Scott-Craig calls it an "ironic countertheme" to Samson's deliverance of Israel and notes that "the Greek word for ransom, *lutron,* appears in the Beza New Testament simply as *redemptio;* while in the Tremellius New Testament it is rendered *redemptionis pretium*" ("Concerning" 47). Hoffman also notes that Manoa's proposal "is, paradoxically, the antithetical parallel of Samson's final deliverance," but she suggests that Milton added this detail to his version of Samson's story so as to emphasize "the importance of individual choice, of human will in determining human fate" (202). Gossman suggests that the word *ransom* for a Christian reader would "inevitably" evoke Christ's redemption (cf. *PL* 12.424); she adds that Milton may here be remembering Crito's offer to ransom Socrates and the latter's reasons for rejecting the proposal ("Ransom" 11–12). Daiches is reminded "somewhat" of *Prometheus Bound* and Oceanus's optimism in thinking he can "arrange everything between Prometheus and Zeus if only Prometheus will behave himself" (240); Marilla is reminded of the Son's temptations in the wilderness from *PR:* "these temptations, in both cases,...represent appeals to the tempted to put personal and immediate interests above concern for ultimate and universal good" (73).

481–82. *made way / To:* "approach[ed]" (so *OED* 25h, the only example cited).
  Some Philistine Lords: Verity observes that *lords* occurs often in *SA.*

483–85. *by this:* "by now" (Prince, *Samson Agonistes*); so also 266.
  utmost: "extreme limit" (*OED* 5); cf. 1153.
  pains: editors gloss as "punishment"; so also 105, 501.

486. *no more...harm:* Verity notes the tragic irony.

487–501. According to Wilkes, Samson rejects his father's plan to ransom him because he believes "he is no more use to God, and freedom on these terms is meaningless" (370). Rajan describes Samson's rejection as "the hero's bleak, fierce knowledge that death in chains is better than death by the fireside," but Rajan also finds "a blind rightness in Samson's fortitude. Manoa is not Satan, but deliverance if it comes must come in some other way" (137). Ferry writes that this passage "is full of contempt so exaggerated that it almost seems to be contempt for speech itself: the loathing in the term 'blab' [495], for example, as if it were the worst, the most ignominious name he could be called" (160). Fogle suggests that Samson's will is here the weakest: "his reasons for refusing [Manoa's offer]... do not bear the marks of real renovation, and he is properly admonished by Manoa against such indulgence in suffering" (192). Gossman instead emphasizes the "spiritual promise" and "honor" in Samson's preference for "earning his own bread even among the Philistines" ("Milton's Samson" 537). Gossman elsewhere writes, "Even though Samson concludes in profound anguish of soul his discussion of ransom with Manoa, his reason as well as his virtue has [*sic*] been manifested and perfected through this trial, this dramatic debate" ("Ransom" 14). See also 472–86n, 495n.

    Spare: "refrain from" (*OED* 6).

    spare: "save," "avoid incurring" (*OED* 7).

489. *pay on:* "continue to pay" (cf. *OED* s.v. *on* adv. 11, and Latin *expendere poenas*).

491. *garrulity:* Charles R. Sumner compares *DocCh: loquacitas* (Patterson, *Works* 17:320, 582).

493. *hainous:* "hateful, odious" (*OED* 1); so also 991.

    fact: "deed" or, perhaps, "evil deed" (*OED* 1a, 1c); so also 736. Le Comte (174) compares *PL* 9.928–29, 10.1.

495. *blab:* "tell-tale," "revealer of secrets" (so *OED* 1); cf. *Mask* 138. Adams cites this word to illustrate how Milton inserts "occasional contemptuous colloquialisms" so as to "clash very finely" with *SA*'s "strong, stiff, dignified idiom" (191). Ferry also detects "loathing" in this term, "as if it were the worst, the most ignominious name he could be called" (160). See also 574 and 487–501n.

496–97. A tetrameter line followed by an alexandrine. With Tonson's edition of 1713 and Warton, some editors have transferred *But I* from the start of 497 to the end of 496, making both lines iambic pentameter. Percival discusses the grounds for each reading.

    mark: Percival suggests that Milton was "perhaps thinking" of those who had received the mark of the beast "upon their foreheads, or in their hands" (Rev. 14:11, 16:2, 20:4); he compares the "different signification" of both the "mark upon Cain" (Gen. 4:15) and the "mark upon the foreheads of the men that sigh and that cry for all the abominations that be done" (Ezek. 9:4). Cf. 992.

    fool: cf. 201, 203. Percival compares Proverbs 10:8: "a prating fool shall fall"; and Proverbs 29:11: "A fool uttereth all his mind"; see also Proverbs 18:7.

    front: "forehead" (so *OED* 1). Editors commonly emend the first edition's punctuation, replacing the question mark after *front* with an exclamation point.

498–99. *publish'd:* editors gloss as "revealed"; cf. 777. Haller suggests that this passage may contain an autobiographical allusion: "in Samson's fall Milton expresses his feeling concerning the experience he had been a part of, the self-defeat of God's Englishman" (210).

    Weakly: see 50, 834.

500. *Gentiles:* see 150.

    Parables: the plural suggests that Milton alludes to several myths. Editors agree that one is the story of Tantalus, who, for revealing divine secrets, was condemned to torture in hell (so Ovid, *Ars Amatoria* 2.603; Euripides, *Orestes* 10; and Natale Conti, *Mythologiae* 6.18). Cf. *PL* 2.614. There may also be an allusion to Prometheus; cf. Aeschylus, *Prometheus Bound* 152–54, 349–76, and the catastrophe (Parker, *Milton's Debt* 181); Horace associates Tantalus with Prometheus in *Epodes* 17.66 (Osgood 80). See 501n s.v. *confin'd.* Hanford comments: "The cloak of Prometheus and Tantalus evidently refuses to fit the less majestic Hebrew Titan" ("*Samson Agonistes*" 184). Gossman agrees that "possibly Milton alludes to Prometheus as well as Tantalus when he has Samson blame himself" but she does not find this comparison fruitful: "The parallels between *Samson Agonistes* and *Prometheus Bound* are almost entirely structural, and the motivation of the two heroes is so different that the one possible point of likeness is negligible" ("Milton's Samson" 535). Parker adds that in these lines Samson "reflects that his suffering thus far may be insufficient"—and so answers, indirectly, "Manoa's previous comment [430–33] on unmerited punishment" (*Milton's Debt* 37).

501. *thir:* "the hell in which they—pagans—believe" (Verity).

   abyss: editors gloss as "hell, infernal regions, Tartarus."

   horrid: Parker glosses as "dreadful" ("Variorum"); so also 1542. Grieve writes, "Note the force of *horrid*. In Milton it nearly always includes a reference to Latin *horridus*, bristling."

   pains: "punishment[s]" (*OED* 1).

   confin'd: "fasten[ed]," "[kept] in place," or "banish[ed]" (*OED* 4b, 3). A noun (here, *pains*) both preceded and followed by an adjective is a Miltonic mannerism; e.g., 572, 672, 699; Parker ("Variorum") suggests the line could thus read: "A sin that Gentiles condemn to Tartarus (as in the case of Tantalus) and to horrid, confined punishment (as in the case of Prometheus)." However, editors who comment on this line (e.g., Percival; Wyatt and Collins; Blakeney; Grieve) make *confin'd* agree grammatically with *sin* (499) but agree in sense with *sinner* (understood from *sin*). Warburton (in Newton) suggests that "Milton had here in his eye" Virgil's *Aeneid* 6.617–19: "sedet aeternumque sedebit / infelix Theseus; Phlegyasque miserrimus omnis / admonet et magna testatur voce per umbras"; "hapless Theseus sits and evermore shall sit, and Phlegyas, most unblest, gives warning to all and with loud voice bears witness amid the gloom."

502–15. Manoa, mistakenly, fears that Samson is contemplating suicide, and the passage thus shows Milton's awareness of the long controversy about this problem in Christian hermeneutics. Allen finds Manoa's remark ironic: "By warning Samson against suicide, he puts the thought in his mind" ("Idea as Pattern" 84, 86). See 507–8, 521–22, 575, 630, 650, and 1664–67n. Krouse writes, "This whole conception of a repentant Samson was an extra-biblical Christian theory distributed widely throughout hermeneutic literature" (104). But Gilbert objects that Manoa's exhortation is abruptly introduced, one of a series of "peculiarities" that he believes suggest *SA* was not fully revised before publication ("Is *Samson Agonistes*" 102, 105).

   On Manoa's thought here, Parker ("Variorum") compares several passages from the divorce tracts: *DDD,* "which of *Jobs* afflictions were sent him with that law, that he might not use means to remove any of them if he could?" (Patterson, *Works* 3:425); also *DDD,* "God sends remedies, as well as evils; under which he who lies and groans, that may lawfully acquit himselfe, is accessory to his own ruin" (Patterson, *Works* 3:495); also *DDD,* "Let not therfore the frailty of man goe on thus inventing needlesse troubles to it self, to groan under the fals imagination of a strictnes never impos'd from above; enjoying that for duty which is an impossible & vain supererogating" (Patterson, *Works* 3:509); and *Tetr,* "Were it a particular punishment inflicted through the anger of God upon a person, or upon a land, no law hinders us in that regard, no law but bidds us remove it if we can…to bear with patience, and to seek effectuall remedies, implies no contradiction" (Patterson, *Works* 4:78). Verity quotes both *Areop,* "Why should we then affect a rigor contrary to the manner of God and of nature" (Patterson, *Works* 4:320), and Milton's condemnation of a "perverse hatred of self" in *DocCh* (Patterson, *Works* 17:201).

502. *contrite:* accent the second syllable, "as always in Milton" (Verity).

503. *in:* "in regard to, in the matter of" (Parker, "Variorum").
      affliction: "mortification," "self-infliction of religious discipline" (*OED* 1 [from 1628]). Parker adds, "there is the implication of 'casting down' in this word; see 501 and cf. *PL* 1.186; 4.939; etc. The sense of the line: 'Do nothing to punish yourself'" ("Variorum").

505. *avoid:* according to Gossman, Manoa forgets "that true contrition does not seek to avoid punishment" ("Milton's Samson" 537).

506. Parker wonders, "Is Manoa echoing Samson's words (373)?" ("Variorum").
      execution: "infliction of punishment" (*OED* 8).
      high disposal: "management, *esp.* divine control" (*OED* s.v. *disposal* 1); cf. 210. Le Comte (85) notes that the phrase occurs also in *TKM* (Patterson, *Works* 5:3).

507–8. *exact:* "enforce the payment of" (*OED* 1); cf. 788.
      penal forfeit: "payable…as a penalty" (so *OED* s.v. *penal* d). See 502–15n.

509–10. *quit thee all his debt:* i.e., "release you from (payment of) all the debt due him," "remit to you (dative) all his debt" (so *OED* s.v. *quit* 4). Cf. *PL* 4.51–52; editors also compare *Merchant of Venice* 4.1.381: "To quit the fine for one half of his goods." Hill finds here the essence of Manoa's temptation: he sinfully "presumes that Samson's mission is over and that God has no further need of his services, and he asks his son to *act* on this assumption" (160).

   approves: Parker glosses as "commends, pronounces to be good" (cf. 421) and/or "tests, tries" ("Variorum").

512. One example would be David (Ps. 51; 2 Sam. 12), according to Keightley (*Poems*), Percival, and Verity; another would be Hezekiah (2 Kings 20:1–6), according to Verity and Jerram.

513. *death as due:* cf. 1225.

514. *Which argues:* editors gloss as "which (attitude) proves, indicates" (with "him to be" understood). Cf. 1193.
   over-just: cf. *DDD:* "the great Law-giver . . . never likes when mortall men will be vainly presuming to out strip his justice" (Patterson, *Works* 3:490).

515. Editors gloss as "displeased with himself more for the offence against himself (i.e., through his failure) than for the offence against God (through disobedience)."

516–17. The construction poses difficulty for editors. Keightley (*Poems*) puts a period after *means* and makes the rest of the sentence an interrogation: "Reject not then what(ever) means (may be) offered. Who knows" etc. Following Hurd (in Todd), Percival, Wyatt and Collins, Edmund K. Chambers, et al. instead read: "Reject not then (those) offered means (which), who knows but God" etc. Verity and Grieve read: "Reject not then (such) offered means as God—who knows?—may have set," with *means* as the object of *set*. Roy Battenhouse (in a letter to Parker) finds "deliberate ambiguity" in the passage, with a second meaning "imbedded prophetically" but not really understood by the speaker, so that the passage becomes a commentary on the meaning of *Nazarite:* "Reject not what the concept 'offered' means, for may it not mean that, in whatever God sets before us, we acknowledge Him as setting out before us to lead us to our spiritual homeland?" (Parker, "Variorum"). Cf. 519 (*off'rings*).
   who knows / But: cf. *PL* 9.1146, 10.787–88.

517–18. *set before us:* "put before [us] for use" (*OED* 18c; cf. 1624 and *PR* 3.380), "made it our task" (Keightley, *Poems*), "proposed to us" (Church), or "placed within our reach" (Percival). Madsen suggests that these lines have "Christian overtones" (197).

 Home: cf. 1733.

 his sacred house: "the Tabernacle" (Parker, "Variorum"). See 1674 (*Sanctuary*), and cf. *PL* 1.496.

520. *vows renew'd:* presumably the Nazarite vows; Parker ("Variorum") notes that there was an elaborate ceremony prescribed for renewal by one who had violated them (Num. 6:9–12). See also 31n, 318n, 634n, 1199n.

521–31. Woodhouse writes, "here a second step is taken" in Samson's recovery ("*Samson Agonistes*" 164); for the first step, see 373n. Bush similarly suggests that Samson's reaction to Manoa's offer "marks another upward step in his relations with himself and God" ("John Milton" 509n). Cf. 410–19, 448–71, and for Samson's one relapse, according to Bush, see 606–51n. Rajan (133) suggests that the first lines of this speech are "redeemed" at 1169–73.

 implore: see 512. Adams comments on the passage's syntax: Milton "derives some fine effects from a mode of writing English as if it enjoyed the grammatical advantages of Latin or Greek.... These clauses, strung loosely and episodically together, audacious and blustering in content but aimless and weakly extended far beyond English usage without any major verb at all (unless one supplies a verb for the subordinate clause 'when *I was* in strength'), may achieve dramatic propriety" (192–93). Church proposes that 522–40 would seem to be one long and complicated sentence (despite the period at 531), with the protasis, or introductory clause, ending in 531 and containing two verbs, *excell'd* (523) and *walk'd about* (530); various clauses beginning with *great in hopes* (523) depend on the second of these verbs.

524. On the prosody, see 122n.

 magnanimous: "heroic for God's greater glory" (Shawcross, *Complete English Poetry*).

525. *birth from Heav'n foretold:* so also 23.

 exploits: cf. 32, 1221, 1492, and *PL* 2.111 (see Le Comte 45, 174). Percival accents the second syllable.

526. *instinct:* "impulse, prompting" (*OED* 1); so also 1545; cf. 223, 422, and *PL* 10.263. Percival and Verity accent the second syllable.

    proof: Parker find this perhaps reminiscent of the "proven knight" of the romances ("Variorum").

527–28. *acts indeed heroic:* Steadman notes that Samson compares himself to the giants of Numbers 13:33 who in the Hebrew text are called Nephilim; the only other occurrence of this word in the Bible is in the account of the giants of Genesis 6:4, who were often regarded as false types of heroic virtue ("'Men of Renown'" 584–85). See 1272n. Parker comments on the wordplay in "acts in*deed*"; he thinks the wording of this boast makes us doubt it ("Variorum"). Le Comte (174) compares the "heroic acts" in *PR* 1.216. See 529n.

    Sons of Anac: "the Anakim"; see 148n, 1080n, and cf. the spelling *Anak* in 1080. Rosedale believes that Milton here "thinks of the triumph of the late King's sons" (163).

    famous now: Church asserts that this description probably does not belong to the "Sons of *Anac*"; but editors disagree whether it belongs to *I* (Church; Verity) or to *acts* (Wyatt and Collins; Blakeney; Grieve).

    blaz'd: "made famous" (so *OED*); editors also gloss as "proclaimed, trumpeted," hence "made widely known"; cf. *Arc* 74; *Ps 86* 43; *Ps 136* 5.

529. *Fearless of danger:* Tillyard (*Milton* 297) writes that, in context, this phrase means "criminally slack and negligent," adding that Samson is guilty of "mental slackness," like the Israelites he condemns (241–50, 265–67, but cf. 268–76n). Hanford identifies this failure with classical hubris and compares it with Mark Antony's fault ("*Samson Agonistes*" 184; see also below s.vv. *petty God*). A. B. Chambers suggests that Samson was never truly heroic before the play begins, "for the fearless man is a fool, either ignorant of danger or presumptuously proud. The second of these causes is the relevant one here" (318); see 532. Bowra similarly traces Samson's fall to his pride: "Samson's feeble submission to Dalila is due immediately to a weakness of the flesh, but this rises from a weakness of the spirit, which assailed him when in the flush of victories he ceased to remember that he was only a man" (119).

    petty God: editors and commentators offer various origins for this phrase. Percival thinks the notion more Greek than Jewish. Hanford agrees: "Samson describes his behavior in terms of the Greek *hybris*, the arrogant pride of mortals who have forgotten their true position with relation to the gods" (*Poems*). Buchanan instead argues that the expression is "pure Italian" (214); Thaler is reminded of Shakespeare's *Julius Caesar* 1.2.135 ("Shakespearian Element" 148); and Carson finds the passage "remarkably reminiscent of St. Augustine's description of those for whom the Sun is not risen" (175). Krouse notes that Samson's undue pride was introduced into the story by Josephus (*Antiquities of the Jews* 5.8.9), and as a reason for Samson's fall it was repeated by many late writers (83, 99). See 532.

531. *my affront:* editors gloss as "an encounter with me, to meet me (face to face)"; Hunter suggests, "my confronting attitude"; Grieve writes, "to stand up to me."

    affront: editors gloss as "attack, assault, hostile encounter" (so *OED* 3). Cf. 343–44.

532. The apodosis begins (Church); see 521–31n. Cf. the clergy "swoln with pride" in *HistBr* (Patterson, *Works* 10:111), and the conquerors in *PR* 3.81. See also 572n.

533. Dunster (in Todd) quotes Fairfax's translation of Tasso's *Gerusalemme liberata* 4.26.2: "snares, of looks; trains of alluring speech."

    fallacious: "deceitful," "deceptive" (*OED* 2); cf. 320; Le Comte (138) also compares *Eikon:* "a sentence faire . . . but fallacious" (Patterson, *Works* 5:137).

    venereal trains: editors gloss as "snares of love (Venus)," or "tricks or artifices associated with sexual desire" (see *OED* s.v. *train* 1b, 2). Cf. 932; cf. also 388–89, 536. To Martin W. Sampson, Milton's use of the word *venereal* "shows the futility of rigid objections to anachronism. It would be idle to object to the adjective, which, nevertheless, presupposes the noun [Venus] whose use would be an anachronism." Wyatt and Collins compare *Macbeth* 4.3.117–19: "Devlish Macbeth / By many of these trains hath sought to win me / Into his power."

534. *Softn'd:* B. A. Wright emends to make this two distinct syllables, as the rhythm would seem to require. Cf. 540.

    voluptuous life: Parker ("Variorum") notes that the phrase occurs also in *HistBr* (Patterson, *Works* 10:74).

535. The construction: "I fell...(so as) at length to lay" (Percival; Blakeney), or "so softened as to lay" (Verity). On 535–37, Todd, Mitford, and Browne compare Spenser's *The Faerie Queene* 2.6.14.6–7: "She set beside, laying his head disarm'd / In her loose lap, it softly to sustaine." Editors also cite Judges 16:19 and *PL* 9.1059–62. Huntley writes, "This vision of himself as a sinner, not as one sinned against by God or nature, releases Samson from his inner blindness and begins his slow progress toward inner freedom" (135).

    hallow'd pledge: his hair; cf. 378, 1144. Percival reads as hendiadys for "the hallowed pledge of my head" (see also 105n).

536. *lascivious:* "inciting to lust" (*OED* 1b); Wyatt and Collins call "lascivious lap" an example of hypallage or transferred epithet; see 552n.

    lap: see 537n.

537. *Concubine:* Krouse writes: "the question most often discussed in the Renaissance was whether Dalila had been Samson's wife or his concubine" (76). Jerram suggests this word is "here used for 'partner of my bed,' without any special significance." Lockwood (s.v. *concubine*) proposes instead that Dalila is Samson's "secondary wife" with an inferior legal status, "a kept mistress." Cf. "The strumpet flatteries" (*RCG* [Patterson, *Works* 3:276]) and "the Harlot-lap / Of *Philistean Dalilah*" (*PL* 9.1060–61). Milton's notes on *Concubinatus* in his *ComBk* appear to throw no light on this passage (Patterson, *Works* 18:152–53).

    who shore: Parker observes that in Judges 16:19 "Dalila calls for someone else to shave off Samson's hair"; Milton's change, he concludes, causes the narrative to gain "in dramatic effectiveness" (*Milton's Debt* 8). McCall both recalls that "Freud denotes hair-cutting a dream symbol of castration" and notes that Samson emphasizes that he has sacrificed his manhood in submitting to Dalila (e.g., 408, 410, 417); she concludes, "Milton himself desired to infer the dissolution of Samson's sexual powers" (59).

    me: editors gloss as an ethical dative, "from me (to my hurt)"; cf. 439.

538. *Like:* cf. 1403.

    Weather: "castrated ram" (so *OED* 1), but *eunuch* is perhaps connoted; see 537n s.vv. *who shore*. Prince writes, "often used depreciatingly" (*Samson Agonistes*); Parker describes Samson's self-contempt as "scathing" ("Variorum").

Several commentators compare *Julius Caesar* 4.1.19–26 (e.g., George Coffin Taylor 194). Bush (*Milton*) compares *Merchant of Venice* 4.1.114. Parker adds that " 'Bell-wether' may be implied, although this would add the idea of a leader who talked too much" ("Variorum").

all my precious fleece: Meadowcourt (in Newton) glosses, "*of* all my precious fleece" (so also Stebbing).

539–40. *ridiculous:* cf. 131, 1361, 1501; see 131n.

despoil'd, / Shav'n, and disarm'd: Buchanan (139) suggests that these are disgraces to knighthood: *Shav'n* connotes, beyond its obvious meaning, the head of such a recreant as Braggadocchio (*The Faerie Queene* 5.3.37.5) or of a bondslave (*The Faerie Queene* 5.2.6.7). Grieve adds that *shaven* is "more contemptuous than 'shorn.' " *Shav'n* may also mean "castrated"; see 537n s.vv. *who shore.* On *despoil'd,* cf. 469.

disarm'd: with this word, Ricks objects, the simile of the shorn sheep, so admirably built up (537–40), "is virtually annihilated" (*Milton's Grand Style* 53–54).

541–46. For the Nazarite vow of abstinence see 31n, 318n. Commentators disagree about the efficacy of these remarks by the Chorus. Verity explains that the Chorus's goal is "to mitigate Samson's extreme self-contempt by reminding him that if he had been weak and self-indulgent in one thing, he had been temperate and strong in another." Huntley finds fault with the Chorus for such "protective maneuvers.... It is as though a man should finally see the blackness of his soul and cry out, 'I have betrayed my father for a whore.' Then his true friends cluster around to say, 'Well, don't worry; at least you never smoked or drank' " (138). Of the speech and 553–57, Gilbert remarks: "The Chorus do not allude to Samson's words [521–40].... It seems as though Milton had written various passages on topics of interest to himself—such as temperance—and suitable for the theme of *Samson,* but had not carefully articulated them" ("Is *Samson Agonistes*" 102–3). But Rajan suggests that this exchange reinforces "Samson's progress from the physical to the symbolic recognition... by pointing out how the lower teetotalism is meaningful only in conjunction with the higher abstemiousness" (132). Mueller similarly thinks this exchange hints at "the mystery of the Nazarite's intimate communion with the divinity" by associating purity with water and impurity with wine: "Impurity is disorder and excitement. 'The dancing ruby...' [543] contrasts with the limpid tranquility of the 'cool crystalline stream' [546]. The liquor is 'turbulent' [552] whereas the brook has direction and flows 'towards the Eastern ray' [548]" (*"Pathos"* 165–66). See 553–57n. For Milton's views on abstinence and drunkenness, see *Tetr* (Patterson, *Works* 4:132); on the poem's dietary imagery, see 633–51n s.v. *nursling*.

543–44. Parker cites these lines as an example of a passage "where the exact meaning is unclear (and where one meaning or another emerges with changes in punctuation)." See also 516–20, 652–59, 701–4, 982–84, 1156–57, 1443–44, 1468–71, 1616–19, 1623–24, 1646–52, 1663–68, 1697–1707, and 1711–12 (*"Notes"* 698). E.g., Keightley inserts a comma between *Rubie* and *Sparkling* (*Poems*); Tickell, Verity, Edmund K. Chambers, William Aldis Wright, et al. insert this comma but also omit the comma after *Sparkling*.

    dancing Rubie: cf. Proverbs 23:31: "Look not thou upon the wine when it is red, when it giveth his colour in the cup, when it moveth itself aright." Editors also compare *Mask* 671–72 and *PL* 5.633. Peck cites this word to illustrate Milton's "exceeding *bold*" figures of speech: here, he notes, the color of wine is a metonymy for the wine itself (sig. Q3v).

    flavor: "aroma" (Lockwood), or "savour," "element in the taste...which depends on the co-operation of the sense of smell" (*OED* 2). Parker also glosses as "golden color," because Milton apparently here distinguishes *flavor* from both *taste* and *smell;* Parker adds, "Latin *flavor* ('yellowness') is a correctly formed word, though without classical authority. Possibly Milton's recollection of Prov. 23.31 (*Ne intuearis vinum quando flavescit*) led him to use the word in what he may have imagined to be its etymological sense (*OED* 2, note)" (*"Variorum"*).

545. *cheers...Gods and men:* cf. Judges 9:13: "And the vine said unto them, Should I leave my wine, which cheereth God and man...?"; also Psalm 104:15: "And wine that maketh glad the heart of man." Edmund K. Chambers calls this "a curious instance of the mixture of scriptural and pagan in Milton's thought," because he apparently, "with the feasts of Olympus in his mind," turns *God* into *Gods*. Cf. *Arc* 67 and *Mask* 444. But Warburton (in Newton) thinks that Milton, recalling the context of the passage in Judges, alludes to the hero-gods of the heathen; Keightley also points out that in the original Hebrew the substantive in this passage is plural, *gods,* and that Milton is carefully accurate (*Poems*).

546. *Crystalline:* "clear and transparent like crystal" (so *OED* 2). Verity writes that Milton always accents the second syllable (as in *PL* 3.482; 6.772; 7.271).

547–49. With ruby-colored wine (543) Samson contrasts pure water touched by the morning sun; see 541–46n. Commentators discuss possible origins for this speech and admire its imagery. Percival (echoed by later editors) discovers here an allusion to Ezekiel 47:1, 8–9: "behold, waters issued out from under the threshold of the house eastward:...These waters issue out toward the east...which being brought forth into the sea, the waters shall be healed...and every thing shall live whither the river cometh." Thyer (in Newton) suggests instead Tasso's *Del Mondo Creato* 3.133–40, which says that, of all pleasant waters, the most wholesome is that which springs out of the clayey soil in the face of the rising sun. For another possible source, cf. Burton's *Anatomy of Melancholy* 2.2.1.1 (Carey, *Complete Shorter Poems*). Bodkin recalls hearing lines 547–51 spoken on the stage: "Amidst the remorse and anger of Samson's speeches this passage...stood forth poignantly. One felt peace descend for the moment on the suffering hero, as his thoughts wandered back over the pure pleasures of his life" (109). To Menzies, this speech is the only passage in the entire play that "attracts the eye by its brightness and serenity" while also evoking "in a distant way...the tempered raptures of Milton's earlier days" (82); Cumberland also cites these lines (547–52) as a passage of "striking beauty" (337). Clark notes that the "keen delight in nature" that Samson seems to take here is absent from the account in Judges (94). Carey cites this passage to illustrate how Milton often — and, as here, elaborately — disrupts English word order by promoting adverbial phrases to the start of a sentence (*Complete Shorter Poems* 334–35).

548. *Against:* "towards" (*OED* II.5 [1634]).
  Eastern ray: editors gloss as "rising sun." Percival, followed by other editors, suggests that *Eastern* alludes to the holy waters in the vision of Ezekiel; cf. Ezekiel 47:1, 8, 9. Percival also quotes Burton's *Anatomy of Melancholy* 2.2.1.1: "Rain water is purest...next to it fountain water that riseth in the east and runneth eastward, from a quick running spring." Verity adds that Sir Thomas Browne's *Vulgar Errors* 6, 7 includes various contemporary claims about the value of facing eastward, including the footnote, "The waters of those springs are held to bee most medicinal (of all others) which rise in the easte: hence in

the west parts of England, to difference such from all others, they call them by a significant name, East-up-springs, intimating by that proper name, a proper kind of excellencye, above other springs." Cf. *L'All* 59.

pure: "clear, transparent," or "unadulterated" (*OED* 1c, 4), or "bright" (so Church; Grieve); cf. 1727; see 541–46n. Wyatt and Collins note, "without a comma after 'pure' the meaning seems to be 'purified by the touch' or 'rendered translucent and pure by the touch.'" The period in the first edition (Patterson, *Works,* has a comma in error) should probably be omitted.

549. *touch...rod:* editors (e.g., Percival; Grieve; Hunter) suggest a possible reminiscence of Exodus 17:5–6 and Numbers 20:11, where Moses smites a rock with his rod and water flows. Cf. 581–82.

ætherial: "celestial" or "impalpable" (*OED* 2, 4). Parker ("Variorum") notes that the spelling in *PL* (twenty occurrences) is *ethereal;* cf. *Æthereal* (*PR* 2.121) and *Ætherial* (*PR* 1.163, 3.28).

Heav'ns: Parker writes that this "probably" should be emended to "'Heavens,' though the reading of this line offers problems" ("Notes" 693).

fiery rod: "the ray of the sun" (Lockwood, s.v. *fiery;* not in *OED*). Cf. Euripides, *Suppliant Women* 650: Λαμπρὰ μὲν ἀκτὶς ἡλίου, κανὼν σαφής, / Εβαλλε γαῖαν; "Bright the sun's beam, true-levelled shaft of light, / Smote on the earth" (Lucas 184). Hunter suggests, too, an allusion to "the rod of Moses which made water start into view out of the dark bosom of the rock." Cf. also *Mask* 339 and *PL* 3.583–86.

550. *clear milkie juice:* editors think this an odd expression for "fresh or sweet water" but try to explain it. The word *juice*—although to Keightley (*Poems*) and Browne "a strong oxymoron"—can be glossed as "liquid" (*OED* 3) but can also be justified as contrasting water with the juice of the "grape" (551). For *milkie,* editors recall the "nectarous draughts between, from milkie stream, / Berrie or Grape" of *PL* 5.306–7 and conclude that Milton means "sweet (as milk)"; because Milton uses the adjective *clear* ("translucent, free from sediment"), *milkie* may refer, not to the appearance, but rather to the taste or quality of the water. But Verity suggests, "*milky* might point to the white froth one often sees in the side-currents of a brook." Parker ("Variorum") notes that *OED* 4 offers the additional possibilities of "soft," or "gentle" (said of persons), which would

provide a contrast with the "turbulent liquor" of the grape (552). Carey (*Complete Shorter Poems*) suggests as a possible source Song of Solomon 5:12: " 'doves by the rivers of water, washed with milk,' where the last phrase can be translated 'Splashed by the milky water'"; Carey also compares Sir John Davies, *Orchestra* 52, where hills are called, "The Earth's great duggs: for every wight is fed / With sweet fresh moisture from them issuing." Also, Josephus describes as "sweet" the water of the spring at Lehi (*Antiquities of the Jews* 5.8.9). Bodkin argues that "the aptness of the word must spring, not from any appeal to the eye, but from some overtone of organic emotional response," and as a clue she suggests that "stepdame Nature" can show poets "the breasts of a mother's tenderness" (109–10). Parker further notes in the Christian literature (e.g., Augustine, *De agone Christiano* 33), milk connotes simple faith ("Variorum").

551. *refresht:* "refresh[ed] oneself," "[took] refreshment" (*OED* 7 dates this meaning from 1650 as applying to drinking). Church suggests it is a participle dependent on *drank;* Verity writes that it is parallel to *allaying.* For other words or phrases that Milton seems to use uniquely, see 373, 424, 803 (Prince, *Samson Agonistes* 108).

    nor…grape: Percival compares Ovid, *Metamorphoses* 15.322–23: "Clitorio quicumque sitim de fonte levavit, / vina fugit, gaudetque meris abstemius undis"; "Whoever slakes his thirst from Clitor's spring shuns the wine-cup and abstemiously enjoys pure water only." Verity and Edmund K. Chambers find it "perhaps worth noting that Milton himself seldom drank wine" ("rarely dranke between meales" is Aubrey's testimony [Darbishire, *Early Lives* 6]). In *DocCh,* Milton defines temperance as consisting first in sobriety or "abstinence from *immoderate* eating and drinking" (Patterson, *Works* 17:213; emphasis added). See also the "rule of not too much" in *PL* 11.531–32.

552. *turbulent:* "causing disturbance or confusion, making trouble" (Lockwood), "having a disturbing effect" (so *OED* 1b); cf. 1040. Wyatt and Collins identify "turbulent liquor" as an example of hypallage, "consisting of a transference of attributes from their proper subjects to others"; see 536n.

    fumes: "something which 'goes to the head' and clouds the faculties," or "a noxious vapour supposed formerly to rise to the brain from the stomach" (*OED* 6, 4). Cf. *PL* 9.1050.

553–57. Parker observes that in 541–46 the Chorus addresses Samson; here it speaks of him as though he were absent ("Variorum"). Edmund K. Chambers suggests that "this rebuke is obviously less dramatic than didactic, intended for the roisterers of the Restoration." Regarding the emphasis on *strongest* in 553–54, Landor objects that "wines were the 'strongest drinks' in those times; perhaps they might have been made stronger by the infusion of herbs and spices" (5:300). Parker notes that Samson's Nazarite vows involve abstinence from any kind of wine ("Variorum"); for the prohibition of both wine and "strong drink," see, e.g., Judges 13:4, 7, 14; Leviticus 10:9; Luke 1:15. For Milton's own views on temperance, see 551n. According to Percival (xlvi), 553 has a pyrrhic in the second foot, a spondee in the third.

556. *Champion:* Parker glosses as "one who fights on behalf of another"; he adds, "Milton's concept of Samson as God's champion (so also in 705, 1751) was solidly based on the Christian tradition" ("Variorum"). See 1152, where Harapha is spoken of as Dagon's champion, and cf. 1 Samuel 17:4, 51. To Nash, this idea (plus the ideas of Samson as deliverer and as a prisoner of love) suggests the inclusion in the poem of many words and themes from Renaissance chivalric poetry (24); see 468–71n. Cf. *PL* 1.763–66.

above compare: editors gloss as "beyond comparison" (*OED* B.7); cf. *PL* 6.705.

557. *liquid:* Latin: *liquidus;* "clear, transparent" (*OED* II.2), or "flowing" (Lockwood).

558. *temperance:* Parker ("Variorum") writes *self-restraint* (not *moderation* or *sobriety*); see *OED* 1b. Cf. 637.

compleat: "fully equipped"; cf. *PR* 4.283.

560–61. Note the military metaphor again; see 235n, 403–5n, 845–46n, 906n. Cf. *Areop:* "that single endeavour they knew would be but a fond labour; to shut and fortifie one gate against corruption, and be necessitated to leave others round about wide open" (Patterson, *Works* 4:317).

What boots it: editors gloss as "What use is it, or good does it do?"; cf. *Lyc* 64–65.

562. *Effeminatly:* "weakly" (Lockwood) and/or "through degrading passion for a woman" (so *OED* 2, with a question mark); cf. 410.

563–76. Tillyard sums up this passage: "That is Samson in the Protestant-Stoic citadel; utterly isolated, for his friends are powerless to help him; hard pressed but still unconquered" (*Miltonic Setting* 86). Rudrum writes here that Samson, above all, desires to be useful: "Born and raised a hero, he can think only in heroic terms" (37). Blakeney notes in 563 "the piling up of epithets," which he calls "very effective," and compares 365, 417.

   disheartn'd: B. A. Wright emends to make three distinct syllables.

563–68. Editors find an autobiographical overtone in this passage: e.g., Church, Collins (who writes it "must be obvious to everyone" [8–9]), Jerram, and Hedley Vicars Ross (61) and Grieve (who both call it "intensely autobiographical"). Thyer (in Newton) comments, "The similitude of their circumstances...has enrich'd the poem with several very pathetic descriptions of the misery of blindness." Rosedale goes the furthest with this argument: "This could never be, strictly speaking, said of Samson, though true of Milton" (164). Bullough and Bullough concede that "Milton may sometimes have thought of himself thus," but they also recall John Aubrey's description of Milton as a cheerful, social man who had many visitors in his later years (see Darbishire, *Early Lives* 5–7).

564–65. *useful:* some editors (e.g., Keightley, *Poems*) replace the comma after this word with a question mark.

   wherein: Parker accents the first syllable ("Variorum"); cf. 780.

   serve: for the possible pun with *servile* (574), see 411–19n.

   work: governed by *serve* understood, which by zeugma means "perform" (Keightley, *Poems;* Percival). On Samson's feeling of uselessness, Parker ("Variorum") compares *DDD:* "from the depth of sadnes and distresse, utterly unfitted...to serve God or man" (Patterson, *Works* 3:510); also *Tetr:* "such a dull dejection, as renders him either infamous, or useles to the service of God and his Country" (Patterson, *Works* 4:121).

   imposed: some editors (e.g., Tickell; Bohn) replace the comma after this word with a question mark.

566. *But to sit idle:* Percival writes, "grammatically depending upon 'serve' or 'be useful,' understood in an ironical sense." Bullough and Bullough call it "a fate which no doubt Milton dreaded" (54). Manoa echoes this in 1500.

567. *burdenous drone:* "burdensome" or "oppressive" (so *OED* 1b) "idler," "sluggard" (*OED* 2). Cf. 54. Probably pronounce *burdenous* as a disyllable; Parker proposes *burd'nous* ("Notes" 693). For knowledge of bees in the Renaissance, see Bartholomaeus, who writes, "Drones be without sting, as it were unperfect bees, and be servaunts to the very bees: and very Bees commaundeth them to worke, and stingeth, and punisheth without pity the Drones that be slow in working, and also in bre[e]ding" (Batman sig. Rrr1v).
    gaze: see 34.

568. *redundant:* "superfluous" (*OED* 1), and/or "exuberant," "abounding to excess or fulness," "copious" (so *OED* 2a), and/or the Latin sense of "waving, flowing" (Verity; Hughes, *Complete Poems* and *John Milton;* et al.). Wyatt and Collins note that "this and the next two lines, together with what Manoa says in lines 586–7, are the first indication not only that Samson's hair has been allowed to grow long again, but also that his strength has returned to him with the new growth." Cf. 1354–55, 1496, and see Judges 16:22: "Howbeit the hair of his head began to grow again after he was shaven." Whiting calls attention to the Geneva Bible's marginal comment on this verse: "Yet had he not his strength againe, til he had called upon God, and reconciled himselfe" (*"Samson Agonistes"* 216). See also 1646–59n.

569. *Robustios:* "stout and strong or healthy-looking" (so *OED* 1b), "vigorous, flourishing" (Lockwood). Edmund K. Chambers (144) thinks that Milton may be recalling *Hamlet* 3.2.9: "a robustious periwig-pated fellow."
    clustring: cf. *PL* 4.303 and *Mask* 54.

570. *Vain:* Parker comments: "because Samson has no hope of using his strength again in God's work; tragic irony" ("Variorum").
    monument: Percival writes: "merely a memorial of past exploits, and not a pledge of future achievements." Cf. 586–89; Jerram finds an inconsistency here.

571. *sedentary:* "slothful, inactive" (so *OED* 2b), "caused by sitting" (Verity); see 566.

   craze: "impair or break down in health; to render infirm" (so *OED* 5). Cf. *PL* 12.210.

572. *old age:* the phrase recurs in 700, 925, 1487–88; cf. *PL* 11.538. See 938n. Carey argues that Samson's "instant equation of an 'obscure' life in his father's house with a 'contemptible' one" reflects the same "pride" on which he had earlier blamed his downfall (*John Milton* 141). See 532. Hill similarly suggests that Samson out of pride refuses Manoa's offer to return him home: "Samson rejects Manoa's temptation, but he does not *overcome* it. He does the right thing for the wrong reason" (161).

   obscure: Newton emends the comma after this word to a question mark.

573. *earn my bread:* cf. 1260, 1365–67 and see 1261n, 1366n. "A remarkably stubborn small fact of existence and a sign of his character" (Stein, *Heroic Knowledge* 158). "Neither suicide nor sloth are [*sic*] in his mind" (Allen, "Idea as Pattern" 87).

574–76. *draff:* "refuse, dregs" (so *OED* 1a), especially "hogwash" (Browne); cf. *PL* 10.630. Adams cites this word to illustrate how Milton inserts "occasional contemptuous colloquialisms" so as to "clash very finely" with *SA*'s "strong, stiff, dignified idiom" (191). See also 495.

   servile: for the possible pun with *serve* (564), see 411–19n.

   Consume: "destroy" (*OED* 1).

   oft-invocated death: cf. 32, 513, 521–22, 630, 650. See 502–15n.

   Hast'n: Parker suggests that the rhythm requires *Hasten* ("Notes" 693); B. A. Wright also emends this word to *Hasten*.

577. The reading of this line offers difficulty. See 122n. Lockwood suggests the pronunciation "Phil-is´-tine" but notes that elsewhere it is "Phil´-is-tine´."

578. *expresly:* Patterson, *Works,* misspells this word.

   annoy: editors gloss as "molest, injure" (*OED* 4); cf. *PR* 3.365; *PL* 6.369.

579. Jerram writes: "A harsh line, as regards scansion." Edmund K. Chambers (127) calls it "a clear instance" of unstressed rhythm in the middle of the line—although, he adds, forced elisions would sustain the regular iambic meter; he similarly describes 122, 399, 429, 748, 842.

    bed rid: "confined to bed through sickness or infirmity" (*OED* 1); emphasized, in contrast with Samson's "to sit idle" (566).

581–82. See 145n and also Judges 15:18–19. Rajan finds evidence of Manoa's limited understanding "in the use of the fountain image…to suggest outward rather than inward sight, a limited view of regeneration which is reiterated in 1502-[3]" (180–81). Robertson discusses the various images associating Samson with fresh water (323–24).

    From the dry ground: i.e., in Lehi. Editors note that Judges 15:19 (Authorized Version and Vulgate) has, "But God clave an hollow place that was in the jaw, and there came water thereout"; however, Milton follows Josephus (*Antiquities of the Jews* 5.8.9), the Targum, and those others who have taken *Lehi,* the Hebrew word for *jaw,* to mean the name of the place. Cf. Judges 15:9, 14, 17. The phrase "dry ground" (after the Flood) occurs in *PL* 11.861.

    spring: a play on the word. Cf. 584.

    allay: cf. 550. Overlooked by Lockwood.

583–84. *brunt:* "shock, violence" (*OED* 3a), or "heat of an onset" (Lockwood), or "the heat or burden of the battle" (Verity).

    spring: "begin to appear" (so *OED* 7b). Cf. 582.

585. Cf. *Sonn 19* 4–5.

586. *I perswade me so:* editors gloss as "I believe it will be so." Manoa repeats this expression in 1495, where "those locks" (1493) and "to sit idle" (1500) echo 587, 566. Cf. *FInf* 29.

587. *miraculous:* Hughes writes that Milton "in general…did not intend to syncopate many syllables," and thus in this case the *u* should not be elided (*John Milton* 424–25).

588. Editors and commentators discuss the dramatic irony. Mickle suggests that Manoa's hopes are "truly in the spirit and conduct of the Grecian tragedy, in leading on the minds of its heroes, so as in the most natural manner to produce the catastrophe" (403). Muldrow writes that "what is needed now is not the miraculous sort of divine intervention which Manoa has suggested might occur with Samson at home, but for Samson to discover within himself some new light marking God's acceptance of the steps which he has been taking" (188). Gossman finds in Manoa's optimism "limitations like those of Job's friends.... [H]e cannot get beyond the material and prudential outlook" ("Samson, Job" 219). Stein similarly describes Manoa's remark as "a facile hopefulness, all right for a father but impossible for a tragic hero, and it emphasizes again the gap between their moral natures"; Stein adds, "But...Manoa is voicing, for the first time in the drama, the present fact of remaining strength as a fact that belongs to the future as well as the past" (*Heroic Knowledge* 159).

> *not for naught:* Percival notes the "play upon words"; see 1118n.
> *wondrous gifts:* the phrase occurs also in *PL* 12.500 (Le Comte 66).
> *frustrate:* Verity notes that participles ending in *ate* are common in Elizabethan English, equivalent to the Latin ending *atus;* "render[ed] ineffectual" (*OED* 2); cf. 1149.

590–98. *All:* "quite" (*OED* C.2). Editors and commentators isolate this passage for praise. Percival find these lines "The most affecting passage in the drama"; Johnson (*Rambler* 20 July 1751) also compliments this section: "It is not easy to give a stronger representation of the weariness of despondency" (222). Masson lauds "the peculiar melancholy that breathes through this speech..., the singularly sorrowful cadence of the last five lines" (*Poetical Works*). Tillyard comments, "Not only are [these lines] hushed in tone but eight out of the nine are end-stopt in flat contradiction of Milton's supposed invariable habit of sustaining rhythms" (*Studies* 4). Collins asserts, "He would be a bold critic who would offer any other comment on such a passage than reverential silence."

Editors also discuss these lines' autobiographical significance. Newton, Collins ("who can doubt it?"), Percival, et al. are sure that Milton is here speaking in propria persona; "He could not have wrote so well but from his own feeling and experience" (Newton); but see 597n. Menzies (83–84) instead identifies this passage as Samson's "lowest pitch of dejection...in the whole story" and finds here an "echo" of this speech in Satan's words in *PR* 3.203–11; James Waddell Tupper agrees: "This is the nadir of his afflictions" (380). Of Samson's

resignation here, Ellis-Fermor remarks: "though seeming at first glance a rever-
sion to the dejection of the earlier part, [it] is as clearly distinguished from it
prosodically as it is psychologically. This is a slow and even movement—lacking
variation...and strong emphases, but musical and not formless" (151).

As a possible source, Carey (*Complete Shorter Poems*) suggests the exchange
between Jason and Phineus in Apollonius Rhodius's *Argonautica* 2.438–48:
"Assuredly there was then, Phineus, some god who cared for thy bitter woe...and
if too he should bring sight to thine eyes, verily I should rejoice.... Thus he
spake, but Phineus replied to him with downcast look: 'Son of Aeson, that is
past recall, nor is there any remedy hereafter, for blasted are my sightless eyes.
But instead of that may the god grant me death at once, and after death I shall
take my share in perfect bliss.'"

591. Cf. *Sonn* 22 3–4.
   dark: see 2.
   treat: editors gloss as "deal, negotiate" (*OED* 1a); cf. 482.

592. *other light:* see 90–93n.
   continue: "endure"; Parker compares 588 and wonders whether it is an ironic
echo ("Variorum").

593. *double darkness:* Verity explains *double* because it is of blindness and death.
Cf. *Mask* 334.
   nigh at hand: the phrase occurs also in *PR* 1.20.

594. *genial:* "natural," "pertaining to 'genius' or natural disposition" (so *OED* 6);
Prince comments that Samson's genial spirits are his innate vital powers, his will
to live (*Samson Agonistes*). Church, followed by other editors, detects "an allusion
to the Roman notion of a tutelary demon attending on each person, and living
and dying with the life and death of the man." McCall instead suggests that "the
word has a second meaning of 'nuptial' or 'relating to the generative faculties'"
and thus points to Samson's "annihilated masculine powers" (63). Cf. *RCG:*
"the genial power of nature" (Patterson, *Works* 3:235). Cf. *Hamlet* 1.2.133–34
(Verity; Thaler, "Shakespeare and Milton" 84). Verity adds, "Coleridge recol-
lected these lines when he wrote his 'Ode on Dejection.'"

595–98. Pattison senses in these lines the author's own tiredness and "consciousness of decay" (193)—an interpretation that Ker dismisses. To Ker, they are "the noblest lines in English poetry" (58); to Belloc also, "perhaps the strongest thing in the whole poem.... That last line is of oak" (277); to Broadbent, "the most expressive...and the most viable for the reader's experience and imagination" (*Milton* 46). Masson calls the last line "among the most pathetic in the English language" (*Life* 6:673) and is here reminded of *Hamlet* 1.2.129–46 (*Poetical Works*). Thaler instead hears an echo of Macbeth's despair, 5.7.49–50 ("Shakespearian Element" 166).

596. *functions:* "activit[ies] of the intellectual and moral powers" (so *OED* 3b).
     weary of her self: cf. *Tetr:* "weary of himself" (Patterson, *Works* 4:127).

597. To Brinkley, "This line and the following form one of the finest examples of the power of the simple style" (*Samson Agonistes*).
     race of shame: cf. *PL* 12.505. Regarding biographical readings of this exchange, Collins cautions that the sense of this phrase "is not to be pressed too closely, for though in its literal sense it would be applicable to Samson, it could not in its literal sense be applicable to Milton." Mitford compares act 4 of Thomas May's *Tragedie of Cleopatra* (1639): "My race of life and glory is not run" (sig. C12v). Parker comments that the figure is biblical ("Variorum").

598. See 595–98n.
     rest: "lie in death" (so *OED* 1b, with many examples). Percival quotes both Job 3:17: "There the wicked cease from troubling; and there the weary be at rest" (Wyatt and Collins call it "a reminiscence"), and Sophocles, *Women of Trachis* 1173: τοῖς γὰρ θανοῦσι μόχθος οὐ προσγίγνεται; "For with the dead there can be no more toil."

599. *suggestions:* "the act of prompting one to a particular action" or, perhaps, "prompting or incitement to evil" (*OED* 2, 1); cf. *PL* 3.129.

600. *humours black:* editors explain this as a reference to black bile, one of the four chief fluids or cardinal "humours" of ancient physiology, too much of which was

supposed to cause melancholy or extreme depression of spirits. Some editors have long notes here on the four humours (the others: blood, phlegm, and choler) and quote from Burton et al. Milton alludes to this physiology often: see, e.g., Preface 9–10; *Mask* 809; *PL* 11.544. That Manoa ascribes his son's depression partly to physiological causes prompts the imagery of Samson's reply. Cf. also Aeschylus, *Prometheus Bound* 333–35 (Dunster [in Todd]; Fleming).

601–4. Commentators note that it was Milton's own idea to have Manoa try to ransom his son from the Philistines; see 481–86n. Because the fallen hero rejects his father's offer, the chief effect, Carey argues, "is a demonstration of Samson's perversity" (*John Milton* 141). Madsen writes that these lines have "Christian overtones" (197). Hedley Vicars Ross finds instead "an ominous prefiguration of the catastrophe" (121).

602. *timely:* "early" (Percival), or "opportune, seasonable" (*OED* 1, 2; Lockwood 1). On the phrase "timely care" cf. *PL* 10.1057 (Le Comte 67). Nicolson finds "unconscious irony" in Manoa's reference to a "father's timely care" (360).

603. *prosecute:* "follow up, pursue . . . (some action, undertaking, or purpose) with a view to completing or attaining it" (*OED* 1).
    deliverance: Oras identifies this word as one of the poem's dactylic endings that "require the suppression of a vowel between two consonants if they are — in theory or reality — to be reduced to the trochaic norm" (thus, pronounce "deliv′rance"). Oras infers from Milton's use of fewer contractible forms for dactylic endings in *SA* that his technique was becoming "bolder and freer" and that *SA* was likely one of his later works ("Milton's Blank Verse" 168). See also 445, 603, 868, 1361. Manoa's futile efforts to deliver the Deliverer (cf. 1505, 1575) echo ironically Samson's own ironic destiny (Parker, "Variorum"); see, e.g., 40, 225, 246, 274, 279, 292, 1214, 1270.

604. *how else:* "in (some, any) way or manner" (so *OED* V.16).
    mean while: Parker ("Variorum") observes that the adverb echoes the noun (479).
    calm: cf. 964, 1758.

605. Manoa's parting advice turns out ironically, for the words that follow are the great choral outburst against God's injustice (Parker, *Milton's Debt* 162). On Milton's adherence to Aristotle's principles of tragedy, Baum writes, "Manoa's exit does not demand Dalila's entrance.... [E]ach scene follows naturally *after* the one before, though not *from* it, and advances the action in something like due proportion" (362). An early-twentieth-century production of the play by Nugent Monck inserted an intermission at Manoa's departure (Stephenson 915).

    healing words: so also *PL* 9.290. The metaphor, which had been elaborated in *SA* 184–86, is probably Greek in inspiration; see, e.g., Aeschylus, *Prometheus Bound* 180, *Suppliant Maidens* 477 (Collins), *Eumenides* 846 (Percival); Euripides, *Hippolytus* 478: λόγοι θελκτήριοι (Todd; et al.); but Statius et al. have *verba medentia* (Parker, "Variorum").

606–709. Baum suggests that this passage is a kommos (354–55). Parker objects: it is "extremely doubtful... calling only two lyrical passages a *kommos*"; he proposes instead that it is "a simple case of a *stasimon* being preceded by a 'stage lyric'" (*Milton's Debt* 107–8). Parker writes that this practice "is not unusual in Greek tragedy" and cites the precedent of Euripides' *Hecuba* 59–97, where "the monody, sung by Hecuba..., is only seven lines shorter than Samson's, and the *stasimon* which follows is only two lines shorter" than that of Milton's Chorus (108).

606–51. The second μονωδια ("solo"); cf. 1–114. Lucas calls the "lyric" monodies of *SA* Euripidean (116); Timberlake also finds this sudden introduction of a lyrical passage Euripidean in inspiration, which, he says, Milton uses here "to heighten the emotion of Samson in his interview with Manoa" (336). Cf. 80–109n. This latter assertion is echoed by various editors and commentators—including Parker, who adds that Milton's monodies are also indebted to Aeschylus's *Prometheus Bound* and Sophocles' *Oedipus at Coloneus* (*Milton's Debt* 108–9).

    Regarding the versification, Thyer (in Newton) suggests that Milton changed the meter to a rapid, irregular rhythm for fear that the drama would grow "tedious to the reader.... These sudden starts of impatience are very natural to persons in such circumstances, and this rough and unequal measure of the verses is very well suited to it." Lines 606–7, 610, 614 are in falling (trochaic) rhythm, according to Bridges (*Milton's Prosody* 55–56). Beum notes the rhyming in 606,

610–12, 615–16, which, he suggests, Milton uses to heighten the "universal-ized nature of the expression here, as well as its depth.... As soon as the speech turns to a more purely personal note [618], the rhyme vanishes" (179). Per-cival, however, thinks these rhymes "accidental or, at least, of doubtful import" (xlvii). See also the annotations for the individual line numbers in this passage.

On the nature of Samson's suffering, Tillyard writes: "Adam [in *PL*] and Samson both suffer so terribly because they can see no possible course of action; and they are both unaware that because they have searched their souls to the bottom and really know themselves and admit every scruple of guilt they are even now saved men" (*Studies* 37). Bullough and Bullough comment that Samson "is suffering from an 'inverted Hubris' for he is as self-centred in his nullity as he was in his pride" (54). Bush suggests that Manoa's news about his negotia-tions with the Philistines "deepens Samson's misery," and initiates a "prolonged reversal" in the play's "upward movement—which, if wholly steady, might have come to seem contrived" (*John Milton* 197; "John Milton" 510; *Milton* 514). Sadler detects in Samson's speech "evocations of the lassitude of noon-day *acedia*" (202). On 606–32 (cf. 599–601), Hanford comments: "The idea which Milton here develops with somewhat shocking explicitness is obviously the same as that which underlies his conception of catharsis—the idea, namely, that the passions operate in precisely the manner of bodily poisons, which, when they find no outlet, rage destructively within. Samson is given over to pity and fear.... The intensity of [his] pain lasts only so long as he remains inactive. His lyric elaboration of his inward woe is immediately followed by the unexpected visits of his foes" ("*Samson Agonistes*" 188). Hawkins adds that Milton uses "like against like" to cure Samson homeopathically: "he is not cured of sin by opposites, by being freed from prison and regaining sight, as Manoa hopes.... Samson's suffering becomes his cure, blindness the means to inner vision, prison the 'house of Liberty' [949]" (221, 222). Parker finds "exceptional" Milton's "knowledge of medical terminology," here put to "poetical use," which Parker associates with the poet's friendship to Charles Diodati (*Milton* 884).

606. *O:* Keightley compares this interjection with the φεῦ ("alas") of Greek drama, "which did not count in the iambic line" (*Account* 326); see 1268. Parker asserts that 606 is without parallel, metrically, in Milton's other poems ("Vari-orum"). Sprott (132) thinks it difficult to determine whether Milton thought of the line as "trochaic with the last foot catalectic, or as iambic with the first foot catalectic" (see 116n).

607. Weismiller notes this line's "rhythmic strangeness," which he assumes is intended: "but we do well to recognize it as a strangeness produced in the first place by a kind of controlled metrical-rhythmical disorientation, and persisting as a strangeness of proportioning—a complex effect for which the reading of stanzaic verse, even Milton's own stanzaic verse, has hardly prepared us" (136). Edmund K. Chambers suggests that this line is iambic but begins with an anapest (129).

609. Ferry argues that the reader's "peculiar awareness of Samson is encouraged by the way in which his language characteristically calls attention to the presence of his body, usually not by making us visualize its shape...but by making us sense its physical properties and its enclosing limits. Reminders come in the frequent references to parts of the body which are obsessively named without being visually described" (137). Cf. 614; *PL* 6.346.

    brest: Patterson misspells (*Works*); cf. 1722, 1739.

    reins: editors gloss as "kidneys" (the supposed seat of the feelings or affections); Church adds, "including the *membra genitalia.*" Cf. Proverbs 23:16, Psalm 7:9.

610–11. For these rhymes (and 615–16), see 606–51n. Bridges remarks that 610 is in trochaic rhythm (*Milton's Prosody* 55); see also 606–51n.

    inmost mind: cf. *PL* 11.418.

612. *his:* editors gloss as "its," with the antecedent "torment" (606); Latin *tormentum* is neuter. Blakeney adds that the word *its* occurs but three times in Milton's verse, only once in the Authorized Version of the Bible, and "very rarely" in Shakespeare's works.

    accidents: "unfavourable symptom[s]" of disease (so *OED* I.3); Verity glosses, "pains, tortures"; Hanford suggests, "properties or concomitants" (*Poems*). Percival writes, "torment" is like "substance" in Aristotelian logic, "invisible, without manifestation: but when it puts forth its 'accidents' or properties, and preys upon the spirit of man, it then becomes visible in its effects, manifests itself in pain inflicted." Northrop Frye adds, "The imagery suggests an allegorical reading of the torments of Prometheus" (Paradise Lost *and Selected Poetry*). Cf. also *Macbeth* 5.3.40–45 (Thaler, "Shakespearian Element" 164).

613. *her:* Parker notes that the antecedent is *mind* (611) and Latin *mens* is feminine ("Variorum"); see 71–72n.

purest spirits: the phrase also occurs in *PL* 5.406 (Le Comte 67). Svendsen discusses the concept from Renaissance physiology: "The faculties are exercised by the soul through the instrumentality of *spirits:* natural, located in the liver; vital, in the heart; animal, in the brain"; thus, Samson here seems to refer to "animal" spirits (*Milton and Science* 181).

614. A line in trochaic rhythm (Bridges, *Milton's Prosody* 55–56); see 606–51n. Sprott (132) thinks it difficult to determine whether Milton thought of the line as "trochaic with the last foot catalectic, or as iambic with the first foot catalectic" (see 116n). Macaulay believes this line and the next reveal that Milton was "agonisingly...haunted" by "the torturing deaths of the regicides" (132).

entrails: "inner parts," e.g., intestines (*OED* II.3), or "the flesh," in the sense of Latin *viscera* (Collins; Prince, *Samson Agonistes*).

joint, and limbs: cf. "joynt or limb" in *PL* 1.426; 2.668; 8.625. Cf. also 953, 1142.

615–16. For these rhymes (and 610–11), see 606–51n.

answerable: editors gloss as "corresponding," i.e., to physical pains (*OED* II.4).

corporal: "bodily" (*OED* 1); so also 1336.

617–27. Ellis-Fermor suggests that "the prosody, following the inner turmoil, returns to a restless movement, fiercer than the corresponding earlier passages, just as the steadier movements now are firmer" (151).

618. Sprott suggests the first two feet are inverted (trochaic) followed by an iamb (132); Weismiller (148) instead suggests that the first two syllables are unstressed, followed by a trochee, then an iamb (see 81n). Edmund K. Chambers suggests that this line is iambic but begins with an anapest (129).

620–28. Todd detects here an echo of *The Faerie Queene* (3.2.39 or 6.6.5); see, too, Greenlaw, Osgood, and Padelford (6:212). Greenlaw et al. (7:272) also note a similar sentiment in March of *The Shepheardes Calender* 100–3.

wounds immedicable: Todd, Browne, Verity, et al. quote Ovid, *Metamor-phoses* 10.189: *immedicabile vulnus;* "the wound is past all cure"; and Tasso, *Aminta Englisht* (1628), 2.1.9–10: "So deadly and immedicable wounds" (sig. D3r [Todd, Fleming]). In *Colas* Milton speaks of "immedicable disaffection" (Patterson, *Works* 4:251). Peck cites this word to show that Milton naturalizes "almost innumerable" Latin words (sig. O4r).

621–22. Percival thinks that the change of meter and "harsh rhythm" are meant "to convey a repulsive idea" (xlvii, 110). Blakeney agrees, "The harshness of these two lines...is made an echo of the sense."
 ranckle: "fester, *esp.* to a degree that causes pain" (*OED* 1b).
 fester: Svendsen notes that this word, like "gangrene" in the same line, is a verb, but he quotes Bartholomaeus's *De proprietatibus rerum* (fol. cviii r) to suggest that "like gangrene, fester had a particular meaning as a noun: 'For a fester hath a deepe wounde within, and a streyghte and narowe withoute'" ("Milton and Medical Lore" 177).
 gangrene: "become mortified" (so *OED* 1). Cf. *DDD:* "inwardly fester with repining and blasphemous thoughts" (Patterson, *Works* 3:510).
 mortification: "death of a part of the body while the rest is living" (*OED* 2).

623–24. Although the comparison is sometimes noticed, Maxwell finds "very little resemblance" between 623–32 and Aeschylus, *Prometheus Bound* 878–86 ("Milton's Knowledge" 368).
 Tormenters: cf. *PR* 4.130.
 deadly stings: cf. 19–21, 1007.
 apprehensive: "pertaining to, or fitted for, the laying hold of sensuous or mental impressions" (so *OED* 2), "sensitive" (Verity; Hughes, *Complete Poems* and *John Milton;* et al.); "the apprehending mind, with its delicate organization" (Moody). Carey suggests that "the physical reference stabs excruciatingly at the area of sexual betrayal" (*Complete Shorter Poems* 339); see also 1037–38.

625. *exulcerate:* "exasperate, irritate," "aggravate (a disease, sorrow)" (so *OED* 2). Kermode (62) identifies an imperfect rhyme in 625–627; see 110–14n.

626–27. Block thinks this passage refers to Milton's own gout "and indicates that it had by now become a major affliction" (210). Banks identifies it as the "only figurative reference to herbs" in Milton's writings (54). See also 698n.

627. *medcinal:* editors note this spelling (hence a likely key to pronunciation) occurs in *Mask* 635 (in both the Trinity Manuscript and printed editions) and also in Milton's prose of 1642–49 (e.g., Patterson, *Works* 3:253, 254, 257, 266; 4:137, 315; 10:17, 317).

   liquor: so *Mask* 846.

   asswage: cf. 184 and *Ps 7* 22.

628. *Vernal Air:* Stein (*Heroic Knowledge* 228) suggests this phrase is a "recollection" of the "breath of Heav'n" (10). Le Comte (64) compares *PL* 4.264. Banks comments, "This sudden jump from a cool draught of medicine [627] to a cool mountain breeze is totally unexpected and highly effective" (136). Tillyard cites this line to show that Milton never "lost his power over the simply sensuous"; he praises here "the suggestion of delicate sense of touch" (*Miltonic Setting* 103; see also 93–93n). A possible rhyme with *despair* (631); see 629–31.

   Alp: "any high, esp. snow-capped mountains" (*OED* 2; Verity); cf. *PL* 2.620. Johnson (*Rambler* 20 July 1751), however, finds this word anachronistic (220); Blakeney agrees, "Strictly speaking, Milton is guilty of an impropriety in putting the word 'Alp' into Samson's mouth." Banks reminds us that "Milton breathed such Alpine air when he journeyed from Italy to Switzerland in the spring of 1639" (137). Parker adds that Milton may have known that snow is found on Mount Lebanon and lies throughout the year in the ravines of the peaks of Mount Hermon at the northern limit of the territory of Israel beyond the Jordan ("Variorum").

629–31. *giv'n me o're:* see 121.

   o're...cure...despair: Edmund K. Chambers remarks "the curious musical effect of the imperfect triple rhyme, 'O'er,' 'cure,' and 'despair.'" Parker observes that there is much assonance in the whole monody and notes, e.g., the recurring *er* sound in 624–33 ("Variorum").

630. A twelve-syllable line (alexandrine) without any break (see 118n).

   deaths benumming Opium: cf. 571. Church thinks "there may be an allusion to the influence of mortification [see 622] in putting an end to pain." Verity quotes Shakespeare's *Winter's Tale* 5.3.102: "Bequeath to death your numbness." George Coffin Taylor recalls *Othello* 3.3.330–31: "Not poppy, nor mandagora, / Nor all the drowsy syrups of the world" (194); so does Edward J. Thompson, who adds that in this speech, "the short, irregular lines turn and writhe like a body in torment" (247). Belloc supposes that Milton here remembers "his own trouble of insomnia" and the drugs he took "to get a little artificial rest" (273).

631–35. Bush interprets the rhythm of these lines: "the smooth flow and strong endings of the third and fourth lines sustain the idea of Samson's former glory and assurance; in the other lines feminine caesuras and feminine line-endings suggest failure and loss" (*John Milton* 195; cf. "John Milton" 412). Rajan suggests that Samson's "sense of abandonment," expressed in these lines (as well as at 460–62), is "reversed in the encounter with Harapha" (133).

faintings, swoundings: Buchanan (139–40) finds an echo of Spenser's despondent knights, e.g., Redcross in *The Faerie Queene* 1.9.48.9.

despair: cf. 1171. In *DocCh*, Milton writes that this vice "takes place only in the reprobate" (Patterson, *Works* 17:58–59).

632. Bullough and Bullough write, "in mystical practice this sense of abandonment by God often precedes regeneration, as here."

633–51. Thyer (in Newton) thinks 633–40 "little more than a repetition [of 23–32]," but stops short of finding fault with these lines: "Grief though eloquent is not tied to forms, and is besides apt in its own nature frequently to recur to and repeat its source and object." Macaulay suggests that this lament "reads like one of the autobiographical passages from the pamphlets" (131). Tillyard also comments: "If Milton is thinking of his own case here, he would be referring with more propriety to the first months of blindness [i.e., 1651–52] than to the period of the Restoration, when his pen was by no means helpless" (*Milton* 160).

nursling: "child in relation to its nurse" (so *OED* 1); Lockwood defines, "one who is highly favoured and tenderly cared for"; see 636–37. Fell writes that this image of childhood care expresses the "isolation of the individual from the source of grace," an essential and tragic part of the suffering required for Samson's atonement (151). Parker comments, "the suggestion that God was 'nurse' to Samson, stated after the 'sense of Heav'ns desertion' [632], is a new and striking thought" ("Variorum"); on other references to nursing, cf. 924, 1487–88. Hawkins (220) sees this line as part of a larger pattern of "dietary imagery" that he traces to Judges 13:4–5, where Samson's mother is instructed to "drink not wine, nor strong drink, and eat not any unclean thing"; see also, e.g., 541, 558–59, 934.

 choice delight: "[a baby or child] select," or "of special excellence" (*OED* 1), and, adds Parker, "affording unusual gratification" ("Variorum"). On *choice*, cf. 264, 1654.

634. *His destin'd:* "destined (to be) his" (so Percival; Blakeney), or, "[his child] set apart in intention for a particular purpose" (*OED* 3). Cf. 226.

 womb: Judges 13:5, 7; 16:17: "the child shall be a Nazarite unto God from the womb.... [T]he child shall be a Nazarite to God from the womb to the day of his death.... I have been a Nazarite unto God from my mother's womb." Krouse finds this line "heavily laden with rich connotations for a reader acquainted with the Vulgate or the Latin Bible of Junius and Tremellius and with any part of hermeneutic literature, throughout which the phrase 'ex utero matris' recurs...as evidence that Samson was a special sort of Nazarite...not an ordinary, voluntary, temporary Nazarite" (95). Percival notes, "Samuel and John the Baptist were, like Samson, 'perpetual Nazarites.'" See also 31n, 318n, 520n, 634n, 1199n.

635. *Heavenly:* Darbishire emends to *Heav'nly* (*Poetical Works*); B. A. Wright does not follow this change; Parker says the change should "probably" be made ("Notes" 693).

 message: editors note, "messenger" (by metonymy); cf. *OED* 3. Wyatt and Collins cite other examples in 464, 677, 1512; Blakeney calls it a Latin usage.

 twice descending: mentioned earlier in 24, 361.

636. *eie:* cf. *Sonn 7* 14.

637. *Abstemious:* "away from intoxicating liquor" in its strict Latin meaning (Collins; Verity; Blakeney; et al.).

 amain: "greatly," "exceedingly" (*OED* 3; Lockwood; cf. *PR* 2.430), or "without delay" (*OED* 2b; cf. 1304), or "vigorously" (Collins; Percival; Prince, *Samson Agonistes;* Blakeney; et al.). Cf. Josephus (*Antiquities of the Jews* 5.8.4): "And the child grew apace and it was plain from the frugality of his diet...that he was to be a prophet."

638. *mightiest deeds:* Tillyard conjectures that Milton might be thinking of his *Defensio* against Salmasius (*Milton* 160); see 633–51n.

639–40. *nerve:* "muscle" (Verity); "sinew" (Wyatt and Collins; Blakeney) and so "energy," "strength" (so *OED* 3); cf. 1646.
 the: Darbishire (*Poetical Works*) and B. A. Wright emend to *th' uncircumcis'd.* See 315–20n.

641. *as never known:* Church interprets "in such a way as never has been known"; Percival, "as never having distinguished myself"; Blakeney compares Matthew 7:22–23: "Many will say to me in that day, Lord, Lord, have we not…in thy name done many wonderful works? And then will I profess unto them, I never knew you: depart from me, ye that work iniquity." Wilkes suggests that Samson's despair arises "not because of his blindness and captivity, but because of the now insupportable conviction that through his own fault he has failed in his appointed task, and that his failure is irreparable" (370). Carey instead describes this passage critically: "Samson is having nothing more educative than a tragic sulk" (*John Milton* 142).

643. Empson emphasizes that Samson boasts about provoking the Philistines: "In effect, he is what the 1890s called a Nihilist, so that few of the literary critics who praise him would be on his side if they met him nowadays" (*Milton's God* 213).
 appointment: "direction, decree, ordinance" (*OED* 6). See 237, and cf. *Bucer:* "the secret purpose of divine appointment" (Patterson, *Works* 4:7).

644. A twelve-syllable line (alexandrine) without any break (Bridges, *Milton's Prosody* 60–61; see 118n). Broadbent notes a pattern of *-loss, -less,* and *re-* words here and in 648 (*Milton* 47).
 irreparable: accent the fourth syllable (Percival). Cf. *PL* 2.330–31.

645. *repeated:* the word causes difficulty: *OED* 2d gives the meaning "celebrate[d], [spoken] of (as)"; Keightley (*Poems*), Collins, and Bullough and Bullough suggest *repeatedly* (the adverb); Hughes suggests "made to repeat the experience of being over and over" (*Complete Poems; John Milton;* cf. *OED* 4), which is close to

the meaning proposed by Lockwood, Masson (*Poetical Works*), Percival, Verity, Prince (*Samson Agonistes*), et al.: "repeated (as), made again and again."

646. *The subject of thir cruelty:* see "cruel enemies" (642).

647. Cf. *PL* 1.66–67 (Verity).
    the list: cf. 290; cf. also 463.

647–51. Commentators mostly agree that Samson here reaches his nadir. E.g., Allen writes, "So Samson reaches the bottom level of despair; he will never again sink so low" ("Idea as Pattern" 87). So also Harris: "he reaches the nadir of *tristitia*" (115); so, too, Huntley (135) and see 650n. (But cf. Nash, who argues that Samson does not experience an isolated nadir [27].) Gohn observes: "much of the tragic effect depends on the re-establishment of order in the soul of Samson. Were this order not regained, Samson would not be able to act" (266–67). Steadman writes that Samson's "hope in God stands...in striking contrast to the absence of personal hope" ("'Faithful Champion'" 19). Lawry cautions that critics should not judge Samson's wish too harshly: "Samson's death is not only the end that his pain and despair wrongly seek but also the rightful gateway both to his championship of God and to the tragic realizations of the drama" (367–68). Cox suggests that "it is ironic that Samson—defined repeatedly as a dead man, calling himself a 'moving Grave' [102]...—should see death as cure. It is doubly ironic that his words are true" ("Natural Science" 69). Alden Sampson thinks these lines may be autobiographical: Milton's "final lament of all" (163).

648–49. A twelve-syllable line (alexandrine; see 118n). Bridges comments that it could be reduced to ten syllables "by reckoning the last two syllables as extra-metrical" (*Milton's Prosody* 61).
    remediless: accent the second syllable, as in *Circum* 17 and *PL* 9.919 (Lockwood; Blakeney; Edmund K. Chambers); but Prince (*Samson Agonistes*) accents the first syllable. Cf. *Colas:* "a remediless thraldom" (Patterson, *Works* 4:239).
    prayer: cf. 520, 581.

650. Hanford calls this "the darkest moment of Samson's suffering" and adds, "Henceforth we have recovery" ("*Samson Agonistes*" 176). Percival similarly

claims that "the reply to this petition for death is the sudden inspiration Samson feels prompting him to accompany the Officer" (1381–84). He also cites Job 6:8–9: "Oh that I might have my request.... Even that it would please God to destroy me"; Gossman instead cites Job 3:17–18: "the wicked cease from troubling; and there the weary be at rest. There the prisoners rest together; they hear not the voice of the oppressor" ("Samson, Job" 217). Steadman ("'Faithful Champion'" 26–27) compares this outburst as well to the "outcries of impatience" by Elijah in 1 Kings 19:4 and in Jonah 4:3. Whiting thinks these lines autobiographical, "the logical and final utterance of Milton's melancholy, the natural outcome of his character, habits, and untoward circumstance" (*Milton's Literary Milieu* 175).

651. *miseries:* Verity would elide *er* to make it a disyllable, but Parker notes the word may be three syllables, as at 64, 107, 1469 ("Variorum"). Bridges includes this among the lines that would not have been admitted into *PL* (*Milton's Prosody* 48); see 122n.

　　balm: cf. 186, where the word is capitalized. Percival (255) quotes a fragment of Aeschylus 141: ὦ θάνατε παιάν...μόνος γὰρ εἶ σὺ τῶν ἀνηκέστων κακῶν / ιαρός; ἄλγος δ' οὐδὲν ἅπτεται νεκρῶν; "O Death the physician!...for thou alone art the healer of incurable ills; no sorrow reaches the dead." Blakeney adds six other quotations illustrating the idea of Death as the "all-healer," e.g., Job 3:13–19 and Sophoclean fragment 626: ἀλλ' ἔσθ' δ θάνατος λοῖσθος ὑατρὸς νόσων; "(But) Death is the ultimate doctor of (all) ailments." Parker ("Variorum") notes that this is the final medical reference in Samson's long response to Manoa's suggestion of "healing words" (605).

652. Sprott (132) thinks it difficult to determine whether Milton thought of the line as "trochaic with the last foot catalectic, or as iambic with the first foot catalectic" (see 116n).

652–709. Editors identify this passage as the second *stasimon* (see 293–325). Epps (193) calls this the third chorus and divides it into four parts: strophe (652–66), antistrophe (667–86), strophe (687–704), and antistrophe (705–24). Stroup (60) argues that the speech, composed "largely" from Scripture, has a strong "liturgical character"; he finds echoes of Psalms 37 and 38, Hebrews 1, Ecclesiastes 7, and Job 7. Larson proposes that these lines on the inscrutability of God express "the final religious ethic of Milton" (196). Brewer instead notes a parallel here with *Prometheus Bound*: "each chorus moralizes on the sad vicissitudes of the hero's career and the ephemeral nature of man" (916). Hanford also writes, "If anything in Milton or indeed in all modern literature deserves to be called a reproduction of antiquity it is this passage" ("*Samson Agonistes*" 185).

652–66. Masson (*Poetical Works*), Wyatt and Collins, and Blakeney, offer this gloss: "Many are the sayings...extolling patience...and, for the bearing well of all calamities (and) all chances..., (many are the) consolatories writ with studied argument..."; Newton suggests, "consolatories *are* writ with study'd argument, and much persuasion *is* sought" (see also Edmund K. Chambers; Prince, *Samson Agonistes*). See 543–44n. Blakeney adds that the passage is "fidgety" and "too classical in mould to be altogether clear to an English reader." To Hanford, who finds the whole drama Milton's "unconscious confessional," this stanza contains "the record of his fruitless endeavor to achieve serenity through the human wisdom of the ancients" (*John Milton* 218); elsewhere he compliments the paragraph's "even flow of rhythm as the philosophic reflection is carried steadily through a single complicated sentence" (*Poems* 552). Parker thinks the speech contains mere "platitudes about patience" (*Milton's Debt* 39), but Harris argues that the speech "must represent the poet's own Christian belief," despite the Chorus's rejection of patience (see 661–62n). Harris adduces examples to show that "Patience as the highest manifestation of Fortitude" is a "traditionally Christian pattern of ethical thought" and represents "the doctrinal concept which informs the play" in opposition to the sin of *tristitia* and despair (107, 109, 116; see 631–35n). Gossman, in comparing Samson's story with Job's, writes that here "Milton seems to be deliberately differentiating his Chorus...from Job's comforters" ("Samson, Job" 222). Parker (*Milton's Debt* 63) comments that this stanza is exactly balanced by the fifteen-line speech announcing the arrival of Dalila (710–24).

    sayings... / In antient and in modern books: Keightley observes that Milton "seems to have forgotten that Samson's was not a literary age" (*Poems*); but see 653n. Bush writes, "Milton has in mind the essays of consolation written by classical moralists, which are inadequate without divine help" ("John Milton" 510; *Milton*). Collins instead suggests, "Innumerable illustrations of the sayings alluded to will crowd on the memory of every well-read student, but what Milton is particularly alluding to is doubtless the Cynic doctrine of καρτερία, τλημοσύνη" ("patience and endurance"). Hughes (*Complete Poems; John Milton*) proposes as an example Henry More's chapter in *An Account of Virtue* (1690), which quotes Aristotle, Andronicus of Rhodes, and Cicero "in its consideration of 'Fortitude' as a 'Branch of Patience.' Elsewhere...More calls Christian patience 'the highest Perfection of Man's Will [2.3].'" Bullough and Bullough add, "Cicero's essay *On Grief of Mind* describes how different philosophers sought to console sufferers (sect. 31–33)." As examples of "antient" books Percival suggests Seneca's *Consolatory Treatises,* Boethius's *De consolatione philosophiae,* and Plutarch's consolatory letter to his wife; of "modern books," the many English translations and adaptations of Boethius, Petrarch's sonnets and canzones on Laura's death, and Simon de Fresne's "Inconstancy of Fortune." Verity suggests that Milton may also be thinking of the praise of "fortitude" in Chaucer's *Parson's Tale.*

653. *enroll'd:* Parker glosses as "written on a roll" (presumably of skin or parchment), "recorded" ("Variorum"). On the spelling see also 1736, and cf. 290, 1224, and *PL* 12.523.

654–55. Twelve-syllable lines (alexandrines; see 118n).
    Patience: cf. 755, 1287, 1296, 1623. Carey interprets this line as Milton's insertion of his own opinion in contrast with Samson's notion of heroic violence (*John Milton* 138); Rudrum, however, disagrees: "In fact, if we read the whole Chorus carefully, we see that the Danites are by no means delivering a homily on patience. While at the end of the Chorus they pray to God on Samson's behalf, through much of its length they empathise with Samson's mental sufferings" (40). To Tung, "it is obvious" that this passage differs from *PL* 9.31–32, "the better fortitude / Of Patience and Heroic Martyrdom"; here, in contrast, the Chorus speaks with "contempt...This 'patience' is a kind of stoic apathy," which the wise may extol but is ultimately ineffective (480–81). In *Educ,* Milton speaks of "Lectures and Precepts...of true Fortitude and Patience" (Patterson, *Works* 4:288).
    truest: Parker ("Variorum") notes, "compared with physical strength and valor. The Chorus later makes clearer what it is saying here (1268–72, 1287–91)."
    fortitude: editors gloss as "moral strength or courage" (*OED* 2)—Grieve adds, "here a more active meaning than in modern English"; see also Verity. The word also meant "physical or structural strength" (*OED* 1). Cf. 1288.

655. See 652–66n.

    to: "for" (Percival); "to help towards" (Church); "(with a view) to" (Verity).

656. The period at the end of this line in the first edition is ordered struck out by the *Errata*.

    chances: Parker ("Variorum") glosses as "mishaps"; so also 918 (and perhaps 1076); cf. 4, 1295.

    incident to: "liable to befall" (*OED* 1; Verity); cf. 774. Cf. Shakespeare's *Timon of Athens* 5.2.203–5 (George Coffin Taylor 195).

657. *Consolatories:* "writings containing topics of comfort" (so *OED* B and Johnson, *Dictionary*), "devotional books" (Blakeney). See 652–66n.

658–59. Notice the rhymes, and the alexandrine in 658 (see 118n).

    argument…perswasion: Percival thinks that Milton, borrowing the language of Roman rhetoric, has in mind Quintilian's twofold division of oratory into "controversial" and "suasory" (*Institutio* 2).

    sought: this word presents difficulty. Warburton (in Newton) thinks it an error for *fraught,* as does Stebbing. But most later editors think it an adjectival participle parallel to *studied* and meaning either "carefully collected" (Verity); or, in the sense of French *recherché,* "curious, refined, far-fetched" (Dunster [in Todd]; Percival); or "ingenious (sought for)" (Bullough and Bullough). Alternatively, Prince (*Samson Agonistes*) gives the meaning as "much persuasion is sought" (the verb supplied from 652: "are").

    Lenient: "softening, soothing" (so *OED* 1, which dates the appearance of the word from 1652). Cf. 184–85. Editors compare Horace, *Epistles* 1.1.34–35: "sunt verba et voces, quibus hunc lenire dolorem / possis"; "there are spells and sayings whereby you may soothe the pain."

660. *with:* the text of the first edition has *to,* corrected in the *Errata*.

    th' afflicted: "a distressed person" (grammatically, an absolute; Lockwood). Parker ("Variorum") compares the friends of Job, who, Milton comments, had no "true sense of a good man in his afflictions" (*Colas* [Patterson, *Works* 4:239]).

    sound: Percival writes, this "implies that to the ears of the afflicted they are but empty sound, sound without meaning." Blakeney compares Tennyson's "In Memoriam," stanza 6.

661–62. Thyer (in Newton), Collins, Percival, and Prince (*Samson Agonistes*) quote Ecclesiasticus 22:6: "A tale out of season [is as] musick in mourning." Todd quotes from "The Wofull Life and Death of King Edward the Second" in *A Mirror for Magistrates* (1610): "The sage instructions of the wise man's mouth, / Do sound harsh musike in the eares of youth" (sig. Aaa2v). Harris emphasizes the difference between the successive verbs, *prevails* and *seems:* "so assertive a judgment is immediately supplanted by a less certain one. That it '*seems* a tune / Harsh, and of dissonant mood' to the afflicted does not mean that it is so of itself" (117); he concludes, "The subtlety of Milton's diction and syntax in framing the Danites' rejection of patience suggests that [Milton intends]...that rejection to contain a truth ironically unapparent to them but implicit in the drama of which they are a part" (116–17).

    prevails: "succeed[s] in persuading" (*OED* 3c); so also 869.

    tune, / Harsh: cf. *DDD:* "grating in harsh tune together, may breed some jarre and discord" (Patterson, *Works* 3:427).

    mood: "mode," i.e., a kind of scale, associated with thought or feeling (so *OED* 3d). Fletcher discusses this musical term as it relates to *PL* 1.550, *L'All* 136, *PR* 4.257, and *Lyc* 87: *mood* or *mode* refers to the diatonic scales (Dorian, Ionian, Lydian, Phrygian, etc.) of Greek music and to the belief that each scale harmonized with (or produced) certain emotions; thus, "of dissonant mood" means "out of harmony (with)" (see Fletcher, *Intellectual Development* 1:349–52). Wyatt and Collins add, "in modern music there are two *moods,* or *modes*—major and minor."

663–66. Harris (117) notes that this is an ironic foreshadowing of 1381–83 and "the ultimate victory through patience and divine sustenance." Gohn writes, "the Chorus specifically compares a Stoic ethic to the Christian ethic of the poem" (264).

666. *fainting spirits:* according to Edmund K. Chambers (123), the word *spirit* is a monosyllable here and in 1269, 1435, 1675, but a disyllable in 594, 613, 1238.

667–709. Some commentators discuss the significance of these lines for Samson's suffering and alleged regeneration. Woodhouse writes, "here the words are given to the Chorus instead of Samson, lest they should be thought of as the effect merely of his despair. They are a reasoned though incomplete comment on life, which will be corrected by the Chorus itself in the final words of the poem" ("*Samson Agonistes*" 165). Allen instead suggests that Samson's sickness "begets a similar disease in the chorus.... The complaint is artistically ironic because it exactly marks the point in the tragedy where the regeneration of the protagonist begins. The former emotional fluctuations of the hero will cease with the last note of the choral song and Samson will move steadily upward towards the elected event" ("Idea as Pattern" 87). Mahood (238) agrees that this speech marks "the turning-point of the play, the moment when Milton begins to demonstrate his belief that *vincit qui patitur*—'who best / Can suffer best can do'" (*PR* 3.194–95). Ellis-Fermor sees in this passage "an indication of mystical experience," surprising because it is not found in *PL* or elsewhere in Milton's works (28). See 632n. Thyer (in Newton) thinks this passage "an imitation" of the chorus in Seneca's *Hippolytus* 4.971; Collins thinks that these lines, compared with the last chorus (1745–58), especially resemble Euripides in their mingling of optimism and despair (6).

But Warburton (in Newton) and many subsequent editors and commentators believe, instead, that the lines are "a bold expostulation with Providence for the ill success of the *good old cause*"; that, as Collins writes, Milton's "own experience was his inspiration"; and that, as Grieve asserts, the passage reveals what Milton "thought of the Restoration." Masson accordingly calls it a "distinct glance" (*Life* 6:673), and Bailey writes, "This is Milton undisguised speaking of and for himself" (221). Collins adds, "It is difficult to believe that Milton is here speaking merely as a dramatist, and that in the last Chorus only we find his authentic philosophy."

Some editors (e.g., Percival; Verity; Blakeney; Collins 9) focus on 678–96 as an allusion to the political changes in England in 1659–60, in particular the overthrow of the republican party. In this view "some great work" (680) becomes the establishment of a commonwealth, temporarily ("in part") effected by the overthrow of monarchy. Warburton (in Newton) first works out the details of the supposed allusion. Hence, commentators see in 686 an allusion to God's helping the republicans in their struggle for independency in religion and a commonwealth in politics; 691 becomes an allusion to the dissensions among republican leaders and their neglect in reform of the constitution; 694 ("captiv'd") is seen as an allusion to the imprisonment of John Lambert and Henry Marten; and 695 ("unjust tribunals") is seen as an allusion to the trials of republican leaders after the Restoration and particularly to the trial and execution of Sir Henry Vane in June 1662 (e.g., Fleming; Muir 176; Hayley, *Life* 1:xci). See also 693–94n, 697n, 698n. Cf. Milton's prediction of what a restoration of kingship would bring (*REW* [Patterson, *Works* 6:138–39]).

Among other responses to these lines, Broadbent writes, "the ode has a peculiar confused muted air of dry-eyed prose assertion exalted into a hymn of defiance on waves of fluctuant rhythm which bounce against heaven and drop back again" (*Milton* 48). Editors also offer various ways to punctuate 667: e.g., Masson transposes the exclamation point and comma, so that the former appears after *Fathers* and the latter appears after *man* (*Poetical Works*); Tickell makes them both commas; Fenton makes them both exclamation points.

667–86. Parker observes that this second stanza, of twenty lines, is nearly balanced by the following one (687–704), of eighteen lines (*Milton's Debt* 62). Cf. 652–66, 710–24.

what is man!: Huntley argues that the Chorus and Samson are exchanging positions: "As Samson gives way to the inward vision of reality, the Chorus are struggling to regain their own false security" (138). Gossman suggests, "the Chorus is led, in its honest search for greater comprehension and stronger faith, to raise questions that are nearer than Samson's to the questions raised by Job" ("Samson, Job" 222). Cf. "What is man, that thou shouldest magnify him?" (Job 7.17); "What is man, that thou art mindful of him?" (Ps. 8:4 [*Ps 8* 12–13]; Heb. 2:6); and "Lord, what is man, that thou takest knowledge of him!" (Ps. 144:3). Steadman notes that the biblical question was originally associated with "man's native dignity," a context that Milton here intentionally omits, according to Steadman, so as to suggest that the Chorus's speech about "the misery of man's estate" is "a half-truth" and to imply that humankind's dignity and misery are closely related ("Tragic Glass" 110–11). Hughes suggests that Milton recalled the same question as put to Prometheus in the second choral hymn of Aeschylus's *Prometheus Bound* (*Complete Poems; John Milton*); Thaler instead detects an echo of *Hamlet* 2.2.309–22 ("Shakespearian Element" 154).

668–70. Belloc terms these lines "the most unforgivable piece of rubbish in all the collected works of Milton...a gem of absurdity...the very depth of bad verse" (279). Roberts W. French is similarly critical: "The rhyme of 'various' and 'contrarious' is surely one of the most superficial and facile attempts at cleverness in all the speeches of the Chorus. From the noble beginning of line

667, the passage by line 669 has moved dangerously close to bathos, if indeed it has not passed over" (64). Martz suggests that this quality may be deliberate: "the contrast between Samson's grandeur of despair and the ordinary, commonplace musings of the chorus is enforced by some of the flattest lines and flattest rhymes that Milton ever wrote" (125). Cf. 658–59, and see 672n, 1118n. Ebbs, by comparison, uses this passage to show that, "for Milton, Providence is the main influence in men's affairs and lives, that Providence is the carrying out of God's will, and that God's will is supreme in the universe." Ebbs goes on to identify Milton's concept of Providence with "poetic justice" in the text (382). Buchanan (326) finds this same description of fortune and "exactly Milton's jingling rhyme" in Giraldi Cinthio, *Didone,* Choro Quinto (*Tragedie* [1583] 128): "Et ella [Fortuna], per natura è così varia, / Che à chi si mostra amica, è al fin contraria."

various: "acting in many different ways" (so *OED* 6b), hence "changeful" (*OED* 1b; Blakeney).

contrarious: editors gloss as "inconsistent" and/or "adverse, untoward, vexatious" (*OED* 2, 5). Le Comte (85) compares *DDD* (Patterson, *Works* 3:471): "But this it is to embroile our selves against the righteous and all-wise Judgements and Statutes of God; which are not variable and contrarious, as we would make them, . . . but are most constant and most harmonious each to other."

670. *Temperst:* editors gloss as "dost guide, regulate" (and see *OED* 7).

671. *evenly:* "equably, uniformly" (so *OED* 4).

rul'st: Malcolm MacKenzie Ross observes that "not once in *Samson* is God referred to as 'King'" (134). In this connection notice also the references to a crown (175, 1296, 1579), and to God as Lord (477).

672. A twelve-syllable line (alexandrine; see 118n). Jerram says the rhymes in 672–75 add variety, "though scarcely dignity"; Roberts W. French suggests that these rhymes, as well as those in 687–91, "strive to give the pronouncements of the Chorus the formal authority of an unmistakably true declaration, but their speech has been undercut from the start by their purposeless playing with 'various' and 'contrarious' [in 668–69]" (64). See 668–70n.

The: Darbishire (*Poetical Works*) and B. A. Wright emend to *Th' Angelic.* See 315–20n.

Angelic orders: the nine ranks or grades: seraphim, cherubim, thrones; domi-
nations, virtues, powers; principalities, archangels, and angels. Cf. *PL* 1.737;
5.587; etc.

673. Editors disagree about the end punctuation mark—a period (so the first
edition), exclamation point, or question mark.

674–77. Larson detects in this passage evidence of Milton's "revulsion" and "fiercest contempt" for "the common people" in England who preferred tyranny
and superstition over a republican government (182–83). Daniells (76) instead
argues that Milton, as in *PL* 3.173–202, is here dividing humankind into three
classes according to God's decree: the "solemnly elected" (678), the "common
rout" (674), and the "heathen and profane" (693).
　　rout: see 443n.

676. *Grow up:* cf. 637.
　　summer flie: "typifying short life" (Verity); equivalent to the *ephemerae* of
Aeschylus, Aristophanes, and Pindar; editors also mention Shakespeare's *3
Henry VI* 2.6.8; *Othello* 4.2.66; *Love's Labour's Lost* 5.2.408. Verity compares
as well George Herbert's "Complaining." Parker notes, too, that flies evoke
filth ("Variorum").

677. *Heads without name:* Blakeney glosses as "nameless persons"; Prince offers,
"without regard to individuality" (*Samson Agonistes*); Wyatt and Collins write,
"mere individuals without fame." Some editors (e.g., Blakeney; Verity; et al.)
also think that Milton recalled such familiar classical phrases as *ignota capita*
("men of no note" [Livy, *Ab urbe condita libri* 3.7]) and/or ἀμενηνὰ κάρηνα
("nameless persons" [Homer, *Odyssey* 10.521, 536; 11.29, 49]). Church suggests an allusion to "the Roman constitution called after Servius Tullius, by
which the lowest class in the Commonwealth was called the *capite censi;* their
property was not sufficient to classify them by, and they were reckoned as so
many 'heads.'"

678. *solemnly:* "formally" (Lockwood).
　　elected: "chosen, selected." Cf. *Call'd* (226); *PL* 3.183–84; *DocCh* (Patterson,
Works 14:99). According to Parker, the idea of "solemn election" gradually

disappears from Milton's writing; that the idea plays such a prominent role in *SA* indicates to Parker that the poem was composed before the Restoration ("Date" 228). Hanford suggests instead that Milton uses this term "not in the Calvinistic sense of those predestined to salvation but of those whom God has chosen as special recipients of his favor" (*Poems*).

679. Cf. *PR* 2.137 (Verity), and also *Areop:* "those whom God hath fitted for the speciall use of these times with eminent and ample gifts" (Patterson, *Works* 4:351).

   graces: "favours" (cf. 360) or "individual virtue[s] or excellence, divine in...origin" (*OED* 11e).

   adorn'd: Lockwood defines as "made beautiful or attractive." Cf. 357.

680. See 667–709n.
   work: see 226.

681. *peoples:* Parker glosses as "(thy) people's" ("Variorum"); cf. 317, 1158, 1533.

   safety: cf. *PL* 2.481.

682–84. Todd thinks Milton "perhaps now remembered" a fragment of Euripides: Πολλοῖς ὁ Δαίμων, οε κατ᾿ ἔυνοιαν φέρων, / Μεγάλα δίδωσιν ἐυτυχήματ᾿, ἀλλ᾿ ἵνα / Τὰς συμφορὰς λάζωσιν ἐμφανέστερας; "To many, God brings great prosperities, not out of good will, but only to make misfortunes appear greater to them."

   toward: Parker observes that elsewhere (334, 668, 772, 792, 911) Milton instead uses *towards* ("Variorum").

683. *highth of noon:* "culminating or highest point [of their good fortune]" (so *OED* s.v. *noon* 5). In *PL* 4.564 the phrase is used literally for "midday"; here it is used figuratively. Todd finds parallels in Sandys; Church, one in Shakespeare, *Henry VIII* 3.2.225. Parker recalls that it was also at the height of noon (1612) when Samson pulled down the building upon his enemies (*Milton's Debt* 162). On the spelling *highth*, see 384n.

684. A twelve-syllable line (alexandrine; see 118n). Verity asserts, "The Restoration of the Stuarts is meant"; see 667–709n.

countenance: "demeanour or manner towards others as expressing good or ill will" (*OED* II.7 [1632]). B. A. Wright emends to *count'nance;* Parker agrees ("Notes" 693).

hand: Percival dismisses the possibility of a zeugma in *changest,* as both *countenance* and *hand* occur in opposite senses in Scripture; he compares Psalm 80:16 and 89:15, Job 2:10, and 1 Samuel 5:11.

686. Carey notes that the repetition in this line approaches *antimetabole* (repetition with inversion); see also 423–25, 462–63 (*Complete Shorter Poems* 335). Blakeney calls 685–86 an example of chiasmus.

or them: Grieve, and Wyatt and Collins gloss as "or (from) them," i.e., "(no regard of) service from them (to thee)." See 667–709n.

service: see 411–19n.

687–704. Adams suggests that the Chorus, which began with "that wonderfully vivid and searching exclamation" (see 667–86n), here "falls to describing the sad fate of men once eminent for virtue; and here the alternatives are enumerated in a solemn processional which neither generates nor seems eager to generate any tension built on contrasts" (194). Adds Hanford, "The personal note here is too distinct to be mistaken" ("*Samson Agonistes*" 185).

remit: "put back *into,*" "to admit or consign again *to* a previous position, state, or condition" (so *OED* 11b). Cf. 1470.

688–91. Jerram thinks the rhyming "not far removed from doggerel." See 672n. Kermode (62) identifies a "doubtful" imperfect rhyme in 688–91; see 110–14n.

life obscur'd: cf. 572. Prince glosses as "hidden from public view" (*Samson Agonistes*); Bullough and Bullough remark, "Milton does not complain about his own obscure life."

fair: "gentle," "not violent" (so *OED* A. IV.15) or "impartial, just" (so Lockwood I.6; *OED* A.III.10). Parker writes, "much depends upon how this simple word is here interpreted" ("Variorum").

dismission: "discharge from service," or "deprivation of office, dignity, or position" (*OED* 3). Blakeney and Meiklejohn note this word is used only here in Milton's works but was the common form (as opposed to *dismissal*) in the seventeenth century.

689. A twelve-syllable line (alexandrine; see 118n). Blakeney quotes Luke 10:15: "And thou, Capernaum, which art exalted to heaven, shalt be thrust down to hell." Percival quotes Horace, *Odes* 1.34.12–14 — "valet ima summis / mutare et insignem attenuat deus, / obscura promens"; "Power the god does have. He can interchange the lowest and the highest; the mighty he abases and exalts the lowly" — and also the similar sentiment in Homer, *Odyssey* 16.212.

690. *Unseemly:* Parker glosses as "unbecoming" or "unfitting" (*OED* 1) and wonders whether the word indicates that the falls are unbecoming to God or that they are unbecoming because they are undeserved ("Variorum"). Blakeney argues it is the latter. Cf. 1451.

691. Curry infers here, "Divine prediction with respect to individual is, therefore, always contingent upon the will; any man may . . . determine his own fate as he pleases" (340–41). Adds Hanford, "The sense of tragedy arises from the disproportion between the error and its consequences" (*Poems*). See 431n.

 trespass: "transgression," "offence," "breach of law or duty" (*OED* 1). The allusion is to "sins of omission and commission." See Warburton's interpretation in 667–709n.

692–700. Jerram believes these lines allude "to the fate of the regicides; they could not refer to Samson."

693–94. *Heathen and prophane:* "members of the Established Church," according to Percival; "the Restoration party," according to Blakeney. See 451, 1362.

 carkasses . . . prey: Newton notes an allusion to the opening lines of Homer's *Iliad* (1.4–5), which describe the fate of the Achaian heroes: αὐτοὺς δ'ἑλώρια τεῦχε κύνεσσιν / οἰωνοῖσί τε πᾶσι; "and made themselves to be a spoil for dogs and all manner of birds." But, also following Newton, most editors read this clause as a historical allusion to the disinterment and disgrace of the remains of Cromwell, Bradshaw, and Ireton in January 1661. Bullough and Bullough add that the image of God's "elected" being slain and their bodies then left to dogs and fowls recalls the fate of crusaders and pilgrims. Parker ("Variorum") thinks this description evokes, too, Old Testament Hebrews, such as Moses: "The Lord shall cause thee to be smitten before thine enemies. . . . And thy carcase shall be meat unto all fowls of the air, and unto the beasts of the earth. . . . The Lord will smite thee with the botch of Egypt, and with the emerods, and with the scab, and with the itch, whereof thou canst not be healed" (Deut. 28:25–27). Cf. also God's punishment of the erring Hebrews in Jeremiah 15:2–3: "Thus saith the Lord:... such as are for the captivity, to the captivity. And I will appoint over them four kinds, saith the Lord: the sword to slay, and the dogs to tear, and the fowls of the heaven, and the beasts of the earth, to devour and destroy." For similar passages see Jeremiah 7:33, 16:4, 19:7; 1 Kings 14:11, 16:4, 21:24; cf. *Eikon* (Patterson, *Works* 5:113).

694. *captiv'd:* editors scan as "cap-tived'"; see 33, and 667–709n.

695. A twelve-syllable line (alexandrine; see 118n).

   the: Darbishire (*Poetical Works*) and B. A. Wright emend to *th' unjust*. See 315–20n.

   unjust tribunals, under change of times: Grieve (v) and Browne detect in these lines a contemporary allusion to Vane's execution; see 667–709n. Phillips expresses a similar sentiment in the dedicatory preface to *Theatrum:* "in human affairs some Men never so vertuously, never so bravely acting are pass't by unvalew'd, unrewarded, or at least not deserving ill fall by unhappy lot into unreasonable hands and miseries, far worse then death" (sig. *3v–*4r). Parker also compares the first chapter of Isaiah ("Variorum").

696. A twelve-syllable line (alexandrine) without any break; see 118n.

   the: Darbishire (*Poetical Works*) and B. A. Wright emend to *th' ingrateful*. See 315–20n.

   multitude: Parker ("Variorum") observes that Milton elsewhere terms it "rude" (*RCG* [Patterson, *Works* 3:247]; *Apol* [Patterson, *Works* 3:348]; *REW* [Patterson, *Works* 6:131]; *HistBr* [Patterson, *Works* 10:105]), or "mad" (*Eikon* [Patterson, *Works* 5:70, 101]; *REW* [Patterson, *Works* 6:134]; *Def 1* [Patterson, *Works* 7:246–47]), or "dizzy" (*PR* 2.420).

697. Following Newton, editors believe that in these lines Milton refers to himself (Collins: "plainly"; Wyatt and Collins: "undoubtedly"; et al.). Bullough and Bullough, however, warn that "Milton was not given to self-pity and we should not exaggerate the autobiographical element here."

poverty: cf. 69, 366, 1479. Parker ("Variorum") suggests that while Milton suffered severe financial loss through the Restoration, and later lost a house in the Great Fire of 1666, he never experienced "real poverty"; see Masson, *Life* 6:718, 743–44. Saurat, however, writes that here "Milton's own old age is bitterly described," including his illnesses and "the loss of his fortune" (202). Parker suggests that in these lines Milton may (also?) recall the trials of Job—"his sudden poverty, his affliction with leprosy, his premature old age" ("Variorum"). See also Gossman, "Samson, Job" 212–24.

698. *sickness and disease:* editors read these lines as autobiographical, and Milton did suffer somewhat from ill health as blindness approached and was incapacitated for a time by sickness in 1651–52. According to Carey (*John Milton* 85), these lines suggest that Milton disagreed with Michael's assertion in *PL* that people can avoid disease if they follow "The rule of not too much" (11.515–37).

bow'st them down: Verity suggests that Milton "is glancing at his own ill health." Aubrey in his *Life* of Milton comments, "He was very healthy, & free from all diseases, and only towards his later end he was visited with the Gowte spring & Fall: he would be chearfull even in his Gowte-fitts; & sing" (Darbishire, *Early Lives* 5). See 701–2n. Block thinks the reference here to Milton's gout is "unmistakable" and reasons that, because Milton began to suffer from the gout circa 1664–66, the traditional dating of *SA* is correct (210). See also 626–27n. Earlier in *Tetr* (1645) Milton speaks of "the gout and dropsy of a big margent" (Patterson, *Works* 4:234–35); also, in *HistBr* he writes of Severus "much weak'nd with Age and the Gout" (Patterson, *Works* 10:85). Parker ("Variorum") adds that Salmasius also suffered from gout (*Defpro Se* [Patterson, *Works* 9:118]).

699. *Painful diseases:* Parker observes that "many are mentioned in the Old Testament: leprosy, boils, scab and scurvy, etc." ("Variorum"); see 693–94n.

deform'd: "that mar the appearance, disfiguring" (Verity; Lockwood; et al.; not in *OED*) or "misshapen" (*OED* 2), or "disgusting, odious" (Wyatt and Collins; Grieve; cf. *OED* 4). Cf. *PR* 3.86.

700. A four-syllable line; Timberlake (336) compares the meter with a similarly short line in Euripides' *Alcestis* 94: νέκυς ἤδη ("She is but a corpse").

crude: editors gloss as "unripe, premature" (cf. *OED* 5, 6); cf. Homer's *Odyssey* 15.357: ἐν ὠμῷ γήραϊ ("untimely old age"); Hesiod's *Works and Days* 5.703:

ὠμῷ γήραϊ δῶκεν ("raw [premature] old age"); Statius's *Thebaid* 9.319: "cruda funera nepotis" ("the premature obsequies of a grandchild"). But in Virgil's *Aeneid* 6.304 — "cruda deo viridisque senectus" — *crude* means "hardy, robust, hale" (Church). Cf. *Lyc* 3.

    old age: see 572n.

701–2. *disordinate:* "unrestrained, immoderate," "not conforming to moral order" (so *OED* 1b); Verity suggests, "irregular in their lives." The sense: "Though not intemperate or immoral, (they) suffer without cause the punishment (which is the usual result) of dissolute days." See 543–44n. Commentators point out that Milton himself suffered from the gout, presumed a result of intemperance; see 697n, 698n, 699n. Hanford thus writes: "We recollect how ardently he had maintained the idea that his blindness was not a punishment for sin but a special mark of the divine favor. It was more difficult to rationalize the gout" (*John Milton* 220). But Prince suggests that Milton may have associated the two conditions: "Milton's blindness, total after 1652, may . . . have been connected with the gout which afflicted him later" (*Samson Agonistes*). The general assumption that Milton here refers to his own gout leads Adams to comment on this ode, "the misfortunes of the just are anticlimactically arranged, with Milton's gout (a hurt both intimate and bitter, but not after all very dignified) occupying the position of supremacy" (195).

    causless: "causelessly" (so *OED* B).

    suffering: Parker proposes *suff'ring*, as regular meter would seem to require ("Notes" 693). See 445.

    dissolute: Parker writes, "wanton, debauched," e.g., like Belial in *PR* 2.150 ("Variorum").

    in fine: "in short," "to conclude" (*OED* I.1b; Prince, *Samson Agonistes*).

703–4. Hanford notes "it is the Chorus and not Samson who says this. In spite of the unrelieved misery of his preceding speech no such expression escapes him. We have reached the darkest point in the drama" (*Poems*). But some editors and commentators do not think the Chorus believes what it says here. Hurd (in Todd), echoed or quoted by Church, Grieve, et al., declares: "We are not to consider the sentiment simply in itself, but as adapted to present circumstances. The purpose of the Chorus was not to calumniate Providence, but to soothe the unhappy sufferer." Steadman also qualifies this passage: "These lines are rather a complaint to Providence than a protest against it. They question, rather than challenge, the ways of God to men." And Steadman finds "another theological commonplace—the misery of the *condition humaine*. Here, however, there is a concealed ambiguity or equivoque, for the misery of the just and the unjust is not the same. It only 'seems' to be" ("Tragic Glass" 110). Alternately, Percival writes: "Sympathy for Samson is the only explanation of this bitter charge.... It is not the ideal chorus of Greek dramatic art, but the living and suffering Milton, that here speaks."

For this sentiment, commentators find various precedents. Percival, e.g., notes a similar idea in Euripides, *Suppliant Women* 226, and Theognis, *Elegies* 337. Bullough and Bullough find it in Job's lament and in the final chorus of Sophocles' *Oedipus Rex*. Parker ("Variorum") adds that it can also be found in other places, including other works by Milton: in *Eikon* he writes of David "suffering without just cause" (Patterson, *Works* 5:278); in *Tetr* he writes of "causeles" punishment and denies that "all affliction comes for sin" (Patterson, *Works* 4:77); his *HistBr* closes with the statement: "And as the long suffering of God permits bad men to enjoy prosperous daies with the good, so his severity of times exempts not good men from thir share in evil times with the bad" (Patterson, *Works* 10:316). In *DocCh*, Milton quotes more than a dozen passages of Scripture to prove that "Generally speaking,...no distinction is made between the righteous and the wicked, with regard to the final issue of events, at least in this life" (Patterson, *Works* 15:60–61).

705. A ten-syllable line with an extrametrical ending (Bridges, *Milton's Prosody* 61).

   Champion: see 556n.

706. A twelve-syllable line (alexandrine; Bridges, *Milton's Prosody* 61; see 118n). Charles Williams asks of this line, "is there a better description of Milton's work?" (*English Poetic Mind* 148).

   Image: "semblance" (*OED* 3), or "embodiment of strength" (Lockwood); cf. Genesis 1:26–27. Cf. also 164. Percival finds it "a very bold epithet for the superhuman strength of Samson; but although applied to the Messiah [*PL* 3.63], it is also applied to Adam [4.292]."

   minister: "agent" (*OED* 2) or "servant" (Verity et al.); cf. *PL* 1.170 etc.

707. Parker comments, "in this line the Chorus explicitly makes Samson an illustration of its generalizations about God's seeming injustice" ("Variorum"). The first edition ends this line with a question mark; some editors emend it to an exclamation point.

708. A twelve-syllable line (alexandrine; see 118n).
    turn: Lockwood defines "to use in bringing about." Landy thinks this word is significant for Samson's conversion: "the Chorus is asking that God grant Samson the 'call,' so that he may know what it is he has to do, and he may, thus, find peace" ("Of Highest Wisdom" 173).

709. *labours:* "mental toil…esp. when painful or compulsory" (*OED* 1), or " 'troubles,' a not uncommon sense of the Latin *labores*" (Church).
    peaceful end: cf. 704 ("evil end"). Summers thinks this prayer "is one of the most significant turning points of the drama. At this moment we share an immediate insight with the Chorus: the resolution lies within the will of God. And, as imaginative spectators…, we are also convinced that, with *this* Samson, God must behold" (166). Radzinowicz also finds in this and the next lines "the faintest note of hope, manifested in the humanity and pity of their [the Chorus's] words as well as in their faith as they pray" ("*Samson Agonistes*" 469). But to Parker, "the picture of violent death flashes across our minds as we hear the choral prayer" (*Milton's Debt* 162), and Raleigh writes that the prayer is "heard and answered with Divine irony on the very day of their asking" (*Milton* 173). Alternatively, Hayley finds, "The concluding verses of the beautiful Chorus…particularly affecting, from the persuasion that Milton in composing them addressed the two last immediately to Heaven, as a prayer for himself" (*Life* 1:xciv); so, too, Percival comments, this "is also a prayer offered by Milton for himself."

710–24. Dalila enters and the third epeisodion begins. Commentators generally praise this speech. To Coleridge (14:317), it was one of "the only two pictures" that he remembered in Milton (the other: Adam bending over the sleeping Eve). To Belloc, "it is one of the finest things in the English language" (276); Brydges calls it "among the finest passages in this grand poem"; and Steiner compliments the fusion of music and dance, "as complete as it must have been in the choral lyrics of Aeschylus" (32).

Commentators also discuss how this speech marks a shift in the poem. To Rajan, it is "a relieving simile where relief is needed" (138); to Tinker, it is "the one moment of comedy" (67). Moody more fully describes the effect: "a subtle change in the metre and color of the verse heralds her approach; the movement becomes more vivacious, evanescent vowel rhymes appear, and epithet and imagery take on a more opulent hue" (286). Edmund K. Chambers also notices a change here: "the elaborate description of the sumptuous appearance of Dalila is meant to emphasize the contrast between her fate and that of the broken-down world-weary Samson in his prison garb" (also Bush, *Milton*). But Gilbert objects to Dalila's introduction here, which he finds abrupt; it is one of a series of "peculiarities" that he believes suggest *SA* remains unfinished. Gilbert also complains that this speech, contradicting Milton's claim about mixing genres in the Preface, introduces Dalila as a comic character: she "is a *thing*, and is called *it* [711], rather than *she*" ("Is *Samson Agonistes*" 100, 101, 105); see Preface 32–34n. Brewer, however, writes that the unexpected appearance of Dalila — as well of Samson's other visitors — follows the precedent established in *Prometheus Bound* (913).

Among other responses to this passage, Gossman argues that Dalila seeks "to appeal to the lust and weakness that were part of Samson's undoing": she notes here that Dalila's "beauty, [though] not visible to Samson, is described by the Chorus and doubtless remembered; she is deliciously perfumed; and she seeks to touch his hand" ("Milton's Samson" 537–38). Percival observes that the pomp of Dalila's approach, and "the studied gracefulness of her affected sorrow, are a striking contrast to the humiliation and wild grief of Eve when seeking Adam's pardon [*PL* 10.910–36]." Fox finds points of resemblance between this passage and the description of the sinful woman in Marco Girolamo Vida's *Christiad* (370–72); J. Macmillan Brown detects a contemporary allusion and thinks the Chorus might be "quoting from some satire on the court of Charles the First" (128). Parker adds that this speech exactly balances the first stanza (652–66) of the stasimon (*Milton's Debt* 63).

But who is this: Mitford compares Plautus, *Epidicus* 3.3: "Sed hic quis est."

what thing of Sea or Land?: Daiches writes, "in the ironic pretence not to know [what]...this dressed-up creature can be, there is a world of criticism of female vanity" (241). Blakeney thinks "the Chorus is not really in doubt that it is a woman," but does not at first recognize Dalila. Percival notes that the expression occurs in Greek poetry in connection with women: e.g., Euripides, *Hecuba* 1181: γένος γὰρ οὔτε πόντος οὔτε γῆ τρέφει τοιόνδε; "Nor sea nor land doth nurture such a breed"; Menander, *Fragment:* πολλων κατὰ γῆν κὰι ματὰ θάλατταν θηρίων ὄντων, μεγιστόν ἐστι θηρίον γυνή; "Of all wild things on land or in the sea, the greatest is woman."

711–13. Kermode (62) identifies possible imperfect rhymes in 711–717–720–722 and 713–718; see 110–14n.

    Femal: Darbishire holds this to be Milton's spelling (*Poetical Works*); B. A. Wright also retains it; but cf. 777, 1055, 1060.

    ornate: "elaborately adorned" (so *OED* 2). Peck cites this word, among others, to show how Milton naturalizes "almost innumerable" Latin words (sig. O4r).

    gay: "showily dressed" (*OED* 4); the word also has the meaning "of loose or immoral life" (*OED* 2). Dalila's costume reminds Gohn (265) of Spenser's description of Excesse at the porch of the Bower of Bliss (*The Faerie Queene* 2.12.4, 43–45).

714. Line 714 is in falling (trochaic) rhythm (cf. 116), unless it is taken as one line with 713, as Bridges suggests (*Milton's Prosody* 55), or unless, as Edmund K. Chambers suggests, the first foot is an anapest (129). Parker, comparing 714 with 1436, asserts that 713 has no parallel elsewhere in the poem ("Variorum").

    Like a stately Ship: the comparison is arguably appropriate in a story about a sea-people who worship a sea-idol (13). Cf. Samson's nautical description of himself in 198–200; cf. also 1044–45. Banks writes, "for anyone a seventeenth-century ship must have been a thing of beauty, in particular when equipped with its long and purely decorative pennants" (123). Broadbent suggests that the association of maritime imagery to "bad subjects" was traditional, but, he adds, "Milton's frequent use of it represents...his horror of the limitless and unmanageable—of, we should say these days, the unconscious" (*Milton* 52). More specifically, the comparison of a woman to a ship is a frequent subject of sexual jest in drama (e.g., *Othello* 1.2.1), and editors and commentators frequently refer to this passage as "comic." The simile is traced by Newton back to Plautus, *Poenulus* 1.2.1–2: "Negoti sibi qui volet vim parare, / navem et mulierem, haec duo comparato"; "A man that wants to make himself a world of trouble should get himself a ship and a woman, just those two"; see also Carr. Todd mentions parallels in other works, e.g., Beaumont and Fletcher's *Wit without Money* (1639), Barnaby Rich's *Roome for a Gentleman* (1609), and Henry

Parrot's epigrams, *Laquei Ridiculosi* (1613). Gilbert cites ten other examples in commenting on this "comic scene" ("Milton's Defense" 68–69; *Literary Criticism* 587); he observes that the comparison of a woman with a ship is "generally derogatory and sexual"; Muldrow agrees that this image "does little to suggest the approach of a repentant woman" (191). Mitford in 1832 (anticipating McManaway in 1937, see reference below) quotes a long, appropriate passage from Robert Wilkinson's sermon, *The Merchant Royall* (1607), which has as its text Proverbs 31:14: "She [a virtuous woman] is like the merchants' ships; she bringeth her food from afar." Young notes the figure (applied to the Commonwealth) in James Harrington's *A Word Concerning a House of Peers:* "In comes the Commonwealth...with all its tackling, full sail, displaying its streamers, and flourishing with top and top-gallant" (28); McManaway agrees that "there can be little question of Milton's indebtedness" (131), but emphasizes that the comparison of woman to a ship was a Renaissance commonplace. (Adds Parker, "Variorum": "So, apparently, was comparison of a Commonwealth to a ship" [see, e.g., *REW* in Patterson, *Works* 6:126].) Wilson (44) remarks that certain details suggest Shakespeare's description of Cleopatra's barge (see 719n) and seem to have inspired Congreve's description of Millamant in *The Way of the World* (see also Williamson 94). Ure suggests Lady Pecunia in Jonson's *Staple of News* 2.5.42–45 and Mrs. Fitzdottrell in Jonson's *Devil is an Ass* 2.2.109–14 as crowning examples of this satirical imagery (298). Lewalski notes that the imagery here is integrated "into a larger pattern of ship and tempest imagery closely related to the basic themes of the poem" and she finds a debt to Giles Fletcher's description of the Lady Presumption in stanzas 35–36 of *Christ's Victory on Earth* ("Ship-Tempest" 372–73). In the preceding year (1958), Bullough and Bullough also suggest that Milton is "probably" remembering Fletcher's description. Carey discusses how this simile describing Dalila's entrance fits within the poem's larger pattern of marine imagery: it is "the major indication of her power. She is able to control the sea, that element which had overcome Samson [198–200], with effortless ease: 'stately,' 'trim,' decked with streamers and 'courted' by the winds, she moves upon its surface. The simile also connects her with the Philistines, worshippers of the 'sea-idol' [13]" (*Complete Shorter Poems* 337). Milton is elsewhere fond of nautical imagery; cf. *PL* 2.1043–44; 4.159–65; etc. In *Ref* he writes of prelates "under Sayl in all their Lawn, and Sarcenet, their shrouds, and tackle" (Patterson, *Works* 3:74); Le Comte (136–38) discusses this parallel, first noted by Todd.

715. *Tarsus:* a city of Cilicia on the river Cydnus, associated with St. Paul and also with the den of Typhon (Parker, "Variorum"). Gilbert (*Geographical*) notes that Milton mentions it in *PL* 1.200; *Colas* (Patterson, *Works* 4:249); and *HistBr* (Patterson, *Works* 10:169)—to which Parker ("Variorum") adds *PE* (Patterson, *Works* 3:88). Gilbert (*Geographical*) further observes that here, like Josephus and others (*Antiquities of the Jews* 8.7.2, 9.10.2; cf. Jon. 1:3), Milton identifies Tarsus with Tarshish of the Old Testament: Isaiah 23:1; Psalm 48:7; 2 Chronicles 9:21; Ezekiel 27:25. Parker comments that in these biblical passages "ships of Tarshish" are frequently mentioned as symbols of pride and hence objects of God's anger ("Variorum"). Editors also note that Tarshish was more probably the Phoenician Tartessus or Gadier in southern Spain, since, as Verity explains, "Tartessus is known to have been an emporium of the Phoenicians, and it is generally in connection with the Phoenician city of Tyre that 'ships of Tarshish' are mentioned." Wyatt and Collins add that the phrase "ships of Tarshish" had come to mean merely "large ships for long voyages"; Prince suggests, "In any case Milton wishes to avoid the harsh 'sh' sounds in *Tarshish*" (*Samson Agonistes*).

Isles: Parker observes that Milton's spelling (after 1634) seems to have been *Iles,* but notes also *PR* 4.71, 75; *PL* 1.521; 8.631; 10.527 ("Variorum"). Gilbert comments, "It is not necessary to think of actual islands..., for in the Bible 'isles' is a term applied to lands bordering on the sea as well as to islands" (*Geographical* 161).

716. *Javan:* i.e., "Greece"; cf. Genesis 10:2, 4–5; Isaiah 66:19; Ezekiel 27:12–15. Noah's grandson, Javan (or Ion), son of Japhet, was the traditional ancestor of the Ionians or the Greeks generally; cf. *PL* 1.508 (see Osgood 46).

Gadier: i.e., "Cadiz," which Gilbert describes as a "very ancient city built on an island on the southern coast of Spain, west of Gibraltar" (*Geographical*). Cf. *Eikon,* where it is *Cales* (Patterson, *Works* 5:153), and also *PR* 4.77, where the Latin (*Gades*) rather than the Greek form of the name is used. Gilbert writes, "Though Cadiz does not appear in Scripture, it is fittingly introduced...because of its ancient commercial importance, its connection with the Phoenician merchants so often mentioned in the Bible, and its association by scholars with Tarshish, which was sometimes identified with it" (*Geographical*); see 715n s.v. *Tarsus.* Gilbert also notes that in *PR* 4.77 "Cadiz appears as the most western city of the world"; Parker concludes, "Javan and Gadier here represent the eastern and western Mediterranean (i.e., extreme positions). They also connote commerce" ("Variorum").

717–18. *bravery:* editors gloss as "display," "finery, fine clothes" (*OED* 3); Verity (143) and Meiklejohn add, "not elsewhere in Milton." Blakeney, Wyatt and Collins, et al. compare Isaiah 3:18: "The Lord will take away the bravery of their tinkling ornaments." Kranidas writes, "Dalila charges on the scene, with all the equipment, not for battle, but for transaction" (127); cf. 1243 ("braveries").
　　tackle: "rigging or ropes used in working the sails" (so *OED* 2).
　　trim: "in good condition or order" (*OED* 1).
　　streamers: "long and narrow pointed flag[s]" (so *OED* 1).

719. *Courted...winds:* Todd notes that this expression is applied to Eve in Pona's *Adamo:* "corteggiata da' venti." Church compares Shakespeare's *Antony and Cleopatra* 2.2.193–94: "Purple the sails, and so perfumed that / The winds were lovesick with them." Nicolson (361) also compares the Nurse's entrance in *Romeo and Juliet,* presumably 2.4.102: "A sail, a sail!"
　　hold them play: "keep them in play" (see *OED* s.v. *hold* 7b), "keep them exercised" (see *OED* s.v. *play* 4c). Also glossed as "keep them moving or in action" (Lockwood I.a); "hold play (to) them, i.e., offer pleasure to them" (Percival; Blakeney); "sport with them" (Wyatt and Collins; Grieve; Bullough and Bullough; Blakeney); and "play or dally with them" (Prince, *Samson Agonistes*). Church suggests "hold them (in) play," but adds that "it is not easy to understand the construction, unless we suppose it in some way to resemble the phrase 'to give a thing play.' " Verity has "make play for them." Grieve compares Shakespeare, *Henry VIII* 5.3.85–86: "I'll find / A Marshalsea shall hold ye play these two months." Kermode adds that 712 (*gay*) and 714 (*play*) contain the only perfect rhyme in *SA* separated by more than three lines (62).

720. Watkins (25) contrasts the description of Eve "Veild in a Cloud of Fragrance" (*PL* 9.425).
　　Amber sent: "scent of ambergris." Verity (140) et al. identify this as a wax-like substance found floating in tropical seas and as a morbid secretion in the intestines of the sperm whale; used in perfumery. Todd, Percival, and Hughes (*Complete Poems; John Milton*) quote evidence of its popularity with women in the seventeenth century. Church, followed by Parker (*Milton's Debt* 181),

quotes the words of Prometheus on the entrance of the chorus of women in Aeschylus, *Prometheus Bound* 115: τίς ὀδμὰ προσέπτα μ ἀφεγγής; "What scent wingeth to me, its source invisible?" Cf. *PR* 2.344. Cox writes that the whale was "commonly in beast lore a figure for Satan" and thus indicates that Dalila "is primarily a thing of the evil element in which the fish-god reigns." Cox adds, "even Dalila's golden scent... implies a trap when joined to Samson's contention that *she* conceived treason by the 'sent' of gold [389–91]" ("Natural Science" 64). Carey writes that ambergris, like the ship simile, further connects Dalila to the sea (*Complete Shorter Poems* 338); see 714n s.vv. *Like a stately Ship*. Rudrum notes that "in Milton's time amber was thought to be the sperm of a whale" and thus may also represent Dalila's sexuality (43).

721. *harbinger:* "forerunner" (*OED* 3).

    a damsel train: Parker notes that *train* can mean either a "trailing skirt or robe" (cf. *IlPen* 34) or a "retinue" (*OED* II.5, III.9): "the former contrasts with 'harbinger' and completes the picture of an elaborate costume. If a retinue is meant (cf. 1732), they remain silent and take no part in the action" ("Variorum"). In this latter regard, Parker elsewhere adds, "since they serve no real dramatic purpose,...one infers that, despite his pronouncement, Milton had a fair sense of stage-craft" (*Milton's Debt* 143). But Verity conjectures that Dalila's retinue does not come on the stage. Commentators note that Greek tragedy provides a precedent for such a silent group: e.g., the suppliants in *Oedipus Rex,* the captive women in *Women of Trachis,* the attendants in *Ion,* Agamemnon's retinue and Clytemnestra's attendants in *Agamemnon,* and the judges and populace in *Eumenides.* Little alternatively suggests that Dalila's damsel train represents the influence of Italian neoclassical tragedy, which made "frequent use of mute choruses" (22, 57–58). Durling observes that Dalila was given three attendant damsels in Nevill Coghill's production of *SA* in July 1951 at All Souls College, Oxford (63).

722. *rich:* see 389n s.v. *Gold,* and cf. 1072.

    Philistian: cf. 380, where she is called a Canaanite. It is not stated in the Bible that Dalila was a Philistine, but, Verity writes, it is natural to suppose that she was, despite the large bribe offered her (see Judg. 16:5: "every one of us eleven hundred pieces of silver"). See 877–78.

    may seem: "would seem (to be)" (Parker, "Variorum").

723. *nearer view:* the phrase occurs also in *PL* 6.81 and *PR* 4.514 (Le Comte 50). *certain:* "certainly" (*OED* C.1); cf. *Mask* 265.

724. *thy wife:* see 227–30. Verity explains Milton's repeated use of this apposition here: "no doubt,...he wished to emphasise the resemblance to his own case." But James Waddell Tupper objects to such a "long-distance reflection": "Mary Milton was not a Dalila any more than Milton was a Samson" (380–81). Hughes and other editors believe that Milton made Dalila Samson's wife instead of his mistress "to stress the depth of her treason and of Samson's infatuation" (*Complete Poems* 534); Radzinowicz adds that this change guarantees that Dalila's "betrayal would be fully spiritual and psychological, not merely commercial" ("Eve" 177). Empson thinks instead, "the marriage is essential to the poem, because it yields a peculiarly moral paradox" and because Milton "wanted to save the lady's dignity, not the hero's" (*Milton's God* 218–19, 224). See 227n, 228n, 231n. Interestingly, Milton included "Samson marriing or in Ramath Lechi Jud. 15" among the possible subjects for tragedy listed in his Trinity Manuscript notes (see Parker, "Trinity Manuscript" 228).

725. While Tillyard emphasizes Samson's emotional response to the approaching Dalila ("We feel him wince and start sweating" [*Milton* 289]), Ellis-Fermor notes that Dalila's entry not only "provokes Samson to wrath and self-determination" but also "concentrates his imagination...on the matter-of-fact, the practical, the petty, everyday things that have deflected the currents of the mind" (28). Bowra writes that Samson is here "unsure of himself" (123); Rajan instead notes "an animal tension lacking in the discussions with Manoa and the Chorus" (138). Parker adds that Samson's impulsive reaction ignores the important truth later uttered by the Chorus (1050–52): "he *must* be tempted again, and resist, in order to be 'acceptable above'" ("Variorum"); see also 401. Thaler compares Samson's response to Dalila with both Antony's harsh reaction to Cleopatra's "peace overtures" in Shakespeare's play (4.12.30) and Adam's similar reply to Eve in *PL* 10.867 ("Shakespearian Element" 167).

726–31. Thyer and Jortin (both in Newton) notice the similarity to the choral description of Ismene's entrance in Sophocles' *Antigone* 526–30, and Collins thinks this classical allusion "plainly in Milton's mind."
    fixt: "fixedly" (Parker, "Variorum").

727–28. Cf. *PR* 4.433–34. Editors posit various sources for the simile. Todd, followed by other editors, refers to Homer, *Iliad* 8.305–6: μήκων δ' ὡζ ἑτέρωσε κάρη βάλεν, ἥ τ' ἐνὶ κήτῳ, / καρπῷ βριθομένη νοτίησί τε εἰαρινῆσιν; "And he bowed his head to one side like a poppy that in a garden is laden with its fruit and the rains of spring." This was imitated by Virgil, *Aeneid* 9.436–37: "lassove papavera collo / demisere caput, pluvia cum forte gravantur"; "or as poppies, with weary neck, bow the head, when weighted by some chance shower." While Todd also notes a similar image in Phineas Fletcher's *Purple Island* (1633), 11.30, 38, and Edmund Waller's "To My Lord Admiral, of His Late Sickness and Recovery" (1645), 33–34 (which Todd misidentifies as Thomas Carew's), Verity notes that Shakespeare often compared dew to tears. Banks reminds us that Milton's own experience may have influenced this image, for "a flower heavy with dew is a common enough sight" (139). Collins observes that the simile became a poetical commonplace. E.g., Dryden appropriates Milton's language almost verbatim in *Aureng-Zebe* 3.74–75 (see Langbaine and Gildon sig. H2v). J. Macmillan Brown notes more generally that the Chorus's diction becomes "more sensuous" with Dalila's approach (61). Carey suggests that "this image, like that of the ship [714–19], emphasizes Dalila's dangerous potentiality, and it does this not only through the attractiveness implied by 'flower' but also through the coolness implied by 'dew'" (*Complete Shorter Poems* 339). In addition to tracing other evocations of "healing coolness" in *SA,* Carey notes that the flower image allies Dalila with the Philistines, who are associated with flowers (144, 1652, 1654), and with Samson, who is also associated with this word (938, 1576–77, 1742): Carey argues that the flower's beauty is thus an emblem of externality, both Dalila's appearance and Samson's physical strength (*Complete Shorter Poems* 340).

    with head declin'd: editors detect here an allusion to the literal meaning of Dalila's name. Edmund K. Chambers, Grieve, and Verity (97), e.g., say that the name *Dalila* is from a root meaning "the drooping one," or "to droop like a palm." Hughes similarly claims that the root meaning of her name is "feeble or declining" (*John Milton*). But cf. 229n. In the seventeenth century, the supposed root was translated as *exhausit,* "to take from one all that he has, to destroy." See, e.g., *Linguae Romanae dictionarium luculentum novum* (1693), which made use of Milton's manuscript materials (Parker, "Variorum").

729. *addrest:* editors gloss as "prepared, made ready"; cf. 731. Newton and Todd note that this line, although printed correctly in the first edition, is mistakenly printed without *into* in subsequent early editions.

730–31. *silk'n:* B. A. Wright emends to *silken,* as the rhythm would seem to require; see also Parker, "Notes" 693.

   But now: Muldrow interprets this phrase to mean "that Dalila has been caught off guard and that she adopts a more hesitant approach than that of a stately ship" (191).

   address: editors gloss as "preparation" (*OED* I.1); cf. 729. Landor thinks the echo of line 729 "inelegant" (5:300).

732–951. Following Johnson's attack on Dalila's scene with Samson, early commentators address the scene's value and significance; later, commentators focus instead on Milton's portrait of Dalila as strong or weak, well intentioned or purely evil. Johnson (*Rambler* 16 July 1751), although he compliments Samson and Dalila's dialogue as "elegant and instructive," complains that her visit ultimately has no "effect but that of [raising] the character of *Samson*" (219). In response, Burnet finds that the dialogue (along with other examples from *PL*) compares favorably "even with Demosthenes in strength, and beauty of composition," particularly in the scene's "vehemence of altercation" and "strength of reasoning" (261–62). Objecting to Johnson's broader assessment that the play has no middle, Mickle cites this scene with Dalila—as well as the subsequent exchange with Harapha—to illustrate that "Samson's perturbation of mind and dark forebodings...are gradually heightened" (403). Cumberland similarly argues that this scene—"moral, affecting, and sublime"—increases our interest in Samson and, significantly, introduces "the cause and origin of all the pathos and distress of the story" (336). Bailey describes the episode as "the most dramatically effective in the poem" (235), and Penn writes that "this scene is perhaps worth all the rest of the play" (2:241).

   Johnson's assessment of Dalila's character and the poem's middle finds some later supporters. E.g., Wordsworth reportedly agreed that the drama has no middle (Robinson 2:479), and, in the early twentieth century, various commentators develop Johnson's thesis—such as Highet, who criticizes the poem's "shadowy" subordinate characters (295), and James Waddell Tupper, who argues that the incident with Dalila is "purely personal" and "does not bear upon the spiritual course of the drama" (380–81). See also Knowlton 335–36; and Beerbohm, *"Samson Agonistes"* (489). Wilkes finds the scene "much less introspective than the earlier ones.... Samson still does not know *what* he is to do, [but] he at least knows that he is not to do what Dalila urges" (372). Fish also downplays the encounter's significance for Samson: "the only visible effect...is a slight backing away from his insistence on reserving all the blame to himself" (241). Tung thinks the scene has a modest function, namely, "to bring Samson's impatience into bolder relief by contrasting it with Dalila's initial patience. It also shows that Samson's lack of patience threatens his repentance" (482).

Most commentators, however, develop Mickle's reading and find this encounter crucial for Samson's repentance. Curry describes the scene as the center of Milton's play, "the pivot . . . about which turns the entire dramatic action" (343). Prince agrees that the scene is "the turning-point in his hero's fluctuating state of mind" (*Samson Agonistes* 115), as does Edward J. Thompson: "from this point [Samson's] triumph begins" (248); Lawry: "the 'middle' [is] exactly in this episode" (376); and Carey: "Dalila's entrance is . . . the hinge of the drama" (*Complete Shorter Poems* 338). Ebbs similarly says that, in this exchange, "Samson undergoes a marked inner development, a growth in strength and faith" (386) that will culminate in his meeting with Harapha, while Woodhouse argues that Dalila's "powerlessness to reassert her sway" indicates "the completeness of Samson's repentance" ("*Samson Agonistes*" 165; "Tragic Effect" 211). Hill also argues for this scene's significance in Samson's regeneration: "the encounter with Dalila . . . succeed[s] in raising him out of the apathy, hopelessness, and despair into which Manoa's visit had thrown him." Hill adds that Dalila's temptations "prepare Samson spiritually for the encounters which follow" (164). Fogle similarly argues that Dalila is "a means, not of his recovery of strength, but of his recovery of a will to use that strength" (193); see also Grenander (386) and Jebb ("*Samson Agonistes*" 342). Clark writes that the episode "is less significant as a portrayal of dramatic struggle than as an exhibition of integrity restored" (96).

Ultimately the terms of debate turn away from Dalila's significance and to Milton's depiction of her character. E.g., Ellis-Fermor emphasizes that Dalila is not entirely without power: "as she engages him closer and closer we notice how severely logical is the argument . . . , how nobly clear and sustained the survey over their past as they uncover layer by layer the conduct and motives that brought it about" (28–29). Goethe reportedly found Dalila "nobly conceived" and exclaimed "Das ist herrlich — Er hat ihr Recht gegeben" (qtd. in Robinson 1:371, 373); Ker observes in response that Dalila is "so far in the right that Samson cannot be thoroughly in the right when he argues against her" (67). Thyer (in Todd) compliments Dalila's speech: "One cannot conceive a more artful, soft, and persuasive, eloquence," which Thyer (and later Prince, *Samson Agonistes* 115–16) finds a beautiful contrast with Samson's "stern and resolute firmness." Bailey also notes that "Dalila makes very good points" (236); Ebbs thinks her "very persuasive arguments...would have prevailed on an ordinary husband who had been wronged by his wife" (386; see also Wilkes 371); J. Macmillan Brown writes that she is false and wicked, but she "puts her case with marvelous power...that would have soon convinced the modern reason with its capacity for seeing all sides of a question and its eagerness to be impartial" (82); and Allen cautions that Dalila's final remarks should not undermine her genuine contrition and the force of her preceding argument—although he still thinks Dalila "shallow" and suggests that Samson knows her "contrition and remorse...are but thinly part of her and that the real impulsion is lechery.... By rejecting her, Samson expiates, among other evils, his own history of lechery" ("Idea as Pattern" 88). Among early-twentieth-century commentators, Baum may take the complimentary reading of Dalila the furthest, emphasizing her humility, patience, and persuasiveness: "we are inclined to award her the better of the argument" (360). He believes that "Dalila returns to Samson with a passionate woman's desire to renew the old life and a proud woman's pique at having lost what she had won" (360).

Other critics, however, continue to find fault with Dalila—such as Watkins, who calls her "transparently shallow, subtle like Satan" (144), and Kranidas, who describes her as "firmly culpable, in certain areas self-deluding, but in general quite deliberately wrong" (126); see also Muldrow, who disagrees specifically with Allen's reading: "it is more than an issue of lechery, important though that is. The 'real impulsion' is Dalila's desire for power" (200). Lawry suggests that Dalila's "speech is an open parody of liberal theology," and, although she winningly claims to have acted out of love, "her Satanic will glints through such verbiage like a serpent" (379, 380).

Various critics conclude that Dalila is a complex character. Curry addresses the "complexity" of Dalila's motives for visiting her husband—"an entirely human curiosity," "a certain tenderness for him whom she possibly still loves, and a sympathy for his suffering." Curry ultimately finds Dalila's characterization ambiguous, which he calls "a stroke of genius": "one cannot ever be quite sure about the character of this Dalila; she has about her a tantalizing mystery" (344). Martz also states that Dalila "remains an enigma.... Her speeches suggest a complex tissue of motives and impulses" (128); Woodhouse agrees that Dalila's "motives are left by Milton obscure," but he asserts that "They do not matter; she is there for the sake of Samson and the action, not in her own right" ("Tragic Effect" 211). Williamson speculates that Dalila may remain an "equivocal" character "because she is the bridge between sympathy and antipathy in the visitors" (94). Landy emphasizes that Dalila "is no mere abstraction," and "Like all humans, she is a bundle of contradictions" ("Character" 246); Moody similarly finds her Milton's "one really dramatic creation, endowed with Shakespearean reality of life" (286). Mollenkott suggests that Milton means for readers to view Dalila (and the play's other characters) on two levels, the human and divine: "Dalila as the instrument of Dagon is clearly in the wrong. But on the human level, Dalila's reasons for betraying Samson are valid in their own way.... Milton uses the Dalila episode to demonstrate that although various points of view may all possess a certain human validity, nothing can actually procure an individual's salvation except obedience to the One God" (96, 101).

Among other critical responses to this passage, Parker compares Samson's conversation with Dalila to Euripides' *Troades* 914–1059 as Menelaus seeks revenge on Helen (*Milton's Debt* 126–28). Collins notes more generally that the scene seems "thoroughly Euripidean" in both "the cast of the language" and "the quality of the sentiment." Lucas also finds this and the poem's other "rhetorical debates" Eurpidean (116). Timberlake agrees: "the whole scene ... is not unlike that between Jason and Medea, with the man this time on the side of the better reason" (337). Moss similarly cites this exchange to illustrate how Milton used the "forensic pattern that occurs in almost every Greek play"; Moss concludes, "in this connection, the relevant meanings of the term *agonistes* are 'debater' and 'contender'" (297, 298). Hughes is instead reminded of the conflict readers experience in *Antony and Cleopatra:* "our sympathies are divided. They go out to both Samson and Dalila, but more strongly to her than to him" (*John Milton* 432; also *Complete Poems* 532–33). J. Macmillan Brown compares Dalila's visit with the return of Milton's first wife (40, 101), as does Rosedale (161). Gohn discusses how various Renaissance writers identify "Dalila with the passions and Samson with the reason; the Samson story was evidently thought of as a kind of psychological allegory" (261).

732–91. About the dramatic function of the versification, Ellis-Fermor writes: "the prosody, like the thought, shows a steady increase of firmness and form. The verse becomes tough and resilient; it hardens as the moods and tempers harden" (151).

732–33. Blakeney notes a "delicate metrical effect produced in these two lines by the extra syllable. Dalila wishes to make a favourable impression at the outset; and her words are cunningly chosen, and set as cunningly, to produce the desired effect." Kranidas more emphatically deems these opening words of Dalila a "scene-governing lie" (127). Radzinowicz follows Blakeney in noting that Milton reveals Dalila's guilt through the verse's rhythm: "She speaks a curiously seductive cadence, hesitation embodied in feminine lines, the unaccented last syllables and plentiful caesuras of which emphasize lightly breathed dubiety" ("Eve" 172).

doubtful: see 740; cf. 477.

wavering: Parker proposes *wav'ring,* as regular meter would seem to require ("Notes" 693).

734. *without excuse:* cf. 829. Percival notes that Dalila's speeches in fact contain "quite a string of excuses." Radzinowicz similarly observes that the lines immediately following (735–39) contradict Dalila's promise here: "Amid penitence she slips in a self-justification, so that rather than grieving that she unnaturally asserted her will against Samson, she grieves that she miscalculated the effect" ("Eve" 173). Timberlake writes that Dalila begins with "that same preface which Aristotle advises for those who have a bad case" (337). Church notes that the infinitive is the object of "acknowledge" in 735. Landor suggests, "The comma should be expunged after *excuse,* else the sentence is ambiguous" (5:300); so also Blakeney who asserts that the words "without excuse" belong to the next line.

735–37. On the use of enjambment in *SA,* see 190n.

fact: editors gloss as "action, deed"; Parker ("Variorum") also suggests, "crime" (*OED* 1a, 1c); cf. 493.

more evil drew: "had more evil consequences" (Prince, *Samson Agonistes*).

perverse: "contrary to expectation" (Edmund K. Chambers 143), or "adverse, unpropitious" (so *OED* 3b); cf. *PL* 9.405, where the adjective follows the noun.

event: editors gloss as "outcome, issue, result," from the Latin *eventus* (*OED* 3).

738–39. *penance:* editors gloss as "penitence, repentance," or, possibly, "punishment" (*OED* 1, 5).

though...assur'd: Verity and other editors note that Milton's "peculiar" diction here resembles a Latin absolute construction, with "be" understood after "pardon." Cf. *PL* 1.140–41.

conjugal affection: Milton uses this phrase also in *ComBk* (Patterson, *Works* 18:151); cf. *DocCh* (Patterson, *Works* 15:177).

742. *estate:* editors gloss as "condition" (*OED* 1). Parker suggests that the period is probably an error for a comma ("Variorum").

743–47. Adams writes that this sentence "suggests, by the omission of a main verb, the wavering of her approach" (193).

744. *light'n:* B. A. Wright emends to *lighten,* as the rhythm would seem to require; see also Parker, "Notes" 693.

appease: "pacify, quiet" (*OED* 1; Lockwood); "desirous to appease" (Hunter).

745. *amends is:* Blakeney, Percival, and Wyatt and Collins explain the construction as "amends (it) is in my power (to make)." Parker responds, though, that Milton could have used the word as a collective singular with a singular verb ("Variorum").

746–47. *recompence:* editors gloss as "make compensation or atonement for" (*OED* 2b); cf. 910.

rash: cf. 907.

unfortunate: "unlucky," "marked by, or associated with, misfortune or mishap" (*OED* 2). Verity explains, "She means that she never anticipated such an evil result of her rash act."

748–58. Johnson (*Rambler* 20 July 1751) admires Samson's response to Dalila's flattery as "a just and striking description of the stratagems and allurements of feminine hypocrisy" (222). Curry instead suggests that "[Samson's] replies to her are so harsh and so winged with a venomous but quite unconvincing hatred as to suggest that he is merely walling himself about with a defence of vituperation and vociferation. He protests too much and too loudly; most of his arguments against her representations are specious" (345). These lines are also quoted in a 1697 antifeminist tract to support that "a True Wife's Incorrigible" (Dutton sig. L9r–v). See also 1053–60n. J. Macmillan Brown alternatively finds in Samson's distrust of Dalila a contemporary allusion to the English civil wars: "the Cavaliers...would hesitate at no lie, however direct or gross," and "the Parliamentarians ceased to trust their words, however eloquent or seductive or plausible" (129).

748–65. Parker (*Milton's Debt* 63) notes that Samson's response, of eighteen lines, nearly balances Dalila's speech of sixteen lines (732–47). Cf. 907–27 and 928–50, where Samson is again given two more lines than his wife. But, Parker adds, in the whole scene, Milton "chivalrously allows Dalila about fifty more lines than he gives his hero" (*Milton's Debt* 63).

748. Bridges scans this line with the second and third feet inverted (trochaic), making a prosodial synaloepha of the *yæ* of *Hyæna*, since there is no other example of an extrametrical syllable within the line in all of *PL, PR,* and *SA* (*Milton's Prosody* 50). Shakespeare, Bridges notes, has *hien;* Chaucer, *hyene.* Edmund K. Chambers (127) describes the middle of this line as an unstressed rhythm—although, he adds, forced elisions would sustain the regular iambic meter; he similarly describes 122, 399, 429, 579, and 842.

Other commentators address here Samson's ferociousness. E.g., Kranidas suggests that the "hammerblows" in the opening of Samson's speech contrast with the "sinuousness" of Dalila's language (128). Belloc comments: "one must be in two minds.... It makes one laugh, but it is vigorous and natural, nor is this naturalness quite on the level of the ridiculous...[if] one would rather stare in horror than grin" (279). Hanford alternatively observes, "It is characteristic of Milton that he cannot represent his hero as victorious...save by making him harsh and hostile" (*John Milton* 220). Carey thinks this sudden harshness undermines the conviction of Samson's earlier claim that he himself, not Dalila, "was not the prime cause" of his fall (*John Milton* 142).

Out: Parker describes this as an "exclamation of abhorrence or indignant reproach" ("Variorum"); cf. *PL* 10.867.

Hyæna: "cruel, treacherous, and rapacious person" (so *OED* 2); in the first edition, this word is followed by a semicolon; early editors, beginning with Fenton, often emend it to an exclamation point. For this metaphor, commentators offer various possible sources. Most often, they quote or cite references to the commonplace that the hyena was a wild animal supposed to lure men to destruction by imitating the human voice; see, e.g., Jeremiah 12:9. Carey (*Complete Shorter Poems*), working specifically from Pliny, *Naturalis historia* 8.44 and 28.27, also notes that the hyena was capable of changing its sex and was believed to have other magical powers—traits which help, he claims, "to give point to Samson's abuse." Onions (79) cites Blount's *Glossographia:* "It is the subtillest (as some say) of all beasts" (sig. U6v). Svendsen adds that the hyena was unclean, and, according to one tradition, most cunning when in mourning (*Milton and Science* 164–65). Todd thinks that Milton had in mind Jonson's *Volpone* 4.6.2–3: "Out, thou *Chameleon* harlot: now, thine eyes / Vie teares with the *Hyaena*." (On Dalila's tears, see 51, 728–30, 735.) Van Kluyve offers the fullest survey of medieval and Renaissance historians but thinks that Ovid's description in *Metamorphoses* 15.408–10 "may have been the most influential" (99).

   Addressing how such beast lore applies to Milton's depiction of Dalila, Cox emphasizes the moral implication of the hyena's ability to change sex: Dalila not only had "assumed the prerogative of the man in desiring mastery over Samson" but also is "not properly woman" and her "misuse of the senses or the will reveals a beast nature" ("Natural Science" 66). Van Kluyve suggests instead that Samson applies the term to Dalila because "she has come to glut herself on his flesh"; because she hides her true intentions just as a hyena hides its "viper neck" beneath its mane; and because she lacks "perspective on the enormity of her crime" just as a "rigid-spined hyena" cannot look back (100). Nicolson (364) compares this and other animalistic descriptions of Dalila (see 936, 997, 1001) with the animal imagery describing Satan's degeneration in *PL*. In *Defpro Se* Milton calls Alexander More a hyena—"or if there be any other brute equally destructive, and equally infamous for the blackness of its guile" (Patterson, *Works* 9:125).

   wonted arts: Todd quotes Ovid, *Heroides* 2.51–52: "credidimus lacrimis—an et hae simluare docentur? / hae quoque habent artes, quaque iubentur, eunt?"; "I had faith in your tears—or can these also be taught to flow where bidden?" Keightley remarks that in the remainder of this speech Milton evidently had in mind the conduct of his first wife (*Poems*); Percival (121) and Edmund K. Chambers (96) quote Edward Phillips on Milton's reconciliation with Mary Powell (see also Darbishire, *Early Lives* 66–67). Rowse finds this parallel to Mary Powell in the very beginning of this episode (102), but Grieve suggests that Milton's "bitter memory" of his first marriage influences the whole speech (v). See also 759–63n.

749. *every woman:* Edmund K. Chambers argues that "Samson's contempt is for women as women, and not merely for Dalila among women" (85), but Parker

claims, on the basis of the passage's syntax, that "Samson is speaking of arts common to those women who are false like Dalila—not all women" (*Milton's Debt* 131; see also *Milton* 317–18). Thaler detects an echo of *Pericles* 2.5.20–32 ("Shakespearian Element" 197).

750. As Percival remarks (and illustrates), "literature, unhappily, abounds with this sentiment." Todd specifically recalls that Dryden borrows most of this verse in *Aureng-Zebe*, act 1 (see also Langbaine and Gildon, *Lives* sig. H2v).

752. *move*: editors gloss as "propose" (*OED* 14); Prince suggests "beg" (*Samson Agonistes*). Cf. *motion'd* (222).
　　remorse: "pity, a sense common in our older writers" (Collins). Cf. *PL* 1.605.

754–56. *chief*: cf. 1452. Peck cites this word to illustrate how Milton sometimes uses substantives as adverbs (sig. P1r). Verity breaks down this passage grammatically: "*husband* is the direct object after *try*, while the clauses *how far*…and *which way*…are indirect questions dependent on *try*."

755. The sense here is "how far his patience will bear urging" (Edmund K. Chambers).

756. *assail*: "to tempt to evil" (Lockwood b); cf. 1165, 1396.

757. *instructed*: "inform[ed]" (so *OED* 1); "prepared, designed" (Percival); "trained" (Lockwood); or "experienced" (Bullough and Bullough; Prince, *Samson Agonistes*).

759–63. *That*: editors gloss as "(so) that."
　　wisest and best men: a similar phrase recurs in 210, 867, 1034, and cf. *DDD* (Patterson, *Works* 3:394, 461); *Tetr* (Patterson, *Works* 4:87, 120); *Colas* (Patterson, *Works* 4:256). Le Comte discusses all these verbal echoes (45, 87–88); cf. also *PR* 2.169–70. Some editors, such as Bullough and Bullough and Masson (*Poetical Works*), agree with Hayley's assertion (*Life* 1:cxiii; and in Todd) that this passage is "a forcible allusion" to Milton's reconciliation with his first wife and its supposed unhappy consequences; see also 748n. But Tinker argues

against reading the poem too biographically: "These utterances are appropriate enough in the mouth of Samson...but they are surely no fair statement of the poet's wedded experiences, for, however unhappy had been Milton's first marriage, his second, as he himself tells us in his most exquisite sonnet, had been one of serene beauty and domestic love" (72).

760. *principl'd:* "taught, actuated" by the principle of goodness (*OED* 1; Blakeney; Hughes, *John Milton*); Edmund K. Chambers defines as "having good principles" (132). Cf. *Mask* 366, *Apol* (Patterson, *Works* 3:311), *RCG* (Patterson, *Works* 3:250), *Educ* (Patterson, *Works* 4:279), and *TR* (Patterson, *Works* 6:172).
    reject: "rebuff," "refuse to accept" (so *OED* 6).

762. Church and Todd quote *DDD:* "what folly is it still to stand combating and battering against invincible causes and effects, with evill upon evill, till either the best of our dayes be linger'd out, or ended with some speeding sorrow" (Patterson, *Works* 3:418–19).

763. *Entangl'd:* Parker ("Variorum") writes, "mixed up in such a manner that a separation cannot easily be made" (so *OED* II.3a).
    bosom snake: cf. *DDD:* "bosome affliction" (Patterson, *Works* 3:404). The idea of the treacherous snake cherished in one's bosom, a symbol of ingratitude, is as old as Aesop's fable (Blakeney). Carey (*Complete Shorter Poems*) cites the proverb from Tilley (V68) "to nourish a snake (viper) in one's bosom." Verity cites examples in *2 Henry VI* 3.1.343, *Richard II* 3.2.131, and Webster's *Duchess of Malfi* 2.2. Cf. also 1001. Parker notices the sibilants and the potentially "undulating rhythm of Dalila's answer" ("Variorum").

764–65. Parker comments, "Samson more than suggests that Dalila's treachery has cost him, not only his eyesight and freedom, but also his life" ("Variorum"). See 888, 958, 1002, 1009; cf. also 32, 575, 592, 630, 650; and see 1225n.
    cut off: "[brought] to an untimely end" (*OED* 55d); as Verity notes, the expression is common in the Bible (e.g., Milton's *Ps 83* 13, 39), implying utter destruction. Verity also compares Harapha's words at 1156–57 as an ironic echo.

765. *example:* "warning," "a person whose fate serves as a deterrent to others" (*OED* 3); see also 166.

766–80. Tillyard finds in these lines the worst "lapse in style" in the poem: "No analogy with Euripidean dialectic can justify such inhuman speech in a play" (*Milton* 284–85). Daiches, however, finds it "an impressive piece of pleading... a real temptation, because sex and a plausible if distorted view of love are involved" (242–43).

    Yet hear me: Landy finds this request "painfully ironic" because it "recalls Samson's earlier description of her 'tongue-batteries'" ("Language" 187).

768–69. *on th' other side:* see 246.

    aggravations: "exaggeration[s]" or, possibly, "accusation[s]" (*OED* 5, 2); Lockwood defines "extrinsic circumstance increasing the guilt of a crime" (cf. *OED* 7b). Cf. *DDD* (Patterson, *Works* 3:475) and *Tetr* (Patterson, *Works* 4:124).

    surcharg'd: see 728. Parker writes that the use of this word so soon after 728 may be considered a blemish ("Variorum").

770–808. Oras notes Milton's lyrical use of pyrrhic endings here and writes that "it may be because of the calculated oratory of Dalila that we find more of them in her speeches than anywhere else." He adds, "the effect of these passages is sober and carries no suggestion of Milton's youthful manner," and thus does not support *SA*'s early composition ("Milton's Blank Verse" 189). See also 975–96; and 270–71n, 315–20n, 1604n.

770–71. *counterpois'd:* that is, the "aggravations" balanced by "just allowance," like a weight on the opposite side (Wyatt and Collins). Cf. *Bucer* (Patterson, *Works* 4:19), *Eikon* (Patterson, *Works* 5:79), and *PL* 4.1001.

    if possible: cf. 490.

773–77. Editors paraphrase as follows: "granted that it was a weakness (to be) curious and to publish secrets, both common female faults, was it not weakness...." As Hughes explains, "*Curiosity* [775] is in apposition with *weakness* in 773, while the two adjectives following it modify *sex* in 774" (*Complete Poems; John Milton*). Rudrum contrasts Dalila's "dispersal of her 'weakness' among all her sex" with Samson's acceptance of sole responsibility (44); cf. 375–76.

granting: Masson writes: "the nearest approach to an actual case of misrelated or unrelated participle that I have observed in Milton.... *Granting,* however, is one of a small group of participial forms...to which custom concedes this slovenliness; and it says much for Milton's care that instances like the above are rare in his verse. It may be taken as an elliptical case-absolute" (*Poetical Works* 3:200–201).

774. *incident:* "naturally appertaining" (*OED* 1); cf. 656.

775. *importune:* "persistent or pressing in solicitation" (*OED* 4); "formerly an alternate form of 'importunate'" (Verity; Prince, *Samson Agonistes*), which Grieve describes as "a less correct form." Cf. 51, 397, 779, 1680. Scansion of this line causes difficulty; cf. *PL* 9.610 and *PR* 2.404. Collins suggests that Milton is using the accent of the Latin and deriving the word from the late Latin, *inquīsītīvus* (see also 341n); Percival thinks that the change of meter is "meant to indicate contempt" (xlvii). Carey (*Complete Shorter Poems*) notes that the use of *importune* with *of* does not occur in the *OED*.

776–77. Hunter finds this construction "harsh" and suggests "the most convenient way...for analysis is to supply the pronoun *this,* as a nominative absolute: 'this, and then to publish, &c., being both common female faults.'"

 like: Percival explains, "because both kinds of weakness [infirmity] are due to...want of self-restraint."

 publish: "make publicly or generally known," "tell or noise abroad" (*OED* 1); cf. 498. Verity, Blakeney, Wyatt and Collins, et al. note that *curiosity* (i.e., "to be curious") and *to publish* are coordinate and both modify *weakness* (773).

 female: Darbishire (*Poetical Works*) and B. A. Wright emend to *femal;* see 711–13n.

778–80. Masson (*Poetical Works*) and Verity note that this argument echoes Eve blaming Adam in *PL* 9.1155–61. Cf. Samson's self-recriminations at 200–2, 235, and 499. Kranidas believes that here Dalila's "false innocence is demonstrated in her pretending that Samson would not have thought of his guilt" (129).

 importunity: see 51.

 naught: "nothing," i.e., no reason (*OED* 1); cf. 1215.

 strength and safety: Dalila repeats the phrase (799).

781. Stein suggests that Dalila "is brazenly right, as right as Eve was when she too used the argument she had lost the moral right to use. It is a maneuver to undermine justice in a relativism of injustice" (*Heroic Knowledge* 168). Mollenkott disagrees: "Dalila is hardly trying to undermine justice; rather, she is trying to get Samson to grant her the human mercy which is part of true justice and which can come only as a result of awareness of one's own shortcomings" (97).

782. *But:* "but you will say" (Verity). Cf. 799. For other anticipated replies to the argument, see 836, 895, and 1208.

783. An alexandrine in trochaic rhythm? Blakeney suggests, "the line is not only hypermetric (*fraility,* last syll.), but requires the slurring of 'thou have.'" See 118n.
    womans frailty: cf. 369; *PL* 10.956; *Hamlet* 1.2.146: "Frailty, thy name is woman!" (Percival; Thaler, "Shakespearian Element" 153). For the general sentiment, Percival quotes Micah 7:5; Homer, *Odyssey* 11.441; Seneca, *Hippolytus* 876; Jean de La Bruyère; and François La Rochefoucauld. Editors commonly supply a colon or semicolon at the end of this line.

784. *to thy self was cruel:* cf. 401, 824. Verity quotes *Mask* 678; Shakespeare's Sonnet 1.8 ("Thyself thy foe, to thy sweet self too cruel"); More's *Utopia* ("not to be cruell and ungentle to the selfe"); and Proverbs 11:17 ("The merciful man doeth good to his own soul; but he that is cruel troubleth his own flesh").

785. *parl:* "parley," "discussion, debate; *spec.* a meeting to discuss terms (between enemies or opposed parties)" (so *OED* 2); cf. 403 (*parlies*), *PR* 4.529, and *HistBr* (Patterson, *Works* 10:274). Here the sense seems to be "agreement" (Collins); Shakespeare often similarly uses both *parle* and *parley* (Verity). Percival notes that Dalila is insidiously placing herself on Samson's level in degree of guilt. By hearing Dalila's plea, Christopher adds, Samson is thus able to purge his own tendency to excuse his betrayal; Christopher also suggests that Dalila "is really asking for excuse, not forgiveness" (367). See 1168–77n.

787. Verity glosses, "Let thy weakness be an excuse for mine." The first edition is punctuated, "kind, / Thine forgive mine; that men may censure thine." Some editors (e.g., Keightley; Verity; William Aldis Wright) transpose these two

punctuation marks; Edmund K. Chambers retains the semicolon after *mine* and emends the comma to a second semicolon.

censure: editors gloss as "judge" (*OED* 1); cf. 948.

790. "The position here assumed by Dalila is exactly that of Deianira in the *Trachiniae* of Sophocles" (Collins; see also Percival 124).

791. *jealousie:* Percival quotes Euripides, *Andromache* 181–82: ἐπίφθονόν τι χρῆμα θηλείας φρενὸς / καὶ ξυγγάμοισι δυσμενὲς μάλιστ᾽ ἀεί; "In woman's heart is jealousy inborn, / 'Tis bitterst unto wedlock-rivals aye."

powerful: pronounced as a disyllable (Parker, "Variorum"); editors identify "powerful of" as a Latin idiom.

794. *fancy:* editors gloss as "amorous inclination, love" (*OED* 8b). Verity and Wyatt and Collins note that in Judges 15:2, the father of Samson's first wife charges him with inconstancy such as Dalila accuses him of here; see also 795n. Cf. "maiden meditation, fancy-free" in Shakespeare's *Midsummer Night's Dream* 2.1.161 (Carey, *Complete Shorter Poems;* Hughes, *Complete Poems* and *John Milton*); and "tell me where is fancy bred" in *Merchant of Venice* 3.2.63 (Meiklejohn; Blakeney).

795. *As her at Timna:* cf. Judges 14:19–20; 15:1–3. On Samson's first wife, see 219–25n. Parker comments, "Dalila's charge, not denied by Samson, that he left his first wife (rather than that she left Samson) could be an inconsistency in the play—hence possible evidence of interrupted composition" ("Variorum"). But Hughes (*John Milton*) suggests that Samson was simply "neglectful, . . . for, when he visited his first wife after an absence, 'her father said, I verily thought that thou hadst utterly hated her; therefore I gave her to thy companion' (Judg. 15.2)"; see also 794n.

796. *endear:* "win the affection of," or "deepen (affection)" (so *OED* 6), or "bind by ties of affection, attach" (Lockwood). Verity suggests that the sense here is "endear myself," although grammatically the object is *thee.*

797. A twelve-syllable line (alexandrine) without any break (Bridges, *Milton's Prosody* 61).

importuning: see 775 and 779. Oras identifies this word as one of the poem's dactylic endings that "require the suppression of a vowel between two consonants if they are—in theory or reality—to be reduced to the trochaic norm" ("Milton's Blank Verse" 168). See 603n.

800–2. Hughes (*Complete Poems; John Milton*) notes that Milton could expect his readers to recognize a lie here: cf. Judges 16:5: "And the lords of the Philistines...said unto her, Entice him, and see...by what means we may prevail against him, that we may bind him to afflict him." (The margin has *humble* next to *afflict,* and the Vulgate reads *affligere* [Carey, *Complete Shorter Poems*].) Krouse (77, 102) identifies Cajetan (Tommaso de Vio Gaetano) as apparently "the only writer who made any attempt to defend Dalila," and, in his *Opera* (London, 1637), he offered this same explanation of Dalila's conduct.

802. *custody:* editors gloss as "safe keeping, care," and/or "imprisonment."

hold: "restraint" and/or "imprisonment," "confinement" (*OED* 5, 4), the meaning of the word in 796. Parker suggests that both words are "carefully ambiguous" ("Variorum"); but cf. 808.

803. *made for me:* editors gloss as "suited my purpose, aided me, was to my advantage" (*OED* 78a), or, perhaps, "(argument) weighed heavily with me" (Prince, *Samson Agonistes;* cf. *OED* s.v. *make* 25). Prince cites this phrase (along with phrases in 373, 424, and 551) to illustrate that Milton "achieves a consistently unusual quality in his diction" (*Samson Agonistes* 108). Blakeney finds parallels in Matthew Arnold's "the Eternal not ourselves that *makes for* Righteousness" (*Literature and Dogma* [1873]) and in Francis Bacon's "[these things] *make for* the advantage of England" (*Considerations Touching a War with Spain* [1629]).

805. *cares and fears:* Parker compares Mary's "Motherly cares and fears" in *PR* 2.64 ("Variorum").

806. *widow'd bed:* Church recalls that Ovid's Penelope speaks of her *viduus lectus* (*Heroides* 1.81). Thaler is reminded of Lady Hotspur in *1 Henry IV* 2.3.40–67

("Shakespearian Element" 177). Parker observes, "the bed as the place of conjugal union occurs again in 1021 and may be alluded to in 916" ("Variorum").

807. *enjoy:* Parker suggests, "take delight in" and (cf. 915) "have sexual intercourse with" ("Variorum"). See Samson's reaction in 836–37. Bullough and Bullough note: "Her idea that Samson might live with her in confinement may come from Luther's note (based on Jerome for Judg. 16.21: 'grinding'), in which he interprets the Hebrew as meaning that Samson was to be kept to breed strong children by a Philistine woman (who might be Dalila)." Cf. *DDD:* "to grind in the mill of an undelighted and servil copulation" (Patterson, *Works* 3:403).

808. *Mine:* Verity notes that this word was commonly used for *my* when separated from its noun (so also Hughes, *Complete Poems; John Milton*).
    Loves prisoner: B. A. Wright emends to *pris'ner,* as the rhythm would seem to require; cf. 1308, 1460. Daiches remarks: "This is not Milton's concept of marriage.... Milton is attacking here a variant of the courtly love tradition...which he attacked in other ways in *PL*" (241). Muldrow agrees and finds Dalila's concept of love "disturbing" (194). Summers adds, "her argument would justify any woman's maiming and enslaving any lover who wished to engage in heroic action—or even leave the house" (167). See also Kranidas (130). On this chivalric concept, see 556n.

809. *Whole:* "wholly" (Blakeney).
    abroad: "out of one's house" (*OED* A.3); so also 919; cf. 1600.

810. *Fearless:* Parker ("Variorum") comments that this word, though rhythmically parallel to *Whole* and *unhazarded,* belongs grammatically to *I* (807) or (so Edmund K. Chambers) to *my self* (809), not to *thee.*

811. *Loves law:* Verity paraphrases this line as, "these reasons have been approved according to the code of right that love recognises." Editors quote or cite various sources and parallels. Verity cites Shakespeare's *3 Henry VI* 3.2.153–54: "love forswore me.../ I should not deal in her soft laws." See *PL* 4.750; cf. *Educ:* "the laws of any private friendship" (Patterson, *Works* 4:275). Cf. also Euripides,

Troades 945–50 when Helen blames Aphrodite; and Petrarch, *Trionfo d'amore* 3.148: "Dura legge d'Amor" (qtd. by Carlo Dati in his letter to Milton of 1 November 1647 [Patterson, *Works* 12:298]). Hughes also observes that "Milton thought of the law of Love as traditionally administered in the medieval Courts of Love, such as Chartier's *Parliament of Love*" (*John Milton*).

812. *fond:* editors gloss as "foolish" (as in 228, 1682).
  to: editors gloss as "in the eyes of, in the opinion of."

817. *in strength all mortals:* an echo of 522–23, not heard by Dalila (Parker, "Variorum"). Cf. *PL* 5.458–59.

819–42. Hedley Vicars Ross argues that this passage is "unconsciously autobiographical" (71).
  sorceress: cf. 937. Parker notes that Exodus 22:18 commands the death penalty for a sorceress ("Variorum").

820. *upbraid:* "censure" (*OED* 1). The expression is usually "to upbraid *with* a thing." Here *me* is the indirect object—"to me"—(Verity; Grieve), and the direct object is *mine* (Hughes, *John Milton*); see also Wyatt and Collins.
  mine?: see 1356. Tickell, followed by many editors, replaces the question mark with an exclamation point.

821. *malice not repentance:* Samson's explanation of Dalila's visit may not satisfy the reader; e.g., Carey calls it "wildly improbable" (*John Milton* 143). See 732–951n; and cf. 754–56, 930–32, 999–1000. A. B. Chambers identifies within Dalila's explicit appeals to Samson an implicit temptation for him to experience her "own dangerous condition of the soul"; Chambers describes this condition as "*malitia,* sometimes defined as 'peccandi studium' but frequently implying the classical meaning of the word as a perverse love of causing harm" (318).

824. Cf. 376, 401. Thaler recalls Polonius at this point ("Shakespearian Element" 150).
  e're: Patterson has *e'er* in error (*Works*).

825–40. Percival writes that, although this striking utterance of Samson turns Dalila's argument against herself, it also exhibits the "over-just" (514) self-condemnation for which Manoa had reproved him. Dunster (in Todd) instead suggests that the "wonderful dignity" of Samson's sentiments reflects "all the noble and resolute virtue of the poet's own highly-principled mind." Daiches thinks that Samson needs to believe Dalila was weak and driven by greed to "maintain his moral position," whereas Milton, standing apart, actually creates a "subtle portrait of sincere but perverse love" (244). Carey, however, thinks that Samson's "brutally simple" explanation is "probably nearer the truth"; for evidence he points to Dalila's elaborate equipage (*John Milton* 142). Carey also notes how Samson repeats *love* and *weakness* four times in ten lines (829–38), which compares with Dalila's four uses of these words (766–818): thus, "Moments of tension, introspective or argumentative, are screwed tighter" (*Complete Shorter Poems* 335). Ellis-Fermor writes that the passage's "steady metallic rhythm is the fitting accompaniment to the hard mood of dispute and debate, and gives stability to the prosodic foundation from now onward" (152).

Such pardon: the sense here is "only so far as I pardon my folly, shall you have pardon for your sin" (Verity). Watkins writes that Samson's pardon of Dalila is thus "precisely none, for Samson does not forgive himself" (145). See 826n.
my folly: see 377.

826. *which:* Verity, Grieve, et al. note that the antecedent is *pardon* (825), i.e., the *un*pardoning judgment that Samson passes on his own folly. Wyatt and Collins suggest that "there is an implied oxymoron, for the 'pardon' is really no pardon at all." See 825–40n.

827. Peck cites this line to illustrate Milton's characteristic use of a "continuative epithet," that is, three epithets to compose a single line of verse (sig. P4r). See also 417n and 1364, 1422.

828. *thy seeking:* "what thou seekest" (Hughes, *John Milton*).

829. *feign'd, weakness:* early editors, beginning with Tickell, agree the comma seems an error for a period; but Carey (*Complete Shorter Poems*) and Shawcross (*Complete English Poetry*), e.g., retain the original punctuation.

830. *weakness to resist:* Blakeney calls this an "explanatory infinitive"; see also 1274–75n.

831. *gold:* see 389n. Writing in 1924, Kilgo uniquely uses this accusation to speculate, "[I]s money the most alluring thing that can be offered to woman?" (314).

832. *Parricide:* Parker notes that this addition seems odd with *Murtherer* and *Traytor* ("Variorum"). Cf. 1180.

834. A few commentators find fault with this line. Menzies writes, "We have here clearly the voice of the author himself; nothing could be more characteristic" (82–83). Hales comments about this passage: "He writes for the most part like some inexorable logician, and not like a man conscious of the infirmities of his kind" (218).

   weakness: Percival notes how this word, first used by Samson (756), then turned into an excuse by Dalila (773, 778, 785), is given "contemptuous emphasis" by Samson as he uses it four times within six lines. Cf. *PL* 4.856. Parker ("Variorum") adds that the final comment on Samson's weakness is Manoa's (1722).

   plea: editors gloss as "excuse" (*OED* 4); so also 843. Parker suggests a defense in court is implied ("Variorum").

835. *remission:* editors gloss as "pardon or forgiveness" (*OED* 2).

836. *But:* see 782n.

   thee: some editors (e.g., Masson, *Poetical Works;* Verity; Edmund K. Chambers; William Aldis Wright) emend the semicolon after this word to an exclamation point.

   rage: "vehement passion *for,* desire *of,* a thing" (so *OED* 7) or "sexual passion" (*OED* 6B). The phrase occurs also in *PL* 8.244, with a very different meaning (Le Comte 62).

837. *Love seeks:* this thought has many classical parallels; editors quote from Martial, Cicero, Dante, and Seneca, as well as George Herbert.

   to have: B. A. Wright emends to *t' have;* cf. 727.

838. *hope:* "hope *for*" (Verity); "desire with expectation" (*OED* 3a).
tookst the way: cf. 1591.

840. Editors identify this as a Greek construction: "knowing (myself, or that I was) betrayed by thee"; cf. *PL* 9.792 and see 1549n.

842. Bridges (*Milton's Prosody* 56) and Sprott (132) suggest that the first two feet are inverted (trochaic; see 81n). Edmund K. Chambers (127) describes the middle of the line as an unstressed rhythm—although, he adds, forced elisions would sustain the regular iambic meter; he similarly describes 122, 399, 429, 579, and 748. Weismiller suggests that "the initial vowel of 'evasions' [ought] to blend with and as it were disappear into the vowel of 'by,' leaving what is in effect an aphaeretic form" (118).

    Or: the reading of the first edition; some editors, from 1705 on, have emended to *For.* Percival summarizes the case for each reading, although he confuses the two and wrongly asserts that *For* was the original reading. Keightley suspects that Milton dictated *And* (*Poems*).

    crime: cf. 490.

843. *determinst...for:* "decide *a thing* to be" (Lockwood; cf. *OED* 5b). Prince suggests that the line also means "since you bring to a close my plea of weakness as being no plea" (*Samson Agonistes*). See 834.

844–48. Saurat (197) and other commentators observe that Samson fell for reasons very similar to Adam's at the moment of the Fall. If Dalila is not lying, Parker adds, then her being actually tempted before she tempts Samson would have the artistic and theological merit of making her case analogous to Eve's ("Variorum").

    though to: "though it result in" (Blakeney).

845–46. *assaults:* "temptation[s] to evil" (so *OED* 6 and Lockwood), and/or "sudden charges of an attacking force" (Parker, "Variorum"); cf. 846 (*sieges*). Cf. 331, 365. For the military metaphor, see also 235n, 403–5n, 560–61n, 906; Parker finds the imagery here to be a mocking echo of Samson's earlier explanations (unheard by Dalila).

847–48. *men:* emphatic (so Percival and Blakeney).

    to have: B. A. Wright emends to *t' have* and puts a comma after *constantest* (as does the 1680 edition).

849. *as . . . lay'st:* i.e., "as you charge" (see *OED* 16b). See 830–31, and see 992n.

850–51. *wrought with:* "influenced" (cf. *OED* s.v. *work* 23).

    Magistrates: Percival notes that Judges 16:5 says the "lords," but Josephus (*Antiquities of the Jews* 5.8.11) says "the presidents of the Philistine confederacy." Todd is reminded of Sallust's account (*Bellum Catilinae* 23.3, 26.3) of Cicero using the harlot Fulvia to gain information about Catiline's plots from Q. Curius: "A principio consulatus sui, multa per Fulviam pollicendo, effecerat, ut Q. Curius (cui cum Fulvia stupri vetus consuetudo) consilia Catilinae sibi proderet"; "immediately after the beginning of his consulate, by dint of many promises made through Fulvia, Cicero had induced Quintus Curius (who had a long-standing intrigue with Fulvia) to reveal Catiline's designs to him." Whiting (*Milton's Literary Milieu* 262–63) notes that Dalila in Quarles's *Historie of Samson* (sig. Q3r–Q4r) similarly is moved by "patriotic considerations." Rudrum emphasizes this line in describing the relative morality of Samson's and Dalila's positions: "we should not gloss over the ethical issue between Samson and Dalila by inertly accepting that Samson's God is the true God, and Dagon a false god"; instead, for Rudrum the contrast lies in the state-imposed religious morality of Philistia, which was anathema to Milton, versus Samson's individual trust in God (47).

    Princes: they are nowhere else referred to; see 857n.

853. *adjur'd:* "solemnly charged, earnestly . . . appealed to" (so *OED* 2).

    bonds: "obligations" (Parker, "Variorum").

    Duty: cf. *duty* (870). Meiklejohn glosses as "my duty as a citizen."

854–55. *press'd:* editors gloss as "impressed, urged, insisted (upon the belief), emphasized" (*OED* 11).

    honourable: on the pronunciation, cf. 1108.

856. *common:* "public," "of or belonging to the community at large" (*OED* 5), or "shared alike by . . . all" (so *OED* I.1a). Samson uses Dalila's phrase in his last speech in the play (1416).

857. *the Priest:* cf. 1419–20. Given that the scriptural account makes no mention of the clergy, editors debate whether Milton deliberately added this word as an allusion to seventeenth-century priests. E.g., Dunster (in Todd) thinks this "obviously a satire on the ministers of the church"; Blakeney has "little doubt" that "a side thrust is aimed here"; Church and Grieve find "Milton's religious prepossessions" responsible; Percival finds "perhaps" a "direct reference to the Restoration clergy" (xli); Prince believes that "Milton is colouring the story with his own anti-clerical convictions" (*Samson Agonistes*). But Collins disagrees with such readings: "There is no need to suppose it intended as glancing at the clergy, though Milton had no affection for that body." Bullough and Bullough instead focus attention on Dalila's religion: "Milton makes her the agent of the false god." Fletcher notes the word *Priest* is misspelled *Pirest* in four copies of the first edition that he examined (*John Milton's Complete* 4:33).

858. *ever at my ear:* cf. *PL* 4.800 (Percival; Verity; Blakeney). Landy notes that Dalila's description "contrasts ironically with the silent affirmation Samson receives from his God before his final act" ("Language" 187).

860–61. *ensnare:* cf. 365.
    Dishonourer: OED cites this as its first example of the word's use.

862–65. Commentators observe that Dalila contradicts herself: earlier she claimed to have acted out of love for Samson in divulging his secret (791–93), but here she says that only her love for Samson prevented her from immediately giving in to patriotic and religious motives and turning him over. Mollenkott, however, observes that "this is not an inescapable indication of duplicity when one considers the complexity of human motives and the conditions under which Dalila is arguing" (96–97). Landy asserts that "Milton is no misogynist, because implicit in Dalila's speech is the suggestion of what the good and true woman would have done. A good woman, above all, would have respected Samson's allegiance to God, his pledge to secrecy" ("Character" 246; "Of Highest Wisdom" 201).

863. *debate:* "consideration" (Verity), or "wrangling," "resistance," or "strife" (*OED* 1c, 1a); so *PL* 9.87, but cf. *PR* 1.95; *PL* 2.390 (Le Comte 67).

864. *these reasons:* Newton notes—and rejects—a change to "*their* reasons" by some early editors.

865. *contest:* Verity accents the second syllable; see 461n.

   grounded: editors gloss as "established" (*OED* 1) or "long-established" (Wyatt and Collins). Cf. *Animad:* "to count that only praise-worthy, which is grounded upon thy divine Precepts" (Patterson, *Works* 3:146).

866. *rife:* "frequently employed" (so *OED* 2b) or "prevalent, current" (Lockwood). Cf. *PL* 1.650–51.

867–68. *wisest men:* Le Comte (45, 87–88) notes that a similar phrase recurs in 210, 759, 1034, and in *DDD* (Patterson, *Works* 3:394, 461); *Tetr* (Patterson, *Works* 4:87, 120); and *Colas* (Patterson, *Works* 4:256).

   public good: Le Comte discusses Milton's other uses of this phrase and suggests that here it sounds as if Dalila is describing Milton's own efforts (84).

   that...yield: commentators disagree about the origin of this sentiment. "There is no particular allusion, the maxim is of the essence of ancient politics" (Collins). Percival cites Ovid, *Tristia* 4.2.74, and Pliny, *Epistles* 7. Charles R. Sumner connects this passage with the discussion of oaths in *DocCh* (Patterson, *Works* 17:122–23, 572). Line 868 may be an alexandrine (Bridges, *Milton's Prosody* 61). See 118n. Calton (in Newton 86) calls it a hypercatalectic line.

   respects: editors gloss as "ends, considerations" (*OED* 14), or, possibly, "interests" (Parker, "Variorum"). Hughes (*Complete Poems; John Milton*) notes that "the reasoning is like Satan's justification of his attempt upon Eve [*PL* 4.389]."

   authority: Oras identifies this word as one of the poem's dactylic endings; he finds it "difficult" to think of it "as even theoretically contractible" ("Milton's Blank Verse" 168–70). See 603n.

869. Stein writes, "The bawdy image is more revealing than honest; for this is a monstrous public seduction by the 'grave authority' of common, public morality, which commands hard cash and a cold passion" (*Heroic Knowledge* 170). Percival notes that in the normal "order of thought the sentence would be reversed thus: 'prevailed [i.e., "overcame my opposition"] and took full possession of me [i.e., "enlisted me entirely in their service"].'"

871. *circling:* "approaching in a roundabout way" (Lockwood 2.c); "devious, slow to come to the point" (Verity; not in *OED*); or "arguing in a circle"

(Parker, "Variorum"). Wyatt and Collins note that the metaphor is from a bird's flight.

    end: "He is not entirely right; her circle has not closed yet" (Stein, *Heroic Knowledge* 171).

872. *hypocrisie:* see *PL* 3.682–89.

874. *bin:* this spelling recurs in 1297, but cf. *been* in 45, 98, 211, 377, 493, 932, 1077, 1098, 1440; both spellings occur in the Preface. Darbishire (*Poetical Works*) comments that *Bin* was Milton's normal spelling in manuscript (nine occurrences); Parker suggests the use of *beene* in *Arc* 85 is arguably needed for a rhyme with *greene* ("Variorum"). See 1440n.

875. *Far other...other:* cf. the similar repetition in *Mask* 611, *Lyc* 174, *Canz* 7–8, and *PL* 4.84.

876. Cf. 1192.

    before: "in preference to" (*OED* B.III.11). Verity states, "We must remember that Milton's first wife came of a Royalist family."

877. *chose:* cf. 1193.

878. *lov'd thee:* see 228n, 231n. Commentators disagree over whether this assertion contradicts Samson's earlier reference to the "divine impulsion prompting" him to marry Dalila (422). E.g., Tung reasons that if Samson "did marry Dalila out of love as he says here, then he was lying earlier; otherwise, he is lying now and trying to put all the blame on Dalila" (482). Dunster (in Todd), also finding "an inconsistency" in these passages, conjectures that Milton "imagined Samson in his marriage with Dalila acting merely from inclination, and (as people, who do so, are apt to reason falsely in their own vindication) *falsely* attributing and ascribing it to divine impulse." Percival instead minimizes Samson's "supposed inconsistency" by observing that "there is nothing in scripture, or in human nature, to prevent the two motives from acting together." Frank offers three possible explanations: "Either Samson is a casuist or Milton is careless — or these contradictions and ambiguities are deliberately intended to suggest that Dalila,

despite her traditional reputation, does have a case and that an argument based on chauvinism can cut two ways" (106).

879. *Too well:* some editors (e.g., Todd) insert a semicolon after *knew'st* (878) so that this "Too well" either modifies *unbosomed* or is a repetition of the previous line with *loved* here understood. Other editors retain the first edition's comma after *knew'st* so that this "too well" goes with "lov'd thee." Both groups of editors then change the first edition's comma after "Too well" to a semicolon. Editors also compare Shakespeare's *Othello* 5.2.344: "one that lov'd not wisely, but too well" (cf. 974n s.v. *wild*, and see 881n s.vv. *deny thee nothing*). Carey notes that this is an example of anadiplosis, the rhetorical figure in which the word (or phrase) occurring at the end of one line of poetry is used also to begin the next (*Complete Shorter Poems* 335); see 18n.

880–90. On the spelling of *their* versus *thir*, Beeching claims that the word is "certainly spelt upon a method" in this passage (along with *PR* 3.414–40), "and it is noticeable that in the choruses the lighter form [*thir*] is universal" (x–xi). See 190n s.v. *their*.

880. *levity:* "want of serious thought" (so *OED* 3a). As Hughes (*Complete Poems; John Milton*) and Verity notice, Milton in *DocCh* opposes levity to gravity, which "consists in an habitual self-government of speech and action, . . . befitting a man of holiness and probity" (Patterson, *Works* 17:321). Perhaps, Verity suggests, Samson is replying now to Dalila's accusation of "weakness" (778–89). Parker ("Variorum") adds that, since *levity* can mean "fickleness, inconstancy" (*OED* 3b), Samson may instead be alluding to her charge that he was "mutable / Of fancy" (793–94).

881. *who:* Parker identifies the antecedent as *I* (876); this is the causative use of the relative: "(because I) could deny" ("Variorum").
   deny thee nothing: Thaler ("Shakespeare and Milton" 87) notes that the phrase occurs twice in speeches of Othello to Desdemona (*Othello* 3.3.76, 83).

882–86. Tillyard thinks that this is the "one place" where Milton "may have been thinking of [his first wife] Mary's sin in preferring her Cavalier parents to his Puritan self" (*Milton* 294).
   now . . . enemy: see 856.

883–84. The first edition ends 883 with a question mark and 884 with a colon; some editors (e.g., Tickell; Bohn; Verity) put a comma at the end of 883 and a question mark at the end of 884. Verity paraphrases the sense as "the avowed enemy *then,* as since: the change has been with Dalila, not with *him.*"

   receive: "take or accept" (so *OED* 13).

   profest: "avowed, declared" (Verity; Grieve; et al.), or "self-acknowledged" (*OED* 2); cf. 385.

885–86. Editors observe that Samson reverses Adam's words after the creation of Eve: "Therefore shall a man leave his father and his mother, and shall cleave unto his wife" (Gen. 2:24; Matt. 19:5; Mark 10:7; Eph. 5:31). Percival remarks that Samson presumably lived in the Philistine country after marrying Dalila, so that she had no occasion to leave. Grieve detects here Milton's "bitter memory" of his first marriage (v); see also Brydges. Rajan wryly suggests, "it is apparent that this particular Samson has done some of his thinking in the sixteen forties" (141). Mollenkott notes that "Samson is very absolute" in this lecture on marriage, "but apparently it does not occur to him that using women as a means to his own end—and that end the destruction of everything that these women have ever loved apart from himself—entails anything immoral" (98).

   thou wast: "it was thy duty" (Parker, "Variorum").

   countrey: *Thy* understood from 884. Parker notes that Milton always uses a possessive pronoun with this word ("Variorum").

   their subject: Percival suggests that "Samson contrasts his case with that of Israelites who had emigrated to Canaan, married Canaanite women, and adopted the Canaanite religion [see Judg. 3:5–8; cf. Ruth 1:4, 16]."

888. *mine:* "my (subject)," or "(under) my (protection)"; Edmund K. Chambers suggests, "perhaps both." On the first possibility, Parker ("Variorum") compares Ephesians 5:24: "Therefore as the church is subject unto Christ, so let the wives be to their own husbands in every thing." See 1053–60n.

   against my life: see 764–65.

890. Bullough and Bullough note that, legally, "a wife cannot be forced to bear witness against her husband."

   law of nature: God's will with regard to human conduct, as implanted in the mind by nature or as demonstrable by reason—what Milton elsewhere calls "the only law of laws truly and properly to all mankinde fundamental; the beginning and the end of all Government" (*REW* [Patterson, *Works* 6:113]). Milton's tracts on divorce contain multiple references to the law of nature.

law of nations: Ridley in 1634 suggests, "The law of Nations, is that which common reason hath established among men, and is observed alike in all Nations, as distinctions of mens rights, building of houses, erecting of Cities, societie of life, judgements of controversies, war, peace, captivity, contracts, obligations, succession, and the like" (sig. B1v–B2r). Wyatt and Collins summarize the law of nature and law of nations: "the laws of holding good (1) for all men as individuals, (2) between different nations." Percival compares Exodus 22:21, Leviticus 19:33–34. Hughes (*Complete Poems; John Milton*) suggests that this line would have reminded Milton's contemporaries of John Selden's *Of the Law of Nature and of Nations,* as Milton in *DDD* (Patterson, *Works* 3:505) translated the title *De iure naturali et gentium, iuxta disciplinam Ebraeorum* (1640). Carey (*Complete Shorter Poems*) finds here an echo of Shakespeare's *Troilus and Cressida* 2.2.184–85.

891. Verity paraphrases, "He means that she should have ceased to regard the Philistines as her countrymen."

   impious: "wicked" (*OED* 1).

   crew: "gang, mob" (*OED* I.4). Verity and other editors note that Milton's use of this word—"a favourite"—is almost always pejorative.

892. *state:* Lockwood defines "the people united under one government as well as the government itself, the body politic" (I.6); cf. 1465. Empson explains, "In modern English, 'their state' chiefly means their country, but in Milton's time it still chiefly meant their position of rule, over Hebrews and lower-class Philistines alike presumably; though Milton could have wanted to leave open for Samson the modern meaning" (*Milton's God* 214).

893. Sprott (131) identifies this as a twelve-syllable line (alexandrine; see 118n). Prince suggests that if "violating" is elided, the line can be read as pentameter (*Samson Agonistes* 135).

   hostile deeds: the phrase occurs also in *PL* 11.796 (Le Comte 174). Cf. 1210.

   the ends: Edmund K. Chambers glosses as "the preservation of family life in peace, whereas the Philistines were trying to break up a family." B. A. Wright emends to *th' ends.*

894. *our countrey:* having picked up Dalila's mention of "my countrey" (851), Samson uses the word *countrey* or *thy countrey* four times (884, 886, 889, and 891), but finally changes it to *our countrey*. Empson suggests that within this *our,* Samson intends to include Dalila: "it must be meant as an appeal to her knowledge of what they have both grown up among, the moral traditions of the land of Palestine" (*Milton's God* 214). Cf. 1425.

    name so dear: is Milton thinking of patria? Cf. the Latin proverb *Patria [cara,] carior libertas* ("Nation is dear, but liberty dearer"). Parker thinks it can hardly be Israel ("Variorum").

895. A difficult line to scan; Edmund K. Chambers's solution is to pronounce *obey'd* as three syllables (122). Empson proposes "an ironical stress on *thee,* implying 'You claim to be dedicated, do you; but I really am'"—an argument, Empson notes, which may preserve "the logic of justice between Delilah and Samson. But it cannot do the same between Jehovah and Dagon" (*Milton's God* 215). Verity also paraphrases Samson's claim: "He gives her objection and then answers it"; Hughes thinks "the words refer ironically to Dalila's plea" in 1857–61 (*John Milton*). Some editors (e.g., Masson, *Poetical Works*) emend the line by inserting an exclamation point after *thee;* other editors (e.g., Edmund K. Chambers) omit the first edition's semicolon after this word.

    But: see 782n.

    zeal: cf. 1420. Editors note Milton's various uses of this word. In his *DocCh* Milton has a chapter "De Zelo," in which he explains that the opposite of true zeal is an ignorant and imprudent zeal (Patterson, *Works* 17:152–53). In *Areop* he condemns "a precipitant zeal" (Patterson, *Works* 4:352). In *PL* 2.483–85 he writes of "bad men" who do "specious deeds" through "clos ambition varnished o'er with zeal," and in tempting Eve, Satan makes "shew of Zeale" (9.665). In *PR* 3.175–76 Satan urges Jesus to hasty action for reasons of "Zeal of thy Father's house, Duty to free / Thy Country from her Heathen servitude"; and, later, Jesus mocks Satan's "zeal" (see 3.407–13).

    mov'd: cf. *PR* 3.171.

896. Some editors (e.g., Masson, *Poetical Works;* Verity; Edmund K. Chambers; William Aldis Wright) insert an exclamation point after *it;* the first edition has a semicolon.

896–900. Carey (*John Milton* 143) writes that Samson's "casuistry about gods who sanction 'ungodly deeds' not being real gods" is "question-begging at best" and recalls Satan's conversation with Eve in *PL* 9.700–1.

897. *acquit themselves:* "avenge themselves, vindicate themselves, clear themselves (of an obligation or accusation)" (so most editors), or "act like gods" (Keightley, *Poems*). Cf. 1709 and *PL* 10.53, 827.
    prosecute: "pursue" (*OED* 5); cf. 603.

898–99. *ungodly deeds:* Parker ("Variorum") notes that the phrase occurs also in Milton's 1642 translation of Sophocles, *Electra* 625 (*Apol* [Patterson, *Works* 3:319]). Todd finds a parallel with the description of the Babylonian idols in 2 Baruch 6:44, "Whatsoever is done among them *is false:* how may it then be thought or said *that they are gods?*"
    deity: see 464.

900. Parker calls attention to this line as making clear "Samson's attitude toward God" (*Milton's Debt* 221); he thus challenges Baum's finding that *SA* contains a "pervading awareness of the divine love" (370).

901. *pretexts:* Parker accents the second syllable ("Variorum").
    varnish'd: "laid on as varnish"; hence editors define as "gloss[ed] over," "cover[ed]...with a specious or deceptive appearance" (*OED* 3). Todd, Verity, and Bullough and Bullough quote *Animad:* "painting his lewd and deceitfull principles with a smooth, and glossy varnish" (Patterson, *Works* 3:163); cf. also *PL* 2.485; *PR* 4.344; *Ref* (Patterson, *Works* 3:12); *RCG* (Patterson, *Works* 3:190). Todd detects as well a possible allusion to St. James's calling the tongue ὁ ΚΟΣΜΟΣ τῆς ἀδιχίας; "the *varnish* of iniquity."
    colours: editors gloss as "shows of reason," "excuses," "specious or plausible reason[s] or ground[s]" (*OED* 12). Wyatt and Collins add, "the word is here a conscious metaphor, as *varnished* shows." Cf. *Tetr:* "fals colours, fals pretences" (Patterson, *Works* 4:127).

902. Editors insert an exclamation point after *appear;* the first edition has a question mark.

Bare: cf. 842 and *PL* 9.1062.

foul: "morally or spiritually polluted," "detestable" (*OED* 7).

903–4. Cf. 861–62. Edward J. Thompson believes that Dalila here "shows her hypocrisy" by her "nonchalant composure…when her arguments are torn to shreds" (248).

    Goes by the worse: "is worsted" (so *OED* s.v. *go* 57c and s.v. *worse* 4c).

    cause: "question for debate" (Lockwood I.5). Stein calls 903–6 "a little transition…of some domestic comedy, the mere he and she of it" (*Heroic Knowledge* 173).

905. A line of monosyllables, ironically spoken; see 1401–7n. Some editors insert a stronger punctuation mark at the end of this line; they replace the first edition's comma with either a semicolon (e.g., Bohn) or exclamation point (e.g., Masson, *Poetical Works*).

906. *Witness:* introduces a clause exemplifying the preceding statement; cf. Latin: *teste.* Verity comments, "An extension of the idiom in phrases like 'witness Heaven'…where the order is inverted. Here we must supply *time,* i.e. 'witness the *time* when I.' This imperative or optative use of the subjunctive was more common in Elizabethan England than now."

    peals: "volley of words (as of gunfire)" (Shawcross, *Complete English Poetry*); see 235n and cf. *PL* 2.920. Greenlaw, Osgood, and Padelford (5:244) note this image's precedent in Spenser's *The Faerie Queene* (5.9.39.7). For the military metaphor, see also 235n, 403–5n, 560–61n, 845–46n.

907–27. Commentators dispute whether Dalila is sincere. Nash compares Dalila with Satan in *PL:* "Milton has let her present her case so skillfully that she actually wins adherents among readers persuaded to believe that blinding and imprisoning her husband is after all a venial affair" (29). But most commentators and editors believe that Dalila genuinely feels for Samson here. Percival, cited approvingly by Wyatt and by Grieve, thinks that she "displays for once a touch of natural feeling that for a short while relieves her artful character." Wyatt adds: "Though Samson but too naturally suspects in this only a new snare, it is hard to think that this offer concealed malice, and was not prompted by a sincere, though fleeting, pity." Wyatt also finds "a counterpart in the mother's feeling that Clytaemnestra betrays when she hears of the death of Orestes. Dramatists seldom fail to bestow on their monsters some relieving touch, to remind us that they are still human." Parker also thinks Dalila is here sincere: "She then abandons argument and, with apparent honesty, admits her folly" (*Milton's Debt* 42). Kilgo suggests that Dalila switches to "womanly pleading" after having argued "most adroitly" and with "consummate skill" (313, 314). Allen adds, "One can reasonably doubt whether a woman who came, as the critics say, to gloat over the misery of the husband whom she hated...would make such a selfless proposal to a broken and blinded man" ("Idea as Pattern" 90). Cf. 927n.

907–8. Maxwell finds a "certain" echo of Sophocles, *Women of Trachis* 666–67 ("Milton's Knowledge" 370).

908–9. *succeeded:* see 1454n.
  obtain: cf. 814.

910. *Afford:* see 1109.
  place: "occasion, opportunity" (*OED* 12b).
  recompense: "restitution," "reparation" (*OED* 1).

912–13. *Misguided:* in apposition to *I* (Parker, "Variorum").
  only: "the only thing to be added being" (*OED* B.1); Blakeney suggests "in any case."
  cure: cf. 630. Parker ("Variorum") notes that the phrase "past cure" occurs also in *Tetr* (Patterson, *Works* 4:162) and *Eikon* (Patterson, *Works* 5:260).
  sensibly: "acutely, intensely" (*OED* 2b); "sensitively" (Verity; Blakeney; Patterson, *Student's Milton*); "passionately" (Shawcross, *Complete English Poetry*).

914. *afflict thy self:* so Manoa had exhorted him (503); Gilbert finds the repetition a flaw ("Is *Samson Agonistes*" 105). For the sentiment, Dunster (in Todd), Church, and Fleming quote Cicero, *Tusculanae quaestiones* 5.38: "Animo autem multis modis variisque delectari licet, etiam si non adhibeatur aspectus."

915. *solaces:* "comfort[s]," but also "delight[s]," "amusement[s]" (*OED* 1 and 2).
  enjoy'd: apart from the obvious meaning, Parker writes ("Variorum"), "there

may be the suggestion of 'to have one's will of (a woman)'"; see 807 and cf. *PL* 9.1032.

916. *Where:* "whereas, since, seeing that" (Lockwood 2.i).
 other senses: "Dalila slyly reminds Samson of the pleasures of her bed" (Carey, *Complete Shorter Poems*); see 388–89, 533, 536, 806–8, 923.
 want not: i.e., "are not without" (*OED* 2); cf. 315.

917. *At home:* cf. 579 (also 805, 810). Steadman ("Dalila" 562) points out that this appeal has a classical analogue in the Horatian conception of the Siren as idleness (*Satires* 2.3.14: "improba Siren desidia").

918–19. Parker detects an ironic echo of 75–76, 103–7 ("Variorum").
 abroad: see 809.

920. Editors paraphrase: "I will (go) to the Lords (and) will intercede (with them on your behalf)." Wyatt and Collins note similar omissions of a verb of motion in 1250, 1370, and 1445. Landy is reminded of Manoa's attempts to ransom Samson (see 1457), of the Son's offer in *PL* to intercede on humankind's behalf, and of Samson's own later supplications to his Lord ("Language" 188). Hill (163) also notes that this temptation—"to sloth and physical ease"—is the same as Manoa's earlier offer (with the important exception that Dalila adds "the note of carnal indulgence"). Van Kluyve observes that Dalila's proposal reverses her and Samson's positions and "takes the masculine role from him, which is neatly analogous to the hyena's reputed change of sex. And it is precisely the insult that would most infuriate a man whose virility had been so far beyond doubt that it proved his downfall" (101); see 748n s.v. *Hyæna*. Kranidas interprets Dalila's offer as a "retreat to a base, non-passive, non-active, . . . vegetative existence, the direct opposite of both the active hero and the truly patient hero" (133).

921. Editors paraphrase as "not doubting to obtain a favorable hearing."
 favourable: for the pronunciation, cf. *PL* 11.169.
 ear: "voluntary hearing, listening, attention" (*OED* 6), "audience" (Parker, "Variorum"). Cf. 1172 (Landy, "Language" 188).
 fetch: cf. 1731.

922. *this loathsom prison-house:* Verity observes, "it was close at hand"; i.e., the scene of the tragedy is "before" and "nigh" the prison; cf. 949 and the Argument.

    abide: Parker ("Variorum") notes the rhyme with *suppli'd* (926).

924. Editors paraphrase, "With diligent nursing, to me (a) pleasant task or service." For other references to nursing, see 633, 1487–88.

925. *tend about:* Meiklejohn glosses as "attend, watch over and wait upon" (not in *OED*); cf. 1490.

    old age: see 572n.

926. *grateful:* "agreeable," "pleasing to the mind or the senses" (*OED* 1).

    chear'd: perhaps "comfort[ed] as food does" or "feast[ed]" (*OED* 5a, c); cf. 1613.

    suppli'd: in addition to the obvious definition, Parker ("Variorum") notes the word can mean "supplemented" (*OED* 3b).

927. *what:* sight. Some commentators believe that this statement confirms Dalila's status as the poem's villainess. Stein (*Heroic Knowledge* 174) declares: "That comes close to pure human evil, a naked desire to have power over another, regardless. (And it makes impossible any sympathetic interpretation of Dalila as behaving so because her sincere first approach was harshly spurned; no one could conjure up this horror out of mere anger: it had to be there.)" Muldrow agrees, adding, "she seems to have understood nothing of Samson's repentance" (198). Nash compares Dalila with another "wanton dame," Armida in Tasso's *Gerusalemme liberata:* above all, "Dalila is the tool of God's enemies and our judgment of her is to be affected accordingly" (24, 30).

    least: "not at all"; see 195n.

928–29. Collins comments that the first words of Samson's reply "show in their milder tone that he was not insensible to the charmer; but reflection comes to his aid and he gradually returns to his former ferocity, his wrath gathering with his words" (see also Martz 127; Carey, *John Milton* 143). Hanford suggests, "The momentary softening of Samson's tone as he rejects Dalila's kindly proposal is as subtle as it is moving" (*Poems*).

care: cf. 923. Parker ("Variorum") notes the rhyme with *snare* (931).

fits: "befit[s]" (*OED* 3) or "[is] seemly, proper" (*OED* 2; Meiklejohn); so also 1236, 1318.

long since: see 4n, 938n.

twain: cf. Genesis 2:24: "and they shall be one flesh."

930. *accurst:* "lying under a [divine] curse" (*OED* 1). Church, Verity, Hughes (*Complete Poems; John Milton*), et al. suggest that Milton is thinking of the Greek notion of ατη, a "Divine curse that brings madness with it." See 1675n.

931. *To bring:* "(as) to bring" (Parker, "Variorum").

932–46. Hanford thinks that "there is new light here on Milton's attitude toward women" (*John Milton* 221).

   trains: see 533n.

933. *dearly:* cf. 1660.

   ginns: editors gloss as "snares, traps" (*OED* 4). Broadbent compares this language with "the tangles of Neaera's hair" (*Lyc* 69), "the blind mazes of this tangled Wood" (*Mask* 180), and, more generally, "Satan and his tempting" in *PL* (*Some Graver Subject* 259).

   toyls: editors gloss as "nets" or "snares" (*OED* 1, 3).

934. *fair enchanted cup:* commentators generally agree that this line alludes to the cup of the enchantress Circe; she turned into swine Odysseus's companions who drank of it (Homer, *Odyssey* 10.210–50); cf. *Mask* 50–53, 524; *Eikon* (Patterson, *Works* 5:204); *Apol* (Patterson, *Works* 3:305); Le Comte (138) notes that Eve is also linked to Circe (*PL* 9.521). Only Stebbing claims that there is no specific allusion to Circe here. Percival suggests that the allusion to Greek myths is "too palpable to admit of any forced allusion to Hebrew or Biblical sorcery," such as the magic cup of Joseph. For a possible biblical allusion, Northrop Frye compares Jeremiah 51:7 (*Paradise Lost and Selected Poetry*), and Lewalski thinks this cup associates Dalila with both Circe and the Great Whore of Babylon, "having a golden cup in her hand full of abominations and filthiness of her fornication" ("*Samson Agonistes*" 1058–59; see Rev. 17:3–7).

Regarding the significance of Circe, commentators disagree about the allusion's efficacy. Although Milton and his contemporaries believed that the voyage of Odysseus ended shortly before Samson's time, Thyer (in Newton), Johnson (*Rambler* 20 July 1751, 220), Todd, et al. deplore the "impropriety" and "objectionable" nature of this alleged anachronism. Collins defends Milton's choice, as the poem does not actually mention Circe and the Sirens. Newton also somewhat defends the allusion: Samson "might as well be supposed to know the story of Circe and the Syrens, as of Tantalus, &c.... and there is no more impropriety in the one than the other."

Among other discussions of this passage, Parker suggests the potentially deliberate irony in having the wine-abstaining Nazarite defeated by a cup; Parker also notes that Josephus had supposed that Samson violated his vows by drinking wine with Dalila ("Variorum"). Banks traces the changing implications of this allusion in Milton's various works (here, Banks says, the cup signifies "seduction" [211]). Hawkins (220) sees this reference to Dalila's cup as part of a larger pattern of "dietary imagery" that he traces to Judges, where Samson's mother is instructed to "drink not wine, nor strong drink, and eat not any unclean thing" (13:4–5); see also, e.g., 541, 558–59, 633.

warbling charms: editors recall that as Eurylochus and his companions approached the palace of Circe, they heard her singing so sweet a song that Polites wondered whether it was the voice of goddess or woman; cf. *Mask* 251–60. Alden Sampson (71) comments that *charms* could also mean "verses," *carmina,* as Milton uses it in *PL* 4.642. Keightley (*Poems*) et al. find here an allusion to the Sirens' "charms" (*Odyssey* 12.166–200). Verity instead suggests that *charms* may refer to "the spells...spoken over the cup at its brewing"; he compares the witches' incantations over the cauldron in *Macbeth* 4.1. Steadman more generally discusses Milton's debt here to Renaissance mythography ("Dalila" 560); he finds the cup and charms "strongly reminiscent" of Horace, *Epodes* 1.2.23: "Sirenum voces et Circae pocula." Horace gives Circe the label of *meretrix* (1.2.25); cf. 537. Steadman also calls attention to "the close relationship between Renaissance allegorizations of the Odysseus myth and Milton's characterization of Dalila" (561). Of *warbling,* Blakeney writes, "Milton's use of this word is exquisite, here as elsewhere in his poems."

935. *null'd:* editors gloss as "annul[ed], cancel[ed]," or "reduce[d] to nothing" (*OED* 3, 2); cf. 72.

936. *Adders wisdom:* The allusion, Newton notes, is specifically to Psalm 58:4–5: "[The wicked] are like the deaf adder that stoppeth her ear; Which will not hearken to the voice of charmers, charming never so wisely." Dalila would thus be likened to a snake charmer. Prince explains that the psalmist refers "to an exceptional individual, a willfully deaf adder, which is not, like the rest of the species, amenable to music" (*Samson Agonistes*). Edmund K. Chambers recalls the counsel of Jesus: "be ye therefore wise as serpents" (Matt. 10:16), i.e., in avoiding danger. In *Tetr,* Milton seems to assume that all adders are deaf (Patterson, *Works* 4:98). Svendsen, working from Edward Topsell's *Historie of Serpents* (1658), notes that deaf adders "signifie unrepentant men"; that Samson's rejection of Dalila seems to invert this traditional pejorative association, Svendsen suggests, is "not unusual in Milton" (*Milton and Science* 166). Shawcross (*Complete English Poetry*) glosses the expression as "knowledge of evil" and recalls that Satan is called an adder in *PL* 9.625.

937. *fence:* "shield" (*OED* 2a). Steadman finds a link between Samson and Odysseus: Samson's new knowledge will enable him to "fence" his ear against Dalila's "sorceries," just as Odysseus had to learn how to guard himself in his encounters with the Sirens and Circe ("Dalila" 564); see 934n.
   sorceries: cf. 819 and *PL* 2.566.

938. *my flower of youth:* cf. 524, 1489; Judges 14:10; *PR* 1.67. Samson feels prematurely old; "between his present and his past lay a space of such suffering as would make his youth seem remote" (Verity). As Percival notes, Ussher's *Chronology* suggests that all the events from Samson's marriage with Dalila to his death fell within the space of one year (1120 BC, according to Ussher; 1199 BC, according to Salianus). Verity gives Samson's age as forty (cf. Judg. 13:1), noting that his life fell between 1156 and 1116 BC. Robertson cites this line's reference to a flower as part of the drama's larger metaphorical pattern associating Samson with vegetation (323).

939–40. Oras notes that the "conspicuous accumulations of asyndeta" such as in these lines are part of *SA*'s "abruptness, or even breathlessness, of manner," what he also calls the poem's "angry choppiness" (*Blank Verse* 29). See, e.g., 1323–25, 1361–62.

could: presumably a subjunctive after *if,* but some editors alter to *could'st.* Percival notes "the bitterness of the reproach conveyed in the repetition of 'me,' and in the heaping up of the verbs into two antithetic groups."

forgo: editors gloss as "give up, forsake" (*OED* 4) or "go against" (Edmund K. Chambers 141); cf. 1483.

942–43. *Deceiveable:* Verity notes that Milton uses this word only here and in 350; he adds that it means "liable to be deceived," whereas Shakespeare used it to signify "deceiving"; see *Twelfth Night* 4.3.21 and *Richard II* 2.3.84. Church finds a personal allusion in this passage.

Helpless: see 644.

944. *last:* "after all others," "at the end" (*OED* B.1).

neglected: cf. 481.

insult: see 113.

945. *uxorious:* "submissive to a wife"; but cf. *OED,* where the element of excessive affection is inseparable from the definitions. Phillips defines this word as "belonging to a wife: also fond, doting upon a wife" (*New World*). On Milton's hatred of uxoriousness, see Le Comte 133–34. Meiklejohn calls "uxorious to" an "unusual idiom."

946–48. James Waddell Tupper thinks Samson argues "rather lamely" here: "What would the lords care now that the champion is a broken man?" (383). Tung agrees: "Samson's suspicion that Dalila might again betray him once she has him is totally unfounded" (483).

perfect: "complete." Wyatt and Collins have a long note on Milton's spelling of this word. Cf. *Verdit* (324). Although Milton wrote *perfect* in manuscript (all instances before 1638), the printed editions consistently contain *perfet* (Parker, "Variorum").

948. *gloss:* "comment" (so *OED* 1b).

censuring: editors gloss as "judging, criticizing" (*OED* 1); cf. 787.

949. *Gaol:* Parker ("Variorum") compares the spelling *jail* in *Nat* 233; *Jayle* in *Animad* (Patterson, *Works* 3:164); *jaylor* in *DDD* (Patterson, *Works* 3:381) and *Areop* (Patterson, *Works* 4:328).

count: see 250.

the house of Liberty: cf. *Areop,* where London is described as "the mansion house of liberty" (Patterson, *Works* 4:340), and *Bucer,* where Parliament sits in "that house of justice and true liberty" (Patterson, *Works* 4:3).

950. *To:* editors gloss as "compared to" or "in comparison with."

951. Freedman ("*All for Love*" 516; "Milton" 107) notes that this passage is echoed in Ventidius's "passionate advice" to Antony about touching Cleopatra's gift in Dryden's *All for Love* 2.1. See also 115–75n, 183–86n.

   approach: Parker thinks this may be a double entendre: "the word was a euphemism for sexual relations" ("Variorum").

   touch thy hand: Percival writes that this is "Dalila's last resource. Where words have failed she hopes that her touch might succeed." Kranidas emphasizes the scene's "inversion": "Samson, who has been groping toward physical and spiritual contact with man, with God, . . . is offered a parody of meaningful contact, a return to the touch which ruined him" (134). Tillyard also suggests that Dalila wants "to arouse physical passion" (*Milton* 290); Bush calls it "a direct appeal to Samson's senses" ("John Milton" 513n; *Milton*); and Landy similarly thinks Dalila "is subtly seeking . . . to revive his physical memories of her. She is hoping to lure him by sexual means" ("Character" 245). Verity believes Dalila is successful: "It is easy to see the force of this appeal . . ., at which the emotion of Samson rises to its highest point." Watkins comments: "Touch frequently, almost inevitably with Milton, sweeps sensuousness into sensuality. . . . [Samson] cannot bear that betraying touch again, knowing too well how thoroughly she has earlier subdued him by touch" (29–30). According to Rajan's count, Dalila tries four times to persuade Samson in this scene: "In seeking to discover Samson's secret, Delilah prevailed only with the fourth attempt"; correspondingly, "There must be four efforts and four failures to make it evident that history will not be repeated" (138).

952–53. To Northrop Frye, this scream of the blind Samson is "one of the most terrible passages of all tragic drama" (*Anatomy* 223; Paradise Lost *and Selected Poetry* xxix). Commentators are divided about whether the violence of Samson's response indicates his strength or weakness. Ebbs thinks that Samson's angry reply represents the "apex" of his growing strength and shows he is ready to meet Harapha (386); Allen ("Idea as Pattern" 90) believes that Dalila is now "physically repellent" to Samson (for a wife or mistress, "the ultimate insult"); and Lewalski sees Samson's forceful resistance to Dalila's "lures and blandishments" as a sign of his "tenacious adherence" to his vocation as judge, specifically the execution of God's wrath ("*Samson Agonistes*" 1058). Nicolson writes of a more physical reaction: Dalila has made Samson "conscious of his manhood.... Vigor returns to his body" (364).

Other commentators suggest instead that Samson is genuinely tempted in this moment. Martz interprets Samson's fierceness toward Dalila here (and at 725, 748) as "a sign of the powerful attraction which she still holds" (128; also Mollenkott 100). Fogle similarly argues, "It doesn't always indicate growth in moral stature when one refuses to touch the hot stove a second time.... [O]ne might wonder whether the savagery of his repulse of Dalila did not evidence his continued weakness, or at least his moral insecurity" (183).

Not for thy life: Todd, Church, and Bullough and Bullough find a parallel in blind Polymestor's impulse to tear Hecuba limb from limb (Euripides, *Hecuba* 1125), but Hughes (*Complete Poems; John Milton*) thinks that Samson's "wish" is "less ferocious," as his hatred is a religious duty in Milton's belief (e.g., *DocCh* [Patterson, *Works* 17:259]). Cf. also *Romeo and Juliet* 5.3.35: "By heaven, I will tear thee joint by joint" (George Coffin Taylor 195). A. B. Chambers is reminded here of St. Paul's advice to "be angry, but not sin" (Eph. 26), which would require that Samson remain compassionate and direct his anger at Dalila's sin, not her person; according to Chambers, both of these qualifications are met, and Samson's rage provides a useful "prop" for his subsequent fortitude (318–19).

rage: Parker glosses as probably "anger" or "indignation" ("Variorum"); but cf. 836.

tear: cf. 128.

954. *At distance I forgive thee:* Samson earlier suggests he would not pardon her; see 825–26. On forgiveness, see also 759–61, 787, 909. Hawkins argues that here Samson's "forgiveness is not much more convincing than her [Dalila's] penitence," whereas Samson's rage in this same exchange "is far easier to believe" and it is his "burning resentment [that] makes Samson invulnerable to Dalila's charms" (224). See 952–53n. Cf. *Colas:* "Charity indeed bids us forgive our enemies, yet...is contented in our peace with them, at a fair distance" (Patterson, *Works* 4:243–44).

955–59. Jerram finds these lines inconsistent with 954, "which perhaps might well have been the conclusion."

pious works: Parker writes, "As though suspecting his charitable gesture to be another weakness, he dismisses her ironically" (*Milton's Debt* 42). Blakeney calls it "bitter irony"; Todd adds that "this irony may have been suggested by Homer [*Odyssey* 11.431]." See 957n.

957. *illustrious...faithful:* these words, Percival notes, may be read in their natural sense, with *memorable* meaning "notorious" and *Among* meaning "in the opinion of"; or they may be read ironically for "infamous" and "faithless"; he prefers the latter reading. See 968.

958. Weismiller scans this line as "Cher'-ish | thy hast' | 'n'd wid' | w'ood with | the gold'" (a sequence of trochee, iamb, iamb, pyrrhic, iamb) (117).

hastened widowhood: i.e., by her (Verity). Cf. 806, and see 764–65n.

959. On the line's rhythm and punctuation, see 205n.

treason: cf. 391.

farewel: perhaps ironic; see 955–59n. Cf. 1413.

960–96. Some early commentators interpret Dalila's final speech as a confirmation of her wickedness. E.g., Verity believes that in this speech Dalila shows "her true colours" and "reveals the hard restlessness of her character, unbending and keen as steel of the ice-brook's temper" (lix). Percival similarly writes: "Whatever good feeling Delilah's last two speeches may have inspired in us toward her disappears at this self-satisfied panegyric on her own conduct." See also J. Macmillan Brown 108–9. Radzinowicz, reading Dalila's final speech in light of Milton's depiction of Eve, his divorce tracts, and *DocCh,* concludes that the gradual hardening of Dalila's heart is now complete even as her presence has effected Samson's rejuvenation: Dalila "speaks her final lines transparent with self-satisfaction. She sees herself as she is and admires her own reflection.... Dalila has left herself no other alternative but to go forward happily seeking her own vain glory, proud of her victory, scornful of Samson" ("Eve" 174). Edward J. Thompson adds that Dalila's "cynical impudence...is only equalled by its splendor as poetry. Even Milton has done nothing grander (though many things as grand)" (248–49). Writing in 1942, Knight suggests that Dalila's argument here "corresponds to the overleaping and unmoral nationalism ardent in modern Germany" (*Chariot* 89).

Other commentators use Dalila's speech to praise her fortitude and sympathize with her circumstance. Edmund K. Chambers calls this "a fine speech, in an impassioned strain, contrasting with the frigid rhetoric of the rest of the scene"; moreover, he believes that Dalila, discovering Samson obdurate, "finally triumphs over him" (95, 98). Empson, also finding this "one of the noblest speeches in Milton," writes: "She does speak up for herself a little; she can at least save her pride. But even then she does it with such large-mindedness, such inability merely to call the kettle black, that she gives us no excuse for calling her earlier professions of love insincere" (*Milton's God* 220–21). Garnett (cited by Wyatt 107) calls this speech an example of "perfect grace . . . united to perfect dignity" (182).

Still other critics question whether Dalila is truly "self-satisfied" and instead suggest that she is rationalizing her rebuff. As Allen comments, "If we are to question any one of Dalila's announcements, it is the last one. . . . [S]he leaves the scene escorted by her wounded pride. The reward of a footnote in the history of the Phoenicians . . . is sorry consolation, indeed, for the sort of woman who had been an international beauty" ("Idea as Pattern" 90). Mollenkott describes Dalila's final words as "the face-saving device of a woman whose every advance has been scorned" and notes that the "human validity" of Dalila's speech "is underlined by the fact that Manoa dreams of a tomb for Samson . . . very similar to the one Dalila envisions for herself" (99). George Coffin Taylor (195) is reminded of Cressida in Shakespeare's *Troilus and Cressida* 3.2.183–96. Hughes (*Complete Poems* 534) notes that Dalila's final speech, containing "something like despair as well as pride," makes her "an incomparably richer character" than Quarles's portrait of Dalila in *Historie of Samson*. See also 732–951n.

960–61. *more deaf . . . seas:* editors quote or cite various sources and parallels for this figure of speech. Todd notes that Dryden borrowed the simile in the first scene of *Aureng-Zebe* (1675) and he finds "the same classical allusion" in Henry Glapthorne's *Albertus Wallenstein* (1640): "I am deafe, inexorable as Seas / To th' prayers of Mariners." Blakeney and Meiklejohn quote Shakespeare's *Merchant of Venice* 4.1.71–72: "You may as well go stand upon the beach / And bid the main flood bate his usual height." Percival quotes *Richard II* 1.1.19: "In rage deaf as the sea" (cf. 1284n, 1472n) and Aeschylus, *Prometheus Bound* 1001:

ὀχλεῖς μάτην με κῦμ'ἄπως παρηγορ'ν; "You tease me to no purpose, for you might as well try to talk over a wave." Among other responses to this passage, Peck compliments the Homeric repetition of *seas* in Dalila's opening lines: "the first of these instances... may be called a *return* of the same words, the latter a fine *turn* of words" (sig. Q2r). Hughes cites 960 to show that often in the poem "light feet... are immediately compensated by spondees" (*John Milton* 424).

    prayers: cf. 392.

961–64. Carey (*Complete Shorter Poems* 338) notes that Dalila as "stately Ship" (714) encounters Samson as "Eternal tempest," which tends "to draw the two of them into an implied, and disturbing, parallelism" and aligns Samson also with Harapha who enters as a "tempest" (1063). Cox discusses the various images of storm in *SA:* "storm is... evoked to define the struggle between good and evil, order and chaos" ("Natural Science" 55–56); see also 962n.

962. *reconcil'd:* Percival writes that "a storm in common metaphor is said to be 'a conflict of the elements,' and waves are said 'to beat angrily on the shore.' Hence the idea of 'reconciliation.'" Gossman adds about Dalila, "Even as she goes she speaks beautifully of the reconciliation that might have been" ("Milton's Samson" 539).

963. *still:* "without change, interruption, or cessation" (*OED* 3).
    rages: "[has] a high degree of intensity" (so *OED* 4b).

965–66. *suing... reap:* Percival wonders if a pun is intended. The first edition ends 966 with a question mark; some editors (e.g., Masson, *Poetical Works;* Verity; Edmund K. Chambers) prefer a comma; Bohn prefers a semicolon.

967. *Bid:* editors gloss as "bidden."
    evil omen: see 955–59.
    brand: cf. *Sonn 15* 12.

969. *concernments:* editors gloss as "affairs, interests" (*OED* 2, 3).

970. Parker describes this line as litotes or light irony: what Dalila means she expresses by negation of the contrary ("Variorum"); cf. 180, 420, 1642.

971. *Fame:* cf. *QNov* 205–12. Edmund K. Chambers calls this "a passage of ornament and metaphor, such as occur rarely in the play." Chambers, followed by
other commentators, also finds Milton's description possibly influenced by book
3 of Chaucer's *House of Fame,* Jonson's *Masque of Queens,* Ovid's *Metamorphoses*
12.39–63, Silius Italicus's *Punica* 15.95, and Virgil's *Aeneid* 4.173–90. Hughes
adds Boccaccio's interpretation of this passage from Virgil in *Genealogy of the
Gods* 1.9 (*Complete Poems; John Milton*).

   double-fac't: editors detect a reference here to Janus, the Roman gatekeeper
of heaven, who had two faces (Virgil's *Aeneid* 7.180: *bifrons*) so that he might
simultaneously look east and west (or, according to Macrobius, in token of his
knowledge of past and future [*Saturnalia* 1.9.4]). Editors compare *PL* 11.129;
Areop: "*Janus* with his two *controversal* faces" (Patterson, *Works* 4:347 [Ver-
ity]); *Animad:* "Your faction then belike is a subtile *Janus,* and ha's two faces"
(Patterson, *Works* 3:120 [Hughes, *Complete Poems; John Milton*]). Meiklejohn
adds that Sin in *PL* 2.741 is "double-formed."

   double-mouth'd: in *QNov* 207 Milton assigns only one trumpet to the goddess. But editors (Masson, *Poetical Works;* Percival; Verity; Edmund K. Chambers; et al.) note that in Chaucer's *House of Fame* (3.485–92, 582–98) she is
attended by Aeolus, god of the winds, who bears two trumpets, one black and
brass with which to "defame," the other made of gold and used to announce
good deeds.

972. *contrary:* "different," "opposed in nature," or "opposite in position or direction" (*OED* A.1, 5). Collins, Todd, Grieve, et al. put the accent on the second
syllable, "as often in our old writers, and still in provincial dialects"; cf. 1037.
Percival and Verity compare Chaucer's *House of Fame* 3.539–40: "For thou
shalt trumpe al the contraire / Of that they hav don wel or faire." Verity adds,
however, that Milton's Fame gives two contradictory reports of the same thing;
thus, Dalila's reputation will seem infamous to some and glorious to others.

973. Beum finds the proverblike effect of the rhymed couplet, 973–74, "certainly
right for this most expressive and epigrammatic metaphor" (179); Percival feels
this rhyming is "accidental" (xlvii).

   his: cf. *Lyc* 19–21. Jortin traces Milton's description of Fame as a deity to
Hesiod (*Remarks* sig. Bb1r), but, as Verity and other commentators note,
Milton seems "alone among poets in making Fame masculine." Commentators

accordingly suggest various explanations. Dunster (in Todd), Percival, Verity, et al. think that "to some degree he connects her [*sic*] with *Rumor*"; Thaler thinks the "family resemblance...unmistakable" between Milton's Fame and Shakespeare's Rumor in the induction to *2 Henry IV* ("Shakespearian Element" 179). Church writes that the "alteration suits the cast of Hebrew thought, which would certainly not have personified any idea of power in a female shape." Collins conjectures that Milton was thinking of Fame "for the moment in the abstract, and 'his' for the neuter." Hughes thinks it possible that Milton "confused her with her trumpeter, Eolus" (*Complete Poems; John Milton*). Jortin (*Remarks* sig. Bb1r–v; and in Todd) associates Fame's gender here with Milton's "very bold" decision to refer to *Muse* as masculine for "poet" in *Lyc*. To these possibilities Parker adds two others: either Milton visualized Fame as a kind of Janus or he allowed Dalila the irony of making masculine the fickleness of Fame ("Variorum").

   wings: in giving Fame one black wing and one white, Milton apparently has no warrant from the classical tradition; but his invention could easily have been suggested to him by the black and golden trumpets of Fame's Aeolus in Chaucer (see 971n s.v. *double-mouth'd*), or, as Dunster (in Todd) notes, by the black wings of Infamy and the white wings of Glory and Victory in Silius Italicus's *Punica* 15.95–100. Verity attributes Fame's white and black wings to her two aspects, *Fama mala* and *Fama bona*. The notion of Fame as winged is classical; e.g., Virgil, *Aeneid* 4.180–85: "pernicibus alis,...nocte volat caeli medio terraeque per umbram, / stridens"; "fleet of wing...by night, midway between heaven and earth, she flies through the gloom."

   th' other: Darbishire (*Poetical Works*) and B. A. Wright emend the meter with *the* here; Parker also thinks elision in this line "mars the rhythm" ("Notes" 694).

974. *Bears greatest names:* cf. Horace, *Odes* 2.2.7–8: "illum aget pinna metuente solvi / Fama superstes"; "him shall enduring fame bear on pinions that refuse to droop" (Jortin [in Newton]), and Chaucer, *House of Fame* 3.320–22: "On her shuldres gan sustene / Bothes armes, and the name / Of thoo that hadde large fame" (Percival; Verity).

   wild: perhaps an error for *wide*, according to Jortin (in Newton); but Todd quotes Shakespeare's *Othello* 2.1.62: "That paragons description and wild fame" (cf. 879n).

   aerie flight: so Virgil's Fame is described (see 973n), and cf. *QNov* 208–10.

975–76. *Circumcis'd:* i.e., "the Israelites" or "Jews" (so *OED*). Robertson suggests that the rite of circumcision "is a sort of symbolic castration — but in affirmative terms, a pledge of restraint, a dedication of animal energy to higher purposes. The uncircumcised and drunken Philistines, anyway, seem to acknowledge no restraints; and the circumcised Samson, who did, and does, has all the less excuse" (328); see 144, 260, 640, 1100, 1364.

  Dan: see 332.

  Judah: see 265.

977–78. *To all posterity:* editors gloss as "forever" or "to all eternity." On the phrase, Le Comte (98) compares *Ref* (Patterson, *Works* 3:61); *RCG* (Patterson, *Works* 3:278); *HistBr* (Patterson, *Works* 10:33); and *DDD:* "stand so black upon record to all posterity" (Patterson, *Works* 3:465). Verity compares *Animad:* "he...may then perhaps take up a Harp, and sing thee an elaborate Song to Generations" (Patterson, *Works* 3:148).

  blot: "imputation of disgrace" (*OED* 2d); cf. 411.

979. Blakeney as well as Wyatt and Collins paraphrase as "and slandered (with) the blot of most unwifely falsehood." See 955.

  unconjugal: Parker ("Variorum") notes the word occurs twice in *DDD* (Patterson, *Works* 3:389, 480).

981. *Ecron:* "Ekron...was the most northern of the five cities of the Philistines (1 Sam. 6.17), about twenty-five miles west of Jerusalem" (Gilbert, *Geographical*). Verity notes that *PL* 1.466 has *Accaron* (the Vulgate spelling). See also 1231n.

  Gaza: the southernmost city; see 41.

  Asdod: also known as Ashdod, this city near the Mediterranean was about halfway between Gaza and Joppa, and was a center of the worship of Dagon (Gilbert, *Geographical*). Editors note that *Animad* has *Ashdod* (Patterson, *Works* 3:122); *PL* 1.464 has *Azotus* (the Vulgate spelling). Wyatt and Collins suggest that "Milton doubtless used the form Asdod...to avoid the combination of consonants."

  Gath: see 266. Gilbert notes, "its site has not been certainly identified" (*Geographical*). Cawley (110–11) points out that these four place-names all occur in an account of Samson in Thomas Fuller's *Pisgah-Sight of Palestine* (1650). Dalila does not mention the fifth city, Ascalon; see 138, 1187.

982–84. Dunster (in Todd), Keightley (*Poems*), Collins, Masson (*Poetical Works*), Jerram, Verity, et al. cite Euripides, *Heracleidae* 598–99: Πασ῾ν γυναικ῾ν, ἴσθι, τιμιωτάτη / καὶ ζ῾σ῾ ὑφ῾ ἡμ῾ν καὶ θανοῦσ᾽ ἔσθ πολύ; "Above all women, know, in life, in death, / Most chiefest honour shalt thou have of us."
    Women, sung: cf. 203.

984. *recorded:* "remember[ed]" (*OED* II.4; Percival), or "set down in writing," "put on record" (*OED* 9; Lockwood), or "celebrated in song" (Wyatt and Collins).
    to save: either the direct object of *chose* (Church; Percival; et al.) or meaning "in order to save," with *chose* intransitive (Verity). Empson describes this as dramatic irony, "because she will be remembered for a disaster to the Philistines and not as she now thinks for having saved them from one" (*Milton's God* 223). Mollenkott thinks this irony is "beside the point," for "it does not change the fact that Dalila speaks the truth from her own chronological position" (99).

985. *fierce:* cf. 952.
    destroyer: cf. 856.

986. *Above the faith:* "in preference to (keeping inviolate) the faith" (Percival); the meaning here given *Above* seems to have no exact parallel in *OED* (Parker, "Variorum").
    faith: Parker ("Variorum") glosses as "duty of fulfilling one's trust, obligation" (so *OED* III.9). Cf. 388, 750, 1115.

987. See 1733–44. Cf. Judges 11:39–40: "And it was a custom in Israel, That the daughters of Israel went yearly to lament the daughter of Jephthah the Gileadite four days in a year" (Thyer [in Newton]; Church; et al.). Cf. 1 Esdras 1:32 (Percival).
    odours: editors gloss as "spices, ointments, incense" (*OED* 2; cf. *Nat* 23). Cf. Jeremiah 34:5: "But thou shalt die in peace: and with the burnings of thy fathers,...so shall they burn odours for thee"; also 2 Chronicles 16:14: "And they buried him...and laid him in the bed which was filled with sweet odours and divers kinds of spices...and they made a very great burning for him" (Verity; Blakeney; et al.).
    flowers: see 1742–44n. Todd, Jerram, and Percival quote Shakespeare's *Cymbeline* 4.2.218–20: "With fairest flowers.../ I'll sweeten thy sad grave."

988–90. Parker ("Variorum") notes that the story of Jael and Sisera is told in Judges 4:17–22 and celebrated in the song of Deborah (Judg. 5:24–31). Cf. *Ps 83* 35.

Mount Ephraim: "that portion of the central highlands of Palestine inhabited by the tribe of Ephraim" (Gilbert, *Geographical*); cf. 282. Parker adds that it is mentioned immediately after the end of Samson's story in Judges; Verity, Prince (*Samson Agonistes*), et al. note that Deborah dwelt there (Judg. 4:5).

Jael: B. A. Wright emends to *Jaël,* as the meter would seem to require. Commentators note that Dalila, in her final self-justification, throws at Samson this allusion to one who was a heroine among the Israelites for what an enemy might consider treachery, cowardice, and barbarism. Mollenkott calls this speech a "powerful statement of relativism" (98); Frank (105–6) also finds this reference significant: because "Jael's murderous exploits...are favorably commented on in the poem," the similarity between the tomb Dalila envisions for herself and the one Manoa plans for Samson (1733–44) cannot be "explained away by the hypothesis that Milton's putative anti-feminism automatically puts the woman in the wrong." Cf. *DocCh,* where Milton defends Jael (Patterson, *Works* 17:309). Empson declares: "To recall the Israelite Jael is a telling stroke; Shelley could have said here too that the decisive proof of Milton's genius is that he alleged no moral superiority for Jehovah's religion over Dagon's" (*Milton's God* 221).

991. *count:* see 250, and cf. 949.

hainous: see 493, and cf. *PL* 9.929, 10.1.

992. *marks:* "token[s]" (*OED* III), but also, possibly, "money" (Parker, "Variorum"). Cf. 849–50, where Dalila does not deny receiving gold but denies that the offer of it influenced her.

honor: Buchanan writes that Dalila's use of this word "as a kind of public gratitude for a benefit conferred shows that she considers it external" (175). See 372n.

993. *piety:* editors gloss generally as "faithfulness to the duties naturally owed" (*OED* 3); in this case, as editors assert, "patriotism, loyalty" (Latin: *pietas*); Percival suggests that the word "has also the ordinary sense of reverence to the gods." Cf. 955.

994. *to have:* B. A. Wright emends to *t' have.*

shewn: cf. 1475 ("shown").

995–96. Blakeney finds the "expression of settled conviction" in these lines a fine close for Dalila's speech and a clear indication that "Milton…imitates a trait of Greek tragic style." But other commentators are here critical of Dalila: Stein comments, "And so she leaves with one final snappy flip of the skirt" (*Heroic Knowledge* 175); see also Edward J. Thompson (249). Parker thinks it perhaps significant that Milton gives the woman the last word, a word made chilly by the use of the third person and the indefinite *who ever* ("Variorum"). Calton (in Newton), followed by Keightley (*Poems*), Browne, Church, Collins, et al., notes a parallel in Sophocles, where Teucer tells his opponents to love their opinions, as he intends to love his own (*Ajax* 1038–39). On Milton's adherence to Aristotelian principles of tragedy, Baum comments that Dalila's exit does not demand Harapha's entrance: "each scene follows naturally *after* the one before, though not *from* it, and advances the action in something like due proportion" (362).

997–98. While a few critics accept the Chorus's authority (e.g., Kranidas writes, "We must agree with the chorus" [135]), other commentators argue that Milton does not necessarily agree with Samson and the Chorus's ultimate assessment of Dalila. E.g., Empson notes that "the Chorus are Israelite patriots, and she has just said, at last, that she too had been actuated by public spirit.… The Chorus is merely giving firm support to Samson, who feels greatly revived by the whole incident" (*Milton's God* 222–23). Daiches similarly believes that both Samson and the Chorus misjudge Dalila: "Milton is subtler than they, and can see that she may well be sincere and yet represent something evil" (243).

   She's gone: cf. 1350.

   manifest: see 122n.

   Serpent: "a treacherous, deceitful, or malicious person" (*OED* 3b); cf. *PL* 10.867.

   sting: on Dalila as a snake, see 763, 1001, and cf. 936. On her sting, cf. 1007.

   discover'd in the end: some commentators pursue this metaphor in terms of a scorpion: e.g., Todd, who cites Ecclesiasticus 26:7, "He that hath hold of her is as though he held a *scorpion*"; Martin W. Sampson, who thinks that the Chorus locates the serpent's sting in its tail—"in the end"—like a scorpion's; and Blakeney, who comments, "From a natural-history point of view this is inaccurate enough, as the poison of a snake is secreted in a bag at the root of the venom-fang." John Maplet, however, writes in 1567 that the adder can hurt "both with tooth and mouth, and also with his hinder part or taile" (121).

Svendsen finds this "an outrageous but irresistible double-entendre," because "the weight of tradition in herpetological lore" shows "that scorpions are classed with serpents, that they are deceptive, and that their sting is concealed in the tail" (*Milton and Science* 150). According to *The Ancrene Riwle,* the scorpion also symbolizes lechery (91–92). Empson observes that "a niggling reader" might interpret the Chorus's reference to "the end" as signifying Dalila's final four words ("and like my own" [996]), but Empson thinks not: "This interpretation would have to fight all along against the cool sad dignity of the words, and in a play so genuinely not meant to be acted they deserve even more priority than usual" (*Milton's God* 223).

999. Baum suggests that these lines, along with the Chorus's speech, "plainly" express Milton's own dramatic intentions here (361).

 So: "thus (discovered, found out for what she really is)" (Blakeney).

 debase: "abase" or "lower in position, rank, or dignity" (so *OED* 1). Fogle thinks that Samson's attitude reveals he has not "gained a significant moral victory" from Dalila's visit: "why should Samson say that God sent her to debase him unless he felt debased, and why to aggravate his folly unless he felt his folly actually aggravated?" (183). Gossman suggests that Samson "does not know yet that God sent her to try him, [to] educate him spiritually by forcing him to use his reason, and hence to prepare him for new tests" ("Milton's Samson" 539).

1000. In other words, according to Hanford, "to show my folly in a worse light by making Dalila reveal her worthlessness" (*Poems*).

 aggravate: editors gloss as "to increase, make worse or more offensive" (*OED* 6; literally, "add to the gravity of"). Cf. *PL* 10.549.

 my folly: see 377.

 committed: cf. 47.

1001. *viper:* a reptile that destroys her mate in the act of love (Allen, "Idea as Pattern" 90). See 763.

 sacred trust: see 428.

1002. *and my life:* see 764–65n.

1003–7. Commentators, beginning with Newton, compare 759–62 and *PL* 10.940–65, and are again reminded of Milton's reconciliation with his first wife. E.g., Alden Sampson thinks that here Milton "has lifted the veil from a passage of his own biography, one very intimate indeed" (55); Moody similarly writes, "the strophes quiver and groan under the weight of personal bitterness" (287). Hanford also infers from this passage that Milton "retains a vivid memory of the temptation" of sensuous beauty, "but he has, presumably, like Samson ceased himself to feel its power" ("Temptation Motive" 178). See 1008–9n. Tillyard instead is reminded of "Homer's old men speaking of Helen" (*Milton* 290); and Hughes (*John Milton*) associates this scene with Tasso's depiction of the wizard Hildraort sending Armida to trick her host (*Gerusalemme liberata* 4.35). Alternatively, Curry compliments here the Chorus's "calm, penetrating analysis" (346).

strange: "exceptionally great" (*OED* 9) and/or "surprising," "difficult to take in or account for" (*OED* 10).

1006. *passion:* "emotion" (Wyatt and Collins); or "vehement predilection," "tender passion" (*OED* 10, 8); or "suffering, violent grief" (Church; Percival; Blakeney; Prince, *Samson Agonistes;* Bullough and Bullough; *OED* 3 [last entry dated 1656]). Cf. 1758.

1007. *sting:* cf. 997.

remorse: editors gloss as "pity, compassion" and/or "regretful recollection" (*OED* 3, 4).

1008–9. To Newton and subsequent commentators, 1008 seems an adaptation of Terence, *Andria* 3.3.23 [555]: "amantium irae amoris integratio est"; "lovers' quarrels are love's renewal." But Wyatt objects, suggesting "that both the thought and its expression may have occurred to Milton independently of any source." On the popularity of this sentiment, see Edwards 214–15. Percival and Verity gloss these lines to mean that wedlock treachery, unlike love quarrels, does not end in pleasing concord—although, adds Parker, the lines could also mean that love quarrels do not often end in wedlock treachery ("Variorum"). Hughes (in a letter to Parker) suggests that "the failure of a lovers' quarrel to end in reconciliation is clear proof that the love was never genuine" (Parker, "Variorum"). Watkins calls 1008 "a flash of unwonted wistfulness" (145); Parker asks, in defense of Milton, "could any sentiment be further from misogynous?" (*Milton's Debt* 131). Ellis-Fermor comments on the close of this scene: "its work done, the work of disciplining and welding together the faculties of Samson, the episode ends and leaves him lifted above even that degree of self-despair which had remained, roused by anger and disciplined by logic into a mood resolute and ready for inspiration" (29).

1010–60. Editors identify this as the third stasimon (see 293–325n); Epps (193) numbers it the fourth chorus and offers the following tentative divisions: strophe (1010–33), antistrophe (1034–45), strophe (1046–52), and antistrophe (1053–60). Note the intricate rhyming in 1010–22, 1024, 1030–33, 1038, 1040–42, 1051–60 (and see notes to individual lines). Beum attributes the start and stop of rhyme in this passage to an "almost imperceptible shifting back and forth" between the Chorus's two roles, as friends and commentators: the use of rhyme "marks the symbolic, the interpretive, as distinguished from the dramatic, presence of the chorus" (180). See 1525–26n. Prince writes that the rhyme in this speech increases its "lyrical impetus" (*Samson Agonistes* 138). Masson (*Poetical Works*) is reminded of the meter in Goethe's *Faust;* see also 301n.

The ode contains 36 consecutive lines (1010–45) that various commentators label "misogynistic." E.g., Collins refers to the play's "all-pervading misogyny" (5); Grieve thinks Milton alludes to the "bitter memory" of his first marriage (v); Masson claims that 1010–45 sum up Milton's "incurably perverted opinion of women" (*Life* 6:674); and Macaulay describes "the bitter invective against practically all women and wives which runs through *Samson Agonistes*" (127). This reading begins at least as early as Newton's edition (1752), in which Warburton remarks that Milton seems to have written about Samson "for the sake of the satire on bad wives" (1:211). Newton suspects that because Milton "had suffer'd some uneasiness through the temper and behaviour of two of his wives" he here "indulges his spleen a little" and gives "these sentiments the greatest weight" by having the Chorus speak them. In 1900 Raleigh also asserts, "When he came to write *Samson Agonistes*, the intensity of his feelings concerning Dalila caused him to deviate from the best Greek tradition and to assign inappropriate matter to the Chorus" (*Milton* 143). In 1939 Knight finds *SA* "one massive tirade against feminine wiles and guiles" ("Frozen Labyrinth" 81)—a criticism that Hughes directly challenges, calling it "gross exaggeration" and "fancy." Hughes notes that "it is not Milton but the chorus speaking to the victim of a wily woman" (*Complete Poems* 534); adds Wyatt, "the Chorus is made to utter sentiments that could only fitly come from the mouth of Samson" (7). In Wyatt and Collins's later edition, however, the editors assert that Milton "attempts to give added weight to his own sentiments with regard to women by putting them in the mouth of the Chorus" (27; see also Wyatt 13). Stroup also believes that Milton endorses the Chorus's speech: here and following the Harapha episode, Stroup argues, the stasima "serve a purpose somewhat like" Michael's instruction of Adam (*PL* 11 and 12) and can also "be thought of as roughly analogous to the sections of Morning and Evening Prayer of instruction and praise following the Absolution and leading to the affirmation of the Creed" (60). Saurat describes the Chorus's speech as "astonishing invective, in which a rich humour mixes with fierceness, there is the bitterness of the man who has suffered, and the resentment of the philosopher who has not understood.... The chorus closes the episode on a doubting and half angry mood. Here again Milton is more human, and has looked more closely into human weakness" (139, 202).

Among defenders of Milton's attitude toward women in this passage—and throughout *SA*—Parker is probably unrivaled. He argues at length that the "misogyny" of *SA* is "entirely confined" to this passage and, even here, is dramatically intended (*Milton's Debt* 129–35; *Milton* 317–18). He also insists that we cannot fairly call "misogynous" Samson's hatred of the particular woman who wronged him, or Milton's ideas on the place of women in marriage (see 1053–60n). Moreover, Parker asserts, *all* the generalizations about women in 1010–45 (like the generalizations on other subjects in the other choral odes) are made with Samson's experience in mind, and here are addressed to Samson: "the more misogynistic the Chorus becomes, the greater is its implied praise of the suffering hero" ("Variorum").

Other commentators also believe that the Chorus does not speak for Milton in these lines. Mollenkott suggests that the Chorus's estimate of Dalila is rhetorical: "the angry outburst of the Chorus after Dalila's retreat is merely a sympathetic expression of what they perceive to be Samson's state of mind" (94). Lawry writes, "what at first seems a statement of misogyny" by the Chorus "surely is instead a reflection of its increasingly libertarian awareness that the self finally must decide what is fit and good—if necessary, in the face of all necessities, compacts, and unions"; Lawry adds that Dalila represents "all tyranny, all legalism, all false compact, whether they appear in the family, the state, or the church" (383–84). Martz more forcefully criticizes "the chorus's wholly inadequate commentary" on the scene between Samson and Dalila. In what Martz deems "the feeblest lines and the weakest rhyming of the entire play," the Chorus has taken Samson's anger toward Dalila and "driven it to the point of comical caricature. The effect is to relieve the violent tension of the previous scene by a touch of satirical humor, and thus to prepare the way for the next scene [with Harapha], which develops a robustly comic tone" (129, 130); Roberts W. French, focusing on the rhymes in 1010–17, makes a similar point: "It is not the first time the Chorus has attempted to fill verse with vain disquisitions, but it is perhaps the first in which the poverty of their minds and imaginations is immediately apparent. The Chorus is characterized by the very ineptness of their verse" (65). See also 1044n, 1053–60n. Huntley argues that Milton uses Samson's conversation with Dalila in part to "confirm the Chorus's blindness and bondage": whereas the episode inspires Samson, it "has the opposite effect on the Chorus" who "twist Dalila's visit to support their own masculine vanity" (140, 141). Rudrum (49) also doubts that the Chorus speaks for Milton and recalls Milton's own assertions regarding the problem of identifying authors with their characters: e.g., in *Apol,* he writes, "the author is ever distinguisht from the person he introduces" (Patterson, *Works* 3:294).

Editors and commentators also discuss this passage in terms of its classical precedents—but again they dispute whether the Chorus's misogyny reflects Milton's own beliefs. Parker asserts that the sentiments expressed here can easily be fitted into a long literary tradition of satire on women; they occur in the great Attic tragedians chosen as "best example," and occur also in many other classical—and English—writers. After making these points, Parker asks: "What subject, other than woman, was appropriate in the circumstances?...Was John Milton (who had good reason to think ill of women, if ever poet had) inspired, in his imitation of Greek tragedy, to subject a personal bias to truly classical restraint?" (*Milton's Debt* 133–35). Hanford, however, replies: "Milton is too fond of giving voice to such sentiments for us to believe...that they are purely conventional or dramatic" (*Poems* 579). Thyer (in Todd) similarly notes that "What the Chorus here says, outgoes the very bitterest satire of Euripides, who was called the *woman-hater*. It may be said indeed in excuse, that the occasion was very provoking, and that these reproaches are rather to be looked upon, as a sudden start of resentment, than cool and sober reasoning." Landor similarly asserts that "the invectives of Euripides are never the outpourings of the chorus, and their venom is cold as hemlock; those of Milton are hot and corrosive" (5:301). To Sheppard it is more simple: "The brooding of the Chorus...is, of course, inspired by memories of the Helen-Clytaemnestra Chorus in the *Agamemnon*" (163). Krouse believes that commentators judge Milton unfairly: "This [antifeminist] element had always been persistent in the Samson tradition, had been stressed by many writers.... It was particularly characteristic of late medieval poetic treatments of the Samson story.... This medieval conception ... is even more purely set forth by Shakespeare, Spenser, Gascoigne, Burton, Phineas Fletcher, and Quarles. Do we argue from such evidence that all these writers were misogynists? Or, if not, do we measure the autobiographical content of Milton's poetry by a unique standard?" (103).

1010. Cf. *PR* 2.431 (Le Comte 66). Martin W. Sampson compares Jonson's *Staple of News* 4.2.119–20: "The bridegroom [hath] virtue, valour, wit, / And wisdom as he stands for it"; Thaler instead hears in the Chorus's lines an echo of *Hamlet* 1.2.129–46 ("Shakespearian Element" 153). Sprott suggests that the rhyme here is used to "indicate a contempt beneath high style to express" (133).

    wisdom ... wit: Parker ("Variorum") comments, "the Chorus by implication attributes to Samson what he has found lacking in himself (53–54, 207)." See 1018n.

1011. Landor complains that the beginning of this line is untrue and the end tautological (5:301). Of 1010–17 he writes: "Never has Milton, in poetry or prose, written worse than this."

1012. *womans:* see 202.

    inherit: "hold as one's portion" (so *OED* 3); cf. Luke 18:18 and Psalm 37:29.

1013–15. Broadbent finds these lines "rhythmically flippant ... as though [the Chorus was] embarrassed, as your Edwardian clubman would be, by the problem of 'the sex'" (*Milton* 51).

1014. *hit:* "light upon," "get at" (*OED* 11b); thus editors propose, "guess, discover"; Verity and Hughes (*John Milton*) specifically note the metaphor of "strike a target." Prince writes that the word "suggests the uncertainty of any conclusion, as in 'to hit upon' an idea" (*Samson Agonistes*). Jerram suggests τυχεῖν. Cf. *Mask* 285.

1015. *refer:* "relate, recount, report," or "assign *to* a thing, or class of things" (*OED* 9, 3), or "look at" (Verity, Blakeney), or "explain" (Percival), or "assign, ascribe" (Lockwood), or "consider, trace out" (Edmund K. Chambers 144; Latin: *referre*).

1016. *riddle:* see 382–87. The sense, "it is as hard to guess as your riddle was, Samson, even though one should sit and muse over it for seven days" (Blakeney). Verity notes that "riddles were held in high estimation in early ages, especially in the East, so that there was nothing remarkable in Samson's propounding one."

    in one day: editors note it is joined with *hit* (1014).

1017. *seven:* B. A. Wright emends to *sev'n*, as regular meter would seem to require; Parker agrees ("Notes" 693). Parker also notes that "Milton avoids almost all [cf. 1122] reference to the symbolic number seven" (*Milton's Debt* 5). Editors suggest that here the word indicates "a long time" as contrasted with "one day" (*OED* 1d), and Milton follows Judges 14:12, 15.

1018. *these:* editors note that the Chorus here refers to qualities named in 1010–11. Verity paraphrases the sense: "If . . . any of these [qualities] could keep a woman's love." Parker emphasizes that the Chorus thus ascribes *all* these qualities to Samson ("Variorum"); see 1010n.

1019. Kermode (62) identifies an imperfect rhyme in 1019–1020; see 110–14n.

1020. *Paranymph:* "groomsman" (so *OED* 1); "best man" (Bush, *Milton;* Shaw-cross, *Complete English Poetry*); "he, or she, that is joyned with the Bride–groom, or Bride, to see all things well ordered at a Wedding" (Phillips, *New World;* also Wyatt and Collins) and "to conduct the bride to the bridegroom's house" (Collins; Todd); see John 3:29. Cf. Judges 14:19–20, 15:1–2: "And his anger was kindled, and he went up to his father's house. But Samson's wife was given to his companion, whom he had used as his friend. But it came to pass within a while after, in the time of wheat harvest, that Samson visited his wife with a kid; and he said, I will go into my wife into the chamber. But her father would not suffer him to go in. And her father said, I verily thought that thou hadst utterly hated her; therefore I gave her to thy companion." Parker observes that Milton, like Josephus, omits the role of the father in this event (and the "fairer" younger sister whom the father offered Samson as a substitute); Milton infers instead that the Timnian bride herself "preferr'd" one of Samson's groomsmen and thus was unfaithful ("Variorum"). Percival notes that Josephus (*Antiquities of the Jews* 5.8.6) speaks of "the girl, scorning him for his wrath." Cf. 219–20n, 320n, 321n.

1022. *Both:* Hunter glosses, "Nor had both; nor would both thy wives have."
    disally'd: OED cites this line as its first example of the use of the word.

1024. *shorn:* cf. 537.
    fatal: "ruinous" or "fateful" (*OED* 6, 5).
    harvest: Parker suggests it is probably only coincidence that Samson tried to return to his first wife "in the time of the wheat harvest" ("Variorum").

1025–33. Parker claims that "The Chorus is puzzled by these questions; it expresses male bewilderment and does not generalize" (*Milton's Debt* 44); Langdon concurs: "the Chorus proves incompetent to solve the problem of woman's beauty" and thus responds "with a resigned perplexity" (12). Other editors and commentators, such as Collins, instead suggest that the "bitter misogyny" of the entire passage (1010–60) is intensified by the Chorus delivering these words "as cool and well-weighed truths"; see 1010–60n. Le Comte compares *PL* 10.891, 897 and writes that Samson's "struggle...was Milton's own, and sometimes...the bitterness of it breaks through" (140). Carey alternatively observes, "Samson's regret that he has strength without wisdom [52–54] links him with the chorus's opinion of Dalila—'outward ornament' but 'judgment scant'" (*John Milton* 145). Kermode (62) identifies an imperfect rhyme in 1025–1027; see 110–14n.
    for that: editors gloss as "because."
    outward ornament: cf. *PL* 8.538. Todd, Keightley (*Poems*), and Percival quote Tasso, *Aminta* 3.1: "E tu, natura / negligente maestra, perchè solo / alle donne nel volto e in quel di fuori / ponesti quanto in loro è di gentile, / di mansueto, e di cortese; e tutte / l' altre parti obliasti?"; "And thou, Nature, careless artist, wherefore in the face and exterior alone of woman placest thou all that is gentle and mild and courteous in her, and forgettest all the rest?"

1026. *that:* "i.e., that therefore, on those grounds" (Blakeney).
    inward: cf. *PL* 8.538–42.

1027. *for:* editors gloss as "by reason of, through" (*OED* 22).

    judgment scant: Percival quotes Euripides, *Hippolytus* 644: γυνὴ / γνώμη βραχεία; "woman of short sense." Bullough and Bullough observe, "some Christian writers went further": e.g., in the commentaries on St. Paul's epistles ascribed to St. Ambrose, "there is a doubt made, whether the woman was created according to God's Image."

1028. *Capacity:* "mental or intellectual receiving power" (so *OED* 4), "mental ability" (Parker, "Variorum").

1030. *affect:* "aim at, seek" (from Latin *affectare;* to Wyatt and Collins, "less probably"), and/or "love," "show preference for" (*OED* 1, 2d), "to adopt by preference, choose, prefer" (Lockwood; Verity; Shawcross, *Complete English Poetry*). Parker notes the rhymes in 1030–33 ("Variorum").

1032–33. *root:* "source" (so *OED* 7).

    nothing: "not at all" (*OED* B.1). Fletcher examined three copies of the first edition that omit the comma here (*John Milton's Complete* 4:33). Percival contrasts the proverb "Love me little, love me long."

1034–45. Commentators dispute whether the origin of these remarks is personal or literary. Masson finds this passage "full of reference to Milton's own experience" (*Poetical Works*). But Parker notes that in *PR* 2.192–228 the very opposite of the sentiment expressed here is argued ("Variorum"). Hughes remarks that 1034–37 and, "less distinctly, the entire chorus may stem from Euripides' outburst against women" in *Hippolytus* 616–18 (*Complete Poems; John Milton*); Bullough and Bullough also quote these lines. Timberlake (337) adds another source: *Oresteia* 604–5. Thaler proposes *Pericles* 2.5.20–32 as a possible influence ("Shakespearian Element" 197); see also 749n. Larson suggests that here and subsequently in 1053–60 Milton anticipates Rousseau, Schopenhauer, and Nietzsche (179). Fish believes that the passage reveals the Chorus's flaw: "The Chorus are forever trying to categorize Samson, first as an example of the tragic fall-from-a-high-place (167), now as a major figure in the antifeminist mythology. If they can place him, they are no longer obliged to understand him" (242). Cf. *PL* 10.888–908; *Tetr:* "the best and wisest men...doe dayly erre in choosing" (Patterson, *Works* 4:87); also *Colas:* "wisest, sobrest, justest men are somtimes miserably mistak'n in thir chois. Whom to leav thus without remedy, tost and tempested in a most unquiet sea of afflictions and temptations, I say is most unchristianly" (Patterson, *Works* 4:256). Masson (*Poetical Works*) and Percival quote *DDD:* "The sobrest and best govern'd men are least practiz'd in these affairs; and who knows not that the bashfull mutenes of a virgin may oft-times hide all the unlivelines and naturall sloth which is really unfit for conversation" (Patterson, *Works* 3:394). Le Comte (45, 87–88) notes that a similar phrase recurs in 210, 759, and 867, and, in addition to the preceding prose works, suggests *DDD* (Patterson, *Works* 3:461) and *Tetr* (Patterson, *Works* 4:120).

1035. A twelve-syllable line (alexandrine) without any break (Bridges, *Milton's Prosody* 61; see 118n)—to Landor, a "very ugly mis-shapen" one; he would omit either "Seeming" or "at first" (5:301).
    virgin veil: cf. Genesis 24:65: "therefore she [Rebekah, meeting Isaac] took a veil, and covered herself" (Percival; Blakeney). Verity thinks "there may be an allusion to the Oriental custom of the women (especially, among the Jews, maidens) being veiled" (see also Todd). Cf. *DDD:* "the sober man honouring the appearance of modesty, and hoping well of every sociall vertue under that veile" (Todd [Patterson, *Works* 3:395]); and *DDD:* "the sequestr'd and vail'd modesty of that sex" (Verity [Patterson, *Works* 3:502]).

1036. *demure:* "serious," "reserved or composed in demeanour" (*OED* 2); cf. *IlPen* 32 (Blakeney).

1037. *join'd:* editors gloss as "united in marriage" (*OED* 6); cf. Matthew 19:6.
    thorn: "source of continual grief, trouble, or annoyance" (*OED* 2); cf. 2 Corinthians 12:7: "there was given to me a thorn in the flesh"; Genesis 2:24: "they shall be one flesh" (Verity; et al.). Parker adds that in Judges 2:3 an angel of the Lord tells the Israelites that the Canaanites and others "shall be as thorns in your sides, and their gods shall be a snare unto you" ("Variorum"). Cf. also *Tetr,* where a bad wife is described as "a thorn in his heart" (Patterson, *Works* 4:93). Carey suggests that "the physical reference stabs excruciatingly at the area of sexual betrayal" (*Complete Shorter Poems* 339); see also 623.

1038. *Intestin:* editors gloss as "inward" and also "domestic" (*OED* 2, 1); to Prince (*Samson Agonistes*) it suggests "the metaphor of civil war" (cf. *PL* 2.1001, 6.259). Discussing divorce in *DocCh* Milton speaks of *malum...intestinum,* which Charles R. Sumner translates as "intestine evil" (Patterson, *Works* 15:156; see also Verity).

far within defensive arms: Todd notes that one of Tonson's early editions replaced *far* with *war,* a change that was generally accepted until Newton's edition (1752). Editors differ widely in interpretation of this phrase: Collins and Blakeney take it to mean "while nestling in her husband's protecting embraces"; Prince, "having penetrated all defences" (*Samson Agonistes*); Masson (*Poetical Works*), Verity, Edmund K. Chambers, and Grieve suggest "underneath his protecting armor" — and thus, adds Grieve, "no protection against it"; Church, Percival, Wyatt and Collins, and Martin W. Sampson interpret it as a metaphor from fencing: "inside his guard," i.e., too near to give him a chance of warding it off.

1039. *cleaving:* editors gloss as "clinging" (*OED* 2, 3; Lockwood); Edmund K. Chambers suggests an ironic echo of Genesis 2:24: "a man . . . shall cleave unto his wife."

cleaving mischief: on the general sentiment expressed in this line, Todd, Percival, Carey (*Complete Shorter Poems*), and Verity compare Euripides, *Oresteia* 605–6: ἀεὶ γυναῖκες ἐμποδὼν ταῖς ζυμφοραῖς / ἔφυσαν ἀνδρ'ν πρὸς τὸ δυστυχέστερον; "women ever stand in the way of men's destiny on the side inclining to unhappiness." Following Meadowcourt (in Newton), most editors also find an allusion to Sophocles' *Women of Trachis,* which describes Hercules' death by the poisoned shirt which his wife, Deianira, sent him in the hope of regaining his love; cf. *Procan* 11; *PL* 2.542–46. So Dryden evidently interpreted Milton's phrase, which he borrows in *Aureng-Zebe* 2.1 (Todd; see also Langbaine and Gildon sig. H2v). Prince, however, objects that "the allusion, if it is present, is very obscurely given. 'Cleaving' may be used in its other sense of 'dividing' or 'penetrating,' and the expression would then continue the metaphor of 'the thorn in the flesh,' which Milton has just used" (*Samson Agonistes*). Bullough and Bullough suggest that Milton "combines the thorn image with that of a sword, and the idea of division in the home." Todd notes that marriage is "a familiar and co-inhabiting mischiefe" in *DDD* (Patterson, *Works* 3:381) and a "begirting mischief" in *Tetr* (Patterson, *Works* 4:173). Bodkin uses this passage to address Milton's total depiction of women: "To such a man as Milton the passionate nature of women — or rather his own sense both of oneness with the passion he recognizes in women and of superiority to it — makes her image the very projection of the weaker, more vulnerable part within himself" (169–70).

his: cf. 1041 (*him*). Parker ("Variorum") suggests the singular antecedent is to be inferred from *Once join'd* and *defensive arms*—less probably from *men* (1034). Cf. *PL* 9.1183–86.

1040. *Adverse:* Parker ("Variorum") accents the second syllable (as in 192).
     turbulent: see 552.

1041. *awry:* Blakeney glosses as "*on wry* = on the twist—i.e., out of the straight course into a wrong direction." Cf. *PR* 4.313.
     enslav'd: OED 2b traces this use of the word from circa 1645.

1043. *folly:* see 377.
     ruin ends: i.e., "downfall puts an end to" (see *OED* 6), or "end in ruin" (so Percival; Verity; Blakeney). Parker suggests that the word *ruin,* which also means the "falling down...of some fabric or structure" (*OED* 1), foreshadows the catastrophe ("Variorum").

1044. The Chorus remembers Samson's shipwreck figure in 198–200, 209; cf. also 111, 1063 (Parker, "Variorum"). Roberts W. French finds it ironic that the force of the rhymes in the preceding lines (1018–45) "serves only to lead up to an absurd rhetorical question about the way in which a woman enslaves and ruins her husband" (65); see also 1010–60n.
     Pilot: "the master of a ship" (so Percival and Verity, who compare *PL* 1.204 and *Lyc* 109, respectively); Parker ("Variorum") thinks "steersman" (*OED* 1) is also possible with *expert* and *Stears-mate* (1045).
     wreck: "suffer[s] or undergo[es] shipwreck" (so *OED* 5a). Parker ("Variorum") compares *PR* 2.228, where the same metaphor is used to express an opposite sentiment about women; *DDD,* where "shipwrack" and unhappy marriage are linked (Patterson, *Works* 3:400); and *Tetr:* "if we do but erre in our choice...this divine blessing that lookt but now with such a human smile upon us, and spoke such gentle reason, strait...brings on such a scene of cloud and tempest, as turns all to shipwrack without havn or shoar but to a ransomles captivity" (Patterson, *Works* 4:90).

1045. *Embarqu'd:* "These French spellings are not Milton's" (Darbishire, *Poetical Works*); cf. 1113 and *PL* 11.753. Cf. also *DDD:* "two persons ill imbarkt in wedlock" (Patterson, *Works* 3:418).

Stears-mate: Lockwood defines as "the assistant of the pilot"; Meiklejohn suggests "companion in steering." Percival glosses as "fellow steersman," but remarks that as a masculine term it "would be out of place here." Cf. *PL* 9.513. Most editors ignore the apparent inconsistency of *Pilot* (1044) and *stears-mate.* The latter suggests "helpmeet" (cf. *Tetr* [Patterson, *Works* 4:88]), and perhaps also "copes-mate" (*Colas* [Patterson, *Works* 4:266]). For the figure in general, Parker ("Variorum") compares Milton's description of Martin Bucer as "such a pilot . . . as ye would soon find the difference of his hand and skill upon the helm of reformation" (*Bucer* [Patterson, *Works* 4:18]).

1046–47. Kermode (62) identifies an imperfect rhyme in 1046–1048; see 110–14n.

Favour'd of Heav'n: the phrase occurs also in *PL* 1.30 (Le Comte 66). Editors compare Proverbs 18:22: "Whoso findeth a wife findeth a good thing, and obtaineth favour of the Lord"; also Proverbs 19:14: "a prudent wife is from the Lord"; also Proverbs 31:10: "Who can find a virtuous woman? for her price is far above rubies"; also Ecclesiasticus 26:1–2: "Blessed is the man that hath a virtuous wife, for the number of his days shall be double. A virtuous woman rejoiceth her husband, and he shall fulfil the years of his life in peace." The rarity of a good wife is also a sentiment expressed frequently in Greek tragedy; editors (e.g., Blakeney; Verity) notice in particular Euripides' *Alcestis* 473–75; Percival also suggests *Iphigenia in Aulis* 1162–63. Verity, citing Aubrey, suggests that Milton may have been "thinking of his own third wife, 'a genteel person, of a peaceful and agreeable humour'" (see Darbishire, *Early Lives* 3). Newton notes that if Milton in *SA* "satirizes the women in general," he also "commends the virtuous and good." Saurat similarly comments: "Even here, four lines remain . . . as a geological survival of a lost continent, traces of an ideal" (139). Todd adds that Milton, unlike Euripides, "harshly esteems such an one a *rarity.*"

1048. *domestic good:* cf. 917, and see *PL* 9.232–34, 11.616–17. Parker ("Variorum") notes also *Tetr:* "both in the Scriptures, and in the gravest Poets and Philosophers I finde the properties and excellencies of a wife set out only from domestic vertues" (Patterson, *Works* 4:106).

combines: editors gloss as "unites" (with her husband), i.e., acts in harmony with him for the sake of domestic goodness (*OED* 5). Masson (*Poetical Works*) and Blakeney suggest "agrees with him," while Hughes recommends "unites herself perfectly." Hughes adds that this ideal resembles Sir Thomas Overbury's in *A Good Woman* (*Complete Poems; John Milton*).

1049. *Happy that house!:* cf. *PE:* "O happy this house that harbour'd him" (Patterson, *Works* 3:93). Cf. Euripides, *Oresteia* 602 (Percival).

1050–52. Editors paraphrase as "Virtue which overcomes all opposition (by a wife to its exercise)...is more acceptable to God (than even the virtue of domestic goodness)." Parker thinks the clear implication is that Samson has now thus won divine approval (*Milton's Debt* 44, 134). Hanford finds the basic idea in this passage "a strange perversity of thought" (*John Milton* 221). Editors compare the final six lines of *Mask* and Aristotle, *Nicomachean Ethics* 2.3.1105a.8–10.

    But: Tung emphasizes this "all-important" conjunction because it "turns the thought of the ode from treacherous women to Samson"; these lines reveal "the Chorus' real purpose" for which all their "misogynistic pronouncements are but prelude" (484).

    temptation: cf. 427.

1052. *acceptable:* pronounce "ac´-cept-a´-ble" (Parker, "Variorum").

1053–60. Parker notes that this stanza of the Chorus's speech exactly balances the first (1010–17) in length, although not in form or rhyme scheme (*Milton's Debt* 63); they and the final choral ode are the only completely rhyming stanzas in the play. The second stanza (1018–33) is the length of this one plus the first (Parker, *Milton's Debt* 63). On the rhyme scheme, cf. *Lyc* 165–72. Roberts W. French complains that the "firm and confident" tone implied by the rhyming "clashes with the matter," for the Chorus here contradicts itself in arguing that a man must have "despotic power / Over his female" so that he is not led astray: "The rebuttal is obvious, and the Chorus has already furnished it: the man of strength does not need despotic power, for his kingdom is within" (66). This passage is quoted and presented as instructive for "She-wits" in a 1697 antifeminist tract (Dutton sig. K9v). See also 748–58n.

    Gods universal law: editors and commentators quote or cite various passages from Milton to show that this view of the relations of man and wife was his personal conviction; some, e.g., Edmund K. Chambers, find it partly "based upon his own unfortunate experience of women." The assumption that it was peculiar and individual is voiced early by Johnson—he refers to Milton's "Turkish contempt of females" ("Milton" 1:157)—and is echoed by critics ever since. E.g., Hanford (*Poems*) asserts that there is no precedent in St. Paul for the "harshness of this utterance" (1 Tim. 2:12; Eph. 5:22–23). Mahood (220) similarly suggests that "modern readers, with the slam of Nora Helmer's door still resounding in their ears, are maddened by Milton's theory of the relationship between man and woman," as expressed most succinctly in *PL:* "He for God only, she for God in him" (4.299). Charles Williams, though, responds more charitably: "Milton had his own views on the relation between the sexes, which (like almost any other views of the relation between sexes) were probably wrong" ("Introduction" xvi). Greenlaw, Osgood, and Padelford (5:223) compare the repealing of women's liberty in *The Faerie Queene* 5.7.42.5–9.

Parker, however, defends Milton's choice in this passage at some length: he argues that (1) the view expressed here was an almost universal belief of his age, that (2) it was solidly based on Scripture, being Pauline as well as Hebraic, and that, (3) even if Milton disagreed with it completely, it would be an appropriate comment in the mouth of an Old Testament male Chorus reflecting on the implications of Samson's marriages (see *Milton's Debt* 133–34). Parker continues, "Although real affection sometimes existed between them, the Hebrew husband did in fact have supreme authority over his wife, who was a chattel legally"; Parker cites as evidence—noting "there are many similar passages"—Genesis 3:16: "Unto the woman he said, . . . thy desire shall be to thy husband, and he shall rule over thee"; also Esther 1:22: "every man should bear rule in his own house"; also Ephesians 5:22–23: "Wives, submit yourselves unto your own husbands, as unto the Lord. For the husband is the head of the wife, even as Christ is the head of the church" ("Variorum"). Blakeney offers a similar defense of Milton: "The 'subjection of woman' (spite of the modern unpopularity of that doctrine) is distinctly taught in Scripture; but whereas the Scriptural doctrine is carefully guarded against abuse, Milton's notions were distinctly Jewish in their rigour." For Milton's view of women and the discussion of misogyny in *SA*, see 57n, 1010–60n.

1054. *despotic:* Parker glosses as "absolute"; he observes that *despot* in its Greek form meant "master" or "lord" (e.g., of a household) but insists that "the later connotation of tyranny and oppression could hardly have been intended here" ("Variorum"). The earliest use of the adjective *despotic* cited in *OED* is by Hobbes

(1650), but Milton uses it in 1649 (*TKM* [Patterson, *Works* 5:37]), whereas in 1641 he had used *despoticall* (*Ref* [Patterson, *Works* 3:59]).

1055. *his female:* "his mate" (*OED* B.1a); the expression was often used of lower animals, and Percival remarks: "One would like to be sure that Milton does not use this unpleasant expression on purpose." Darbishire (*Poetical Works*) and B. A. Wright emend to *femal;* see 711–13n.

    in due awe: i.e., "to keep her in proper or fitting reverence," or "who is to stand in (the) reverence due (from her) to him" (see Wyatt and Collins; so also Percival).

1056. The construction: "Nor (gave to him permission) to part (for) an hour from that right" (Percival).

1057. *lowre:* "frown," "look angry or sullen" (so *OED* 1); Grieve paraphrases as "whether she like it or not," or "willy-nilly." Cf. 948.

1058–59. *confusion:* see 471.

    least: Empson notes that this word "implies a man must expect some degree of confusion if he has anything to do with a woman" (*Milton's God* 219).

    sway'd: cf. *PL* 8.635.

1060. Prince (*Samson Agonistes*) cites 1 Timothy 2:12: "But I suffer not a woman... to usurp authority over the man," which Milton quotes in *DDD* (Patterson, *Works* 3:475). Le Comte (133–34) notes that Milton accused Charles I of being "govern'd and overswaid at home under a Feminine usurpation" (*Eikon* [Patterson, *Works* 5:139]; Le Comte also compares *Eikon* [Patterson, *Works* 5:251] and *Def 2* [Patterson, *Works* 8:204]). Cf. Adam, who was "fondly overcome with Femal charm" (*PL* 9.999). Prince detects a transition in this line: "here we are meant to feel the passage from chanted verse to spoken" (*Italian Element* 156). See also 80–83.

    female: Darbishire (*Poetical Works*) and B. A. Wright emend to *femal;* see 711–13n.

    dismay'd: "paralyzed, rendered powerless" (Percival); but Parker ("Variorum") suggests that it is difficult to know what strength Milton intended for this word, which can mean "defeated" or "disheartened" (*OED* 2, 1).

1061–1267. The fourth epeisodion (see 176–292n). There is no rhyming in this scene. Waggoner observes that this episode has been prepared for *artistically* by Samson's general concern with honor and heroic exploit, by scattered military imagery, and by earlier allusions to the concept of "judicial combat" (proving on the field the truth and the glory of God). Waggoner thus asserts, "It is fitting that the challenge to Harapha should form a central point in the play" (86). Ellis-Fermor points out that the episode has also been prepared for *psychologically:* "Samson's speech reveals the active presence of certain moral qualities; courage, self-respect, self-control, faith, and the intellectual virtue of disciplined and ordered thought. The restoration of these we have traced step by step through the earlier episodes" (29). Parker (*Milton's Debt* 45) adds that giants are several times mentioned before Harapha's entrance (see 148, 528), and he infers that the giant, who lives away from Gaza, is presumably one of the people "attracted to the city by the great holiday" (see 1654–56).

Editors and commentators also emphasize the dramatic significance of Harapha's visit for Samson's spiritual regeneration. Whereas Jerram is one of the few editors who dismiss this character ("Harapha seems intrusive and hardly required for the action of the play" [x]), more representative is Ker, who notes: "The scene with Harapha is necessary for the action, and to save Samson from the mood of dejection in which he begins.... [H]e needs the plain question of courage to put him in possession of his strength; dealing with Harapha he knows where he is, and refuses to be blind" (66–67). Allen similarly writes: "There is no temptation in this scene and no comedy; it is the most important scene of all, for it is the hinge of the tragedy. By the victory over Harapha, who symbolizes all that is valiant in Philistia, God, working through Samson, has put Dagon down. It is, in truth, the final event of the tragedy in miniature" ("Idea as Pattern" 93). Prince also comments: "The battle of words with Harapha is no mere interlude.... It provides a certain relaxation after the emotional and moral tension of the scene with Dalila.... But the true dramatic function of the scene is to display the change which has taken place in Samson since Manoa left him.... [T]he most significant fact is his renewed desire for action" (*Samson Agonistes* 122). Verity, too, considers the Harapha episode "one of the most dramatic parts of the play, vivid in characterisation,... essential to the catastrophe" (xlviii). And Christopher observes that Samson's reaction to Harapha fits within the play's larger homeopathic structure: visitor by visitor, Samson is purged of "his own negative attitudes when he meets them on the lips of others," and Harapha "works the most spectacular part of the cure" (367, 370).

1061–64, 1074–75. Examples of στιχομυθία or "dialogue in single lines." See also 1308–9, 1345–47, 1562–64, 1569–70, 1582–84 (and *Mask* 276–89). Examples of two-line speeches are 903–6, 1104–7, 1515–20; of one-line with two- or three-line speeches, 1178–81, 1233–36, 1319–22, 1365–68, 1531–36, 1552–64 (Parker, *Milton's Debt* 65). Verity notes the comparative absence in *SA* of this device so popular with the Greek tragedians (xlix); Parker responds that Milton "introduces it, as the Greeks do, when there is considerable tension; but on the whole, there is perhaps not enough emotional excitement in *Samson Agonistes* to allow of much of it." Parker adds that Milton may have minimized stichomythia, "obviously a stage device," for the same reason that he avowedly omitted division into acts and division of choral odes into strophe, antistrophe, and epode: *SA* was not intended to be acted on a stage (*Milton's Debt* 65–66).

1061–68. Johnson (*Rambler* 20 July 1751) criticizes this dialogue spoken by Samson and the Chorus as Harapha approaches: "of all meanness, that has least to plead which is produced by mere verbal conceits, which depending only upon sounds, lose their existence by the change of syllable" (221).

1061. Gilbert objects to the Chorus's abrupt question here to introduce Harapha, one of a series of "peculiarities" that he believes suggest *SA* remains unfinished ("Is *Samson Agonistes*" 101, 105). Brewer (913), however, writes that the unexpected appearance of Samson's visitors recalls the chance appearance of Prometheus's visitors in *Prometheus Bound*; cf. 1061–1267n.

    had we: Tickell transposes to read "we had."

    storm: Blakeney, Verity, et al. note this word is metaphorically used, but taken literally by blind Samson (1062). To Johnson's objection that the play upon this word is out of place, Percival replies that the Chorus is remembering its metaphor of Dalila as a ship sailing under fair weather (714); cf. 1063, 1070, 1072, 1075. The first edition reads, "retire, I see a storm?" Fenton emends this line with a question mark after *retire* and a period after *storm,* a reading favored by many early editors.

1062. *Fair days…rain:* Samson responds philosophically to what he takes to be a threat to his physical comfort (Parker, "Variorum"); see also 1061n s.v. *storm.*

    contracted: "become infected with," "incur[red]" (*OED* 5), or "drawn or brought together, collected" (*OED* 7; and so Collins; Percival; Verity; Lockwood;

et al.), or "concentrated in intensity" (Shawcross, *Complete English Poetry*); Percival adds, "we similarly speak...of a 'storm gathering,'" and, one might further add, of "contracting an illness."

1064. *abstruse:* "difficult, recondite" (so *OED* 2; Latin: *abstrusus*); "dark, obscure" (Phillips, *New World*).

    riddling days: see 382–87, 1200, but editors especially compare 1016, which presumably prompts the remark. Verity writes, "The irony of the reference is clear"; Blakeney suggests an allusion to Judges 14:12–19.

1065. *Look...voice:* cf. *PR* 2.158. Todd and Fleming quote Euripides, *Medea* 773: δέχου δὲ μὴ πρὸς ἡδονὴν λόγους; "Nor look I that my words should pleasure thee."

    now: i.e., "this time the new-comer is no Dalila" (Verity).

1066. *bait of honied words:* responding to Johnson's objection to *honied* (he defines it as "sweet; luscious" [*Dictionary*]), Todd shows "it was a common term in our old poetry" and quotes, among other examples, Shakespeare's *Titus Andronicus* 4.4.89–91: "I will enchant the old Andronicus / With words more sweet, and yet more dangerous, / Than baits to fish or honey-stalks to sheep" (cf. 1576–77n). Quarles also has "sugerd words" (sig. R4r). Todd notes, too, that "honied words" is classical; cf. also Psalm 119:103.

    tongue: cf. 1181; also 495.

1067. *draws:* intransitive verb; Blakeney cites similar examples from Tennyson, who "had a special liking for the idiom."

    stride: "long steps," "striding gait" (so *OED* 2); cf. 1245.

1068. *Harapha:* editors and commentators note that for this character and episode Milton had no warrant in either the biblical history of Samson or the Christian tradition; it was his own idea to have the unarmed Samson confront and defeat the father of Goliath (see 1248–49) without even the aid of a sling. Thorpe infers from metrical scansion, Hebrew practices of pronunciation, and the general practice of recessive accentuation that the primary stress of this name (as with "Ma´-no-ah" and "Da´-li-la") should fall on the antepenultimate syllable: it should be pronounced "Ha´-ra-pha" (72, 74). See 229n, 328n.

There may or may not be a person named *Harapha* mentioned in the Old Testament. *Ha* is the Hebrew definite article, and the Authorized Version translates as "the giant" the *raphah* of 2 Samuel 21:16 and the *rapha* of 1 Chronicles 20 (so argue, e.g., Percival; Wyatt and Collins; and Moody). On the other hand, Josephus writes of one "Araphos" (*Antiquities of the Jews* 7.12.1), and Harapha is taken as a proper name by the Vulgate, the Geneva ("Breeches") Bible, John Diodati (sig. O1r), and Edward Leigh (sig. Hh1r). (For this reading, see Newton, Verity, Edmund K. Chambers, and Adler.) Parker ("Milton's Harapha" 12) suggests that what Milton thought is probably reflected in an entry which his nephew Edward Phillips introduced in the third (1671) and subsequent editions of his *New World of Words*: "*Haraphah,* (*Hebr.*) a Medicine, a *Philistim* whose Sons being *Gyants*, were slain, by *David* and his Servants." Parker adds that in Milton's poem Harapha acts as a "medicine" to Samson, whose spiritual sickness had earlier been described with much medical imagery. However, Leveen questions Phillips's authority—"a man...utterly ignorant of the most elementary principles of Semitic philology" (60). Loewe alternatively proposes that the name derives from "*raphah* to be weak" so that the giant's name "was a euphemism for 'the flabby, powerless ones'" (60).

Commentators approach the episode with Harapha in light of various conventions: the dueling code (e.g., Verity; Allen, "Idea as Pattern" 91–93; Carey, *Complete Shorter Poems*) the *miles gloriosus* tradition (Buchanan; Nicolson), and Renaissance tragicomedies (Boughner; Penn); see notes to individual lines.

Other commentators emphasize what Harapha represents. E.g., Hughes interprets Harapha as "a collective representative of the whole court party. He is a monstrous, composite portrait standing opposite to the mass of caricatures of the Commonwealth men in Butler's *Hudibras*" (*John Milton* 427). J. Macmillan Brown similarly writes that he is "a portrait of the champions of the Restoration. He has the haughty airs of the Cavaliers, bedraggled in the mire of long years of vagabondism" (123). Lewalski ("*Samson Agonistes*" 1059) finds here "adumbrations...of an antitype in Revelation: Harapha...evokes the great beast (Antichrist) associated with the kings of the earth and their armies, who combats with the King seated upon the white horse (Christ the Judge)." Daniells argues that the character so effectively fits the drama because he not only reminds readers of "the archetypal Philistine giant, Goliath of Gath," but also, as an Antaeus figure, Harapha "is needed...to round out still another insistent association,...Samson and Hercules" (213). For Landy, Harapha "represents the same physical power which, in the past, Samson had possessed.

He is like a mirror to Samson of what he had been in the past and what he must now reject" ("Character" 247). Landy thinks Harapha is the "most deadly" character in the play "because he holds out no hope to Samson of comfort.... He reminds the reader that the contest in the play is not only between Samson and the individual antagonists, but between two ways of life—the way of God and the way of Dagon" ("Character" 249). Muldrow (202) is reminded of the powerful but unvirtuous men described in *PL* 11.789–90 and Jesus' denunciation of warfare in *PR* 3.386–440. Steadman instead casts this encounter as "the antithesis between trust in God and 'carnal reliance'—between confidence in the unarmed might of God and trust in purely human force and arms" ("'Faithful Champion'" 24).

Among other responses to this episode, Knowlton criticizes the passage for not contributing "to the probability or the inevitability of the catastrophe" and thus bringing about an anticlimax (336); Carey agrees: "It is difficult to believe that Samson would have reacted less violently to Harapha's taunts had they come at the start" (*John Milton* 139). But Ellis-Fermor writes, "The conflict with Harapha, which is the direct result of the state of mind into which he [Samson] has been brought, now transfers a part of the action to the plane of event; what had been purely psychological action begins to express itself simultaneously in thought and in deeds" (29).

1069. *Haughty:* a pun: "high" and also "proud, arrogant" (*OED* 3, 1); cf. *PL* 6.109. Darbishire writes that *Hauty* seems to be Milton's spelling (*Poetical Works*), but cf. *Mask* 33 (especially Trinity Manuscript); *RCG* (Patterson, *Works* 3:218, 221, 244); *Apol* (Patterson, *Works* 3:304); *OAP* (Patterson, *Works* 6:270).

as is his: Blakeney remarks that Milton seems generally to avoid such cacophony.

pile: "a lofty mass of buildings," or, perhaps, "a large building" (so *OED* 4b, which cites this instance as the first figurative usage of the word in this sense, and Lockwood; see also *PL* 1.722, 2.591; *PR* 4.547). Editors take this as meaning "bulk," i.e., as a metaphor for Harapha's huge body, some comparing the *Herculea...mole* of Silius Italicus's *Punica* 12.143. But Gilbert suggests that Milton may have meant the term literally, thinking of the evidently tall dwelling of the giant as it stood on an elevated position in Gath, which Adrichomius says was a city on a hill (*Geographical* 128). Also, Calvin had compared Goliath to a tower (*Homiliae in primum librum Samuelis;* see Steadman, "'Men of Renown'" 581–83). Parker, in view of 1069–72 and 1075 (perhaps also 1061,

1063, 1244), suggests the "pile high-built and proud" may be a ship ("Variorum"). See 1075n. He adds that if *pile* also means "hair" (see *OED*), then we may note that Harapha leaves "somewhat crestfall'n" (1244).

 proud: cf. *PL* 5.907 and *PR* 4.34.

1070–71. While the Chorus here puzzles over the reasons for the giant's visit, Allen suggests that "Harapha's visit to Samson is prompted by a champion's curiosity, and we should accept his first speeches as uttered honestly and generously" ("Idea as Pattern" 92). Hanford suggests instead that Harapha was "sent to threaten him" (*Poems* 549). Fenton inserts a question mark after *hither.*

 wind: cf. *storm* (1061) and *fraught* (1075). The expression was proverbial (*OED* 15).

1072. *sumptuous:* "spending largely" (so *OED* 3), or "richly and splendidly attired" (Lockwood).

 floating: cf. 714. The scansion of this line has caused confusion. Collins writes that it "seems desperate." Wyatt suggests we read it as a line of four feet, an iamb followed by three anapests. Percival thinks that the change of meter is "meant to indicate contempt" (xlvii).

1073. *habit:* see 122.

 carries: "bear[s] as a character, mark, attribute, or property" (so *OED* II.28a).

 peace: "he is dressed as for every-day affairs, i.e., not stripped or armed for combat" (Prince, *Samson Agonistes*); cf. 1119.

 defiance: "a challenge or summons to a combat or contest" (*OED* 2); cf. *PL* 4.873.

1074. Editors paraphrase as "(whether he carries) peace or not (is) equally (a matter of indifference) to me." Samson's cool contempt for Harapha contrasts with his anger when Dalila approached. To Parker, it "suggests, not only his self-mastery, but also the lassitude of the episode with Manoa. It is this lassitude, this soul-weariness, which must be finally removed" (*Milton's Debt* 45).

1075. *fraught:* "cargo," "freight" (so *OED* 2); Verity, Blakeney, et al. thus paraphrase as "charge or business"; Masson (*Poetical Works*) suggests "burden." Meadowcourt (in Newton) emends to *freight;* Wyatt and Collins write in 1932 that the word is still in use in northern Scotland. Grieve observes the ship imagery is continued; cf. 1070, 1072. Northrop Frye notes that Harapha is compared to "tall ships like those in the Armada" (Paradise Lost *and Selected Poetry*). Cf. *Giantship* (1244).

1076–90. Allen suggests that "Harapha's first speech is that of a genuinely valorous man, proud of his famous ancestry and of his long record in the annals of war. We know his counterparts in the romances of chivalry—knights who know their rivals by reputation but who have never competed with them." It is only as the scene progresses, Allen argues, that "a brave and knightly man will change into a coward and a blusterer" ("Idea as Pattern" 91–92). Nash also writes about Milton's allusions to chivalric combat in the exchanges between Samson and Harapha (23–38); Madsen argues that such allusions place the confrontation "at a vast moral distance" from Christ's encounter with Satan in *PR* (190).

1076. Collins compares the entrance of Harapha with the entrance of Creon in Sophocles' *Oedipus Rex* 1422.
  condole: editors gloss as "lament, grieve over" (*OED* II.3).
  chance: "lot," "the way in which things [fell] out" (*OED* 3, 1); "misfortune" (Blakeney; Bullough and Bullough; Wyatt and Collins; et al.); or "mishap" (Shawcross, *Complete English Poetry*).

1077. Editors paraphrase as "As (have) these (the Chorus) perhaps, yet (I) wish it (your misfortune) had not been." Parker thinks *these* sounds contemptuous ("Variorum").

1078. *Gath:* Fletcher notes there are two states of sig. N1v in the first edition, and, in three copies that he examined, there is no comma after *Gath* (*John Milton's Complete* 4:33). The other lines with variants on this page are 1086 and 1093.

1079. *renown'd:* Parker suggests a possible echo of Genesis 6:4: "There were giants…of old, men of renown." He adds, "Milton apparently distinguished between two tribes of giants that were traditional enemies of the Israelites—the Anakims ('longnecked' ones who were bullies, fellers of men) and the Rephaims, to which family Harapha belonged" ("Variorum"). Steadman writes that Harapha's boast about his ancestry's renown has some truth to it, "even though it does embody a false criterion of nobility. According to Calvin, the giant 'men of renown' were the world's first noblemen—a nobility which exalted itself through contempt and dishonour of others" ("'Men of Renown'" 585).

1080. *Og:* Deuteronomy 3:11: "For only Og king of Bashan remained of the remnant of giants; behold, his bedstead was a bedstead of iron; ... nine cubits was the length thereof, and four cubits the breadth." (Church suggests that this bedstead "was probably a sarcophagus of black basalt.") He dwelt at Astaroth (Deut. 1:4); see 1242. Editors also cite, among other sources, Joshua 13:12; Numbers 21:33–35. Milton mentions Og in *Ps 136* 53.

    Anak and the Emims: cf. 528. Deuteronomy 2:10–11: "The Emims dwelt therein [the land of Moab] in times past, as people great, and many, and tall, as the Anakims; which also were accounted giants." Numbers 13:33: "And there we saw the giants, the sons of Anak." Verity notes that in using here the incorrect plural *Emims,* Milton follows the Authorized Version, which treats such Hebrew words as English; but elsewhere in his poetry Milton uses the correct form (e.g., *Cherubim* and *Seraphim* in *Nat* 112–13; *SolMus* 10; *PL* 1.129, 387). Milton uses *Cherubins* in *Ref* (Patterson, *Works* 3:60) and *Seraphim* in *RCG* (Patterson, *Works* 3:241). See also 1242n s.v. *Astaroth.*

1081. *Kiriathaim:* Genesis 14:5: "And in the fourteenth year came Chedorlaomer, and the kings that were with him, and smote ... the Emims in Shaveh Kiriathaim." This was a "town east of Jordan, in territory disputed between Moab and Reuben" (Gilbert, *Geographical*). Pronounce "Kir´-i-atha´-im" (Lockwood).

    thou knowst: Parker ("Variorum") compares Deuteronomy 9:2: "the children of the Anakims, whom thou knowest."

1082. *known:* Parker ("Variorum") glosses as "informed, possessed of knowledge" (*OED* 2 [1655]). But editors prefer the meaning "an object of knowledge" (*OED* 1) and quote Satan's speech in *PL* 4.830: "Not to know mee argues your selves unknown." Daiches, describing the "insolent swagger" of Harapha's speech, notes "this is Satan's idiom reduced to petty proportions" (244).

1086. *encounters:* there is a comma here in the second state of the first edition (Fletcher, *John Milton's Complete* 4:33); see 1078n.

1087. With this line Harapha suggests that he is a pagan knight who recognizes that Samson has been a knightly "champion" of the Hebrews; see Nash (23–38).

camp: "field" (of battle); Percival, Verity, Carey (*Complete Shorter Poems*), Hughes (*Complete Poems; John Milton*), et al. say that the word keeps this Italian (*campo*) or Latin (*campus*) meaning (*OED* IV.9). Parker adds, "in Middle English the word meant 'battle,' perhaps the general sense here intended" ("Variorum"). Cf. 1436, 1497.

listed: "enclosed in or converted into lists for tilting" (so *OED* 1, the first example of this usage). Meiklejohn and Blakeney thus paraphrase: an enclosed space as contrasted with a battlefield. Cf. 463, 1102, 1117, 1220–21.

1088–89. *noise:* editors gloss as "fame, rumour, common talk" (*OED* 2). Cf. "loud report" (1090).

walk'd about: "circulate[d]" (so *OED* 3b). Carey notes that the use of *walk* with such subjects as *report* or *fame* was obsolete by the end of the seventeenth century (*Complete Shorter Poems*).

survey: see 1230. Cf. *PL* 8.268. Blakeney paraphrases as "survey (and find out) if." George Coffin Taylor (195) is reminded of Achilles' "perusing" Hector in Shakespeare's *Troilus and Cressida* 4.5.231–33, 237–38.

1090. *answer:* "come up to," "correspond to" (*OED* III.4).

loud: "current" (Parker, "Variorum"); cf. *Sonn 15* 4.

1091. Parker ("Variorum") notes that the use of monosyllables, in classical rhetoric, was the language of command, the language of master to slave (cf. *DDD* [Patterson, *Works* 3:491]). See also 1104–5.

taste: editors suggest "try, test" (*OED* 2 [last entry dated 1670]) or "experience" (*OED* 3); cf. *PR* 2.131. Wyatt and Collins note that literally the word means "touch" (from Latin *tangere*). But Parker detects a play on words: Samson adds another sense to those of hearing and seeing; cf. *see* and *feel* in 1154–55 ("Variorum"). Blakeney comments, "there is grim humour in Samson's quiet retort that contrasts strongly with Harapha's noisy insolence." Stein writes, "a remarkable piece of brevity.... Something has happened suddenly, a positive new motion in the drama" (*Heroic Knowledge* 179).

1092–1103. Harapha is surprised by the prisoner's show of spirit, but not believing the challenge serious, he starts boasting. Boughner writes that Milton is here "infusing the traditional rôle of the classical blusterer with the newer spirit of mockery of chivalric pretensions and the dueling code," as found in comic continental literature, especially the commedia erudita of Italy (306). Rudrum compliments Milton's dramatic strategy, "using devices from comedy" so as to provide "a challenge for Samson to respond to while ensuring that Samson does not act yet" (56). On the use of enjambment in *SA* (here, 1092–93), see 190n.

single: editors gloss as "pick out" (for single combat), here almost equivalent to *challenge* (so *OED* 4). Parker suggests that this word may also be a "verbal quibble, i.e., recognition that Samson's reply was monosyllabic and a single line" ("Variorum"); see 1091.

me: a second state of the first edition substitutes a question mark for the semicolon after this word; the second edition (1680) also prints a question mark here. Fletcher interprets this as possible evidence of Milton's direct or indirect participation in correcting the text (*John Milton's Complete* 4:250–51). See also 1093–94n s.v. *thee.*

1093–94. *Gives:* "shackle[s], esp. for the leg[s]," "fetter[s]" (*OED* s.v. *gyves*); cf. 1235, 1238, 1410. Keightley (*Poems*), Collins, et al. think *handcuffs* is meant; Masson (*Poetical Works*), Verity, et al. think Samson's restraints are only at his ankles. Cf. 1309.

thee: some copies of the first edition have a question mark; others have a semicolon (Fletcher, *John Milton's Complete* 4:33, 250–51); see 1078n. The second edition (1680) clears up this muddle (see 1092 and 1092n) by substituting a period.

fortune: "chance, luck" (Parker, "Variorum").

fam'd: "reported or reputed" (so *OED* 2).

1095. Cf. 142–45.

To have: B. A. Wright emends to *T' have;* Hughes suggests that the extra syllable in this first foot is deliberate (*John Milton* 423).

Asses: i.e., "Ass's." Lee Sheridan Cox comments (in a private correspondence to Parker): "Literally, Samson . . . had used an ass's jaw as a weapon to overwhelm the Philistines; figuratively, the ass's jaw does not, as manipulated by the tongue-doughty Harapha, amount to much of a weapon; and eventually Samson, the comrade of asses, is to serve as God's weapon" (Parker, "Variorum").

1096. *wish:* all editions from 1671 through 1713 read "wish" (McDavid 89). Gilbert ("*Samson Agonistes* 1096") defends the common emendation to *with*, which is made without comment in Tickell's 1720 edition, in Beeching's 1900 edition "after the Original Texts" (v), and in Patterson, *Works*. Verity was the first modern editor to restore the original reading. Gilbert argues that "the reading *with* gives a line in harmony with Milton's habits of language and versification, suitable to its context, of dramatic value, and of aid in bringing out clearly a thought important in the drama" ("*Samson Agonistes* 1096" 162). McDavid responds: "the passage is awkward whether *wish* or *with* is accepted, and…this awkwardness may be taken as corroborative evidence that Milton wrote it rather early but never got around to revising it" (87). McDavid also notes the possibility that the change to *with* in 1720 could have been an error made at the printing house: the compositor may have inadvertently repeated *with* from the preceding line (89). Editors note in view of the word *Or* that *wish* must imply either "wish (and get)" or "wish (and so leave the scene to get)" other arms.

1097. *carkass…Ass:* Jerram asks, "Is this line a giant's ponderous joke?"
   Or: "The implications are that Harapha would have gladly faced Samson well-armed, and granting weapons to him might involve going to get them to some place afar from the carcass of the ass. If Harapha means he could have beaten Samson with his own arms…he would say '*And* left thy carcass'" (T. O. Mabbott qtd. in McDavid 87; see 1096n).

1099–1100. *Palestine:* see 144n.
   the unforeskinn'd race: "the circumcised Jews" (Parker, "Variorum"); see 144, and cf. 29.

1101. *Acts:* editors sometimes substitute a period or semicolon for the comma.

1102. *mortal duel:* editors gloss as "duel to the death of one of the parties" (see *OED* 3a); it probably translates *joute l'outrance;* cf. 1175 and *PL* 1.766. Allen asserts that Harapha is not here "hedging but talking as a man conscious of the knightly code" ("Idea as Pattern" 92). Verity remarks that it is an anachronism to use language that suggests the medieval duello (cf. 1087, 1117, 1175, 1220, 1222, 1226). But Parker suggests that the monomachy of David and Goliath was a familiar notion ("Variorum"). See also 1104–7n.

1103. *prevented:* Masson notes the Latinism (*Poetical Works* 3:77).

1104–7. Parker notes that this is "the only perfect instance of balance in the actual dialogue between Samson and Harapha"; he adds, however, that 1156–67 and 1168–77 differ in length by only two lines (*Milton's Debt* 63).

   Commentators primarily discuss these lines in the context of the dueling code. Waggoner argues that the challenge to single combat is a "basic plot device" and that "contemporary interest in single combat, especially judicial combat, on the part of both legal writers and the public has important bearing upon this episode" (82, 83). According to Waggoner, the issuing of such a challenge at a comparable point in the plot of *1 Henry IV* (5.1.83–100) and *Antony and Cleopatra* (3.1.25–28) suggests that a challenge to single combat "has a connotation for heroic behavior" (83). Tung, however, reasons that Samson's persistent challenges ignore the knightly code and thus are "wrong and dishonorable," whereas Harapha's repeated refusal to fight (1106–7, 1164–66, 1224–26) "has its source in single-combat tradition" and thus is "an honourable act." Tung concludes that Milton uses "Samson's error in challenging Harapha to reveal his impulsive temper, his impatience with an unpromising future, and above all, his desperate motive—seeking destruction by another's hand" (486). Fogle also finds fault with Samson's attitude here: Samson is "on the verge of wasting his hard-fought spiritual gains by allowing his old warrior's blood-lust to displace the divine mission of freeing Israel in his endeavors" (185). Lawry (387), in contrast, hears in Samson's brief answers the Son's "calm wit" in *PR*. Le Comte (45) notes the verbal echo in 1127–28.

1105. *hand:* editors gloss as "power" (*OED* B.2). Verity paraphrases as "what (as you say) you would have done."

1107. *hast need:* "to need, require," or, perhaps, "to be in straits or in want" (so *OED* 7c, 8; cf. *Mask* 393 and *PL* 2.413–14). Landy explains that Harapha wishes Samson to "feel the full humiliation of his condition" ("Character" 248). Whereas the taunt strikes Edmund K. Chambers as bathos, Percival finds it "another little Euripidean trait." Rajan suggests, "The exterior grime is…meant to remind us that matters are otherwise with the inner man" (140); so also Mueller, "There is…an ironical contrast between inward and outward purity.… [T]he new Samson had been hiding underneath his rags" ("*Pathos*" 165). See also 123n, 415.

1108–13. Parker comments, "Samson's implication is that the Philistine Lords are cowards. If Harapha is not also a coward, let him now accept Samson's challenge" ("Variorum").

Such usage: the sense: "(the dirtiness you mention results from) such treatment as your rulers furnish me" (Parker, "Variorum").

honourable: Blakeney comments, "The irony is intentional." Parker observes that either the line is tetrameter or, more likely, the pronunciation is "hon´-our-a´-ble"; cf. 855 ("Variorum").

1109. Hughes suggests that the extra syllable in the second foot is deliberate (*John Milton* 423).

Afford: "grant," "yield," "furnish" (*OED* 5); so also 910.

assassinated: editors gloss as "treacherously harmed or attacked" (i.e., not actually murdered; *OED* dates the verb from 1618, this meaning from 1626). Johnson writes, "waylaid, taken by treachery. This meaning is perhaps peculiar to Milton" (*Dictionary*); Lockwood proposes, "injured by treachery." Parker ("Variorum") compares *DDD* (Patterson, *Works* 3:422) and *PL* 11.219 (*Assassin-like*).

1110–11. *united powers:* cf. 251, 1190.
withstand...unarm'd: cf. 126–27.

1112. *chamber Ambushes:* editors cite Judges 16:9: "Now there were men lying in wait, abiding with her in the chamber."

1113. *Close-banded:* "secretly leagued" (Johnson, *Dictionary;* and in Todd; Verity).

attaque: Phillips uses this same French spelling (*New World,* and see 1045n). *PL* 6.248 has *attack.*

sleeping: so Judges 16:14, 20. Cf. 990.

1114–15. *hir'd:* "bribe[d]" (*OED* 1b).

a woman: Verity and Blakeney note Samson's contemptuous reference to his wife. See 50.

gold: see 389.

circumvent: "overreach, outwit, cheat" (*OED* 3); cf. *PL* 3.152.

1116–29. Some commentators interpret Samson's challenge in terms of Milton's own life. E.g., Visiak identifies Harapha with Salmasius (*Milton* 99), a view endorsed by Kreipe (54–56) and the German critic Theodor Siebert (67–82). Masson similarly asks: "In the chained Samson's challenge...may we not read Milton's own unabated pugnacity, his longing for another Salmasius to grapple with, his chafing under the public silence to which he is enforced in the midst of repeated attacks and insults?" (*Life* 6:675). But Wyatt is doubtful: "May we not ask, if this is not the extreme limit to which the allegorical interpretation of the play can be allowed to reach?" Hughes more openly dismisses such biographical interpretations as "pure surmise": "it is a long step" from the satisfaction Milton took from his victory over Salmasius "to indulgence of it in naïve identification of himself with the hero of his drama" (*Complete Poems* 535).

Among other responses, Waggoner posits that Milton "readily and naturally" used this device of a duel or "single combat" when he needed "a motive and a symbol for Samson's revived will to act" because "contemporary authority" referred to dueling as if it were "based in the sound experience of both the Greeks and the Hebrews." Waggoner (92) also illustrates that dueling continued to play a part "in English concepts of heroic and honorable behavior," especially in "judicial combat" (for the test of truth). Stein instead focuses attention on Samson's motive in this passage: "The most important fact in the speech is the return of inspiration.... In his challenge he has come to terms with the physical blindness; he has invented conditions that permit him to be a champion again, and in a comic scene of his own setting" (*Heroic Knowledge* 179; see also Rudrum 54). Wilkes takes issue with Stein's claim that Samson acquires "inspired knowledge" (Stein, *Heroic Knowledge* 205); here instead, Wilkes argues, "it is much more like the instinctive awakening of the warrior in Samson, before the derision of a foe" (374). Muldrow more critically comments, "there is an element of humor in this description, and with this wealth of detail, Samson becomes something of a blusterer himself" (204). Dick Taylor also does not think Samson's threat is entirely serious: "he might resume his old reckless course, and in his offer to beat up Harapha, he seems possibly verging toward this course, although not actually" (77). Hawkins discusses how Samson's "passion, not reason, arms him" against Harapha's temptation just as it armed him earlier against the temptations of Manoa and Dalila: "throughout, Samson's arguments and reasonings only confirm...resolutions reached by passionate instinct" (224).

1116–17. *feign'd:* "fictitiously invented or devised" (*OED* 2).

shifts: editors gloss as "tricks, evasions, i.e., excuses"; e.g., 1106–7; cf. 1220.

enclos'd: editors note that it is presumably enclosed with lists or barriers; see 1087. Verity compares *PL* 1.763 ("covered field").

1118. *flight:* Brydges thinks "this play on words is beneath Milton." Keightley quotes passages to suggest that this kind of jingle on words is imitated from the Hebrew Scriptures, e.g., Isaiah and Judges (*Account* 438). Parker suggests that the rhyme with *sight* (1117) points the contemptuous sarcasm ("Variorum"). Mueller (in a letter to Parker) notes two parallels in the *Iliad:* where Apollo tells Diomedes to stop fighting with him (5.440) and in Diomedes' challenge to Glaucon (6.143). For other instances of wordplay, see 301, 588, 668–69, 1134, 1278, 1529.

    on: "over" (Edmund K. Chambers 143; Verity).

1119–23. Belloc compliments this instance of Milton's "vivid visual concept, now at its height after twelve [*sic*] years of blindness...enhanced by the right noise of words" (280). Verity and Grieve suggest Milton is remembering 1 Samuel 17:5–7: "And he [Goliath] had an *helmet of brass* upon his head, and he was armed with a *coat of mail;* and the weight of the coat was five thousand shekels of brass. And he had *greaves* of brass upon his legs, and a target of brass between his shoulders. And the staff of his *spear* was like *a weaver's beam;* and his spear's head weighed six hundred shekels of iron: and one bearing a *shield* went before him" (emphasis added). Steadman develops this comparison in the most detail, adducing various similarities between Harapha and Goliath as well as between Samson and David ("Milton's Harapha" 787–94); see also 1123. Cf. 2 Samuel 21:16, 19; 1 Chronicles 20:5.

1120. The alliteration in this line is probably meant to express contempt (Verity), or belligerency (Parker, "Variorum").

    Brigandine: "coat of mail, corslet"; "body armour composed of iron rings or small thin iron plates, sewed upon canvas, linen, or leather, and covered over with similar materials" (so *OED* 1). See 1119–23n. Parker compares Jeremiah 46:4: "furbish the spears, and put on the brigandines" ("Variorum").

    Habergeon: "sleeveless coat or jacket of mail or scale armour" (so *OED*), or, as most editors suggest, "hauberk, armor for the neck and shoulders" (*OED*; see Dodd sig. I11r); Phillips calls it "a diminutive of *Haubert,*" which he defines as "a Coat of Mail" (*New World*). Parker speculates it may be Milton's version of Goliath's "target" in 1 Samuel 17:5–7 ("Variorum"); Percival and Verity, followed by Buchanan (132), note that, in Coverdale's Bible, *habergeon* is used for Goliath's "coat of mail"; see 1119–23n. Laking, however, writes that the *haubergeon* was invented in 1328–50; that it was a shirt or tunic of mail, with sleeves, but shorter than the hauberk; that it retained the *avant-bras* ("Vant-brass") and *grevières* ("Greves"); and that early in the fifteenth century it was worn over a brigandine (1:35–36).

1121. *Vant-brass:* "vambrace," "armour for the (fore-)arm" (so *OED;* Dodd sig. L9r). Keightley, followed by other editors, emends to *Vant-brace* (*Poems*).
    Greves: "armour for the leg[s] below the knee" (so *OED* s.v. *greave* 1; Dodd sig. I10v); see 1119–23n.
    Gauntlet: "glove worn as part of medieval armour," invented in the mid-fifteenth century, "usually made of leather, covered with plates of steel" (*OED* 1; Prince, *Samson Agonistes*).
    add: from 1680 until 1747 the editions read "and" in error.

1122. *Weavers beam:* a "wooden roller or cylinder in a loom on which the warp is wound before weaving" (Verity; *OED* 4). See 1119–23n. Verity and Percival note that the same comparison occurs in 1 Samuel 17:7 and 2 Samuel 21:19. Todd reads this metaphor in the context of other Renaissance works that depict similarly aggrandized weaponry.
    seven-times-folded shield: editors gloss as "shield made of seven layers" (of leather), and hence very strong. Blakeney adds, "possibly the outer face was strengthened with metal as well." The allusion now shifts for a moment from David and Goliath to classical antiquity: Wyatt and Collins cite Ovid, *Metamorphoses* 12.2, where Ajax's shield is described: "Clipei dominus septemplicis"; Verity et al. suggest Virgil's *Aeneid* 12.925 ("clipei extremos septemplicis orbis"), which, they note, is probably an imitation of Homer's σάκος ... ἐπταβόειον (*Iliad* 7.222). B. A. Wright emends to *sev'n-times-folded,* as regular rhythm would require; Parker agrees ("Notes" 693). See 1017.

1123. *Oak'n staff:* Steadman ("Milton's Harapha" 788) suggests an analogue in 1 Samuel 17:40: "And he [David] took his staff in his hand" (when he went to meet Goliath); see also Percival. B. A. Wright emends to *Oaken,* as the rhythm would seem to require; see also Parker ("Notes" 693).

1124. *out-cries:* "noise[s]" (*OED* 1). Edmund K. Chambers remarks, "there seems to be some confusion of idea between the clatter of blows on the armour and the outcries which the wounded giant will probably raise." Parker suggests this explanation: the outcries are *raised* "produce[d]" (so *OED* 13) *on* the rattling armor; he adds that *clattering* also means rapid, noisy talk and that a pun may be intended ("Variorum").

1125–26. *mee:* Masson writes, "probably...emphatic" (*Poetical Works*); cf. 63, 244, 252, 460, 463, 1264, 1326, 1416. See, however, 219–20n s.v. *Mee. remains:* "continue[s] with" (so *OED* 6c).

1127–28. *boast...done:* Le Comte (45) notes that Samson repeats himself (see 1104).

1130–38. Editors (e.g., Grieve; Blakeney; Prince, *Samson Agonistes;* et al.) find echoes of medieval romance with its notion of protection in battle by spells; these echoes are anticipated by 1087, 1102, 1117, and Samson's description of Harapha's armor. E.g., Joseph Warton (in Todd) suggests that Milton specifically adopted this line from chivalric combat; Thyer (in Todd) thinks it "very probable" that Milton borrowed this idea from the charmed armor that so often is used in Italian epics; Greenlaw, Osgood, and Padelford (1:223) find a possible echo of Spenser's *The Faerie Queene* 1.4.50.5. Parker ("Variorum") argues that Milton "must also have realized that the practice of magic is abundantly evidenced among the Hebrews themselves from their nomadic days to the end of the monarchy in the sixth century BC. E.g., Deut. 18.10–14 forbids a variety of magical practices; magic is regarded as harmful in 2 Kings 17.17, 21.6; Saul visits the sorceress of Endor (1 Sam. 28.3–20); Moses and Aaron vie with the magicians of Egypt (Exod. 7.11–12, 22)"; and see 1139–40n s.vv. *forbidden Arts.* Waggoner, however, insists that the situation in *SA* is more medieval than Hebraic, for in medieval combats champions were obliged to swear that they had not had recourse to magic; he gives examples, including one as late as 1571 (90); see also 1139–40n.

   Among other responses, Verity emphasizes, "this is not merely Harapha's personal opinion. It expresses the view of Samson's power which the Philistines held"; see also 1133n. Mueller adds that Harapha here echoes the unregenerate Samson's own description (59–60) of his gift as a magic charm "hung...in my hair" ("*Pathos*" 163). J. Macmillan Brown instead hears contemporary echoes "from the Cavalier pamphlets of the time; for they accused the Puritans of succeeding in the civil war by diabolic means" (125). Cf. *DDD* where Milton protests, whimsically, that his views on divorce are to "dispell rooted and knotty sorrowes: and without inchantment if that be fear'd, or spell us'd" (Patterson, *Works* 3:386).

1131–32. *battel:* here perhaps "duel, single combat" (Parker, "Variorum"); cf. 287, 583.
    spells: see 1130–38n.

1133. *black:* "malignant," "sinister," or "iniquitous" (*OED* II.8, 9). Parker writes that the reference is to the "Black Art" ("Variorum").
    Art: cf. *Mask* 63, 149. Verity suggests that this term "was specially used of magic" and compares Prospero's description of his powers in *The Tempest* 1.2. Krouse notes that the medieval commentator Rupert of St. Harbert had suggested (Migne 167:1050) "that perhaps Samson wrought his wondrous feats by means of magic, that is, by alliance with Satan rather than by impulsion of the Holy Spirit" (130). Cf. Samson's words to Dalila (819, 934).

1133–70. In the first edition, the leaf containing these lines (sig. N3, pp. 69–70) is a cancel in two copies examined by Parker. Only one difference between the integral and canceled leaf has been discovered: the inserted page is incorrectly numbered "79" instead of "70" on sig. N3v (*Milton* 1137).

1134. *Arm'd . . . charm'd:* Verity thinks this jingle intentional; see 1118n.
    strong: Percival glosses, "predicative and proleptic, 'so that thou becamest strong.'"
    which: the antecedent is *strength,* understood from *strong* (Church; et al.).

1136. *least:* "not at all"; see 195n.

1137. *ridge:* "mark with or as with ridges" (so *OED* 3, the first example cited).

1138. *chaf't:* "angry" (*OED*); cf. 1246.

Porcupines: editors cite "And each particular hair to stand on end / Like quills upon the fretful porpentine" (*Hamlet* 1.5.19–20). Buchanan (142–43) instead proposes that Milton was thinking of the bristling boar and ruffled porcupine that appeared at the top and bottom of a much-used seventeenth-century ornamental title-page border, e.g., in London editions of Sidney's *Arcadia* (1593–1638, except 1605, 1627) and Spenser's *The Faerie Queene* (1611).

1139–40. Todd identifies this as an echo of the oath taken by medieval champions before the judges of the combat; he quotes versions of the oath from Lewis Machin's *Dumbe Knight* (1608, 1633) and John Cockburn's *An History and Examination of Duels* (1720). Carey (*Complete Shorter Poems*) compares Samson's language to oaths from Selden's *Duello* (1610) and *Antiduello* (1632); see 1130–38n. Bush claims, however, that "Samson's grand affirmation transcends" such oaths (*Milton*). Hill notes that here "Harapha's taunts have drawn from Samson, almost unawares, an expression of hope—the first in the poem" (165).

   forbidden Arts: see 1130–38n. Percival remarks that "Jews were forbidden to consult wizards and familiar spirits."

1140–44. See 58–59n. Commentators use this speech to measure Samson's spiritual regeneration (see also 1168–77n). Parker suggests that Samson realizes "that here, at last, might be an opportunity of serving again," and "his faith grows stronger as the call to action assumes reality" (*Milton's Debt* 46). Landy similarly notes that here Samson's "earlier fears have been surmounted" ("Language" 189). Grenander also emphasizes that "Samson sees himself once more as God's champion," and "this faith in his ultimate restoration to divine favour is the last step necessary . . . before he can be chosen again as God's agent" (387). But Fish finds Samson's affirmation of faith unexpected: "The surprise we experience at this sudden shift in levels of discourse should alert us to the fact that what we see here is not the end of a linear and charitable progression or the conclusion to a chain of inferences, but an illumination; an illumination which surely has antecedents and therefore causes; but as to what they are exactly—well, that is 'hard to hit'" (252). Knight detects a political allusion here: Samson's strength "is God-given, yet proudly physical, corresponding to the armed strength of the Cromwellian revolution" (*Chariot* 87).

   My trust: cf. Jeremiah 17:5, 7: "Cursed be the man that trusteth in man, and maketh flesh his arm. . . . Blessed is the man that trusteth in the Lord, and whose hope the Lord is" (Steadman, " 'Faithful Champion'" 24).

living God: cf. 1673. Editors note that the expression occurs frequently in Scripture; cf. *PL* 12.118 and *Ps 84*8 (Le Comte 67). In *DocCh,* Milton associates this expression with God's vitality and eternity (Patterson, *Works* 14:54–55).

diffus'd: Lawry (386) notes that the Chorus had earlier described Samson as "carelessly diffus'd" (118) but "now a far different meaning swells in the word," indicating Samson's "spiritual progress."

1143–44. *while:* "so long as" (Verity).

vow: cf. 1151 (*Avow*); also 319, 378–79 (*pledge / Of vow*), 1386.

1145–55. Blakeney is reminded of Elijah's address to the priests of Baal in the scene enacted upon Carmel (1 Kings 18).

For proof hereof: Steadman suggests, "For the first time in the drama, Samson appears once more in his ordained role as 'Defensor Fidei'" ("'Faithful Champion'" 21). He adds that "it is actually faith which makes Samson's final exploit an heroic act—a deed acceptable to God" (16). See *DocCh* (Patterson, *Works* 17:6–10).

if Dagon be thy god: Parker observes that Harapha later swears by "Baal-zebub" (1231) and "Astaroth" (1242); he wonders if, in fact, Dagon *is* Harapha's god ("Variorum"). Tung, noting that Samson challenges Harapha three times before mentioning Dagon or God, suggests that the idea of receiving divine assistance to defeat Harapha only now occurs to Samson: "To say, then, that his challenge is motivated by his renewed hope in God's pardon and his restored will to act is not entirely accurate" (486). Hyman interprets Samson's challenge as a reflection of his inability to understand "a kingdom that is not of this world.... He is also challenging God to give him a visible sign of His power" ("Unwilling Martyrdom" 93).

1146–47. *invocate:* editors gloss as "invoke, pray for" (*OED* 1); cf. 575. Verity and Meiklejohn observe that Milton does not use this word elsewhere in his poetry.

devotion: "worship," "prayer and praise" (*OED* 2).

spread: "open out or lay out" (so *OED* 1a), i.e., explain fully. Cf. 2 Kings 19:14 (Keightley, *Poems*).

1149–50. *frustrate:* "counteract" (*OED* 2); cf. 589.

dissolve: "undo," "destroy the binding power, authority, force, or influence of" (so *OED* 11).

    Israel's God: so also in 1527.

1152. *Offering:* B. A. Wright emends to *Off'ring,* as regular meter would require; Parker agrees ("Notes" 693). See 343–44n.

    Champion: see 556n, 1175n.

    bold: Parker ("Variorum") finds this ironic but notes that it may also mean "audacious, presumptuous" (*OED* 4); cf. 138.

1153. *utmost:* see 484.

    Godhead: "divine nature" (*OED* 1); cf. 464.

1154–55. For Samson's diction, see 1091n.

    strongest: Blakeney notes that Milton uses the superlative where modern writers would use the comparative.

1156–67. Parker writes, "Harapha now—very significantly for the plot—echoes Samson's and the Chorus's hitherto unanswered complaint of God's desertion. We are now at the heart of the drama" (*Milton's Debt* 46). Allen also observes, "To defend his own declining courage, Harapha uses some of the old arguments that had earlier cast Samson into despair.... But Samson knows better now" ("Idea as Pattern" 92). Woodhouse makes this same point ("Tragic Effect" 211), and Christopher similarly comments, "It is precisely when Samson's 'sense of heaven's desertion' comes to him in a bald taunt from the enemy that Samson rejects his negative identity as a God-forsaken man and at last makes an emphatic, unequivocal declaration of faith" (369). See 1168–77n. Harris observes: "he speaks a part long traditional in English literature—the tempter to ultimate despair of God's forgiveness" (117).

    Line 1156, with commas after both *God* and *be,* offers a problem in punctuation for the modern editor (Parker, "Notes" 698; see 543–44n). Verity observes that the single comma after *God* in the first edition means "that the words 'whate'er he be' may be taken either with what precedes or with what follows." Grieve prefers the single comma—"even at the risk of introducing ambiguity" (xiv). Keightley changes the comma after *God* to a period (*Poems*).

    what e're he be: cf. 1034.

1157–58. *cut off Quite:* Parker glosses as "completely excluded" ("Variorum"). See 764–65n and cf. *Ps 83* 39: "quite cut off." Hughes notes that the expression resembles "the sanctions pronounced against disobedient Hebrews in the Old Testament" (*Complete Poems; John Milton*); cf. Exodus 30:33: "shall even be cut off from his people."

> *delivered:* Parker proposes *deliver'd,* as regular meter would seem to require, as in 437 and 1184 ("Notes" 693–94).

1161–62. According to Dunster (in Todd), "there can be no doubt" that Milton was here recalling Apuleius's description of a *pistrinum* from *Metamorphoses* (or *Golden Ass*) 9.

> *Asses:* see 37n.
>
> *comrades:* accent the second syllable (Newton; Masson, *Poetical Works;* Verity).

1164. *boyst'rous:* "coarse-growing" (so *OED* 6) or "strong in growth, luxuriant, rank" (Lockwood). Percival suggests the meaning "strong, indicating strength" (not in *OED*). Cf. 569. The word occurs often in Milton's prose works, "always with the bad sense 'violent,' 'turbulent'" (Verity; also Hunter); cf. 1273. Prince adds, "There is a sarcastic allusion to Samson's hair as the seat of his strength" (*Samson Agonistes*).

> *match:* cf. 346.

1165. *valour:* "a brave man" (Hughes, *John Milton*).

> *nor by:* i.e., "unworthy of a noble warrior's sword, that he should stain his honour by accepting your challenge" (Blakeney).

1167. *subdu'd:* "conquer[ed]" and, probably, "[brought]…into mental, moral, or spiritual subjection" (*OED* 1, 2). Cf. 174. Blakeney notes the "coarsely personal insult"; cf. 1107.

1168–77. Commentators use this speech to measure Samson's spiritual regeneration (see also 1140–44n, 1156–67n). Here, Parker writes, "Samson *finds his faith completely;* all his doubts disappear. He admits every one of Harapha's allegations concerning himself, but asserts God's eternal justice. This is the final spiritual victory. Samson is ready at last" (*Milton's Debt* 46; see also Dick Taylor 77–78). Similarly, Broadbent calls this Samson's first expression of hope

(*Milton* 53), and Bush suggests that "Perhaps the most impressive testimony to Samson's renewed faith is this humble confession to a contemptuous enemy" ("John Milton" 515n; *Milton*). Woodhouse also writes: "Nothing surely could be psychologically more true, or dramatically more effective.... Till the hope [of God's forgiveness and of further service] was uttered, he did not dream that it existed: and utterance was born of the perfectly natural union of repentance and indignation" ("*Samson Agonistes*" 166; "Tragic Effect" 212). Allen, too, observes, "With this speech we know that Samson will not die an apathetic death. Life has returned to him; and though he does not yet know how it will all be brought about, he is God's champion once more" ("Idea as Pattern" 93). Gossman notes the irony that Manoa, "pathetically wishing to help, should cause despair, whereas Harapha, selfishly wishing to cause Samson despair, should unintentionally help Samson to overcome his evils" ("Milton's Samson" 539); Stein also comments, "Samson's answer is the old one of justice, and the important new addition that has appeared only with the coming of Harapha" (*Heroic Knowledge* 181). Landy thinks this speech, combined with Harapha's taunts, is "the clearest indication thus far of the widening gap between Samson and the world which was once so important to him" ("Language" 189). Powell finds this speech the clearest statement "in all of Milton's writings" of "God's obligations to man," namely, that Samson "has a *right* to final pardon if he can prove himself worthy" (181).

Among other responses to this speech, Hill thinks that, "as was the case in his marrying Dalila, Samson's motive here is, in itself, good," but, Hill cautions, "his defiant and almost selfless challenge to Harapha puts him on the verge of committing another act of presumption, of sacrificing all the spiritual headway he has made through one negligent, though well-meaning, act" (166). Tung is more critical: "in challenging Harapha to a duel, Samson exemplifies the false fortitude of rashness" (477). Alternatively, Tinker comments: "this is more like King David than the strong, self-confident bully of Judg[es]. In his words there is something of the spirit of the penitential psalms" (70). Bowra instead compares Samson in this speech to "a Crusader or a Covenanter" (124). And Rosedale suggests that Milton is here "aptly alluding to himself" (154).

indignities: "unjust taunts; unjust, that is, from the Philistines" (Hughes, *John Milton*).

1169. *From thine:* editors paraphrase as "(coming) from thy countrymen"; cf. 291. Edmund K. Chambers suggests "from thy indignity, or worthlessness."
deserve: cf. 489.

1171. For the meter, see 122n. Parker suggests synaloepha of a final vocalic *y* with initial consonantal *y* ("Variorum").

    despair not…pardon: editors compare Manoa's words (510–12) and Samson's (521).

1172–73. *ear…eye:* Percival remarks the echoes of Scripture, e.g., Psalm 17:1: "give ear unto my prayer"; Genesis 6:8: "Noah found grace in the eyes of the Lord." Cf. *Ps 81* 1: "Thy *gracious* ear, O Lord, encline."

    suppliant: Parker ("Variorum") compares *Ref:* "nothing is readier then *grace* and *refuge* to the distresses of mortall Suppliants" (Patterson, *Works* 3:76).

1175. *trial or mortal fight:* editors and commentators primarily address the medieval origin of this line. E.g., Verity, Blakeney, Bullough and Bullough, and Hughes (*Complete Poems; John Milton*) again find an allusion to the medieval custom of "trial by combat" to determine the merits of a cause. Todd calls it "another phrase in chivalry"; Dunster (in Todd) finds a parallel with canto 2, stanza 90 of Tasso's *Gerusalemme liberata:* "Ed a guerra mortal, disse, vi sfido"; "In mortal combat, I shall take you on." Cf. 1102 and *PL* 1.766. Waggoner suggests that such terminology remained current during the Renaissance: "Samson's language in the successive challenges is not that of Goliath but resembles the language of the antiquarians and legal theorists of the seventeenth century as they discuss various forms of judicial combat…. Harapha's part in the challenges also has no source in I Samuel…. [A]ll these references have their source in the later tradition of single combat" (84). Parker insists, however, that beneath the terminology of chivalry lies the spirit of such Old Testament contests as those recorded in 1 Kings 18 and 1 Samuel 17:4, 8–9, 45 ("Variorum").

1176–77. *god is god:* Fletcher examined four copies of the first edition that use all lowercase letters for this clause; he notes that all other copies he examined have "god is God" (*John Milton's Complete* 4:33). See 1183n for another line printed on this page (sig. N4r) that survives in two states. Parker discusses the generally inconsistent use of capitalization in the first edition ("Notes" 694–96).

    Israel's Sons: the phrase occurs also in *PR* 3.406 (Le Comte 67).

1178–80. Buchanan relates this to the code of the duello, listing the crimes that, under the code, destroy a man's honor: Harapha is saying that Samson, having committed three of these crimes, is ineligible to challenge a gentleman (242–43).

Krouse observes that this accusation "creates an occasion for the hero to reply to commentators who regarded him as an unauthorised privateer" (130); Carey writes that the accusation (1180) justifies Samson's challenge to fight Harapha in single combat (*Complete Shorter Poems*). Steadman suggests that *trust* and *confidence* (1174) are "key words" in this scene and are especially "important to Milton's delineation of his hero of faith" ("'Faithful Champion'" 21). Knight instead finds more evidence of the poem's political context; he suggests that Harapha levels "an accusation directly fitting the regicide party" (*Chariot* 87).

   Fair: Lockwood suggests "specious, plausible." Blakeney observes that this line is spoken with bitter irony.

   trusting: for Milton's concept of "trust," see *DocCh* (Patterson, *Works* 17:52–53).

1180. Peck (sig. P4v) cites this line (along with examples from *PR*) to illustrate how Milton "heaps the *substantive*," which Fenton specifically calls the "continuative substantive." Peck notes that Milton similarly uses a list of epithets or verbs to compose a single line of verse. See 417n.

1181. *Tongue-doubtie:* editors gloss as "brave in words (not deed)." The second edition (1680) has *Tongue-doughtie;* but cf. *Colas:* "our doubty adversary" (Patterson, *Works* 4:246); *RCG:* "your doubtiest reasons" (Patterson, *Works* 3:216). On the thought editors cite Aeschylus, *Agamemnon* 1399 and *Seven against Thebes* 617: θρασύστομος; "over-bold of tongue, insolent"; also Beaumont and Fletcher's *Pilgrim* 2.3 (*tongue-valour*) and *Little French Lawyer* 5.1 (*tongue-valiant*). See 404n. Peck writes that the use of this kind of "complex epithet" is characteristic of Milton and Shakespeare (sig. P3r–P4r). Ferry suggests that this "satirical epithet" reveals Samson's "characteristic contempt for 'talk'" (164).

1182. See 240 and 251–64n s.vv. *Thir Lords.* Verity, Grieve, et al. comment that Harapha first tries to prove Samson a "Revolter" (1180).

   thy nation: Empson observes that Harapha here refers to the Philistines and Hebrews as separate nations, "but that does not prove he would admit it in more diplomatic moments. The reader is evidently meant to imagine the position as like the results of the Norman Conquest; a gradual settlement is in progress" (*Milton's God* 215–16).

1183. *Their:* Fletcher examined four copies of the first edition that contain this spelling; all others that he examined read *Thir* (*John Milton's Complete* 4:33). See 1176n for another line printed on this page (sig. N4r) that survives in two states.

1184. *League-breaker:* cf. 1189–1209. Although the biblical story of Samson says nothing about a league, Percival notes that Josephus (*Antiquities of the Jews* 5.8.8) speaks of the Israelites paying tribute to avoid hostile raids by the Philistines. Parker adds that a covenant existed between Isaac and the Philistines (Gen. 26:28; cf. Gen. 21:32), and "it would be natural to suppose that some league existed between Samson's people and their rulers" ("Variorum"). Cf. Judges 2:2–3, where an angel of the Lord said to the children of Israel: "And ye shall make no league with the inhabitants of this land; . . . but ye have not obeyed my voice: why have ye done this? . . . they shall be as thorns in your sides, and their gods shall be a snare unto you."

    deliver'd bound: Judges 15:13: "And they bound him with two new cords, and brought him up from the rock." Cf. 261.

1186. *murder:* cf. 1180 (*Murtherer*). Judges 14:19: "and he went down to Ashkelon, and slew thirty men of them, and took their spoil, and gave change of garments unto them which expounded the riddle." Parker notes that Josephus has Samson encounter some Ascalonites on the road and despoil them (*Antiquities of the Jews* 5.8.6); Josephus says nothing about murder, or a trip to Ascalon ("Variorum"). Cf. 138.

1187. *Askalon:* on the spelling cf. 138 (*Ascalonite*); *PL* 1.465 (*Ascalon*); *Animad* (*Ascalon* four times [Patterson, *Works* 3:169]). Phillips has *Askalon* (*New World* s.v. *Derceto*). Parker ("Variorum") notes that the Authorized Version has *Ashkelon* (Judg. 14:19) but also *Askelon* (Judg. 1:18).

1188. *Robber:* see 1186n.

    robes: the Authorized Version's marginal reading for *spoil* is "apparel." See 1203n.

1190. *Went up:* Judg. 15:9.

armed: pronounce with two syllables, as in 1617; cf. 20, 347. Oras notes that there are only five instances in *SA* of the syllabized *ed* ending: see 1283, 1617, 1634, 1693, and cf. 1568. In *PR* there are only two (3.311; 4.191); in *PL* 7–12, seven; in *PL* 1–6, forty-seven; in *Mask,* seventeen. Because the *ed* ending occurs frequently in Milton's early verse, Oras considers these facts evidence of the late composition of *SA* (*Blank Verse* 12–19; "Milton's Blank Verse" 173–80).

  powers: cf. 251, 1110.

1191. *spoil:* "spoliation, plundering" (Wyatt and Collins), or, in view of "To others," perhaps "harm," "injury" (*OED* 2, 7c); see 1188, 1203n. Percival and Blakeney think *did* a case of zeugma and thus gloss this as "nor (took) spoil (from them)."

1192. Judges 14:2: "I have seen a woman in Timnath of the daughters of the Philistines: now therefore get her for me to wife."

1193. *which argu'd me no foe:* Samuels calls Samson's opening reply "a repulsive bit of hypocrisy... a cynical quibble" (500); Prince less critically terms it a "somewhat disingenuous argument" (*Samson Agonistes*); cf. 223–25, 884. Stein attempts to defend Samson's apparent dishonesty: "His intention, we know, was to provoke, but he stands on the timing, and not without some justification. He may have known that the rascals would respond with the first hostile move, but they did not *have* to give him the 'occasion' he wanted. It is a small point, and legalistic, but it anticipates the larger disregard of justice by the persuaders of Dalila" (*Heroic Knowledge* 182). Parker also offers a defense: Samson argues with his opponent because he feels powerless to act immediately and wishes to satisfy his sense of personal integrity ("Variorum").

  argu'd: see 514.

1194. *City:* Milton spelled the word *Citty* in manuscript (Parker, "Variorum").
  Nuptial Feast: Judges 14:10.

1195–1204. Judges 14:11–15; Josephus, *Antiquities of the Jews* 5.8.6. Masson comments, "Milton follows Jewish tradition in supposing the thirty bridal friends there mentioned to have been spies appointed by the Philistines" (*Poetical*

Works). But Carey finds fault with Samson's argument: Harapha's "accusations of murder and robbery are just," and "all Samson's reply amounts to is that it seemed reasonable to him to kill thirty innocent men because thirty quite different men had outwitted him" (*John Milton* 144).

Politician: editors gloss as "crafty, intriguing" (cf. *OED* 1 and 5); they note the word had a pejorative implication. Cf. *politic* used contemptuously in *PR* 3.400 (Verity).

Lords: commentators observe that this is Milton's addition to the story; Judges 14:11 has, vaguely, *they,* and Josephus mentions the *Thamnites,* i.e., the people of Timnath (*Antiquities of the Jews* 5.8.6).

pretense: Josephus says "ostensibly as companions" (*Antiquities of the Jews* 5.8.6); Judges 14:11 speaks simply of "thirty companions." On the phrase cf. *Mask* 160.

Bridal: "wedding" or, possibly, "of the bride," as Samson evidently brought no friends to the wedding (see Verity; Wyatt and Collins). Todd notes that the word is also Saxon for "the nuptial feast" so that the phrase here might mean "friends and guests invited to the bridal."

1197. *await:* "watch stealthily with hostile purpose" (so *OED* 1), and also "attend" (*OED* 5); evidently a pun (Parker, "Variorum").

spies: Judges does not refer to the thirty as "spies"; they are instead called "companions" (14:11) and "men of the city" (14:18). Editors suggest that Milton took this idea from Josephus. See 386n, 1195–1204n s.v. *pretense.*

1198. *threatning cruel death:* Judges 14:15: "lest we burn thee and thy father's house with fire." Le Comte (174) compares *PR* 4.388.

1199. *my secret:* Judges 14:6–9. Percival points out that Samson kept secret, even from his own father and mother, the fact that by touching the dead lion he had violated one of his vows as a Nazarite. See also 31n, 318n, 520n, 634n.

1200. *riddle...propos'd:* cf. *PR* 4.572–73.

1201–2. *set on:* "intent on"; so also 1462, 1679.

chanc'd: "an opportunity offered" (Lockwood), or "come (upon) by chance" (*OED* 2). See 1186n.

1203. *took thir spoil:* cf. 1191. Judges 14:19: "and slew thirty men of them, and took their spoil." Verity notes that the Septuagint reads τὰ ἱμάτια αὐτῶν, and the Vulgate has *ablatas vestes dedit.*

1204. *pay…in thir coin:* Tilley cites "To pay one in his *own* coin" as a proverbial phrase and dates it from the late sixteenth century: "to give…tit for tat," "to treat [one] as he has treated you" (C507; and *OED* s.v. *coin* II.7b). But Percival, Wyatt and Collins, and Grieve observe that Samson does *not* repay undermining with undermining, but rather pays the Philistines with spoil taken from Philistines. Cf. Judges 15:11: "As they did unto me, so have I done unto them."
   my underminers: editors gloss as "secret plotters against me" (*OED* 2). Parker ("Variorum") finds a suggestion here of mining for gold or silver ("coin"); Verity detects "the metaphor of sapping the walls of a fortress."

1205. Editors note that here (and 1208–10) Samson ironically repeats Harapha's charges (1182) and answers them. Knight writes, "the contrast of 'nation' with 'lords' suggests an opposition bearing directly on Milton's political experience. Thus Samson appears as the revolutionary cause" (*Chariot* 87).

1206–13. Samuels argues that this passage "is confused" because Samson first validates rebellion according to "the law of nations," then "claims the more particular right of private rebellion," and finally "returns to the argument that he was not a private person" (500–1). But editors propose that the intervening gesture (1208–10) is an argument put rhetorically by Samson into Harapha's mouth and inferred from 1184, 1189–91; see 782n, 1205n. Visiak infers, "force may justly be employed against military aggressors" ("Notes" 186).

1207. *well:* "justly, properly" (Blakeney; et al.).
   Conquer'd can: see 168–271 and *PL* 11.797–804.

1209. *league-breaker:* cf. 1184; Le Comte discusses such repetitions (44).

1211–19. *command from Heav'n:* Blakeney writes, "Samson often returns to this," and he cites 30, 273. Bullough and Bullough note that "most commentators from Theodoret to Calvin and Paræus" emphasize God's guidance of Samson but Milton "makes more of" Samson's patriotism (216). Lewalski observes that, according to Protestant exegesis, the Israelite judges had two functions, deliverance of God's people and execution of divine vengeance. In this speech, she argues, "Samson justifies his whole course of action against the Philistines in terms of his vocation as Judge and deliverer of his people" ("*Samson Agonistes*" 1058). But see 1216n.

1211. Prince paraphrases, "but, you say, I, though only a private person, &c." (*Samson Agonistes*).
  private: "person . . . who does not hold any public office or position" (so *OED* B.1); see 1208.
  rais'd: "[brought] into existence" (*OED* 9). Percival interprets the word as a case of zeugma, i.e., necessarily having two meanings: "endowed with strength sufficient" and "(sent forth) with command."

1213–14. *servile minds:* thus Samson had earlier described himself (412).
  their: the second edition (1680) has *thir;* see 190n s.v. *their.*

1215. *for nought:* "without good cause" (*OED* 5d) or "without payment" (so *OED* 5c).

1216. Parker addresses an inconsistency between Judges and Milton's poem: "Echoing as it does the phrase 'to this day' in the Chorus's account of Samson's victory at Ramath-lechi (145), as well as their later '*Israel* still serves' (240), this line makes it clear that Milton either did not believe Samson to have 'judged Israel twenty years' (Judg. 15.20, 16.31) or he chose to ignore the fact—as he did some others—as quite incompatible with his conception of Samson as a champion who *never* enjoyed the support of his people. The 'judges' were all temporary administrators or leaders in war. Milton's Samson was neither" ("Variorum"). Cf. *PL* 12.320 and 1211–19n.

1218. *my known:* Martin W. Sampson would emend to *mine own,* as giving a more pointed antithesis with "your force." Prince finds the conjecture tempting (*Samson Agonistes*), while Verity explains *known:* Dalila had informed the Philistines that Samson had revealed his secrets.
  offence: cf. 767, 1004.

1220. *shifts:* see 1116.

    appellant: "one who challenges another to single combat" (so *OED* B.1b). Verity explains, "strictly...one who *appealed* (i.e. charged) another man of treason or felony, and offered to prove the charge upon his body by single combat"; e.g., *2 Henry VI* 2.3.48–49: "This is the day appointed for the combat; / And ready are the appellant and defendant." Again some editors note an anachronistic allusion to a term in chivalry; see 1102n, 1221n, 1222n.

1221. *maim'd:* "disable[d], render[ed] powerless" (*OED*); Verity adds, "technically...through loss of limb." Cf. *PL* 1.459.

    high attempts: "great enterprises" (Parker, "Variorum"); so also *PR* 3.26 (Le Comte 66). Hughes notes that the phrase belongs to the language of romance and heraldry (*Complete Poems; John Milton*); Verity lists other instances and concludes, "It would seem that the phrase was traditional; perhaps it was taken from the Italian." Cf. 32, 525, 1492.

1222. *thrice:* Samson three times challenges Harapha, each time hoping he will accept; for the previous challenges, see 1151–55, 1174–77. Editors, following Newton, find an anachronistic allusion to the medieval ritual, familiar through coronation ceremonies, of challenging and sounding the trumpet three times in judicial combats. Newton also compares Shakespeare's *King Lear* 5.3.108–18; Parker ("Variorum") suggests that Milton may also be remembering the *Iliad*, where Achilles chases Hector three times around the walls of Troy (22.165). Percival remarks that "Samson has in reality challenged Harapha more than thrice"; but the earlier challenges (1091, 1104–5, 1116–29) were not to determine a religious *cause*.

1223. *enforce:* editors gloss as "difficulty, effort, exertion" (so *OED* [last entry dated 1671]); "not elsewhere in Milton and not in Shakespeare" (Verity).

1224. *Slave enrol'd:* see 653. Finding no mention in Scripture of such a class of slaves, Percival conjectures that Milton recalled the criminal slaves among the Romans (*servus poenas* in Justinian's *Institutiones* 1.12.3) who were condemned to labor in chains in prison workhouses (*ergastula*) and were called *inscripti* or *inscripta ergastula*.

1225. *Due...capital punishment:* Parker comments that the belated revelation of this fact would, if it is accepted (cf. 513), throw a different light on earlier statements (e.g., 32, 485, 575, 650) and on subsequent events ("Variorum"). See also 764–65n, 1470n.

    capital: "always dissyllabic in Milton by elision of *i*" (Verity). See 394.

1226. *man of arms:* "one practised in war, a fully-armed knight" (*OED* s.v. *arm* 3; cf. *man-at-arms:* "soldier, warrior"). Editors again find reference to the laws of single combat, and some, following Todd, quote from the second book of Vincentio Saviolo's *His Practice...of Honor and Honorable Quarrels* (1595) to show that the privilege of trial by combat was expressly denied to men guilty of treason, robbers, and "all other persons, not liuing as a Gentleman or a Souldier"; indeed, "whosoeuer should fight with them, should iniurie himselfe, making himselfe equall with dishonourable persons" (sig. cc3v–cc4r). See 1178–80n. Thaler ("Shakespearian Element" 168) suggests that Samson's challenge to Harapha "resembles in its dramatic point that which the baffled Antony sends to Octavius" in *Antony and Cleopatra* 4.1.4–6.

1227. *survey:* see 1089, 1230.

1228. *descant on:* editors gloss as "comment on" (*OED* 2); Parker ("Variorum") thinks more likely it means "carp at" (cf. *OED* 3); Meiklejohn and Blakeney scan with the accent on the first syllable. Hughes (*Complete Poems; John Milton*) compares the opening sentence of *Eikon:* "To descant on the misfortunes of a person fall'n from so high a dignity,...is neither of it self a thing commendable, nor the intention of this discours" (Patterson, *Works* 5:63).

    verdit: "finding, conclusion" (so *OED* 3); cf. 324.

1229–30. Verity paraphrases, "you say you come to survey me: do not let my *hand* (since my eyes may not) survey *you.*"

    slight: "slightly" (so *OED* B.3, the first example cited).

    survey: "examine" (*OED* 4), or here, Parker finds more probable, "take the measure of" ("Variorum"); cf. 1089, 1227.

1231. *Baal-zebub:* cf. 1 Samuel 17:43. Pronounce *Baal* as two syllables, with accent on the first as in Hebrew (Darbishire, *Poetical Works;* B. A. Wright). Editors note he was one of the "Baalim" (*PL* 1.422) and the Philistine god at Ekron (2 Kings 1:2–3, 6, 16); Verity and Blakeney suggest this was probably a local name of Baal, the supreme male deity (cf. 1242) of the Philistines, Canaanites, and Phoenicians. The name means "lord, or god, of the fly." Except for *DocCh* (Patterson, *Works* 17:56–57), this is Milton's only mention of him; unlike Diodati (sigs. P6v, A8v), he evidently distinguished between Baalzebub and Beelzebub (*PL* 1.81 etc.) or Beelzebul (*DocCh* [Patterson, *Works* 14:396–97]), who was later known in Palestine and whom Milton mentions at least nine times (Parker, "Variorum"). Phillips (*New World*) lists only *Belzebub* (so *DDD* [Patterson, *Works* 3:437]), as does Dodd (sig. H7v).

> *unus'd:* "unaccustomed" (*OED* 1).

1232. *dishonours:* "indignit[ies]" (*OED* 1), "insult[s]" (*OED* 1b); cf. 452.
> *render:* "give in return," "make return of" (so *OED* 2).

1234. *incurable:* Parker detects a learned pun on Harapha's name: *rapha,* meaning "medicine" ("Variorum"); see also 435n, 1235n.
> *van:* editors gloss as "vanguard, foremost division of an army" (*OED* 1). Parker notes three levels of meaning: (1) "begin the fight," (2) "you'll need help, you coward," and (3) "I am ready for an army of Haraphas, just as I fought whole armies before" ("Variorum"). Carey writes that "Samson is mockingly grandiloquent" (*Complete Shorter Poems;* see also Blakeney).

1235. *heels:* Parker comments, "there may also be punning here on Harapha's name" ("Variorum"); see also 1234n.
> *fist is free:* Summers cites this image, among others, to illustrate how the poem often suggests attitudes and physical gestures for readers to imagine, even though Milton claimed that he never intended the drama to be staged (153–75). Cf. 1–2, 115–16, 951–54. Huntley notes that Samson, having begun the drama lying down (118–21), must be standing to deliver this speech, thus signifying his "spiritual development" (142). Cox suggests that this speech "symbolically establishes the victory of the will over the senses which had once fettered it" ("Natural Science" 67).

1236. *insolence:* Blakeney scans as a disyllable.
> *other kind of answer:* see 1243 and cf. 1250–52.
> *fits:* "[is] proper for" (so *OED* II.3).

1237. *baffl'd:* "disgraced, dishonoured" (so *OED* 1) or "frustrated" (Shawcross, *Complete English Poetry*). In chivalry "baffling" was a punishment of a perjured knight, part of which might be hanging him up by his heels (Percival; MacCaffrey; et al.). Stein finds this episode "a comic inversion of Dalila's final proposal that she touch his [Samson's] hand. Samson threatens the warrior's loving touch" (*Heroic Knowledge* 182). Parker notes the contemptuous effect of the iterated "b" sound in Samson's speech ("Variorum").

    run: cf. 129.

1238. *bulk without spirit:* the construction: "lest I, though in these chains, run upon thee, vast bulk without spirit." Prince suggests " 'without spirit' is used adverbially, and is best spoken rapidly, as if hyphenated" (*Samson Agonistes*); Masson (*Poetical Works*) suggests that the first three words almost form a compound noun. Lawry (388) compares this description with Death's "vast unhide-bound Corpse" (*PL* 10.601).

    bulk: Parker thinks this could be an extension of the ship imagery ("Variorum"); e.g., see 1070, 1075.

    vast: "the epithet to *bulk*" (Verity). Cf. 54.

1239. *structure:* "a pile of building of some considerable size" (*OED* 5a); cf. 1069 (*pile*).

    low: as, later, he will "lay . . . low" the temple of Dagon (Parker, "Variorum").

1240. Percival recalls Hercules and Antaeus.

1241. *the:* B. A. Wright emends to *th' hazard.*

    shatter'd: Wyatt and Collins identify this as a proleptic construction: "to the hazard of thy sides (which would be) shattered (by the fall)"; for other examples, see 439, 1430. Cf. *PL* 1.232. Fogle argues that the "relish" Samson shows here at the prospect of hurting Harapha physically "does not seem the mark of the tempered, triumphant, and inspired champion of God" (185).

1242. *Astaroth:* probably the idol, rather than the place, a town in Transjordan. Evidently treated here, as in *Nat* 200 and *PR* 3.417 (*Ashtaroth*), as a singular; but in *PL* 1.422, 438, Milton explains that *Ashtaroth* is a plural form and *Astoreth* a singular (Parker, "Variorum"). G. Ernest Wright traces the possible plural form to "one of the dangers of polytheism," namely the construction of "rival temples, making rival claims, [which] tended to split up a god's or goddess's personality.... The plural must have come into being to designate the totality of the god's appearances, attributes and personalities; it was a way of emphasizing the one in the many" (110). See also 1080n s.vv. *Anak and the Emims.* For references to Ashtaroth and Baalim, see Judges 2:13, 10:6; 1 Samuel 7:4, 12:10; to Ashtoreth, see 1 Kings 11:5. Percival thinks that Milton is specifically remembering 1 Samuel 31:10 — "And they put his [Saul's] armour in the house of Ashtaroth" — which suggests that she was looked upon as a goddess of war and, Verity notes, explains why the warrior Harapha swears by her. Cf. also 1 Samuel 17:43. Editors comment that Ashtoreth, the mother goddess and embodiment of the generative principle, was the consort and counterpart of Baal (see 1231). Paton notes that she was evidently the Astarte of the Greeks (so *PL* 1.439), the Ishtar of the Assyrians and Babylonians, the Ashtart of the Phoenicians, and so on; he adds, "The fact that her name makes all the proper phonetic changes in passing from one dialect to another proves that it is primitive Semitic and that she is the most ancient of the greater Semitic divinities" (27).

1243. *These braveries:* "bravado," "boasting" (so *OED* 1). Dunster (in Todd), echoed by later editors, says that this threat "connects Harapha with the business of the drama, by making his revenge . . . the cause, why [Samson] is to be brought before the publick assembly"; Cumberland similarly argues that the Chorus's prediction (1250–52) demonstrates that the scene with Harapha "leads to the catastrophe" (336). But Johnson (*Rambler* 16 July 1751) thinks that Samson's subsequent remarks (1253–56) determine "that no consequence good or bad will proceed from their interview" (219). Hyman similarly interprets Harapha's exit and refusal to fight: "God is refusing to satisfy Samson's plea for the 'invincible might' with which to overcome the heathen" and prove by combat God's divinity ("Unwilling Martyrdom" 93).

   loaden: Darbishire emends to *load'n* (*Poetical Works*).

1244–52. Parker notes the balancing of these three three-line speeches (*Milton's Debt* 63).

   His Giantship: Percival calls this "a mock title of honor on the analogy of 'his lordship'"; the first instance of this word in *OED*. Verity notes, "[Abraham] Cowley coins words with the suffix *-ship* very freely; they are always depreciatory." See also 1075n.

somewhat: cf. *PL* 6.616.

crest-fall'n: Prince comments, "The expression implies that too great a confidence has gone before" (*Samson Agonistes*).

1245. *unconsci'nable:* "unreasonably excessive" (so *OED* 2b); Verity notes that literally, "an *unconscionable* thing was one which went beyond your *conscience,* i.e. which your thoughts could not grasp." Lockwood, Collins, Percival, Wyatt and Collins, et al. define as "enormous, vast"; Hughes, "absurdly insolent" (*Complete Poems; John Milton*). Prince writes that the elision of this word allows the line to be read as pentameter (*Samson Agonistes* 135).

1246. *sultrie chafe:* i.e., "hot rage" (so *OED* s.v. *sultry* 2a). Cf. 1138.

1247. *Giantbrood:* cf. *PL* 1.576 (also 1.511).

1248. *Fame:* "report, common talk" (*OED* 1); cf. 971.

    divulge: editors gloss as "publish," "make commonly known" (*OED* 1). The first edition has *divulg'd,* corrected in the *Errata* to *divulge.*

    five Sons: according to 2 Samuel 21:16–22, four of these were Ishbi-benob, Saph (or Sippai), the brother of Goliath (Lahmi), and an unnamed "man of great stature, that had on every hand six fingers, and on every foot six toes." Church notes that the words *the brother of* are inserted by translators. Wyatt and Collins explain, "Lahmi is distinctly stated to have been 'the brother of Goliath the Gittite,' and as 'these four were born to the giant in Gath (2 Sam. 21.22)' it is evident that all five were brothers." Regarding the roughly one hundred years, according to biblical chronology, that elapsed between the death of Samson and the slaughter of the sons as related in 2 Samuel 21, Masson writes, "it is only on the supposition that the giants were unusually long-lived that Milton's accuracy in making the five sons of Harapha, who were all slain in David's time, full-grown in Samson's time, can be defended" (*Poetical Works*).

1249. *Goliah:* so Phillips (*New World*); spelled *Goliath* in the Authorized Version. This is Milton's only direct reference to him (Parker, "Variorum"); see 1119–23n, 1175n.

1250–52. Mickle writes that Samson's "prophetic hope…strongly marks the progress of what is passing in his mind" (403). See 1243n.

He will: editors gloss as "he will (go)." Percival calls attention to the gradual foreshadowing of the catastrophe in 1252, 1265–67, 1300, 1346–47, 1379, 1387–89, 1426; see also Grieve; Wyatt and Collins.

1253. *allege...cause:* cf. *PL* 4.921–922.

    offer'd fight: editors gloss as "(my) offer of fight"; cf. 344. Stein remarks that now "a new quality appears in Samson. The gap between him and the Chorus begins to demonstrate itself as a superiority in practical grasp.... Samson has emerged into the world of practical action after the long descent into the darkness of self" (*Heroic Knowledge* 182). Scott-Craig similarly claims, "the exploration and martyrdom of the 'Agony' are over" ("Concerning" 49); and Parker writes that Samson gives his friends "cool, logical reasons which had not occurred to them" (*Milton's Debt* 47). Rudrum recalls here "the enhanced practical ability which students of mysticism see as the mystic's reward for surviving the 'dark night of the soul'" (57). To Buchanan, 1253–55 are Milton's "clearest confession" that he is using the dueling code throughout the Harapha episode (293).

1259. *intend advantage of:* "mean (to reap) advantage (from)" (Blakeney).

1260. Blakeney paraphrases: "work which would naturally require many men to get through."

    keeping: "maintenance" (so *OED* 5, where the earliest example is dated 1644). Cf. 573, 1365–67.

1261. *owners:* Parker notes that although Samson speaks of himself as a slave, he takes pride in his work ("Variorum"); see 573n, 1366n.

1262–67. Harris writes, "[Samson's] attitude toward death has undergone change. No longer invoking it, praying for it, he patiently awaits it" (118). So other commentators interpret the passage, but Tung argues that Samson remains impatient until the drama's climactic reversal and this "death wish...represents a stoic resignation to fate rather than patient submission to God's will" (485). Wilkes also suggests that this passage proves Samson not really a victor over his despair, hence not a regenerated soul. Wilkes would make the essential theme of the tragedy, not regeneration, but "how the fallen Samson is to serve God's 'uncontroulable intent'" (366, 370–71). Cf. 1381–89n.

But come what will: the first edition has a comma after this phrase ("in any case"); Masson (*Poetical Works*) and Percival replace this with a semicolon. Verity writes that such a change is unnecessary: " 'come what will' is a subordinate, adverbial phrase meaning 'under any circumstances.'"

1263. Editors paraphrase: "if he rids (delivers) me hence by death." Parker notes that the thought of death ending mortal woe is a commonplace ("Variorum").

1264. *me:* Darbishire emends to *mee* as a "clear use of the emphatic form" (*Poetical Works*); B. A. Wright does not make this change; cf. 1125; see 219–20n s.v. *Mee*. Some editors omit the comma after *give* so as to create the sense, "the worst that he can give *is* to me the best." Verity again prefers the original punctuation and suggests that this verse is in apposition to the previous line: thus, "my foe will rid me hence, the worst (i.e. thing) that he can give, the best that I can receive."

1265–67. Verity describes this passage as tragic irony, for at this stage Samson could not have realized the full significance of his words. But Hanford feels that Samson "is given an intimation of what actually will happen. A forward movement of the inner action of the drama is markedly felt at this point. Samson is clear-headed and calm" (*Poems*). Ellis-Fermor similarly writes, "From the exit of Harapha the mind of Samson enters upon a phase in which it is resolute, clear, and steady. The process of rehabilitation is complete and energy of spirit and power of continuous thought return. From now onward Samson's speech...is illuminated with prophetic flashes of exultation" (29). Parker adds that Samson "threatens vengeance because he has just been cheated of action; it is a new note in his character, and gives us the key to how he will act at the feast" (*Milton's Debt* 47). Cf. 1347, 1381–83.

1266. Editors paraphrase: "it (the attempt) may with my (ruin)."

1267. *Draw:* cf. 736.
    thir: "In this position, where the pronoun is antecedent to the relative, Milton spells *their*" (Darbishire, *Poetical Works*); B. A. Wright does not adopt this change; cf. *PR* 3.55; see 190n s.v. *their*.
    ruin: Verity suggests that this word (along with *Draw*) accentuates the tragic irony; see 1515–20n.

1268–99. Editors identify this as the fourth stasimon (see 293–325n); Epps (193) numbers it the fifth chorus and divides the lines as follows: strophe (1268–86), antistrophe (1287–96), and epode (1297–1307); see also 1292n. Parker notes "a certain symmetry: the first stanza is of nineteen lines [1268–86]; the second, of ten—or almost half (1287–96)" (*Milton's Debt* 63–64). Gilbert finds it "almost a repetition of the first ode...rather than directly applicable to what precedes" ("Is *Samson Agonistes*" 101). Stroup describes it as "a canticle of praise,...full of Scriptural echoes such as that from Isaiah 57, Ephesians 6, and Revelation 14" (61).

Commentators disagree about the relative significance of active and passive heroism in this episode. Nash argues that "if the choric speech...is really presenting two alternatives," then Samson's final act "is in the spirit of the first alternative, befitting the strenuously active, quasi-military career of Israel's champion and deliverer, but not attaining to the saintly patience whose exercise makes each his own deliverer" (35). Both Tillyard (*Milton* 278, 282; *Miltonic Setting* 85–88) and Stein (*Heroic Knowledge* 178–91, 198) agree that Milton is ultimately endorsing active heroism in *SA*. Tillyard says that this passage "not only sums up the main thought of the play, but...gives in brief the thought that was most characteristic of Milton's whole mind," namely, "the reconcilement of action with the inner paradise" (*Milton* 296). Eleanor Gertrude Brown (100) also thinks these lines of the Chorus are "more suggestive of Milton than those of Samson" (see also 166–69, 293–99); and Saurat, noting the implications of the Samson story for Milton's philosophy, observes that "it is not enough for man to attain wisdom for himself; he must help the course of the world, become the instrument of God's will, and act greatly" (202).

Other commentators, however, believe that Milton in *SA* favors heroic martyrdom. E.g., Harris argues that, although the Danites in the first part of this passage clearly endorse "the heroic aggressiveness of magnanimity," Milton in *SA* and his other works espoused "the martyring endurance of patience" as the higher manifestation of fortitude (118). Emphasizing differences between the views of Milton and the Chorus, Huntley here paraphrases the "bitter meaning" of the Chorus's words: "in a fickle world, run by a lawless, unreasonable God, whom it pleases to break promises, to betray chosen heroes, and to endow enemy women with irresistible attractions—in such a world as this, unless he can muster despotic power, passivity is man's highest virtue" (141). See also see 652–66n, 1287–88n.

Still other commentators suggest that Milton brings together both active and passive heroism through Samson's final act. E.g., Low comments: "[Samson] conquers in defeat, suffers and inflicts, slays and is slain, is reborn and dies. Thus he combines Christian and non-Christian, or two kinds of Christian, heroism.... The pulling down of the temple is a return to action that explicitly surpasses the active deeds of his youth, made possible only by the return of his strength; and it is also the culmination (not merely the product) of his inner development and regeneration, made possible by his new self-knowledge and humility, his victory over despair, and his confirmation in Christian patience" ("Action" 518). Summers similarly suggests that the Chorus is mistaken and these categories of heroism are not mutually exclusive: "a major point of Milton's Christian tragedy (and of his thought elsewhere) is that the active hero is only truly heroic if he has first triumphed over 'all / That tyranny or fortune can inflict' [1290–91]. Every hero is a hero of patience. The question whether patiently crowned heroism shall proceed to active public deliverance depends upon the will of God" (169). Mahood also writes that the Chorus "celebrate[s] both active and passive heroism as if both were now within Samson's reach. The champion is now ready for the promptings of those 'rouzing motions' which impel him to a final act that embraces and transcends the two kinds of heroism" (238). Lewalski sees in the Chorus's generalizations a foreshadowing of the apocalyptic victory: "they describe the mighty deliverers raised up by God as bearers of the Divine might, quelling God's enemies in an instant in spite of all material weapons—though rather by abashing and amazing the wicked than by overpowering them physically" ("*Samson Agonistes*" 1059). Adams also discusses the relationship between these two types of heroism: he contrasts these "strikingly Stoic" two lines with the "notably Christian" tenor of the first part of the Chorus's speech (cf. 1268–71). Adams argues that the conflict "is nicely resolved in Samson's final action, which irresistibly combines action and passion; the confusion as to which prevails may be taken as evidence that the two elements are pretty well balanced; and one may usefully think of the style itself as combining in dramatic fashion energy and lassitude, exhausted patience and invincible might" (196–97). Visiak more critically remarks that Milton here confuses superhuman physical force with spiritual power; he nevertheless infers "that natural, or material, force may in excess become supernatural, or spiritual...and that a man thus supernormally empowered is a direct instrument of God" ("Notes" 186). See also 1292n, 1295–96.

Other commentators emphasize this episode's political implications. Warton suggests that Milton was "writing a panegyric to the memory of Cromwell and his deliverance" (sig. Yy2r [1785 ed.; omitted in 1791 ed.]). Percival explains that the "deliverer" (1270) would thus become "Cromwell overthrowing the monarchy" and he finds it "strange that the unmeasured terms in which Milton, here and elsewhere, speaks of the monarchy, both before and after the Commonwealth, did not raise the scruples in the mind of the Licenser, which a much less pronounced passage in *PL* [1.599] is said to have done." Parker responds that some of the lines in this passage discourage a topical reading: e.g., he argues, "the feats of the *unarmed* Samson against armed men, celebrated once more in 1279–81 (cf. 130–34), make a highly dubious allusion to the military prowess of Cromwell" ("Variorum"). Writing in 1942, Knight instead turned to his own contemporary circumstances: "the lines may most perfectly serve to blend the Messianic victory of *Paradise Lost*…with the cause of Great Britain in the World War" (*Chariot* 100, 167–68).

1268–71. Sprott (132), Bridges (*Milton's Prosody* 56), and Weismiller (121) all read the first two feet in these lines as trochaic (see 81n). Of the meter, Raleigh exclaims, "To try to explain this marvel of beauty is to beat the air" (*Milton* 196); Broadbent also compliments this passage: "more subtly incantatory than anything before 'Tiger, tiger, burning bright[,]'…this unheard-of, unprecedented verse clashes against the ancient authority of the form; their clash echoes the collision of the terrible Old Testament myth with Christian doctrine" (*Milton* 37). Arguing that the poem is not more Stoic than Christian, as some critics claim, Adams cites these lines as an example of the "flashes of grim and terrible exultation which are highlights of its poetic expression" (196). Cf. 1287–88n.

O: Keightley compares this interjection with the φεῦ ("alas") of Greek drama, "which did not count in the iambic line" (*Account* 326). See 606.

comely: "becoming," "pleasing or agreeable to the moral sense, to notions of propriety, or aesthetic taste" (*OED* 3), or "pleasing, agreeable" (so *OED* 2; Lockwood).

just men long opprest: "presumably the Chorus refers thus indirectly to itself and to its emotions upon witnessing the rout of the Philistine giant" (Parker, "Variorum"). Le Comte (67) notes that the phrases "just man" and "just men" occur in *Mask* 767; *PL* 7.570, 11.577, 681, 818, 890; *PR* 3.62. The first edition punctuates this line with an exclamation point after *opprest;* Tickell emends to a semicolon; other early editors emend to a comma.

1270. *thir deliverer:* in view of 40, 225, 246, 274, 279, 292, and especially 1214, the Chorus presumably refers to Samson; but see 1268–99n. Verity, Grieve, et al. detect a possible allusion to Cromwell. In Milton's prose works, he uses *deliverers* both for Parliament (*Apol* [Patterson, *Works* 3:337–38]; *DDD* [Patterson, *Works* 3:371]; *Tetr* [Patterson, *Works* 4:72]) and for the leaders—including Cromwell—who delivered England from tyranny (e.g., *Def 2* [Patterson, *Works* 8:4, 8, 248, 250]; *Defpro Se* [Patterson, *Works* 9:2–3]). Cf. *HistBr* (Patterson, *Works* 10:323).

1271. Sprott (132) suggests the first two feet are inverted (trochaic; see 81n). Cf. *Ref:* "joyn your invincible might to doe worthy, and Godlike deeds" (Patterson, *Works* 3:61).

1272–76. *quell...Earth...brute...violent...Tyrannic power...Truth:* cf. *PR* 1.218–20 (Le Comte 66).

1272. *the mighty of the Earth:* cf. Genesis 6:4: "There were giants in the earth in those days; and also after that, when the sons of God came in unto the daughters of men, and they bare children to them, the same became mighty men which were of old, men of renown." Parker comments that the choral reference seems to be to these giants of Genesis and to Harapha, who are false types of the "hero" ("Variorum"). Steadman argues that conventional interpretations of Genesis 6:4—including Calvin's—probably influenced Milton's distinction between military prowess and true heroism ("'Men of Renown'" 580–86). Cf. *PL* 11.638–99; Le Comte (174) compares *Mask* 612.

1273. *violent men:* cf. *Ps 86* 50. See also 1268–99n.

1274–75. Weismiller writes that 1274 could be read as an acephalous pentameter or as a tetrameter, depending on whether *Hardy* and *and* should be elided (124).

   Hardy: "vigorous" (*OED* 4), or "strong, enduring" (Lockwood); cf. *PL* 4.920.

   industrious: "zealous" (*OED* 2; cf. *PL* 2.116).

   raging to pursue: i.e., "vehemently passionate" (so *OED* 7), "to persecute" (Parker, "Variorum"); Blakeney calls this an "explanatory infinitive"; see also

830n. Darbishire (*Poetical Works*) and B. A. Wright emend to *peruse* in keeping with the first edition's spelling of this word in 1544; see 1544n.

1277. *He:* the deliverer (1270). Darbishire (*Poetical Works*) and B. A. Wright emend to *Hee;* see 219–20 s.v. *Mee.*

    Ammunition: "military stores or supplies" (so *OED* 1), or, more generally, "warlike preparations" (Percival; Wyatt and Collins), or "in the widest sense of preparations" (Grieve). Parker suggests the rhyme with *expedition* (1283) might be intentional ("Variorum"). Cf. other possible rhymes in 1288, 1293, 1298, 1300, 1343, 1432, 1439, 1639.

1278. *feats of war:* "military duties or exercises" (*OED* 5), or "deeds" (Grieve).

    defeats: Parker paraphrases: "he undoes what has been done" ("Variorum"). Todd thinks the *"feats"/"defeats"* play on words is an "unpleasing jingle"; Baum also calls it "cheap" (370); Percival suggests that Milton imitates Hebrew usage (149); see 1118n. Hughes thinks these lines recommend comparison with Milton's sonnets to Cromwell, Fairfax, and Vane (*Complete Poems; John Milton*); Verity finds in these lines an echo of Joshua Sylvester's *Divine Weekes and Workes of Du Bartas* (Alexander B. Grosart's ed., 1:205).

1279. *plain:* "unassisted, unaided" (Lockwood). Percival remarks that "this epithet is fitly applied to Cromwell"; see 1268–99n.

    magnitude of mind: cf. *PL* 8.557 and *PR* 2.139. Parker comments that "it is with this, presumably, that Samson conquered Harapha" ("Variorum").

1280. Sprott (132) suggests that the first two feet are inverted (trochaic; see 81n, 116n) but thinks it difficult to determine whether Milton thought of the line as "trochaic with the last foot catalectic, or as iambic with the first foot catalectic." Bridges counts it as one of 17 lines of falling rhythm (*Milton's Prosody* 55).

1281. *Armories:* "place[s] where arms are kept" (so *OED* 3).

    Magazins: "munitions of war," "military equipment" (so *OED* 3a); Blakeney observes, "This word has come to us from Arabia by way of the Spanish peninsula."

1283. Sadler detects in this part of Harapha's speech "terms anticipating the eagle and dragon images of the phoenix crux" (208); see 1692–1707.

winged: pronounce with two syllables (Parker, "Notes" 691; Oras, *Blank Verse* 15 and "Milton's Blank Verse" 176). See 1190n.

expedition: "speed" (so *OED* 5). Cf. Shakespeare's *Richard III* 4.3.54: "Then fiery expedition by my wing" (Todd). See also 1277n s.v. *Ammunition.*

1284. Meiklejohn compares Shakespeare's *Richard II* 1.3.79: "Be swift like lightning in the execution" (cf. 960–61n, 1472n).

1285. *errand:* "purpose" (*OED* 3). Hughes suggests a commission of vengeance (*John Milton*).

1286. *defence:* "capacity of defending [themselves]" (*OED* II.3b [last entry dated 1654]), or "resistance against attack" (*OED* II.3a). Cf. 560.

distracted: "confused" (cf. 1556) and/or "driven hither and thither" (*OED* 2) and/or "crazed" (*OED* 5).

amaz'd: editors gloss as "stunned, confounded, or terror-stricken"; Verity, Grieve, et al. observe, "a much stronger word then than now." Cf. 1645 and *PL* 1.281, *PR* 4.562.

1287–88. To Nash, "The announcement of this possibility is perhaps the furthest point Milton could attain in transforming the old legend into something nearer his conception of the better fortitude of patience and heroic martyrdom" (33; see also 35). Harris also believes that "Victory through patience was to Milton the nobler triumph" (119). For the relative significance of active and passive heroism, see 1268–99n.

patience...fortitude: Hughes notes the echo of 654, where Milton was evidently "thinking of Stoic virtue rather than of Christian patience" (*John Milton*). Radzinowicz argues that "by patience is meant something well beyond passive endurance. Extolled as 'the truest fortitude,' patience is the courageous obedience to the will of God which comes from some sort of prophetic understanding or faith" ("*Samson Agonistes*" 468). Edmund K. Chambers detects irony in the Chorus's preaching patience to Samson just at the moment when he is no longer called upon to exercise patience (but see 1623). Lewalski finds here an allusion to "the embattled suffering saints" in Revelation 13:10 ("*Samson Agonistes*" 1056); Percival quotes Euripides, *Phoenician Women* 393: τὰς τῶν κρατούντων ἀμαθίας φέρειν χρεών; "We should submit in patience to the dispensations of the gods." For Milton's definition of patience, see *DocCh* (Patterson, *Works* 17:66–67, 252–53), and see Baumgartner 205, 207. Cf. *PL* 9.31–32: "the better fortitude / Of Patience and Heroic Martyrdom"; also 12.569–70: "suffering for Truths sake / Is fortitude to highest victorie." Verity also finds a related sentiment in the sonnet "To Mr. Cyriack Skinner."

exercise: "practice for the sake of training or improvement, either bodily, mental, or spiritual" (*OED* 6); or, perhaps, "painful mental struggle" (*OED* 6c); Grieve glosses as "discipline."

1288. *Saints*: Parker glosses as "true believers, holy persons" ("Variorum"). Cf. *PR* 4.348–49. Dunster (in Todd); Percival; Verity; et al. comment here that the republican Independents called themselves "saints." But, Verity adds, "it is a favourite word with M[ilton] in the general sense 'holy men.'" In *DocCh*, Milton accepts that all true believers are called saints, though their holiness is imperfect in this life (Patterson, *Works* 16:14–15); he also writes in *DocCh* that Old Testament personages who believed in the true God were saints (Patterson, *Works* 15:150–51; 17:308–9). Parker ("Variorum") adds that Milton believed in living saints (*DocCh* [Patterson, *Works* 17:146–47]); that several times in his prose works he referred to his contemporaries as such (e.g., *Ref* [Patterson, *Works* 3:18–19, 148]); that several times he referred mockingly to the "saints" of the turncoat Presbyterians (*Eikon* [Patterson, *Works* 5:6, 24]; *Def 2* [Patterson, *Works* 8:164]); and that once, when Salmasius had sneered at "Saint Independency," Milton accused him of creating saints at pleasure, like a pope (*Def 1* [Patterson, *Works* 7:420–21]). Madsen accepts "saints" and "patience" (1287, 1296) as "vaguely Christian" but emphasizes that these connotations "should not blind us to the essentially Stoic quality of the idea of victory over 'fortune,' 'lot,' and 'chance'" (188).

1289. *Deliverer*: see 1270n. Nash observes, "He becomes, indeed, his own deliverer, but not in the manner implied in the Chorus's speech" (34). Broadbent comments that this line "ignores the Christian doctrine that no man is saved (Biblical deliverer = saviour) but by grace. Milton is asserting what had long been for him temperamental axioms: that 'they also serve who only stand and wait'; that public defeat need not obviate private victory; indeed private must precede public victory" (*Milton* 54).

1291. Parker comments, "Samson's 'fortune' has subjected him to Philistine 'tyrannie'" ("Variorum"). (The spelling "tryrannie" is a typographical error in Patterson, *Works.*)

1292. Blakeney marks this line as the beginning of the fourth stasimon, 1292–1309; cf. 1268–99n.

    Either of these: Verity paraphrases, "i.e. Samson may be either the warrior or the patient saint, though probably the latter." Parker ("Variorum") finds tragic irony in the Chorus's phrasing of this, which leaves open the possibility of Samson's using his strength once more to bring swift destruction "on" the wicked (1284–85). Robertson describes instead the dramatic irony: "Samson is not to be *either* the invincible warrior *or* the martyred saint, but both, at once" (329). Daniells similarly observes, "Samson was enabled to follow the archetype of the Son of Man (though not in time) and to fulfil both destinies" (217).

    lot: see 1743.

1294. *sight bereav'd:* editors gloss as "loss of sight." Cf. 85.

1295–96. Some commentators think the Chorus wrong here (Bush, "John Milton" 517) and "still blind to what is to come" (Hanford, "*Samson Agonistes*" 176). Others argue that the Chorus's prediction is right (Krouse 15–16, 98). Harris thinks the Chorus "wrong in its understanding of patience" but "ironically right" because the winning of patience is for Samson a "victory over despair" and the necessary prelude to his final action (119–20). Cf. *Mask* 9. Tung, emphasizing the "all-important" use of *but* at the beginning of this passage, argues that the Chorus is not offering a real alternative for Samson (1287–94): "without sight Samson will have to be among those 'whom Patience finally *must* crown'" (488). See also 1268–99n.

    crown: "endow with honour, dignity" and/or "complete worthily" (*OED* 11, 9); "the crown of victory and everlasting life" (Verity); cf. 1579. Verity compares Revelation 2:10: "be thou faithful unto death, and I will give thee a crown of life." Percival quotes (as does Augustine in the opening of *De agone Christiano*) 2 Timothy 4:7–8: "I have fought a good fight, I have finished my course, I have kept the faith: Henceforth there is laid up for me a crown of righteousness." In *DocCh*, Milton writes that this "crown of righteousness" will not be conferred on the saints until "the appearance of Christ in glory" (Patterson, *Works* 15:224–27).

1297. A twelve-syllable line (alexandrine) without any break, or, possibly, four-four-four (Bridges, *Milton's Prosody* 61; see 118n).

   bin: see 874n.

   day of rest: "Sabbath, Lord's day," i.e., as contrasted with "Idols day" (Percival).

1298. Parker suggests, "the new stanza more properly (and probably) begins with 1300, and the period in 1300 and the comma in 1299 should be reversed. As it stands, 1297 is the only example (out of seventeen) of a stanza in a *stasimon* ending in a comma" ("Variorum"). Weismiller writes that 1298 could be either a dimeter or an acephalous trimeter (124–25).

   Labouring: editors note that this word is used intransitively, i.e., "causing thy mind to labour" (e.g., Prince, *Samson Agonistes*). Blakeney defines as "exercising"; it also means "caus[ing] to undergo fatigue" (*OED* 9b); or, possibly, "use ... in some work" (so *OED* 9).

1300–1426. The fifth and last epeisodion (see 176–292n). Parker comments, "this is Samson's final test or temptation: he is challenged to withstand not a giant but a whole nation" ("Variorum"). A. B. Chambers interprets it as a test of both his wisdom and his fortitude (320); see 1372–75n.

   behind: "yet to come" (Prince, *Samson Agonistes*).

1301. *descry:* "espy," "catch sight of, *esp.* from a distance" (*OED* III.6).

1302–6. To Percival, "the frequent ellipses ... give a hurried movement to the words, well depicting the idea of the hurrying messenger."

1303. *quaint:* Verity et al. gloss as "fanciful, curious" (*OED* 7)—he adds, "implying perhaps that the staff was ornamented." Hughes thinks that the reference here is to an ornamental rod symbolizing authority as carried by Greek messengers

(*Complete Poems; John Milton*). Blakeney instead suggests the word's literal sense, "known" (Latin *cognitus*), i.e., "the staff known to be used on such occasions." Wyatt and Collins also suggest "skillfully worked," "neat" (so *OED* 4); they add, "The meaning 'neat' or 'pretty' was influenced by a false derivation of *coint* from the Lat. *comptus*. The modern meaning 'odd' was beginning to come in by Milton's time, and may be glanced at here." Cf. *Nativity* 194; *Arc* 47; *Mask* 157; *PL* 9.35.

1304–5. *amain:* "without delay," "at full speed" (*OED* 2); cf. 637. See also 1343–44.

    habit: see 122.

1306. Parker thinks the iteration of *hands* (1299), *hand* (1302), and *hand* (1306) may be thought a blemish ("Variorum"). See 1n.

    A public officer: Bullough and Bullough observe that this type of character was common in Greek tragedy. Parker specifically compares him to the heralds in *Troades* and *Prometheus Bound,* but adds "actually any of a dozen plays might have furnished the parallel" (*Milton's Debt* 137–38, 182). Baum dismisses the Officer, along with the Messenger (1541), as "mere traditional conveniences of technique" (358). Landy defends the lack of character development: the Officer "may be thought of as a mouthpiece for his people, and for this purpose does not need to be dramatically individualized" ("Character" 250; see also "Of Highest Wisdom" 209). Verity notes the Officer's "contemptuous abruptness...verifying what the Chorus have just predicted"; however, Parker describes the Officer as "the most likable of three Philistines whom we meet. His duty is performed efficiently, but with a kindness that is surprising in the circumstances" (*Milton's Debt* 137). Ellis-Fermor suggests that the Officer's entrance is necessary to "assemble" and "give...direction" to the "prophetic flashes of exultation" that have begun to illuminate Samson's speech: "from this moment the play sweeps up easily to the triumphant climax" (29). Tung takes this idea further, arguing that previously "there is no progression, no gradual process of regeneration" and that it is the Officer's arrival which initiates "a breath-taking climactic reversal" (476, 477).

1307. *voluble:* editors gloss as "characterized by great fluency or readiness of utterance" (*OED* 6); Northrop Frye thus suggests, "concise" (Paradise Lost *and Selected Poetry*); Grieve writes, "fluent (but with more emphasis on rate than length)."

1308. *Ebrews:* editors note that Milton here follows the medieval Latin and Middle English (*Ebreu*) form of the word, which omitted the *H*. Masson (*Poetical Works*) conjectures that Milton in his poetry writes *Hebrew* for the adjective, *Ebrew* for the substantive; Verity responds, "but it is not easy to see what distinction was meant." Belloc has a long comment on this spelling (279–80). Parker ("Variorum") thinks it may provide a clue to *SA*'s date of composition: *Ebrews* is so spelled in 1319, 1540, and Argument 25; also in parts of two tracts published in 1645, *Tetr* and *Colas* (Patterson, *Works* 4:110, 178, 225, 235, 258); also so spelled in *SA*'s second edition. Elsewhere (*PR* 4.336; *Ps 136* 39; prose of the period 1641–59) the spelling is *Hebrew,* after classical Latin and Greek.

1309. *manacles:* see 1093, 1235, 1238, 1410. Masson (*Poetical Works*) writes, "fetters at the legs, not handcuffs."
 remark: "mark out, distinguish" (so *OED* [the earliest occurrence of the verb is dated 1633; the last entry is dated 1671]).

1310. Judges 16:25: "And they called for Samson out of the prison house." Percival notes that Milton follows the practice of Greek tragedy in making the Officer deliver his message in indirect narrative.

1311. The line echoes 12 (Le Comte 45); see 12n.

1312. *Triumph:* "pomp," "magnificence" (so *OED* 3) and/or "public festivity," "spectacle or pageant [in honor of a victory]" (*OED* 4; Lockwood I.b); cf. *L'All* 120 and *PL* 11.723. Joseph Warton (in Todd), Percival, et al. quote many illustrative passages. Cawley suggests George Sandys's *Relation of a Journey Begun An. Dom. 1610* as the source for the "magnificent alchemy of Milton's lines on Dagon" (119).
 Pomp: see 436.

1313. *rate:* editors gloss as "degree, extent" or "measure, calculation, estimation" (*OED* 11, 2b). The text of the first edition reads *race,* corrected in the *Errata* to *rate.*

1314. Parker writes, "this is superbly—indeed doubly—ironic. Not only does Samson give them more proof (demonstration) than they had expected; their attempt to humiliate him gives him the proof (confirmation; cf. 1145) that he has at last the strength necessary to do so. He knew his strength to be returning (586–88, 1355) but had no way to know the *extent* to which it had returned. Harapha's cowardice deprives him of one means of learning the truth, but the tests to which the Philistines put him (1624–27) tell him all that he needs to know" ("Variorum").

1315. *Assembly:* "gathering of persons for religious worship" (*OED* 6); cf. *PR* 1.34.

1317. Broadbent writes of this and the following seventeen lines, "the verse could not...nearer approach what was then prose, yet still so assertively be verse" (*Milton* 36).

   Where: "(to a place) where" (Parker, "Variorum").

   heartn'd: "strengthen[ed] with food or nourishment" (*OED* 3a); editors also gloss as "cheered" or "encouraged." Lockwood defines as "to inspirit, animate."

1319–21. Landy argues that this delay makes for suspense but also makes Samson's eventual decision more credible because accepting the first invitation "would not have been in keeping with his newly won knowledge, the wisdom which tells him he must not serve Dagon or the Philistines, that he must wait for God to give him the sign to act" ("Character" 241). Gossman also writes: "In refusing the Philistines' command, he shows that he will obey his conscience though the result be martyrdom, and that he knows he must not use his consecrated gift of strength except in the service of God" ("Milton's Samson" 540). Steadman, too, suggests that Milton intends "to emphasize...that Samson is actually conforming to the law of the Spirit in contradistinction with the written law" ("'Faithful Champion'" 17). Mueller adds, "Samson regains his status as a Nazarite by his initial refusal to attend.... His obedience to the law is a sort of purification, which is not yet the final *katharsis*, but points towards it" ("*Pathos*" 165). See 1347n.

1320. *Our law forbids:* editors cite Exodus 20:4–5: "Thou shalt not make unto thee any graven image.... Thou shalt not bow down thyself to them, nor serve them"; and Exodus 23:24: "Thou shalt not bow down to their gods, nor serve them, nor do after their works."

Religious Rites: Parker observes that the expression is neutral ("Variorum"); see *PL* 12.231 (Le Comte 67) and cf. 1378.

1323–32. Stein discusses the metrical effectiveness of this speech and 1334–42: "this passage is ... individual and assertive in effect, and seems to put a very great strain upon the meter, as if the strength of the personal passion were tearing at the bonds of the impersonal form" ("Note" 455–56; see also Stein, *Heroic Knowledge* 229–30); on the rhythm, see also 939–40n. Hill finds evidence in 1323–28 that Samson's wounded pride prompts his refusal to perform: "Once again, he is on the verge of doing the right thing for the wrong reason" (167).

Sword-players: "[persons] skilled in sword-play" (so *OED*). Parker glosses as "gladiators" ("Variorum"). Hughes prefers "professional fencers" on the basis that "Milton's contempt for the sports of Restoration London made him abandon historical consistency" (*John Milton*); see 1324–25n.

1324–25. About this list of entertainers, Landor complains, "the jugglers and the dancers they probably had, but none of the rest" (5:302); see also 1323–32n s.v. *Sword-players*. Todd thinks that in this passage Milton perhaps introduces—"not without contempt"—the usual performers in English festivities or "holiday sports." Keightley (*Poems*), Browne, Edmund K. Chambers, Bullough and Bullough, et al. agree that the list of entertainers belongs to Milton's own time. To Collins, they are "the rabble of harlots, rope-dancers and buffoons who crowded the court of the second Charles" (9); J. Macmillan Brown similarly sees an allusion to the "professional pleasure-makers" of Charles II's court (36, 121); Percival also thinks that Milton alludes contemptuously to the spectacular drama of the Restoration in his mention of mummers and mimics. Scholes, however, does not support an allusion to the Restoration; he describes this list as "the pleasures of life" that continued under the Protectorate in the form of masques, operas, puppet-plays, fairs, dancing schools, horse-races, and tight-rope walking (875). Parker instead favors a possible biblical allusion: "The Hebrews had no public games such as the Greeks and Romans did (cf. 1 Macc. 1.14–15 and 2 Macc. 4.12–16, where Jason's introduction of a gymnasium is denounced), but competitive foot-racing seems to be referred to in Ps. 19.5; Eccles. 9.11; etc. The apostle Paul refers often, of course, to the Greek games"

("Variorum"). Mueller, noting in this catalogue the absence of the tragic actor, detects a "grim literary joke": Samson "agonistes" or "actor" (see the note to the title) is filling this role as he appears with these other performers and, by destroying the Philistine "theatre" (1605), brings the audience into his own tragedy ("*Pathos*" 170); see 1645n.

   Gymnic: "gymnastic" (so *OED* A). Peck cites this word to support his claim that Milton "naturalizes many *Greek* words" (sig. O3v); see also 1619n.

   Juglers: "conjurer[s]," "performer[s] of legerdemain" (*OED* 2). Todd comments, "*Juglers* were anciently included under the general name of *minstrels.* . . . They sang, to their instruments, verses composed by themselves or others."

   Antics: "clown[s]," "mountebank[s]," "performer[s] who [play] a grotesque or ludicrous part" (so *OED* B.4). Todd describes their appearance in old English farces with a "blacked face and a patch-work habit." Verity glosses as "buffoon . . . because they practised odd gesticulations and antics, like clowns; or perhaps from their patch-work dresses which might be described as *antic* = fantastic" (141). Blakeney notes the word originally meant "ancient" (Latin *antiquus*).

   Mummers: "actor[s] in a dumb show" (*OED* 2), "masked buffoon[s]" (Lockwood). Todd identifies them as "A set of persons, who went about at Christmas, in disguise, to get money or good cheer. . . . [They] were so called, because they made it a law among themselves, to say nothing but *mum*." Greenlaw, Osgood, and Padelford (4:208–9) compare *The Faerie Queene* 4.7.44.5: "And unto every thing did aunswere mum."

   Mimics: "mime[s], burlesque actor[s]," "performer[s] . . . skilled in mimicry" (*OED* B.1). The text of the first edition has *Mimirs,* corrected in the *Errata* (but nevertheless admitted into Johnson's *Dictionary* as *mimer,* which he defines as "a mimick; a buffoon"); Fenton also emends to *Mimers.*

1326. *me:* Darbishire (*Poetical Works*) and B. A. Wright emend to *mee;* cf. 1125; see 219–20n s.v. *Mee.*

   tir'd: Parker ("Variorum") suggests a possibly ironic pun: "wearied" and also "dressed, adorned" (*OED* 2b).

1327. *publick:* this is also the spelling in the list of "the Persons" and in the Argument 17, 19, but elsewhere in the text of *SA* (867, 992, 1306, 1314, 1393, 1615) it is *public*—which Parker identifies as Milton's preference from about June 1644 onward ("Variorum").

Mill: Le Comte suggests that Milton refers to Samson's work at the mill three times so as to emphasize Samson's "agonizing present" (45); see 37, 1393.

1328. *make them sport:* "provide entertainment [to them]" (*OED* 3a); cf. 1614, 1679, and Judges 16:25: "Call for Samson, that he may make us sport." Cf. *Tetr:* Adam had all creatures "to make him sport" (Patterson, *Works* 4:83).

    blind: Parker glosses as "not directed by sight" ("Variorum"). Diodati in 1648 thinks it possible that Samson "did indeed do some ridiculous acts, as blind men use to do" (sig. L6r).

1329. *occasion:* see 224n. Stein suggests that the word makes this line an odd echo of Samson's own alleged motive for his first marriage (*Heroic Knowledge* 186).

1330. *me:* Parker glosses as "myself" but notes that a comma after *refusal* would alter the sense ("Variorum").

1331. *make a game of:* Parker detects a pun: "turn into ridicule" (so *OED* 2b) and "make an athletic exhibition of" ("Variorum"); cf. 1312, 1602.

1332. *Return the way thou cam'st:* editors compare *Ps 6* 23: "They shall return in hast the way they came." Parker (*Milton's Debt* 182) compares *Prometheus Bound* 961–62: σὺ δὲ κέλευθον ἥνπερ ἦλθες ἐγκόνει πάλιν; "Quickly return the way thou camest." Of this and the following two lines, Broadbent writes, the "speech-rhythms emphasise meaning against the metrical pattern. . . . These tensions symbolize or complement the strain that Samson's roused individuality is now putting on his captivity—the strain the Messenger will directly mime [see 1648–51]" (*Milton* 36).

1333. *Regard thy self:* Verity et al. gloss as "look to, have a care for yourself; consider your own interests" (so *OED* 3); Shawcross suggests, "beware" (*Complete English Poetry*). Todd and Percival compare the advice of Mercury to Prometheus in *Prometheus Bound* 1041, but Maxwell objects that "there is no verbal similarity" ("Milton's Knowledge" 369).

1334. Editors paraphrase: "What! regard myself? nay, rather, I ought to regard my conscience." Verity compares "To Mr. Cyriack Skinner," lines 9 and 10.

Bush notes that the parallel structure of 102 helps to measure, by comparison, Samson's developing confidence ("John Milton" 517; *John Milton* 199). Some editors (e.g., Keightley, *Poems*) alter the question mark after *My self* to an exclamation point.

    internal peace: Parker comments, "the phrase is most significant: Samson now makes explicit what he has finally achieved" ("Variorum").

1335–36. Stein calls attention "to the controlled shaking of Samson's wrath in exact time with the meter in this line. . . . This metrical variation in the last two feet . . . would markedly decrease the emphasis by making it more common and general, less specific to Samson. . . . [T]he meter requires and sanctions the dislocation of stressing *my* more than *mind.* . . . This is the last flare-up of the self before he accepts the role as Fool of God" (*Heroic Knowledge* 229–30).

    corporal: see 615–16.

1337. *commands:* Fletcher examined three copies of the first edition that have a period instead of a question mark (*John Milton's Complete* 4:33).

1338. *drudge:* so Samson in 573; cf. 1393.

    fool: "jester, clown" (*OED* 2).

1339. *in my midst: OED*'s editors cite this line to illustrate the use of *midst* with a poetical transposition of the possessive adjective (so *OED* 2d).

    heart-grief: cf. Shakespeare's *Henry V* 2.2.27: "in heart-grief and uneasiness" (Verity). Percival compares the *cordolium* of Plautus, *Cistellaria* 1.1.65.

1340. Cf. 1601–2.

    feats: Fletcher examined three copies of the first edition that omit the comma here (*John Milton's Complete* 4:33).

    play: so also 1448 and Argument 18.

    god: Keightley changes the first edition's comma after this word to a question mark (*Poems*); other editors (e.g., Verity) replace the comma with a dash.

1341. *all indignities:* cf. 371, 1168.

    me: Darbishire (*Poetical Works*) emends to *mee,* but Bridges would scan the line recognizing an enclitic accent on *on* (*Milton's Prosody* 48), as in 241, 1118;

see 219–20n s.v. *Mee*. Krouse suggests that Samson realizes he is being asked to take part in the celebration of his own ruin (107). See 12n.

1342. Some editors (e.g., Masson, *Poetical Works*) alter the first edition's question mark after *contempt* to an exclamation point; Keightley changes it to a period (*Poems*).

Joyn'd: "united or combined" (Lockwood); "enjoined" (so Church; Verity; Grieve; Hughes, *Complete Poems* and *John Milton;* et al.); "fastened" (Edmund K. Chambers 142). *OED* cites no example later than the sixteenth century. Cf. 6 (*enjoyn'd*) and the spelling in 265, 1037.

I will not come: so *Julius Caesar* 2.2.64 (George Coffin Taylor 196). Hill (168) notes that "Until God commands otherwise, Samson is prepared to pass the remainder of his days in patient waiting; at last he has become a true hero, a hero of patience, and one who exemplifies that 'better fortitude / Of Patience and Heroic Martyrdom' (*PL* 9.31–32)." See 1268–99n, 1287–88n.

1343. Editors paraphrase: "imposed on me (to be dispatched) with speed." Blakeney adds, "The construction imitates the Greek (*constructio praegnans,* where two clauses are compressed into one)."

1344. Sellin suggests that the Officer feigns haste and does not dispute further with Samson because the Philistines "in fact are attempting to force him upon the horns of a dilemma—if he avoids indignity and pollution by refusing to come, then they can make him suffer for disobedience" ("Milton's Epithet" 153).

Brooks: "tolerate[s]," "put[s] up with" (*OED* 3); cf. *PL* 9.675–76.

1346. *sorry what:* editors paraphrase: "sorry (for) what," or "sorry to imagine what."

stoutness: Percival, Meiklejohn, Verity, Grieve, Hughes (*Complete Poems; John Milton*), et al. suggest "overbearing spirit," "stubbornness," "defiance," "arrogance," or "pride"; editors cite in particular Isaiah 9:9 and Shakespeare's *Coriolanus* 3.2.125–27 "let / Thy mother rather feel thy pride than fear / Thy dangerous stoutness." Verity, though, notes that "both the noun and adjective could be used in a good sense, and this would not be unsuitable here: the officer has some sympathy with Samson and may admire his *courage*." *OED*

(3, 2) has "firmness, resoluteness" and/or "courageousness." On the Officer's sympathy, cf. 1410, and see Parker (*Milton's Debt* 137).

1347. *sorrow indeed:* commentators discuss whether Samson dismisses the Officer's avowed sympathy incredulously, or begins to realize, at this moment, that the great opportunity for further service may have come. Newton leans toward the latter reading: "such anticipations are usual with the best dramatic writers. . . . The speaker himself can only be supposed to have some general meaning, and not a distinct conception of all the particulars." Verity observes here how the notion of revenge gradually occurs to Samson; Parker imagines the Officer leaving at 1346, and Samson then speaking these words slowly and thoughtfully, as if to himself ("Variorum"). But Fish instead suggests that Samson treats the Officer poorly: he writes that Milton's depiction of such a "solicitous" Officer complicates readers' reactions to the Philistines' destruction, and that here Samson's "irony, local and final, is at the expense of someone we know and like. This is not the Nazarite's finest moment" (257, 258).

1348–70. Parker finds great irony in the Chorus's begging Samson to go to his death, and in failing utterly to understand his thoughts ("Variorum"); see 1347n, 1380n. Fish suggests instead that this open-ended exchange illustrates one of the drama's main points: the reader "acknowledges the justness of one of the Chorus's arguments only to find himself agreeing no less emphatically with an objection raised by Samson in the following line; and then he enters the cycle again." The reader, Fish argues, thus arrives at an "insight the play has been urging on us all along: no firm—that is, external—basis for action exists in this world" (253).

    strain'd . . . break: Percival thinks this metaphor is of a bent bow; Verity, of a bow or "some mechanical contrivance"; Edmund K. Chambers and Bullough and Bullough, of a "taut rope." Cf. *PL* 8.454.

1350. *He's gone:* cf. 997. The Officer may exit here; some editors have him exit earlier, at 1346 or 1347.

1351. *adding fuel to the flame: OED* finds this expression used by Michael Drayton in 1596 (s.v. *fuel* 1b); Parker comments, "It was common in Italian drama"

("Variorum"). Johnson (*Rambler* 20 July 1751) objects to its use here because the consistency of Milton's metaphors "is not accurately preserved" (221). Cf. *Ps 2 27*.

1352. *imperious:* "urgent, absolute, overmastering, imperative" (*OED* 4).

1353. Jerram calls this "a line bigger in words and sound than its sense will well bear."

    Lordly: Parker thinks this may be a pun on *loudly* ("Variorum").

1354–60. Landy thinks this speech, not the episode with Harapha, indicates that "Samson has been fully regenerated. There is no longer any question of regression on his part" ("Character" 251).

    this gift / Of strength: Wilkenfeld pinpoints Samson's use of the word *this:* "the past has finally been exorcised; it has finally given way to the realities of the present" (163). Samson also uses the phrase in 47.

    strength, again returning: Verity and Stein point out that "Favour renew'd" and returning strength have not hitherto been linked, except by Manoa (586–87) and "then without the sense of dynamic immediacy conveyed by the return*ing*" (Stein, *Heroic Knowledge* 186). Jerram finds Samson's statement here "not quite consistent" with 1260, 1313, but adds, "nor need they be, perhaps." See also 568n, 570n, 1314n; this line echoes 1496 (Le Comte 45).

    again: "anew," "back in a former position" (*OED* A.3).

    transgression: the first edition has a comma after this word; some editors (e.g., Keightley, *Poems;* Verity) change it to a question mark.

1358. *Idols:* plural here but elsewhere singular; cf. 1297, 1672.

1360. *Vaunting:* editors gloss as "displaying proudly" (*OED* 4 [last entry dated 1592]).

1361. A twelve-syllable line (alexandrine) without any break (Bridges, *Milton's Prosody* 61). See 118n; on the rhythm, see 939–40n.

    Besides: a comma follows this word in the first edition; the construction and sense change when it is removed, as in the editions of Percival, Verity, et al. Percival discusses the implications of this punctuation.

ridiculous: cf. 131, 539, 1501; see 131n. Oras identifies this line as one of the poem's dactylic endings which "require the suppression of a vowel between two consonants if they are — in theory or reality — to be reduced to the trochaic norm" ("Milton's Blank Verse" 168). See 603n. Thus, as in *PL* 12.62 and *PR* 4.342, *ridiculous* is probably a trisyllable.

1362. Hughes scans this line: "two heavy feet, which are better treated as spondees than as iambs, close the line after a very light foot of *three* syllables" (*John Milton* 424).

    execrably: Keightley would emend to *execrable* so that it would correspond with 1361, 1364 (*Poems*).

    unclean: cf. 1320; the word is used in the legal sense (Prince, *Samson Agonistes*). Cf. 321.

1364. Peck cites this line to illustrate Milton's characteristic use of a "continuative epithet," that is, three epithets to compose a single line of verse (sig. P4r). See also 417n, 827, and 1422.

1365. *Idol-worship:* *OED* traces the expression to *PL* 12.115. Bush here compliments Samson's "quiet Socratic rationality, fortitude, and fearlessness" and notes that Samson's reply to the Chorus echoes Socrates' response to "the friends who wished to arrange his escape from prison and death" (*John Milton* 199). Johnson (*Rambler* 20 July 1751) also admires this passage (1363–75): Samson "destroys the common excuse of cowardice and servility, which always confound temptation with compulsion" (222).

1366. *honest:* "free from disgrace" (*OED* 2b), or "faithful, genuine" (Lockwood).

    deserve: editors gloss as "merit by service" (the Latin sense), "earn." Collins thinks that in these lines Milton may be "alluding to his own position in submitting quietly to the power of the Royalists." Parker asserts that Samson's pride in his daily labor is a significant part of his characterization ("Variorum"); see 573n, 1261n.

    food: cf. 574.

1367. *civil power:* as opposed to religious (cf. 1365); so also 853. Northrop Frye notes that "Samson's position in Philistine society is based on a clear separation of spiritual and temporal authority"; he compares *Sonn 17* 10–11 (Paradise Lost *and Selected Poetry*).

1368. Church and Verity suggest that this line is Milton's variation on Euripides, *Hippolytus* 612: ἡ γλῶσσ᾽ ὀμώμοχ᾽ ἡ δὲ φρὴν ἀνώμοτος; "My tongue hath sworn: no oath is on my soul." Hughes (*Complete Poems; John Milton*) thinks the line may refer to Aristotle's doctrine that "it is only voluntary feelings and actions for which praise and blame are given; those that are involuntary are condoned, and sometimes even pitied" (*Nicomachean Ethics* 3.1.1). Alden Sampson thinks this line expresses the "inward spirituality of Quakerism" (183). Archer Taylor (in a letter to Parker) finds here the legal maxim (3 Inst. 107): *Actus non facit reum nisi mens sit rea* (Parker, "Variorum"); see also Rushton (40) and Broom, Pease, and Chitty (256), who translate this maxim as, "The act does not make a man guilty unless his intention were guilty."

1369. *outward force:* the phrase occurs also in *PL* 9.348.
    sentence: editors gloss as "maxim, aphorism, proverb" (*OED* 4); Blakeney suggests, "your opinion" (*OED* 2); see 1368n.
    holds: Verity glosses as "holds good." Most editors supply punctuation after this word; the first edition has none.

1372–75. A. B. Chambers discusses how Samson here resists his final temptation and demonstrates his worthiness to receive the divine inspiration that immediately follows: "the fear of God is the beginning of wisdom, but he who fears man more than God is a fool. By one deceptively simple act—the mere refusal to obey the Officer's command—Samson concisely demonstrates that neither fear nor folly can sway him now," and "the moral action of the play concludes" (320). Dick Taylor writes that this speech "constitutes the turning point of the play" (78); cf. 1381–89n. Alden Sampson instead suggests that Samson's reply to the Chorus "might well have been spoken by Lucifer, the champion of liberty" (212).

1374. *prefer:* editors gloss as "give precedence to"; see 464n.

1375. *which:* "i.e., an act which" (Blakeney); editors note this "act" is "preferring man to God."

jealousie: "having a love which will tolerate no unfaithfulness or defection" (*OED* 4c). Editors cite Exodus 20:5: "for I the Lord thy God am a jealous God."

1377–79. *Yet:* Mickle, responding to Johnson's criticism, claims that "the middle is here pointedly drawing to a conclusion" (403). Parker observes, "with this thought the whole difficult problem is solved for Samson. But the Chorus is still in the dark" ("Variorum"); see 1380n.

dispense with: editors gloss as "excuse," "grant a dispensation for" (*OED* 15), or "to do without, forego" (Lockwood); cf. 314. Parker ("Variorum") compares *DocCh:* "A question here arises, whether it be lawful for a professor of the true religion to be present at idol-worship, in cases where his attendance is necessary for the discharge of some civil duty. The affirmative seems to be established by the example of Naaman the Syrian [2 Kings 5:17–19]" (Patterson, *Works* 17:145); Charles R. Sumner (trans., 1825)—followed by Verity, Grieve, et al.— first connects this passage to *SA* (see Patterson, *Works* 17:573). Bullough and Bullough also note *DocCh,* but add: "here the idea is Luther's, that God may dispense with all other commandments but the first." Muldrow finds another connection with *DocCh,* specifically Milton's description of a "good conscience" (Patterson, *Works* 17:41), which, Muldrow proposes, Samson is finally using (210–11). Edmund K. Chambers notes, "the limits of obedience to the civil authority was . . . a much-discussed point of 17th century casuistry."

1378. See 122n. On the pronunciation of *Idolatrous,* cf. 443, 1364.

1380. Edmund K. Chambers writes, "the Chorus gives it up, as the Greek chorus generally does when a difficult problem has to be solved." E.g., Sheppard compares the Chorus here to "the followers of Ajax, when he went to settle his account with heaven" (164). Parker adds that the Chorus's failure is especially ironic because it had earlier (310–21) seemed to understand how God can prompt his servant to disobey a law of God for "some important cause" ("Variorum").

come off: Prince glosses as "extricate yourself from danger" (*Samson Agonistes*); *OED* cites the first such usage in *Mask* 646. Summers suggests that this verb also implies the Chorus's sense of "'get away with it,' 'come off' with one's skin intact" (171).

reach: see 62, and cf. *PL* 5.571.

1381–89. Most editors and commentators agree that this is the turning point in the action. E.g., Brydges calls "this change of purpose...the hinge on which the whole catastrophe turns." Northrop Frye similarly writes that "[Samson] is right in refusing but has come to the end of his own will. At that point he appears to change his mind, but what has happened is that God has accepted his efforts, taken over his will, and changed his mind for him.... Samson is now certain to die, though also certain of redemption" ("Typology" 238). Frye compares this moment to the "temptation of the pinnacle" in *PR* 4.551–61. Allen instead compares *PR* 1.290–93 ("Idea as Pattern" 94), as does Baumgartner: "Samson has come to feel that, with or without him, God will set things right.... The words Samson speaks...indicate clearly that he, without heroic plan of his own, is relying on Divine Providence" (209). Grierson also thinks that Samson now "feels that he is led by the Spirit" ("Note" 337); and Tung remarks: "God's spirit, coming at this crucial moment, represents a special dispensation; it commands Samson to do an about-face; it convicts him and makes him into a new being; for the first time Samson becomes patient and submissive" (489). Daiches similarly writes: "Samson has at last reached the state which Milton describes at the end of the sonnet on his blindness, at the end of *Lycidas* (by implication), and early in *Paradise Regained,* in the self-communings of Jesus: he is waiting for God to reveal what He has in store for him. It is not enough to repent, to absolve God of blame, to avoid despair, to resist the various temptations...; one must also resign oneself patiently to the will of God, whose purpose...will be revealed in due time" (245).

Among other responses to this passage, Ellis-Fermor notes that the rhythm correspondingly becomes "firmer and more even, passing into a grave, majestic movement which increasingly reflects the growing assurance and clarity of Samson's spirit" (152). Bridges also finds this speech's "exceptional and forceful rhythm" expressive of Samson's new resolve ("Extraordinary" 93). Ferry notes Samson's growing heroic reticence: this speech, in contrast to his earlier emotional revelations, "is full of vague terms with unspecified references," and, "although he claims to be describing his 'thoughts,' he actually tells only how he will immediately act" (169–70). Parker adds that 1381–83 have been ironically foreshadowed in 663–66 ("Variorum"). Arthos cites the same lines from this passage among the many "tantalizing" similarities between *SA* and Girolamo Bartolommei's *Polietto* (194–99).

Still a few commentators find fault here with Samson's change of purpose. E.g., Tillyard writes, "There is a dramatic improbability about Samson's final

regeneration. His sudden resolution . . . is too abrupt to be convincing: it seems
to be taken too lightly" (*Milton* 291). Wilkes similarly describes "an unmistakable discontinuity" between Samson's decision to perform at the feast and the
preceding events — but for Wilkes that in itself is significant: he believes that
grace here operates beyond human capacity and effort; it comes undeserved to
an uncomprehending Samson and reverses his course of action. *SA,* as Wilkes
interprets it, "demonstrates rather the sovereignty of providence, undistracted
by man's errors and deserts, moving invincibly toward the objective proposed"
(377–78). Cf. 1262–67n.

 Be of good courage: Baumgartner suggests that with these words Samson suddenly assumes the role of the Chorus as comforter, which marks the drama's
"turning point" (210).

1382. *rouzing motions:* "awakening" (so *OED* 3); "inward prompting or impulse"
 (*OED* s.v. *motion* 9); or "stirrings of excitement" (Bullough and Bullough). Cf.
 222–23, 422, 526, 638; cf. also Argument 20: "perswaded inwardly that this
 was from God" (and see the note on this). Cf. also *PR* 1.290.

 Commentators discuss the divine and human nature of Samson's promptings.
A. B. Chambers writes that this "inspiration [was] from God"; he identifies it
as "the last requirement — as even Cicero knew [*De natura deorum* 1.2] — for a
great heroic act" (320); see 1372–75n. Mollenkott agrees that these "motions"
are divine: "The triumphant conclusion proves that this time, as on the occasion
of Samson's first marriage, the inspiration is genuine, is God-inspired rather
than ego-inspired" (93). Fogle instead argues that the two words "surely have
primary meaning in terms of Samson's *response* to his enlightened mind. . . . They
represent an impulsion to act, a free response by his receptive but nonetheless
dynamic will. It was the moment when the divine and human will became one"
(195). Mueller suggests that this illumination occurs so suddenly that Samson
and the Chorus do not fully understand it. Mueller adds that the swiftness with
which the play concludes is by design: "at the end of a seemingly loose plot it
is shown that the events did fulfill a supreme design" ("*Pathos*" 159). Christopher suggests that this moment represents a "hiatus" in the play: "Given his
dramatis personae, Milton can show a free response to God only as a puzzling,
isolated response, which disrupts the established pattern of dramatic interac-
tion. The exact nature of the 'rousing motions' as well as the decision to attend
the feast remain a mystery" (371). Haller writes, "The irrepressible, tough,
resilient arrogance of spirit which so often repels us in Milton the revolutionary

pamphleteer...comes to full poetic expression" (210). Marilla suggests that Samson's "inner compulsion" constitutes "an implicit assertion of the moral obligation that is always contingent in the challenges which life is capable of extending to great though erring man" (76).

1383. *extraordinary:* Bridges finds "good reason" for this irregularity: "It may at first seem childish to assert that 'something extraordinary' in the sense determined 'something extraordinary' in the prosody; yet to deny this requires the acceptance of an unlikely alternative:...that at the crisis in the poem...there occurs by accident a violent rhythmical jar in the verse" (*Milton's Prosody* 49, 116). Bridges scans: "To something extr'órdinary my thoughts" (48). Hughes scans: "the first foot iambic, the second and third trochaic, the fourth a very light trochee and the fifth a heavy iambus with the first element, *my,* given almost as much emphasis as should be laid upon *thoughts,* so that the last foot comes only a little short of being a spondee" (*John Milton* 424). Verity suggests, instead, scanning the last foot in this line as trisyllabic (anapestic). The pronunciation *extraornary* has also been suggested, but Bridges gives detailed reasons against what he calls this "threefold blunder—in philology, in literary, and in textual criticism" ("Extraordinary" 93).

1384. Todd and Church note that "it was not expressly said before that the messenger was coming"; they conclude that the blind Samson evidently expected the Officer to return. See 1352. Newton suggests that Samson may "know that the messenger was coming by the same impulse that he felt rousing him to something extraordinary." Bridges writes that "the easy rhythm and diction" in this line express Samson's readiness ("Extraordinary" 93).

1385. *be sure:* see 465.

1387–89. Editors and commentators discuss the extent of Samson's knowledge in this passage and his resemblance to Christ. Collins finds these lines significant and cites Brydges: "This change of purpose from a sudden internal presage of the mind is magnificently imagined." Goldsmith concedes that Samson "speaks truer than he knows" but similarly calls this passage "the moment of self-discovery (*anagnorisis*)" as Samson "hears and heeds the inner voice that prompts him to go to the Temple of Dagon" (82). J. Macmillan Brown finds a paradox here in Samson: "He is now drunk with revenge, that most primitive of passions.... And yet he is filled with the spirit of the prophet, too, whose one trust is in the God he serves" (84). Edmund K. Chambers points out "that the exact nature of what [Samson] is to do is not clear to him yet," and, Madsen argues, "there is no indication...that Samson attaches any moral or spiritual significance to his willingness to suffer public humiliation." Because Samson lacks this insight, Madsen concludes, the poem's hero only "dimly" prefigures Christ: Samson primarily serves as a counterexample, remarkable for "his inability to measure up to the heroic norm delineated in *Paradise Regained*" (200–2). But Rajan argues that such a comparison oversimplifies Samson's character: "His faith is primarily that men and nations bring ruin on themselves and that God will triumph despite the fallibility of his agents. He is not perfect man but he is Miltonic man, a creature of error, dignity and blindness, descended from the hill of Christ's detachment. His reinstatement as God's champion conveys more than an individual act of forgiveness" (140). Christopher accepts that Samson is ultimately identified with Christ but also rejects Samson as a Christ figure in the play: "Samson's new identity is a metaphysical identity with Christ" (372–73). Maxwell observes that Samson's specific prophecy suggests the ambiguous oracle in Sophocles' *Women of Trachis* 79–81, which warns that Heracles is destined either to death or "release from toils"; as with Samson's prophecy in *SA*, the destinies are not alternative but complementary ("Milton's Samson" 90–91). See 1389n.

   aught of: Parker glosses as "anything of," i.e., "any truth in" ("Variorum").

   presage: Todd, Fleming, and Percival quote Euripides, *Andromache* 1072: πρόμαντις θυμὸς ὥς τι προσδοκᾷ; "O my prophetic soul, what ill it bodes!"

1389. *or:* Parker (*Milton's Debt* 163) writes, this "little word...is tremendously effective here. It helps us to appreciate 'And for a life who will not change his purpose?' (1406) and 'The last of me or no I cannot warrant' (1426)." Summers observes that Milton presents various either/or constructions in the play that appear mutually exclusive, when in fact, as with this scene, both prove true (158–59). Low also analyzes this ironic technique, which he refers to as the "irony of alternatives"; he argues that it "is...basic to the play's method and meaning" ("Action" 514–19). See also, e.g., 1073, 1516–17, 1537, 1545–46, 1636–38, 1587n. In *Log,* Milton calls this technique *axioma disjunctum contingens* (Patterson, *Works* 11:365). Fish instead thinks that Samson may here be speaking ambiguously on purpose: "The conditional 'If there be aught of presage in the mind' (1387), is a deliberate hedging, a recognition perhaps, of his earlier presumption in rushing too quickly to conclusions about the divine will and his responsiveness to it" (254). Ellis-Fermor finds "the accident of physical death...clearly separated now in Samson's mind from significant experience. It is hardly important, one way or the other" (30).

1390. *the man returns:* McCall attaches a secondary significance to this description of the Officer's second entrance: "the phrase can...[also] refer to Samson's return from his living death to a world of action and participation" (65). Parker comments that "the Chorus, without having the remotest idea of what has been passing through its friend's mind, is much relieved" ("Variorum").

1391. *this second message:* Percival observes that, unlike the first, this "is delivered in direct narrative," peremptorily, after the manner of "the heralds in Homer, who repeat their message word for word as it had been delivered to them." The Argument describes this short speech as "great threatnings." Sellin writes that from this moment "Samson dons his mask and begins his histrionic performance," and "all of Samson's actions are not to be taken literally but to be viewed as part of his feigning" ("Milton's Epithet" 156).

1393–94. *drudge:* so Samson himself (1338); cf. 573.
   And: "and yet" (Parker, "Variorum").
   our sending and command: Percival reads: "our command sending (for thee)," or "our sending (message) commanding (thy presence)," thus considering the phrase a case of hendiadys, or expression of a complex idea by two nouns connected by *and.* Cf. 105, 535, 1654.

1396. *Engines:* some editors gloss as "means, contrivances" (*OED* 3; cf. 5b); others prefer "machine, instrument" (e.g., Lockwood; Verity); still others recognize both meanings (e.g., Prince, *Samson Agonistes*).

1397–98. *hamper:* "bind, fetter" (*OED* 1; Verity), "mutilate, maim" (Percival; Grieve), or "render powerless" (Wyatt and Collins); cf. *REW:* "our liberty shall not be hamperd" (Patterson, *Works* 6:134).
   of force: "by force," i.e., "unavoidably" (Wyatt and Collins).
   rock: "a large rugged mass of stone" (*OED* 1); cf. 253.

1399–1400. *content:* "pleased" (*OED* 2); cf. 1322, 1403.

   try: Blakeney glosses as "test" (*OED* 7).

   pernicious: "ruinous; fatal" (*OED* a); Verity glosses as "full of destruction" (Latin *perniciosum*).

1401–7. In this speech, Samson is enjoying his own irony: Fish comments, "His is a special kind of irony, an irony of humility which operates at his own expense, since it allows those around him to attribute to him motives he would consider base" (262). Stein also writes, "He jokes with what would be a facile irony if the right to say it had not been so terribly earned" (*Heroic Knowledge* 189). As various editors note, we are not misled because we have learned that Samson's true sentiments are the very opposite of these. Furthermore, Parker emphasizes that he has previously displayed a fondness for simple irony, e.g., in 14–18, 22, 40–42, 558–59, 905–6, 955–59 (*Milton's Debt* 158). Parker is especially complimentary of this passage: "More than any visible act . . . these four lines make us realize the degree of self-mastery which Samson has won. To hear this man who despaired of his own life pretending a respect for power and a concern for his own safety—this is a glimpse of human character that only genius can give! The concluding touch of platitudinous moralizing completes the revelation" (*Milton's Debt* 158). On the other hand, Parker ("Variorum") compares *DocCh:* "That it may be the part of prudence to obey the commands even of a tyrant in lawful things, or, more properly, to comply with the necessity of the times for the sake of public peace, as well as of personal safety, I am far from denying" (Patterson, *Works* 17:402–5). For the irony, see also the notes to individual lines.

1402–3. *Because:* "so that" (*OED* B.2); Shawcross explains the sense as "because I do not desire them to" (*Complete English Poetry*).

   content: "willing, ready" (*OED* 3 [last entry dated 1709]); cf. 1322, 1399. Hill compares Samson's decision to perform at the feast with his earlier decision to marry the woman of Timna: in both cases, Samson "transgresses the law out of respect for the Lawgiver" (168). Hyman adds to the reasons Samson gives for attending the Philistine games "his unconquerable desire for action," which is "the deepest impulse of his character" ("Unwilling Martyrdom" 95).

1404. *Masters commands:* Edmund K. Chambers finds this "ironically double-edged. Samson is indeed obeying a master, but not the Philistines." Warburton (in Newton) comments, "This was a feint, but it had betray'd itself had it not been cover'd [in 1408]." Dunster (in Todd) writes, "the most indignant spirit of irony"; Sellin calls it "wily irony" that Samson uses to allay further the Officer's suspicions ("Milton's Epithet" 156). Cf. 1215.

1406. As Dunster (in Todd) and Verity remark, this is said lest his sudden compliance and heavy irony arouse the Officer's suspicion.

   change: cf. 684.

1407. *So mutable:* Stein (*Heroic Knowledge* 190) observes that Samson "hauls up for our startled recognition two moral clichés that sounded thin when we first heard them and are positively ridiculous now": the Chorus's "O mirror of our fickle state" (164) and Manoa's "oh what not in man / Deceivable and vain" (349–50). Cf. also 793.

   ways of men: the phrase also occurs in *PL* 3.46 (Le Comte 67). Some early editors follow Masson (*Poetical Works*) and insert an exclamation point after *men*.

1408–9. Cf. 1385–86. Editors note these words depend on "I am content to go" (1403), and are perhaps addressed only to the Chorus, lest it be misled by the irony. Dunster (in Todd) comments, "The Officer certainly answers Samson's speech, as if he had not heard these words." Keightley thus refers to the intervening lines (1404–7) as parenthetic (*Poems*).

1410. *thy resolution:* Richardson (in Newton) notes that "to come with me" is understood.

   doff: "take off" (*OED* 1); "a contraction of *do off*" (Hunter).

   links: "fetters" (so *OED* 1). Cf. 1093, 1235, 1238, 1309.

1411–12. Stein observes that the Officer's apparently kind suggestion does not alter Samson's detachment; "Manoa and Dalila had played that tune before to uninterested ears" (*Heroic Knowledge* 190). Lawry notes that the "painful oxymoron involved in the phrase 'compliance: set...free' stamps such ransom as fraudulent" (391).

   compliance: cf. Adam's "compliance bad" at the moment of the Fall (*PL* 9.994).

favour: either a verb ("to favour [thee]") or a noun (Parker, "Variorum").
to set thee free: tragic irony; Verity calls it "verbal 'irony' as in l. 1267."

1413–26. Parker (*Milton's Debt* 64) notes that Samson's final speech is exactly balanced in length by the fifth stasimon (1427–40). With Samson's departure, Bailey is reminded of *Oedipus at Coloneus:* Samson "leaves the scene, like Oedipus, to return no more, but to be more felt in his absence than in his presence" (238). Brewer also discusses the resemblance to Sophocles' play: "each hero, receiving a mysterious divine intimation, leaves the stage and walks to the place which the intimation appoints. He departs confident that his act will have great significance for the two states with which fate is involved" (919–20). Mueller observes that "Samson deliberately severs his connexions with his fellowmen; when he leaves the stage he has done with Manoa, Dalila, and the Danites" ("*Pathos*" 157). Low suggests that this "progressive isolation" is "part of the essence of tragedy" and culminates with Samson, "entirely alone with God," performing for the Philistines: "Here and in his death the twofold movement toward God and away from man reaches its completion" ("Tragic Pattern" 918, 919). Mickle uses this scene to refute Johnson's claim that nothing happens in the middle of the drama: Mickle argues that it "is so self-evident on attentive perusal" that "Samson's mind is in a very different state when he bids the Chorus farewell, from that in which they found him" (404). Hanford adds that by this point Samson "has, in a sense, regained his own lost Paradise, and in his story Milton, by vindicating the power of a free but erring will to maintain itself in obedience and be restored to grace, has again asserted eternal Providence and justified the ways of God to man" ("*Samson Agonistes*" 177).

Commentators disagree, however, about Samson's intentions in this passage. Verity thinks that these lines prove "that Samson has not yet conceived the plan which he afterwards carries out" (123), and Gray notes that "We never know whether he has made any plan or not, but that action allows the poet to follow the classical custom of having the catastrophe occur offstage and be reported" (143). Parker, however, argues that "Samson could scarcely have been more definite than this in the presence of the Officer" (*Milton's Debt* 50). Flatter goes even further, arguing that Samson's final line is "an obvious hint at what he intends to do: to pull down the temple" (7 August, 443). But Farnham-Flower insists that Samson could not realize that he is specifically going to destroy the Philistine temple because the necessary situation has not yet presented itself (471).

1414. *wish:* "request" (so *OED* 5a).
    offend them: cf. 1333.

1416. *me:* Darbishire (*Poetical Works*) and B. A. Wright emend to *mee;* cf. 1125;
see 219–20n s.v. *Mee.*
    common: see 856.

1418–22. Following Joseph Warton (in Todd), most editors point out that this is
"a concealed attack" on English society: the nobility, the opulent clergy, and the
people observing pagan holy days and participating in public sports. See 1421n.
Carey writes that the imagery used to describe Dagon's worshipers—here,
fired (1419), *unquenchable* (1422), and, earlier, *flame* (1351)—foreshadows
Samson's own fiery inspiration (1688–92): "An equivalence between the religious
fervour of the Philistines and that of the protagonist is momentarily revealed" that
"sharply question[s]" the imagery's "elevatory force" (*Complete Shorter Poems*
340–41). Parker ("Variorum") adds, "Dramatically the speech is necessary to
explain why it is safe for the Chorus to remain (and not empty the stage)."
    Lordliest: editors gloss as "most like their true selves," and/or "most impe-
rious, haughtiest." Parker adds, "ambiguity may be intended because of the
presence of the Officer" ("Variorum"). Cf. 1353.
    in thir wine: editors gloss as "intoxicated, in their cups." Bullough and
Bullough note that Luther (*On Psalm 59*) and others "take 'Philistines' to mean
'falling in drink.'"

1419. *well-feasted Priest:* editors note that Milton attacked the luxury of the clergy
in many places, from *Lyc* on. Cf. 857.
    then: Edmund K. Chambers suggests, "when he is well-feasted"; Percival
offers, "when he is in his cups."

1420. *zeal:* see 895n.
    aught: "in any respect" (*OED* C); editors cite the Latin *si quid.*

1421. *the people:* see Argument 17.
    Holy-days: editors gloss as "religious festivals" and suggest that Milton is
referring to the public sports in England on holy days and is implying that these

festivals are of heathen origin. They go on to discuss the Puritan opposition to the *Book of Sports* and quote Milton's opinions as expressed in, e.g., *Ref* (Patterson, *Works* 3:53) and *RCG* (Patterson, *Works* 3:239). See 1422 and cf. 1323–25.

1422. Parker notes that "with these adjectives Samson emphasizes the danger to the Chorus if it accompanies him" ("Variorum"). Peck cites this line to illustrate Milton's characteristic use of a "continuative epithet," that is, three epithets to compose a single line of verse (sig. P4r). See also 417n, 827, 1364. Keightley (*Poems*), Church, Percival, Browne, Verity, Carey (*Complete Shorter Poems*), et al. quote Horace, *Ars poetica* 224: "spectator, functusque sacris et potus et exlex"; "the spectator [at the Satyric drama], who, after observance of the rites, was well drunken and in lawless mood." Greenlaw, Osgood, and Padelford (6:309) compare *Hamlet* 1.5.77 and *The Faerie Queene* 7.7.46.5: "Unbodied, unsoul'd, unheard, unseene." Blakeney notes the "striking" effect produced, in this line, by the juxtaposition of "three sonorous words, unconnected by participles." Broadbent observes: "It is one of the less-remarked themes of *Samson Agonistes* that he is the persecuted protagonist of a culture more civilised at all levels of society than its Asian aggressors" (*Some Graver Subject* 90).

    Impetuous: "acting with or marked by great, sudden, or rash energy"; "violent" (*OED* 2).

    insolent: "offensively contemptuous" and/or "immoderate, going beyond the bounds of propriety" (*OED* 2, 3).

    unquenchable: Parker ("Variorum") glosses as "not to be suppressed or cooled down (perhaps with an implication about thirst)."

1423–26. Goldsmith (82) compares Samson's combination of ignorance and faith in this passage with Hamlet's belief in a "divinity that shapes our ends, / Rough-hew them how we will" (5.2.10–11). Flatter suggests that Milton, identifying with Samson, implied here that he himself intended to "collapse another temple," the Church of England, by having his heretical *DocCh* published posthumously (7 August, 443; 4 September, 499). Kelley (471) and Farnham-Flower (471) challenge this assertion.

1423. *Happ'n:* B. A. Wright emends to *Happen,* as the rhythm would seem to require.

1424–25. Samson reassures the Chorus about the problems expressed in 1320–21, 1338, 1357–62, 1377–79, 1385–86, 1408–9 (see Blakeney).

1425. Parker notes the repetition: "Our…our…my…my" ("Variorum").

1426. Editors paraphrase: "I cannot say for certain whether or not you will see me again" (i.e., in contrast to the assurances just given). Commentators offer slightly different interpretations of this line. To Fell, Samson's "calm, dignified statement" is "an almost casual dismissal of his own importance" and "consummates the course of rehabilitation, of complete and trustful self-sacrifice to God's design" (149, 152). Fish instead describes this line as "a tour de force of non-committalness, establishing consecutively the mutually exclusive alternatives — 'the last of me or no' — and disassociating the 'I' from the influence that will determine them" (256). See 1413–26n.

Bullough and Bullough claim that Samson exits at this line because "Greek practice did not allow bloodshed on the stage"; Verity similarly asserts "scenes of violent suffering or crime may not be enacted in the presence of the audience" (122). Arthos addresses the function of Samson's departure: this "contrivance" not only allows the audience "to imagine the extent of the destruction as beyond what could appear upon a stage" but also "allows us to think with less distraction upon the significance and consequences of this final effort, and especially since there is something mysterious about it" (182). Gohn adds, "Samson has fulfilled his mission as saint — by withstanding the temptation of his faith — before he goes to the temple. As man, however, he must offer this rational act as proof of his humanity" (267). From here to the poem's end, Ellis-Fermor finds "a gradual lowering of tension from the sublimity of Samson's final mood towards the conversational tempo of verse in the drama of everyday life" (153).

1427–40. Editors identify this as the fifth and last stasimon (see 293–325n). Parker observes that the fifth stasimon exactly balances in length Samson's final speech (*Milton's Debt* 64). Edmund K. Chambers explains that it is brief so that "the action once begun may not be delayed." Ralli thinks that in it — and 1687–1707 — "something is captured of the rhythm of the Hebrew prophets" (141); Stroup suggests that the passage "echoes both the familiar '*Ite*' of the '*Ite Missa est*' of the Mass" as well as Psalm 89, Judges 13, Malachi 1, and other biblical passages (61). Sheppard comments: "[Samson] goes, amid the prayers of the Chorus, who have not understood" (164), but Huntley detects signs of the Chorus's development: "For the first time their words amount to 'Thy will, not mine, be done,' and imply a growing trust in God's treatment of His champions" (142). Bush thinks that the Chorus, "in pronouncing a benediction" for Samson, "recall the angel who attended his birth" (*Milton* 199). Parker adds that this passage "has an element of irony, for it invokes God's guidance for Samson, unaware that the guidance has begun" ("Variorum").

    the Holy One / Of Israel: the phrase (reminiscent of Isaiah: see Broadbent, *Milton* 56) occurs also in *DDD* (Patterson, *Works* 3:371, 437); cf. *PL* 6.359, 12.248; and see 2 Kings 19:22.

1429. A twelve-syllable line (alexandrine; see 118n).
    spread: cf. *Sonn 87.*
    name: cf. 467, 475.

1430. Bridges thinks that this is one of seventeen lines of falling (trochaic) rhythm (*Milton's Prosody* 55); Sprott (132) thinks it difficult to determine whether Milton thought of the line as "trochaic with the last foot catalectic, or as iambic with the first foot catalectic." See 116n.
    Great: editors note that the adjective is proleptic: "so that it becomes great."
    among the Heathen round: the Chorus echoes Samson's early phrase about the honor he had brought Dagon (451); see also *PL* 10.579, *PR* 2.443 (Le Comte 67).

1431. *Angel:* Verity, Edmund K. Chambers, Alden Sampson (49, 216), and Hughes (*Complete Poems; John Milton*) find here the idea of a guardian angel, an idea evidently congenial to Milton (see, e.g., *PL* 2.1033; *DocCh* [Patterson, *Works* 15:99–103]). Whiting notes that Milton ignores the commentary in the Geneva Bible, which explains that the angel of Samson's birth "was Christ the eternall word" ("*Samson Agonistes*" 210). Penn in his edition of *SA* omits lines 1431–40 because he deems "Samson's history...unnecessary" (2:253); see 1–11n.
    Birth: see 1434–35n.

1432. *Fast:* "firmly" and/or "close" (*OED* 1a, 4).
    field: Judges 13:9: "and the angel of God came again unto the woman as she sat in the field."

1433. Cf. 25, 27–28.

flames: Wilkenfeld finds a foreshadowing of the poem's conclusion in the angel's prophecy: "these flames will appear at the end of the action, connecting Samson with the 'lightning glance' of the heroic saint [1284], the destruction of the Philistian temple, and most importantly, with the all-embracing emblem of the fiery phoenix [1687–91], the image of Samson's regeneration" (164).

after...told: editors gloss as "after telling his message." Verity explains, "it is an imitation of the Latin idiom in *post conditam urbem* and such-like phrases, where the participle does the duty of a noun followed by a genitive case"; see also Hunter.

1434–35. *now:* Parker ("Variorum") suggests that Milton may have intended an ironic contrast with *Birth* (1431).

shield Of fire: cf. *Mask* 657. Cf. Exodus 13:21: "And the Lord went before them...by night in a pillar of fire, to give them light" (Church; Percival); also Zechariah 2:5: "For I, saith the Lord, will be unto her [Jerusalem] a wall of fire round about" (Percival); also Psalm 84:11: "A sun and shield is the Lord God" (Parker, "Variorum").

that Spirit: cf. Judges 14:6: "And the Spirit of the Lord came mightily [Vulgate: *irruit*] upon him" (Verity).

1436–37. Either an anapest followed by an iamb (Edmund K. Chambers 129), or a line in falling (trochaic) rhythm (Bridges, *Milton's Prosody* 55–56). Sprott (132) thinks it difficult to determine whether Milton thought of the line as "trochaic with the last foot catalectic, or as iambic with the first foot catalectic." See 116n.

In the Camp of Dan: cf. Judges 13:25: "And the Spirit of the Lord began to move him at times in the camp of Dan." See 332n. Diodati (sig. L5r) identifies this with Mahaneh-dan, mentioned in Judges 18:12. Bridges proposes that the line "should have been printed with contraction *i'th* or *ith'*" (*Milton's Prosody* 117).

efficacious: Steadman ("'Faithful Champion'" 17) calls this word "especially apt, inasmuch as the 'primary efficient cause of good works...is God'" (see *DocCh* [Patterson, *Works* 17:26–27]).

1439. *seed:* "progeny" (*OED* 4); Prince suggests, "the human race" (*Samson Agonistes*).

1440. *been seen:* Darbishire calls this an "impossible collocation" and writes that *bin* is Milton's spelling and pronunciation (*Poetical Works*); B. A. Wright also makes this change. See 874n.

1441–1758. Editors identify this as the exodos. Aristotle defines the ἔξοδος as "that entire part of a tragedy which has no choric song after it" (*Poetics* 12.2). Parker notes that "this definition can be slightly misleading, because in almost all of the extant tragedies the chorus has the concluding word. Perhaps it is simpler to define the exodos as that part of the play after the last stasimon.... [T]he exodos, as in *Samson Agonistes,* sometimes includes a κομμός or dirge [1660–1758]" (*Milton's Debt* 16). Penn in his edition liberally reduces this section of the drama (e.g., omitting lines 1470–71, 1475, 1478–89, 1500–3, 1532–40); he acknowledges, though, that these cuts do not "leave much time for Samson to do what is afterwards related" (2:255); see 1–11n. Verity notes that 1441–42 are in intentional contrast with 327, 336–37 (the "e're while" referred to). He adds, "Against this last act criticism cannot hint a fault or hesitate the faintest dislike" (xlviii).

    old Manoa: see 328n. On Milton's decision to have Samson's father return, Hoffman writes, "Milton ties the drama together and relates the eternal visionary experience to the humdrum world of everyday living" (205).

1442. *With youthful steps:* Hoffman notes that Manoa's stride is here "deliberately and ironically contrasted with the lagging steps of the first scene" (205). Cf. 1520 (*Run*).

1443–44. See 543–44n. The first edition ends 1444 with a question mark; some editors (e.g., Tickell; Bohn) change it to a period.

1445. Commentators and editors note that Manoa's hopes and plans, announced just as the catastrophe nears, provide dramatic irony. Mueller argues that the entire scene (1445–1758) is "almost certainly" based on *Oedipus Tyrannus* and "should be interpreted as a little complex tragedy with Manoa as the tragic hero, Samson's death as the *pathos,* and the messenger's arrival as the *peripeteia* through *anagnorisis*" ("*Pathos*" 170). Bailey is also reminded of *Oedipus Tyrannus* (238); Collins compares Sophocles more generally (6); and Hoffman echoes Mueller in arguing that Manoa "enacts his own personal tragedy within the greater drama" (205). Gossman attributes "much of the tragic irony" in the drama's conclusion to both Manoa's "touching human tenderness" and Milton's "allowing the audience to learn of Samson's death from Manoa's point of view" ("Ransom" 14).

Peace: expression of salutation in Hebrew and Arabic form, in and after biblical use (Keightley, *Poems*).

you: the word is used only here and in 1511, 1644. See 193 (*Yee see*).

hither: Prince glosses as "what has led me here" (*Samson Agonistes*); the verb of motion is understood.

1447–48. *new parted:* editors gloss as "just departed, just gone."

come: some editors (Keightley, *Poems;* Percival; Blakeney) call this an archaism for *go.* But Parker suggests, "it may be read with 'By order of the Lords'" ("Variorum").

1449–50. *rings:* "resound[s]," "[is] filled with talk or report" (so *OED* B.I.3; cf. *Sonn* 22 12; *PL* 2.723).

I had no will: editors supply "to go to the feast."

1451. *unseemly:* Parker notes that Manoa shows no real concern over the legalistic issue that had exercised Samson and the Chorus; his mind is on practical matters (*Milton's Debt* 50–51). Bush describes Manoa's hope as "that 'false dawn' which in some Greek tragedies precedes the catastrophe" ("John Milton" 519n; *Milton*). See also 1476–84, 1490–1503.

1453. *To ... part:* Meiklejohn et al. gloss as "impart to you."

ye: "you" (*OED* 3 dates its use in the objective case from circa 1449; Parker notes that "it seems originally to have been restricted in usage to the nominative plural" ["Variorum"]). Verity and Hughes (*John Milton*) say it is dative here; Church says it is a "common but incorrect" use of the accusative.

1454. *success:* editors note that this word was neutral during the seventeenth century and generally meant "fortune" or "consequence," favorable or otherwise (*OED* 2); cf. *PL* 2.123; *PR* 4.1; and *CharLP:* "in good or bad Success" (Patterson, *Works* 18:254).

1455. Blakeney paraphrases: "to partake (share) with thee that hope would rejoice us much."

1457. *attempted:* editors gloss as "to try to move or persuade" (so *OED* 7) or "to seek to influence" (Lockwood 2.c). Although Manoa speaks as though there were more, there seem to have been only five "Lords" (Judg. 3:3), one in each of the chief cities. Of Manoa's recital, Stein observes, "the gap between Samson and the ordinary values of the world is displayed. . . . The account has an irrelevance that challenges nothing but offers a relaxed comedy of gratuitous contrast" (*Heroic Knowledge* 193). But Rudrum, while acknowledging the "ironic gap" between Manoa's efforts and Samson's final act, finds here a parallel between father and son: "we see Manoah's willingness to undergo humiliation: the account humbly mirrors Samson's willingness to play the fool at Dagon's games while he awaits God's final revelation" (61–62).

 Following Thyer (in Newton) and Masson's suggestion (*Life* 6:676; *Poetical Works*), some editors find in 1457–71 an allusion to Milton's own situation at the Restoration and to his friends' efforts to save him. In lines 1461–71 Masson detects "the different shades of feeling among the men in power in England after the Restoration" (*Poetical Works*). Verity says "possibly"; Thyer (in Newton) and Hughes (*John Milton*), "perhaps"; Wyatt and Collins, "considerable probability"; Grieve, "probable"; Bullough and Bullough, "could be paralleled"; etc. Some editors (e.g., Verity) have gone so far as to identify the first group of enemies (1461–63) with the High Church party and the second (1464–66) with Presbyterians who had joined the Royalists. Bush notes the possible contemporary allusion but adds that "such attitudes of course have appeared after any revolution" (*Poetical Works*). Parker asserts more adamantly, "To find a personal allusion here adds only confusion to the poem, and makes but an ambiguous contribution to biography"; he adds, "a small amount of dramatic invention accounts sufficiently for the lines in question" ("Variorum").

1459–60. Gossman detects in Manoa's "pathetic eloquence" a similarity to Priam's speech in *Iliad* 24.484–502 where the king must ransom his son Hector from disgrace, through the magnanimity of Achilles. This association, Gossman suggests, contributes to the scene's "dignity and beauty" ("Ransom" 15).

 supplication prone: Parker compares Ruth 2:10 for this attitude of humble entreaty ("Variorum").

prone: "bending forward," "lying face downwards," or "eager" (*OED* 1, 7).

To accept of ransom: B. A. Wright emends to *T' accept,* as a completely regular meter would require. Patterson describes as a partitive genitive construction (*Student's Milton*).

1461. For the possible allusion, see 1457n.

1463. Thyer (in Todd) thinks that Milton here alludes to his own situation after the Restoration or indulges his "inveterate spleen, which he always had against publick and established religion"; other editors, including Masson, find a specific reference to High Church Royalists (*Poetical Works*).

1464. For the alleged allusion to the Presbyterians (stemming from Dunster [in Todd] and Masson, *Poetical Works*), see 1457n.

1465–66. *Private…sale:* Percival cites Ovid, *Ars amatoria* 3.653: "Munera, crede mihi, capinunt hominesque deosque"; "Bribes, believe me, buy both gods and men." "Private reward" is presumably a bribe to an individual rather than ransom given the state; cf. 868. Parker ("Variorum") suggests that Milton may have been remembering those later judges of Israel, Samuel's sons, who "walked not in his ways, but…took bribes, and perverted judgement" (1 Sam. 8:3).

1466–70. Percival comments: "It is probable that Milton's escape was partly due to the indifferent attitude of the king himself and of Clarendon." On the alleged allusion, see 1457n. Primarily, commentators discuss these lines in relationship to readers' reactions. Tinker argues that readers "must feel nothing but satisfaction" when Israel's enemies are destroyed according to Jehovah's will: "This is the one concession which must be taken over from the ancient legend, like the mythical elements common in the plots of Greek tragedy. These are among the conditions 'given,' under which the author must work and which the reader must accept" (65). But Ricks objects: "elements of a plot are different in kind from moral judgments. There are limits to what a *donnée* in great literature can be asked to encompass, and genocide is beyond them" ("Milton" 315). Fish specifically suggests that these lines "reveal the Philistine lords to be no worse, and indeed somewhat better, than any other cross section of humanity…. In short, on the evidence—that is, on the visible and merely human evidence—they do not deserve the destruction that is about to be rained down on them.... By granting the Philistines the status of human beings, and insisting that we so acknowledge them, Milton...evidences his disinclination to allow us a comfortable perspective on Samson's action" (258–59).

1467. *generous:* "magnanimous, noble-minded" (OED 2b); Parker adds, "the meaning is not 'liberal, munificent'" ("Variorum").

    confess'd: Parker ("Variorum") notes that the normal Miltonic spelling is *confest* (1183). Cf. 266 (*possess'd*).

1468–69. *reveng'd:* the first edition has a comma after this word; Parker suggests that a colon would clarify the syntax ("Variorum").

    beneath: "unworthy of" (*OED* B.7), "to a greater degree than" (Lockwood 2.d).

1470. Some editors explain the construction: "To remit (refrain from exacting) the rest (i.e., of their revenge) would be magnanimity" ("they said" understood). See 543–44n. Other editors interpret "the rest" as the remainder of men whom Manoa petitioned so that the line would mean "the rest were so magnanimous as to remit." Verity, however, finds this reading "very awkward." Penn in his edition omits this line and the next; see 1–11n. For the syntactic inversion, cf. 1455. Milton often associates magnanimity with justice (see, e.g., Patterson, *Works* 3:341; 4:280; 5:5; 6:112).

    magnanimity: Oras cites this word as one of two in *SA* (for the other, see 1480) where an "unstressed *i* before *t* seems to undergo elision" ("Milton's Blank Verse" 170).

    remit: Parker ("Variorum") compares *Apol:* "he hopes they will remit what is yet behind" (Patterson, *Works* 3:333).

1471. *convenient:* "suitable," "appropriate" (*OED* 4b).

1472. Cf. *PL* 1.542. Verity notes also *Richard II* 3.3.56–57: "their thund'ring shock / At meeting tears the cloudy cheeks of heaven" (cf. 960–61n, 1284n). Lawry calls it a "parodic Palm Sunday shout" (394). The shout of the people when Samson enters the theater is noted again in 1620.

1474–75. *dread:* so also 342, 1622. Cf. 1673.
   proof of strength: cf. 1313–14, 1602.

1476. Percival observes that, if necessary, Manoa is resolved to give up all his wealth; therefore, Percival conjectures, "Milton does not make the work of ransoming Samson an accomplished fact." To have done so, Parker responds, "might have deepened the irony both here and in the tragedy as a whole. On the other hand, to have done so would have inspired an irrelevant sympathy with Manoa, drawing attention away from Samson" ("Variorum").

1477. *compass:* "accomplish" (*OED* IV.11); cf. *PL* 3.342.

1478. *numberd down:* "count[ed] out, [paid] down," i.e., into the hand (so *OED* 3b). Patterson has *numbered* in error (*Works*).

1479. *richest:* Milton's addition to Judges, perhaps (as Percival notes) encouraged by Josephus: "among the most notable of the Danites and without question the first in his native place" (*Antiquities of the Jews* 5.8.2). Prince suggests that by making Manoa wealthy, Milton not only enables him to play a part of some importance, but also increases "the dignity of the story" (*Samson Agonistes* 94–95).

1480. *and he…left:* editors gloss as "while he…is left." Verity calls this idiom "peculiar"; cf. 149 and *PL* 2.609.
   calamitous: Oras cites this word as one of two (for the other, see 1470) where an "unstressed *i* before *t* seems to undergo elision" ("Milton's Blank Verse" 170).

1481. *fixt:* editors gloss as "firmly resolved" (*OED* 2), and they note the irony: as Parker puts it, "Manoa spoke truth here: he did not 'part hence without him,'" for he takes away Samson's body (*Milton's Debt* 166–67). The full irony of this statement becomes evident only with Samson's final speech (1725–33).
   part hence: cf. 1229.

1482. Cf. 1486.

> *redemption:* "ransom" (so *OED* 2): but, Parker suggests, possibly also with echoes of Jewish law (Num. 18:15) and Christ's atonement ("Variorum"). See 483, 604, 1459–60n.

1483–84. *forgo:* "give up," i.e., "sacrifice" (*OED* 6).

> *quit:* "give up," "cease to enjoy" (*OED* 5).

> *not . . . nothing:* the sense: "having him (back) will be riches enough"; Hunter glosses the first phrase as a subjunctive, "If I be not without him." Hoffman hears in this line "the poignant tones of a father who loves his son too much" (206).

1485–86. *lay up . . . lay out:* Johnson (*Rambler* 20 July 1751) finds fault with this "despicable" play on words (221). But Prince notes the "gnomic concision" of these comments (*Samson Agonistes* 128); and Parker suggests that the Chorus is echoing the spirit of Manoa's "wanting him . . . want nothing"; Parker also notes a pun on *wont* ("Variorum").

1487. *wont:* "[are] wont or accustomed" (so *OED* 3).

> *nurse:* "take care of" (*OED* 3). For other references to nursing, see 633, 924.

1488. *Son:* the period after this word in the first edition is a typographical error; editors typically change it to a comma.

1489. Cf. Samson's speech, 938–43.

1490–1503. Commentators praise Manoa's speech, both as an example of dramatic irony (Edmund K. Chambers; Parker, *Milton's Debt* 51) and as a characterization of a fond parent ("particularly natural and moving," says Thyer [in Newton]). Daiches compares Manoa's growing optimism before the final tragedy with the irony in works by Shakespeare and Sophocles (246). Hedley Vicars Ross detects "a consciousness of the poet's own days . . . behind these verses" (79).

1491. *house:* Parker ("Variorum") notes, "it was during the settlement of Canaan that the Hebrews gradually gave up dwelling in tents and adopted the Canaanite custom of living in houses (Deut. 6:16[–19])"; cf. *PL* 12.333–34.

1492–93. *high exploits:* Manoa echoes Samson in 525; cf. also 32, 1221, and *PL* 2.111. Le Comte (84) also finds an echo here of *Areop* (Patterson, *Works* 4:344).

   those locks: see 586n.

1494. Editors think Milton here remembers Ovid's description of Nisus in *Metamorphoses* 8.8–10: "cui splendius ostro / inter honoratos medioque in vertice canos / crinis inhaerebat, magni fiducia regni"; "[This Nisus] had growing on his head, amidst his locks of honoured grey, a brilliant purple lock on whose preservation rested the safety of his throne." But Steadman argues that Milton cannot be referring to this myth, for to do so "would have seemed anachronistic"; the myth was generally regarded in the Renaissance as derived from the Samson story ("Samson-Nisus" 450–51). See also 58–59, 1496–97.

1495. Cf. 586: editors note that Manoa repeats his earlier thought.

   had not: Verity et al. gloss "would not have"; the second edition (1680) has *hath not,* a reading noted by Fletcher (*John Milton's Complete* 4:278) et al.

1496. This line echoes 1355 (Le Comte 45) and see 568n.

1497. Collins explains, "Samson's hair is as it were a fort of strength, the single hairs corresponding to single soldiers." He calls this "a conceit which savours more of Donne than of Greek tragedians"; Percival defends it as a metaphor "suggested naturally enough in the case of Samson, whose hair was his stronghold"; Raleigh thinks it "perhaps some faint reminiscence" of Milton's earlier comparison, in *RCG,* of Samson's hair to the strength of the law (*Milton* 51). Bullough and Bullough ask: "is there some trace here of the allegorical interpretation of Samson's hair as 'the people of the Church' (Gregory the Great), or as 'the virtuous deeds which a man does by gift of the Holy Spirit'...(Rabanus, *De Universo*)?" Parker notes that this passage is an extension of the military imagery in 235–36, 402–5, 560–61, 845–46 ("Variorum").

   Garrison'd: "furnished with or defended by a garrison," i.e., stationed for defensive purposes (so *OED* 3; cf. 1).

1498. *Souldiery:* "soldiers collectively" (*OED* 1). Milton uses the word also in *PE* (Patterson, *Works* 3:102) and *Educ* (Patterson, *Works* 4:289).

1499. Tragic irony: editors (e.g., Verity) observe that Manoa does not realize how right he is.

1500. *Not to sit idle:* Edmund K. Chambers notes, "according to strict grammatical construction, it is God, and not Samson, who is 'not to sit idle.' Milton has...shifted his thought...to a new grammatical subject; and the whole is equivalent to, 'Samson is to do some further service, and not to sit idle'" (138). Parker notes that Manoa echoes Samson's words in 566; cf. 579 ("Variorum").

1501. *Useless:* cf. *Sonn 19* 4.
    ridiculous: cf. 131, 539, 1361; see 131n. Edmund K. Chambers remembers Puritan mockery of the flowing locks of the Cavaliers.
    about: "carried by, attached to, possessed by" (Lockwood 2.g).

1502–03. Percival calls this "The logic of affection," anticipating another miracle.
    to: Blakeney et al. gloss as "in addition to, to cooperate with."

1504–07. Newton observes that the Chorus joins in the hopes for Samson's "delivery" but gently intimates that Manoa's other hopes are ill founded and vain. He adds that the Chorus, like Manoa, is most optimistic just before the catastrophe so as to render the sudden change "more striking and affecting." See 1508n.
    ill founded: hyphen omitted apparently in error in the first edition; cf. 122 (*ill-fitted*) and 1195 (*ill-meaning*).
    thereon...love: Parker glosses as "conceived on the basis of your hopes, befitting a father's love" ("Variorum").

1506. *Conceiv'd:* Parker suggests that Milton is deliberately punning on this word and *delivery* ("Variorum"); cf. 390. The punning continues in 1574–76.
    agreeable to: editors gloss as "suitable to," or "corresponding to."

1507. *we:* B. A. Wright emends to *wee.*
    next: "nearest [after yourself] in respect of kinship, intimacy" (*OED* 12); "next in interest" (Masson, *Poetical Works*). Editors note that the Chorus, Danites like Samson, are his friends and neighbors; cf. 180, 187.

1508. Thyer (in Newton) praises Milton's art in this abrupt transition from Manoa's growing optimism, encouraged by the Chorus, to feelings of horror and mounting suspense. Gilbert notices that the noise of the catastrophe is not mentioned in the Argument ("Is *Samson Agonistes*" 98–99; see Argument 24–35n). Edmundson compares this passage with a similar description in Vondel's *Samson* (187–88); on Vondel, see 115–75n. On the line's rhythm and punctuation, see 205n.

1509. *Mercy:* cf. *Mask* 694. The first edition ends this line with an exclamation point; some editors change it to a question mark and insert an exclamation point after *Heaven*. Bohn inserts a comma after *Heaven* and omits the end punctuation.

1510. *former shout:* in 1472.

1511. *you:* one might expect *thou;* see 1445n s.v. *you.* Lawry writes, "Good Friday is again intimated" (393); see 41n.

1512. *inhabitation:* "population" (so *OED* 3). Browne, Church, and Collins, following Richardson (in Newton), think Milton means οἰκουμένη; "the inhabited world." Blakeney and Grieve comment, "abstract for concrete." In the first edition, this line ends with a comma; some editors change it to a question mark; Fenton changes it to an exclamation point; Shawcross (*Complete English Poetry*) changes it to a semicolon.

1513. *death:* "slaughter" (*OED* 6). Todd notes a resemblance to the reply of the chorus in Euripides' *Electra* 752: οὐκ οἶδα πλὴν ἕν, φόνιον οἰμωγὴν κλύω; "I know but this, I hear a cry of death."

1514. *Ruin:* see 1267 and 1515–20n.
        at: "(of degree) up to" (Parker, "Variorum").

1515–20. Parker notes the symmetry of these three successive two-line speeches (*Milton's Debt* 64).
        ruin: editors gloss as "the falling or crashing down of a building" (see *OED* 1). Some editors (e.g., Wyatt and Collins) note the word can also mean "that

which causes destruction" (*OED* 8), perhaps its meaning in 1514, made more literal (Latin *ruina*) by Manoa. Editors cite *PL* 6.868; see also 1267 and 1514. Peck notes that Milton "partly *melts* & partly *cuts* off the latter syllable of the word *ruin*, by the first syllable of the word *indeed*" (sig. O4v).

1517. A twelve-syllable line (alexandrine) without any break (Bridges, *Milton's Prosody* 61).

1518. *ascend:* cf. *PL* 1.499.

1519. *dismal accident:* "dreadful disaster" (*OED* s.v. *dismal* 4; s.v. *accident* I.1c); Percival has a long note on *dismal* meaning " 'disastrous' in a stronger sense than its modern one of 'gloomy.'" Commentators disagree about Milton's use of rhyming here. Jerram thinks the couplets "surely in questionable taste"; Prince (*Samson Agonistes*) thinks the couplets "convey the excitement of the moment" (see also Beum 179). Cf. 1525–26n.

1520–22. Hughes writes, "So, in moments of crisis Euripides's choruses [e.g., *Hippolytus* 782–85] question what to do" (*Complete Poems; John Milton*). Following ancient practice, Milton gives a reason for the Chorus continuing on the stage (Joseph Warton [in Todd]). Edmund K. Chambers notes, "the Greek Chorus is always timorous in presence of danger"; see 1716.
   dangers mouth: cf. "Mouth of death" in *Richard III* 4.4.2. (Verity). Watkins detects here the "primitive fear of being eaten" (18).

1525–26. Masson (*Poetical Works*) wonders whether the rhyming here is intentional. See 1010–60n, 1519n.

1527–35, 1537. In the text of the first edition, these ten lines were omitted and 1536 was given to the Chorus instead of to Manoa. The corrections—or additions—were made in the *Omissa*. Although an amanuensis or compositor may have been responsible for the omissions, the transfer of line 1536 to Manoa suggests that Milton added these lines at the last minute. Verity believes this latter explanation is "more probable." Masson (*Poetical Works*) finds the ten additional lines "certainly an improvement" and suggests that Milton may have written them "so as to prolong the suspense before the messenger arrives." Noticing that in their excitement Manoa and the Chorus now reverse their previous positions—the Chorus entertaining a hope that Samson's eyesight has been miraculously restored, Manoa doubting—Newton writes: "Such changes of our thoughts are natural and common, especially in any change of our situation and circumstances. Fear and hope usually succeed each other like ague and fever. And it was not a slight observation of mankind, that could have enabled Milton to have understood and describ'd the human passions so exactly." Kaufmann, however, criticizes this passage: "What is tragic here save the narrowing of a great, though always partisan intellect, to joyous fantasies of treading on broken bodies?" (378). Percival points out that in describing an outburst of wild hope before the catastrophe, Milton is imitating Sophocles: *Ajax* 693–704; *Antigone* 1115–51; *Oedipus Rex* 1086–1109; *Women of Trachis* 205–23. See also 1532–33n.

1528. Kermode (62) identifies an imperfect rhyme in 1527–28; see 110–14n.
    miracle: Parker ("Variorum") notes that such a miracle was performed by Augustine, according to *HistBr* (Patterson, *Works* 10:147).

1529. *dealing:* "giv[ing] forth," "deliver[ing]" (*OED* 6c).
    dole: editors gloss as "grief, sorrow" (*OED* 1; cf. *PL* 4.894). Many editors—e.g., Browne, Church, Masson (*Poetical Works*), Percival, Wyatt and Collins, Grieve, Prince (*Samson Agonistes*), Hughes (*Complete Poems; John Milton*), Shawcross (*Complete English Poetry*)—see a pun here (see 1118n), with *dole* also meaning (so *OED* 5b) "distribution, delivery (of blows)," in which case Milton would be saying "deal a dealing"—a phrase Verity thinks "not...very felicitous." Cf. *Apol:* "who made you the busie Almoner to deal about this dole of laughter and reprehension...?" (Patterson, *Works* 3:318). Editors cite examples of both senses of *dole.* Todd notes that the expression "deale his balefull dole" occurs, among other places, in William Warner's *Albions England* (1602 ed.) and Robert Tofte's translation of Boiardo's *Orlando innamorato* (1598). *OED* cites other examples. Percival notes a punning use of *dole* (without *deal,* however) in Nicholas Udall's *Ralph Roister Doister* (1566?). Bullough and Bullough call "dealing dole" a "favourite phrase about heroes in romances." Greenlaw, Osgood, and Padelford (4:191) note that the idea (not the phrase) occurs in *The Faerie Queene* 4.4.32.4. About the grammar, Hunter observes that a verb governs a cognate noun.

1530. Todd cites *The Faerie Queene* 5.7.36: "the heapes, which he did make, / Of slaughtred carkasses." Edmund K. Chambers finds irony in the hope expressed here: "the Chorus realize their triumph before they realize their calamity."

1532–33. On God's ability to have "wrought things as incredible," Parker ("Variorum") recalls Elisha, aided by God, striking blind and restoring sight (2 Kings 6:18–20). An unsigned entry in a Sotheby auctioneer's catalog from 1866 reports the sale of a manuscript where these lines are changed to read, "For God of old hath for His people wrought / Things as incredible; what hinders now?"; the catalog suggests the lines "may be in the handwriting of the poet," and, it should be noted, they are among the lines added as part of the *Omissa* ("Milton's *Samson Agonistes*" 332). The emendation would remove the difficulty about reading 1533: e.g., Lockwood accents the second syllable of *people*. Sprott (132) and Bridges (*Milton's Prosody* 56) describe the first two feet of 1533 as trochaic.

1534–35. *doubt:* "hesitate" (*OED* I.3). Hoffman comments, "Manoa sees for the first time the distinction between divine power and divine will" (207).
    fain subscribe: "gladly" (*OED* B) "support" (Prince, *Samson Agonistes;* et al.).

1536. See 1527–35n. Calton (in Todd) argues that this line should be given to the Chorus (as in the 1671 text as printed) rather than Manoa (as the *Omissa* direct), and that Manoa should be given most of 1537–38: "Of bad the sooner! / For evil news rides post, while good news bates."
    notice: "information" (so *OED* 1).

1537. See 1527–35n. The reference is to the "notice" that will come of Samson's death *or* triumph. Percival writes, "The stiffness of the construction" is due to the fact that the line is an afterthought." Low suggests that the Chorus posits a false alternative, for the Messenger will bring both good *and* bad news: that Samson has defeated the Philistines, and that Samson is dead ("Action" 516). For this type of irony, see 1389n.

1538. Johnson (*Rambler* 20 July 1751) objects to these remarks by the Chorus as lacking "elevation" (221). Banks identifies this as one of only a few images in Milton's writings that "actually visualize riding" (72).

news: here singular, as in *PR* 1.64; but cf. 1569.

post: adverb; "With speed" (*OED*).

baits: "make[s] a brief stay" as at an inn for refreshment (so *OED* 7b); thus editors gloss as "travels slowly" or "dawdles." Cf. *PL* 12.1. Carey (*Complete Shorter Poems*) cites the proverb from Tilley (N147), "Ill news flies faster than good"; Verity and Hughes (*Complete Poems; John Milton*) trace the expression to the practice of stopping to feed horses during a journey; Todd cites Statius, *Thebaid* 9.33–34: "Fama per Aonium rapido vaga murmure campum spargitur in tumas solito pernicior index / cum lugenda refert"; "Fame, traveling in swift rumours about the Aonian Plain, is spread from troop to troop, a more rapid messenger than of wont when her tidings are evil."

1539. *to our wish:* Blakeney paraphrases: "in accordance with our wish, in answer to"; Parker suggests that this is ironically ambiguous in view of what has just been said about bad news ("Variorum").

1540. *Ebrew:* Percival writes, "A Hebrew is with propriety made the messenger.... [E]ven if truthful, [a Philistine] would lack that feeling with which the Hebrew tells the story." On the spelling, see 1308n.

guess: "judge, suppose" (*OED* 4).

1541–1659. Editors and commentators compare these lines to the introduction and exclamation of messengers in Aeschylus's *Persians* (Todd) and Euripides' *Hippolytus* (Todd) and *Phoenician Women* (Hughes, *Complete Poems; John Milton*). Timberlake says, more generally, that the Messenger's "distracted incoherence" is "characteristically Euripidean" (338); Moody writes that here "Milton has caught, perhaps more completely than anywhere else, the very form and pressure of Sophoclean dialogue" (285). Hanford observes: "Milton never breaks into the natural dramatic expression of the Elizabethans, as he sometimes does in *Comus*. The more exciting passages [e.g., 1539–70]... are phrased in the artificial Greek manner" (*Poems* 551). Arthos notes that the use of the Messenger establishes "the relevance of that which happens away from the stage to that which we actually see, and by extension relat[es] the life the play tells of to life outside the theatre.... Manoa and the Chorus and ourselves become one, one imaginary onlooker.... The events of the play thus seem to merge with the life we ourselves are living" (182). Grenander also compliments this device: "the

Hebrew messenger's narration of the catastrophe dignifies it and concentrates attention on its dramatic significance, rather than on its sensational aspects" (388). Percival writes that the Messenger's "first utterances are most skillfully managed by Milton so as to revive Manoah's hopes once again, before [in 1570] they are dashed for ever…, whereas the calmer Chorus never speaks until they have heard all the messenger has to say." J. C. Smith points out that the thickest cluster of unstressed endings in Milton's three major poems occurs in this dialogue (1541–95), in contrast to their rarity in *SA* as a whole: "We may fairly conclude that Milton uses this type of verse deliberately to express agitation" (1016). See 172n. Cf. also *PL* 1.38.

1541. *flie:* "flee," "run away from" (*OED* 11). Cf. Argument 25: "an Ebrew comes in haste confusedly at first."

1542–43. *horrid:* editors gloss as "dreadful"; see 501n.
    earst: "not long ago" (so *OED* 5b); so also 339 and *PL* 6.187, 308.
    behold: a semicolon follows this word in the first edition; some editors prefer a question mark, which was first used in the 1688 edition.

1544. *pursues:* Parker explains, "implying that he vainly wishes to escape the results of his reproductive imagination" ("Variorum"); cf. *PL* 10.783. The first edition reads *persues;* the second edition reads *pursues;* Darbishire (*Poetical Works*) and B. A. Wright believe that *persues* is Milton's spelling; cf. 1275n.

1545. This line may offer difficulty in scanning; see 122n. Percival suggests reading *providence* as a disyllable, "in-stinct'" with its Latin accent.
    instinct of nature: Milton uses this phrase in *RCG* (Patterson, *Works* 3:237); *Apol* (Patterson, *Works* 3:30); *DDD* (Patterson, *Works* 3:500). See 526.

1546. Low suggests that the Messenger posits another of *SA*'s false alternatives: "the reader knows that the hidden workings of providence and the promptings of right reason are the same" ("Action" 515). For this type of irony, see 1389n.

1548. *reverend:* so also 326, 1456.

1549. *knew remaining:* editors call this a Latin (Edmund K. Chambers) or Greek (Percival; Meiklejohn; Verity; Wyatt and Collins; Grieve) construction. Cf. 840n.

1550–51. *As…So:* some editors (Percival; Wyatt) suggest the Latinism *tum…quum:* "although (if)…yet." Edmund K. Chambers instead suggests "both…and," which he admits offers no real antithesis; Verity and Grieve suggest that *so* implies a concern proportionate to distance from the event. Cf. *OED* s.v. *as* B.II.7c.

> *event:* see 737, 1756; Le Comte (174) compares *PL* 4.716.
> *too much:* Parker notes this may mean "intolerably" (cf. *OED* 5b) or *too* may simply mean "also" ("Variorum").

1552–95. Parker writes, "Manoa's eagerness and dogged hope fill this incident with moving pathos" (*Milton's Debt* 51).

1552–53. *accident:* cf. 1519.

> *here…hear:* a play on words. The text of the first edition had *heard* for *here*, but a correction was made in the *Errata* to *here*. (This correction is missing in the second edition.) Editors note that "reached here" is implied.
> *rueful:* "expressive of sorrow" (so *OED* 1b).
> *cry:* cf. 1517, 1524.

1554. *needs:* editors gloss as "is necessary" (*OED* 3); so also *PL* 11.251. Blakeney compares the impersonal construction in *PL* 4.235.

1555–95. Hoffman suggests that the dialogue between Manoa and the Messenger "delineates Manoa's purgative movement toward the light of all-encompassing truth. For the Messenger's answers to Manoa's agitated questions are all in the half-truths so characteristic of Manoa himself" (207).

1556. *distract:* "confused in mind by having the thoughts drawn in different directions" (so *OED* 3); cf. 1286.

1557. *sum:* most editors gloss as "upshot, conclusion" (*OED* 12); Blakeney suggests "essence, epitome" (*OED* 9a).

> *circumstance:* "details" (so *OED* III.9a).

1560–64. *Sad:* Manoa uses the Messenger's word (1551); a comma follows this word in the first edition; some editors (e.g., Masson, *Poetical Works;* William

Aldis Wright) change it to an exclamation point. Finding in *SA* "a settled ferocity," Tillyard remarks on the "cool, ironical gloating of Manoa's answers" (*Milton* 283).

1562. Editors cite *Two Gentlemen of Verona* 3.1.219–20: "O, I have fed upon this woe already, / And now excess of it will make me surfeit." See also Thaler ("Shakespeare and Milton" 95). And see 1708–17. Todd finds the idea of feeding on grief or woe in Petrarch, Sonnet 104: *Pascomi di dolor;* in the comedy *The Rare Triumphs of Love and Fortune* (1589): "there feed upon thy woe"; and in Thomas Carew's "To the Countess of Anglesey" (line 23): "Yet since you surfeit on your Grief." Cf. also *PL* 3.3.7.

1563. Blakeney paraphrases: "relate to (us) by whom (the city was overwhelmed)."

1565. *Ah:* the sole use of this exclamation in the poem; cf. *PL* 4.42, 366; 10.822. Joseph Warton (in Todd) suggests, "The reader cannot fail to observe, and to feel, the art of the poet in very gradually unfolding the catastrophe." Editors explain the construction: "I refrain from uttering too suddenly."
   suddenly: "without preparation" (Lockwood); cf. *OED* 4a.

1567. *evil tidings:* cf. 1538.
   irruption: "bursting or breaking in" (*OED*). Parker ("Variorum") thinks this may be a pun on *ear* (1568).

1568. *aged:* pronounce with two syllables (Parker, "Notes" 691).

1569. *news:* here plural (unless the antecedent of *them* is *tidings*); cf. 1538 and *PR* 1.64.

1570. For the stark, affecting brevity of this announcement, Milton had possible models in Jesus' statement about Lazarus (John 11:14, cited by Blakeney), Homer's *Iliad* 18.20: κεῖται Πάτροκλος; "low lies Patroklos" (cited by Todd and Church), and Sophocles' *Electra* 673 (Todd) and *Oedipus Rex* 1234–35 (Mueller, "*Pathos*" 170–72). Mueller further notes that the line may be thought of as marking a peripeteia for Manoa, whose tragedy the play has, by now, also become (172).

take: "receive information of, to hear" (so *OED* 34c).

1571. *indeed:* a comma follows this word in the first edition; some editors (e.g., Fenton) change it to an exclamation point; Bohn alters it to a colon.

hope's: so the first and second editions; but, beginning with Fenton, some editors emend to *hopes.* Cf., however, the use of the apostrophe in 997, 1350.

defeated: "cause[d] to fail, frustrate[d]" (*OED* 5); so also 1278. Edmund K. Chambers writes, "As Manoa has been unduly exultant, so now he is unduly depressed. There is a harmonious rise and fall of emotion throughout this scene." Parker adds that Manoa thinks first of the frustration of his personal hopes (*Milton's Debt* 51).

1572. Blakeney here compares the concluding paragraphs of Walter Raleigh's *History of the World* (1614).

sets all free: cf. 1412 (and 317). Samuel hears in this line (and lines 102, 155–59) an echo of Plato's dualistic view that the soul is imprisoned in the body and only released through death: "apparently even after he [Milton] had discarded the belief that the body and soul are separate entities, he could make dramatic use of it" (158). Robertson instead finds in this language a resolution for the metaphor of the body as a tomb; he explains somewhat cryptically that "In the death of Samson's body of death, as in the death of Christ, is the death of death" (331).

1573. McCall observes, "even at this instant of greatest crisis Manoa continues to think first in terms of payment and ransom and yet, for the first time, to think of them apart from a strictly financial sense" (83). This metaphor is followed by one of childbirth and then by a figure of a flower killed in winter. Parker comments, "the successive imagery of 1572–79 blends the imagery of the Petrarchan, metaphysical, and Cavalier traditions of English poetry" ("Variorum").

ransom: Verity notes that here Milton emphasizes the irony that death has done what Manoa intended to accomplish for his son; see Manoa's earlier uses of *ransom* in 483, 604, 1460.

discharge: "liberation" (so *OED* 4d); cf. *Ps 88* 17.

1574. *windy:* "empty," "vain" (*OED* II.5); "fleeting, unsubstantial, empty" (Lockwood); and/or, in view of the metaphor that follows, "unproductive" (Percival; Verity). Collins finds the Homeric epithet ἀνεμώλιος "more probably" relevant, but Percival urges the double meaning and traces the idea to Plato's *Theactetus* 151 and Aristotle's *Historia animalium* 6.2, 10. Verity notes that the metaphor had already been introduced by the Chorus (1504–6); Manoa echoes it and caps it with *Abortive* (1576) and *first-born* (1576). Cf. *wind-egg*, "an unfertile egg," as in *Colas* (Patterson, *Works* 4:237) and *Eikon* (Patterson, *Works* 5:185). Cf. also *Apol:* "windy ceremonies" (Patterson, *Works* 3:345).

    conceiv'd: see 390n, 1506n.

1575. *Delivery:* a pun (see Percival; Verity); see 1506n.

1576–77. *bloom:* "blossom or flower," or "flowers" (*OED* 1). The metaphor again changes; see 1573n. The much admired "Shakespearean" quality of these lines—sounding, "perhaps, the very last authentic note of Elizabethan poetry" (Blakeney), and "much more like early Shakespeare than the latest Milton" (Tillyard, *Milton* 293)—has led editors to *Love's Labour's Lost* 1.1.100–1: "Berowne is like an envious sneaping frost / That bites the first-born infants of the spring"; *Henry VIII* 3.2.353–58: "to-morrow blossoms / ... The third day comes a frost, a killing frost, / And ... nips his root, / And then he falls"; and *Titus Andronicus* 4.4.70–71: "These tidings nip me; and I hang the head / As flowers with frost" (cf. 1066n). Cf. also *FInf* 1–4; *EpWin* 35–36. On *first-born*, cf. 391; on *lagging*, cf. 337. Banks associates this image, conveying "the dashing of a brief hope," with the death of Lycidas (106). Thyer (in Newton and in Todd): "One cannot possibly imagine a more exact and perfect image of the dawning hope ... and its being so suddenly extinguished by this return of ill fortune." But Brydges comments: "I think this comparison, though poetical in itself, is out of place, as coming from Manoah in his state of distraction."

    frost: a period follows this word in the first edition; some editors (e.g., Newton) change it to an exclamation point; Tickell changes it to a question mark.

1578. Manoa, significantly, does *not* give way to grief; in 1708–24 he explains why.

    rains: see 302n. Ricks complains that this phrase is a dead metaphor into which Milton should have breathed some life (*Milton's Grand Style* 54).

1579. *crown:* "honourable distinction or reward" (*OED* 1b); also "consummation, completion, or perfection" (*OED* 33); Lockwood suggests "that which adorns as a crown, chief ornament" (1.c). Cf. 175, 1296. Buchanan cites eight examples of this sentiment from Italian drama (352–53); Parker compares *corona agonistica:* "a crown of martyrdom" ("Variorum"). Thaler detects in this and the following nine lines a parallel with Siward's reaction to his son's death in *Macbeth* 5.8.46–50 ("Shakespeare and Milton" 88). See also 1708–17.

1580. *he:* Darbishire emends to *hee* (*Poetical Works*); B. A. Wright does not make this change; see 219–20n s.v. *Mee.* A comma follows this word in the first edition; some editors (e.g., Fenton; Bohn; Verity; William Aldis Wright; et al.) change it to a question mark.

1581. *glorious:* Parker ("Variorum") notes that the meaning may be "eager for glory" or "entitled to renown, possessing glory" (*OED* 2, 3a).
   deaths wound: the expression occurs also in *PL* 3.252, 12.392 (Le Comte 174) and *HistBr* (Patterson, *Works* 10:136).

1582. *of:* editors gloss as "by."

1583–85. On these lines' rhythm and punctuation, see 205n.
   self-violence: euphemism for *self-murder* (so *OED,* which cites this as its earliest example). Carey argues that this final act "rounds off an almost unwavering self-absorption on Samson's part, which makes the chorus's confidence that self-love is a womanly failing (1031) rebound upon them ludicrously" (*John Milton* 140).
   at variance with himself: "in a state of discord" (so *OED* 8b), a euphemism for *suicide* (Blakeney). Verity instead suggests, "what brought him among his foes so soon after his refusal to go."

1586–89. Gossman argues that here Milton "is careful to indicate" that Samson's death was "not suicide, but heroic martyrdom" ("Samson, Job" 218); however, Empson disagrees: "the Messenger hardly does more than report the facts" (*Milton's God* 212). With this "both…and" statement, Low suggests, the play's various contradictions are finally reconciled: "Milton presents a whole series of difficulties and conflicting alternatives before the catastrophe, then solves them with a stroke of action that is calculated to reveal the simplifying and resolving power of God's providence" ("Action" 516). See 1389n.

    Inevitable: cf. 1657.

1590–95. Keightley (*Poems*) suggests that this speech "probably belongs" to the Chorus (e.g., the use of "*we* know" [1592]); Verity explains the plural pronoun as Manoa speaking for both the Chorus and himself. Cf. 1520, 1553–54, 1557, where Manoa also uses *we.*

1590. To Percival, Hunter, and Blakeney this line implies "in the beginning over-weak against thyself"; Verity sees the emphasis on *thyself,* i.e., "till then it had always been Samson's enemies who had suffered from his superhuman strength."

    lastly: editors gloss as "at the end, ultimately" (*OED* 1).

1591. *revenge:* Roston emphasizes the differences between Samson's death and Christ's crucifixion, noting in particular that Milton's Samson personally seeks vengeance as he destroys the theater. Roston argues that Milton's familiarity with rabbinical writings "deepened the sense of identity he felt" with the poem's Old Testament characters, which, Roston believes, also reflects the "distinctly philosemitic tendencies" of political and religious culture in seventeenth-century England (156–57, 160).

1592. *we know:* see 1590–95n.

1594. *Eye-witness:* "a report," "the result of actual observation" (so *OED* 3 and Lockwood). But Church, Masson (*Poetical Works*), Percival, et al. read "one who has seen a thing done" (*OED* 2), with the line in apposition to *thou.*

    first or last: the phrase occurs also in *PL* 9.170 (Parker, "Variorum").

1595. *Relation:* editors gloss as "account, report."

1596–1659. *Occasions:* "affairs, business" (*OED* II.6). Parker observes that this is the longest speech in the play (sixty-four lines): "in the tragedies of Euripides there

are eleven speeches by messengers which average ninety-three lines in length"
(*Milton's Debt* 9). For Verity, "There are, perhaps, few pieces of more essentially
Sophoclean narrative in English" — "with its refrain of the old, unhappy, far-off
things of the *Electra* or *Oedipus at Colonus*" (xlii, xlix). Stein writes, "Milton has
constructed the scene so that it can stand alone, independent and complete. If it
had been published separately, or had been discovered in manuscript, we should
regard it as an extraordinarily successful dramatic poem" (*Heroic Knowledge*
194–95). Thyer (in Newton) also compliments this speech: "It is circumstantial,
as the importance of it requir'd, but not so as to be tedious or too long to delay
our expectation. It would be found difficult…to retrench one article without
making it defective, or to add one which should not appear redundant.… [T]he
poetry rises as the subject becomes more interesting.… [T]he poet seems to
exert no less force of genius in describing than Samson does strength of body
in executing." Rudrum discusses the "natural progression" of the Messenger's
evolving perspective: "The movement of the Messenger's account beautifully
exemplifies the way in which the individual ego is transcended in face of the
high tragic event" (63). To Macaulay, however, this is a "rather flat narration
of a diffuse and wordy messenger with little dramatic sense" (134).

1597–98. Cf. other references to "popular noise" (16) and the "popular feast"
and "Great pomp" (435, 436). Cf. also *PL* 6.526.
    Sun-rise: Verity notes that this description and "with day-spring born" (11)
establish when the drama begins.

1599. *little:* editors supply "of my business."
    dispatch'd: "[got] done," "dispose[d] of" (*OED* 5a).

1600. Mueller notes an inconsistency: the Messenger suggests here that Samson's
appearance at the festival was planned in advance, whereas other references imply
that he was summoned on a whim (1314, 1343, 1675–79). Mueller reconciles
the two accounts by suggesting that "God had decided on this sign long before
Samson was ready" ("*Pathos*" 158–59).

1601. Sprott (132) suggests that the first two feet are inverted (trochaic; see
81n).

1602. *Proof...strength:* cf. 1313–14, 1475.

1603. *minded:* "purpose[d], intend[ed]" (so *OED* 6b). Parker comments, "In just such simple fashion are puppets transformed into people" (*Milton's Debt* 137).

1604. *at:* the word is substituted for *from* (by synesis) because "Not to be absent" means the same as "to be present" (Percival).

    spectacle: Oras notes this and other pyrrhic endings in the speech reporting Samson's death, perhaps intended to enhance the passage's "slow stateliness" ("Milton's Blank Verse" 189). He adds that the effect "is sober and carries no suggestion of Milton's youthful manner," and thus does not support *SA*'s early composition. See also 1605, 1612, 1614, as well as the pyrrhic endings in Dalila's speech, 770–808n.

1605–10. Cf. Judges 16:27–30: "Now the house was full of men and women; and all the lords of the Philistines were there; and there were upon the roof about three thousand men and women, that beheld while Samson took hold of the two middle pillars upon which the house stood, and on which it was borne up.... And he bowed himself with all his might; and the house fell upon the lords, and upon all the people that were therein." Editors and commentators discuss how Milton changes this account: he makes the building an amphitheater seating the lords and other persons of rank, with the common people standing safely outside. Following Verity (xxx, 130), some editors (e.g., Grieve vii) try to explain Milton's deviation from Scripture by inferring a debt to the account of the supposed "theater of Sampson" described in detail by Sandys in *A Relation of a Journey* (sig. O3r). Verity (xxx–xxxi) notes that the idea certainly did not come from Francis Quarles's *Historie of Samson* (1631), where the scene is a "common Hall" (sig. S4v). Krouse (opposite 68) instead reproduces Arias Montanus's design of the temple in *De varia republica* (Antwerp, 1592) and explains that this, like Milton's "unlovely expository passage," was an attempt to show how it was possible for Samson to destroy the entire structure (and, in *SA,* to account for the survival of an eyewitness): "It reflects also a tendency to explain the marvelous which is characteristic of rationalistic exegesis" (90). Newton finds Milton's exposition helpful and adduces examples "of far more large and capacious buildings than this, that have been supported only by one pillar." Martin W. Sampson terms the comments of some of his fellow editors "wasted erudition," because Milton is not trying to follow descriptions of any ancient buildings but is simply trying "to bring before the eye a building that might architecturally comply with the needs of the situation." The description, he says, "is its own ample warrant; it needs no inner meaning." Masson (*Poetical Works;* and Verity) describes the theater in some detail: "There is a large semicircular *covered* space or amphitheater, filled up with tiers of seats; the roof of which semicircular building is supported by two great pillars rising from the ground about mid-point of the diameter of the semicircle. There is no *wall* at this diameter, but only these two pillars; standing near which Samson would look *inside* upon the congregated Philistine lords and others of rank, occupying the tiers of seats under the roof. *Behind* Samson was then an uncovered space where the poorer spectators could stand on any kind of benches under the open sky, seeing Samson's back, and, save where the pillars might interrupt the view, all that went on inside." See also 1634n.

1606. *Half round:* Percival and Blakeney note that the shape of a Roman theater was a semicircle; that of Greek theater was a segment larger.

> *main:* see 1634.

> *vaulted:* "construct[ed] with . . . a vault or arched roof" (*OED* 2, 1); see 1634n. Probably because there is no mention of the arch in the Hebrew Bible (the translation *arches* in Ezekiel 40:16 is incorrect), Landor calls Milton's expression an anachronism (5:302); but Percival, noting that "arches were known in ancient Egypt," raises the possibility that "Jews *may* have introduced the arch from Egypt into Canaan."

1607–08. *degree / Of sort:* "stage or position" (*OED* 4) of social "rank, class" (so *OED* 15), as enumerated in 1653; "mark, distinction" (Masson, *Poetical Works*).

> *in order:* "in proper rank" (Prince, *Samson Agonistes*) or "with purpose" (Parker, "Variorum"); see also 1694.

> *behold:* editors substitute a period or semicolon for the comma in the first edition.

1609. *other side:* editors supply "of the arena."

> *op'n:* B. A. Wright emends to *open,* as the meter would seem to require; see also Parker ("Notes" 693).

1610. *banks:* editors gloss as "benches."
    scaffolds: "raised platform[s] or stand[s]" (so *OED* 5).

1611. *obscurely:* "inconspicuously" (*OED* 3). Percival explains that, as a Hebrew, he did not wish to attract attention. Cf. 1631.

1612. *grew high:* Wyatt and Collins identify here "a rather daring zeugma": "grew high" can modify *Feast* and *noon*—that is, "the feast neared its height (of merriment) and the day neared full noon." Wilkenfeld, noting the connection with the poem's opening reference to "blaze of noon," argues that the "conjunction" between these two lines reveals "how swiftly Samson meets his doom" and "marks Samson's transformation as a mythical event by obliterating temporal distinctions" (165). Sadler instead interprets such temporal references according to the typology of the "Scriptural-temporal sequence" (199), which puts Christ's crucifixion at noon and revelation at midnight: Dagon's noontime feast accordingly "parodies the supper of the Lamb of Revelation.... Christ meets doubt at the noon of the Crucifixion and is simultaneously exalted; Samson's noontime despair mingles with the consolation of Revelation" (203). Cf. 80–109n. Broadbent, however, describes Samson's destruction as "the self-punitive revenge of personal phantasy" and writes that the Chorus's lines, representing Samson's final act "as a type of crucifixion, a justification of the ways of God to men, seem false" (*Some Graver Subject* 284).

1613. *hearts:* cf. 1669 and Judges 16:25: "And it came to pass, when their hearts were merry, that they said, Call for Samson." Parker ("Variorum") compares Josephus, who writes: "Samson at their summons was led to the banquet, that they might mock at him over their cups" (*Antiquities of the Jews* 5.8.12).
    high chear: "cheerfulness, gladness, high spirits" (Lockwood), or "godly entertainment" (Percival), or, in view of the mention of wine, "food rich in flavor or quality" (Parker, "Variorum"; *OED* 5). Cf. 545, 926.

1614–19. Sellin observes that Milton invents this description of Samson's entrance (it is not included in any of the biblical versions) but "in his choice of detail, Milton indicates clearly that he is presenting to us the passive Samson of the Alexandrine codex and the Geneva Bible" ("Milton's Epithet" 149).

1616. *Livery:* "distinctive badge or suit worn by a servant or official" (so *OED* 2); cf. 1317–18. Verity adds that Milton "often uses it of any kind of clothes"; e.g., *L'All* 62; *PL* 4.599. Sellin suggests that this detail "is a wonderful touch for indicating the vindictiveness of the Philistine taunting" ("Milton's Epithet" 149–50).

1617. *Timbrels:* "musical instrument[s] of percussion," "tambourine[s] or the like" (*OED;* Prince, *Samson Agonistes*).

    armed: presumably to be pronounced with two syllables (as in 1190; Oras, *Blank Verse* 15; "Milton's Blank Verse" 176). See 1190n.

1618. *horse:* "horse soldiers" (*OED* 3b). For the phrase, Le Comte (174) compares *PL* 11.645.

    before him: Parker notes there is a problem about punctuating this line so that its sense becomes clear: a comma could be placed after *foot,* after *him,* or after *behind* ("Notes" 698). See 543–44n.

1619. *Archers:* "bow[men]" (*OED* 1); cf. *PR* 3.330. Todd notices that the invention of the bow and arrow has been ascribed to the Philistines.

    Slingers: "soldier[s] armed with...sling[s]" (so *OED* 1).

    Cataphracts: "soldier[s] in full armour" (so *OED* 2). Editors and Lockwood emphasize that these are mounted soldiers whose horses also wear heavy armor; Todd quotes from William Lisle's translation of Heliodorus's *Faire Æthiopian* (1631), which also lists archers, slings, and cataphracts. Peck cites this word to support his claim that Milton "naturalizes many *Greek* words" (sig. O3v); see also 1324–25n s.v. *Gymnic.*

    Spears: "spear[men]" (*OED* 4).

1620–21. Cf. 1472.

1621. *Rifted:* "split," "rent apart" (so *OED* 2).

    clamouring: "disturb with clamour; to din" (so *OED* 3a), "to salute noisily" (Lockwood). Percival adds, "the word is used contemptuously."

1622. *thrall:* see 370.

1623. *He:* Darbishire emends to *Hee* (*Poetical Works*); B. A. Wright does not make this change; see 219–20n s.v. *Mee.*

    patient: Stein writes, "Here finally the ridicule is faced and mastered in a total victory of patience" (*Heroic Knowledge* 196); cf. especially 1296, 1338. Landy notes that this image of Samson contrasts with the people's loud shouts, "a contrast which reinforces the constant antithesis between noise and silence, words and action" ("Language" 191).

    undaunted: "undismayed," "intrepid" (*OED* 3).

    where…place: Parker paraphrases: "He came to the place where they led him" ("Variorum"). See 543–44n.

1624–25. *what:* editors gloss as "whatever, as much as."

    assay'd: editors gloss as "attempted"; cf. 392.

1626. Bullough and Bullough write, "there are six strong stresses in this line."

    draw: Parker ("Variorum") tentatively suggests "stretch, distend" (*OED* IV.54) so as to distinguish this action from *pull* in the same line.

    still: "without change, interruption, or cessation," "continually," "invariably" (*OED* 3). Krouse points out that some biblical commentators, troubled about a saint and a Nazarite behaving indecorously, suggested that Samson pulled down the columns *before* the time came for his performing (98–99). But, Krouse notes, Milton chose to take literally Judges 16:25 ("and he made them sport"), and he enlarged upon it. To show that Milton was acquainted with the discussion of the problem, Krouse cites 1310–42, 1408–9. Sellin proposes that Milton here "follows the Vatican codex in presenting Samson as the willing entertainer of the Philistines" ("Milton's Epithet" 150).

1627. *All:* Parker notes that it is to be joined with *what* (1624) as the object of *perform'd* ("Variorum").

    stupendous: "amazingly large or great" (*OED*); cf. *PL* 10.351. The original spelling is *stupendious,* which, as Bullough and Bullough, Carey (*Complete Shorter Poems*), Prince (*Samson Agonistes*), and Hughes (*Complete Poems; John Milton*) note, was the common form through most of the seventeenth century.

1628. *Antagonist:* "[in the character of] one who contends with another in an athletic contest, a battle, or struggle"; "an opponent, an adversary" (*OED* 5, 1).

Parker ("Variorum") observes that the use of this word suggests Samson's role as *Agonist* in its sense of "champion" (in athletic games); see the note to the Title, 1324–25n, 1645n.

1629. *intermission:* Parker ("Variorum") detects here a possible triple meaning: although the primary meaning is "temporary cessation, respite, relief, rest" (*OED* 1b; see 1632), Samson has just been identified as an actor (see 1605, 1628, 1645n; cf. 1646), and as a term in architecture *intermissions* meant "the spaces between the Wall and the Pillars, or between Pillars and Pillars" (see Phillips, *New World*). Wyatt and Blakeney remark that "Milton is generally regular in his construction of possessives" but does not use *'s* before *sake* "to avoid a cacophony"; Wyatt cites *PL* 1.782; 11.514; *PR* 2.184; cf. also *RCG* (Patterson, *Works* 3:239).

1630–34. Judges 16:25–26: "and they set him between the pillars. And Samson said unto the lad that held him by the hand, Suffer me that I may feel the pillars whereupon the house standeth, that I may lean upon them." Tung writes, "It is while resting between the two massive pillars that Samson receives the full revelation of how he is to accomplish his mission" (490).

1631. Parker emphasizes here Milton's concern for verisimilitude ("Variorum").

1633. This line echoes 1648 (Le Comte 45).
      massie: see 147n. In Quarles's description of the scene of the catastrophe, the roof "was all / Builded with massie stone" (sig. S4v).

1634. *arched:* pronounce with two syllables (Parker, "Notes" 691; Oras, *Blank Verse* 15 and "Milton's Blank Verse" 176). See 1190n. Todd notices that Milton is fond of the arch and cites *Nat* 175, *IlPen* 157, and *PL* 1.726; Le Comte observes that it "consistently refers to a heathen temple" (64). Bullough and Bullough, Verity, and Hughes (*Complete Poems; John Milton*) suggest that Milton may have taken this image from either Quarles, who describes a theater with an "arched roofe" (sig. S4v), or Sandys, who describes Gaza's "ruins of huge arches sunke low" (sig. O3r). See 1605–10n, 1606n, 1633n.
      main: "strong" (so *OED* 1a); so also 1606.
      support: *OED* 4 dates this sense of the word from 1663.

1635. *He:* B. A. Wright emends to *Hee;* see 219–20n s.v. *Mee.*

1636–38. See 1389n. Woodhouse notes that the Messenger's either/or is incorrect here: Milton combines and harmonizes the human and providential, as Samson is doing both, praying *and* revolving "some great matter in his mind" ("Tragic Effect" 213). Mollenkott similarly suggests that "the natural and supernatural levels" of the catastrophe "are welded together in the description of Samson's posture.... The fall of the Philistine temple is thus the result of divine direction...but equally the result of Samson's far-from-perfect motives" (90). Mollenkott further argues that the ambiguity about whether Samson is praying or thinking in the Messenger's account "seems to imply that for Milton the precise dividing line between human and divine will was at this time mysterious and perhaps irrelevant: God's will is right, and it is man's responsibility, with the help of his inner motions, to discern what is right and to do it" (94).

1637. *eyes fast fixt:* cf. 726. Is Samson pictured with eyes tightly closed, or with eyes imagined as "staring" fixedly at the ground? Verity objects that "it is not a very appropriate description of the blind Samson"; Parker defends this mention of eyes, when Samson bows his head in prayer, as ironically pathetic ("Variorum"); Blakeney adds, "We need not suppose that his eyes had actually been reft from their sockets, but that they had been cruelly deprived of their sight." Some editors, finding the phrase classical, cite Homer, *Iliad* 3.217 (κατὰ χθονὸς ὄμματα πήξας); Virgil, *Aeneid* 6.156 (*defixus lumina*) and 8.520 (*defixique ora tenebant*); Persius, *Satires* 3.79 (*Obstipo capite et figentes lumine terram*); Horace, *Epistles* 6.14 (*defixis oculis*).

    pray'd: in Judges 16:28 Samson prayed aloud at the last for strength to revenge his blindness. Parker explains this omission: "Milton, keeping ever in mind the spiritual development of his protagonist, makes the prayer silent. In his final act Samson is again God's champion—not a private individual seeking revenge" (*Milton's Debt* 8). Krouse identifies the speech that Milton omits as one of the primary reasons commentators have difficulty regarding Samson as a saint. He notes that scholastic commentators excused Samson's suicide as inspired by the Holy Spirit (47–49, 75–76, 106–8).

1638. Grierson believes that this is Samson's epiphany: "And then he saw what it was" (*Milton* 144).

some great matter: i.e., "something important, weighty; distinguished, promi-nent; famous" (*OED* III.11). The phrase occurs also in *PL* 9.669.

1639. *cryed:* Parker proposes *cry'd,* as regular meter would seem to require ("Notes" 694).

1640–45. *Lords:* for the tone, Parker compares 251, 267, and 477 ("Variorum").
commands...obeying: an ironic echo of 1372.
impos'd: cf. 565. There is no warrant for this speech in Scripture; moreover, editors note that Milton ignores Samson's final prayers for revenge as reported in Judges 16:28–30—but cf. 1591, 1660, 1712, where Manoa and the Chorus refer to Samson's revenge. Parker finds this speech a masterpiece of conscious irony: "Notice how carefully he chooses his words: 'delight' is contrasted with 'amaze'; 'commands,' with 'own accord.'... Samson's last words are as impres-sive, in their own way, as his last act. His speech is completely disarming. Its full meaning 'struck' the Philistines only when the roof did" (*Milton's Debt* 158–59). Ferry similarly observes that Samson's "detached, controlled irony...in the final episodes is a measure of his progress toward his heroic goal of silence. He uses words with his characteristic sense of their inappropriateness to his inward experience, but now he chooses them *because* they are irrelevant, and therefore can mislead men who belong to the outward world and who apprehend only the immediate, ordinary human references of language" (172). Sadler specifically suggests that Samson "feigns...in the application of the term *strength,* now syn-onymous with God's strength and Samson's faith" (209). Sellin concludes that in this scene the title *agonistes* no longer refers to Samson "being sported with" but to Samson "playing upon" the Philistines ("Milton's Epithet" 150).

1641. *as reason was:* Percival glosses, "as (there) was (good) reason." Tillyard asks: "Who but Milton in English literature could have slipped in this 'as reason was' at the very height of excitement?" (*Milton* 291). See Preface 43n.

1642. Verity notes the litotes or light irony (see 420n); he paraphrases: "(my performance) beheld with (great) wonder or delight."

1644. *you:* see 1445n s.v. *you.*

1645. Mueller describes how Samson "agonistes" or "actor" (see Title) is actually performing a tragedy for the unwitting Philistines: here he offers to give an encore that will "amaze" his audience, "that is, he will fulfill the requirement for a good tragedy, which should cause *admiratio,* a major critical term of the period, roughly equivalent of Aristotle's *ekplêktikon* and *thaumaston* (*Poetics,* 9.52a4; 14.54a4). Then he proceeds to draw the audience into his tragedy..." ("*Pathos*" 170). See also 1325n.

    amaze: "extreme astonishment, wonder" (*OED* 4), also "consternation" (Parker, "Variorum"). Cf. 1286; *Nat* 69; *Sonn 15* 3 (Le Comte 174); *PR* 2.38.

    strike: "cause...to be overwhelmed" (so *OED* 47c) and "hit" and "kill" (*OED* 25, 45). Editors note that this word has an ironic triple meaning (see 1640–45n; see Sellin, "Milton's Epithet" 150), although some editors (Dunster [in Todd]; Collins; Blakeney; Grieve) sound only half convinced. Dunster (in Todd) and Prince (*Samson Agonistes*) are reminded of Satan's ironic puns in *PL* 6.558–67. Parker adds, "Samson, like Mercutio, dies with a jest on his lips" ("Variorum").

1646–59. Percival describes this passage as the catastrophe or *lusis* ("solution") of the action—also its "το φοβερόν or the circumstance that rouses the feeling of terror in the spectator. According to Aristotle's distinction [*Poetics* 2.14] it may be inferred to be of the highest order," the perpetrator of the dreadful deed being also its victim. Cox interprets the elemental imagery in this passage as part of a larger, "ready-made symbolism" that Milton uses in *SA* to invest "the matter of Samson's rebirth with the magnitude of cosmological movements" and to illustrate a "universal climate...of conflict and harmony, within which human choice must operate" ("Natural Science" 51–52). Alternatively, Radzinowicz suggests that Samson can pull down the pillars "because of the perfect obedience of his will to the return of divine inspiration—or, to put it another way, [he is] able to act when action and patience are perfectly in accord in him" ("*Samson Agonistes*" 470). Dick Taylor prefers to describe Samson's final act as miraculous: he is finally "an instrument of miraculous accomplishments through God's power. The miracle is still of God, even though accomplished in the natural world by Samson" (78–79). Whiting finds "the key to the last hours of Samson's life" in the marginal commentary of the Geneva Bible: "Yet had he not his strength againe, til he had called upon God, and reconciled himselfe." Here, Whiting argues, is the idea of spiritual regeneration absent from the account in Judges and "implied" in *SA* ("*Samson Agonistes*" 215–16). Hyman instead thinks that that this passage "impresses us with the self-defeating nature, the futility of action"; whereas God requires that Samson "exercise the patience of a saint, Samson's final action represents his own ineradicable desire to act like a military hero" ("Unwilling Martyrdom" 95, 92). Fish proposes that readers ultimately cannot know whether Samson's spiritual regeneration prompts his act of destruction: "The fact that a regenerate Samson pulls down the temple is important—for Samson; but despairing Samson would have also pulled down the temple, if God had willed it" (260). Ellis-Fermor suggests that the catastrophe is, in fact, "purely subsidiary to the real action.... The earlier phases do not lead consistently towards it because it is not, in itself, the significant climax of the action. What they do lead to...is the resolution of the spiritual conflict which the apparent catastrophe serves only to image in terms of event" (33).

   nerves: "sinew[s]," i.e., "mak[ing] the utmost (physical) exertion" (so *OED* 1); cf. 639.

   bow'd: see 1647–48n.

1647–48. *As with...tremble:* the punctuation leaves it uncertain whether this comparison belongs with "he bow'd" (e.g., B. A. Wright inserts a semicolon after *tremble*) or with "He tugg'd," etc. (Darbishire inserts a semicolon after *bow'd* [*Poetical Works*]); see 543–44n. Jerram writes, "Perhaps it is hypercriticism which has prevented commentators making 'bowed' [1646] govern 'pillars' [1648]," a reading he supports on the grounds that it sounds more musical. Ferry recognizes Samson in this passage "as the ancestor of a kind of Wordsworthian hero, a poetic celebration of wordless and immutable non-human nature" (177). Carey instead suggests, "The destructive and amoral power of the sea which, at the opening of the drama, was specifically associated with the Philistines, has now been transferred to Samson. His last bloody act of vengeance, which the surface voice of the drama invites us to applaud, is condemned, at a deeper level, by the progression of the imagery" (*Complete Shorter Poems* 338).

   pent: editors gloss as "shut up, confined within narrow space" (*OED* 1). This supposed cause of earthquakes occurs in Ovid, *Metamorphoses* 25.296–306, 346, and editors note that this simile also appears in *PL* 1.230–37, 6.195–98. Cf. Shakespeare, *Venus and Adonis* 1046–47: "As when the wind, imprison'd in the ground, / Struggling for passage, earth's foundation shakes" (Percival).

   those two massie Pillars: this echoes 1633 (Le Comte 45).

1649. *with…convulsion:* "wrenching" (so *OED* 1) or "violent agitation" (*OED* 2c). Cf. *PL* 6.328. Wyatt and Collins comment, "*with* denotes accompaniment, not the means or cause as in line 1647." Newton notes that some early editions change *convulsion* to *confusion.*

1652. *He tugg'd, he shook:* Newton writes that some early editions "absurdly" change this to read, "He tugg'd, he took".

    Upon the heads: cf. Judges 16:27: "and there were upon the roof about three thousand men and women." Milton visualizes it otherwise: as Masson writes, the deaths in *SA* are "caused by the falling in of the roof upon those seated in the *covered* part of the theatre" (*Poetical Works*). Le Comte (152) finds an echo here of *Mask* 798–99 and "A Letter to a Friend" (see Patterson, *Works* 6:103).

1653. These are "the Lords and each degree / Of sort" (1607–8). Verity et al. think that Milton here alludes to Restoration court society, as does Masson (*Life* 6:676). See 1659n.

    Ladies, Captains: Parker wonders whether Dalila and Harapha are included: he notes, "It would have been easy to have the Messenger provide answers but Milton elects otherwise" ("Variorum").

    or Priests: Keightley (*Poems*) and Verity conjecture that Milton dictated "and Priests"; see 182n.

1654. *choice nobility and flower:* hendiadys: "the choice flower of their nobility" (Percival; Wyatt and Collins). Cf. *PR* 3.314, and see 144, 264; for the construction, see 1393–94n.

    nobility: "the body of persons forming the noble class" (so *OED* 3).

1655. *round:* "on all sides" (*OED* 3), perhaps "in the vicinity" (Parker, "Variorum").

1657. *immixt:* "intermingled" (*OED*); Parker adds that the word can also mean "not mixed, pure" ("Variorum").

    inevitably: Percival remarks that with this word Milton distinguishes the death of Samson from the suicides of either Ajax or Cato: Samson's earlier "prayer for death [649–50] shows that he did not presume to take the matter into his own hands, and his present action towards himself is unavoidably bound up with that other towards his enemies, to which he felt himself called by divine inspiration [1381–83]." Percival also notes the silence of Jewish law on the subject of suicide, even in the accounts of Saul, Ahithophel, and Zimri. On Samson's death, see also 1664–67n.

1659. *The vulgar:* editors gloss as "the crowd" or "the common people" (*OED* 3). Parker writes, "by this addition to the tale in Judg., Milton accounts plausibly for his Messenger's survival" ("Variorum"). But Verity (with Grieve and Hughes, *John Milton* agreeing) conjectures that Milton's purpose was allegorical, i.e., to prophesy vengeance falling on the Restoration court but "not on the nation at large."

　without: editors explain, "outside" of the theater (1609–10).

1660–1758. Parker (*Milton's Debt* 103–9) defines these last 99 lines of the exodos (not mentioned in the Argument) as a kommos or "joint lamentation of chorus and actors" (Aristotle, *Poetics* 12.2). Earlier editors assert that the kommos is limited to 1660–1707 (e.g., Edmund K. Chambers 108; Wyatt and Collins 28; Percival xiii, 20, 187; Collins 5; Page 20). Parker cites various Greek parallels for Milton's handling of the kommos in *SA:* the use of a single actor with the chorus (Aeschylean); the intermixture of emotional speech with lyrical passages (also Aeschylean); the irregular structure of the choral odes (Euripidean). Parker finds a "possible precedent" for the ending of *SA* in the *Suppliant Maidens* of Aeschylus (*Milton's Debt* 103–09). Among other responses to this passage, Arthos writes that these final lines, not Samson's destruction of the temple, represent the drama's "conclusion, the climax . . . in the discovery of the formalities of consolation and benediction, in the most perfect beauty of speech and through that beauty in the communication of the faith that speaks of blessedness" (177).

1660–1707. The Chorus breaks the respectful silence it had preserved while Manoa asked his anxious questions of the Messenger. Woodhouse discusses this sequence of events: "It is of the first importance" that "the reconciliation, the mitigating of the sense of disaster, is worked out in purely human terms [1660–1744] before the larger rhythm of the divine comedy is invoked, lest that rhythm should not only resolve the tragic irony of the action, but dissolve the whole tragic effect" ("Tragic Effect" 213, 222; "*Samson Agonistes*" 168). Joseph Warton (in Todd) and Verity note that Manoa is now speechless, presumably crushed by what he has heard, struggling with his personal loss and frustration of hopes. Parker ("Variorum") adds that "Milton may have visualized him wailing and beating his breast (1721–22)."

The tone and substance of the choral response to the catastrophe disturb some commentators. Hanford suggests that "neither the spirit nor the reception" of Samson's last act is Christian (*John Milton* 222). Adams similarly writes that "for the morally uncommitted general reader," *SA*'s "vindictive exultations…are barbaric and hysterical" (207). Martz (132) specifically suggests that the Chorus fails "to grasp the deeper meaning of Samson's triumph," a failure suggested in part by the "heavy rhyme" of its initial speech (1660–68). Baruch notes that the Chorus, like Manoa, seems to have misunderstood the "true lesson" of Samson's final action, "appearing instead both generally perplexed about corporeal and mystical matters and intent on leaving themselves very much out of the pictures that evolve from their thoughts, however imperfect." Through the Chorus's final lines, Baruch continues, Milton thus illustrates the "trouble [that] awaits the men who stop at the level of admiration, who remain passively dependent on a foolish idea of vicarious regeneration" (326, 320). Bush similarly notes that although at the end Manoa and the Chorus "pronounce heartfelt and noble eulogies, they appear to have seen only the outward proof of God's continued trust in his champion, not the way in which Samson had regained trust in God and in himself as God's agent" ("John Milton" 521; *John Milton* 200; *Milton* 515; *Portable Milton* 23). Barker suggests that Manoa's and the Chorus's limited understanding highlights the reader's participation: "the reader is left to decide…what is happening and is meant. Manoa and the Hebrew chorus do not quite tell us the meaning, but only that the moment is to be remembered and the meaning of its new aquist sought after the event" (178).

Among other responses to the Chorus's assessment, Goldsmith suggests "the sense of tragic waste in Samson's death is more excruciating because, as Auden says of the Christian hero: 'What a pity it was this way when it might have been otherwise'" (83). Williamson writes that Samson's death "appears to be an act of shame, and is indeed a consequence of the penalty for his original lapse. Thus his death is tragic in one sense and a moral victory in another" (101). But Parker predicts that "readers will some day agree…that the poem is intensely, almost unbearably pessimistic, with Samson's 'victory' a final irony, since—in the perspective of Biblical history—Samson dies in vain…and with no promise of immortality" (*Milton* 937). Burke instead discusses the similarity between Samson and Milton: "In saying, with fervor, that a blind Biblical hero *did* conquer, the poet is 'substantially' saying that he in his blindness *will* conquer" (153). But, Burke cautions, "a poet's identification with imagery of murder or suicide, either one or the other, is, from the 'neutral' point of view, merely a concern with *terms for transformation in general*" (160).

glorious: Landor suggests that Milton typically makes syllabically weak vowels "either coalesce with or yield to others. In no place but at the end of a verse would he protract *glorious* into a trisyllable," a tendency that Landor attributes to the Italian influence on Milton's versification (5:302).

1661. Edmund K. Chambers glosses as, "Life or death matters little, since thou hast fulfilled"; Percival, Verity, Blakeney, et al. read "in life and death alike." Parker instead suggests, "whether living (as was thought) or (by) dying" ("Variorum").

Living or dying: the phrase occurs also in *PL* 10.974 (Le Comte 67).

fulfill'd...foretold: the Chorus expected that Samson's act would lead to the Israelites' deliverance but, as Verity observes, the angel had only said: "he shall *begin* to deliver Israel out of the hand of the Philistines" (Judg. 13:5); see 225–26, 1714–16, and cf. 38–39. Historically, Samson did not free his nation; see 1715–16n.

1664–67. "Milton thus challenges the view of those biblical commentators who argued that Samson's death was perilously like suicide" (Parker, "Variorum"); see 1586–87, 1657–58, and Argument; see also 1657n. Krouse provides a detailed account of the controversy on this point (37, 48–49, 75, 107). Todd cites Moore's *Full Inquiry into the Subject of Suicide* (1790): Samson's "own death was an accidental circumstance connected with his point in view, but not the first and direct aim of the action." Hughes (*Complete Poems*) cites Burton's *Anatomy* 1.4.1 and also Donne's *Biathanatos* (1644): " 'the very text... is against those who, like St. Augustine, equally zealous of Samson's honor and his own conscience,' argue that Samson acted simply by divine prompting, 'for Samson dyed with these words in his mouth, *Let me lose my life with the Philistins.*'" Allen notes that in Judges 16:30, but not in Milton, Samson says: "Let me die with the Philistines"; the authoritative Hebrew text, modified in vernacular translations, has "Let my soul die with the Philistines"—suggesting that Samson either did not believe in the afterlife or was praying, as a self-convicted suicide, for release from the pains of hell ("Idea as Pattern" 83). Nicolson finds the poem's ending "predominantly Hebraic" except for the Christian overtones of these lines (371).

self-kill'd: Grierson suggests that Milton here remembers Augustine's phrase *mors voluntaria* from *De civitate Dei* (*Milton* 139, 144).

1665. *Not willingly:* Grierson writes that Milton is endorsing the Chorus's view here and was "bound by the Faith" to think that God directly inspired Samson's destruction (*Milton* 139). Huntley instead comments that the "Chorus' initial reaction to the messenger's speech is totally wrong in a typically Manoan sense" (143); see also 1660–1707n.

fold: "clasp," "embrace" or "winding" (*OED* 4, 1c), or "toil, snare" (Lockwood). Cook argues for "coil" or "toil(s)" on the basis of Sophocles' *Antigone* 343–47, Aeschylus's *Prometheus Bound* 1076–79 and *Choephori* 998–1000, and Euripides' *Orestes* 25–26, 1315 ("*Samson Agonistes*" 78). Editors do not explain this figure; why has "necessity" a "fold"? Muldrow (220) admits his uncertainty: "the reference...must be to some law of inevitable physical causation and not to any mysterious power of fate in the universe"; he compares Milton's concept of "compulsory necessity" (Patterson, *Works* 14:73). Cf. 763, and *PR* 2.162. Le Comte discusses at length Milton's conception of entanglement, but without reference to *SA* (6–7).

1666. A twelve-syllable line (alexandrine; see 118n) and the only unrhyming line in this nine-line song (Parker, "Variorum"). Cf. *Lyc* 1, 13, 15, 22, etc.

dire necessity: Todd, Browne, Collins, Hughes (*John Milton* 438–39), et al. infer Milton's approval of Horace's expression *dira necessitas* (*Odes* 3.24.6). Cf. also "strict necessity": *PL* 5.528; 10.131. Cook notes parallels in Aeschylus's *Prometheus Bound* 1076–79 and Sophocles' *Antigone* 343–47 ("*Samson Agonistes*" 78). Frederick Tupper adds a parallel from "a comic fragment, the *Boutalion* of Xenarchus, preserved by Athenaeus (II, 64)"—although ultimately he dismisses this likeness as "certainly accidental" (47). Osgood (61) notes, more generally, that this personification "was especially common among the Greek dramatists" and that they emphasize necessity's strength: "according to a fragment of Sophocles...not even Ares can withstand Necessity, and Aeschylus speaks of 'the resistless might of Necessity'" in *Prometheus Bound*. Editors also find an allusion to the Greek Ἀνάγκη ("necessity") and some are troubled accordingly, for this was a common synonym for Μοῖρα ("fate") and Αἶσα ("destiny") in Greek tragedy (Parker, *Milton's Debt* 213). While Prince in fact defines *necessity* as "fate" (*Samson Agonistes*), Edmund K. Chambers writes, "this sounds like an echo of Greek fatalism, but it may possibly be only equivalent to the 'inevitable destruction' of lines 1657, 1658." Percival, after quoting Aeschylus's *Prometheus Bound* 105 and Euripides' *Helen* 514, and citing Plato's *Laws* 5.10, concludes: "these Hebrews here speak in the language, though not in the spirit, of the Greek chorus.... Milton would hardly make his Hebrews say...that necessity has on this occasion overruled the providence of God. This, however, is what the Greek dramatists mean when speaking of fate." Verity also comments, "Milton's desire to reproduce the form and conventions of classical tragedy has led him to use language which, if interpreted literally, would be inconsistent with his belief as a Christian." Mueller, too, discusses this apparent inconsistency: "Between the revelation of God's plan as something ultimately good and the horror and bewilderment it causes in the survivors, there remains a tension, an element of terror and fear, than cannot be explained but has to be accepted" ("*Pathos*" 162).

whose law: Percival writes: "the law of nature, as modern science would call it, which acts uniformly, no matter whether its action affects the good or the bad.... Samson had won this moral freedom...but this could not save him from the operation of the unalterable decree of fate, or, as the scientist would say, of the physical laws of nature. It is in this contrast that the pathos of the tragedy lies."

in death: Landor would omit these words to improve the verse "and the sense too" (5:302).

1667–68. Judges 16:30: "So the dead which he slew at his death were more than they which he slew in his life." Blakeney interprets 1668 as "than all (that thou in) thy life (time)"; Percival, "than (thou in) all thy life (hadst)." See 543–44n. Robertson finds here evidence of "the fortunate fall," a theory that he thinks fits *SA* better than *PL:* "by Samson's fall, compared with Adam's, things are much more obviously better in the end than the beginning" (334).

1669–86. Hanford argues that this passage shows that the Philistines—more than Samson—embody the classical conception of *hubris* and *Ate*. Along with Samson's recollection of his earlier pride (529–33), this speech illustrates "the degree to which Milton has grasped the central motive of Greek tragedy and the pains he was at to bring his own material under the ethical, religious, and artistic formulae afforded by it" (*John Milton* 225–26; "*Samson Agonistes*" 184–85). Tillyard adds that peripeteia also pertains to the Philistines: "The *peripeteia* consisted in the fact that by calling Samson in to make them sport they were really calling him in to destroy them…while the actual recognition [*anagnorisis*] must be supposed as taking place after Samson has addressed the Philistines or in the brief interval between his tugging at the pillars and the catastrophe. The broader recognition by the audience is brought about by the messenger's speech" (*Milton* 292). Mueller objects to the former claim: "But such an *anagnorisis* would not be the recognition of a tragic situation which radically alters the relationship of the characters involved…[cf. *Poetics* 11.52a30]; it would merely be the realization that the tables are turned" ("*Pathos*" 157). Gossman detects in the words describing the Philistines' pride an echo of the wicked in the book of Job 21.12 ("Samson, Job" 220).

1669. Bridges thinks the line in falling (trochaic) rhythm (*Milton's Prosody* 55); Sprott (132) thinks it difficult to determine whether Milton thought of the line as "trochaic with the last foot catalectic, or as iambic with the first foot catalectic." See 116n.

   Semichor[us]: OED gives 1797 as the earliest use of this word, which recurs at line 1687. Percival explains, "The chorus now divides itself into two, one half taking for the subject of its ode the fate of the Philistines, the other half, the triumph of Samson"; to Lawry, the semichoruses resemble "two inward eyes, cleared gradually across the play from an original blindness like that of Samson" (395). Williamson writes that the semichoruses "give antiphonic development to the contest between Samson and the Philistines" (101). Parker notes that the first semichorus is exactly twice the length of the outburst by the whole Chorus (1660–68); "the second semichorus…is three lines longer than the first; but the effect of symmetry is there" (*Milton's Debt* 64). The first semichorus (1669–86) is without rhymes.

   hearts: see 1613n.

   jocund: Darbishire (*Poetical Works*) and B. A. Wright emend to *jocond.*

   sublime: editors read "uplifted" (Church; Verity; Blakeney; Northrop Frye, Paradise Lost *and Selected Poetry;* Hughes, *Complete Poems* and *John Milton;* cf. *OED* 1)—i.e., the Latin *sublimis* (cf. Horace, *Ars poetica* 195; Livy 1.16)—or "exalted in feeling, elated" (so *OED* 3b; Lockwood; Percival; Wyatt and Collins; Prince, *Samson Agonistes;* Bullough and Bullough; Shawcross, *Complete English Poetry*); this latter meaning, according to *OED,* occurs only in Milton. Cf. *PL* 10.136–37.

1670. Editors cite Isaiah 29.9: "they are drunken, but not with wine." Hawkins notes the contrast between the Philistines' "gluttony and drunkenness" and "Samson's final act of self-emptying" as well as the contrast between "the idolatrous offering of bulls and goats [see 1671]" and "the true sacrifice Samson now performs, offering himself in the likeness of one who is both priest and victim" (226). Percival observes, "although 'drunk' is repeated in the text, the constr[uction] is substantially a *zeugma*"; see 1671n. Verity states that *Idolatry* is "a trisyllable by elision of *a;* cf. ll. 443, 1378"—but see 122n, and cf. *PL* 1.456, 12.337; *PR* 3.418.

1671. Parker ("Variorum") compares Deuteronomy 32:38: "Which did eat the fat of their sacrifices, and drank the wine of their drink offerings."

fat: Parker suggests it may be a typographical error for *sat* ("Variorum"). Edmund K. Chambers terms this an "adjective used as an adverb," i.e., making the sense "stuffed to fatness" (132).

regorg'd: "gorge anew" (not in *OED;* Parker, "Variorum"), or "disgorge or cast up again" (*OED* 1). Lockwood defines "to devour to repletion," and Church, Percival, Blakeney, Prince (*Samson Agonistes*), et al. read "swallowed, ate, gorged to excess" (not in *OED*), making the prefix *re-* intensive, as in Latin. In any case, the construction is difficult. Are "they" (understood from "thir hearts" [1669]) drunk with wine *and* fat (if so, "an exceedingly bold zeugma," write Percival, and Wyatt and Collins, who are undecided), or should we read 1670 as semiparenthetic and construe 1671 as "and (while they) regorg'd (the) fat of Bulls and Goats"? Keightley (*Poems*) suggests, "and (the) fat of bulls and goats (was) regorged (by them who had eaten too much)."

Bulls and Goats: the phrase occurs also in *PL* 12.292 (Le Comte 67).

1672. *Chaunting:* editors gloss as "singing praises to, celebrating in song" (*OED* 3).

preferring: see 464.

1673. *Dread:* "object or cause of fear, reverence, or awe" (*OED* 2); cf. 1474. Blakeney cites Isaiah 8:13: "Sanctify the Lord of hosts himself; and let him be your fear, and let him be your dread." Alden Sampson refers to these as "terms of highest reverence and praise" (203).

1674. *Silo:* "Shiloh" or (Greek) "Silous." Masson (*Poetical Works*), Verity, Blakeney, and Prince (*Samson Agonistes*) remark Milton's dislike of the *sh* sound; see also 138, 715, 981, 1187. Parker ("Variorum"), however, observes that Milton used the spelling *Shilo* in his outlines for possible dramas circa 1641 (Patterson, *Works*, 18:237); cf. also 181 (*Eshtaol*) and 289 (*Shibboleth*). Wyatt and Collins note, "the form 'Silo' is that of the Prayerbook version" of Psalm 78:60; it is also that of the Vulgate. Editors explain that during the period of Samson's exploits the chief sanctuary of the Hebrews was at Shiloh, a place north of Bethel, south of Lebanon, on the east of the road from Bethel to Shechem (Judg. 18:31; 21:19). The sacred ark was kept there from the time of the conquest of Judah until the Philistines captured it (Josh. 18:1; 1 Sam. 4:11), and religious festivals were held there annually (1 Sam. 5:2–5).

    bright: Parker ("Variorum") finds here an allusion to the Shekinah or visible glory of God, a refulgent light (Exod. 40:34; 1 Kings 8:11; etc.). Milton refers to it in *Animad* (Patterson, *Works* 3:147).

1675. See 1682–84n.

    he: Darbishire (*Poetical Works*) and B. A. Wright emend to *hee;* see 219–20n s.v. *Mee.*

    spirit: a monosyllable by elision of one *i* according to Verity and Grieve, who are uncertain about which *i;* Bridges believes it to be the second, "following the Italian" (*Milton's Prosody* 34).

    spirit of phrenzie: Edmund K. Chambers writes, "the ἄτη so often spoken of in Greek tragedy, leading men on to ὕβρις or overweening pride, and thence to νέμεσις or divine retribution." Todd cites *Ref* (Patterson, *Works* 3:75): "unless God have smitten us with frensie from above, and with a dazling giddinesse at noon day"; cf. also Deut. 28:28–29: "the Lord shall smite thee with madness, and blindness, and astonishment of heart: And thou shalt grope at noonday, as the blind gropeth in darkness." Hughes (*Complete Poems*) suggests that the semichorus's thought parallels Milton's discussion in *DocCh* (Patterson, *Works* 14:90–175) of "reprobation" as the "self-punishment of hard-hearted men, though several biblical passages (e.g., Isa. 6:10) speak of God as hardening the hearts of the doomed. Milton significantly closes this chapter by quoting the *Od[yssey]* (1.32–34), where Zeus protests to the gods that men accuse them unjustly of responsibility for the woes that blind mortals bring upon themselves." Svendsen cites instead *Batman uppon Bartholome* (f. 88v), a Renaissance encyclopedia of popular science: "this disease of phrensie is a token of a deepe displeasure from God, when it remaineth vnto the end in the possessed, as plainly appeareth" ("Milton and Medical Lore" 172).

1676. *Who:* Percival glosses as "the 'spirit of phrenzie,' which is here personified like the Greek Furies and Erinyes."

    hurt: cf. βλάπτω, specially said of the gods distracting or perverting men's minds, e.g., in *Odyssey* 14.178 (Verity) or in *Iliad* 15.724 (Bush, *Milton*).

1678. *call in hast:* see 1316, 1343–44, 1395.

    destroyer: see 1587.

1679. *only:* Blakeney says this word "is strictly out of place; it should come after 'set,' as it qualifies 'sport and play.'"

1680–81. *Unweetingly:* "unknowingly" (so *OED*).

    importun'd: "ask[ed] for (a thing) urgently and persistently" (*OED* 4). Parker explains, "through their Public Officer" ("Variorum").

    come...upon: see 205.

1682–84. *fond:* "foolish" and/or "mad" (*OED* 2, 3). On this passage and 1675, editors quote the familiar maxim: *Quos deus vult perdere, dememtat piruis*—"whom God wishes to destroy He first drives mad"—and also the similar sentiment in Sophocles' *Antigone* 620–23. Todd adds that he finds the same idea expressed in one of the supposed fragments of Euripides. Lawry observes, "Samson ultimately was his own deliverer, so ultimately were the Philistines their own executioners.... 'Wrath divine' is seen to be in part mere noninterference with the ends men choose" (394).

    mortal men: the phrase recurs in 168; see also *DDD* (Patterson, *Works* 3:490); and *PL* 1.51; 3.268; 12.248 (Le Comte 67).

    wrath: Darbishire emends to *wrauth,* the spelling in *PL* (*Poetical Works*).

1685. Editors paraphrase: "left (either) without a sense (understanding), or (with respect) to sense, depraved, morally corrupt" (so *OED* s.v. *reprobate* 2); cf. 1042. Editors interpret *reprobate* variously as "lost, past all feeling or power to perception" (Church—although Grieve protests that this makes it equivalent to "insensate left"); "abandoned, lost to all grace and virtue" (Blakeney; cf. *OED* 3b); "ill–judging" or "erroneous" (Edmund K. Chambers 108, 144); "perverse-thinking" (Verity); "(abandoned to) wicked (thoughts)" (Percival); "condemned" (Shawcross, *Complete English Poetry*); and "abandoned to the enjoyment of the outward senses," with a play upon the word *sense* (Wyatt; Grieve). Editors quote Romans 1:28–29: "And even as they did not like to retain God in their knowledge, God gave them over to a reprobate mind, to do those things which are not convenient; Being filled with all unrighteousness." Here *reprobates* translates ἀδόκιμος, which means "rejected as spurious or base." The Vulgate has *in reprobum sensum,* which may be translated "reprobate sense" (*OED* s.v. *sense* 7b). Parker ("Variorum") notes that the phrase "reprobate sense" occurs in *Animad* (Patterson, *Works* 3:157) and *TR* (Patterson, *Works* 6:170); in *Eikon* Milton speaks of the "madness" of "reprobate thoughts" (Patterson, *Works* 5:272); in *RCG,* of "a reprobate conscience in this life, and hell in the other world" (Patterson, *Works* 3:254); and in *DocCh* he writes, "the object which reprobation has in view is the destruction of unbelievers" (Patterson, *Works* 14:99).

1686. To Northrop Frye, this line "marks the final transfer of the tragic catastrophe from Samson to the Philistines" (Paradise Lost *and Selected Poetry* 1675n). Sprott (132) and Bridges (*Milton's Prosody* 56) read the first two feet as inverted (trochaic). Prince cites this line (and 1685) as an example of a passage in which the absence of rhyme "is a particularly striking effect" (*Italian Element* 167). Broadbent writes that "the verse and the sense clang and muddle" before they "clarify ferociously" in the next line (*Milton* 37). Edmundson finds in these lines a verbal echo of Vondel's *Samson* (173–74); on Vondel, see 115–75n.

    blindness internal: cf. 418. Todd thinks Milton is remembering "O cecità de le terrene menti" ("O blindness of earthy souls") in Battista Guarini's *Il pastor fido* 5.6. Percival quotes Ephesians 4:18: "being alienated from the life of God…because of the blindness of their heart"; Lucretius, *De rerum natura* 2.14: "o pectora caeca" ("O blind intelligences"); Ovid, *Metamorphoses* 6.472–73: "pro superi, quantum mortalia pectora caecae / noctis habent" ("Ye gods, what blind night rules in the hearts of men!"). Parker ("Variorum") cites Deuteronomy

28:28: "the Lord shall smite thee with madness, and blindness, and astonish-ment of heart"; and John 12.40: "He hath blinded their eyes, and hardened their heart" (the latter is quoted in *DocCh* [Patterson, *Works* 15:70]). Keightley suggests that these two words may have been mistakenly transposed, "but there would be a loss of energy" (*Account* 327). Carey notes that the repetition of *blindness* (1686) and *blind* (1687) is an example of *traductio* (*Complete Shorter Poems* 335–36); see 38–42n.

    struck: Wyatt writes, "in four cases out of six in his poetry and at least once in his prose works Milton wished this word to be sounded 'strook,' and so spelt it, but not here." See *Nat* 95; *PL* 2.165, 6.863; *PR* 4.576; but cf. *PR* 3.146.

1687–1707. See 1669n s.v. *Semichor.* The second semichorus emphasizes Samson's transformation. Notice the rhymes in 1687–88, 1691–92, 1697–1707; according to Beum, the rhyme underscores the Chorus's passion and wisdom (180–81); Ralli thinks that here—and 1427–40—"something is captured of the rhythm of the Hebrew prophets" (141); Roberts W. French suggests that these rhymes differ from the Chorus's earlier rhyming speeches: "for the first time the Chorus has found the matter with which to fill their forms" (67). See also 1745–58n. Huntley emphasizes the first part of this speech: "Here, Milton represents the light breaking in on the benighted Chorus. This is the first time they have real-ized that Samson might indeed have overcome his blindness" (144). Hanford notes that "the outburst of similes, occurring uniquely here to enhance the climactic episode, reminds us of the similar indulgence in the relatively bare text of *Paradise Regained* at the moment of Satan's downfall" (*Poems*).

    Some commentators—e.g., Masson (*Poetical Works*) and Raleigh—think that Milton is here, in a "marvellous fugal succession of figures" (Raleigh, *Milton* 37), alluding to his own situation after the Restoration: "No one can study the subtle wording and curious imagery without seeing that the secondary idea in Milton's mind was that of his own extraordinary self-transformation, before the eyes of the astonished Restoration world, out of his former character of horrible prose iconoclast into that of supreme and towering poet" (Masson, *Life* 6:677; *Poetical Works*). Marvell, in his commendatory verses for the 1674 edition of *PL,* compared its composition to Samson's destruction of the "Temples [*sic*] Posts" to "revenge his sight" (lines 9, 10); but he writes that, for a time, he thought Milton meant to destroy "the sacred Truths" which are the subject of his epic (lines 6–8). Muir holds it "surely unlikely" that Marvell would have written these lines if *SA* "were already in existence" (175).

1688. *Despis'd:* cf. 272.

   extinguish't: Percival glosses: "thought (to be) rendered powerless." Parker notes that this word introduces the metaphor involving "illuminated," "fierie," and "sudden flame": thus he paraphrases, "he or his vertue is thought extinguished because 'under ashes'" ("Variorum").

1689. Parker comments, "this is the nearest the Chorus ever comes to comprehending what has actually happened" ("Variorum").

   inward eyes: cf. 162 and Milton's own prayer in *PL* 3.51–53: "thou celestial light / Shine inward, and the mind through all her powers / Irradiate, there plant eyes." Cf. also *Def 2* (Patterson, *Works,* 8:71). Allen discusses this theme of the "inner eye that knows only when the exterior sight is gone" within Milton's various works, including *SA* and particularly *PL* ("Milton" 621–30). Jebb writes that "the contrast between physical blindness and inward vision is an undernote" in Sophocles' *Oedipus at Coloneus* (xxii). Todd, followed by Mitford, cites Henry More's use of the phrase "inward eye(s)" in canto 3, stanzas 10 and 11 of *Psychodia Platonica: Or a Platonicall Song of the Soul* (Cambridge, 1642). Alden Sampson finds evidence here of Milton's "reverence" for the Quaker doctrine of the inner light (221). Percival quotes Ephesians 1:18: "the eyes of your understanding being enlightened" (see 1686n), and also Guarini's *Il pastor fido:* "aprir nel ceico senso occhi incei"; "to open piercing eyes within blind sense." Browne and Church compare the expression to Wordsworth's "inward eye."

1690–96. *fierie...Dragon...thunder:* Parker ("Variorum") compares Milton's account of a Danish invasion in *HistBr:* "which many strange thunders and fiery Dragons, with other impressions in the air seen frequently before were judg'd to foresignifie" (Patterson, *Works* 10:188).

   fierie vertue: "ardent" (*OED* 5a) "moral excellence" (see *OED* 2). See 173n. Carey writes that the fire imagery used to convey Samson's inspiration recalls the language describing Dagon's worshipers, e.g., *flame* (1351), *fired* (1419), and *unquenchable* (1422): "An equivalence between the religious fervour of the Philistines and that of the protagonist is momentarily revealed" that "sharply question[s]" the imagery's "elevatory force" (*Complete Shorter Poems* 340–41). Milton also uses this phrase ("fierie vertue") in *DDD* (Patterson, *Works* 3:401).
   rouz'd: cf. 1382.

1692–96. The sense seems to be that Samson "came" upon his enemies as unsuspected as a dragon under a chicken roost at evening, "but" his actual attack came suddenly, not from below, but from above, like an eagle out of a clear sky. This interpretation was first advanced by Thyer (in Newton), and later by Masson (*Poetical Works*); but earlier, and meanwhile, editors (e.g., Keightley, *Poems*; Church; Collins; Hunter), troubled by the *but* in 1695, propose "And *not*" or *Nor* for *And* in 1692. Collins thus glosses the line, "he did not come as a serpent comes in the evening, but as an eagle suddenly descending with the thunderbolt." Or Jerram proposes, "In so far as he attacked men at rest, secure on their benches, he was like a dragon, coming in the evening to attack tame fowls on nests and perches. In so far as he brought destruction unexpectedly on them from above, he was like an eagle."

ev'ning Dragon: commentators disagree about the apparent inappropriateness of describing Samson as a dragon. While Banks accepts *dragon* literally and interprets it as a symbol of Samson's "strength and fierceness" (162), many editors explain that *Dragon* means "serpent, snake." Keightley thinks these editors are mistaken because the image of a serpent would be inaccurate and inappropriate: it implies that Samson steals upon the Philistines to kill them one by one (*Poems*). Moreover, Cox notes, "the change from snake to eagle . . . sounds a grating note; [and] the snake is an incongruous, indecorous choice of a figure for Milton's hero, God's 'faithful Champion'" ("'Ev'ning Dragon'" 578). Carey also suggests that while Milton wishes to elevate Samson through the poem's animal imagery, "the eagle and the Phoenix are undercut by the snake in the henroost, which looks much more like the 'serpent' Dalila [997] than they do, but which is Samson" (*Complete Shorter Poems* 339). But Sellin defends Milton's description: "it is perfectly in keeping with the *hypokrites* interpretation of Samson's activity, for the emphasis is . . . upon the nature of the method used for destroying the Philistines" ("Milton's Epithet" 159). MacCaffrey also finds this tag apt: "to the enemies of God he seems a dark satanic force . . . , but this simile serves only to measure their own condition" (xxxii). Sellin adds "a long tradition . . . exists in Rabbinical literature" comparing Samson and the serpent ("Milton's Epithet" 159).

Various Renaissance writers collected lore about dragons. E.g., the naturalist Topsell records that dragons live in dens unless they are hungry; then they come out at evening and eat fowl, eggs, fruit, and herbs (Batman sigs. Ooo3r–Ppp4v). Bartholomaeus describes dragons as flying, stinging, and biting (they "hath teeth lyke a saw"); possessing keen sight; devouring "beasts and fowles"; and setting "the ayre on fire, by heate of his venime, so that it seemeth that he bloweth and causeth fire out of his mouth" (Batman sig. Ppp6r–v). The natural philosopher

Maplet similarly writes, "The Dragon is the heade and chiefest of all other Serpents, and flieth from his Den or Cave in the earth his [*sic*] holownesse up to the top of the brode ayre, and of *Dragon* in Greeke, is Englished flight" (138). Milton's dragon is *saliant* (see 1693 and cf. 139), it has two forefeet up, two hind feet on the ground, and is about to *assail* ("leap at") the "perched roosts" of its enemies; 1690 encourages us to imagine a "fierie dragon" (see 1690–96n).

Some of the confusion among commentators arises from the different uses of *Dragon* in the Bible, where the word means, in various contexts, a serpent, Satan, a whale (leviathan), and even a jackal. E.g., Stollman detects an allusion to Genesis 49:16–18 ("Dan shall judge his people, as one of the tribes of Israel. Dan shall be a serpent in the way, a horned snake in the path.... I wait for Thy salvation, O Lord"), a passage that would cast "the history of Samson as a fulfillment of divine prophecy" (188, 189). Le Comte discusses Milton's numerous references to dragons (e.g., *IlPen* 59; *Eli* 58) without, however, addressing this particular line (57). Commentators also note here a succession of figures involving *winged* creatures (fowl, eagle, phoenix), a fact that encourages readers to imagine the dragon, too, as winged (as Jerram writes)—if not the "mighty saile-wing'd monster" of *RCG* (Patterson, *Works* 3:275). Cox notices a "progression of winged-figures" that "echoes the progression in Samson's act as a movement of earth (mountain), air (winds), water, and eventually fire, a description which evokes the lore of elemental transmutation and which, like the images of dragon, eagle, and phoenix, suggests Samson's spiritual metamorphosis" ("Natural Science" 74). Working in part from a parallel passage in Philostratus's *Life of Apollonius of Tyana,* Cox argues that Milton knew the Greek meaning of *dragon* to be "the seeing one," as in "'to have a particular look in one's eyes' .... [It] refers not so much to the function of the eye as to its gleam *as noticed by someone else.*" Cox concludes that when Milton opposes Samson as "the seeing one" to the Philistines as "villatic Fowl" (1695), he is "showing the terrible, blind Samson commanding the fascinated attention of the onlookers" and contrasting Samson's "inward eyes illuminated" with the Philistines' "blindness internal" ("'Ev'ning Dragon'" 583; see also Rudrum 65). Svendsen argues that "'dragon,' commonly pejorative, fits the context and harmonizes with 'eagle' as dynamic energy exploded in righteous violence upon the enemies of God.... The rapid change here from dragon to eagle to phoenix typifies Milton's way of capitalizing upon accepted associations, then altering their image to make a new point; for the shift expresses Samson as a force expending itself, like his passion, and leaving the mind purged as by fire but renewed" (*Milton and*

Science 149). On the implications of the dragon and eagle for Samson's changing role, Sadler writes: "The dragon image first effects the completion of his initial role as a saviour of his people from the Philistines; then he becomes the eagle whose insight moves him closer to God's ways" (208).

Regarding the description *ev'ning*, Cox notices that Milton not only evokes "the expression 'evening wolves'" (Hab. 1:8), but also punningly suggests that "the ev'ning Dragon" will "bring down the order he sees before him, will make all even—balanced, just, calm" ("'Ev'ning Dragon'" 583). Sellin finds this word "absolutely necessary as a designation of time in order to establish a valid comparison between the vulnerability of the Philistines and of villatic fowl" ("Milton's Epithet" 159). Sadler believes the word fits within the drama's temporal typology: "Revelation is the evening of a sequence whose dawn is Genesis and whose noon is Redemption" (206).

1693–94. *Assailant on:* "attacking" (so *OED*), probably with the sense of "intending to leap at" (Blakeney).

perched roosts: editors gloss as "roosts made of perches"; Blakeney adds, a "contemptuous comparison of Philistine lords—by whom Milton wished to signify the courtiers of the Restoration—to mere barn-door poultry." Parker suggests a possible allusion to one of the prophecies of Calchas ("Variorum"). Flatter believes that Milton here and in 1695 refers to his "old enemies, the clergy" (4 September, 499). Parker and Oras write that *perched* is pronounced with two syllables (Parker, "Notes" 691; Oras, *Blank Verse* 15 and "Milton's Blank Verse" 176). See 1190n.

in order: see 1607–8n s.vv. *in order.*

1695. *tame:* "domesticated" (*OED* 1). Parker also suggests "unafraid" ("Variorum").

villatic Fowl: "rural, rustic [birds]" (so *OED*, the first example cited; Latin: *villaticus:* "of a villa or farmhouse"); Dodd writes, "belonging to villages" (sig. L9v). Editors cite Pliny's *Naturalis historia* 23.17: "villaticae alites."

but: see 1692–96n.

Eagle: commentators have little to say about Milton's choice of this bird or his immediate shift to a metaphor of a thunderbolt. Both eagle and thunderbolt are emblems of Zeus, and Topsell (sig. Ooo5v) notes a story where Zeus also metamorphosed into a dragon (see 1692n). On eagles, Topsell writes that they and dragons are natural enemies—although, according to one tradition, the dragon "took beginning from the unnatural conjunction of an Eagle and a she Wolf" (Batman sigs. Ppp2v, Ooo5v). Bartholomaeus notes that "all foules have dread of the Eagle," that the eagle possesses keen sight above all other fowls, and that the eagle has the ability to renew youth (Batman sigs. Hh2v–Hh3v; also Maplet 142; and see Dodd sig. I6r). According to Pliny, the phoenix was of the size of an eagle (Parker, "Variorum"). In *Areop*, Milton likens England both to Samson and to "an Eagle...kindling her undazl'd eyes at the full mid-day beam...while the whole noise of timorous and flocking birds, with those also that love the twilight, flutter about, amaz'd at what she means" (Patterson, *Works* 4:344). The word *eagle* (Latin: *Aquila;* Greek: ἀετός) also meant "the gable of a house," or "the pediment of a temple" (*OED* 7 cites a 1682 usage). Jortin (in Newton) quotes from Sophocles, *Ajax* 167–71, a simile of the sudden fear of birds at the appearance of a vulture. Malcolm MacKenzie Ross calls the eagle and phoenix Milton's "final substitutes for the symbol of royalist power" (137); alternatively, we might recall that Milton's birthplace and seal had the sign of the spread eagle.

1696. *cloudless thunder bolted:* Grieve paraphrases, "bolt from the blue"; Wyatt and Collins add, "Thunder from a clear sky was thought portentous by the ancients." Cf. 1651. Editors cite various classical writers. E.g., Dunster (in Todd) notes, "The ancients described heroes of great prowess and activity in war as *thunderbolts*." Todd and Percival quote *RCG:* "they [Samson's locks] sternly shook, thunder with ruin upon the heads of those his evil counsellors, but not without great affliction to himselfe" (Patterson, *Works* 3:276–77). Svendsen suggests that behind this image lies "the association of the eagle with the sun, with Jupiter." He specifically cites a theory from Milles's *Treasurie of Auncient and Moderne Times* (1613), "that the eagle cannot 'bee smitten with lightning or thunder'" (*Milton and Science* 100). Hughes wonders whether Milton "thought of Horace's professed conversion by the portent of a thunderclap from a clear sky (*Odes* 1.34.6) to a belief that the gods concern themselves in the affairs of men" (*John Milton*). Shawcross compares *PL* 6.762–64 and concludes, "The lines refer the victory over the Philistines and their god to the Providence of God" (*Complete English Poetry*).

1697–1701. Masson notes the intricate rhyme scheme (*Poetical Works*).
     vertue: the verb is found in 1704, but see 1703n. Percival notes the attribute here stands for the person possessing it, Samson (193).

giv'n for: "consider[ed], set down as" (*OED* 31b); cf. *PL* 2.14. Parker suggests that the Chorus "expresses the essential issue of the play" in 1697–98, 1704–6 (*Milton's Debt* 52).

1698. *Deprest:* "put down by force," "vanquish[ed]" (so *OED* 1a).
    overthrown: cf. 463.

1699–1707. The phoenix was mentioned by so many writers, ancient and modern, that it is impossible to ascertain Milton's source or sources for this account (and that in *PL* 5.272). Osgood (69) describes various sources for Milton, in particular Ovid's *Metamorphoses* 15.391–402 and Herodotus's *Histories* 2.73 (where the phoenix is said to resemble the eagle). Hughes (*John Milton*), Murry (132–33), and Tillyard (*Milton* 293) hear the meter and style of *The Phoenix and the Turtle*. Murry further suggests that these "falling rhythms" disrupt the Chorus's "stately rhythm" and evoke "a poetic delicacy quite alien to the massive and artificial style of *Samson*" (133). Cf. 1576–77 and see the note for these lines. Charles Williams has written a presumably ironic footnote on this reminiscence of Shakespeare, suggesting that Shakespeare must have composed this passage in *SA*—and that "Bacon may have had a hand in the political parts, and perhaps Jonson in the classical allusions" (*English Poetic Mind* 149). Editors also quote or cite Pliny's *Naturalis historia* 10.2 (Verity), Bartholomaeus Anglicus (Edmund K. Chambers), Rabelais and Sir John Mandeville (Blakeney), Tacitus's *Annals* 6.28 (Church), Claudian (Collins), Vaughan's *Resurrection and Immortality* (Hughes, *John Milton*), Tasso's *Phoenix* (Hughes, *John Milton*), and Sir Thomas Browne's *Vulgar Errors* 3.12 (Verity).

    Editors and commentators often discuss this image in terms of Samson as a Christ figure. Dunster (in Todd), Percival, et al. note that the phoenix, long in use as a figure in Christian literature, had been discussed as a type of the Resurrection by Tertullian, Ambrose, Cyril, and other writers. Percival adds that the phoenix of Cynewulf, based on the *Carmen de phoenice* of Lactantius, is an allegory on Christian life and death; Scott-Craig also thinks Lactantius a likely source and calls this passage in *SA* "a *carmen saeculare* of Resurrection" ("Concerning" 50). Rudrum adds, "The freedom and the rebirth of the Phoenix arise from entombment and apparent extinction, just as the regained freedom of Samson arises from imposed imprisonment and voluntary extinction of self" (65). Low believes the emblem specifically represents "the death and resurrection, or the triumph in defeat, of a sacrificial victim," which Low traces to both an "ancient pattern of ritual sacrifice" and "the Christian ideal of the way of humiliation and self-sacrifice" ("Tragic Pattern" 926, 927). Northrop Frye similarly argues that Samson's death would not "lead to 'calm of mind, all passion spent,' if Samson were not a prototype of the rising Christ, associated at the appropriate moment with the phoenix" (*Anatomy* 215). Mueller interprets the equation of the phoenix with the holocaust as an indication that "the purifying power of water has failed" and "Only the violence of fire can heal Samson, since fire alone can penetrate below the surface" ("*Pathos*" 167); Mueller adds, "there is no better comment" on this passage than T. S. Eliot's "Little Gidding" 4.200–6.

Among other interpretations of this passage, commentators alternatively treat the phoenix as a symbol of England, earthly fame, human life, and sexual experience. E.g., Knight (*Chariot* 100–1, 120–21) compares this passage on the phoenix and the allusion to Samson in *Areop* (Patterson, *Works* 4:344). Muir agrees that Samson is here "a symbol of England" (181). Woodhouse suggests instead that the symbolism is "carefully confined" to the immortality, not of Samson himself, but of Samson's fame ("Tragic Effect" 215; see also Madsen 198); Bush, noting the "'metaphysical' density" of these lines, concurs that the symbol "is limited to human regeneration and earthly fame" (*Milton* 516); and Henn writes, "The long decorative excursion on the Phoenix, from one point of view cumbrous and artificial, is designed to provide...[an] expansion and re-alignment of Samson's death into a mythology of its own" (264). Wilkenfeld goes further in asserting that the "phoenix emblem," signifying "eternal fame, the conjoining of knowledge and power, and a transcendent freedom born in transformation," is the culmination of the poem's "important thematic and structural motifs" (168). Robertson instead approaches the phoenix as a "conventional symbol of sexual experience" and suggests that it "conforms" both to Samson's "victory in death" and "defeat by Delilah" (332).

Shaping early discussion of this image, Johnson (*Rambler* 20 July 1751) censures Milton's introduction of the phoenix as his grossest anachronism, the legend being a product of Greek imagination, though placed in the East. Johnson explains that it "is faulty, not only as it is incongruous to the personage to whom it is ascribed, but as it is so evidently contrary to reason and nature, that it ought never to be mentioned as a fable in any serious poem" (221). Some editors accept Johnson's criticism; e.g., Verity. But Parker thinks it may be significant that Milton does not name the bird here; rather, he has the Chorus speak of it as living in nearby Arabia ("Variorum").

1699–1701. Acephalous lines in falling (trochaic) rhythm (Bridges, *Milton's Prosody* 55); Sprott (132) thinks it difficult to determine whether Milton thought of the lines as "trochaic with the last foot catalectic, or as iambic with the first foot catalectic." See 116n.

    begott'n: Parker suggests that the meter requires *begotten* ("Notes" 693).

1700. *the:* pronounced *th'Arabian.* See 1699–1701n.

    Arabian: so *EpDam* 186; cf. *PL* 5.274. The tradition agrees that the home of the phoenix is in Arabia (Parker, "Variorum").

    woods: Percival, Verity, and Prince (*Samson Agonistes*) point out that the tradition often emphasizes a single tree, and they cite Shakespeare's *Tempest* 3.3.22–23 ("in Arabia / There is one tree, the phoenix' throne"); and *Phoenix and the Turtle* 2 ("the sole Arabian tree"); Florio's *Dictionary* ("a tree in Arabia, whereof there is but one found"); and Lyly's *Euphues* ("there is but one tree in Arabia, wherein she buyldeth").

    embost: "imbosked," i.e., "hidden" (so *OED* 1b), "take[n] shelter" (*OED* 1a; Darbishire, *Poetical Works*), or "enclosed in a thicket" (so many editors, following Johnson, *Dictionary*). Hughes notes, "The word originally applied to hunted animals" (*Complete Poems*); Todd adds, "applied more particularly to the hart," and he supports this sense of hunting by citing passages from Chaucer, Chapman, and Phineas Fletcher.

1701. *no second knows:* the legend asserted that there was but a single specimen. Cf. *EpDam* 187 (*unica terris*) and *PL* 5.272. Percival and Verity cite Ovid, *Amores* 2.6.54: "unica semper avis"; "bird ever alone of its kind."

    nor third: Landor calls this addition "nonsense" (5:302–3).

1702. *a Holocaust:* "complete consumption by fire" (so *OED* 2c; the first usage, according to *OED*, where the word is not applied to burnt sacrifice). Editors cite Psalm 51:19. Parker suggests that a sacrifice to God (as in a Jewish burnt offering) is implied: "Samson's death would thus be interpreted as a pious sacrifice with a certainty of resurrection" ("Variorum").

1703. *her:* the phoenix is a male according to the ancients (and in *PL* 5.273–74). Osgood suggests that here "the new phoenix is not represented as a young bird, but as the old one rejuvenated by the fire" (69). Agreement with this assertion—and whether Milton makes the phoenix female—apparently depends on whether the simile is concluded with 1702; in other words, is *vertue* (1697) or *that self-begott'n bird* (1699) the subject of 1703? Verity favors *vertue* as the subject; Newton, Percival, and Wyatt and Collins favor *that self-begott'n bird*. Edmund K. Chambers and Hughes (*John Milton*) think that the phoenix is used in 1699–1702 as a simile for virtue but now becomes a metaphor. Verity notes, though, that the phoenix is female in Lyly's *Euphues* and in Shakespeare's *Phoenix and the Turtle; Sonnet* 19.4; and *Henry VIII* 5.5.411–43. See also 144n.

    teem'd: editors gloss as "brought forth, produced" (*OED* 1; a transitive past participle).

1704–05. Grieve thinks this is "a faithful picture of the poet." See 1687–1707n.

    then...when: "the demonstrative gives emphasis" (Verity); cf. *Mask* 188.

1706. *her:* virtue's (Latin: *virtus,* feminine; see 71n); the phoenix of course survives in body. For the sentiment Percival cites Homer's *Odyssey* 24.196 and Tyrtaeus's *Elegies* 2.8, 31.

    survives: Newton, following Calton (and cited by Todd), would omit the comma after this word, as breaking the construction. But *survives* may be read as "live[s] on" (so *OED* 1b), and, as Church suggests, the following line may revert to the simile. Church continues, "it seems better to take 'survives' as intransitive than to suppose that it governs 'a secular bird,' as meaning that virtue outlives the Phoenix...by ages of lives. We should expect to find *the,* not *a,* 'secular bird.'"

1707. *secular:* "living or lasting for an age or ages," "centuries old" (so *OED* 6; Latin: *saeculum:* "century, generation, age"). Herodotus's *Histories* 2.73 and Ovid's *Metamorphoses* 15.391–402 described the phoenix as completing five secles, or centuries, of life before rebirth; Pliny's *Naturalis historia* 10.2 made it 660 years; some writers made it a thousand. Osgood (70) writes that this line is a direct adaptation of *Metamorphoses* 15.395: "Hæc ubi quinque suae complevit secula vitae." Bush (*Milton*) also compares Claudian, *Phoenix* 104–5, "te saecula teste / cuncta revolvuntur." The sense of this line is: "(As) a secular bird (during) ages of lives" (Percival), or "(Like) a real Phoenix (for) ages of lives" (Wyatt). Masson (*Poetical Works*) takes issue with Newton, Todd, et al. for omitting the comma after *survives* so that the passage means " 'Virtue, like the Phoenix, teemed out of its own ashes, revives, etc.; and, though her body die, her fame outlives for ages of lives any ordinary phoenix or bird living a few centuries.'" Masson finds this reading "singularly languid" and suggests that the original text, with the comma, is correct. The passage thus reads, " 'Virtue, like the Phoenix, etc., revives, etc., and, though her body die, her fame survives, a real phoenix, ages of lives'" (*Poetical Works*). Prince suggests, "The omission of many grammatical links in these last lines is in keeping with the triumphant rapidity of the chorus" (*Samson Agonistes*). See 543–44n.

ages: perhaps "centuries," considering the preceding meaning of *secular*. Parker compares *RCG* (Patterson, *Works* 3:246, but also 3:208), where an age seems to be two hundred years ("Variorum").

1708–58. Ellis-Fermor writes that the concluding rhythm's "compactness and stability" contrast sharply with the "unmusical and formless" lines in the play's opening phases. Here, especially 1711–14 and 1745–48, the "extreme simplicity, of blank verse and choric ode alike, mirrors the serenity" (153).

1708. *Come, come*: so Euripides' Hecuba (591) "checks her grief" at news of the death of her daughter Polyxena (Dunster [in Todd]; Browne; Collins; Percival). Percival comments on "the impatience with which Manoah breaks upon the lament of the Chorus"; however, Parker, noting that the Chorus has just been rejoicing (not lamenting), suggests that Manoa is pathetically exhorting himself (*Milton's Debt* 52; and see Mollenkott 101). See 1660–1707n. Mahood calls it "the finest exequy in the language" (239). Mickle writes that the speech "is truly grand, very worthy of the father of a patriot hero" (405). Edward J. Thompson suggests that only *King Lear* can compare with Manoa's "superb words...for stoicism raised to such a pitch that it braces the spirit beyond the power of hope and joy" (250). Hamilton pronounces it "completely Sophoclean in substance and in style," and, quoting from it, adds: "It is hard to believe that Sophocles did not write that" (194). Parker adds, it "is a wonderful summary, but it is the Hebrew father's—not necessarily Milton's" (*Milton's Debt* 52).

no time: Parker explains, "because there is work to do" ("Variorum"); see 1715–16, 1725–37.

1709–11. *Samson*... / *Like Samson:* in rhetoric, a *traductio* or repetition of a word in an altered or pregnant sense, or for the sake of emphasis (Carey, *Complete Shorter Poems* 335–36); note also here, "heroicly... / ...heroic"; see 38–42n. Blakeney writes that Milton here "seems to ascribe to Samson a faith or repentance to which he has no real claim," and therefore is rather describing himself. Low instead suggests that this formulation expresses Samson's isolation and uniqueness: "As a man, he is something greater than a king, a knight, a leader, or a judge. *He has become himself*" ("Tragic Pattern" 929).

    quit: "do[ne] one's part," "behave[d]" (*OED* 3); editors often gloss as "acquitted" or "discharged his duty"; cf. 509, 897. Prince finds "also present here the idea that Samson has quitted his life" (*Samson Agonistes*).

    himself: cf. 1423–25.

    Like Samson: Parker describes Manoa's eloquent summary as a final irony, for Samson has acquitted himself like a new man, and his genuine heroism is in contrast to his unheroic past ("Variorum"). Mollenkott instead locates the irony in the statement's truth: "Samson died not only like God's champion but like a bragging strong-man" (91). But Daniells reads this line as unironic and accordingly describes the play's "philosophic conclusion" as "ambivalent": on the one hand, if Samson endured as the old Samson might have, the "suggestion is never dispelled that the hero has been unjustly treated by Providence"; on the other hand, we are later reassured that God assisted Samson to the end (216). See 1720.

1711–12. The first edition has a comma after *Heroic* and after *revenged;* some editors change one of these commas to a semicolon. See 543–44n.

    A Life Heroic: Parker comments, "it was this rather than saintly" ("Variorum"); cf. 1279, 1287–88.

1713. *Sons of Caphtor:* editors identify as "Philistines." See Deuteronomy 2:23; Jeremiah 47:4; Amos 9:7. Gilbert notes that this land "from which the Philistines came" has been "variously identified" with Crete (see 1 Sam. 30:14–16; Zeph. 2:5), the Nile Delta (see Gen. 10:14), and Cilicia. In Milton's time, he adds, "Cappodocia, the form used in the Vulgate, was also suggested" (*Geographical*).

1714. *Through all...bounds:* cf. *PL* 1.518.

Israel: B. A. Wright (*John Milton's Poems*) emends (as in 240 but not elsewhere) to *Israël,* as the meter would seem to require.

1715–16. Editors and commentators observe that they do not "lay hold on this occasion," and this is the final irony; see 1661n. In fact, Philistine control steadily increased until, in the battle of Aphek, they overwhelmed the Hebrews and even captured the sacred ark of the covenant (1 Sam. 4). As Diodati in 1648 puts it: "*Samson* did never quite free the people from the Philistims yoak: that being reserved for *David* to do, who was the figure of Christ, who shall accomplish the delivery of his Church, at the last glorious appearing of his kingdome" (sig. L5v). Northrop Frye also writes: "the Israel who triumphs is not the Israel that reluctantly followed and then deserted Samson: they have little part in his victory, and will be enslaved many times again. It is the Christian Israel, the city of God, whose power to destroy tyranny Samson has vindicated,...though nothing can actually be seen but bewildered slaves with no masters, a city wailing to its helpless gods, and a dead giant in a pile of broken stones" (Paradise Lost *and Selected Poetry* xxi). Percival alternatively suggests that 1715–16 be read as Milton's prophecy of the Glorious Revolution.

Honour: "victory" (Buchanan 174).

let but them: meaning "let them but," i.e., "if they only" (Blakeney).

courage: cf. 1521–22, where even the Chorus had, as if prophetically, shown lack of courage (Parker, "Variorum").

this: Percival writes, "emphatic," as "the Israelites had neglected former opportunities."

occasion: see 224n.

1717. An ironic echo of 447. As parallel sentiments Todd cites Pindar's *Isthmian Odes* 7; Percival, Euripides' *Rhesus* 758 and Tyrtaeus's *Elegies* 2.9.23. Hoffman finds this passage evidence of Manoa's limited understanding: "despite the ennobling catharsis of grief, human beings remain self-centered, concerned with the ephemeral dream of earthly repute" (208).

eternal fame: the phrase occurs also in *PL* 6.240 (Le Comte 66).

1718–19. Manoa, observes Parker, once again "takes a practical view of events, leaving generalization to the Chorus. He comes closest to a real [i.e., 'valid'] interpretation [in these lines]" (*Milton's Debt* 52). Hanford adds, "This doubt and its resolution are evidently important in the meaning of the drama" (*Poems*). Verity asserts that Manoa could not have spoken these lines if Samson had "premeditated his destruction." Stroup suggests that the passage "is wrought out of the prayer at the opening of the Service of the Burial of the Dead 'suffer vs not at our last houre for any paines of death to fall from the [*sic*]'" (62).

    which: "that which, what, something that" (see Blakeney; et al.).

    parted: Judges 16–20: "the Lord was departed from him." Cf. 632.

1720. *assisting:* Parker glosses as "helping, supporting" and/or "standing by, accompanying" ("Variorum"). Daniells argues that the "explicit nature of God's dealings" with Samson "make impossible the normal effect of tragedy, either Greek or Elizabethan" (166).

1721–24. Commentators generally agree about the excellence of these lines but offer differing views about the passage's implications for Manoa's character. Raleigh calls this "the loftiest epitaph in the language" (*Milton* 9). Bush thinks this passage "may represent the last phase of Milton's 'classical' art" (*John Milton* 199) and quotes it as a "great example" of blank verse "which in its irregularities is much more colloquial and 'prosaic,' much more closely molded to the natural movement of thought and feeling, than the blank verse of epic speeches and dialogue" (*Milton* 516; *Portable Milton* 28). Bullough and Bullough claim that "in this superb epitaph Manoa achieves great nobility." Arthos suggests that Manoa's speech "characterizes perfectly" the audience's feelings at the end of the drama: "This is the formula of funeral benediction rather than of the terrible state of the purged" (178). Northrop Frye compares the "serene quiet" of the poem's conclusion to the "solemn troops and sweet societies" in *Lyc* (Paradise Lost *and Selected Poetry* xxi). But Mollenkott suggests that Manoa is "obviously trying to convince himself that there is nothing to cry about since he urges the Chorus to stop lamenting when they have not been lamenting, but exulting…; and his callousness about the grief of Gaza need not be taken as a directive to the reader" (101); see 1708n. Baker describes this passage as "a vision of erring man wrestling with the infinite justice of God" and uses it to place Milton "securely within the central tradition of Christian humanism"; he writes that in *SA* (as well as *PL*) Milton was "seeking to preserve both human responsibility and divine sovereignty" (41). Daniells similarly notes that the play here has a "double resolution, one Greek (or at least classical) and one Hebraic, so deftly compounded as to produce a single effect of remarkable depth" (213). Baum notes that "The happy ending is in large measure hostile to greatly tragic effectiveness; but 'averted tragedy' was not unknown to the Greeks" (366). Fell finds in this statement evidence that Manoa "does attain to an understanding in the end" and achieves "reconciliation to the ostensibly merciless divine" (152). Martz, however, argues that in this passage Manoa, as does the Chorus, misses "the true greatness of Samson's achievement," and, "Like everything else that Manoa has said in the play, this [speech] is at best a half-truth, a partial understanding" (131, 132). Lewalski notes, though, that "this [statement] does not mean that nothing is here to promote tragic effect"; she adds that "the adumbrations of...that perfect conquest and victory of the Saints over their enemies which can only come after the end of time...may seem to mitigate the tragic effect by reference to the Apocalyptic hope, but at the same time they enhance it in regard to individual human lives, like Samson's, which must be lived out in such conditions" ("*Samson Agonistes*" 1062).

Nothing: "nought" (so *OED* A.1); Parker thus paraphrases: "(there) is no (cause) in this event or circumstance" ("*Variorum*"). Church and Bush (*Milton*) quote Tacitus's *Agricola* 46: "quas neque lugeri, neque plangi fas est"; "which it were impiety to lament or mourn." Dunster (in Todd) comments that the remainder of Manoa's speech "gradually rises in beauty, so as to form one of the most captivating parts of this admirable tragedy." Blakeney is reminded of the passing of Oedipus. Charles Williams writes that this line "is here no Stoic maxim, but something beyond—something 'comely and reviving.' The phrase would cover most of Milton" ("Introduction" xxi–xxii).

wail: see 66.

1722. *knock the breast:* editors supply *for.* Cf. Luke 23:48 for this sign of grief among the Hebrews. Haigh notes that the kommos (see 1660–1758n) or "dirge" in Greek tragedy was "in its origin an artistic development from the old national custom of lamentation at funerals, and derived its name from the beating of the breast by which lamentation was accompanied" (359).

contempt: Parker glosses as "disgrace, contemptible action" ("*Variorum*").

1723. *Dispraise:* "cause of blame, discredit, or disgrace" (*OED* 2b).

but: editors gloss as "but (what is)."

well: "good," "of a character or quality to which no exception can be taken" (so *OED* 8c).

fair: "desirable," "propitious," or "suitable" (*OED* I.3, IV.14). Meiklejohn notes the use of adjectives for nouns; cf. 324.

1724–25. *quiet us:* Parker glosses as "free us from agitation" but suggests that a pun is intended: *quietus,* meaning "death" ("Variorum").

    noble: Dunster (in Todd) is reminded of the rites paid to the corpses of Sarpedon, Patroclus, and Hector in *Iliad* 16, 18, 24. Thaler finds Manoa's tribute "strikingly like" that of Brutus in *Julius Caesar* 5.5.68–75 ("Shakespearian Element" 148).

1726. See 122n.

1727. *lavers pure:* Wyatt and Collins gloss as "washing vessels (full of) pure (water 'from the stream')." Verity notes that lavers in the Old Testament were used for the ablutions of the Jewish priests and victims (150). Cf. *Mask* 838; *PR* 1.280; *RCG* (Patterson, *Works* 3:191). *OED* 3 cites this line and defines "a process or mode of ablution"; Lockwood suggests, "water used in the bath." On *pure,* cf. 548.

1728. Editors paraphrase: "I wish what speed (I can) meanwhile."

1729. *Gaza:* Parker suggests, "presumably the 'throng' (1609) of 'vulgar' (1659) who survived" ("Variorum").

    plight: editors gloss as "state, condition" (*OED* 4a); Verity notes it was originally neutral (153); cf. 480.

1730. So Judges 16:31: "then his brethren and all the house of his father came down, and took him, and brought him up, and buried him"—a passage that Newton says Milton "has finely improved."

1731. *fetch:* cf. 921.
    solemnly: "gravely" (so *OED*).
    attend: "accompany" (*OED* II.4).

1732. *silent:* Percival, Verity, and Wyatt quote Todd on the custom of silence at Jewish funerals: "all the near relations of the deceased came to the house in their mourning dress, and sat down upon the ground *in silence;* whilst in another part of the house were heard the voices of mourners, and the sound of instruments hired for the purpose."

   obsequie: "funeral rites or ceremonies" (so *OED*), or, in the literal sense, "following, train" (Percival; Wyatt and Collins; Grieve).

   train: "procession" (Prince, *Samson Agonistes;* cf. *OED* 11). Parker comments, "Presumably all these words refer, not to the actual burial ceremonies, but to the carrying of Samson's body from *Gaza* 'Home to his Father's house,' where the burial took place" ("Variorum").

1733–44. Parker ("Variorum") finds here a possible echo of Jewish culture: Jacob set up a pillar at the grave of Rachel, making it a sanctuary (Gen. 35:20; cf. 1 Sam. 10:2); other sanctuaries were the graves of Joseph at Shechem (Josh. 24:32; cf. Gen. 12:6; 35:4), Sarah (Gen. 13:18; 18:1, 23), Miriam (Num. 20:1), and Deborah, Rebekah's nurse (Gen. 35:8). Bowra instead detects an echo of Greek culture: "Much as Milton disliked all outward forms of religion and anything that savoured of ritual, he was in this case prepared to make some concession and to allow to his Jewish hero the kind of posthumous survival which the Greeks accorded to their great men" (115); Mickle also writes that the speech is "in the genuine spirit of the first of the Greek tragedies" (405). But Jebb contrasts Manoa's plans for a monument with the consecrated mountain that marked Herakles' apotheosis: whereas Samson's grave "was long visited by the men of his tribe and people with the remembrance only of a triumph—of a victory which his successors had perpetuated," Herakles' mountain did not convey the same continuity: for the Greeks, "it was…a lonely instance of superhuman strength towering above the rugged, low range of human history, and confronting, though not vanquishing…the awful malignity of fate" ("*Samson Agonistes*" 348). Baruch notes the "loveliness and inappropriateness" of Manoa's future plans for his son, which unfortunately remain "rooted firmly in the material world" (325). Bush (*John Milton* 200; *Milton*) notices the parallel with Dalila's image of her posthumous fame (986–90); according to Frank, the similarity is one of the drama's paradoxes that "indicate Milton's intellectual and artistic daring" (105); according to Huntley, this "echo suggests that…Manoa [is] advancing from a self-centered to nationalistic view of events" (143). See 1741n. Wilkenfeld instead finds here a connection with Samson's choice of "Sun or shade" at the poem's start: "It was as a result of this choice to accept 'ease' in the 'Sun' that Samson ultimately finds a 'resting place' in the 'shade'" (168).

Home to his Fathers house: in very different fashion the victorious Jesus returns "Home to his Mothers house" (*PR* 4.639; cf. *PR* 3.175; 4.552); Barker writes that Jesus' and Samson's respective returns "and their contexts are related in the right order" in the 1671 volume (176). See 1481n, and cf. 518. Citing both *PR* and *Lyc,* Broadbent suggests that Milton's longer poems "end with abrupt dismission to the everyday while the poet or his persona steps off into privacy...as though trying to disengage himself from the work's moodiness and relegate it to the reader's contemplation as an artifact" (*Some Graver Subject* 288). Bush, remembering John 14:2, wonders if "an ambiguous overtone" is intended here ("Ironic" 634).

1734–35. *shade / Of Laurel:* hendiadys for "shady laurel" (Percival; Wyatt and Collins). See 105n.

    branching Palm: it has no branches; thus, Milton here and in *PL* 4.139 and 6.885 refers to the head or tufted crown of fan-shaped leaves and their stalks (Percival; and see Le Comte 64). Parker ("Variorum") compares Ovid, *Metamorphoses* 15.395–400. Verity notes that the laurel and palm symbolize victory or triumph; the laurel "being 'ever green,' is also emblematic of undying fame"; cf. *Lyc* 1 and *SolMus* 14.

1736. *Trophies:* editors gloss as "spoils, tokens of victory, valor, or strength" (*OED* 2), i.e., to be hung on the "monument." Le Comte (174) compares *IlPen* 118: "Of Turneys and trophies hung." Some editors, following Todd, suggest that Milton is thinking here, as in *IlPen,* of the age of chivalry. Parker ("Variorum") adds that the custom was also one of Greek and Roman antiquity (cf. *PR* 4.37). The Philistines put the dead Saul's armor in the temple of Ashtaroth (1 Sam. 31:10). See 1740n.

    enroll'd: editors gloss as "recorded, celebrated" (*OED* 6); cf. 653.

1737. *copious:* "abounding in information," "full of matter" (*OED* 2).

    Legend: "story, history" (so *OED* 3), or "epic poetry" (Wyatt and Collins). Verity, however, writes, "the sense 'false story' had become the usual one when Milton wrote." Grieve refers to this term (along with "Trophies" [1736]) as a "mediævalism"; cf. also 1740n. Hughes suggests that the term refers to "either an inscription over the tomb or a literary record like the lives of the saints in the Golden Legend" (*John Milton*). Krouse notes that there is no mention of an epitaph in Judges, but thinks that "some seventeenth-century readers would probably have found [here] an allusion to exegetical writings": an epitaph for Samson is included in Salianus's *Annales ecclesiastici veterus Testamenti* (1620), 2:441–72 (reprinted in Cornelius à Lapide's *Commentarius in Ioshue, Iudicum, Ruth* [1664]). Krouse adds that *Legend* in *SA* "was the name of a literary genre...and designated a saint's life—another indication that Milton did not depart from the conception of Samson as saint" (108). Cf. *PE* (Patterson, *Works* 3:82) and *HistBr* (Patterson, *Works* 10:5, 128, 155, 179, 193, 231).

 sweet Lyric Song: Percival, Verity, and Blakeney suggest as examples the songs of deliverance and victory sung by Moses (Exod. 15), by Deborah and Barak (Judg. 5), and by David (2 Sam. 20:1–51; Ps. 18, 68). Todd quotes Pindar's *Pythian Odes* 1. Le Comte notes that *sweet* is Milton's "favorite word for music" (63).

1738–40. Percival supposes that the youths would honor Samson's memory with "athletic and martial exercises" and recalls Homer's *Iliad* 23 and Plutarch's *Alexander*.

1739. *inflame:* cf. 1690–91 (also 25, 1433–35).

1740. *matchless valour:* Parker ("Variorum") notes that the phrase occurs also in *RCG* (Patterson, *Works* 3:275) and *TKM* (Patterson, *Works* 5:37); cf. *PL* 6.457.

 adventures high: Todd and Percival note, "this is a term in chivalry and romance," and give examples. Quarles had written: "his youth was crown'd / With high and brave adventures" (sig. F1r). Parker adds that *Adventure* is Spenser's usual word for *quest* ("Variorum").

1741. Editors (e.g., Verity and Edmund K. Chambers) note that this is an honor that Dalila had promised herself (986–87). Mollenkott suggests that such a conjunction between Manoa and Dalila supports the "human validity" of Dalila's departing speech (99). See 960–96n, 1733–44n.

 feastful: "festival" (so *OED* 1); cf. *Sonn 9* 12.

1742–44. Commentators disagree about the merit of this passage. To Charles Williams, these lines coming so near the end "(of all places in poetry!) appear almost funny" (*English Poetic Mind* 155). To Belloc, this ending of a "very fine speech" is bathos; he deplores "the horrid shock, the flop" (272). But Parker finds this passage one of the finest ironies of the drama, "a final reminder that Manoa has never really understood the downfall of the son whose death he eloquently celebrates" ("Variorum"). This last reference to women in *SA*, Parker adds in response to Collins's criticism, "far from justifies any charge of 'all-pervading misogyny'" (*Milton's Debt* 134; see 1010–60n). Lawry also defends these lines: "Although Manoa insists (perhaps self-righteously) that causative sin be remembered, this does not pull down the whole play into a mere protest against unfortunate marriage, any more than the gravestone in *The Scarlet Letter* signals a mere protest against unfortunate love affairs" (395). Percival notes that the ancients and the early Christians had the custom of putting flowers on tombs, but it does not seem to have existed among the Jews.

1742. *only:* Baruch identifies this adverb as a pun: on the one hand, Manoa is describing how the virgins will mourn "only" that part of Samson's story they can appreciate; on the other hand, the word *only* hints that the virgins, like Manoa, are misplacing their sorrow by focusing attention on Samson's worldly status (326). Cf. 1733–44n.

1743. *lot:* "destiny, fortune, or 'portion' in this life" (so *OED* 2d); so also 996, 1292.

1744. Parker comments on Manoa's final words: "they close a speech in which the father takes consolation in distinctly lesser values: revenge, patriotism, family honor, the ritual of burial, earthly fame" ("Variorum"). Percival suggests that Manoa departs after this line.

1745–58. That the final words should be spoken by the chorus was a conspicuous convention of Greek tragedy (the only exceptions being *Agamemnon, Prometheus Bound,* and *Women of Trachis*), and commentators identify obvious resemblances between this speech and the final chorus that Euripides uses in *Andromache, Alcestis, Bacchae,* and *Helen,* all of which are identical; there is a slight variation in the ending of *Medea*. On the sentiment, Thyer (in Newton) cites Aeschylus's *Suppliant Maidens* 90–109; Todd, the "six last verses" of Pindar's twelfth Pythian Ode; and Percival, Plato's *Republic* 10.12. Edmund K. Chambers notes that Euripides frequently ends his plays with some remarks of the

chorus to the effect of "Inscrutable are the ways of God," but Milton alters this
to "The ways of God are past finding out, but always for the best." Chambers
instead compares the end of *SA* with the blessing of the Communion service
of the Anglican church: "the peace of God, which passeth all understanding,
keep your hearts and minds in the knowledge and love of God, and of His son
Jesus Christ our Lord."

Other commentators also discuss how Milton modifies the classical sentiment
in the Chorus's last speech. Epps cites these closing lines to illustrate how Milton adds "the Hebraic idea of God's foreordained purpose" to the Greek idea
of ὕβρις, an addition that shows Milton "was no servile imitator" (195, 196).
Bowra also observes, "we see at once that Milton has provided a purgation different from what he describes in his Preface, or at least applied his doctrine in a
special way. Not only have pity and fear been removed, but...we feel peace and
consolation" (127). Similarly, Kaufmann, noting that both *SA* and *Oedipus at
Coloneus* end with a report of a religious experience, asserts that "the two endings are very different: the former brings humanity up to godhead, and hence
is an apotheosis; the latter shows God reaching into history and performing
His Providential function of making a martyr" (376). Lawry writes that this
passage, together with the phoenix image, "seriously intimates the Apocalypse
as well as present catharsis and the restoration of Israel, thereby impressing massive order beyond that of the immediate artistic action" (397). Alternatively,
Radzinowicz comments that these lines "summarize what the drama revealed.
God resembles the Aristotelian tragic poet, and human existence an Aristotelian
tragedy" ("Eve" 180–81). On the sentiment, Parker ("Variorum") compares
also *Animad:* "Every one can say that now certainly thou hast visited this land,
and hast not forgotten...in a time when men had thought that thou wast gone
up from us to the farthest end of the Heavens" (Patterson, *Works* 3:147). See
also 1745n, 1755–58n, 1758n.

Most commentators think the ending of *SA* beautiful and fitting. E.g., Parker
writes, "The final speech is sublime in its utter brevity. We hear a benediction
after a solemn music" (*Milton's Debt* 53); Edward J. Thompson makes this same
point, adding, "This is the only play of this kind in English that has equalled the
divine reticence of the Greeks, on their own ground" (250–51). Wordsworth
reportedly found the poem's ending, like its beginning, "sublime" (qtd. in
Robinson 2:479); Alden Sampson calls it "a supremely fitting ending for his
last expression in verse" (162); and Ellis-Fermor specifically remarks upon "the
mood of beatitude which is the natural conclusion of religious drama" (80).

Collins attributes these lines to the tragedy's "technical exigencies" and Milton's "righteous confidence in God's justice and wisdom"; he concludes that "Nobler verses never flowed from the pen of man." Tillyard also comments: "I see in Milton little signs of brooding on another life and every sign of an intense concern with the world as it is. His renewed trust in the highest wisdom indicates some sallying out from the Protestant citadel of the individual self, some renewed faith in the goodness of life as lived on earth. Samson has, after all, saved his country" (*Miltonic Setting* 87–88). On Israel's salvation, see 1715–16n.

Some commentators find the use of rhyme in this speech (abab, cdcd, efefef) especially significant. E.g., Beum thinks the rhyme sets off the "metaphysical tenor" of the Chorus's words: "The closing speech is so lofty and universalized that it is at once a summarizing comment on the action and meaning of the poem, and a description and example of the cathartic effect of classical tragedy" (181). Roberts W. French discusses the significance of the rhyme for the Chorus's development: "Just as the contradictions and confusions of the Chorus have been laid to rest, so their lines have been tamed by rhyme" (60). Muir also compliments Milton's choice here: "anything more sensuous or displaying a more lively sensibility would be more shocking than Milton's flat statements in which he weds the Aristotelian theory of tragedy to religious sentiment.... [I]t has the effect, after the occasional rhymes and assonances of the earlier choruses, of rounding off the whole play. The re-affirmation of faith finds its metrical equivalent in the rhymes for which the chorus had seemed earlier to be fumbling" (184). MacCaffrey suggests the speech "calls on gnarled syntax broken by simple phrases...and unorthodox diction to express the bewilderment of human vision confronted by the mystery of tragedy which it has accepted but cannot totally comprehend" (xxvi). Sprott writes that the rhyme here is "for epigrammatic purposes" (133). Parker emphasizes this "intricate rime pattern...reminiscent of a sonnet" to support his argument that Milton must have composed *SA* before he denounced rhyme in the note on "The Verse" in *PL* ("Date" 223).

A few commentators find fault with this final passage. Belloc notes that *SA* ends "at its fine full flow, which would have been more satisfactory had it not lapsed into rhyme" (277). Larson suggests that "the only consolation Milton here can find is to throw himself blindly upon the mercy of God" (174), and says of the final speech: "This is essentially the attitude of surrender which is characteristic of all Puritan thought" (175). Ralli also declares: "if there is a calm, the cause is rather the numbness and exhaustion that follow a catastrophe than increase of spiritual knowledge.... In the last phase the clouds re-gather, and only a Being from beyond can vanquish evil; and the only kind of happiness that survives is the true repentance of a captive in chains.... The last word, therefore, despite his greatness is 'frustration'" (142).

1745–46. Bridges thinks these lines are in falling (trochaic) rhythm (*Milton's Prosody* 55); Sprott (132) thinks it difficult to determine whether Milton thought of the lines as "trochaic with the last foot catalectic, or as iambic with the first foot catalectic." See 116n.

1745. *All is best:* Percival glosses, "All is (for the) best." Mahood here infers that "*Samson Agonistes* is ... the story of a Fortunate Fall.... [A]pparent evil is once more the source of final good" (250–51). Parker, however, doubts that the ending is "fortunate": "it is a hard saying, this final 'All is best' of the Chorus. It was best for them, best for Israel; best for all men, I take it, in the light of God's 'divine disposal'.... But Milton, in *Samson Agonistes,* is a greater artist than he is a philosopher.... Is Samson not a victim of Fate as surely as was Oedipus at Colonus? ... A great figure has suffered greatly, and died to illustrate a great principle. But a great figure has suffered" (*Milton's Debt* 226–28). Kurth similarly argues, "Though Samson was an instrument of Providence, his end was tragic because before Christ's act of Redemption there could be no Christian sense of salvation" (132). Some critics accept this pronouncement as a summation of the poem's overarching meaning and an indication of Milton's inability to sustain *SA* as tragedy; e.g., see Hughes, who interprets the Chorus's speech here to mean that Samson "has redeemed himself by his last act from the passions which were his spiritual tragedy" (*John Milton* 440; see also Baum 365–66). But Hanford argues that "the reality of suffering" and "the pain of the earlier scenes is something which cannot be so easily displaced. Sealed as it is with the hero's death, it outlives all consolation" (*John Milton* 224; "*Samson Agonistes*" 182). He finds the specific pronouncement in this line "of scarcely more avail than the identical formulae which bring Greek plays to their conclusion and from which this one is derived.... Though Providence is proclaimed, its ways are dark and its face, at times, is hardly to be distinguished from the countenance of Fate herself.... [T]here remains an irreducible element in the midst of Milton's faith—a sense as keen as Shakespeare's of the reality of suffering which neither the assurance of God's special favors to himself nor his resolute insistence on the final triumph of his righteousness can blot out" (*John Milton*

224; "*Samson Agonistes*" 182–83). Stroup thinks this consolation "bears the mark of the Christian formulary" and "is closer in doctrine" to the Service of the Burial of the Dead than to "the formulary out of Greek drama on which it is patterned" (62). See also 1745–58n.

though we oft doubt: Percival notes that the Chorus had indeed done so in 667–704.

1746. *unsearchable:* "inscrutable" (*OED* 1). Parker ("Variorum") compares Psalm 145:3: "his greatness is unsearchable"; he also compares *PL* 8.10 and *DDD:* "God indeed in some wayes of his providence, is high and secret past finding out" (Patterson, *Works* 3:445). Saurat writes that God in *SA* "is more mysterious and more dreadful; He is no longer the all-too-clear logician of *Paradise Lost;* He is the incomprehensible and yet just Power that presides over the course of the World. . . . For the first time in Milton's work, there appears an element which is lacking in *Paradise Lost,* the feeling of awe in the presence of God, respectful dread and trust" (198, 200).

dispose: editors gloss as "disposal," "dispensation," or "ordering." Cf. 61, 210, 373, 506. Verity also cites *RCG* (Patterson, *Works* 3:270): "the arbitrary and illegal dispose of any one that may hereafter be call'd a King."

1747–48. *highest wisdom:* the phrase occurs also in *PL* 7.83.

brings about: "cause to happen" (Lockwood).

close: Parker ("Variorum") suggests "end," but also, possibly, "the closing passage (of a drama)." Cf. 651.

1749–54. To Tillyard these lines seem "curiously uncouth" (*Milton* 284). Bridges thinks that 1749 is another in falling (trochaic) rhythm (*Milton's Prosody* 55). Sprott (132) thinks it difficult to determine whether Milton thought of the line as "trochaic with the last foot catalectic, or as iambic with the first foot catalectic." See 116n.

hide his face: "take no heed" (*OED* 1c), or, Verity suggests, "turn away in displeasure" (editors cite, e.g., *Ps 88* 58; also Psalm 27:9, 30:7, 104:29; cf. Psalm 67:1).

1750. *unexpectedly:* Parker comments, "this word emphasizes once more the Chorus's surprise at the providential turn of events" ("Variorum").

1751. *faithful:* Krouse (85) writes that Samson in Milton's period was thought to have fulfilled his vocation faithfully by pulling down the temple; he cites Johann Brenz, "Moritur in fide et vocatione Dei" (*In librum Iudicum et Ruth commentarius* [1535]), and notes "a similar gloss is given in the Geneva ('Breeches') Bible." In Hebrews 11:32, Samson is listed among the heroes of faith.

 Champion: cf. 705, and see 556n.

 in place: editors suggest "in this present place, here" (Edmund K. Chambers, citing Shakespeare's *Measure for Measure* 5.1.500); "opportunely, at the proper moment, in due course" (Blakeney; Grieve); "in the proper place, opportunely," like ἐν καιρῷ and opposed to "out of place" (Percival); "appropriately, fittingly" (Martin W. Sampson); "by his (God's) presence" (Verity); "in the right place, at the right moment" (Prince, *Samson Agonistes*); and "present" (Lockwood I.9).

1752. *Bore:* Blakeney glosses as "borne," and notes this form (the past participle of *bear*) was common in the seventeenth century.

 witness: cf. 239.

 whence: cf. 1216, 1744. Bush (*Milton*) cites Aeschylus's *Persians* 511–12.

1753–54. *band them:* "unite themselves" (Blakeney).

 intent: a comma follows this word in the first edition; editors typically replace it with a semicolon or period.

1755–58. Commentators emphasize the Aristotelian sentiment in these final lines. E.g., Raleigh observes: "[Milton's] last word on human life might be translated into Greek with no straining and no loss of meaning" (*Milton* 30); Gilbert also suggests that Aristotle is "virtually quoted in the concluding lines" (*Literary Criticism* 587); Langdon, too, describes it as "a fine reminiscence of Aristotle" (94); and Gray calls the final line "the most completely classical, and perhaps the greatest, single line he ever wrote" (145).

 Some commentators believe the ending of *SA* refers "to the condition of Milton's own mind after he had fought the good fight of religion and freedom" (so Percival; see also Blakeney, and cf. Macaulay 133). Other commentators suggest that the ending indicates Milton's sense of artistry and of the purpose of great art. Thus, Allen writes: "there is more to the tragedy than the passionate purgation of the Chorus, of Manoa, and of Samson. Aristotle may have laid down the rules and the poet Milton may have obeyed them, but behind them both was a greater critic and a greater poet who made the rules in eternity and supplied the tragic *fabula* for his own glory" ("Idea as Pattern" 94). Hanford terms this final line "the fruit of the experience for actors, audience, and author alike" (*Poems* 549). He also observes: "It is characteristic of the critical self-consciousness which Milton carries with him even in his moments of highest creative inspiration and suggestive also of the vital uses to which he turned aesthetic as well as religious doctrine that the last word of all should be an almost explicit reference to the tragic formula which he had derived from the authority of 'the master of those who know' " ("*Samson Agonistes*" 189).

More generally, commentators here discuss *SA*'s sense of resolution. To Arthos, the final line "seems to mean that all conflict, all fever, has been done with, now there is to be reconciliation and content, the peace of God prevailing" (145). Saurat writes, "Samson is buried in his victory. Such death is not to be dreaded; it is the final liberation from passion, the ultimate triumph of intelligence" (199). Woodhouse finds only in these final words the drama's resolution of "the inner tension between man's freedom and God's Providence" ("Tragic Effect" 207). Landy also suggests that the final lines reflect "the culminating experience of a man's labor, a tremendous reward for man's great effort to be converted and spiritually reborn in God" ("Of Highest Wisdom" 185). And Steadman writes, "this is the Christian equivalent of the Stoic *consolatio*. Like the latter, it attempts to comfort; like the latter, it seeks to moderate the passions and restore tranquility of mind" ("Tragic Glass" 108). See also 1758n.

Some commentators compare the ending of *SA* and the conclusions of Milton's other long poems. E.g., Bailey interprets these final lines as "that peace which follows upon the right understanding of all great experiences," a sentiment he also finds implied at the end of *PL* and *PR*, whereas here it is "almost expressly set forth" (249). Raleigh similarly thinks all three of Milton's long poems conclude "with the same exquisite lull" (*Milton* 158; cf. Raleigh, "Milton's Last Poems" 253).

Among other responses to this passage, Mueller thinks these lines leave the catharsis somewhat ambiguous: "on the one hand, it is 'calm of mind, all passion spent'; on the other hand it is 'new acquist of true experience,' an insight into the perplexing ways of dire necessity, which willing acceptance can mitigate but the terror of which it can never entirely remove" ("*Pathos*" 174). Landy instead notes that the Chorus "finally comes to terms with the nature of sin and the nature of God's justice and mercy. As a result of its spiritual growth, it is able to articulate the final statement of the play, which is one of justification of God's ways" ("Character" 252). Huntley similarly argues that in the end the Chorus's "vision of reality remains less perfect than Samson's" and "their willingness to act well in God's service...is less firm," but here "they see more clearly than ever before who Samson is, what it means to be a son of Israel, and how God orders the world through His just providence" (142–43). Grierson in his old age reportedly pointed to these lines while summing up his sentiments about the author: "Milton is the one great English poet who lasts a lifetime" (qtd. in Nicolson 373). See also 1745–58n.

His servants: editors identify this as Manoa and the Chorus. But, Verity notes, because this is an explicit recognition of the principle of catharsis, it presumably also includes readers. Newton writes that other early editions change it to *his servant*. Parker adds, "the word 'servant' implies obedience" ("Variorum").

acquist: editors gloss as "acquisition" (*OED* 2); Meiklejohn observes it is Milton's sole use of the word, which is listed in Phillip's *New World*. Masson (*Poetical Works*) notes that the word, sometimes spelled *acquest,* is "not unfrequent in the old writers."

1756. Parker (*Milton's Debt* 53) and Le Comte (174) note that this line "strangely echoes Satan's words" in *PL* 1.118.

true: "conveying truth" (cf. *OED* 3d), and/or "of the right kind, such as it should be" (*OED* 4b).

experience: cf. 188, 382.

event: see 737, and cf. 1551.

1757. Commentators note the rhyme scheme would have been that of a Shakespearean sonnet had Milton ended this with a couplet; on the rhyme, see 1745–58n.

peace: cf. 1445.

consolation: cf. 183, where the Chorus thought itself bringing this (Parker, "Variorum").

dismist: "give[n] permission to go," "bid depart" (*OED* 2); note "servants" (1755). Parker comments, "the reader, too, is thus dismissed" ("Variorum"). Cf. 688.

1758. *passion:* editors gloss as "agitation, vehement or overpowering emotion" (*OED* 6). Cf. 1006n. See the account of the purpose of tragedy given in Milton's

Preface, but recall also the quiet ending of *Lyc*. Hughes is reminded of the Italian critic Antonio Minturno's use of passion "in the strong sense" in his *L'arte poetica* (1564), where he compares the soul's "impestuous passions" to poisons in an ill body (*Complete Poems; John Milton*). Hughes explains further: "Milton expected our pleasure in watching the disease of passion run its course in his hero to work as a kind of homeopathic medicine upon us and 'purge' us of the 'pity' and 'fear' by which we are beset" (*John Milton* 440). See also 1755–58n.

Works Cited

Editions

Beeching, H. C., ed. *The Poetical Works of John Milton*. Oxford: Clarendon Press, 1900.

Blakeney, E. H., ed. *Milton:* Samson Agonistes. Edinburgh: Blackwood, 1902.

Bohn, Henry G., ed. *The Poetical Works of John Milton*. London: William Ball, 1838.

Brinkley, Roberta Florence, ed. *Samson Agonistes. English Poetry of the Seventeenth Century,* 326–76. New York: W. W. Norton, 1942.

Brooks, Cleanth. *Complete Poetry and Selected Prose of John Milton*. New York: Modern Library, 1950.

Browne, R. C., ed. *English Poems by John Milton*. 2 vols. 1866. Rev. by Henry Bradley. Oxford: Clarendon Press, 1902.

Brydges, Egerton, ed. *The Poetical Works of John Milton*. 6 vols. London: John Macrone, 1835.

Bullough, Geoffrey, and Margaret Bullough, eds. *Milton's Dramatic Poems*. London: Athlone Press, 1958. Rev. ed. London: Athlone Press, 1965.

Bush, Douglas, ed. *Milton: Poetical Works*. London: Oxford University Press, 1966.

———. *The Portable Milton*. New York: Penguin, 1949.

Carey, John, ed. *The Complete Shorter Poems*. London: Longman, 1971.

Carey, John, and Alastair Fowler, eds. *The Poems of John Milton*. London: Longmans, 1968.

Chambers, Edmund K., ed. *Samson Agonistes*. London: Blackie and Son, 1897.

Church, A[lfred] J., ed. *Milton's* Samson Agonistes. London: Seeley, Jackson, and Halliday, 1872.

Collins, John Churton, ed. *Samson Agonistes*. Oxford: Clarendon Press, 1883.

Cowper, William, and William Hayley, eds. *The Poetical Works of John Milton*. 3 vols. London: John and Josiah Boydell, and George Nicol, 1794–97.

481

Darbishire, Helen, ed. *The Poetical Works of John Milton.* 2 vols. Oxford: Clarendon Press, 1952–55.

Fenton, Elijah, ed. Paradise Regain'd. *A Poem. In Four Books. To Which is Added* Samson Agonistes. London: Jacob Tonson, 1725.

Fleming, I. P., ed. *Milton's Imitation of a Greek Tragedy,* Samson Agonistes. London: Longman, 1876.

Fletcher, Harris Francis, ed. *John Milton's Complete Poetical Works Reproduced in Photographic Facsimile.* 4 vols. Urbana: University of Illinois Press, 1943–48.

Frye, Northrop, ed. Paradise Lost *and Selected Poetry and Prose.* New York: Rinehart, 1951.

Grierson, Herbert J. C., ed. *The Poems of John Milton.* 2 vols. London: Chatto and Windus, 1925.

Grieve, A. J., ed. Samson Agonistes *by John Milton.* London: Dent, 1904.

Hanford, James Holly. *The Poems of John Milton.* New York: Thomas Nelson, 1936. 2nd ed. New York: Ronald Press, 1953.

Hughes, Merritt Y., ed. *Complete Poems and Major Prose.* New York: Macmillan, 1957.

———. *John Milton:* Paradise Regained, *the Minor Poems, and* Samson Agonistes. Garden City, N.Y.: Doubleday, Doran, 1937.

Hunter, John, ed. *Milton's* Samson Agonistes *and* Lycidas. London: Longmans, Green, 1870.

Jerram, Charles S., ed. *Samson Agonistes.* London: Rivingtons, 1890.

Keightley, Thomas, ed. *The Poems of John Milton.* 2 vols. London: Chapman and Hall, 1859.

MacCaffrey, Isabel Gamble, ed. Samson Agonistes *and the Shorter Poems.* New York: New American Library, 1966.

Masson, David, ed. *The Poetical Works of John Milton.* 3 vols. 1874. Rev. ed. London: Macmillan, 1890.

Meiklejohn, J. M. D., ed. *Milton's* Samson Agonistes. *With Church's Introduction and Milton's Preface.* New York: Maynard, Merrill, 1893.

Milton, John. *Paradise Regain'd. A Poem. In IV Books. To Which is Added Samson Agonistes.* London: John Starkey, 1671.

———. *Paradise Regain'd. A Poem. In IV Books. To Which is Added Samson Agonistes.* 2nd ed. London: John Starkey, 1680.

———. *Paradise Regain'd. A Poem. In IV Books. To Which is Added Samson Agonistes.* London: Randal Taylor, 1688.

———. *Paradise Regain'd. A Poem. In IV Books. To Which is Added Samson Agonistes.* London: J. Tonson, 1713.

———. Paradise Regained, Samson Agonistes, *and* Poems upon Several Occasions. London: J. and R. Tonson et al., 1747.

———. *The Poetical Works of John Milton.* 2 vols. London: Jacob Tonson, 1705.

Mitford, John, ed. *The Poetical Works of John Milton.* 2 vols. 1832. Boston: Phillips, Sampson; New York: James C. Derby, 1854.

Moody, William Vaughan, ed. *The Complete Poetical Works of John Milton.* Boston: Houghton Mifflin, 1899.

Newton, Thomas, ed. Paradise Regained, Samson Agonistes, *and* Poems upon Several Occasions. 2 vols. London, 1752. London: J. and R. Tonson et al., 1766.

Onions, C. T., ed. *Samson Agonistes.* London: Horace Marshall and Son, 1905.

Page, Thomas, ed. *Samson Agonistes.* London: Moffatt and Paige, 1896.

Patterson, Frank Allen, ed. *The Student's Milton.* 1930. New York: F. S. Crofts, 1934.

Patterson, Frank Allen, gen. ed. *The Works of John Milton.* 18 vols. in 21. New York: Columbia University Press, 1931–38.

Penn, John, ed. *Samson Agonistes.* In *Critical, Poetical, and Dramatic Works,* 2:213–63. 2 vols. London: Hatchard, Piccadilly, 1798.

Percival, H. M., ed. Samson Agonistes *and English Sonnets.* 1890. New York: Macmillan, 1931.

Prince, F. T., ed. *Samson Agonistes.* Oxford: Oxford University Press, 1957.

Sampson, Martin W. *The Lyric and Dramatic Poems of John Milton.* London: George Bell and Sons; New York: Henry Holt, 1908.

Shawcross, John T., ed. *The Complete English Poetry of John Milton.* 1963. Rev. ed. New York: Doubleday, 1971.

Stebbing, H., ed. *The Complete Poetical Works of John Milton.* New York: Daniel Appleton, 1843.

Tickell, Thomas, ed. *The Poetical Works of Mr. John Milton.* 2 vols. London: Jacob Tonson, 1720.

Todd, Henry John, ed. *The Poetical Works of John Milton.* 1801. 2nd ed. 7 vols. London: J. Johnson, 1809; New York: AMS Press, 1970.

Verity, A. W., ed. *Milton's* Samson Agonistes. Pitt Press Series. Cambridge: Cambridge University Press, 1892.

Warton, Thomas, ed. Poems upon Several Occasions, *English, Italian, and Latin, with Translations, by John Milton.* London: James Dodsley, 1785. 2nd ed. London: G. G. J. and J. Robinson, 1791.

Wright, B. A., ed. *John Milton: Poems.* London: J. M. Dent; New York: E. P. Dutton, 1956.

Wright, William Aldis, ed. *The Poetical Works of John Milton.* Cambridge: Cambridge University Press, 1903.

Wyatt, A. J., ed. *Samson Agonistes.* London: W. B. Clive, 1892.

Wyatt, A. J., and A. J. F. Collins, eds. *Samson Agonistes.* London: University Tutorial Press, 1932.

Commentaries and Reference Works

A. D. "Possible Echoes from Sidney's *Arcadia* in Shakespeare, Milton and Others." *Notes & Queries* 194 (1949): 555.

Adams, Robert Martin. *Ikon: John Milton and the Modern Critics.* Westport, Conn.: Greenwood Press, 1955.

Adler, E. N. "Milton's Harapha." *Times Literary Supplement,* 16 January 1937, 44.

Allen, Don Cameron. "Idea as Pattern: Despair and *Samson Agonistes.*" In *The Harmonious Vision: Studies in Milton's Poetry,* 71–94. Baltimore: Johns Hopkins University Press, 1954. Rptd. in *Twentieth Century Interpretations of* Samson Agonistes: *A Collection of Critical Essays,* ed. Galbraith M. Crump, 51–62. Englewood Cliffs, N.J.: Prentice Hall, 1968.

———. "Milton and the Descent to Light." *Journal of English and Germanic Philology* 60 (1961): 614–30.

Ames, Percy W., ed. *Milton Memorial Lectures 1908.* London: H. Frowde, 1909.

The Ancrene Riwle. Trans. M. B. Salu. London: Burns and Oates, 1955.

Arthos, John. *Milton and the Italian Cities.* New York: Barnes and Noble; London: Bowes and Bowes, 1968.

Atterbury, Francis. Letter to Alexander Pope, 15 June 1722. In *The Correspondence of Alexander Pope,* ed. George Sherburn, 2:124. 5 vols. Oxford: Clarendon Press, 1956.

Bailey, John. *Milton.* London: Oxford University Press, 1915.

Baker, Herschel. *The Wars of Truth: Studies in the Decay of Humanism in the Earlier Seventeenth Century.* Cambridge, Mass.: Harvard University Press, 1952.

Banks, Theodore Howard. *Milton's Imagery.* New York: Columbia University Press, 1950.

Barker, Arthur E. "Structural and Doctrinal Pattern in Milton's Later Poems." In *Essays in English Literature from the Renaissance to the Victorian Age Presented to A. S. P. Woodhouse,* ed. Millar MacLure and F. W. Watt, 169–94. Toronto: University of Toronto Press, 1964. Rptd. in *Twentieth Century Interpretations of* Samson Agonistes: *A Collection of Critical Essays,* ed. Galbraith M. Crump, 74–83. Englewood Cliffs, N.J.: Prentice Hall, 1968.

Baruch, Franklin R. "Time, Body, and Spirit at the Close of *Samson Agonistes.*" *ELH* 36 (1969): 319–39.

Batman, Stephen. *Batman uppon Bartholome.* London, 1582.

Baum, Paull Franklin. "*Samson Agonistes* Again." *PMLA* 36 (1921): 354–71.

Baumgartner, Paul. "Milton and Patience." *Studies in Philology* 60 (1963): 203–13.

Beerbohm, Max. "Agonising Samson." *Around Theatres.* 1924. Rptd. 1953. Pp. 527–31. [Reprint of a review, 19 December 1908.]

———. "*Samson Agonistes* and Zaza." *The Saturday Review of Politics, Literature, Science, and Art,* 21 April 1900, 489.

Belloc, Hilaire. *Milton.* Philadelphia: J. B. Lippincott; London: Cassell, 1935.

Beum, Robert. "The Rhyme in *Samson Agonistes.*" *Texas Studies in Literature and Language* 4 (1962): 177–82.

Block, Edward A. "Milton's Gout." *Bulletin of the History of Medicine* 28 (1954): 201–11.

Blount, Thomas. *Glossographia; or, A Dictionary, Interpreting All Such Hard Words.* 1656. 2nd ed. London, 1661.

Bodkin, Maud. *Archetypal Patterns in Poetry.* London: Oxford University Press, 1934. New York: AMS Press, 1978.

Boughner, Daniel C. "Milton's Harapha and Renaissance Comedy." *ELH* 11 (1944): 297–306.

Bowra, Cecil Maurice. *Inspiration and Poetry.* London: Macmillan; New York: St. Martin's Press, 1955.

Brennecke, Ernest, Jr. *John Milton the Elder and His Music.* Columbia University Studies in Musicology 2. New York: Columbia University Press, 1938.

Brewer, Wilmon. "Two Athenian Models for *Samson Agonistes.*" *PMLA* 42 (1927): 910–20.

Bridges, Robert. "Extraordinary." *The Athenaeum* 3951 (18 July 1903): 93–94.

———. *Milton's Prosody.* Oxford: Clarendon Press, 1921. Rev. ed. Oxford: Clarendon Press, 1965.

Brinkley, Roberta Florence, ed. *Coleridge on the Seventeenth Century.* Durham, N.C.: Duke University Press, 1955.

Broadbent, J. B. *Milton:* Comus *and* Samson Agonistes. London: Edward Arnold, 1961.

———. *Some Graver Subject: An Essay on* Paradise Lost. New York: Barnes and Noble, 1960.

Brooks, Cleanth. *Modern Poetry and the Tradition.* Chapel Hill: University of North Carolina Press, 1939.

Broom, Herbert, Joseph Gerald Pease, and Herbert Chitty. *A Selection of Legal Maxims.* 8th ed. London: Sweet and Maxwell, 1911.

Brown, Eleanor Gertrude. *Milton's Blindness.* New York: Columbia University Press, 1934.

Brown, J. Macmillan. *The* Samson Agonistes *of Milton.* Wellington, New Zealand: Whitcombe and Tombs, 1905.

Buchanan, Edith. "The Italian Neo-Senecan Background of *Samson Agonistes.*" Ph.D. diss., Duke University, 1952.

Burke, Kenneth. "The Imagery of Killing." *Hudson Review* 1 (1948): 151–67.

Burnet, James, Lord Monboddo. In *Of the Origin and Progress of Language.* Edinburgh, 1773–99. *Milton, 1732–1801: The Critical Heritage,* ed. John T. Shawcross, 225–84. London: Routledge and Kegan Paul, 1972.

Burney, Charles. *An Account of the Musical Performances in Westminster-Abbey and the Pantheon ... in Commemoration of Handel.* London: T. Payne and Son, and G. Robinson, 1785.

Bush, Douglas. *English Literature in the Earlier Seventeenth Century, 1600–1660.* Oxford: Clarendon Press, 1945. 2nd rev. ed. London: Oxford University Press, 1962.

———. "Ironic and Ambiguous Allusion in *Paradise Lost.*" *Journal of English and Germanic Philology* 60 (1961): 631–40.

———. "The Isolation of the Renaissance Hero." In *Reason and the Imagination: Studies in the History of Ideas, 1600–1800,* ed. J. A. Mazzeo, 57–69. New York: Columbia University Press; London: Routledge and Kegan Paul, 1962.

———. *John Milton.* London: Collier Books, 1965.

Bush, Douglas, ed. "John Milton." In *Major British Writers,* ed. G. B. Harrison, 1:401–522. Enlarged ed. 2 vols. New York: Harcourt, Brace, 1959.

Buttrick, George Arthur, ed. *The Interpreter's Bible.* 12 vols. Nashville: Abingdon-Cokesbury Press, 1951–57.

Bywater, Ingram. "Milton and the Aristotelian Definition of Tragedy." *Journal of Philology* 27 (1901): 267–75.

Carey, John. *John Milton.* New York: Arco, 1969.

Carr, Frank G. G. "Women and Ships." *Times Literary Supplement,* 27 February 1937, 151.

Carson, Barbara Harrell. "Milton's Samson as Parvus Sol." *English Language Notes* 5 (1968): 171–76.

Cawley, Robert Ralston. *Milton and the Literature of Travel.* Princeton, N.J.: Princeton University Press, 1951.

Chambers, A. B. "Wisdom and Fortitude in *Samson Agonistes.*" *PMLA* 78 (1963): 315–20.

Chatman, Seymour. "Milton's Participial Style." *PMLA* 83 (1968): 1386–99.

Christopher, Georgia. "Homeopathic Physic and Natural Renovation in *Samson Agonistes.*" *ELH* 37 (1970): 361–73.

Clark, Evert Mordecai. "Milton's Conception of Samson." *Texas Studies in English* 8 (1928): 88–99.

Coleridge, Samuel Taylor. *The Collected Works of Samuel Taylor Coleridge.* Gen. ed. Kathleen Coburn. 16 vols. London: Routledge and Kegan Paul; Princeton, N.J.: Princeton University Press, 1971–2001.

Cook, Albert S. "Milton's View of the Apocalypse as a Tragedy." *Archiv für das Studium der Neueren Sprachen und Literaturen* 129 (1912): 74–80.

———. "*Samson Agonistes,* 1665–6." *Modern Language Notes* 21 (1906): 78.

Corson, Hiram. *An Introduction to the Prose and Poetical Works of John Milton.* New York: Macmillan, 1899.

Cox, Lee Sheridan. "The 'Ev'ning Dragon' in *Samson Agonistes:* A Reappraisal." *Modern Language Notes* 76 (1961): 577–84.

———. "Natural Science and Figurative Design in *Samson Agonistes.*" *ELH* 35 (1968): 51–74. Rptd. in *Critical Essays on Milton from ELH,* 253–76. Baltimore: Johns Hopkins Press, 1969.

Cumberland, Richard. *Observer,* no. 76 (1785). In *Milton, 1732–1801: The Critical Heritage,* ed. John T. Shawcross, 333–38. London: Routledge and Kegan Paul, 1972.

Curry, Walter Clyde. "*Samson Agonistes* Yet Again." *Sewanee Review* 32 (1924): 336–52.

Daiches, David. *Milton.* London: Hutchinson University Library, 1957. 2nd rev. ed. London: Hutchinson, 1959.

Daniells, Roy. *Milton, Mannerism and Baroque.* Toronto: University of Toronto Press, 1963.

Darbishire, Helen, ed. *The Early Lives of Milton.* London: Constable, 1932.

Diodati, John. *Pious and Learned Annotations upon the Holy Bible.* 2nd ed. London, 1648.

Dodd, William, ed. *A Familiar Explanation of the Poetical Works of Milton.* London: J. and R. Tonson, 1762.

Durling, Dwight. "Coghill's *Samson Agonistes* at Oxford." *Seventeenth-Century News* 11 (1951): 63.

Dutton, John. *The Challenge, Sent by a Young Lady to Sir Thomas— &c.; or, The Female War.* London: E. Whitlock, 1697.

Ebbs, John Dale. "Milton's Treatment of Poetic Justice in *Samson Agonistes.*" *Modern Language Quarterly* 22 (1961): 377–89.

Edmundson, George. *Milton and Vondel: A Curiosity of Literature.* London: Trübner, 1885.

Edwards, Richard. *The Paradise of Dainty Devices,* ed. Hyder Edward Rollins. Cambridge, Mass.: Harvard University Press, 1927.

Eliot, T. S. "Milton I" (1936) and "Milton II" (1947). In *Selected Prose of T. S. Eliot,* ed. Frank Kermode, 258–64 and 265–74. London: Faber and Faber, 1975.

———. *On Poetry and Poets.* London: Faber and Faber, 1957.

Ellis-Fermor, Una. *The Frontiers of Drama.* New York: Oxford University Press, 1946. 2nd ed. London: Methuen, 1964. Two sections rptd. in *John Milton's* Samson Agonistes: *The Poem and Materials for Analysis,* ed. Ralph E. Hone, 194–211 and 212–17. San Francisco: Chandler, 1966.

Empson, William. "Emotions in Words Again." *Kenyon Review* 10 (1948): 579–601.

———. *Milton's God.* Rev. ed. London: Chatto and Windus, 1965.

———. *Seven Types of Ambiguity.* London: Chatto and Windus, 1930. 3rd ed. London: Chatto and Windus, 1953.

Epps, P. H. "Two Notes on English Classicism." *Studies in Philology* 13 (1916): 184–96.

Éstienne, Charles [Carolo Stephano]. *Dictionarium historicum, geographicum, poeticum.* Oxford: William Hall, 1670.

Farnham-Flower, F. F. "*Samson Agonistes* and Milton." *Times Literary Supplement,* 21 August 1948, 471.

Fell, Kenneth. "From Myth to Martyrdom: Towards a View of Milton's *Samson Agonistes.*" *English Studies* 34 (1953): 145–55.

Ferry, Anne Davidson. *Milton and the Miltonic Dryden.* Cambridge, Mass.: Harvard University Press, 1968.

Fields, Albert W. "Milton and Self-Knowledge." *PMLA* 83 (1968): 392–99.

Finney, Gretchen L. "Chorus in *Samson Agonistes.*" *PMLA* 58 (1943): 649–64.

Fish, Stanley. "Question and Answer in *Samson Agonistes.*" *Critical Quarterly* 11 (1969): 237–64.

Flatter, Richard. "*Samson Agonistes* and Milton." *Times Literary Supplement,* 7 August 1948, 443.

———. "*Samson Agonistes* and Milton." *Times Literary Supplement,* 4 September 1948, 499.

Fletcher, Harris Francis. *The Intellectual Development of John Milton.* 2 vols. Urbana: University of Illinois Press, 1956.

Flower, Annette C. "The Critical Context of the Preface to *Samson Agonistes.*" *Studies in English Literature, 1500–1900* 10 (1970): 409–23.

Fogel, Ephim G. "Milton and Sir Philip Sidney's *Arcadia.*" *Notes & Queries* 196 (1951): 115–17.

Fogle, French. "The Action of *Samson Agonistes.*" In *Essays in American and English Literature Presented to Bruce Robert McElderry, Jr.,* ed. Max F. Schulz, William D. Templeman, and Charles R. Metzger, 177–96. Athens: Ohio University Press, 1967.

Fox, Robert C. "Vida and *Samson Agonistes.*" *Notes & Queries,* n.s. 6 (1959): 370–72.

Frank, Joseph. "The Unharmonious Vision: Milton as a Baroque Artist." *Comparative Literature Studies* 3 (1966): 95–108.

Freedman, Morris. "*All for Love* and *Samson Agonistes.*" *Notes & Queries,* n.s. 3 (1956): 514–17.

———. "Milton and Dryden." Ph.D. diss. Columbia University, 1953.

French, J. Milton, ed. *The Life Records of John Milton.* 5 vols. New Brunswick, N.J.: Rutgers University Press, 1949–58.

French, Roberts W. "Rhyme and the Chorus of *Samson Agonistes.*" *Laurel Review* 10 (1970): 60–67.

Frye, Northrop. *Anatomy of Criticism: Four Essays.* Princeton, N.J.: Princeton University Press, 1957.

———. "The Typology of *Paradise Regained.*" *Modern Philology* 53 (1956): 227–38.

Frye, Roland Mushat. "Theological and Non-theological Structures in Tragedy." *Shakespeare Studies* 4 (1969): 132–48.

Garnett, Richard. *Life of John Milton.* London: Walter Scott, 1890.

Gilbert, Allan H. *A Geographical Dictionary of Milton.* New Haven, Conn.: Yale University Press, 1919.

———. "Is *Samson Agonistes* Unfinished?" *Philological Quarterly* 28 (1949): 98–106.

———. "Milton's Defense of Bawdry." In *SAMLA Studies in Milton: Essays on John Milton and His Works,* ed. J. Max Patrick, 54–71. Gainesville: University of Florida Press, 1953.

———. "*Samson Agonistes* 1096." *Modern Language Notes* 29 (1914): 161–62.

Gilbert, Allan H., ed. *Literary Criticism: Plato to Dryden.* New York: American Book, 1940.

Gohn, Ernest S. "The Christian Ethic of *Paradise Lost* and *Samson Agonistes.*" *Studia Neophilologica* 34 (1962): 243–68.

Goldsmith, Robert H. "Triumph and Tragedy in *Samson Agonistes*." *Renaissance Papers* (1968): 77–84.

Gossman, Ann. "Milton's Samson as the Tragic Hero Purified by Trial." *Journal of English and Germanic Philology* 61 (1962): 528–41.

———. "Ransom in *Samson Agonistes*." *Renaissance News* 13 (1960): 11–15.

———. "Samson, Job, and 'the Exercise of Saints.'" *English Studies* 45 (1964): 212–24.

Gray, F. Campbell. "Milton's Counterpoint: Classicism and Romanticism in the Poetry of John Milton." *Sewanee Review* 43 (1935): 134–45.

Green, Thomas. *Extracts from the Diary of a Lover of Literature*. Ipswich: J. Raw, 1810. In *Milton, 1732–1801: The Critical Heritage*, ed. John T. Shawcross, 401–3. London: Routledge and Kegan Paul, 1972.

Greenlaw, Edwin, Charles Grosvenor Osgood, and Frederick Morgan Padelford, eds. *The Works of Edmund Spenser: A Variorum Edition*. 9 vols. Baltimore: Johns Hopkins University Press, 1932–49.

Grenander, M. E. "Samson's Middle: Aristotle and Dr. Johnson." *University of Toronto Quarterly* 24 (1955): 377–89.

Grierson, Herbert J. C. *Milton and Wordsworth, Poets and Prophets: A Study of Their Reactions to Political Events*. London: Chatto and Windus; New York: Macmillan, 1937.

———. "A Note upon the *Samson Agonistes* of John Milton and *Samson of Heilige Wraeck* by Joost van den Vondel." In *M—langes d'Histoire Litt—raire G—n—rale et Compar—e offerts à Fernand Baldensperger*, 1:332–39. 2 vols. Paris: Librairie Ancienne Honoré Champion, 1930. Rptd. in *Essays and Addresses*, 55–63. Folcroft, Pa.: Folcroft Press, 1970.

Haigh, Arthur Elam. *The Tragic Drama of the Greeks*. Oxford: Clarendon Press, 1896.

Hales, John W. *Folia Litteraria: Essays and Notes on English Literature*. London: Seeley, 1893.

Haller, William. "The Tragedy of God's Englishman." In *Reason and the Imagination: Studies in the History of Ideas, 1600–1800*, ed. J. A. Mazzeo, 201–11. New York: Columbia University Press; London: Routledge and Kegan Paul, 1962.

Hamilton, Edith. *The Greek Way*. New York: Avon, 1958.

Hanford, James Holly. *John Milton, Englishman*. New York: Crown, 1949.

———. *A Milton Handbook*. 1926. 5th ed. by James Holly Hanford and James G. Taaffe. New York: Appleton-Century-Crofts, 1970.

———. "*Samson Agonistes* and Milton in Old Age." In *Studies in Shakespeare, Milton, and Donne*, 167–89. New York: Macmillan, 1925. Rptd. in *John Milton's* Samson Agonistes: *The Poem and Materials for Analysis*, ed. Ralph E. Hone, 170–93. San Francisco: Chandler, 1966. Rptd. in *Twentieth Century Interpretations of* Samson Agonistes: *A Collection of Critical Essays*, ed. Galbraith M. Crump, 14–32. Englewood Cliffs, N.J.: Prentice Hall, 1968. Rptd. in Hanford, *John Milton: Poet and Humanist*, 264–86. Cleveland: Press of Western Reserve University, 1966.

———. "The Temptation Motive in Milton." *Studies in Philology* 15 (1918): 176–94.

Harris, William O. "Despair and 'Patience as the Truest Fortitude' in *Samson Agonistes*." *ELH* 30 (1963): 107–20.

Hawkins, Sherman H. "Milton's Catharsis." In *Milton Studies,* vol. 2, ed. James D. Simmonds (Pittsburgh: University of Pittsburgh Press, 1970), 211–30.

Hayley, William. *A Life of the Author.* In *The Poetical Works of John Milton,* ed. William Cowper and William Hayley, 1:iii–cxxxiii. 3 vols. London: John and Josiah Boydell, and George Nicol, 1794–97.

Henn, T. R. *The Harvest of Tragedy.* London: Methuen, 1956.

Highet, Gilbert. *The Classical Tradition: Greek and Roman Influences on Western Literature.* New York: Oxford University Press, 1949.

Hill, John S. "Vocation and Spiritual Renovation in *Samson Agonistes*." In *Milton Studies,* vol. 2, ed. James D. Simmonds (Pittsburgh: University of Pittsburgh Press, 1970), 149–74.

Hoffman, Nancy Y. "Samson's Other Father: The Character of Manoa in *Samson Agonistes*." In *Milton Studies,* vol. 2, ed. James D. Simmonds (Pittsburgh: University of Pittsburgh Press, 1970), 195–210.

Hone, Ralph E., ed. *John Milton's* Samson Agonistes: *The Poem and Materials for Analysis.* San Francisco: Chandler, 1966.

Hopkins, Gerard Manley. *The Correspondence of Gerard Manley Hopkins and Richard Watson Dixon.* Ed. Claude Colleer Abbott. London: Oxford University Press, 1935.

———. *The Letters of Gerard Manley Hopkins to Robert Bridges.* Ed. Claude Colleer Abbott. London: Oxford University Press, 1935.

Hughes, Merritt Y., gen. ed. *A Variorum Commentary on the Poems of John Milton.* Vols. 1, 2, and 4 in 5 vols. New York: Columbia University Press, 1970–75.

Huntley, John F. "A Revaluation of the Chorus' Role in Milton's *Samson Agonistes*." *Modern Philology* 64 (1966): 132–45.

Hutchinson, F. E. *Milton and the English Mind.* London: Hodder and Stoughton, 1946. Rpt. New York: Collier Books, 1962.

Hyman, Lawrence W. "Milton's Samson and the Modern Reader." *College English* 28 (1966): 39–43.

———. "The Unwilling Martyrdom in *Samson Agonistes*." *Tennessee Studies in Literature* 13 (1968): 91–98.

Jebb, R[ichard] C., ed. *The Oedipus Coloneus. Sophocles: The Plays and Fragments.* 6 vols. Cambridge: Cambridge University Press, 1883–94.

———. "*Samson Agonistes* and the Hellenic Drama." *Proceedings of the British Academy* 3 (1907–8): 341–48. Rptd. in *John Milton's* Samson Agonistes: *The Poem and Materials for Analysis,* ed. Ralph E. Hone, 116–69. San Francisco: Chandler, 1966.

Johnson, Samuel. *A Dictionary of the English Language.* 2 vols. 1755. Philadelphia: James Maxwell, 1819.

————. "Milton." In *Lives of the English Poets,* ed. George Birkbeck Hill, 1:84–200. 3 vols. Oxford: Clarendon Press, 1905.

————. *The Rambler* 139 (16 July 1751). In *Milton, 1732–1801: The Critical Heritage,* ed. John T. Shawcross, 217–20. London: Routledge and Kegan Paul, 1972.

————. *The Rambler* 140 (20 July 1751). In *Milton, 1732–1801: The Critical Heritage,* ed. John T. Shawcross, 220–22. London: Routledge and Kegan Paul, 1972.

Jones, Ernest. *Essays in Applied Psycho-Analysis.* 2 vols. London: Hogarth Press, 1951.

Jortin, John. "Milton." In *Remarks on Spenser's Poems,* sigs. Z2r–Bb1v. London, 1734. New York: Garland, 1970.

Josephus, Flavius. *Antiquities of the Jews.* Trans. H. St. J. Thackeray, Ralph Marcus et al. Vols. 4–9 of *Josephus with an English Translation.* 9 vols. Cambridge, Mass.: Harvard University Press, 1958–65.

Kastner, L. E., and H. B. Charlton, eds. *The Poetical Works of Sir William Alexander.* 2 vols. Manchester: Manchester University Press, 1921.

Kaufmann, R. J. "Bruising the Serpent: Milton as a Tragic Poet." *Centennial Review* 11 (1967): 371–86.

Keightley, Thomas. *An Account of the Life, Opinions, and Writings of John Milton.* London: Chapman and Hall, 1855.

Kellett, E. E. *The Whirligig of Taste.* London: Hogarth Press, 1929.

Kelley, Maurice. "*Samson Agonistes* and Milton." *Times Literary Supplement,* 21 August 1948, 471.

Ker, William P. *Art of Poetry: Seven Lectures, 1920–22.* Freeport, N.Y.: Books for Libraries Press, 1967.

Kermode, Frank. "*Samson Agonistes* and Hebrew Prosody." *Durham University Journal* 14 (1953): 59–63.

Kilgo, J. W. "Hebrew Samson and Milton's Samson." *Methodist Quarterly Review* 73 (1924): 312–16.

Kirkconnell, Watson. *That Invincible Samson: The Theme of* Samson Agonistes *in World Literature with Translations of the Major Analogues.* Toronto: University of Toronto Press, 1964.

Kitto, H. D. F. *Greek Tragedy: A Literary Study.* 1939. London: Methuen, 1966.

Knight, G. Wilson. *Chariot of Wrath: The Message of John Milton to Democracy at War.* London: Faber and Faber, 1942.

————. "The Frozen Labyrinth: An Essay on Milton." In *The Burning Oracle: Studies in the Poetry of Action,* 59–113. London: Oxford University Press, 1939.

Knowlton, E. C. "Causality in *Samson Agonistes.*" *Modern Language Notes* 37 (1922): 333–39.

Kranidas, Thomas. "Dalila's Role in *Samson Agonistes.*" *Studies in English Literature, 1500–1900* 6 (1966): 125–37.

Kreipe, Christian Edzard. "Milton's *Samson Agonistes*." *Studien zur Englischen Philologie* 70 (1926): 54–56.

Krouse, F. Michael. *Milton's Samson and the Christian Tradition*. Princeton, N.J.: Princeton University Press, 1949. New York: Octagon Books, 1974.

Kurth, Burton O. *Milton and Christian Heroism: Biblical Epic Themes and Forms in Seventeenth-Century England*. Berkeley and Los Angeles: University of California Press, 1959.

Laking, Guy Francis. *A Record of European Armour and Arms through Seven Centuries*. 5 vols. London: G. Bell, 1920–22.

Landor, Walter Savage. "Southey and Landor." In *Imaginary Conversations. The Complete Works of Walter Savage Landor,* ed. T. Earle Welby, 5:230–334. 16 vols. London: Chapman and Hall, 1927–36.

Landy, Marcia K. "Character Portrayal in *Samson Agonistes*." *Texas Studies in Literature and Language* 7 (1965): 239–53.

———. "Language and the Seal of Silence in *Samson Agonistes*." In *Milton Studies,* vol. 2, ed. James D. Simmonds (Pittsburgh: University of Pittsburgh Press, 1970), 175–94.

———. "Of Highest Wisdom: A Study of John Milton's *Samson Agonistes* as a Dramatization of Christian Conversion." Ph.D. diss., University of Rochester, 1962.

Langbaine, Gerard. *An Account of the English Dramatick Poets*. Oxford: George West and Henry Clements, 1691.

Langbaine, Gerard, and Charles Gildon. *The Lives and Characters of the English Dramaticke Poets*. London: N. Cox and W. Turner, 1699.

Langdon, Ida. *Milton's Theory of Poetry and Fine Art*. New York: Russell and Russell, 1924.

Larson, Martin A. *The Modernity of Milton: A Theological and Philosophical Interpretation*. Chicago: University of Chicago Press, 1927.

Lawry, Jon S. *The Shadow of Heaven: Matter and Stance in Milton's Poetry*. Ithaca, N.Y.: Cornell University Press, 1968.

Leavis, F. R. "Milton's Verse." In *Revaluation: Tradition and Development in English Poetry,* 42–67. Harmondsworth: Penguin Books, in association with Chatto and Windus, 1936. Rptd. 1972.

Le Comte, Edward S. *Yet Once More: Verbal and Psychological Pattern in Milton*. New York: Liberal Arts Press, 1953.

Leigh, Edward. *Critica Sacra: Observations on All the Radices, or Primitive Hebrew Words of the Old Testament*. 2nd ed. London, 1650.

Leveen, Jacob. "Milton's Harapha." *Times Literary Supplement,* 23 January 1937, 60.

Lewalski, Barbara. "*Samson Agonistes* and the 'Tragedy' of the Apocalypse." *PMLA* 85 (1970): 1050–62.

———. "The Ship-Tempest Imagery in *Samson Agonistes*." *Notes & Queries,* n.s. 6 (1959): 372–73.

Little, Marguerite. "Some Italian Elements in the Choral Practice of *Samson Agonistes*." Ph.D. diss., University of Illinois, 1946.

Lockwood, Laura E. *Lexicon to the English Poetical Works of John Milton*. New York: Macmillan, 1907.

Loewe, H. "Milton's Harapha." *Times Literary Supplement,* 23 January 1937, 60.

Low, Anthony. "Action and Suffering: *Samson Agonistes* and the Irony of Alternatives." *PMLA* 84 (1969): 514–19.

———. "Tragic Pattern in *Samson Agonistes*." *Texas Studies in Literature and Language* 11 (1969): 915–30.

Lowell, Robert. "Poets and the Theater." 1963–64. Rptd. in *Collected Prose,* ed. Robert Giroux, 175–78. New York: Farrar, Straus and Giroux, 1987.

Lucas, Frank L. *Euripides and His Influence*. London: George Harrap; Boston: Marshall Jones, 1923.

Lynch, James J. "'Evil Communications.'" *Notes & Queries,* n.s. 3 (1956): 477.

Macaulay, Rose. *Milton*. London: Duckworth, 1934. 2nd ed. New York: Macmillan, 1957.

Madsen, William G. "From Shadowy Types to Truth." In *The Lyric and Dramatic Milton: Selected Papers from the English Institute,* ed. Joseph H. Summers, 95–114. New York: Columbia University Press, 1965. Rptd. in *Twentieth Century Interpretations of* Samson Agonistes: *A Collection of Critical Essays,* ed. Galbraith M. Crump, 84–95. Englewood Cliffs, N.J.: Prentice-Hall, 1968. Slightly revised as "Samson and Christ," in *From Shadowy Types to Truth: Studies in Milton's Symbolism,* 181–202. New Haven, Conn.: Yale University Press, 1968.

Mahaffy, J. P. *What Have the Greeks Done for Modern Civilization?* New York: G. P. Putnam's Sons, 1909.

Mahood, M. M. *Poetry and Humanism*. London: Cape, 1950.

Maplet, John. *A Greene Forest; or, A Naturall Historie*. 1567. London: Hesperides Press, 1930.

Marilla, E. L. "*Samson Agonistes:* An Interpretation." *Studia Neophilologica* 29 (1957): 67–76. Rptd. in *Milton and Modern Man: Selected Essays,* 68–77. University, Ala.: University of Alabama Press, 1968.

Martz, Louis L. "Chorus and Character in *Samson Agonistes*." In *Milton Studies,* vol. 1, ed. James D. Simmonds (Pittsburgh: University of Pittsburgh Press, 1969), 115–34.

Marvell, Andrew. "On *Paradise Lost*." In *Paradise Lost,* by John Milton, sig. A3. London: S. Simmons, 1674.

Masson, David. *The Life of John Milton*. 7 vols. 1877–96. New York: Peter Smith, 1946.

Maxwell, J. C. "Milton's Knowledge of Aeschylus: The Argument from Parallel Passages." *Review of English Studies,* n.s. 3 (1952): 366–71.

———. "Milton's Samson and Sophocles' Heracles." *Philological Quarterly* 33 (1954): 90–91.

McCall, Lois Anne-Marie Gilbert. "The Imagery and Symbolism in *Samson Agonistes*." M.A. thesis, Mount Holyoke College, 1949.

McCollom, William G. *Tragedy*. New York: Macmillan, 1957.

McDavid, Raven I., Jr. "*Samson Agonistes* 1096: A Re-examination." *Philological Quarterly* 33 (1954): 86–89.

McManaway, James G. "Women and Ships." *Times Literary Supplement,* 20 February 1937, 131.

Menzies, W. "Milton: The Last Poems." *Essays and Studies* 24 (1939): 80–113.

[Mickle, William]. "A Critique on the *Samson Agonistes* of Milton, in Refutation of the Censure of Dr. Johnson." *The European Magazine and London Review* 13 (1788): 401–6. In *Milton, 1732–1801: The Critical Heritage,* ed. John T. Shawcross, 344–49. London: Routledge and Kegan Paul, 1972.

Migne, Jacques-Paul. *Patrologiae Cursus Completus.* 221 vols. Paris: Apud Garnier Fratres, 1844–91.

"Milton's *Samson Agonistes.*" *The Gentleman's Magazine and Historical Review,* 3rd ser., 2 (1866): 332.

Mitchell, Charles. "Dalila's Return: The Importance of Pardon." *College English* 26 (1965): 614–20.

Mollenkott, Virginia R. "Relativism in *Samson Agonistes.*" *Studies in Philology* 67 (1970): 89–102.

Moore, Charles. *Full Inquiry into the Subject of Suicide.* London: J. F. and C. Rivington, 1790.

Moss, Leonard. "The Rhetorical Style of *Samson Agonistes.*" *Modern Philology* 62 (1965): 296–301.

Mueller, Martin E. "*Pathos* and *Katharsis* in *Samson Agonistes.*" *ELH* 31 (1964): 156–74. Rptd. in *Critical Essays on Milton from ELH,* 234–52. Baltimore: Johns Hopkins University Press, 1969.

———. "Sixteenth-Century Italian Criticism and Milton's Theory of Catharsis." *Studies in English Literature, 1500–1900* 6 (1966): 139–50.

Muir, Kenneth. *John Milton.* London: Longmans, 1955.

Muldrow, George M. *Milton and the Drama of the Soul: A Study of the Theme of the Restoration of Men in Milton's Later Poetry.* The Hague: Mouton, 1970.

Murry, John Middleton. *The Problem of Style.* 1922. London: Oxford University Press, 1967.

Nash, Ralph. "Chivalric Themes in *Samson Agonistes.*" In *Studies in Honor of John Wilcox,* ed. A. Dayle Wallace and Woodburn O. Ross, 23–38. Detroit: Wayne State University Press, 1958.

Nicolson, Marjorie Hope. *John Milton: A Reader's Guide to His Poetry.* New York: Farrar, Straus, and Giroux; London: Thames and Hudson, 1964.

O'Connor, William Van. *Climates of Tragedy.* Baton Rouge: Louisiana State University Press, 1943.

Oras, Ants. *Blank Verse and Chronology in Milton.* Gainesville: University of Florida Press, 1966.

———. "Milton's Blank Verse and the Chronology of His Major Poems." In *SAMLA Studies in Milton: Essays on John Milton and His Works,* ed. J. Max Patrick, 128–97. Gainesville: University of Florida Press, 1953.

Osgood, Charles Grosvenor. *The Classical Mythology of Milton's English Poems*. New York: Haskell House, 1964.

Pareus [Paré, David]. *A Commentary upon the Divine Revelation of the Apostle and Evangelist John*. Trans. Elias Arnold. Amsterdam: C. P., 1644.

Parker, William Riley. "The Date of *Samson Agonistes*." *Philological Quarterly* 28 (1949): 145–66. Rptd. in *John Milton's* Samson Agonistes: *The Poem and Materials for Analysis*, ed. Ralph E. Hone, 218–44. San Francisco: Chandler, 1966.

———. "The Date of *Samson Agonistes:* A Postscript." *Notes & Queries*, n.s. 5 (1958): 201–2.

———. *Milton: A Biography*. Oxford: Clarendon Press, 1968. 2nd ed. 2 vols. Ed. Gordon Campbell. Oxford: Clarendon Press, 1996.

———. *Milton's Debt to Greek Tragedy in* Samson Agonistes. Baltimore: Johns Hopkins University Press, 1937.

———. "Milton's Harapha." *Times Literary Supplement*, 2 January 1937, 12.

———. "Notes on the Text of *Samson Agonistes*." *Journal of English and Germanic Philology* 60 (1961): 688–98.

———. "On Milton's Early Literary Program." *Modern Philology* 33 (1935): 49–53.

———. "The Trinity Manuscript and Milton's Plans for a Tragedy." *Journal of English and Germanic Philology* 34 (1935): 225–32.

———. "Variorum Notes and Commentary." Unpublished annotations, Department of English, University of Illinois at Urbana-Champaign.

Patch, Howard R. *The Goddess Fortuna in Mediaeval Literature*. Cambridge, Mass.: Harvard University Press, 1927.

Paton, Lewis Bayles. "The Cult of the Mother-Goddess in Ancient Palestine." *The Biblical World* 36 (1910): 26–38.

Pattison, Mark. *Milton*. London: Macmillan, 1879. New York: Harper, 1902.

Peck, Francis, ed. *New Memoirs of the Life and Poetical Works of Mr. John Milton*. London, 1740.

Phillips, Edward. *New World of Words; or, A General English Dictionary*. 1658. 4th ed. London, 1678.

———. *Theatrum Poetarum*. London, 1675.

Powell, Chilton L. "Milton Agonistes." *Sewanee Review* 34 (1926): 169–83.

Prince, F. T. *The Italian Element in Milton's Verse*. Oxford: Clarendon Press, 1954. Corrected ed. Oxford: Oxford University Press, 1962.

Quarles, Francis. *The Historie of Samson*. London, 1631.

Radzinowicz, Mary Ann N. "Eve and Dalila: Renovation and the Hardening of the Heart." In *Reason and the Imagination: Studies in the History of Ideas, 1600–1800*, ed. J. A. Mazzeo, 155–81. New York: Columbia University Press; London: Routledge and Kegan Paul, 1962.

———. "*Samson Agonistes* and Milton the Politician in Defeat." *Philological Quarterly* 44 (1965): 454–71.

Rajan, Balachandra. *The Lofty Rhyme: A Study of Milton's Major Poetry.* Coral Gables, Fla.: University of Miami Press; London: Routledge and Kegan Paul, 1970.

Raleigh, Walter. *Milton.* London: Edward Arnold, 1900.

———. "Milton's Last Poems." *Living Age* 260 (1909): 251–53.

Ralli, Augustus. *Poetry and Faith.* London: Bodley Head, 1951.

Richardson, J[onathan]. *Explanatory Notes and Remarks on Milton's* Paradise Lost *by J. Richardson Father and Son. With a Life of the Author, and a Discourse on the Poem. By J. R. Sen.* London, 1734. In Helen Darbishire, ed., *The Early Lives of Milton* [199]–330. London: Constable, 1932.

Ricks, Christopher. "Milton: Part III. *Paradise Regained* and *Samson Agonistes.*" In *English Poetry and Prose, 1540–1674,* ed. Ricks, 299–316. Vol. 2 of *Sphere History of Literature in the English Language.* London: Barrie and Jenkins, 1970.

———. *Milton's Grand Style.* Oxford: Oxford University Press, 1963.

Ridley, Thomas. *A View of the Civile and Ecclesiasticall Law.* 2nd ed. Oxford, 1634.

Ritson, Joseph. *Ancient Engleish Metrical Romanceës.* 3 vols. London: G. and W. Nicol, 1802.

Robertson, Duncan. "Metaphor in *Samson Agonistes.*" *University of Toronto Quarterly* 38 (1969): 319–38.

Robinson, Henry Crabb. *Henry Crabb Robinson on Books and Their Writers.* 3 vols. Ed. Edith J. Morley. London: J. M. Dent, 1938.

Rosedale, H. G. "Milton: His Religion and Polemics, Ecclesiastical as Well as Theological." In *Milton Memorial Lectures 1908,* ed. Percy W. Ames, 109–90. New York: Haskell House, 1964.

Ross, Hedley Vicars. "*Samson Agonistes:* Its Autobiographical Character and Its Relation to the Greek Drama." Ph.D. diss., Cornell University, 1899.

Ross, Malcolm MacKenzie. *Milton's Royalism.* 1943. New York: Russell and Russell, 1970.

Roston, Murray. *Biblical Drama in England: From the Middle Ages to the Present Day.* Evanston, Ill.: Northwestern University Press; London: Faber and Faber, 1968.

Routh, James. "The Classical Rule of Law in English Criticism of the Sixteenth and Seventeenth Centuries." *Journal of English and Germanic Philology* 12 (1913): 612–30.

Rowse, A. L. "The Milton Country." In *The English Past: Evocations of Persons and Places,* 85–112. New York: Macmillan, 1952.

Rudrum, Alan. *A Critical Commentary on Milton's* Samson Agonistes. London: Macmillan; New York: St. Martin's Press, 1969.

Rushton, William L. *Shakespeare's Legal Maxims.* Liverpool: Henry Young and Sons, 1907.

Sadler, Lynn Veach. "Typological Imagery in *Samson Agonistes:* Noon and the Dragon." *ELH* 37 (1970): 195–210.

Saillens, Émile. *John Milton, Poète Combattant.* Paris: Gallimard. 1959. Trans. as *John Milton: Man, Poet, Polemist.* New York: Barnes and Noble; Oxford: Blackwell, 1964.

Sampson, Alden. *Studies in Milton*. New York: Moffat, Yard, 1913. New York: AMS Press, 1970.

Samuel, Irene. *Plato and Milton*. Ithaca, N.Y.: Cornell University Press, 1947.

Samuels, Charles Thomas. "Milton's *Samson Agonistes* and Rational Christianity." *Dalhousie Review* 43 (1963): 495–506.

Sandys, George. *A Relation of a Journey Begun An. Dom. 1610*. 1615. 3rd ed. London: Robert Allot, 1632.

Saurat, Denis. *Milton: Man and Thinker*. London: J. Cape, 1924.

Scholes, Percy A. "The Puritans and Music." *Times Literary Supplement*, 6 December 1934, 875.

Scott-Craig, T. S. K. "Concerning Milton's *Samson*." *Renaissance News* 5 (1952): 45–53.

———. "Miltonic Tragedy and Christian Vision." In *The Tragic Vision and the Christian Faith*, ed. Nathan A. Scott, 99–122. New York: Association Press, 1957.

Sellin, Paul R. "Milton and Heinsius: Theoretical Homogeneity." In *Medieval Epic to the "Epic Theater" of Brecht*, ed. Rosario P. Armato and John M. Spalek, 125–34. Los Angeles: University of Southern California Press, 1968.

———. "Milton on Tragedy." In *Daniel Heinsius and Stuart England*, 164–77. Leiden: Leiden University Press, 1968.

———. "Milton's Epithet *Agonistes*." *Studies in English Literature, 1500–1900* 4 (1964): 137–62.

———. "Sources of Milton's Catharsis: A Reconsideration." *Journal of English and Germanic Philology* 60 (1961): 712–30.

Shawcross, John T. "The Chronology of Milton's Major Poems." *PMLA* 76 (1961): 345–58.

———. "One Aspect of Milton's Spelling: Idle Final 'E.'" *PMLA* 78 (1963): 501–10.

———. "The Prosody of Milton's Translation of Horace's Fifth Ode." *Tennessee Studies in Literature* 13 (1968): 81–89.

Shawcross, John T., ed. *Milton, 1732–1801: The Critical Heritage*. London: Routledge and Kegan Paul, 1972.

Sheppard, John T. *Aeschylus and Sophocles: Their Work and Influence*. New York: Longmans, Green, 1927.

Siebert, Theodor. "Untersuchungen über Milton's Kunst von Psychologischen Standpunkt aus." *Anglia* 54 (1930): 67–82.

Sirluck, Ernest. "Some Recent Suggested Changes in the Chronology of Milton's Poems." *Journal of English and Germanic Philology* 60 (1961): 773–85. Rptd. in *John Milton's Samson Agonistes: The Poem and Materials for Analysis*, ed. Ralph E. Hone, 245–57. San Francisco: Chandler, 1966.

Smith, G. C. Moore. "Milton, Samson Agonistes, 373." *Modern Language Review* 3 (1907): 74.

Smith, J. C. "Feminine Endings in Milton's Blank Verse." *Times Literary Supplement*, 5 December 1936, 1016.

Smith, Logan Pearsall. *Milton and His Modern Critics.* London: Oxford University Press, 1940.

Spencer, Terrence, and James Willis. "Milton and Arnobius." *Notes & Queries* 196 (1951): 387.

Spingarn, Joel E., ed. *Critical Essays of the Seventeenth Century.* 3 vols. Bloomington: Indiana University Press, 1908.

———. *A History of Literary Criticism in the Renaissance.* London: Macmillan, 1908. 2nd ed. New York: Columbia University Press, 1924.

Sprott, S. Ernest. *Milton's Art of Prosody.* Oxford: Basil Blackwell, 1953.

Steadman, John M. "Dalila, the Ulysses Myth, and Renaissance Allegorical Tradition." *Modern Language Review* 57 (1962): 560–65.

———. "'Faithful Champion': The Theological Basis of Milton's Hero of Faith." *Anglia* 77 (1959): 12–28. Rptd. in *Milton's Epic Characters: Image and Idol,* 44–57. Chapel Hill: University of North Carolina Press, 1968. Rptd. in *Milton: Modern Essays in Criticism,* ed. Arthur E. Barker, 467–83. London: Oxford University Press, 1965.

———. "'Men of Renown': Heroic Virtue and the Giants of Genesis 6:4 (*Paradise Lost,* XI, 638–99)." *Philological Quarterly* 40 (1961): 580–86. Rptd. in *Milton's Epic Characters: Image and Idol,* 177–93. Chapel Hill: University of North Carolina Press, 1968.

———. *Milton and the Renaissance Hero.* Oxford: Oxford University Press, 1967.

———. "Milton's Harapha and Goliath." *Journal of English and Germanic Philology* 60 (1961): 786–95.

———. "The Samson-Nisus Parallel: Some Renaissance Examples." *Notes & Queries,* n.s. 7 (1960): 450–51.

———. "The Tragic Glass: Milton, Minturno, and the *Condition Humaine.*" In *Th'Upright Heart and Pure: Essays on John Milton Commemorating the Tercentenary of the Publication of* Paradise Lost, ed. Amadeus P. Fiore, 101–15. Pittsburgh: Duquesne University Press, 1967.

———. "'Verse Without Rime': Sixteenth-Century Italian Defences of *Versi Sciolti.*" *Italica* 41 (1964): 384–402.

Stein, Arnold Sidney. *Heroic Knowledge: An Interpretation of* Paradise Regained *and* Samson Agonistes. Minneapolis: University of Minnesota Press, 1957.

———. "A Note on Meter." *Kenyon Review* 18 (1956): 451–60.

Steiner, George. *The Death of Tragedy.* New York: Hill and Wang; Faber and Faber, 1961.

Stephenson, Andrew. "*Samson Agonistes.*" *Theatre Arts Monthly* 22 (1938): 914–16.

Stoll, Elmer Edgar. *Poets and Playwrights: Shakespeare, Jonson, Spenser, Milton.* Minneapolis: University of Minnesota Press, 1930.

Stollman, Samuel S. "Samson as Dragon and a Scriptural Tradition." *English Language Notes* 7 (1970): 186–89.

Stroup, Thomas B. *Religious Rite and Ceremony in Milton's Poetry.* Lexington: University of Kentucky Press, 1968.

Summers, Joseph H. "The Movements of the Drama." In *The Lyric and Dramatic Milton: Selected Papers from the English Institute,* ed. Joseph H. Summers, 153–75. New York: Columbia University Press, 1965.

Svendsen, Kester. "Milton and Medical Lore." *Bulletin of the History of Medicine* 12 (1943): 158–84.

———. *Milton and Science.* New York: Greenwood Press, 1956.

Taylor, Dick, Jr. "Grace as a Means of Poetry: Milton's Pattern of Salvation." *Tulane Studies in English* 4 (1954): 75–80.

Taylor, George Coffin. "Shakespeare and Milton Again." *Studies in Philology* 23 (1926): 189–99.

Thaler, Alwin. "Milton in the Theatre." *Studies in Philology* 17 (1920): 269–308. Rptd. with additions in *Shakespeare's Silences,* 209–56. Cambridge, Mass.: Harvard University Press, 1929.

———. "Shakespeare and Milton Once More." In *SAMLA Studies in Milton,* ed. J. Max Patrick, 80–99. Gainesville: University of Florida Press, 1953.

———. "The Shakespearian Element in Milton." *PMLA* 40 (1925): 645–91. Rptd. with additions in *Shakespeare's Silences,* 139–208. Cambridge, Mass.: Harvard University Press, 1929.

Theresa, Sister Margaret. Review of *Milton's Samson and the Christian Tradition,* by F. Michael Krouse. *Thought* 25 (1950): 137–39.

Thompson, Edward J. "*Samson Agonistes.*" *London Quarterly Review* 125 (1916): 244–54.

Thompson, Elbert N. S. *Essays on Milton.* New Haven, Conn.: Yale University Press, 1914.

Thorpe, James. "On the Pronunciation of Names in *Samson Agonistes.*" *Huntington Library Quarterly* 31 (1967): 65–74.

Tilley, Morris Palmer. *A Dictionary of the Proverbs in England in the Sixteenth and Seventeenth Centuries.* Ann Arbor: University of Michigan Press, 1950.

Tillyard, E. M. W. *Milton.* London: Chatto and Windus, 1930. Rev. ed. Harmondsworth: Penguin, 1966.

———. *The Miltonic Setting, Past and Present.* Cambridge: Cambridge University Press, 1938.

———. *Studies in Milton.* London: Chatto and Windus, 1951.

Timberlake, P. W. "Milton and Euripides." In *Essays in Dramatic Literature: The Parrott Presentation Volume, by Pupils of Professor Thomas Marc Parrott of Princeton University,* ed. Hardin Craig, 315–40. Princeton, N.J.: Princeton University Press, 1935.

Tinker, Chauncey B. "*Samson Agonistes.*" In *Tragic Themes in Western Literature,* ed. Cleanth Brooks, 59–76. New Haven, Conn.: Yale University Press, 1955.

Topsell, Edward. *The History of Four-Footed Beasts and Serpents.* London, 1658.

Tung, Mason. "*Samson Impatiens:* A Reinterpretation of Milton's *Samson Agonistes.*" *Texas Studies in Literature and Language* 9 (1968): 475–92.

Tupper, Frederick. "*Samson Agonistes,* 1665–6." *Modern Language Notes* 22 (1907): 47.

Tupper, James Waddell. "The Dramatic Structure of *Samson Agonistes.*" *PMLA* 35 (1920): 375–89.

Upton, John. *Critical Observations on Shakespeare*. London: G. Hawkins, 1746.

Ure, Peter. "A Simile in *Samson Agonistes*." *Notes & Queries* 195 (1950): 298.

Van Doren, Mark. *John Dryden: A Study of His Poetry*. New York: H. Holt, 1946.

Van Kluyve, Robert A. "Out, Out Hyaena!" *American Notes & Queries* 1 (1963): 99–101.

Visiak, E. H. *Milton Agonistes: A Metaphysical Criticism*. London: A. M. Philpot, 1922.

———. "Notes on Milton." *Notes & Queries* 179 (1940): 184–87.

Wagenknecht, Edward Charles. *The Personality of Milton*. Norman: University of Oklahoma Press, 1970.

Waggoner, George R. "The Challenge to Single Combat in *Samson Agonistes*." *Philological Quarterly* 39 (1960): 82–92.

Watkins, W. B. C. *Anatomy of Milton's Verse*. Baton Rouge: Louisiana State University Press, 1955.

Weekley, Ernest. "'To Appoint': Milton, *Samson Agonistes, 373*." *Modern Language Review* 3 (1907–8): 373–74.

Weismiller, Edward. "The 'Dry' and 'Rugged' Verse of *Samson Agonistes*." In *The Lyric and Dramatic Milton: Selected Papers from the English Institute*, ed. Joseph H. Summers, 115–52. New York: Columbia University Press, 1965.

Whiting, George W. *Milton's Literary Milieu*. Chapel Hill: University of North Carolina Press, 1939.

———. "*Samson Agonistes* and the Geneva Bible." *Rice University Studies* 38 (1951): 16–35. Rptd. in *Milton and This Pendant World*, 201–22. Austin: University of Texas Press, 1958.

Wilkenfeld, Roger B. "Act and Emblem: The Conclusion of *Samson Agonistes*." *ELH* 32 (1965): 160–68.

Wilkes, G. A. "The Interpretation of *Samson Agonistes*." *Huntington Library Quarterly* 26 (1963): 363–79.

Williams, Arnold. "A Note on *Samson Agonistes* ll. 90–94." *Modern Language Notes* 63 (1948): 537–38.

Williams, Charles. Introduction to *The English Poems of John Milton*, ix–xxii. Oxford: Oxford University Press, 1940.

———. *The English Poetic Mind*. Oxford: Clarendon Press, 1932.

Williamson, George. "Tension in *Samson Agonistes*." In *Milton and Others*, 85–102. Chicago: University of Chicago Press; London: Faber and Faber, 1965.

Wilson, J. Dover. "Shakespeare, Milton, and Congreve." *Times Literary Supplement*, 16 January 1937, 44.

Wittreich, Joseph A. *The Romantics on Milton: Formal Essays and Critical Asides*. Cleveland: Western Reserve University Press, 1970.

Wolff, H. T. *On Milton's* Samson Agonistes *Both as Drama and as an Illustration of the Poet's Life*. Berlin: A. W. Schade, 1871.

Wood, Anthony à. *Fasti Oxonienses.* 1691. In *The Early Lives of Milton,* ed. Helen Darbishire, 35–48. London: Constable, 1932.

Woodhouse, A. S. P. "*Samson Agonistes* and Milton's Experience." *Transactions of the Royal Society of Canada,* 3rd ser., 43 (1949): 157–75.

———. "Tragic Effect in *Samson Agonistes.*" *University of Toronto Quarterly* 28 (1959): 205–22. Rptd. in *Milton: Modern Essays in Criticism,* ed. Arthur E. Barker, 447–66. London: Oxford University Press, 1965.

Wright, E. "Samson as the Fallen Champion in *Samson Agonistes.*" *Notes & Queries,* n.s. 7 (1960): 222–24.

Wright, G. Ernest. *Biblical Archeology.* Philadelphia: Westminster Press, 1957.

Young, G. M. "Milton and Harrington." *Times Literary Supplement,* 9 January 1937, 28.